LAW
COURTS &
JUSTICE IN AMERICA

SEVENTH EDITION

HOWARD ABADINSKY

St. John's University

WAVELAND

PRESS, INC.

Long Grove, Illinois

To my wonderful wife, Caralyn Bishop-Abadinsky

For information about this book, contact:
   Waveland Press, Inc.
   4180 IL Route 83, Suite 101
   Long Grove, IL 60047-9580
   (847) 634-0081
   info@waveland.com
   www.waveland.com

Contents

PART II: Courts   87

5 The Appellate Process and the Role of the Judiciary   126

6 The Supreme Court   164

7 Judges, Prosecutors, and Criminal Defense Attorneys   200

PART III: Justice   239

8 Criminal Justice   241

12 Alternative Justice   379

Preface

The Seventh Edition provides an in-depth examination of essential historical and contemporary elements involved in the US legal system. This thoroughly updated edition is designed for courses on law, courts, and judicial process in criminal justice, government, political science, and sociology. I have attempted to take advantage of my background in these disciplines to provide a comprehensive, core textbook.

Coverage in the Seventh Edition is structured around three parts. Part I, Law, chronicles the evolution of the justice system in the United States, highlighting important historical events. It also explains the transformative process of law schools, legal education, and the practice of law. Part II, Courts, provides readers with a clear understanding of the roles and administration of federal and state courts, as well as the Supreme Court. The treatment of the multifaceted judicial branch of government includes historical foundations—discussions of key people, events, and cases—that influenced current court structures and procedures. Part II also provides a close look at the intertwinement of judges, prosecutors, and defense attorneys. Part III, Justice, examines five avenues (systems of justice) to effect fair legal action in civil, criminal, and juvenile cases. Descriptions of each chapter follow.

Chapter 1 explores the meaning of law, the concept of natural law, and capitalism's need for rational law. The chapter examines two rational systems of law: the common/case law system used in the United States and countries with an English heritage, and the civil-law system used in the rest of the democratic world. The chapter examines American codes of procedure and the variety of American law: statutory, administrative, and regulatory.

Chapter 2 reviews the history of legal education from colonial times to the present state of legal education in the United States. The chapter examines the law school curriculum, differences between law schools, criticism of legal education, and the positions offered by the legal realists, critical legal studies, and the law and economics movement.

Chapter 3 addresses the development of bar associations, the practice of law, and the stratification of the legal profession. The chapter ends with a discussion of federal legal services and attorneys practicing public interest law.

Chapter 4 reviews the history and development of court systems, federal and state; the variety of ways in which they are organized; and court administration and reform.

Chapter 5 explores the appellate court process and judicial review, the issue of legitimacy, and the implementation of appellate decisions. There is an examination of the processes involved in interpreting statutes and the Constitution, including plain meaning, originalism, textualism, and legislative intent. This chapter discusses the controversies surrounding the role of the judicial branch and the related issues of judicial restraint versus judicial activism.

Chapter 6 focuses on the history and role of the Supreme Court by examining critical decisions and the policy-making role of the Court.

Chapter 7 is devoted to judges, prosecutors, and criminal defense attorneys. The role of the trial judge is discussed and methods for selecting judges are compared and contrasted. The office of prosecutor is examined, including the ways in which it can be organized and their implications. The discussion of the criminal defense attorney—private counsel, public defender, court-appointed counsel—focuses on the very difficult problems encountered in the practice of criminal law.

Chapter 8 begins with a review of the evidence needed to convict in a criminal case, the due process guarantees to which every criminal defendant is entitled, and the relevant Supreme Court decisions that affect defendant rights. The trial process is examined from pretrial activity, to the *voir dire* hearing, to the judge's charge to the jury. The differences between indeterminate sentencing and various types of determinate sentencing are reviewed as a prelude to the presentence report and the sentencing hearing. The chapter ends with a discussion of probation, parole, and executive clemency.

Chapter 9 provides an in-depth examination of the method most frequently used to decide criminal cases, and the controversy surrounding plea bargaining.

Chapter 10 contrasts the civil trial process with the criminal trial and examines issues surrounding the contingency fee and class action lawsuits.

Chapter 11 examines the system of juvenile justice, important Supreme Court decisions that have affected the juvenile court, and the movement away from *parens patriae* and toward the justice model of responding to juvenile crime.

Chapter 12 surveys alternative, nonadversarial methods and ideologies of dispute resolution in both civil and criminal matters, including mediation, arbitration, community courts, therapeutic justice, and restorative justice.

The Seventh Edition was written to supply readers with an in-depth, timely volume that serves as a window into the US justice system as well as a frame of reference from which they can analyze and critique that system. Throughout each chapter, boxed material supplements or reinforces significant topics. Each chapter ends with an extensive summary, a list of key terms, 15–25 review questions, and a list of relevant websites. The glossary includes key terms used throughout the book, as well as terms commonly used in the study of law, courts, and justice. Boldfaced type alerts readers to the key terms in the text.

I am grateful for the confidence shown in this work by Publisher Neil Rowe. I would like to thank Jeni Ogilvie, an outstanding editor, for her work on this edition.

I welcome comments about this work and can be reached at
Criminal Justice & Legal Studies
St. John's University
8000 Utopia Parkway
Queens, NY 11439
abadinsh@stjohns.edu

PART I

Law

An Introduction to Law

This chapter will explore the meaning of law, the concept of natural law, and capitalism's need for rational law. We will examine two rational systems of law, the common/case law system used in the United States and countries with an English heritage, and the civil-law system used in the rest of the democratic world. We will examine American **codes** of procedure, and the variety of American law: statutory, administrative, and regulatory.

Law

The concept of law is ancient—references to written law date back to about 2400 before the Common Era (BCE) (Draper 1989). According to Richard Epstein (2005: 223), "Law (as a collective noun) is a set of rules that is enforced by the sovereign over some determinate territory. The sovereign is that person or those individuals who exercise the legitimate use of force within the system." According to Max Weber, laws are "norms which are directly guaranteed by legal coercion" (1967: 14). Conduct that violates a social norm may be impolite or perhaps eccentric, and it can cause the violator to be shunned by those who are aware of the norm-violative behavior. But behavior that violates the law draws punishment. According to Benjamin Cardozo (1924: 52), law "is a principle or rule of conduct so established as to justify a prediction with reasonable certainty that it will be enforced by the courts[1] if its authority is challenged."

"Some laws compel conduct while others serve to facilitate voluntary actions by providing guidelines for them" (Lou 1972: 24). Wallace Lou suggests, "It is useful to think of law as comprising a set of authoritative and prescriptive rules for conduct." While "some rules instruct persons in what they must or must not do (for example, 'pay your taxes'; 'do not segregate public school pupils on the basis of race'), others tell people how to do what they wish to do so that their actions are legally enforceable, that is, backed by the power of the state (for example, 'this is how to make a valid contract'; 'follow these steps in setting up a partnership')." There are also laws that create benefits, such as Social Security and Medicare, while others deal with the functions of bureaucratic entities such as a department of transportation responsible for building and maintaining public roads.

---

[1] The term "court" is derived from a time when the king in his court served as a judge. Medieval English judges acted as agents of the king, conducting their business in court (Rabkin 1989).

The Fugitive Slave Act 1850

"When a person held to service or labor in any State or Territory of the United States, has heretofore or shall hereafter escape into another State or Territory of the United States, the person or persons to whom such service or labor may be due . . . may pursue and reclaim such fugitive person."

As we have defined it, law is amoral—witness the laws of Nazi Germany[2] or the Fugitive Slave Act of the United States. The idea of morality in law is associated with the concept of natural law. Before there was law in the form of rules deliberately set forth by a human society—positive law—there was the "law of nature," or natural law.

Natural Law

In the body of law revealed to Moses on Mount Sinai—for example, thou shalt not steal, thou shalt not murder—we can find universal elements that more contemporary observers refer to as **natural law**. "The term designates a theory which holds that law necessarily has a moral basis and its criteria are grounded in something more than ordinary experience—'in nature.' Natural law accepts as viable the quest for an absolute ideal of justice" (Levy 1988: 3). At its core, natural law posits a belief that humans have an inborn notion of right and wrong and, therefore, the very essence of law does not rest on the arbitrary will of the ruler or on the decree of the multitude (Rommen 1998). Natural law, while not requiring a belief in a deity, refers to a higher law, primordial or law of nature[3]—in other words, rules for living that are binding on all human societies.

Natural law was expounded by Aristotle[4] (384–322 BCE) and the Greek Stoics[5] (circa 300 BCE). As derived from Aristotle and ancient philosophy, natural law doc-

---

Natural Law

"We hold these Truths to be self-evident, that all Men are created equal, that they are endowed by their Creator with certain inalienable Rights, that among these are Life, Liberty and the Pursuit of Happiness" (*Declaration of Independence*, July 4, 1776).

---

[2] See Heinrich A. Rommen (1897–1967), an opponent of the Hitler regime (for which he was imprisoned), for a critique of German legal positivism and his espousal of natural law: *The Natural Law: A Study in Legal and Social History and Philosophy* (1998).

[3] Richard Posner (1990) states that the term natural law is an anachronism—nature is amoral.

[4] That natural law could be invoked to defend both freedom and slavery has an early example in the apologetics of Aristotle.

[5] Stoicism, a philosophical movement that lasted about 500 years, emphasized the laws of nature and reason over emotion. Founded in Greece, stoicism flowered in Rome, where it was popularized by Cicero (106–43 BCE).

Natural Law

"Congress shall make no law . . . prohibiting the freedom of speech" (*US Constitution*, Amendment I).

Positive Law

The judge determined that Karlrobert Kreiten had indeed violated paragraph 91b of the German Criminal Code; he sentenced the defendant to death. Kreiten was subsequently executed—for making derogatory remarks to his friends about Hitler's regime (Müller 1991).

trines were united into a Christian framework by Thomas Aquinas (1225–1274). In his *Summa Theologica*, Aquinas asserts that if **positive law** (law derived out of the political process) violates natural law, it is not law but a corruption of law. According to many references in Church doctrine, natural law is rooted in human nature; divine law is written on the human heart (Fuchs 1965), the principles of which are known or at least knowable by anyone (Jos. Boyle 1992). In the language of the Declaration of Independence, natural law comprises truths which are self-evident—a moral consensus.

During the Middle Ages (from the fall of the Roman Empire to the Renaissance), the concept of natural law served the interests of the Church in its dealings with secular powers, and in the hands of the Papacy it was an impediment to the growth of nation-states (Aubert 1983). According to Church doctrine, the source of all natural law is divine and, thus, "the Church in her own Code emphatically refuses to recognize any legislation that contradicts the natural law" (Fuchs 1965: 8). An emerging middle class used the concept of natural law in efforts to counter the power of feudal nobility and later the divine right of the monarch in order "to preserve an area of individual freedom and initiative secure from interference by the state" (MacDonald 1961: 4). Natural law necessarily places limits on political power, and in England it was embodied in the common law (discussed later).

Out of the concept of natural law evolved the idea of natural rights, "certain qualities inherent in man and demonstrated by reason, which natural law exists to secure and to which positive [that is, man-made] law ought to give effect" (Pound

Natural Law in Colonial Virginia

"Now all acts of the legislature apparently contrary to natural right and justice, are, in our laws, and must be in the nature of things, considered void. The laws of nature are the laws of God, whose authority can be superseded by no power on earth. A legislature must not obstruct our obedience to him from whose punishments they cannot protect us. All human constitutions that contradict his laws, we are in conscience bound to disobey."

Source: George Mason's argument for plaintiffs in *Robin v. Hardaway*, found in Thomas Jefferson's *Virginia Reports* 109, 114 (1772). Mason, a wealthy Virginia landowner and delegate to the Constitutional Convention, opposed slavery and inspired the Bill of Rights.

Women According to "Natural Law"

"Civil law, as well as nature herself, has always recognized a wide difference in the respective spheres and destinies of man and woman. The paramount destiny and mission of woman are to fulfill the noble and benign offices of wife and mother. This is the law of the Creator" (*Bradwell v. Illinois* [1873]). The Supreme Court upheld the right of Illinois to deny Myra Bradwell admission to legal practice because of her gender.

1975: 15–16). Thus, natural law transcends all formal human constructs and any law contrary to the natural law is based on the coercive force of the state, not the voluntary compliance of the governed. According to the *Commentaries* of William Blackstone (1723–1780), any human law contrary to natural law has no validity. Positive law, even that approved by a majority of voters, cannot transform evil into justice (Rommen 1998). However, stalwarts of natural law often had no qualms averring that its protections did not apply to certain "nonpersons": Native Americans, blacks, women, and children. Natural law was used as a basis for denying women all political and many legal rights.

The natural law concepts of John Locke (1632–1704), according to which all men are by nature free, equal, and independent, and no one can be subjected to the political power of another without his own consent, were incorporated in the US Declaration of Independence: "all men are created equal" whose "governments are instituted among men, deriving their just powers from the consent of the governed." While Locke referred to the natural law right of "life, liberty, property," Thomas Jefferson enumerated the inalienable right to "life, liberty, and the pursuit of happiness." According to this view, the purpose of government was "largely to protect the natural rights retained by the people." And if "the government invaded these natural rights, the people could not only disobey, but resist and establish a new government as well" (Pohlman 1993: 10). By the middle of the eighteenth century, the legal commentators "had moved from thinking of natural law as a collection of moral abstractions to which conduct should conform, to the more particular assertion that natural law could be expressed in a body of legal precepts against which all positive law could then be measured" (Ferguson 1984: 62). Accordingly, natural law in the United States was expressed not in terms of the nature of man but, instead, in the nature of government, a government restrained by "the principles of natural constitutional law" (Pound 1975: 20) as exemplified by the **Bill of Rights**, the first ten amendments of the Constitution.

Natural law was so deeply embedded in the American psyche that even before the adoption of the Constitution, state judges engaged in **judicial review**, invalidating legislation and overturning convictions, not only on the basis of a conflict with a state constitution, but also on the basis of natural law. As the nation matured, the new federal courts joined state courts in using natural law to invalidate **statutes**, justifying and explaining their actions in the language of natural rights. "Court opinions spoke of such limits on legislation as 'natural rights,' 'inalienable rights,' 'inherent rights,' 'fundamental principles of civilized society,' and the 'immutable principles of jus-

Natural Law ⟶ Natural Rights ⟶ Constitution/Judicial Review

In the United States, the concept of natural law was transformed into something more practical: *natural rights*. The Constitution and judicial review are the instruments by which these rights are guaranteed.

tice.'" They also broadened the definition of natural rights, protecting not only property rights and the right to jury trial, but also the right of representation and rights against retroactive laws or laws granting special **privileges** (Sherry 1998: 16). "Many of the provisions of the Bill of Rights were clearly rooted in natural law thinking" (Atiyah and Summers 1987: 231).

In the United States, natural law was transferred into a secular document for ordering society, and the principles of natural law would be implemented through judicial review: "The judiciary would serve as an overseer to guard against unwarranted governmental usurpation" (Slotnick 1992: 7). "After all, if the Constitution was thought to mirror natural law and natural rights, a politically insulated judge exercising judicial review was not merely enforcing the people's will (i.e., the Constitution) against the popularly elected branch of government, but was also defending the natural order created by God" (Pohlman 1993: 11).

There is an inherent conflict between natural law, which restrains and limits human enactments, and positive law: human enactments resulting from the popular consent of individuals who form themselves into a sovereign people. According to Locke (1952), the people may delegate lawmaking to a governmental agency (legislature), one that is limited to those ends authorized by the people. Natural law, however, limits the ends that the people may authorize. "If legislatures should act beyond or against such ends, even with popular consent, their acts would not be valid. Thus, the laws that must be established by positive human authorities are in turn limited by natural law" (Smith 1985: 68). Natural law stands as a bulwark against totalitarianism, even that brought about by democratic means or the popular will (e.g., Fascist Italy and Nazi Germany). The natural law doctrines limiting the power of government prepared the way for the institution of judicial review (Smith 1985; Sigmund 1971).

Although it may be constrained by natural law, if a society is to advance into a more complex structure, rational law must prevail.

Legal Positivism and Totalitarianism

The nationalist form of totalitarianism arose and flourished in the two countries—Germany and Italy—where legal **positivism** had obtained a dominant position in the universities and the legal profession. Legal positivism conditioned an outlook of unqualified acceptance of the mythical *will of the state*—the state can do anything—as the controlling philosophy of law (Rommen 1998).

Rational Law

Envision a system of law whose judges are scrupulously honest and fair, whose decisions are based on the particular circumstances of each case. Max Weber (1967) refers to this as an irrational legal system—**irrational law**. In contrast to a rational legal order—**rational law**, which is *the application of general norms to specific cases*—an irrational legal system is characterized by case-by-case decisions without recourse to generalized principles of law but, rather, according to what is deemed morally correct in each case. Such a system results in the liberties and fortunes of citizens "left at the mercy of each judge's personal sense of what procedures are fair, what outcome is just, who needs protection, and who deserves compassion" (Glendon 1994: 164). In such a system, since every dispute involves unique facts and parties, it would be difficult to predict the outcome of a given case. Thus, persons and businesses would be unable to adjust their behavior in order to avoid becoming embroiled in legal disputes (Beckerman-Rodau 1999).

Under an irrational legal system a modern capitalist economy cannot develop, "for modern rational capitalism has need, not only of the technical means of production, but of a calculable legal system and of administration in terms of formal rules" (Weber 1958: 25). Modern rational capitalism requires a legal order that is both prompt and predictable, one that is calculable in accordance with rational rules and guaranteed by the strongest coercive power. Weber notes that the development of capitalism occurs under rational legal orders wherein contractual obligations will be enforced between not only the primary parties but also their agents:

> Every rational business organization needs the possibility, for particular cases as well as for general purposes, of acquiring contractual rights and of assuming obligations through agents. Advanced trade, moreover, needs not only the possibility of transferring legal claims but also, and quite particularly, a method by which transfers can be made legally secure and which eliminates the need of constantly testing the title of the transfer. (Weber 1967: 122)

Without such guarantees, an economy must remain on the primitive level of barter or under control of the state.[6] Countries of Eastern Europe and the former Soviet Union are struggling with commercial law that has long been a staple of business relations in the West.

The rational-law systems governing Western nations proceed from five postulates (Weber 1967):

1. Every legal decision involves the application of an abstract legal proposition to a concrete factual set of circumstances.

2. Every concrete case can be decided on the basis of abstract legal propositions derived by means of legal logic.

3. The law constitutes a gapless system of legal propositions, one that can deal with any and all possible concrete cases. In other words, there are no gaps in the legal system that render certain disputes outside the pale of law.

---

[6] John Noonan, Jr. (1976) states that a modern legal system in America also made bearable the institution of slavery. The legal process depersonalized participants to such an extraordinary degree that it was possible to deal with slaves using legal principles and processes that applied to the sale, transfer, and inheritance of property. For a similar rendition of the legal system in Nazi Germany, see Müller (1991).

> **Rational Law**
>
> Rational law involves the application of general principles to specific facts (cases).

4. Every social action of human beings is construed either as an application or a carrying out of legal propositions or as an infringement thereof.

5. Whatever cannot be decided legally in rational terms is legally irrelevant.

In sum, a system of modern or rational law involves the application of general principles to specific facts (cases).

The legal philosopher John Rawls asks what makes a particular case "rational"? The answer, he offers "is that a judgment in a particular case is evidenced to be rational by showing that, given the facts and the conflicting interests of the case, the judgment is capable of being explicated by justifiable principle (or set of principles)" (1999: 10). These principles are encompassed in the two basic systems of Western society for implementing a system rational law.

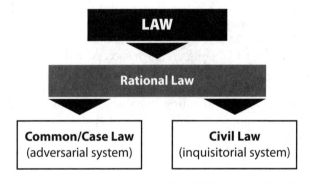

Figure 1.1   Implementing Rational Law

Common/Case Law

England's rational system of law is based on judicial law finding. Prior to the Norman conquest in 1066,[7] principles applied in local Anglo-Saxon courts (fifth to eleventh centuries) broadly reflected the customs of local communities as declared by their freemen or judges. In 1086, William I ("The Conqueror") sent commissioners throughout the realm to record (in *Dooms* or *Domesday Books*—"doom" refers to law/judg-

---

[7] The original Normans were Vikings—Norsemen—who had settled in France and from whom Normandy derives its name. By the time of the Norman conquest, the early Norsemen had integrated with the native Gaulish population, had become Christians, and lost most of their Nordic character. They were well versed in Roman law, a source of the Latin words in common law (Zane 1998).

ment) the names of towns and the number of persons, cattle, and houses, as well as the customs and norms of the population. The Norman kings gradually wielded these local customs into a single body of general principles—**common law**, referring to their application throughout the realm. A legislative body—parliament—would not emerge for several centuries, and royal edicts did not extend to many of the legal issues confronting judges. Thus, in applying these general principles, judges relied on previous judgments given in similar cases, a procedure that generated the doctrine of judicial precedent and **case law** (Tarr 2014). Toward the end of the thirteenth century, arguments of the barristers (trial lawyers) and the rulings of the judges were written down and circulated. These documents became the forerunners of the published *Law Reports* that are the basis for common law,[8] which was revolutionized with the advent of the printing press in the middle of the fifteenth century.[9]

"The common law of England evolved from spontaneously observed rules and practices, shaped and formalised by decisions made by judges pronouncing the law in relation to the particular facts before them" (Central Office of Information 1976: 4). The controlling element is **precedent**: "When a group of facts come before an English Court of adjudication," observed Henry Maine, "it is taken absolutely for granted that there is somewhere a rule of known law which will cover the facts of the dispute now litigated, and that, if such a rule be not discovered, it is only because the necessary patience, knowledge or acumen is not forthcoming to detect it" (1861: 24). If the circumstances of a particular case are unique, the common law resorts to reasoning by analogy from previous cases. The foundation of English common law is judicial decisions handed down from the earliest time to the present, each successive decision being founded on some preceding adjudication or a new application of a judicial principle already established. "The genius of the common law is that it proceeds empirically and gradually, testing the ground at every step, and refusing, or at any rate evincing an extreme reluctance, to embrace broad theoretical principles" (Aldisert 1997: 8). Because common law does not resort to written codes, it is sometimes referred to as "unwritten law" (Abraham 1998).

Basic to understanding common law is the notion that a judicial decision serves a dual function:

> First, it settles the controversy, that is, under the doctrine of *res judicata* [final conclusive judgment] the parties may not relitigate issues that have been decided. Second, in the common-law system, under the doctrine of *stare decisis*, the judicial decision also has precedential value. The doctrine, from *stare decisis et non quieta movere*, "stand by the decision and do not disturb what is settled," is rooted in the common-law policy that a principle of law deduced from a judicial decision will be considered and applied in the determination of future similar cases. [This doctrine]

---

[8] "If the modern layman is bewildered by the language of the legal profession, he can blame William the Conqueror for his confusion, for the Norman Conquest made French the language of the royal household and the language of the royal courts. Anglo-French, or 'law French,' was used in pleading in the English courts, and the lawyer was forced to learn it as a second language. He had to learn Latin as well, for Latin was the language employed in the Middle Ages for formal written records. Anglo-French was a dialect from which the English legal profession first developed a precise vocabulary for the expression of legal concepts" (Hogue 1966: 7). Words such as plaintiff, defendant, *voir dire, en banc*, and *demurrer* are of French origin; *certiorari, subpoena, mens rea, actus reus, mandamus*, and *pro se* are Latin (Schubert 2012).

[9] There is also an Islamic influence in English law via the Crusades and the conquest of Jerusalem in 1099 (Glenn 2010).

refers to the likelihood that a similar or like case arising in the future will be decided in the same way. (Re 1975a: 2; emphasis added)

"The principle of *stare decisis* therefore creates a chain of cases, in which each decision is an interpretation of immediately prior decisions" (Post 1995: 32). Decisions rendered in prior cases enable those trained in law to predict the likely outcome of a legal dispute and thereby enable their clients to avoid the expense of litigation.

However, the common law was not a "gapless system" capable of resolving all concrete cases. Common-law remedies were confined almost entirely to money damages, and the procedures became increasingly complex and inflexible. By about 1300, the common law had become so encumbered with artificial restrictions it was incapable of doing justice in a large number of legal issues, many of them of ordinary occurrence (Zane 1998). As a result, an alternative system of law—equity—developed alongside common-law courts; parallel systems of law.

Equity

The concept of **equity** expresses a concern for fairness that can be found in the Bible: "And thou shalt do that which is right and good in the sight of the Lord" (Deuteronomy VI: 18). Thus, it is not enough to "do that which is *right*," to act in accord with the letter of the law; one must also act fairly—do that which is *"good* in the sight of the Lord." The Hebrew concept of *yosher* is based on this biblical imperative, according to which an individual must act beyond the mere rule of law (*din*) whenever the latter involves harshness or causes hardship (see Kirschenbaum [1991] for a discussion of this issue). As a system for correcting imperfections of positive law, equity is traced to Aristotle, who viewed equity as the application of natural law (Rommen 1998).

In more contemporary times the issue still remains: Should a rule be applied mechanically, no matter how outlandish or unfair the outcome, an approach advocated by Immanuel Kant (1949)—positive law devoid of natural law restraints—or should there be room for ensuring a fair and reasonable outcome? While common law has been associated with rules, the nondiscretionary application of particular precepts (*formalism*), equity has been associated with the more flexible *reasonable standard* (*situationism*) component of law that has its own problems inherent in the exercise of **discretion**. "Standards have the disadvantage of making it harder to predict the outcome of a legal dispute—there are more variables, which makes litigation more likely and also makes it harder for people to plan and to conduct their affairs" (Posner 1990: 45). "Most commonly, an equitable standard exists to counterbalance an overly harsh rule"[10] (Kelman 1987: 48).

"Equity," from the Latin *aequitas*, meaning equality or justice, is an Aristotelian idea (discussed in his best-known work on ethics, *Nichomachean Ethics*) found in the Roman concept of natural law as set forth by Cicero and discussed earlier. It referred to fairness or equality of treatment between Roman citizens and foreigners in matters before the praetor, a powerful legal official in pre-Justinian Rome (Maine 1861). The Roman concept appears to have influenced English custom, particularly the practice of asking the king to intercede in the name of justice—for equitable relief—on behalf of

---

[10] Known in law as **estoppel** (a term derived from French) doctrines.

a petitioner. "English judges have throughout history shown anxiety lest the effect of legal prohibitions should be weakened by equitable modifications designed to show mercy or compassion (or even justice) to those who committed prohibited acts in exceptional situations of stress or ignorance or lack of cognitive understanding" (Atiyah and Summers 1987: 38)—the dilemma exemplified in Melville's *Billy Budd* (1961).

In the early days of English common law, **litigants** were refused a hearing if their suits could not be settled by a narrowly drawn **writ** or order. Petitioners who argued that they could not find justice in common-law courts often begged the king to follow his conscience, rather than cause the petitioner to suffer because of the technicalities of common-law procedures. Medieval kings were warrior princes with little time or patience for such matters; they typically referred **petitions** to the chancellor, a combination executive secretary and chief of staff (Hoffer 1998). In time, petitioners went directly to the chancellor, the "keeper of the king's conscience," for relief. From this practice emerged chancery court or courts of equity. John Zane (1998: 235) declared this dualism absurd: "One system enforced in many legal relations rules which the other system pronounced unjust and unrighteous, and boldly set at naught."

The chancellor, usually an educated clergyman with a staff of scribes, was in a unique position to provide relief for petitioners who could not gain swift justice in common-law courts, which could proclaim duties and rights but could not compel any kind of action other than the payment of money. Equity, on the other hand, had a plethora of remedies. For example, the **injunction** could be used to command a person to do some specific act or to refrain from something he or she might be doing or planning to do. Injunctions were enforced by the chancellor's power to declare someone in "contempt" for which he could order summary imprisonment. Henry Abraham notes that equity "begins where law ends; it supplies justice in circumstances not covered by law" (foreword to McDowell 1982: xii). While the common law provides for money damages, it cannot easily deal with nonmonetary issues such as divorce, administration of estates (trusts), civil rights, and labor disputes. Equity, however, has power over persons, *in personam* jurisdiction (but not over things, *in rem* jurisdiction). The injunction is an order addressed personally to the defendant. For example, while equity could not force a transfer of land, it could jail for contempt the party that refused to make such a transfer (Friedman 1973). Under equity, a judge can require **specific performance**; for example, where damages would be inappropriate or inadequate, a judge can compel the fulfillment of terms of a **contract**. This court is characterized by flexibility and humane realism: "The chancellor peers behind the formalities to seek the real extent of harm" and retains jurisdiction over the case until satisfied with its resolution (Hoffer 1990: 8).[11]

Because the chancellor was empowered to settle controversies on the basis of general notions of fairness—equity—his decisions were often contrary to one of the principles of a rational system of law, the application of abstract legal propositions to concrete cases. The outcome of any dispute became difficult to calculate and predict with any certainty. Toward the end of the sixteenth century, however, the chancellor's decisions were published, and he began to follow the common-law practice of prece-

---

[11] Many of the modern rules of "discovery" are taken directly from the procedures of equity—rules that promote fairness (Hoffer 1998).

Equity

"The term 'equity' refers to a set of rights, remedies, and procedures available ostensibly to ameliorate defects of the common law" (Collins 2010: 267).

dent—in equity, called *maxims*—when rendering decisions. As the role of the chancellor became more judicial, it evolved into a separate court of chancery and, by the eighteenth century, had become similar to common law with decisions formed into technical rules (Zweigert and Kötz 1998). While equity began as an extraordinary intervention against the rigors of the common law, successive chancellors decided "disputes referred to them by consulting the records in order to see how such a question had been dealt with on previous occasions" (Archer 1956: 39). By the 1800s, the High Court of Chancery had become as complex and inflexible as common-law courts, and in 1875 it was dismantled by Parliament (Quillen and Hanrahan 1993).

Equity in America

The American colonists had a philosophical prejudice against royal prerogatives with which chancery courts were associated. Although many colonies had courts of equity, after the Revolution most states abandoned chancery courts and consolidated court jurisdiction so that the same judges would sit in (common) law and equity. An important exception is Delaware that, although it did not have a chancery court before the Revolution, established one in 1792 (Quillen and Hanrahan 1993). As will be discussed later, this proved fortuitous to corporate America.

When rendering decisions judges are aware of the need for continuity and stability; the law must remain certain and predictable. Thus, the paradox:

> This demand for certainty, of course, runs counter to a demand for some flexibility, that the law be accommodated to changed conditions. Thus, when applied to new situations, the law should produce fair results yet still serve its original social purpose. Judges, being sensitive to these apparently contradictory demands and owing fidelity to the institutions of a well-ordered legal system, do not lightly disregard precedents, even though in theory they are free to do so. (Yiannopoulos 1974: 75)

Equity Courts in Tennessee

The Tennessee secretary of state describes the state's chancery court as based on the English system in which the chancellor acted as the king's conscience: "This is still fundamentally the court's role in modern time. Equity is the power to apply moral standards of justice in a given case by allowing the Chancellor the discretion to modify or soften the application of strict rules and thereby adapt or gear the relief in light of the circumstances of the particular case" (cited in Smith 1993a).

Common Law or Equity?

The Constitution (Article III, Section 2) provides that a federal judiciary has power over cases arising in law and equity, and in most states, judges were similarly empowered to hear cases both of law and equity. The *Federal Rules of Civil Procedure*, adopted in 1938, empowers judges to provide a **plaintiff** in a single action with monetary damages (*in rem*) and order the defendant to comply with the law (*in personam*), a merger of law and equity. The Constitution "guarantees the right to a jury trial in all cases that would have been tried in law courts at the time of the Revolution, but not in cases that would have been tried in equity courts at that time" (Neely 1985: 38). Since England did not provide for jury trials in cases of equity, there is no constitutional right to a jury trial in equity cases in the United States, although some states (e.g., Texas and Georgia) provide for such juries, and in some equity cases a judge can order a jury trial limited to specific factual issues. "The presence of a jury can make a significant difference in the way a trial is conducted. For example, evidence rules are more strictly observed in jury trials than in bench trials, and the mode of argumentation will differ somewhat depending on whether the decision-maker is a judge or a jury" (Sward 2003: 358–59). Modern interpretations of constitutional provisions have broadened the right to a jury trial, except when the **remedy** sought is an injunction—equitable relief (Hazard and Taruffo 1993).[12]

In 1988, a group of teamsters brought suit against their union, alleging a breach of **fiduciary** duty (obligation to act for the benefit of others). The Supreme Court had to decide if the case were one of equity or common law; if it were a case of equity, the plaintiffs would not be entitled to a jury trial. Cases involving fiduciary duty are equity determinations. However, the litigants were asking for monetary damages, and money remedies are relegated to common law. The Court has interpreted the language of the Seventh Amendment, which guarantees a jury trial in cases of common law, as requiring historical analysis to "see whether it is the type of case that would have gone before an English jury at the time the Seventh Amendment was adopted" (Greenhouse 1990: 13). However, collective bargaining was unlawful in eighteenth-century England, and the justices were unable to agree on a majority **opinion**, although by a vote of 6–3 they ruled that the litigants were entitled to a jury trial (*Chauffeurs, Teamsters, and Helpers v. Terry* [1990]).

In most states and in the federal system, a judge can make an equity determination "in good conscience," such as granting a restraining order or injunction to prevent further or future harm to the plaintiff. The court may grant a temporary injunction where injury is imminent or continuing, the merits of the case to be determined subsequently at trial. Equity is uniquely suited to deal with matters of corporate law since the outcome is in the hands of experienced judges, rather than jurors who may have difficulty understanding the complex issues typically being litigated.

Some states (e.g., Illinois and Tennessee) have a separate chancery court/division; in Delaware, there is a court of chancery that has historically provided a speedy and clear resolution for corporate litigation, thus attracting major corporations. Almost

---

[12] Other types of litigation not using juries include admiralty (cases arising out of maritime activities), bankruptcy, and family (custody and divorce) matters.

Formalism	v.	**Equity**
rules		standards
legal imperative		good faith
ministerial		discretionary
predictable		uncertain
determinate		indeterminate
inflexible		arbitrary

Formalism is an effort to constrain judgments in advance by reference to a rule of law that advances predictability. As discretion, flexibility and the rule of man (represented by equity) increase, equal treatment and the rule of law (represented by formalism) decrease—a zero sum outcome (Sunstein 1996). The formalist judge is indifferent to the consequences of his or her interpretations—should they be untoward, the role of changing the law is the responsibility of the executive and legislative branches (Posner 2013).

half of the Fortune 500 corporations are incorporated in Delaware, and for jurisdictional purposes a corporation and its stockholders are considered a "citizen" of the state in which it is incorporated, giving the Court of Chancery an importance beyond the borders of the nation's second smallest state (Henriques 1995). Indeed, Delaware's size permits equity to be efficiently managed in a single centralized court. [13]

Corporate takeovers and disputes involving management and stockholders are routinely adjudicated by the Delaware Court of Chancery, whose five members (a chancellor and four vice chancellors) are appointed by the governor for 12-year terms (Grunson 1986). In addition to the injunction, equity is often used in cases of stockholders' derivative suits: "A stockholder brings a derivative suit on behalf of the corporation, not to redress a wrong done him individually, but to obtain recovery or relief in favor of the corporation for all similar stockholders and to compensate the corporation as a collective entity for some wrong done to it by management" (Neely 1985: 39–40). Typically, in such actions, a group of stockholders seeks to enjoin the corporate directors from certain actions such as selling off assets. Corporate directors have a fiduciary responsibility to the corporation, and as trustees—persons obligated to act for the benefit of others—they can be held accountable in equity.[14] "The court is so highly specialized and its decisions so scholarly that corporations' legal counsels refer to Delaware rulings to order their companies' actions to avoid litigation" (Milford 2001: 38).

Toward the end of the nineteenth century, the injunction was frequently used to enjoin strikes, a practice that continued until federal legislation favorable to labor unions was enacted during the New Deal era of the 1930s. Since the 1960s, the courts have used their equity powers to impose themselves in broad policy areas (e.g., they have reorganized the management of mental institutions and welfare agencies, and

---

[13] There are more than 160,000 corporations registered in Delaware that pay the state millions in fees and taxes.

[14] In corporate matters, in the absence of any federal statute or policy to the contrary, the federal courts typically defer to state law (Greenhouse 1991a).

Common Law and Civil Law

"The two most widespread legal systems are the common-law systems, in use in most English-speaking countries, and the civil-law systems, in use in Continental Europe and the many countries around the world influenced by Continental Europe, from Japan to most of Africa and all of Latin America" (Elsing and Townsend 2002: 1).

---

for several years courts presided over the operation of the Alabama prison system and Boston public schools in order to remedy violations of constitutional rights). Equity was used by the Supreme Court in *Brown v. Board of Education* (1954), marking the beginning of the end of *de jure* segregation in the United States.

In contrast to the common/case-law system used in the United States are the civil-law systems of Continental Europe.

Civil-Law Systems

Systems of **civil law** use a detailed enumeration of rules and regulations, typically (but not necessarily) a code that provides the basis for settling all possible disputes. While common law and equity are products of English history and tradition, other European nations (such as France and Germany)[15] use civil law and have comprehensive codes that supersede earlier law—precedent is absent as a legal concept.

The use of civil law (as distinguished from ecclesiastical or canon law) can be traced to Hammurabi, king of Babylonia, 1792–1750 BCE In a quest for legal uniformity throughout his vast realm, Hammurabi authored a code inscribed on a block of diorite nearly eight feet high and about five feet in circumference. It had 8,000 Semitic words, equivalent to about 20,000 English words, comprising 282 clauses dealing with all aspects of Babylonian life, including rents, slavery, marriage and divorce, trade and commerce, adoption, wages, and criminal law (Harper 1904). Punishments were typically harsh, and the law of damages was based on "an eye for an eye." It was not, however, a systematic attempt to cover all possible situations (Draper 1989; Sinha 1990). Many Babylonian laws, especially those dealing with commerce, passed to Palestine and Syria and to Asia Minor and its Greek cities, then to Greece itself where it formed the basis for the commercial code of Athens (Zane 1998).

Draco (circa 621 BCE) authored Athens' first written code of law, whose punishments were so severe that the word "draconian" (derived from Draco) means an unreasonably harsh law. This code was refined by Solon (638–558 BCE), and the courts became more accessible to the citizens of Athens. According to an ancient tradition, a commission from Rome traveled to Athens to study the laws of Solon from which they drafted the Twelve Tables (circa 450 BCE), a code written on wood and bronze tablets that for several hundred years was the basic law of Rome (Kelly 1993). Although comprehensive, like any code, the Twelve Tables could not fit every situation. In fact, "any-

---

[15] Modern civil-code systems can be divided into the French family and the German family, both influenced by Roman law (Glenn 2010).

thing in the nature of a formal code, rigidly interpreted, cannot fully meet the needs of present justice, and without elasticity of application, it cannot afford adequate guidance for the future" (Edmunds 1959: 147–48). This was recognized by the Romans, whose college of pontifices (priests) provided the expert interpretive process enabling the law to meet the changing needs of Roman society (Kunkel 1972).

The most important legacy of Roman law was the compilations of Justinian (van Caenegem 1994). After the Roman Empire became permanently divided, the Emperor Justinian I, reigning in Constantinople (present-day Istanbul) from 527 to 562 CE, appointed a team of scholars to systematize Roman law, which had grown heavy with commentaries and treatises written by legal scholars (jurisconsults): The published commentaries of the jurisconsults were a collection of answers, decisions, or rules derived from particular cases (Zane 1998). Justinian "sought both to abolish the authority of all but the greatest of the jurisconsults of the classical period and to make it unnecessary for any more commentaries or treatises to be written" (Merryman and Pérez-Pedomo 2007: 7). When the resulting *Digest, Corpus Juris Civilis* or Code of Justinian, was published in 533, the emperor forbade any further reference to the works of the jurisconsults as well any commentaries on the *Corpus Juris Civilis* itself, which to all appearances was honored mainly in the breach. Law always needs explaining, and legal scholars of the sixth century in fact produced abundant commentaries on the code even during Justinian's lifetime (McNamee 1998). With the fall of the Eastern Empire in 1453, the Code of Justinian was relegated to relative obscurity, although much of it was adopted by the Roman Catholic Church and the Holy Roman Empire, roughly Germany and Austria in the years 962–1806 (van Caenegem 1994). Both Roman and canon law were ill suited to deal with issues of commerce,[16] "so from the twelfth to the fifteenth centuries, a customary and cosmopolitan commercial law was developed in practice. It was dictated essentially by the needs of commerce and efficacy in commodity and money markets, in trade fairs, corporations, banking operations and means of insurance and credit" (van Caenegem 1994: 83). The commercial law that developed out of the activities of guilds and maritime cities became international in character, extending throughout the commercial world, even into areas such as England where the Roman civil-law system had met with resistance. This private commercial law of Europe was later adopted by the nation-states and eventually incorporated into the commercial codes established throughout the civil-law world in the eighteenth and nineteenth centuries (Merryman and Pérez-Pedomo 2007).

Renewed interest in the study of Roman law emerged during the twelfth and thirteenth centuries at universities, most notably in Italy and France, but until the French Revolution Roman law was largely in the form of a body of academic text and commentary rather than a set of statutory enactments. Nevertheless, "Roman law increasingly affected legal life and practice in Europe in general," providing authorities "solid compelling arguments for reinforcing state power against feudal fragmentation" (van Caenegem 1994: 67; 73; Zane 1998). In Spain, *Las Siete Partidas*, a legal code that was apparently influenced by the Code of Justinian, was extended to Spanish colonies. It became part of the law in colonial Louisiana, remained in force in Texas until 1840, and operated for a decade later in California (Edmunds 1959).

---

[16] Indeed, based on *Exodus* 22: 24 and *Leviticus* 25: 36–37, canon law prohibits the charging of interest.

The idea of a code reemerged during the Enlightenment period of the eighteenth century. With philosophical attachment to the law of nature, universal or natural law, Enlightenment scholars argued that the disorderly and patchy historical growth of law could be reworked into a comprehensible form through deliberate and planned legislation based on a rational system. The law should "be stated in the vernacular, not Latin, and be phrased in clear and ordinary language, so that citizens could consult the code and perfectly understand their rights and obligations, without having to go to lawyers and judges. The codes needed to be organized logically so that people could readily find the relevant laws" (Tiersma 2011: 270).

To implement such an idea, however, required the powerful political impetus of the French Revolution and the authority and decisiveness of Napoleon—a soldier, not a lawyer. Beginning in 1804,[17] the emperor devoted himself to that task, constantly focusing the attention of the lawyers he appointed to the *Conseil d'Etat*, "on the realities of life rather than the technicalities of law; he immediately saw the practical relevance of abstract rules; he put an abrupt end to any hairsplitting discussions, and by clear and simple questions kept bringing the discussion back to the practical and concrete; above all, he insisted on a style of drafting which was transparently clear and comprehensible to a non-lawyer like himself" (Zweigert and Kötz 1987: 195). The resulting code applied civil law to the entire country.

Napoleon's ideas are similar to the idea of those who today propose a "plain English" legal system for the United States.[18] In his egalitarian zeal, Napoleon wanted laws so clear even the peasant with limited education could understand them—the code avoids legal jargon—and there would be no need for lawyers. Civil-law judges were to apply the provisions of the code literally to cases that came before them. "At the beginning of his Civil Code, Napoleon put in a provision forbidding judges from laying down any general rule of law" (Edmunds 1959: 181). Prerevolutionary (*ancien régime*) judges were creatures of the crown, and revolutionary France sought to divide sharply legislative and judicial functions (Baudouin 1974), while putting in place a system that did not promote judicial independence: "Given the ancient régime, nobody wants a 'gouvernement des juges,' so the primacy of codes, and legislation in general, is reinforced by ongoing skepticism towards, and even surveillance of (through control of the career structure [discussed later]) the civilian judiciary" (Glenn 2000: 134). Napoleonic doctrine is antagonistic toward judges, and judicial discretion.

But the Napoleonic Code was never a complete and exhaustive body of statutory law, and during the nearly 200 years of its existence, judges and legislators have adjusted the rules of the code in line with changing economic and social conditions. "The task of the court in this had been made easier because . . . the principles of Code Civil are often unclear and deliberately designed to require completion, the concepts used are frequently indefinite and ambiguous, many individual rules are incomplete,

---

[17] The *Code Civil des Frances* was proclaimed on March 21, 1804. In 1807, the title was changed to *Code Napoléon*, but the original title was restored in 1816 with the fall of the Napoleonic regime. Napoleon III (1852–1870) restored the reference to Napoleon (Weber 1967).

[18] In 1999, Latin legalisms were barred from English civil courts: *in camera* is now "in private," a *subpoena* is a "witness **summons**," and an *interrogatory* is a "request for information." California adopted plain English for criminal jury instructions: "innocent misrecollection" is now honestly forgot, while "willfully false" is simply lied (Murphy 2005).

and the systematic interplay of different provisions is often faulty" (Zweigert and Kötz 1998: 95). In fact, the Napoleonic Code expresses only broad general principles laid down in simple terms. When a judge finds no positive rule in the code on an issue of law before the court, the judge uses principles of equity in reaching a decision (Rommen 1998).

The legislature's failure to keep the codes up to date encouraged judges to rely on their own authority to extend provisions in new situations, while lawyers learned to search for relevant precedents and use them in their arguments (Provine 1996). Nevertheless, the utility of the code has been proven by its continued existence as basic law in France.

In civil-law systems "legislation is considered the one and only authoritative source of law to which all others, including case law, are subordinated" (Baudouin 1974: 7). Civil law is the product of legal scholarship. It is the legal scholar who "molds the civil-law tradition and the formal materials of the law into a model of the legal system. He teaches this model to law students and writes about it in books and articles (jurisprudence). Legislators and judges accept his idea of what the law is, and, when they make or apply law, they use concepts he has developed. Thus, although legal scholarship is not a formal source of law, the doctrine carries immense authority" (Merryman 1985: 60). Indeed, French judges "often cite academic authority to explain their decisions" (Provine 1996: 201). Thus, in civil-law systems it is the text of the law rather than prior judicial interpretation of that text that is authoritative. Although prior judicial decisions may be consulted for their persuasive effect, they are not binding (Scalia 1997). Indeed, in France judges never cite a previous judicial decision as the basis for their judgment (Elliott, Jeanpierre, and Vernon 2006).

The function of the judge is to discover the applicable provisions of the code and apply them to cases under consideration *without discretion* (Murphy and Pritchett 1986; Damâska 1986). Martin Shapiro notes that in practice, however, no civil system is so complete as to make unnecessary judicial discretion: "A code law judge would be almost completely bound by preexisting rules if his code were complete, consistent, specific, produced by a single authoritative legislator, and capable of rapid amendment by that legislator to meet changing circumstances. No code can fully meet these conditions" (1981: 26). A "purely deductive method in which decisions are explained merely by citing some code provision may seem to be simple, but it disguises the real choices that are inevitably involved" (Dawson 1961: 26).

> Although the legislature tries to provide a clear, systematic legislative response for every problem that may arise, legislative practice falls far short of that objective. As a result, judges have a lot of interpreting to do. They frequently find themselves confronted by problems in which the only applicable legislation is so general as to be useless, is unclear or contradictory in application, or is obviously the product of a legislature that did not foresee the problem now facing the judge. (Merryman 1985: 82–83)

In this respect, civil law and common law are similar.

Differences between common law and civil law, Martin Shapiro argues, are often overdrawn. He observes that while the Continental judge "purports to be drawing a series of definitions, doctrines, and conclusions from the code by logical exegesis, in reality he is acknowledging the body of legal doctrines built up around the bare words of the code by previous cases" (1981: 135). Thus, while the civil-law judge may avoid citing previous cases, other judges and lawyers are able to discern which prior cases are being followed, and some decisions will contain references to prior cases. While the importance of *stare decisis* is not given official recognition in civil-law countries, there are hundreds of volumes of published decisions, and Continental lawyers frequently cite them when presenting their arguments in court. But, as in France, there is no system of binding precedent in (Elliott, Jeanpierre, and Vernon 2006).

However, civil courts do not defer to the authority of precedent established by a single case. If precedent is to command a particular outcome, it must be consistent with contemporary standards, not contradict legislation, and entail a continuous line of decisions that create a form of judicial custom or customary law (Baudouin 1974). Decisions of high courts are "not treated as exemplars of how a life situation had been resolved in the past so that the case *sub judice* [before the court] could be matched with these exemplars of earlier decision making" (Damâska 1986: 33). Unlike the common-law judge who has been trained to find law in cases, the civil-law judge is trained to look first at legislation in order to find answers to issues before the court.

> Only if he cannot find a clear-cut answer in the code itself will he then try to deduce one from the broad general principles underlying the basic code rules. Cases will be used only to reinforce his arguments or as illustrations of what other judges have done in analogous situations. In other words, precedent [better expressed as legal custom] may enter only at the end of the second phase of his intellectual process. (Baudouin 1974: 15)

If legislators note that the court has applied a statute in a way they did not intend, they can change the law (Sweet 2007).

Many civil-law countries, however, have adopted constitutions that limit the power of the legislative branch to amend laws by ordinary legislative action and, accordingly, impose some form of judicial review by which a constitutional court can declare a statute void because it conflicts with a constitutional provision (Merryman and Pérez-Pedomo 2007; Volcansek 1996). France has a Constitutional Council—part of the legislative branch—"which reviews legislation before promulgation for adherence to legal and constitutional requirements" (Provine 1996: 179). Germany has a Federal Constitutional Court, whose members are elected by the legislature (*Bundestag*), with sweeping powers of judicial review (Kommers and Miller 2012). Judicial review in Continental Europe, notes Mary Volcansek (1996), is a reaction to the Fascist/Nazi experience that gave unbridled power to the legislative branch. After World War II, "many nations installed constitutional review by courts as one safeguard against oppressive government and stirred-up majorities" (Ginsburg 2012: xi). In rendering decisions, European constitutional courts generate case law that precedential value (Sweet 2007).

Legislative Supremacy

Many civil-law countries have adopted constitutions that limit legislative power.

Danger of Legislative Supremacy

After the Second World War, Nazi judges claimed that they "were merely following the laws [of Hitler's Germany] and that, after all, this was how they had been trained by their democratic professors during the Weimar Republic" (Müller 1991: 220). They enforced laws that created a definition of who was a Jew so they could be deprived of their property and eventually their lives. French lawyers under German occupation performed similar roles; they even wrote briefs to determine if particular individuals could, under Nazi legislation, be defined as a Jew—and thus imprisoned (Weisberg 1997).

> *A great deal of the difference between common-law and civil-law systems can be explained by the role of judges and how they are chosen.*

Judges in Civil-Law Countries and in the United States

In civil-law countries, there is a long history dating back to the seventeenth century of judicial officers being career bureaucrats (Damâska 1986): Civil-law judges "do not differ fundamentally from the state bureaucracy, and reflect the old division of law from politics. Judicial legitimacy rests on technical legal knowledge, and the traditional assumption that judges (like civil servants) simply apply preexisting rules without interfering in the prerogatives of the political branches" (Guamieri 2004: 170).

Continental judges opt for a judicial career early in life, receive specialized education and training for the position, and are appointed by the state after passing the necessary examinations (Zweigert and Kötz 1998). "Students decide to become judges at the end of their professional training, and, if their grades are high enough, immediately enter into a largely anonymous civil service in which promotion is dependent upon a mixture of seniority and professional skill in interpreting the relevant codes" (Murphy and Pritchett 1986: 11).

Whereas judges in the United States are typically drawn from the ranks of practicing attorneys, in a civil-law country judges are specialists, and the largest proportion are recruited directly from law school without professional experience, but they must pass an exam promulgated by the ministry of justice (Guamieri 2004). In France, for example, on completing law school, aspiring judges take a competitive examination to qualify for a special school, *Ecolé Nationale de la Magistrature*, which they attend for at least 28 months and receive a government salary (Abraham 1998). In Germany, candidates must complete law school, two years of practical training, pass two government examinations, and serve as temporary civil servants for which they receive a small salary. The entire process lasts about 10 years, and relatively few succeed. More recently, in many European civil-law countries lateral entry into the judiciary has been opened to experienced lawyers (Guamieri 2004).

The opinions they render are unsigned and there is typically an absence of dissent even in appellate cases. In fact, most Continental systems do not permit the publication of dissenting opinions (Damâska 1986). Civil-law judges are usually independent and cannot be removed for any reason other than **cause** (personal impropriety).

In the United States, judges sit in either trial courts or appellate courts. The trial court is a fact-finding body that has jurisdiction in criminal and noncriminal matters. The fact-finding responsibilities of a trial court may be carried out by a jury or by a single judge in what is known as a bench trial. The trial court has primary responsibility for the enforcement of norms; its decisions respond to the single case at issue. Most cases that are brought to trial courts in the United States do not result in a trial. In civil—that is, noncriminal—cases they are usually resolved by a negotiated settlement (discussed in Chapter 10), and in criminal cases the outcome is often the result of plea bargaining (discussed in Chapter 9). Appellate courts do not use juries (they render decisions on issues of law, not fact), and, except in certain specific cases, they hear cases on appeal only after they have been decided by a trial court.[19]

An appellate court does not consider new evidence. The court's decisions are based on the formal record of the trial court (and any lower appellate court that considered the case) that has been officially transmitted by the court clerk, and the pleadings of attorneys. The major decisions of an appellate court are typically elaborate documents that outline the issues presented by the litigants and the rationale underlying the court's decision, the *ratio decedendi*. These published decisions are available to other judges and lawyers and can be used to buttress cases litigated in other courts. It should be noted, however, that most appellate court decisions are quite brief, often only one word—"affirmed." Sometimes referred to as "unpublished," despite their being available in legal databases, these decisions contain no explanation and therefore have no precedential value. Alan Tarr (2014) notes that while they have generally adhered to precedent, judges in the United States never viewed precedent as binding to the same extent as judges in England, and American judges reveal a greater willingness to **overrule** earlier decisions in response to changing circumstances.

In the United States, appellate courts render policy decisions (discussed in Chapter 5), something very rare in trial courts. There are trial courts and appellate courts on the state and federal levels; the US Supreme Court being the preeminent appellate court.

Continental courts do not use juries in noncriminal cases (and they are rare in England [Kötz 2003; Kritzer 1996; Lloyd-Bostock and Thomas 1999]). But juries have become widely used in criminal proceedings, a custom borrowed from England where criminals retain the right to opt for a jury trial in a superior—Crown—court (Damâska 1986; Lloyd-Bostock and Thomas 1999). In France, as in England, jury trials are reserved for serious crimes, and the jury of nine citizens sits with one or more judges; verdicts are determined by majority vote (Abraham 1998). In contrast to the virtually unlimited discretion of an American prosecutor, Continental prosecutors are subject to great deal of judicial oversight, and plea bargaining does not involve the coercive tactics frequently found in the United States (Ma 2002). The concept of equity is absent from civil-law systems: While civil-law judges may be empowered by statute to ren-

---

[19] One exception is the *interlocutory appeal*, raised prior to the completion of a trial, alleging errors by the judge that must be corrected if the trial is to proceed in a just and proper manner.

der equitable decisions in certain narrowly defined situations, they do not enjoy the power of injunctive relief (Merryman and Pérez-Pedomo 2007).

In Continental Europe, there is no clear distinction between trial courts and appellate courts, and policy issues are typically outside the purview of both. A single judge using simplified procedures has jurisdiction over minor cases, while a second level of courts hears serious cases and appeals from the lower courts. Judges in these courts sit in panels of three, and in some countries their decisions may be appealed to courts at a third level, whose judges sit in panels of three to seven. These higher courts may also conduct trials in special circumstances, or when the matter is particularly serious. At the highest level is a single supreme court, whose judges sit in panels of seven or more. The European appellate process allows for consideration of questions of fact and law; new evidence can be introduced, and often the appellate tribunal will hold a new trial (trial *de novo*) and reexamine witnesses (Elliott, Jeanpierre, and Vernon 2006; Shapiro 1981). France and Italy also have a unique judicial tribunal: the *Cour de cassation* and the *Corte Suprema di Cassazione* respectively.

Established by revolutionary French legislation, the mission of the *Tribunal de cassation* is to ensure that courts do not deviate from the text of laws and thereby encroach on the legislative branch (a major political issue in the United States); it does not have the power of judicial review (discussed in Chapter 5). Napoleon renamed it the *Cour de cassation* and, with six specialized chambers, each with 15 justices, it continues to have the power to *casser* (quash) incorrect interpretations by judges–and remit the matter for rehearing to another court of the same level (Zweigert and Kötz 1998). While the *Cour de cassation* constitutes the French supreme court and frequently provides reasons for its decisions, they are persuasive at best and not binding on the lower court (Merryman and Pérez-Pedomo 2007). The court has no **original jurisdiction** and does not try cases. The original ideal—that law would not need to be interpreted by judges, "since its plain meaning covered all the bases—was eventually dropped in practice" (Tiersma 2011: 273).

Inquisitorial and Adversarial Justice

Civil-law and common-law systems differ in their approach to trials: civil law utilizes an **inquisitorial system** and common law an **adversarial system**. The term inquisitorial (or inquisitional) carries negative connotations about the papal ecclesiastical courts, established in 1233, in which the judge was also the prosecutor, and the notorious courts of the Spanish Inquisition, established in 1478, which resorted to torture in their investigation of Jews whose conversion was not considered sincere, a scrutiny that was later extended to Muslims and any Spaniard suspected of heresy. However,

---

Governing by Code

"If we truly wish to govern by a code of written laws, and if we also limit judges to the task of mechanistically applying those laws to the facts of a case, then every time an interpretive question arises, judges would have to refer the issue to the legislature, which would then have to resolve the matter and amend the statute to reflect its decision" (Tiersma 2011: 282). "Most modern legislatures do not have the time and resources to do so" (2011: 289).

France

Suspects in France may be interrogated by police without being given an opportunity to consult with an attorney. "Expansive pretrial investigation is conducted by a magistrate, and requires that, before bringing a case to trial, there must be witness testimony, fact-gathering, and interrogation of the accused. Because the pretrial investigation is conducted to determine whether criminal charges should even be brought, the pretrial investigation is not open to the public in order to avoid prejudicing the suspect." Pretrial "proceedings can extend for long periods of time, with the suspect often in custody and not formally charged" (Finegan 2009: 464–65).

the inquisitorial system today is a judicial procedure in which judges are at the center of the fact-gathering process. Thus, supporters of this system prefer the term *investigative* (and pejoratively refer to the adversarial system as *accusatorial* [Glenn 2010]).

With some variations, this system is used in civil-law countries on the European continent and throughout Latin America. The parties must provide all relevant evidence to the court, and the judges, not the attorneys for the plaintiff and defendant, call and actively examine witnesses. In German courts, for example, the judge calls witnesses who have been nominated by opposing counsel, and they are invited to narrate what they know about the matter being tried; the court will then ask questions. While there is no cross-examination, attorneys are invited to ask questions, an opportunity they usually decline—to do otherwise would impugn the ability of the court, which Kötz (2003) notes is a dubious tactic. The court, not the attorneys, determines which witnesses and how many to call. In civil-law countries there is a great deal of faith in the fairness and competence of judges, who (as noted earlier) are not political appointees but career technocrats.

Written additions to the file continue as the case proceeds. "The parties have many opportunities to enter new evidence and arguments and to respond to written pleadings filed by the other side" (Shapiro 1981: 149). Finally, the entire process ends with what appears to be a trial; actually, it is simply the time when the court finally decides the case that has been developed by opposing attorneys and lower judges during a series of preliminary proceedings. "In the civil-law system, no distinction is made between pretrial and trial" (Hazard and Taruffo 1993: 125). "There is a brief preliminary

Contrasting Civil- and Common-Law Systems

"In civil-law systems, the judge is expected to have read the dossiers of documents submitted by each party in advance of the hearing. The dossiers may include the written statements of witnesses, or witnesses may appear at the hearing to give an unprompted narrative and to be questioned by the judge. The role of the lawyers for the parties is generally limited to suggesting to the judge questions that should be asked. The idea of a witness being presented by the lawyer for a party in the question-and-answer format of common-law direct examination is vaguely distasteful to civil lawyers. And the idea of a witness being required to agree or disagree with statements by a lawyer in the format the common law calls cross-examination is positively repugnant to them" (Elsing and Townsend 2002: 4).

stage, in which the pleadings are submitted and a hearing judge (usually called the instructing judge) appointed; an evidence-taking stage in which the hearing judge takes evidence and prepares a written summary; and a decision-making stage, in which the judges who will decide the case consider the record transmitted to them by the hearing judge, receive counsel's briefs, hear their arguments, and render decisions" (Merryman 1985: 111–12). Noncriminal cases may be "described as a series of isolated conferences before the judge, some of which may only last a few minutes, in which written communications between the parties are exchanged and discussed, procedural rulings are made, evidence is introduced and testimony taken until the cause is finally ready for adjudication" (Kötz 2003: 72)

"The Continental trial is, then, actually not the doctrinally proclaimed event of paramount importance that generates all material for disposition of the criminal case quite independently from prior (piecemeal) proceedings" (Damâska 1986: 53). Instead, information derived at preliminary hearings is checked independently by judges from material assembled over time and preserved in the written record. Information presented by attorneys is suspect, and thus Continental lawyers rarely engage in independent investigative activities, and expert witnesses are seldom called by private parties; to be credible they must be called by the court and are treated as judicial assistants. In many civil-law countries even plaintiffs and defendants are barred from testifying "on the premise that their interest in the outcome will bias their testimony" (Hazard and Taruffo 1993: 83). Thus, judges in inquisitorial systems perform many of the functions that would be performed by attorneys in adversarial systems.

In France, in criminal cases there is a preliminary inquiry by an investigating magistrate who assigns most tasks to *la police judiciaire*—police investigators (Provine 1996). Then judges "actively, often vehemently and acidly, participate in the courtroom questioning of witnesses as well as of the accused—who incidentally cannot invoke the Anglo-Saxon privilege of refusing to take the stand on grounds of possible **self-incrimination**" (Abraham 1998: 107; emphasis added). In Italy, prosecutors and judges are magistrates, a profession for which they qualify through a national competition. In the course of their career they may easily pass from the role of prosecutor to that of judge and vice versa (Orlando 2001).

"In Anglo-American systems, the crucial event is a trial, and the appropriate metaphor is combat, with the defense taking primary responsibility for articulating the interests of the accused. The civil-law alternative that France represents envisions a more cooperative relationship between participants, with careful investigation at the heart of the criminal process. Plea-bargaining is not part of the process because of the expectation that a trial will occur whether or not the defendant confesses" (Provine 1996: 213). In France, a criminal trial is presided over by a three-judge panel whose members also form part of the jury panel: nine laypersons and the three judges. Verdicts require a majority of eight and ballots are secret (Elliott, Jeanpierre, and Vernon 2006).

In contrast to inquisitorial systems, there is the *laissez-faire* role of the judge in adversarial systems;[20] each side is expected to pursue self-interest to the fullest, a legal

---

[20] There are differences between the roles of judges in the United States and in England. Although both are presumed neutral, in England the judge provides a "'summing up' which can include, in addition to a summary of the evidence and legal instructions, comments on the relevance of pieces of evidence and on the credibility of witnesses" (Kritzer 1996: 106).

correlate to free enterprise economics. In the adversarial system used in Anglo-Saxon countries,[21] an attorney—an advocate—represents each side; the judge is neutral, authorized to play the role of a referee who enforces the rules of "combat." In trial courts, the attorneys, not the judges, control the flow of information to the court, and a jury of citizenry determines issues of fact: guilty or not guilty, or blame in noncriminal cases. In appellate courts, however, justices typically question attorneys (there are no witnesses) directly in a process that resembles an inquisitorial system. In the adversarial system, inequalities in ability between parties often loom larger than in systems that rely primarily on judges: a party assisted by skillful counsel, or capable of expending the costs of pretrial discovery (discussed in Chapter 10) has a significant advantage over a weaker opponent (Damâska 1986). In civil-law countries, noncriminal cases are decided without the use of juries.

The absence of a jury in noncriminal cases accounts for much of the difference between civil- and common-law procedure. Since a jury cannot be kept together indefinitely, the American trial is more concentrated—and dramatic—than in civil-law systems where a case is handled by judges over a series of hearings. Furthermore, since a legally unsophisticated jury can deal with factual issues only if they are presented in a focused manner, there is extensive pretrial activity (pleadings and discovery, discussed in Chapter 10) to sharpen contested issues, something far less compelling in civil-law systems. And the distinction between issues of fact, for which the jury is responsible, and issues of law, for which the judge is responsible, is less relevant when only judges hear the case. Civil law is focused on a search for the truth, while in the United States the focus is on procedure—due process.

While common law has been dominant in the United States, civil law has left its imprint. As Patrick Glenn (2010) notes, the particular genius of American law is the combining of civil and common law. This is clearly seen in the adoption of codes of procedure (Coffin 1994).

Comparative Law

The Anglo-American trial is concentrated, transpiring as a single continuous meeting of the court. This proceeding may adjourn for the evening or the weekend, but is otherwise uninterrupted. "At this continuous proceeding, the court hears all the evidence and all the legal submissions, after which the jurors deliberate and render judgment" (Langbein 2012: 529).

In jury-free civil-law systems, "proceedings are discontinuous, taking place across as many hearings as the court, staffed exclusively with professional judges, thinks necessary. At these hearings the court hears testimony and the submissions of the parties' lawyers. The court records evidence and party submissions in an official file or dossier, which the court will draw upon when writing its judgment" (Langbein 2012: 529–30).

---

[21] The United States, however, is unique with respect to the degree to which the adversarial method is encouraged: "The American legal profession long has stressed the ethic of zealous advocacy, in contrast to the legal professions of England and Western European nations" (Kagan 1994: 37).

Codes of Procedure

The British approach to common law was unyielding—"the law is the law"—and generally devoid of concern for American notions of "justice." The American colonists, and the United States after the Revolution, inherited this English system but found the procedural requirements far too rigid for their purposes. There was also an absence of uniform rules for the commencement of a particular action in law or equity. The language of the pleadings (formal written statements constituting the plaintiff's cause of action and the defendant's grounds for defense, or statements of the litigants' positions outlining the dispute) was antiquated and verbose. An action could be lost for failure to adhere to numerous technical details despite the merits of the case. As one lawyer wrote in 1844: "Its principal characteristics are a great many forms of an antique phraseology, according to which every controversy in the ordinary courts must be carried on; forms, the reasons for which perished long ago, and which are now become inadequate, uncouth, and distasteful" (Field 1965: 34). **Procedural law** was needed; that is, codes of civil and criminal procedure that could simplify and standardize the commencement and resolution of legal actions (much as the development of *Robert's Rules of Order* helped bring procedural order to private organizations). A **code of procedure**[22] could explain how to apply the substantive law to particular cases. Although the substantive law defines certain behavior as criminal and provides for the recovery of damages in the event of a breach of contract or reckless behavior, questions remain concerning how a complaint is to be filed: What information can be received by the judge or jury? How is that information to be presented? What are the standards of proof ("beyond a reasonable doubt," "preponderance of the evidence")? The establishment of such procedural law is largely the result of the efforts of David Field.

David Dudley Field (1805–1894) was the son of a noted Massachusetts family; his brother Cyrus J. Field was responsible for the laying of the first transatlantic cable; brother Stephen J. Field became an influential justice of the United States Supreme Court, serving for more than 30 years; and another brother served as president of the Massachusetts senate. "Field entered the practice of law in New York City in 1828 and soon became known for his expertise in 'pleadings,' the stage of a lawsuit when the procedural complications were at their worst" (Gordon 1991: 18). Despite the handsome living he made as a result of common-law complexity, Field soon became its opponent.

Field advocated codification. He believed law was a science whose elements could be categorized and classified according to central principles that could then be taught more systematically to law students and be more readily available in convenient form to legal practitioners (Hyman and Wiecek 1982). He campaigned vigorously for a uniform code of procedure for both civil and criminal matters and, later in his life, for a code of international law (Miller 1962). Field advocated legislative enactments that would simplify both the substance and the language of pleadings while abolishing distinctions between law and equity. His efforts, however, were opposed by those attached to the common law by education and training, and who favored the slow organic growth of common law as opposed to the swift legislative remedy that

---

[22] Procedure implies structures and rules that endure beyond the controversies of the moment, that permit men and women to make reliable plans, that keep arbitrary discretion at bay" (Glendon 1994: 247).

codes represented. Field's conservative opponents argued that substantive changes in legal development should come from the judicial branch of government and not from the legislature that was prone to follow the whims of an electorate that might be bent on radical social and economic reformulations (Feldstein and Presser 1984). Thus, according to Rufus Choate, a vigorous opponent of codification, writing in 1845, "It is one of the distemperatures to which an unreasoning liberty may grow, no doubt, to regard law as no more nor less than just the will—the actual present will—of the actual majority of the nation" (1962: 264). There were also attorneys who saw codification as a simplification that would be harmful to their economic interests, and they proved a formidable lobby (Herget 1990).

In 1846, Field was able to have a requirement for codification made part of the New York State Constitution and his code of civil procedure was subsequently enacted in 1848. The "Field Code" served as a prototype for other states in codifying their rules of civil, and later criminal, practice. Among other changes, the Field Code removed distinctions between actions at law and suits in equity. Even Great Britain used his code to provide a basis for reforming the common law (Gordon 1991). The codification movement died down about the time of the Civil War (Gilmore 1977). During the 1890s, however, the American Bar Association set up an affiliate, the National Conference of Commissioners on Uniform State Laws, which worked to codify various aspects of commercial law. These efforts resulted in the Negotiable Instruments Law (NIL) that was promulgated in 1896 and eventually enacted in all American jurisdictions. The NIL and other commercial codes drafted by the conference were eventually replaced by the **Uniform Commercial Code**, which is now in force in all jurisdictions except Louisiana, which has adopted part of it. (The Louisiana Civil Code, enacted in 1808, is based on the Napoleonic Code.) Its major architect was the legal scholar Karl Llewellyn (1893–1962). Morton Horowitz points out that codification resulted in the merger of law and equity: "It marks the final and complete emasculation of Equity as an independent source of legal standards" (1977: 265). And it was the ultimate rationalization of civil and criminal procedure, a move away from "natural justice" to formalism.

The National Conference is now a permanent organization whose membership consists of lawyers, law professors, and judges from the 50 states, with each state's delegation being selected by the governor. The conference meets annually in conjunction with the annual meeting of the American Bar Association, while day-to-day activities are conducted by a variety of standing and ad hoc committees. It should be noted that states usually adopt model uniform law packages in modified form, changing or deleting some parts and, in many cases, adding new sections. "In short, by the time uniform laws have been adopted by the various states, they are no longer, strictly speaking, 'uniform'" (Elias 1989: 100).

In 1934, Congress authorized the Supreme Court to write general rules for the federal courts, and pursuant to this legislation, in 1938, the Court promulgated the *Federal Rules of Civil Procedure*, which were heralded for their uniformity and simplicity. However, these rules are general and permissive, failing to cover many topics on which federal courts must have a rule. Because of these shortcomings, the *Federal Rules* have been supplemented or expanded by about 5,000 local rules, undermining their uniformity and *raison d'etre* (Coquillette, Squiers, and Subrin 1989). Nevertheless, most states' procedural rules are modeled on the federal code (Hazard and Taruffo 1993).

Although the United States' legal tradition includes codes, they have a meaning different from those of civil-law countries: They make no pretense of completeness, and a code provision will be interpreted in such as way as to avoid conflict with a common-law precedent. In the United States, codes of procedure are the rules for enforcing substantive law. They prescribe the means of enforcing rights or providing redress of wrongs, the manner of pleading and practice, evidence, appeal, execution of judgments, representation of counsel, costs, transfer of property (conveyance), court costs, and related matters.

In sum, our system of justice has two basic types of statutory law, substantive and procedural, and each is divided into criminal and civil:

- *Substantive criminal law* defines the elements that constitute a crime, e.g., robbery, the unlawful taking of the property of another through the use or threat of force, and the penalties that attach for its commission.

- *Procedural criminal law* controls the manner in which the substantive criminal law is invoked (e.g., **rules of evidence** and due process); thus, in order for a criminal conviction to be lawful, it must follow the rules set out in the procedural law.

- *Substantive civil law* consists of the principles that determine "the rights we are said to have and the duties we are told we must accept" (Rembar 1980: 77), such as exercising care when we operate a motor vehicle. In a typical civil action, the law of torts determines who is **liable** for damages.

- *Procedural civil law* is "the set of instructions prescribing how we redress a violated right, how our neglected duties are imposed" (Rembar 1980: 77), such as how to initiate a tort (suit for damages) action.

Statutory Law

Statutory law is the province of legislative bodies that enact statutes—the Congress of the United States, state legislatures, county boards, and municipal councils. As in civil-law countries, except when constitutional questions are at issue, statutes are superior to judicial decisions, but statutes must also be interpreted by judges at the point of application.

In general, one or more legislators introduce (sponsor) a bill into the house of which they are members. Serious bills (as opposed to those introduced solely to score points with certain constituents and that have no hope of passage) are usually introduced into both houses by a legislator in each body and referred to the appropriate committee (or committees) for consideration. Bills reported out by committee are referred to the entire house for consideration. Legislation that passes both houses (in bicameral legislative bodies) is sent to the chief executive—president, governor, county board chairman, or mayor—for his or her signature or veto. The signing of a legislative enactment, or the overriding of a veto (usually requiring a two-thirds vote), makes the bill a law. Legislative enactments are assembled and ordered in a systematic manner by a state code commission. They are then published.

All federal and state statutes and regulations (rules promulgated by **administrative agencies** pursuant to statutory authority) and all county and municipal **ordinances** are published in full. Federal statutes, the enactments of Congress, appear in several forms, the most convenient being the compilation authorized by Congress in 1925 and referred

Federal Legislation

When a member of Congress, senator or representative, introduces a bill, with few exceptions it is referred to the appropriate standing House or Senate committees. The bill may be referred to a subcommittee or considered by the committee as a whole. The failure to act on a bill effectively kills the legislation. If after hearings the committee fails to act, the legislation is dead. If the committee approves of the bill, it is sent to the House or Senate with a written report describing the intent and scope of the legislation, its impact on existing law and programs, the position of the executive branch, and the views of dissenting members of the committee. It is then placed on the **calendar** for floor action.

The legislation is debated on the House or Senate floor and if approved, with or without amendments, is sent to the other chamber, where it usually follows the same route as a newly introduced bill. If only minor changes are made, the bill is then sent to the president. If there have been significant changes, a House-Senate conference committee is formed to reconcile the differences. A failure to agree on changes kills the bill; otherwise, it is sent back to both houses for a vote, and then sent to the president. If the president signs the bill, or fails to take action within 10 days while the Congress is in session, it becomes law. The president may also veto a bill or, if the Congress is not in session, take no action ("pocket veto") and the legislation dies. A veto can be overridden by a two-thirds vote of the members of the Senate and House who are present in sufficient numbers for a quorum.

to as the United States Code (U.S.C.). There is also the United States Code Annotated (U.S.C.A.), which includes commentary on judicial decisions (case law) relating to the statutes contained in the code. State statutes are first published in volumes called session laws because they are prepared at the end of each legislative session. They are later printed in volumes arranged by subject matter and have different names in different states: statutes/laws/codes at large, compiled, consolidated, revised.

Statutory law is divided between criminal and civil/noncriminal enactments. The criminal or penal law (or code) defines those behaviors that are criminal and prescribes punishment, whereas civil law is concerned with the resolution of noncriminal disputes and the carrying out of government functions (e.g., the budget). The government has an important and direct interest in dealing with crime, so all criminal proceedings have the government (e.g., *United States v. Smith* or *State of California v. Jones*) as the plaintiff, whereas litigation in civil disputes is typically brought by individuals or corporations (*Smith v. Jones*; **private law**), although the government may be a defendant or a plaintiff in a civil action ("public law"). Thus, while the government has a direct interest in whether or not you burglarize your neighbor's home, "it has only an indirect interest in whether you keep a promised contractual agreement with that neighbor. Private law, therefore, encompasses the major categories of substantive legal rules, such as contracts, real property, and torts" (Hall 1989: 7).

In some instances, a criminal violation can result in damages *and* a civil action,[23] while the government can bring a civil forfeiture action against certain defendants in

---

[23] A civil action for behavior that violates the criminal law is permissible even in the absence of a conviction, such as in the case of O. J. Simpson.

Forfeiture

The Comprehensive Criminal Forfeiture Act "creates a rebuttable presumption that any property of a person convicted of a drug felony is subject to forfeiture if the government establishes by a preponderance of the evidence that the defendant acquired the property during the period of violation, or within a reasonably short period thereafter, *and* there was no likely source for the property other than the violation" (President's Commission on Organized Crime 1986: 274). To obtain a seizure order, the government must provide sworn testimony in an affidavit spelling out the property to be seized and why there is reason to believe that it is being used to commit crimes or was acquired with money from criminal activity. The filing of criminal charges against the owner is not required and the owner of the property is not informed of the action until his or her property is seized by US marshals pursuant to the court order. The owner of the property has a right to contest the seizure only after it has occurred; he or she must prove that the money or property was earned through legal enterprise (Abadinsky 2013).

order to seize property that has been secured through the proceeds of or used in furtherance of criminal behavior. And the civil law is frequently used against criminal justice agencies and personnel who (allegedly) act beyond their authority or maintain jails and prisons in a manner that violates constitutional provisions, such as the Eighth Amendment's prohibition of cruel and unusual punishment.

The criminal law grades crimes in descending order according to their seriousness. For example, the Illinois Criminal Law and Procedure classifies all crimes in eight categories in order of seriousness: felonies as class X, 1, 2, 3, 4, and misdemeanors as class A, B, C. The New York Penal Law classifies crimes into seven categories according to seriousness: felonies as class A, B, C, D, E, and misdemeanors as class A and B. Both states also have numerous lesser offenses: violations or infractions, such as local (municipal or county) ordinances prohibiting jay walking or littering, and there are traffic-related violations.

Sentences for Federal Felonies and Misdemeanors

Class A felony—Death or life imprisonment
Class B Felony—25 years or more
Class C felony—Less than 25 years but more than 10 years
Class D felony—Less than 10 years but more than 5 years
Class E felony—Less than 5 years but more than 1 year
Class A misdemeanor—1 year or less but more than 1 month
Class B misdemeanor—6 months or less but more than 30 days
Class C misdemeanor—30 days or less but more than 5 days

Sources of Law in the United States

After the Revolution, the Constitution became the supreme law of the land, and neither statutes nor judicial rulings can conflict with its provisions as construed by the Supreme Court. The rules of English common law were altered by legislation and many states purged the common law of its feudal elements, particularly during the Jacksonian era (1829–1837). While common law continues to provide certain avenues of civil redress, particularly in state courts,[24] the major sources of law governing the United States are the Constitution (constitutional law), legislative enactments (statutory law), and appellate court decisions (case law).

1. US Constitution
2. Federal statutes
3. Federal administrative rules and regulations
4. Treaties
5. Federal court decisions
6. State constitutions
7. State statutes
8. State administrative rules and regulations
9. State court decisions
10. Municipal charters
11. County and municipal ordinances
12. County and municipal administrative rules and regulations
13. Municipal court decisions

---

[24] For example, claims of public services being applied in conflict with the common law duty to serve in an equal and adequate manner; see Haar 1986; Haar and Fessler 1986).

Administrative and Regulatory Law

During the Progressive era of the late nineteenth century, complaints of economic exploitation by railroads and other monopolies led to the passage of state regulatory legislation. These efforts were declared unconstitutional by the Supreme Court—a violation of the exclusive federal jurisdiction to regulate interstate commerce. In response, in 1887 Congress created independent regulatory agencies such as the Interstate Commerce Commission. The number of such agencies multiplied during the era of the New Deal. Another expansion occurred during the years 1960 to 1980 with the creation of the Environmental Protection Agency (EPA), Occupational Health and Safety Administration (OSHA), and the Consumer Product Safety Commission (Pierce, Shapiro, and Verkuil 2014). Statutory law is rarely self-implementing, and federal or state legislators may create an administrative agency to carry out a particular statutory function, for example, at the federal level to administer Social Security (Social Security Administration), to regulate labor management relations (National Labor Relations

Board), to prohibit unfair methods of competition (Federal Trade Commission), or at the state level to regulate such professions as medicine and architecture and trades such as barbering and plumbing. There are liquor boards and zoning boards, and boards of examiners for security personnel and real estate brokers. Some agencies are part of the executive branch, for example, the Internal Revenue Service, and there are also numerous independent administrative agencies—commissions, examiners, and boards—such as the Federal Reserve Board or municipal health board. "Often the statutes that create them, even while placing them in political departments, contain special measures safeguarding against political influence; decisions of the Internal Revenue Service respecting the selection of individual taxpayers for investigation are shielded from political direction, for example" (Strauss 1989: 89). The independent agencies are typically bipartisan, with members who serve staggered terms that overlap (e.g., six years) that of the appointing authority, a governor or the president. Administrative agencies make regulatory law, and the bureaucrats enforcing these laws are governed by **administrative law**. For example, Federal Communication Commission (FCC) rules limit the number of commercial broadcasting stations a company may own, and "the Internal Revenue Service (IRS) by rule determines which groups qualify as 'charities' and therefore need not pay taxes" (Carter and Harrington 2009: 28) The IRS creates tax law, and the FCC makes communications law.

Although the executive branch contains a wide array of departments and administrative personnel capable of regulatory functions, Congress was concerned that partisanship and party politics could slowly but inexorably enter into regulation of sensitive areas such as transportation and communications. Besides, while presidents change frequently, as do their cabinet appointees, responding to technologically complex problems requires continuing expertise and leadership (Carter and Harrington 2009).

But how can legislative authority be delegated to an administrative agency when the Constitution (Article I, Section I) provides that all legislative power is vested in Congress? Indeed, courts have invalidated laws granting too much legislative power to an administrative agency. Nevertheless, the delegation of legislative authority to administrative agencies was gradually accepted by the US Supreme Court as long as the scope of agency discretion was clearly delineated (Pierce, Shapiro, and Verkuil 2014).

Governments in colonial America (discussed in Chapter 4) often combined the executive, legislative, and judicial functions, a practice that came to an end when our Constitution created a delineation of authority. This has become a basic doctrine in American government: "The one who makes or implements a rule ought not be the same as the one who judges its fair application to particular circumstances" (Strauss

Hygiene Jurisprudence

The New York City Administrative Tribunal of the Department of Health and Mental Hygiene handles about 200 cases a day. The tribunal's hearing examiners earn $36 an hour to determine culpability for violating a myriad of city ordinances involving food vendors, barbers, day care centers, funeral homes, et al. Observers note the prime offense is vermin in food preparation, and penalties can cost thousands of dollars (Barry 2006).

> ## On Administrative Due Process
>
> "The vast expansion of this field of administrative regulation in response to the pressure of social needs is made possible under our system of adherence to the basic principles that the legislature shall appropriately determine the standards of administrative action and that in administrative proceedings of a quasi-judicial character the liberty and property of the citizen shall be protected by the rudimentary requirements of fair play" (Chief Justice Charles Evans Hughes, *Morgan v. United States* [1938]).

1989: 14). Nevertheless, many administrative agencies still enjoy a combination of these powers. For example, the EPA

> exercises legislative powers when it issues rules and regulations to minimize industrial pollution of the air. These rules and regulations have the force of laws passed by Congress. The EPA exercises executive powers when it monitors and publicizes pollution levels throughout the nation and subsidizes the construction of municipal waste treatment plants. It exercises judicial powers when it determines whether a business firm has violated certain of its antipollution rules and regulations and then imposes penalties for the violation. (Auerbach 1983: 74–75)

Despite the problems inherent in combining legislative, executive, and judicial powers in a single agency, it has often been seen as the only logical and workable arrangement for the efficient regulation of huge, complex, rapidly changing, and often highly technical enterprises (Lorch 1980). Public agencies organized around specialized technocratic concerns, such as the EPA or the Nuclear Regulatory Commission, typically establish policy based on ad hoc, discretionary powers in response to scientific variables. Causal or scientific reasoning, rather than legal reasoning and the search for precedent and *stare decisis*, predominates (Stryker 1989), thereby reducing predictability. Many administrative agencies provide a mechanism for adjudicating disputes arising out of regulatory law, usually in the form of administrative hearings—the equivalent of a trial court. New York City, for example, employs administrative judges to help regulate the taxi industry (Taxi and Limousine Commission), the environment (Department of Environmental Protection), and street parking (Parking Violations Bureau).

Instead of a trial judge, in the federal system there are about 30 agencies with more than 1,500 administrative law judges (called hearing officers until 1978) empowered to take testimony and either render a decision or make a recommendation to the agency's governing board; about 1,300 work for the Social Security Administration. Administrative law judges are required to have at least seven years' trial experience and pass an examination on general legal knowledge. They are then placed on a merit selection list from which various agencies select judges; appointments are for life. They adjudicate cases according to procedures set out in the Administrative Procedure Act, which was promulgated by the American Bar Association and adopted by Congress in 1946. In most agencies administrative trials are exactly like bench trials heard by federal district court judges.

In the federal system:

> Administrative law judges are paid at the level of the senior executive service but—although formally located within the particular agencies they serve—are virtually beyond agency control. Appointments must be made on a competitive basis, from the top few names on a list supplied by civil service authorities. Once made, appointments are permanent (without [a] probationary period). Within the agency structure, administrative law judges must be free of supervision or direction from agency employees responsible for the cases that may come before them; neither salary, nor assignments, nor any disciplinary measure can be controlled from within the agency, but (if adverse) must be the subject of formal proceedings before the Merit System Protection Board. Any conversations administrative law judges may have with agency employees concerning the outcomes of formal proceedings they are hearing must be on the record—that is, there may be no private consultations. (Strauss 1989: 95)

The decision of an administrative agency may sometimes be appealed to a specialized tribunal, for example, in tax disputes, to the tax court or the courts of appeals: "Congress gave Courts of Appeals special responsibility to review the actions of federal regulatory agencies and to reconcile their conduct with law" (Howard 1981: 6). Courts of appeals may hear petitions to review or enforce the orders of such agencies as the National Labor Relations Board or the Securities and Exchange Commission.

Statutes require that federal agency administrative regulations be published in the *Federal Register*, along with notices of agency meetings or hearings in order to provide interested parties with an opportunity to object. They are then published in the *Code of Federal Regulations* that is organized into 50 separate titles, such as agriculture and energy. State regulations are usually compiled by the agency involved and maintained in loose-leaf form. Copies may be filed with the secretary of state and are also found in law school or central public libraries.

Persons dissatisfied with the decisions of an administrative agency have to exhaust all other remedies, that is, follow agency review procedures, before turning to the courts. "Most statutes setting up administrative agencies provide for or imply the right of courts to review such agency decisions. The Administrative Procedure Act itself provides for review unless Congress firmly and explicitly says otherwise" (Friedman 1984: 118). Any time a statute is ambiguous, it is a general rule that courts should defer to the reasonable administrative agency interpretation of that statute (Breyer 2005).

Administrative Law Judges

Administrative law judges for the New York State Public Service Commission, an independent regulatory agency, preside at formal evidentiary hearings on utility rates, the choosing of sites for electric generation or transmission facilities, and general commission policy. They analyze the hearing record and prepare recommendations for action by the commission.

SUMMARY

- Laws are societal norms guaranteed by legal coercion.

- Some laws instruct persons in what they must or must not do; others tell people how to do what they wish to do so that their actions are legally enforceable. Some laws also create benefits, while others deal with the functions of government agencies.

- The idea of morality in law is associated with the concept of *natural law.*

- Natural law in the United States is expressed in terms of government restrained by the Constitution.

- The Bill of Rights is based on natural law.

- In the United States, the principles of natural law are implemented though judicial review.

- Popular will is limited by natural law.

- *Rational law* entails the application of general norms to specific facts.

- *Irrational law* involves case-by-case decisions without recourse to generalized principles of law but, rather, according to what is deemed morally correct in each case.

- A system of rational law provides a relatively predictable outcome for legal disputes.

- Modern capitalism requires a legal order that is both prompt and predictable.

- In the absence of a system of contract law, an economy will remain primitive.

- Precedent is the controlling element of common law

- The doctrine of *res judicata* means parties may not relitigate issues that have been decided.

- Equity involves a modification of law to promote fairness.

- Common law provides for money damages.

- Equity has power over persons, e.g., injunction, *in personam* jurisdiction, but not over things, *in rem* jurisdiction.

- Common law and equity are products of English tradition; other European nations use civil law and have comprehensive codes that supersede earlier law—precedent is absent as a legal concept.

- Civil-law systems promote legislative supremacy—the judiciary is subservient.

- In civil-law systems the text of the law rather than prior judicial interpretation of that text that is authoritative.

- In response to the unbridled legislative power of Nazi Germany and Fascist Italy, civil-law countries have created constitutional courts.

- While judges in the United States emerge from the political system, in civil-law countries they are trained bureaucrats.

- In the United States, judges sit in either trial courts or appellate courts. The trial court is a fact-finding body; the appellate court does not consider new evidence but renders decisions on issues of law.

- Major decisions of an appellate court are typically elaborate documents that outline the issues presented by the litigants and the rationale underlying the court's decision, the *ratio decedendi*.

- Appellate decisions often involve courts in policy, something that is typically absent in civil-law countries.

- Civil-law and common-law systems differ in their approach to trials: civil law utilizes an *inquisitorial* approach and common law an *adversarial* approach.

- A code of procedure explains how to apply the substantive law to particular cases.

- Statutes are the result of bills introduced in both houses, subjected to committee hearings, approved by both houses, and sent to the chief executive for his or her signature or veto, which can be overridden by a supermajority,

- Administrative law is promulgated by agencies created by the legislative branch to carry out the purpose of specific statutes.

KEY TERMS

administrative agencies	*in camera*	positivism
administrative law	*in personam*	precedent
adversarial system	*in rem*	private law
Bill of Rights	infraction	privilege
calendar	injunction	*pro se*
case law	inquisitorial system	procedural law
cause	irrational law	*ratio decedendi*
civil law	judicial review	rational law
code	legislative supremacy	remedy
code of procedure	liable	*res judicata*
common law	litigant	rules of evidence
contract	natural law	self-incrimination
de jure	opinion	specific performance
de novo	ordinance	*stare decisis*
discretion	original jurisdiction	statute
equity	overrule	summons
estoppels	petition	Uniform Commercial Code
Federal Register	plaintiff	writ
Fiduciary	positive law	

REVIEW QUESTIONS

1. What distinguishes social norms from law?
2. Provide examples of laws that instruct persons what they must or must not do.
3. How does natural law differ from positive law?
4. How is the Bill of Rights an expression of natural law?
5. How does judicial review represent the implementation of natural law?

6. What is the inherent conflict between natural law and positive law?

7. How does natural law serve to restrain popular will?

8. Why is applying what is morally correct in each case, irrational?

9. What is essential about predictable outcomes in legal disputes?

10. Why does capitalism require a predictable legal system?

11. What is the relationship between common law and precedent?

12. What is the legal concept of *res judicata*?

13. Why did the system of common law require a system of equity?

14. What are the legal remedies for a judge using the power of equity?

15. How does *in personam* jurisdiction differ from *in rem* jurisdiction?

16. How does a court of equity differ from a court of law?

17. Why have civil-law countries created constitutional courts?

18. How do judges in the United States differ from those in civil-law countries?

19. In the United States why don't appellate courts consider new evidence?

20. What is meant by the *ratio decedendi* of an appellate decision?

21. How does the role of a trial judge in the United States differ from that of a judge in civil-law countries?

22. In the United States, what is the purpose of a code of procedure?

23. What is the general process for enacting a statute?

24. How does administrative law differ from statutory law?

25. Why do administrative agencies combine powers that are typically assigned to the executive, legislative, and judicial branches?

INTERNET CONNECTIONS

Administrative hearing rules: www.oalj.dol.gov/librules.htm
Global Legal Site: www.hg.org
'Lectric Law Library: www.lectlaw.com/ref.html
Legal Sites on the web: http://ih2000.net/ira/legal.htm
Meta-Index for Legal Research: https://gsulaw.gsu.edu/metaindex
The National Association of Administrative Law Judges: www.naalj.org
National Conference of Commissioners on Uniform State Laws:
    http://uniformlaws.org
United Kingdom Legal Website: www.infolaw.co.uk

Legal Education and Law Schools

Legal education is closely intertwined with the social, economic, and political changes in American history. In this chapter we will review that history from colonial times to the present state of legal education in the United States. We will examine the stratification and criticisms of legal education, and the positions offered by the legal realists, critical legal studies, and the law and economics movement.

Early American Legal Education

No law schools existed in the colonies, and only a small number of attorneys in the American colonies were trained in England. Some aspiring American lawyers traveled to England to attend the **Inns of Court**, companies of barristers in charge of legal training and admission to the upper branch of the English legal profession (solicitors make up the lower branch). The Inns of Court represented a highly centralized and privileged source of legal education and controlled entry into the English legal community (McKenna 1986), a system that was not transferred to the American colonies.

The era of American colonialization was a time when education at the Inns of Court was in decay (Pound 1953; McKenna 1986), thus, many lawyers in colonial America learned through apprenticeship. Numerous lawyers combined their law practice with being innkeepers, soldiers, merchants, or clergymen (Friedman 2005). Only in urban areas could the apprenticeship be described as compulsory, and the quality of the apprenticeship was as diverse as those who acted as lawyer-mentors (Stevens 1971; McKenna 1986).

America's greatest chief justice, John Marshall, had little formal education in law or any other discipline—in fact, he attended law lectures for fewer than three months while on leave from military service (Schwartz 1993). Most American attorneys, however, including such notables as Thomas Jefferson and Alexander Hamilton, gained a legal education through the system of clerkship, serving as an apprentice to an established attorney. The law clerk studied common law as set down by Sir Edward Coke (1551–1634)[1] and, most importantly, by William Blackstone (1723–1780). He read statutes, copied legal documents, and watched his tutor practice law.

---

[1] Sir Edward Coke was the early seventeenth-century English chief justice whose views greatly influenced the American colonists, particularly his assertion that even the king must submit to law as interpreted by the court—a government of laws, not of men.

The first law schools evolved out of this system, as some attorneys found the teaching of law more rewarding than the practice of law. The earliest law office-school was established in a modest one-story building in Litchfield, Connecticut, in about 1784, by a county judge, Tapping Reeve. At Litchfield, legal education/training was comprehensive and systematized. Students were exposed to lectures based on Blackstone's work and were concerned primarily with commercial law. They had to write up their notes, do collateral reading, and take a weekly examination. In later years moot courts and debating societies were part of the curriculum; the full course at Litchfield took 14 months. The largest class (1813) had 55 members. Its success gained Litchfield a national reputation, and by the time it closed in 1833, the result of heavy competition, more than 1,000 students had graduated, 28 of whom became US senators, 101 congressmen, 34 state supreme court justices, 14 governors, three justices of the US Supreme Court, and three US vice presidents. Judge Reeve, however, never considered Litchfield a "law school" and no diplomas were issued, although for students that required it, he gave letters verifying attendance (McKenna 1986).

The first American professorship in law was established by Governor Thomas Jefferson at Virginia's College of William and Mary in 1779, to which he appointed George Wythe, a signer of the Declaration of Independence.[2] Wythe's students included James Monroe and John Marshall (Schwartz 1974). This led to the establishment of other positions in law at major institutions of higher learning: Yale, Columbia, University of Pennsylvania, University of Maryland, and the University of Virginia all established law professorships by the early part of the nineteenth century. "Overall, the efforts by the colleges to develop law as a scholarly study were not a success. Professorships frequently lapsed or remained sinecures. The common law content of courses was normally small, and serious professional training took place at the private law schools" (Stevens 1971: 415). It was not until 1817 that the first university law school was established at Harvard.

Harvard

Isaac Royall, a Loyalist (that is, a colonist who remained loyal to Britain), fled to England during the Revolution and died there in 1781. His will bequeathed an endowed chair to Harvard University for a "Professor of Physick and Anatomy" or a professor of law. The school chose the latter. Harvard had a great deal of difficulty securing the lands Royall left to the university, since there was hostility even toward dead Loyalists who had fled during the war. In addition, the idea of law as a course of study at an institution of higher learning was not universally accepted. Whereas legal education as a legitimate object of university study was never questioned in Continental Europe (Herget 1990), this was not the case in England or America. Here, critics argued that if legal education were to be practical, it would not be academically respectable; on the other hand, if it were to be respectably academic, it would be professionally unprofitable (Sutherland 1967). It was not until 1815 that the Harvard Corporation chose the chief justice of Massachusetts, Isaac Parker, as its first professor of law.

---

[2] Wythe was poisoned in 1806 by his grandnephew who, apparently in debt, was eager to gain his inheritance (Schwartz 1974). Another version reports that a dispute over Wythe's will led to his murder (Noonan 1976). In any event, the only witnesses were two former slaves freed by Wythe. Under Virginia law, blacks were not permitted to testify against whites, and the murderer went free.

Legal education at Harvard was hardly disciplined scholarship; no readings were assigned and there were no examinations. The school offered the degree of bachelor of law (LLB) to students who completed the prescribed 18 months of academic requirements. The degree could be earned by those who had already completed an apprenticeship in the law office of an attorney—a college degree was not necessary to attend law school. Blackstone's *Commentaries* and moot courts were the cornerstone of legal education at Harvard. Professors spent their time preparing cases for argument and classroom questions for their students (Sutherland 1967). Legal education floundered, and by 1828 only one student remained (Newmyer 1987).

In the early 1820s, colleges began to incorporate private law schools that were interested in the prestige of such an affiliation, because in most states only universities were empowered to issue degrees. Yale absorbed a **local law school** in 1824, and in 1829, Harvard reorganized its law offerings, bringing in a professor from the Northampton Law School (Stevens 1971). That same year, Joseph Story (1779–1845), a Harvard graduate and justice of the Supreme Court who rode the New England circuit, accepted an endowed (Nathan Dane) chair. As a result of his efforts the Harvard Law School Library quickly became the largest in the country. By the 1830s Harvard was making a comeback, and there was an increasing study of judicial decisions—case law as analyzed and shaped by the energetic Story in his capacity as justice, professor, and author of legal texts. He helped transfer New England law into a national **jurisprudence** that would dominate the post-Civil War era and help foster an economic revolution (Newmyer 1987).[3] Harvard began to attract students from throughout the country. "By 1844, the school had 163 students—a remarkable number for the period" (Stevens 1971: 418). Declining standards for admission to the **bar**, however, led to a lowering of standards for admission to the Harvard Law School, and students not qualified for admission to Harvard College were allowed into the law school (Stevens 1971).

Other university law schools were established, and by 1840 there were nine university-affiliated law schools. By 1850, there were 15 law schools in 12 states (but none in the remaining 19). In the years just before the Civil War, there was a dramatic growth in formal legal education, "a revival of law teaching in the East (including Columbia, New York University, and the University of Pennsylvania) with the result that, by 1860, there were twenty-one law schools in existence" (Stevens 1971: 425). Despite their university affiliation, like their private law school counterparts, they were primarily trade schools (Stevens 1983), "little more than efficiently organized apprenticeship systems" (Herget 1990: 33). By 1870 there were 31 law schools (Friedman 1973), and in that year Christopher Columbus Langdell became dean of the Harvard Law School.

Langdell and Harvard Law School

The nature of learning and science changed dramatically after the Civil War, and the methods of Charles Darwin became a key element in this change: "The late nine-

---

[3] Story, originally a Jeffersonian, joined with the Federalists in a strong defense of property and capitalism. In his Harvard inaugural address, he argued: "The sacred rights of property are to be guarded at every point. I call them sacred, because, if they are unprotected, all other rights become worthless or visionary. What is personal liberty, if it does not draw after it the right to enjoy the fruits of our own industry? What is political liberty, if it imparts only perpetual poverty to us and all our posterity. . . . One of the glorious, and not infrequently perilous duties of the Bar is the protection of property" (1962: 180–81).

teenth-century scientific method was organic, inductive, and classificatory in its emphasis. Its adherents posited the inevitability of growth and change ('evolution') and argued that continuity and even permanency were linked to change. By examining the growth of an area of knowledge over time one could extract the core principles that had been retained and refined" (White 1980: 23–24). According to its proponents, science "'taught' that knowledge, although infinite, was capable of being reduced to discernible units; science also taught the proper methods of discernment, the proper goals of these methods, and ultimately the proper persons to be using them" (White 1980: 25). This approach was applied to the study of law at Harvard by Christopher Columbus Langdell.

Born to a New Hampshire farming family in 1826, Langdell attended Exeter and Harvard, but due to limited finances, left Harvard before finishing his degree requirements. He clerked in a prominent law office for one and a half years and then returned to Harvard where he was awarded a scholarship as a research assistant and supported himself as the school librarian. Studious and intellectually gifted, Langdell earned an undergraduate degree in law (LLB) in 1853 (Kimball 2002). For the next 16 years he practiced law in New York. A poor trial lawyer, Langdell specialized in research for other attorneys (Sutherland 1967; Cosgrove 1987). Eventually he was appointed as a professor of law at Harvard in 1870 and in 1875 was elected dean of the three-member law faculty, a position he held until his resignation in 1895 (Feldstein and Presser 1984).

Legal education at Harvard "had no relation to Harvard College. Students in general chose either law school or college, not both." Most came directly from high school (Stevens 1983: 36). Under Langdell, however, admission standards were raised; only those who already showed intellect and possessed a bachelor of arts degree or passed a strenuous entrance examination could enter the Harvard Law School. (By 1909, the examination alternative was discontinued.) Langdell required proficiency in French or Latin, although in some cases another language could be substituted. In 1871, the course of study for the LLB was lengthened from 18 months to two years. In 1872, there were prescribed examinations required at the end of the first year as a condition of admission to the second year of study. And by 1899, the curriculum was extended to three years of residence, and examinations had to be passed at the end of each year (Sutherland 1967).

As important as these changes were, it was the method of instruction at Harvard that revolutionized the study of law in the United States. Grant Gilmore refers to Langdell as "an essentially stupid man" who early in his life hit on one great idea—the **case method**—"to which, thereafter, he clung with all the tenacity of genius" (1977: 42). Richard Cosgrove presents a more flattering view: "Langdell united academic ambition with experience of the world, and both elements colored his theories of law and legal education" (1987: 27).

Langdell introduced the case method as the basic pedagogical tool for educating lawyers at Harvard. Textbooks (and lecture-based instruction) were abandoned in favor of casebooks containing appellate court decisions. By reading and analyzing the opinions of appellate judges, the law student learns how to spot similar issues in factually different situations and gains an understanding of judicial thinking. "The new system trained students to understand the sources as a practicing lawyer must understand them" (LaPiana 1994: 26).

Contrary to the older English view of law as a form of custom, Langdell taught that law is a *science* and legal education is a search for the underlying principles of selected cases:

> Law, considered as a science, consists of certain principles or doctrines. To have such a mastery of these as to be able to apply them with constant facility and certainty to the ever-tangled skein of human affairs, is what constitutes a true lawyer; and hence to acquire that mastery should be the business of every earnest student of law. Each of these doctrines has arrived at its present state by slow degrees; in other words, it is a growth extending in many cases through centuries. The growth is to be traced in the main through a series of cases; and much the shortest and best, if not the only, way of mastering the doctrine effectually is by studying the cases in which it is embodied. But the cases which are useful and necessary for this purpose at the present day bear an exceedingly small proportion to all that have been reported. The vast majority are useless and worse than useless for any purpose of systematic study. (Langdell 1871: vi–vii)

Langdell "argued that the law was a science that could be reduced to a finite number of principles embedded in court decisions. Speculation into jurisprudence [the system of justice] and other, loftier disciplines [sociology, political science, psychology, economics] were banished from Dean Langdell's world. Cases, he maintained, were the lawyers' specimens, and law libraries were for them what laboratories . . . are to the chemists and physicists, the museum of natural history to the zoologists, the botanical gardens to the botanists" (Margolick 1983: 22).

Although he attempted to wrap the study of law in the mantle of science, Langdell had little or no scientific education or training. Thus, his view of science, particularly biology, from which he drew many parallels, was limited and lacked sophistication even by the standards of his day (Stevens 1983; Cosgrove 1987). Indeed, as Richard Posner points out, adherence to precedent, a cornerstone of the case method, is in one sense a "refusal to correct errors—a posture that would be thought bizarre in scientific inquiry" (1990: 82). The study of law, Judge Posner argues, has more in common with theological exegesis than science.

The Case Method

The case method teaches students the skill of legal reasoning through cases that are carefully selected since, according to Langdell, the vast majority are useless and worse than useless for any purpose of systematic study. In his pioneering casebook on contracts, Langdell relied almost entirely on sequences of English cases, arranged chronologically, abridged, and organized in a systematic manner. In Langdell's view, the English common law "comprised an internally consistent body of precedents whose systemization proceeded from the application of induction and logic. Once identified, however, legal principles then became subject to a deductive process in which the judiciary used these rules to decide cases" (Cosgrove 1987: 28). Typically, a casebook does not explicitly state the basis for the selection and organization of the cases. Instead, guided by questions in the casebook or from the instructor, the student learns how to dissect an appellate decision and analyze its constituent parts. The student "learns to relate one case to another, to harmonize the outcomes of seemingly inconsistent cases so that they are made to stand together. By taking and putting together different cases, the student acquires a way of thinking and working with cases that constitutes the fundamentals of legal reasoning, as well as knowledge of doctrinal rules presented by these cases" (Loh 1984: 15).

The burden is on the student to make sense of the decisions. "There is no single correct way of analyzing or synthesizing opinions. In the case method of study, it is the process, not the outcome, that counts" (Loh 1984: 16). Each case has to be read several times to make sure nothing of importance has been missed, and students must come to each class prepared to discuss and analyze a group of actual appellate decisions. The role of the law professor is to goad and stimulate, asking questions in a Socratic method to explore the facts of the case, to determine the legal principles applied in reaching the result, and to analyze the method of reasoning used. The professor will often play the devil's advocate, challenging students to defend their reasoning (*Pre-law Handbook 1982–1983*), and "students are given no advance notice of the positions they will be required to defend before their classmates under Socratic interrogation" (Kronman 1993: 111). The goal is for students to learn simultaneously substantive doctrines, analytical reasoning, and the practical skills involved in public speaking.

The **Socratic method** "familiarizes the student with legal materials, most of them written in the profession's standard style, which exaggerates the uniqueness and the power of the analytical methods that lawyers and judges use. And it imbues the student with that style, at the same time training him to exploit, by means of logic wielded as a critical tool, the indeterminacies in legal materials" (Posner 1990: 99). The student learns "to analyze the implications of each case for possible future disputes, and to integrate the lessons from groups of cases into a general understanding of each subject under study. The process of analyzing and synthesizing cases seeks to develop in the student a capacity to predict what the courts will do and persuade the courts to rule one way or the other in possible future cases" (Burton 1985: 15).

For every class session, appellate cases are assigned and the teacher generally begins by asking a student to summarize the facts of a case, the arguments of the parties, the application of the law to fact, the judge's rationale, and the rule of law as contained in the judge's decision. The teacher then asks the student a series of questions about the assigned material. Few questions have definite answers, nor are they designed to stimulate discussion. "Their nature is to probe issues systematically in the classroom, using the question and its answer to structure the information that the student receives, processes, and takes away from the class" (Gac 1988: 3). In the Socratic method there is "focused dialogue." The teacher then asks a series of hypotheticals— questions based on the case as altered slightly, and the student is asked to decide if the results would be the same. Hypotheticals teach the student to explore the limits of law and the boundaries of case law. In law school, using hypotheticals is seen as "the most effective method for teaching critical thought and analysis" (Gac 1988: 3). Students also learn to think on their feet. Unprepared students can be the brunt of ruthless scrutiny:

> In a typical first-year course such as Contracts, the students prepare for class by reading five or six appellate decisions from a variety of courts on the same topic, for example contract formation. During class, the teacher uses the Socratic method to probe the students' understanding of the different facts, law, and legal reasoning used by the different judges. In the future, when practicing law and faced with a new case, they will be able to recognize the relevant facts of the new case, deter-

mine and interpret the law that might be applicable, and then apply that law to the facts to predict the outcome. (Foster 2001: 347)

Absent from Langdell's curriculum was a discussion of statutes, and his casebooks were devoid of explanatory notes or comments—there was nothing to aid the students. Classroom lectures bewildered students as every possible legal principle was extracted from each case. By the end of Langdell's first year as dean, class attendance had dropped considerably, as had student enrollments. In 1872, nearby Boston University opened a law school for students who were not happy with the innovations at Harvard.

Contrary to the expectations of Langdell's critics, by 1874 enrollments at Harvard Law School were increasing, as Langdell's case method gained adherents. "Gradually the advantage of Langdell's technique became appreciated. By teaching students law from court decisions, an original source, Langdell taught legal reasoning more effectively than did the textbook professors" (Seligman 1978: 41). Harvard had "become a national law school freed from the parochial concerns of a particular state jurisdiction"—the case method is generic (Cosgrove 1987: 28). By 1895, the year he stepped down as dean (he continued to teach until his death in 1905), it was clear that Langdell's reforms had brought a large and able student body to Harvard. Enrollments soared, and standards were raised. In 1896, law at Harvard became a graduate education requiring three years of study with vigorous examinations at the end of each year. There was also curriculum innovation: The study of law was divided into patterns of specialization linked to professional training, for example, contracts, torts, and property. By 1895, Harvard Law School had 10 professors and more than 400 students; by 1907, there were 14 professors and more than 700 students (Stevens 1971). "The conversion of the professoriate into cloistered academics, rather than experienced practitioners, was Langdell's next innovation"—experience in a law office work he held is insufficient for teaching law (Spencer 2012: 1975).

Harvard became the model for other university law schools, and the use of the case method spread rapidly. Many hired Harvard professors and law graduates to help them convert to the new system of teaching law. By 1908, there were more than 30 law schools using the case method (Seligman 1978). What started as innovation at Harvard led to a revolution that eventually became the norm for legal education in the United States. The other schools even copied the Harvard approach of required courses (adhering to the case method) during the first year of study, with electives for the next two years. In large part, this was driven by a quest for elite status (Spencer 2012). In 50 years, "one school had, intellectually, socially, and numerically overwhelmed all others" (Stevens 1971: 434–35).

The case method also had economics in its favor, allowing for one professor to educate classes of as many as 150 students: Langdell "proved to the presidents of universities all over America that they, too, could make money by opening a law school and hiring just a few people to teach" (Turow 1977: 122). The case method resulted in a new profession: law professor. Prior to 1870 it was the practicing lawyer who became the teacher, often on a part-time basis. The case method, however, made stringent demands on time and intellect. Part-timers could not devote the time necessary for preparation, and those practitioners with leisure time "lacked the intellectual flexibility to cope with the analytical, inductive process that comprised the core of the case method" (Auer-

---

The Case Method

"The case method reflects the general belief that the primary purpose of law school is not to teach substantive law, but to teach you to think like a lawyer" (Law School Admission Council 1996: 3).

---

bach 1971: 552). Case-method law professors were frequently recruited right out of school without any practical experience in law, a trend that continues: Nearly half of faculty members at top-tier law schools have never practiced law (Segal 2011). "Langdell introduced the idea that full-time academics with little or no experience were to be preferred when staffing a law school faculty." More or less true to this vision, professors who dominate contemporary law school faculties "are less experienced practitioners than they are highly credentialed legal scholars" (Spencer 2012: 2048).

The teachers of law at the major schools came to comprise an influential elite that would affect the legal and political life of the United States. The influence of the new profession was enhanced by "law review," a student-run journal first established at Harvard in 1887, and subsequently copied by all law schools aspiring for national status; today, there are more than 600. At one time, "legal briefs and judicial decisions increasingly came to use ideas expressed by the professors in law review articles" (Hobson 1986: 408). But the import of law reviews has reportedly declined, with fewer federal decisions citing their articles, which are dismissed as obscure and/or irrelevant to real-world legal issues (Liptak 2007, 2013a; Segal 2011).

Harvard Prevails

The model of education at Harvard was uncritical—it was law devoid of any political or social context. The lawyer *qua* scientist was to be rigorously educated to serve the interests of clients without regard to political beliefs or issues—the case method "makes every position respectable" (Kronman 1993: 114). But who could afford the price of such talented "scientists," persons with an undergraduate degree and three years of intensive graduate education? It was apparent that the Harvards of America were preparing lawyers to serve corporate America:

> At about the turn of the century, a number of the new corporate partnerships became convinced that Harvard Law School provided the most effective preparation for their type of practice. As a result, Harvard Law graduates initially received higher salaries than graduates of other law schools. In an unashamedly acquisitive age, such a reputation was no small matter. Harvard Law School could brag that it attracted students from every state of the Union. Law schools desirous of preparing their graduates to serve in the best-paying firms were inclined to follow Harvard's lead. (Seligman 1978: 44)

Entry into law schools, however, did not become truly competitive until the 1960s; as late as 1960, for example, Harvard Law School admitted 50 percent of all applicants (Abel 1989).

| **Law Schools and Law Students** | | | | | |
1870	1880	1890	1900	1910	1920
31	51	61	102	124	143
1,653	3,134 (approx.)	4,518	12,516	19,567	27,000

Source: Hobson (1986).

The jurisprudence that evolved out of the Harvard model, and which would grow to dominate legal education, is summarized by James Herget (1990: 37):

1. Law consists of principles, something apart from the cases themselves.
2. These principles are the proper subject for intellectual study.
3. Law changes over time in unplanned ways, such change being aided by judges.
4. Rigorous legal analysis is the only rational way to understand the law and to make it applicable to new situations.

Contemporary Legal Education

"The shift from apprenticeship to academic education, which began about 1880 and was complete by 1920, had the unanticipated consequence of greatly accelerating the growth of the profession and facilitating entry by immigrants and their sons. The American Bar Association responded by promulgating standards that only some law schools could meet and [by] seeking to persuade states to restrict entry to graduates of approved schools," a campaign that was largely successful (Abel 1989: 71–72).

Robert Stevens summarizes the relationship between legal education and the American Bar Association's (ABA) campaign to restrict the practice of law: "It had begun in the 1870s as a requirement for some period of law study followed by a bar exam. The second stage was recognition of law school as an alternative to apprenticeship. The third stage was the requirement of law school without the alternative of office study; and the fourth was recognition only of ABA-approved law schools" (1971: 505). Thus, the organization that benefits from restricting the practice of law is in a position to restrict the number of law schools (Shepherd 2000). There are about 200 ABA-approved law schools in the United States that graduate between 35,000 and 40,000 students annually (Glater 2005a).

Standardization of First-Year Law Courses

As a result of ABA **accreditation** and the influence of the American Association of Law Schools (AALS), legal education in the United States has become standardized. In fact, the first-year education of law students is fairly uniform across schools, with each student required to take most or all of the following courses (Law School Admission Council 2012):

- *Civil Procedure.* The process of adjudication in the United States: jurisdiction and standing to sue, **motions** and pleadings, pretrial procedure, the structure of a lawsuit, and appellate review of trial results.

- *Constitutional Law.* The legislative powers of the federal and state governments, and questions of civil liberties and constitutional history, including detailed study of the Bill of Rights and constitutional freedoms.

- *Contracts.* The nature of enforceable promises and rules for determining appropriate remedies in case of nonperformance.

- *Criminal Law and Procedure.* The bases of criminal responsibility, the rules and policies for enforcing sanctions against individuals accused of committing offenses against the public order and well-being, and the rights guaranteed to those charged with criminal violations.

- *Property Law.* Concepts, uses, and historical development in the treatment of land, buildings, natural resources, and personal objects.

Harvard University JD Program

The First Year

"Harvard Law School recently undertook a sweeping overhaul of its first-year curriculum. The new curriculum reflects legal practice in the 21st century, adding courses in legislation and regulation and international and comparative law to the traditional curriculum of civil procedure, contracts, criminal law, property, and torts. All first-year students now take a problem solving workshop in which they grapple with real-world challenges involving complex fact patterns and encompassing diverse bodies of law. Students also participate in a legal research and writing course which teaches important skills essential to the practice of law. And students choose electives, in the international law arena and, more generally, from the wide array of courses Harvard offers.

"The first-year class is divided into seven sections of eighty students each. Faculty Section Leaders, generally senior faculty members who teach one of the section's basic courses, provide guidance and support to the students in their sections and develop a program of extracurricular activities related to the law.

"In addition to section activities, students may participate in first-year reading groups—groups of 10–12 students—that offer the opportunity to interact with faculty in informal settings outside the classroom. Led by faculty members who often focus on areas of particular personal interest, these ungraded groups explore such topics as diverse as law and literature, legal responses to terrorism, regulation of climate change, and issues of bioethics."

The Upper-Level Years

"In the second and third years of law school, Harvard students shape their own courses of study, selecting among a wide offering of electives. Students generally take a mix of classroom, clinical, writing and cross-registration credits, selecting courses at the Law School and throughout the University that align with their interests. Five optional Programs of Study—Law and Government; Law and Social Change; Law and Business; International and Comparative Law; and Law, Science and Technology—developed by the Law School faculty provide pathways through the upper-level curriculum."

Source: J.D. Program 2014 Harvard Law School http://www.law.harvard.edu/academics/degrees/jd/

- *Torts.* Private wrongs, such as acts of negligence, assault, and defamation that violate obligations of the law.
- *Legal Method.* Organization and processes of the American legal system.
- *Legal Research and Writing.* Students research and write memoranda dealing with various legal problems.

Uniformity of legal education ensures that attorneys will share an understanding of the law and its application. This is necessary to meet the needs of a rational legal system in which a lawyer is generally able to predict what a court will do, and judges, if they are to earn the respect of the legal community, will treat cases according to these shared understandings. In other words, "the conventions of the legal community can lead the lawyer with a problem case to see the important facts in the case as other lawyers and judges within the same legal system would see them" (Burton 1985: 97).

The first-year curriculum is quite demanding, focusing on the analysis of appellate court opinions:

> [At first] the number of pages of assigned reading is not great, but the beginning student finds it extremely difficult. Not only is one confronted with a baffling array of unfamiliar concepts, but he or she must also master new intellectual skills. The student must learn to make sense out of the sometimes-incoherent syntax of lawyers and judges, to think with analytical precision, and to distinguish legally relevant passages from the marginally relevant or irrelevant. He or she must acquire a new vocabulary, including numerous Latin and French words and phrases, the meaning of which varies according to the context in which they are used.
>
> All of this is made more difficult by the fact that the mastery of each of these skills depends in part upon ability in the others. For example, it is difficult to distinguish the legally relevant from the irrelevant until one understands the simple meaning of the sentences one is reading. But it is often difficult to pierce the nearly impenetrable veil of judicial syntax without some sense of legally relevant categories and some knowledge of legal vocabulary, neither of which is independently taught but instead is supposed to emerge from the cases. (Stover 1989: 46–47)

Advanced Curriculum

Soon, the amount of reading increases substantially, and the student is required to pursue deeper meanings as he or she is drilled in the Socratic method. "The traditional 'Socratic method' of legal instruction continues to be used in first-year law classes as an extremely effective technique for developing analytical skills, but is less dominant today in the upper-class years. It is supplemented by a diversity of teaching methods that, like the 'Socratic method,' are designed to foster fundamental skills and require students to make use of legal materials in performing lawyer-like functions" (American Bar Association 1980: 13). Second- and third-year courses, however, are often taught in seminar-style rather than the confrontational (between instructor and student) manner of the Socratic method. Seminar courses may only be one-third as large as typical first-year case-method courses. Requiring a third year of law school increases the cost and, critics argue, provides little in the way of improving the quality of legal education (Butler 2006).

Changes in Legal Education

Besides an ABA-mandated course in professional responsibility and participation in a moot court and/or clinical experience, there are no additional course requirements common to all schools. Pressure by bar associations to reduce the cost of "on the job training" has led to the rise of clinical and legal skills training in the law school curriculum: "Legal educators have been forced to capitulate on their traditional exclusion of such matters from the curriculum and accept a dilution of the Langdell model geared solely to 'scientific' search for eternal truths found in judicial opinions" (Van Alstyne, Scott, Julin, and Barnett 1990: 72). "Langdell's method was built upon two essential premises, each valid at the time: first, that there was a manageable corpus juris which could and should be mastered by every 'educated' lawyer; second, that this corpus juris was essentially unchanging and thus, once mastered, was mastered forever." While this is no longer accepted legal doctrine, legal education has remained essentially unchanged and the case method remains the dominant model.

The increasing complexity of law, however, has brought changes in legal education. Scholars recognize that the social and behavioral sciences can inform the techniques, content, and conceptual vocabulary of the law. At the same time, initially inspired by the education of physicians, clinical education has found a niche in legal education. Borrowing from other disciplines has often been superficial, but more law schools are taking a more serious approach to interdisciplinary studies and clinical education. Clinical education, however, can be expensive; a traditional class may have 100 students, while clinical students require close supervision and classes are usually limited to 10 or less (Tamanaha 2012).

Many schools have broadened their required course offerings: The University of Virginia requires Agency and Partnership, Family Law, Introduction to International Law,[4] and Law and Economics. Cornell requires Legal Process, and two courses in Practice Training. Harvard requires Problems in Legal Practice and Methods. The University of California at Los Angeles requires Facts, Clients, and Lawyers (product-lia-

---

Prelaw Education

The American Bar Association (ABA) does not recommend any undergraduate majors or groups of courses for legal education. Instead, students are encouraged to pursue areas of interest that can be as diverse as art, music, science, math, economics, and computer science. Courses that offer development of research, analytical/problem-solving, critical-reading abilities, and writing skills are particularly important. The Law School Admission Council points to the need for experience at close reading and critical analysis of complex textual material in literature, political or economic theory, philosophy, or history. Whatever the major, undergraduates are encouraged to prepare for their legal education by developing a high degree of skill in written and oral communication.

---

[4] International law is a growing field that is particularly relevant for those with foreign language skills and familiarity with another culture.

Stanford

At Stanford Law School, the Supreme Court Litigation Clinic provides hands-on experience to students in preparing and arguing cases before the nation's highest court. Despite the enormous amount of work required, competition for one of the clinic's nine slots is intense. Each term, students travel to Washington for at least one oral argument, most often for a case on which they worked. Whereas the Court grants an oral hearing for less than 1 percent of the more than 8,000 annual petitions, since 2004, it has heard five of the eight cases filed by the clinic, and clinic lawyers have won most of their cases (Falcone 2006).

bility and fact investigation). The University of Chicago requires Elements of the Law (legal reasoning and the relationship between law, social, economic, and political issues). The University of Pennsylvania requires Labor Law and offers the student a choice of one of four courses: American Legal History, Economics of Law, Income Security (welfare, Social Security), or Legal Philosophy. The University of Pennsylvania has a public service requirement: "All second- and third-year students perform a total of 70 hours of public service as a condition of graduation." One of the more recent innovations in law school curricula is the addition of courses, sometimes multidisciplinary, on cyberlaw: legal issues involving the Internet (Harmon 1998). A. Benjamin Spencer (2012) points out that law schools are increasingly offering practical skills training courses, adjusting their programs in various ways to improve their ability to produce practice-capable graduates.

Professional Training v. Scholarship

University law schools frequently draw on faculty from other disciplines—business, economics, history, psychology, and sociology—to present separate courses or to team teach such courses as family law, antitrust law, and criminal law. Some observers see this as obeisance to scholarly traditions rather than a genuine liberal arts commitment on the part of law schools. The emphasis remains on professional training rather than scholarship and is reflected by greater student interest in courses that promote career preparation than those of more scholarly interest. Professional legal training emphasizes advocacy, while scholarship implies truth seeking (Kronman 1993).

One important innovation in the direction of scholarship (and legal realism/sociological jurisprudence discussed below) is the joint-degree program offered at a number of universities, combining law with a second discipline. For example, Columbia offers joint degree programs leading to a JD/MBA (Master of Business Administration), JD/MMCJ (Master of Mass Communication and Journalism), JD/MPA (Master of Public Administration), JD/MFA (Master of Fine Arts), JD/MSW (Master of Social Work), and JD/MUP (Master of Urban Planning). The University of Michigan, in addition to a JD/MBA, offers joint degree programs in Law and Economics, Law and Modern Near Eastern and North African Studies, Law and Public Policy Studies, Law and Natural Resources, Law and Russian and East European Studies, and Law and World Politics. A number of universities combine a law degree with a doctorate in these and additional disciplines for a JD/PhD. There are about 20 law schools that

Grueling Workload: Reality or Myth

As a first-year student at Harvard Law School, Scott Turow states: "I keep waiting for things to relent somehow. I'm blown out. I've never experienced mental exhaustion like what I felt by the end of each day this week. The ceaseless concentration on books and professors . . . left me absolutely blithering when I got home each evening" (1977: 61). But Robert Granfield and Thomas Koenig (1992) discount the "paper chase" myth as just that—*myth*. Students at Harvard are quite nonchalant about their grades and, particularly after the first year, feel little or no pressure to answer in, or even attend, class. (Chris Goodrich's [1991] portrayal of his first year at Yale Law falls somewhere between Turow and Granfield and Koenig.)

offer a Doctor of Juridical Science (SJD) degree, and even more that offer a master's degree in some specific aspect of law, for example, an LLM in taxation (Van Alstyne, Scott, Julin, and Barnett 1990).

Legal education appears to dampen a student's commitment to practicing law in the public interest in favor of the narrow interests of corporate America (Foster 1985; Granfield 1986). Robert Stover found a pronounced change between the first and last year of law school with respect to students' desire to work for social and political goals or to help persons or groups with whom they sympathized. "By the end of law school, students had downgraded the opportunities for altruism in public interest law, while upgrading them for business-oriented jobs" (1989: 34). Richard Kahlenberg (1992: 4) recalls his experience at Harvard: "We came to law school talking about using the law as a vehicle for social change, but when it was time to decide what we would do with our lives, we fell over each other to work for those law firms most resistant to change." According to the American Bar Association (n.d.) 5.9 percent of law school graduates in 2012 were employed in the public interest sector, while 39.3 percent took jobs in law firms and 14.9 percent were employed in business and industry.

Chris Goodrich (1991: 4) reflects on his first-year experience at Yale Law School: "Law schools commonly boast that they teach students to 'think like lawyers,' but I learned that some important things are lost, to both the culture and the individual, in the course of this transformation. Legal training doesn't create selfish, aggressive people—but it does provide the intellectual equipment with which recipients can justify and give force to beliefs and actions most people would wholeheartedly condemn."

Stratification of Legal Education

Similarity of required courses does not mean that all law schools are equal. In fact, there is a great deal of stratification in legal education, and it reflects, and is reflected back, by stratification in the legal profession. Of the more than 200 schools approved by the ABA, about two dozen are consistently referred to as the most prestigious law schools in the United States. It is largely irrelevant whether these schools actually provide a superior education—some argue that Harvard actually provides, instead, elitism and fraternalism (Granfield and Koenig 1992)—what matters is that they are perceived by those who employ law school graduates, particularly national law firms, corporations, and investment bankers, as being superior. In this case, perception creates its own reality. Most of these schools are private institutions that are part of prestigious universities, such as Cornell University, Duke University, Northwestern University, University of Southern California, and Vanderbilt University. Some are church affiliated, such as Boston College, Georgetown University, and the University of Notre Dame; and state universities are also prominent on any list of elite schools, such as the University of

Figure 2.1   Stratification of Legal Education

California at Los Angeles, University of Minnesota, and University of Texas (see figure 2.1). There is a certain amount of homogeneity across elite schools, since their faculties are generally graduates of **elite law schools**.[5]

Elite Law Schools

Entry into these institutions requires an exceptionally high undergraduate grade point average (GPA) and score on the **Law School Aptitude Test (LSAT)**:

- University of California at Berkeley, over 7,000 applications; about 900 admits
- University of Chicago, about 5,000 applications; about 800 admits
- Columbia University, about 6,000 applications; about 900 admits
- Harvard University, about 6,000 applications; about 800 admits
- University of Michigan, about 5,000 applications; about 1,000 admits
- New York University, about 7,000 applications; about 700 admits
- University of Pennsylvania, about 5,000 applications; about 900 admits
- Stanford University, about 4,000 applications; about 400 admits
- University of Virginia, about 7,000 applications; about 700 admits
- Yale University, about 3,000 applications; about 250 admits

(In most instances the number that actually enroll is considerably smaller than the number of admits; many top students are admitted to several schools.)

"Because of variations from college to college in academic standards, law schools tend to favor applicants from undergraduate schools whose marks have proved reliable in the past." At law schools like Harvard, that means a continued influx from the Ivy League colleges, with students from less prestigious schools at a disadvantage. "The sole leveler is the LSAT—the only measure common to all applicants" (Turow 1977: 28).

---

[5] In 2013, every member of the US Supreme Court was a graduate of a "top ten" law school—mostly Ivy League.

The LSAT

The Law School Aptitude Test (LSAT) is a post-World War II addition to the law school admissions process and is administered by the Law School Admission Services (LSAS) four times a year. This standardized examination comprises five 35-minute multiple-choice sections—reading comprehension, analytical reasoning, logical reasoning (two sections), and an experimental section (the examinee does not know which section is experimental). There is also a 35-minute writing sample. The experimental section and the writing sample are not included in the scoring. The writing sample is sent to each law school to which the LSAT score is reported for the school's own use, if any. A candidate's score is based on the number of questions answered correctly—no penalty for guessing—and through a statistical calculation it is then equated with other LSAT tests, resulting in a scale that ranges from 120 to 180. The average (mean) score is about 150, while more than half of those taking the test score above (the median of) 151. According to the LSAS, the exam "is designed to measure skills that are considered essential for success in law school: the reading and comprehension of complex texts with accuracy and insight; the organization and management of information and the ability to draw reasonable inferences from it; the ability to reason critically; and the analysis and evaluation of the reasoning and argument of others." Many take the LSAT more than once since law schools are allowed to consider only the highest score.

The Law School Admission Council advises students that a broad liberal arts curriculum is the preferred preparation for law school: "Enrolling in courses that are designated as part of a prelaw curriculum or major tends to be a less effective means of preparing for law school than enrolling in a diverse college program."

National, Regional, and Local Law Schools

Next in the law school stratification system are national law schools that are part of a state or private university, and a number of them are church affiliated. These schools draw their student body from the nation as a whole. Then there are **regional law schools** whose students are primarily from the geographic region in which the school is located. At the bottom of the stratification system are law schools that are not part of a doctorate-granting university, commuter (local) schools that tend to educate local students for a local practice. Graduates of these schools are overrepresented in the ranks of solo practitioners and local government. There are also law schools that have not been approved by the ABA[6] but whose graduates can be admitted to the practice of law in eight states if they pass the bar examination (Holmes 1996). California, for example, has experienced a growth industry in such schools since it has a very liberal policy with respect to qualifications for taking the bar examination. In 2013, Arizona became the first state to permit law students to take the bar exam in their third year, and there is support for no longer making the third year of law school mandatory (Tamanaha 2012).

---

[6] In 1996, the ABA reached a settlement with the Department of Justice, which had accused the association of anti-competitive practices in its accreditation practices. Among other practices, the ABA dropped its policy of denying accreditation to "for-profit law schools" (Holmes 1996).

Employment Opportunities

The economic recession beginning in 2008 has impacted law schools, causing the number of applications to decline, and 2012 experienced a 30-year low. The decline is a reflection of the disappointing job market for law school graduates who are saddled by debt exceeding $125,000 (Bronner 2013a). While the ABA sought to restrict access to legal education and the practice of law by the poorer classes in the early twentieth century, the rising cost of legal education in the twenty-first century is having the same, albeit unintended, effect (Tamanaha 2012).

Graduates of elite law schools, no longer assured of employment with big-name law firms, are moving down the food-chain, taking positions traditionally filled by graduates of less prestigious law schools with smaller firms, government, and public interest groups (Shih 2009). About 45 percent of law school graduates are unable to secure law-related employment in the nine months following graduation, in part because firms are outsourcing legal work to India and using software for routine chores (Timmons 2010). The title of an article in the *New York Times* (Markoff 2011: 1) points out: "Armies of Expensive Lawyers, Replaced by Cheaper Software." In response, a number of law schools operate their own law firms or arrange a clinical placement (externships) for their graduates, a practice analogous to the postmedical school internship (Bronner 2013b).

Criticisms of Legal Education

Langdell's career at Harvard coincided with an era of unbridled growth for American capitalism. The wheels of industry were greased with the labor of waves of immigrants: men, women, and children whose welfare was not a governmental concern. Positivism and social Darwinism were popular among the educated classes, and the theories of Herbert Spencer provided an aura of science to doctrines that were inimical to the interests of the "huddled masses yearning to breathe free." Like biological evolution, case law was an evolutionary process that placed the brakes on legislatures' statutory interventions into natural legal processes. The preoccupation with judicial decisions and opinions of the past meant that this legal science, generally referred to as *legal formalism*, would be distinctly conservative, and it was bitterly criticized by the proponents of sociological jurisprudence and legal realism.[7]

Sociological Jurisprudence and Legal Realism

About the time of the First World War, some national law schools began to revise their curricula in a way that challenged the case method of instruction.[8] Instead of the exclusive use of cases that focused only on the *ratio decedendi* of appellate court decisions, a number of law schools, most notably Yale and Columbia, introduced courses on legislation, comparative law, and the social sciences. This represented an attempt to "under-

---

[7] Gregory Alexander (n.d.) connects sociological jurisprudence and legal realism to the American Progressive movement and its aftermath: the late nineteenth century until the New Deal.

[8] The conservative nature of the case method is offset by legal education's stress on the adversarial method. The legal profession's ethic of zealous advocacy serves to expand the reach of precedent and renders the case law approach more flexible.

stand the law in terms of its factual context and economic and social consequences" (Kalman 1986: 3). The changes had wide implications. Well-known jurists and legal scholars asserted that deciding cases on the narrow grounds of precedent was both reactionary and illogical. Critics, such as Oliver Wendell Holmes, Jr. (1841–1935) and Benjamin N. Cardozo (1870–1938), both justices of the Supreme Court, became known as legal realists who favored a **sociological jurisprudence**—expanding the study of law beyond the case method to include social realities. The realists were critical of the proposition that judges are simply engaged in law-finding, that they merely apply the facts as presented by litigants to known and certain principles of law. Instead, realists argued, judges exercise considerable discretion in rendering decisions. Legal realists "asserted, with varying degrees of emphasis, that judges make law rather than find it" (Schur 1968: 43).

Proponents of **legal realism** had no patience for "the attempt by traditional jurists to reduce law to a set of rules and principles, which they insisted guided judges to their decisions" (Kalman 1986: 3). It is one of the curious features of Anglo-American case law, states Richard Wasserstrom, "that regardless of the way in which a given decision is actually reached, the judge apparently feels it necessary to make it appear that the decision was dictated by prior rules applied in accordance with the canons of formal logic" (1961: 17). Even when a judge decides to overrule a previous case—to disregard precedent—he or she often finds it necessary to confine the case to its particular facts—to **distinguish away**, a legal device that allows the judge to ignore precedent without stating that the previous decision was incorrect. To do this, the judge finds that the case whose precedent is being urged is not similar enough to the case at hand for the precedent to be relevant.

Realists argued that this is simply an effort to protect the dogma of the infallibility of the courts. The skillful judge will not be bound by the past but will use precedent to maximize freedom of decision making (Llewellyn 1951). Judges "need to find a way to impose their own views on the text without thinking of themselves as doing so, and they disguise their role by attributing what they say not to who they are but to what they read" (Frug 1986: 28). Posner notes that case citations can make "an opinion look more solid than it really is" (1990: 93).

Holmes and Cardozo argued that the proposition that judges merely find law was ludicrous—judges, they argued, choose between competing political, social, and economic values. Law, they concluded, is not a pure doctrine uncontaminated by practical affairs, nor can it be separated from social forces. Instead, law acts as a controlling and stabilizing force in a changing society. Thus, law has to be understood in the context of the social sciences: sociology, political science, economics, and history. "The realists did not object to legal rules and concepts per se; they believed that they could be useful in predicting judicial decisions. But they found other factors equally relevant to their understanding of the judicial process" (Kalman 1986: 6). *Social* justice must be recognized alongside the older *legal* justice (LaPiana 1994).

The realist position is that judges, in effect, *create* law (Murphy and Pritchett 1986). Indeed, the judge, as lawyer, is schooled in disregarding precedent that does not support his or her case, while citing in capital letters cases that do (Llewellyn 1951). Roscoe Pound (1870–1964), who received a PhD in botany before becoming dean of the Harvard Law School (1916–1936), argued for a sociological jurisprudence that complemented the realist critique:

Often formulas are conveniently elastic so that they may or may not apply. Often rules of contrary tenor overlap, leaving a convenient no-man's-land wherein cases may be decided either way according to which rule the court chooses in order to reach a result arrived at on other grounds. Occasionally a judge is found who frankly acknowledges that he looks chiefly at the ethical situation between the parties and does not allow the law to interfere therewith beyond what is inevitable. (Pound 1975: 59–60)

The legal realists, particularly legal scholar Karl Llewellyn (1893–1962) and Judge Jerome Frank (1889–1957), believed that judicial decisions are not controlled by prior rules of jurisprudence but are simply value-laden choices of the judges. Rather than search for precedent to determine the outcome of a case, Frank (1970) reasons that judges arrive at a decision first, no matter how tentative, and then seek the justification for it. If sufficient justification cannot be found, that decision will be dropped, unless that judge is arbitrary or mad, and the process of seeking a justifiable decision continues. Conclusions determine a judge's reasoning, and, according to Frank, the stimuli that lead a judge to justify a particular decision are what need to be studied and explained. In addition to variables such as the economic and political background of the judge (items stressed by judicial realists), Frank pointed to individualistic elements, that is, the personality factors that influence a judge's decisions, an idiosyncratic jurisprudence: "By attributing the cause of their actions to others." Jerry Frug (1986: 28) asserts, "These lawyers and judges establish legal rules without taking responsibility for what they are. They hide—even from themselves—the extent of their own role in choosing what these rules are. And by presenting themselves as experts, they reinforce the average reader's sense that only a professional can make legal judgments." Frank states that personality factors that can influence a decision are usually beyond discovery except by the judge's own introspection—psychoanalytic jurisprudence: "The conscientious judge will, as far as possible, make himself aware of his biases . . . and by that very self-knowledge, nullify their effect" (Frank 1970: xxiii).[9]

The legal realists urged a system of law based on the social sciences and designed to meet the needs of contemporary society. They "hoped to force students to see the interrelationship between law and policy and to make them want to reform the law" (Kalman 1986: 68). Instead of organizing and teaching law along conceptual lines that emphasize "black letter" rules and legal principles, they stressed a living law or law in action (Macaulay 2005). According to this view, law would be organized along the lines of factual situations, for example, building and construction contracts as opposed to mutual assent and consideration. "They tried, however inadequately, to integrate law with the social sciences, adopt the functional approach, and make legal education more clinical" (Kalman 1986: 52).

Appellate court justices, cognizant of the realists' critique, often provide reasons for the policies that underlie the legal rules they fashion and use (Feeley 1984). David Kairys points out, however, that "*stare decisis* neither leads to nor requires any particular results or rationales in specific cases. A wide variety of precedents and a still wider variety of interpretations and distinctions are available from which to pick and choose. Social and political judgments about the substance, parties, and context of the

---

[9] For a more recent attempt to apply a psychoanalytic approach to the legal process, see Shaibani (1999).

> **Precedent and Property**
>
> Judicial adherence to precedent is particularly important to the law of property: "Without certainty as to rules and their application, owners could not determine what they have acquired, how they can use it, and what they might convey. Without adherence to precedent, these private determinations could not be made; instead there would be constant litigation, resulting in significant costs to the interested parties and to the entire community" (Becker 1998: 856).

case guide such choices, even when they are not the explicit or conscious basis of decision" (1982: 14). As Posner points out: "We now know that if we give a legal problem to two equally distinguished legal thinkers chosen at random we may get completely incompatible solutions" (1987: 767).

Harold Berman (1958: 373; edited) places the arguments of those who stress the importance of precedent and the legal realists in perspective:

> Not only is *stare decisis* not absolute but it also has no clear meaning. The *ratio decedendi* of a case is never certain. Moreover, the doctrine of precedent has different values in different fields of law. In dealing with questions of property law or commercial law, a court is reluctant to overturn the holdings of previous cases, since the community relies upon the stability of court decisions in making property or business transactions. In dealing with questions of tort law, on the other hand, courts have less reason to be reluctant to overrule precedent or to "distinguish away" past cases; presumably if a driver of a car proceeds carelessly through an intersection when another careless driver is approaching from the opposite direction, he does not do so in reliance on a rule that the **contributory negligence** of the other driver will bar the latter's recovery. Nevertheless, predictability of judicial decision is a factor to be considered in tort cases as in any other, if only for the reason that the lawyers for the parties rely on past decisions in bringing suit or in defending.

The Impact of Legal Realism

The impact of legal realism is ambiguous; while it succeeded in pointing out that law and lawyers need more than "pure" law when seeking answers to legal problems, it failed to significantly affect the way lawyers are educated (Cosgrove 1987). While the notion of sociological jurisprudence was increasingly accepted, it proved to have little content, and "proved virtually meaningless for legal education" (LaPiana 1994: 156). Columbia University's attempt to expand legal education with an infusion of legal scholarship and the social sciences failed. Yale University was unable to create a sociological jurisprudence. Although Pound expounded the view that law should be treated as one of the social sciences and, as such, a tool for social reform, as dean of the Harvard Law School "he never attempted to meet the demands of his own sociological jurisprudence"; rather, Pound subscribed to the method established by Langdell (Kalman 1986: 46). By the 1930s and the New Deal, Pound had moved away from his earlier "radical" view of law, becoming increasingly conservative, a defender of the status quo in both law and politics, and even an admirer of Adolph Hitler (Stevens

1983). While Fascism and Nazism were gaining strength in Europe, proponents of natural law attacked the realists because of their advocacy of *legal relativism*: "The Realists had difficulty articulating a consistent ethical and moral position; instead, with each situation a different set of facts influenced the course of the law" (Hall, Wiecek, and Finkelman 1991: 469).

By the end of the Second World War, legal realism as a "movement" was history, although its impact on legal education remained. According to Stevens, the primary contribution of the legal realists "was to kill the Langdellian notion of law as an exact science, based on the objectivity of black-letter rules. When it became acceptable to write about the law as it actually operated, legal rules could no longer be assumed to be value-free. This change inevitably caused the predictive value of doctrine to be seriously questioned" (1983: 156). The modern realist remains skeptical of the formalist view and, while emphasizing consequences, is cognizant of the need for predictability. The realist judge believes interpretation "should be guided by a sense of purpose of the text (contract, statute, regulation, constitutional provision) being interpreted, if the purpose is discernible, rather than the literal meaning of the text if purpose and literal meaning are at odds with one another" (Posner 2013: 120).

The *Yale Law Bulletin* (YLB) notes that in some areas "the appellate opinion as the exclusive source of 'case' material was found to be too limited a vehicle for learning about legal rules, much less about the legal system." The bulletin points to the realists' effort to make the "science" of law more useful "by infusing it with the social sciences, locating law and legal institutions in the context of the entire social process, with attention not only to courts but also to legislatures, administrators, and the consumers of law—the people" (1985–1986: 16). An American Bar Association publication on law schools also describes the realists' challenge: "The movement infused certain law schools with intellectual excitement. At Yale and Columbia, particularly, inquiring and challenging minds were busy comprehending the function of law and evaluating its effects. The Columbia law faculty, reflecting the pragmatic, technological orientation of this era undertook the Herculean task of reorganizing its entire curriculum along functional lines with the goal of teaching law as an integral part of the social sciences" (1980: 7).

"Since World War II," notes the *Yale Law Bulletin*, "there has been a development of casebooks made up of 'cases and materials' where once there were only appellate opinions. There have been efforts to blend sociological and realist views, to move them on to 'policy science,' or to portray law in terms of context and process" (1985–1986: 16). In addition, as noted earlier, there has been an expansion of the law school curriculum, adding social science faculty and courses on jurisprudence, legal history, and legal philosophy. At elite law schools, as many as one-third of faculty have PhDs but not law degrees (Tamanaha 2012).

"Legal education in most law schools today focuses upon private rather than public conflict. Its emphasis is on private practice of law in a firm. Law school downplays legislation, public service, judicial or administrative law" (Gerber 1989: 38). Ted Gest (1993) reports, however, that in the 1990s, an increasing number of students had been motivated to enter the field of public service, and about 50 law schools had started programs to ease the debt burden of graduates who enter legal services or government agencies. Several states have created loan forgiveness programs that pay off

> ## To Advance Social Justice?
>
> Many students enter law school "with idealistic notions about advancing social and eco-
> nomic justice, yet our system of ethics instructs lawyers that the broader social implications of
> legal work are subverted by the goals of individual representation. The repeated focus on just
> one client rather than the lofty ideals of systemic change can be disappointing—especially
> when the outcome in a particular case is adverse to a larger group of disenfranchised peo-
> ple—since our system privileges the absolute right of clients to dictate the goals of represen-
> tation" (Carasik 2011: 751).

some or all of a lawyer's student loans if he or she is employed in low-paying public service positions (Kendall 1991). Law schools have been slowly modifying the basic curriculum to cover problems of the poor.

Critical Legal Studies

A more recent attack on legal education (and legal formalism) in the United States is known as **critical legal studies** (CLS), which became popular during the 1970s, a time when Americans were struggling with issues of civil rights and the Vietnam War. Allan Hutchinson (1989) credits the "official birth" of CLS to a conference in 1977 at the University of Wisconsin in Madison. The CLS movement is an attempt to revive the legal realist claims that *law is politics* (Manza 1990).

Many who take the CLS approach view law from a neo-Marxian perspective. Law, they argue, is part of an ideological system that legitimates the social order "by pre-senting existing social relationships [capitalism] as normal, desirable, and just" (New-man 1983: 19). Laws and their application are, thus, not neutral but represent the interests of a dominant elite to the disadvantage of the less powerful masses. CLS stal-warts ("crits") challenge the ability of the judicial system to dispense "true justice." They point to the prevailing probusiness climate of the nineteenth century, when judges interpreted tort law governing cases of personal injury in a manner that clearly favored business and industry at the expense of the public, and to the routine use of courts to harass and weaken the ability of workers to organize and strike (discussed in Chapter 6). Instead of being neutral, the courts allowed corporate America to reign free from legal liability in their quest for profits, while workers were kept under strict legal control (Michalowski 1985).

CLS goes against the formalist view of law, pointing to the uncertain nature of meaning in language as the source of the indeterminacy of deciding cases. Thus, legal rules are so far from clear, with regard to where and how they should be applied, that there is no possibility of their being applied consistently or objectively (McCormick 1999). Not only is the law inconsistent, but it is radically indeterminate, capable of producing opposite results in similar cases depending on the outcome the judge desires or the system requires. Furthermore, legal principles are not neutral, but biased in favor of certain economic and social arrangements that are themselves nei-ther inevitable nor just—the law is not apolitical but in fact the instrument and enforcer of the ideology of liberal capitalism (Menand 1986). By pretending that legal outcomes are the product of apolitical and neutral modes of argument rather than the imposed preferences of those with wealth and power, the rule of law legitimizes current political and economic arrangements (Hutchinson 1988): *legal elites protecting monied elites*. The case law system "legitimates things by seemingly withdrawing matters of substantial ideological controversy from legislative and political debate. Fundamental issues are instead put into courts where they are translated into less transparent vocabulary that conveys the basic rightness of the status quo" (Paul 2001: 714).

The elite law schools, in particular, have been criticized for turning out narrowly educated technocrats dedicated to the perpetuation of corporate interests at the expense of the urban and rural poor, workers, farmers, consumers, and the environment. A leader in the critical legal studies movement, Duncan Kennedy of Harvard, refers to legal education as "ideological training for willing service in the hierarchies of the corporate welfare state" (1982: 40). He offers a critical description of contemporary legal education:

> [Students] learn to retain large numbers of rules organized into categorical systems (requisites for a contract, rules about breach, etc.). They learn "issue spotting," which means identifying the ways in which the rules are ambiguous, in conflict, or have a gap when applied to particular fact situations. They learn elementary case analysis, meaning the art of generating broad holdings for cases so they will apply beyond their intuitive scope, and narrow holdings for cases so that they won't apply where it at first seemed they would. And they learn a list of balanced, formulaic, pro/con policy arguments that lawyers use in arguing that a given rule should apply to a situation despite a gap, conflict, or ambiguity, or that a given case should be extended or narrowed. These are arguments like "the need for certainty," and "the need for flexibility," "the need to promote competition," and "the need to encourage production by letting producers keep the rewards of their labor." (1982: 45)

David Margolick points out, "For many students, law school has become more a conduit to lucrative positions in large law firms than an opportunity to ponder the larger questions about law and justice" (1983: 21). To Derek Bok, a former president of Harvard University and an attorney, the overwhelming preference among top law graduates for such positions represents "a massive diversion of exceptional talent into pursuits that often add little to the growth of the economy, the pursuit of culture or the enhancement of the human spirit" (1983: 573). As noted earlier, many law schools are offering courses designed to broaden the education of their students, and there are law clinics through which students receive a more realistic legal experience and sometimes have the opportunity to serve the interests of the poor. However, the bulk of legal education is narrowly focused to meet the needs of business, not the public interest, and the heavy recruitment at the elite schools by national law firms tends to provide reinforcement for the status quo.[10] (For a further discussion of CLS, see James Boyle 1992; Cardarelli and Hicks 1994. For an in-depth critique, see Whitehead 1999.)

---

[10] Despite their criticism of the legal profession, the "crits" generally do not support opening up the practice of law, something supported by many political conservatives who want to break the legal profession's monopoly over the practice of law. "The rise of the paralegal," notes Posner, "has demonstrated that much of the traditional work of lawyers can be done by nonlawyers" (1995: 66).

Researchers v. Lawyers

Companies in the United States spend an estimated $194 billion on research and development and $205 billion on tort litigation (Newman 2006).

Law and Economics

At the other end of the political spectrum from critical legal studies is the law and economics movement, according to which "the overriding goal of law, as of economics, should be that of efficiency" (Schwartz 1993: 201)—a *consequentialist* or pragmatic approach. Economics as a scholarly discipline has impacted on the study and teaching of law as evidenced by specialized journals and the founding of the American Association of Law and Economics. (It has also impacted on other disciplines, such as sociology.) The law and economics movement received its impetus at the University of Chicago when Edward H. Levi teamed with an economist to teach his course in antitrust law (Lewis 2000). Indeed, the law and economics perspective is sometimes referred to as the "Chicago School." Levi, who would become the dean of the law school, president of the University of Chicago, and attorney general of the United States in 1975, founded the school's *Journal of Law and Economics* in 1958 (Lewis 2000). The **law and economics** perspective argues that while common-law judges feign obeisance to common-law principles, in practice they decide their cases "as though they were trying to bring about the outcome that a free market would have produced" (MacFarquhar 2001: 87).

The development of a legal focus determined by economics is, of course, not surprising; Chapter 1 noted that modern/rational law is intertwined with capitalism. Anthony Kronman states, "In almost every area of law a working knowledge of economics is now required to keep abreast of scholarly developments" (1993: 166). He sees this as an extension of the Langdellian view of law as a scientific endeavor—law as amoral. Of all of the various social sciences, why economics? Kronman points to the discipline's abstractness and its tendency to have "indifference to the content of human interests" (1993: 228)—it is closest in appearance to the ideological neutrality of the natural sciences. "These days, many law teachers now have supplemented (or in some cases replaced) the science of legal reasoning with the science of economics" (Roithmayr 2005: 84).

Although the law and economics movement "can be regarded, in crude terms, as the right wing of modern American Jurisprudence, critical legal studies being its left" (Kelly 1993: 436), this would be an oversimplification: "The libertarian inclinations of most law-and-economics scholars place them to the right of most Americans on economic issues, but to the left on social questions. Cultural conservatives and Republicans of any stripe are a decided minority" in the law and economics movement (Glendon 1994: 216).

One of the foremost proponents of the economic approach to law is Richard Posner, a federal appellate judge, law professor at the University of Chicago, past president of the American Law and Economics Association, and a prolific author. He considers law and economics consistent with legal realism (2013). Wealth maximization, Judge Posner argues, should be the guiding principle in common-law adjudication. Issues should be stripped of their ideological or ethical implications and, instead, legal decisions should be based on "the costs to be incurred and the benefits to be reaped from alternative courses of action" (1995: 16). The common law, Posner states, serves to maximize wealth by imbuing judges with concern for promoting efficiency.[11] A failure to promote efficiency results in appeals and/or new legislation that conforms to the dictates of productivity. Thus, laws and legal decisions can be subjected to economic analysis along the lines of wealth maximization. Common-law judges, he argues, are especially well equipped to promote prosperity: "The rules of the common law that they promulgate attach prices to socially undesirable conduct," thereby creating incentives to avoid such conduct (Posner 1990: 359). Instead of *stare decisis*, however, law and economics, like the discipline of economics, discards theories that are falsified by data—it is pragmatic (Posner 1995). Law and economics studies have influenced a number of legal subjects, most importantly, antitrust law—Judge Posner was a key player in the Microsoft antitrust case of 1999–2000.

The economic view of human behavior presumes that the pursuit of self-interest will guide decisions ranging from purchases and production to whether to break the law (Blackstone and Bowman 1999). Law and economics views human behavior as rational, driven by incentives to which people respond in accord with their own self-interest. This is the basis of *rational choice theory*, the presumption that individuals act to maximize their self-interest. Accordingly, legal rules, which create incentives or disincentives for people to act, should conform to the goal of wealth maximization. However, while sound legal policy must recognize these incentive effects and be responsive to them, there is a great deal of evidence indicating that individuals frequently act in ways that are incompatible with the assumptions of rational choice theory (Korobkin and Ulen 2000). And is it reasonable to expect judges with little or no understanding of statistics-based research to routinely interpret economic data? And there is the problem of predictability: How does a business organize activities that avoid the consequences of litigation when the rules change according to economics-based pragmatism?

There are, of course, some legal issues beyond the pale of economics—not all issues that arise in law can be recast as economic questions. Economics has difficulty, for example, with cases involving sexuality and reproduction (Posner 1995: 22). "The costs of forcing a woman to bear an unwanted child are readily analyzed within an economic framework, but what of the costs to the fetus of being aborted?"[12] Furthermore, "some legal rules are defensible even if they are shown to impose costs and inefficiencies," as do a host of due process requirements (Winick 1997: 191).

In this chapter we examined the development of legal education and law schools. In the next chapter we will turn to the parallel development of the practice of law, bar associations, and the stratification of the legal profession.

---

[11] For a discussion of intricacies of applying cost-benefit analysis to policy issues, see Adler and Posner (2000); Sunstein (2000b).

[12] For a discussion of the varied traditions that make up law and economics, see Mercuro and Medema (1997).

Summary

- There were no law schools in colonial America; a few attorneys were trained in England.
- Most American attorneys, including Thomas Jefferson and Alexander Hamilton, gained a legal education serving as an apprentice to an established attorney.
- Chief Justice John Marshall had little formal education in law or any other discipline.
- Efforts by the colleges to develop law as a scholarly study were not a success.
- There was disagreement over whether the study of law should be academic or practical.
- The first law school was established at Harvard, which offered a degree earned in 18 months—a college degree was not necessary.
- Colleges incorporated private law schools that were interested in the prestige of such an affiliation, because in most states only universities were empowered to issue degrees, but they remained primarily trade schools.
- As dean of the Harvard Law School, Christopher Columbus Langdell raised standards at Harvard and introduced the case method and Socratic method.
- According to Langdell law was a science that could be reduced to a finite number of principles embedded in court decisions.
- Requirements for graduation from Harvard Law School were increased to three-years of full-time study, a requirement eventually followed by other law schools.
- The case method is generic and thus not dependant on the case law of any particular state.
- The case method has economics in its favor, allowing for one professor to educate classes of as many as 150 students.
- The changes instituted at Harvard increased the cost of becoming an attorney.
- The American Bar Association sets standards for law schools and is the reason that legal education is relatively uniform throughout the country.
- Uniformity of legal education ensures that attorneys will share an understanding of the law and its application. This is necessary to meet the needs of a rational legal system in which a lawyer is generally able to predict what a court will do, and judges will treat cases according to these shared understandings.
- Legal education is stratified into four levels: elite, national, regional, and local.
- The prestige of a law school is determined by student grades on the LSAT and the geographic range of its applicants.
- Legal education has been criticized for failure to pay sufficient attention to the social and economic consequences of legal decisions.
- Criticism of law schools has been expressed in sociological jurisprudence, legal realism, and critical legal studies.
- The law and economics perspective advocates considering the economic consequences in rendering a court decision.

KEY TERMS

accreditation	elite law schools	legal realism
bar	Inns of Court	motion
case method	integrated bar	regional law schools
contributory negligence	jurisprudence	sociological
critical legal studies	law and economics	jurisprudence
distinguish away	Law School Aptitude Test (LSAT)	Socratic method

REVIEW QUESTIONS

1. What was the educational background of most prominent attorneys in colonial and post-Revolutionary America?
2. What was the disagreement over the nature of the study of law?
3. What changes did Christopher Columbus Langdell bring to Harvard Law School?
4. What is the case method approach to legal education?
5. What is the Socratic method in legal education?
6. What is the advantage for students of using the case method in legal education?
7. What is the economic advantage of using the case method?
8. Why does uniformity of legal education promote predictability in law?
9. What are the four levels of legal education stratification?
10. How are national law schools distinguished from local law schools?
11. Why is the geographic range of applicants an indication of its prestige?
12. What is sociological jurisprudence?
13. What are the arguments of Critical Legal Studies?
14. What does the law and economics view advocate?

INTERNET CONNECTIONS

American Law and Economics Association: http://amlecon.org
Law Links: http://www.washlaw.edu
Law School Admissions Council: http://lsac.org
Legal Research: http://www.ilrg.com
Meta-Index for US Legal Research: https://gsulaw.gsu.edu/metaindex

Lawyers and the Practice of Law

Chapter 2 examined the development of legal education and law schools. In this chapter we will turn to the parallel development of the practice of law, bar associations, and the stratification of the legal profession.

Lawyers in Revolutionary America

Throughout the colonial era, there was hostility toward lawyers. Some colonists had had negative experiences with lawyers in England, and the poor often viewed lawyers as part of the ruling merchant and propertied class. There was also opposition to lawyers from the landed gentry of the South and the clergy of the North, both of whom saw attorneys as competitors for power and influence (Pound 1953). Legislation hostile to the practice of law was enacted in many colonies (Schwartz 1974). "In most societies at most periods," notes Grant Gilmore, "the legal profession has been heartily disliked by all non-lawyers: a recurrent dream of social reformers has been the law should be (and can be) simplified and purified in such a way that the class of lawyers can be done away with. The dream has never withstood the cold light of waking reality" (1977: 1).

A majority of colonial lawyers appear to have sided with the king and either left America for Canada or England or were forced to retire from practicing law after the Revolution. In some states, a loyalty oath was required before an attorney was permitted to practice law. The loyalty test required by the state of New York in 1779 resulted in so many attorneys retiring from practice "that the bar of the state Supreme Court had almost ceased to exist" (Chroust 1965: 10). Kermit Hall refers to the conflict between the colonists and the Crown as a conservative revolution under the influence of lawyers: "No heads rolled in America; loyalists were tarred and feathered but not hung. Patriot leaders permitted them to flee with their lives and they confiscated their lands only after proper legislative and judicial proceedings" (1989: 50). Many of those who left because of the Revolutionary War were the better trained lawyers, so the post-Revolutionary bar was one of limited ability. And most judges were as unfit by training and education as the lawyers who practiced before them (Pound 1953).

Ambitious young men flocked to the practice of law as the dislocation of the Revolution expanded the need for attorneys at a time when the number of attorneys had dwindled. However, "a large segment of the young American bar was made up of men who had but a sketchy acquaintance with the law and with the standards required of an honorable profession" (Chroust 1965: 35). Yet, even those with little formal education were frequently quite literate. Patrick Henry was admitted to the practice of law in Virginia at age 24, and "what law he knew was self-taught" (Handlin and Handlin 1982: 71); Alexander Hamilton's preparation for the bar consisted of three months of law reading (Ferguson 1984).

Economic disarray was widespread in the years following the Revolution, and the lawyer was despised in debtor areas as a tool of monied interests. A major part of his (there were no female lawyers) practice typically involved legal action against debtors, many of whom were Revolutionary War veterans who had left their farms and businesses unattended to serve in the military. They quickly found that patriotism had an economic price: Unable to pay their debts, veterans found their property foreclosed and sold at auction by the sheriff. If this was insufficient to pay off the debt, the debtor was imprisoned (Chroust 1965). In 1786, these conditions brought about a farmers' rebellion in western Massachusetts led by Revolutionary War veteran Daniel Shays (Hurst 1950). The newspapers regularly castigated lawyers, and legislation was proposed in a number of states to curtail the practice of law or otherwise open it up to anyone who wished to practice (Chroust 1965).

In spite of the antagonism against lawyers, the profession thrived. Anton-Herman Chroust notes that "highly effective in the gradual conquest of public opinion and the common mind was the consistent and clever barrage of self-serving propaganda which lawyers levied in their own behalf" (1965: 30). The portrait presented to the public was that of the noble lawyer eager to assist those who could not afford his services. They were also great exponents of the republic whose "voice and pen served both culture and country in a seemingly endless stream of works instructing and strengthening the American people in the meaning of republicanism" (Ferguson 1984: 26).

> The lawyer's status in this period was determined by his effort to rise above the level of a trade and reach that of a profession. The effort ran into opposition from those forces in American life which wanted no part of the specially trained and specially privileged elites who were trying to map out for themselves a broad control over society. . . . At the same time, the egalitarian "folk" ethos gave way to the realities of a complex society where the lawyer's skills and discipline were needed. With its usual disregard for consistency, the public, while deprecating practitioners of law for inattention to truth and fairness, continued to bestow upon them offices of trust. (Haar 1965: 12–13)

Thus, despite the low status of the bar, lawyers continued to be prominent in American government. In fact, lawyers were the most prominent members of colonial legislatures and the Continental Congress. Of the 56 signers of the Declaration of Independence, 25 were lawyers. Of the 55 members of the Constitutional Convention, 31 were lawyers, as were 10 of the 29 senators and 17 of the 56 representatives of the first Congress (Schwartz 1974); 13 of the first 16 presidents were lawyers (Ferguson 1984). Being aligned with the merchant and propertied class was obviously not a political handicap. "Economic necessity stimulated a demand for skilled interpreters of the labyrinth of provincial and local economic regulatory legislation" (Hall 1989: 23). Law-yers were articulate and active in community affairs, available to help with the myriad of increasingly complex issues affecting the newly independent United States. "If law-yers were an evil, they were, however, a necessary evil" (Friedman 1973: 83). In the 109th Congress (2006), 170 members of the House and 58 senators were law school graduates (Amer 2006). Seven years later in the 113th Congress, 156 members of the House and 58 members of the Senate were law school graduates (Manning 2013).

Admission to the Bar

In colonial times, each colony set its own standards for admission to the bar, and requirements usually involved a long period of apprenticeship. Traditional English differences between solicitors and barristers, for all practical purposes, did not exist. In some colonies each court admitted attorneys to practice before it, and admission to the higher courts was more difficult than admission to the lower courts. In others, admission by one court granted an attorney the right to practice in all courts of the col-ony. In some colonies admission to practice was centralized through the royal gover-nor or an examining body appointed by the court (Pound 1953). "Bar associations created by the leading lawyers soon gained the approval of the colonial legislatures, themselves increasingly penetrated by members of the legal profession. Bar examina-tions went hand in hand with licensing examinations by judges, the result of which was a more influential profession as well as a more English one" (Hoffer 1998: 96).

However, lawyers were extremely unpopular in the years following the Revolu-tion and particularly during the era of Jacksonian democracy (1828–1836). Strong democratic feelings and concurrent opposition to monopolization of legal practice led to the demise of standards for entry into legal practice. During the first third of the nineteenth century, there was a legislative breaking down of educational and training requirements necessary to be admitted to the practice of law (Pound 1953). In 1800, a definite period of preparation for admission to the bar was prescribed in 14 of the 19 states or organized territories that made up the Union. By 1840, it was required in only 11 out of 30 jurisdictions. In New Hampshire (in 1842), Maine (in 1843), Wisconsin (in 1849), and Indiana (in 1851), any citizen and voter could enter into the practice of law with no other evidence than that of having good character. By the eve of the Civil War, only nine of 39 jurisdictions had standards, and they were usually quite low: "Good natured lawyers gave certificates of 'regular and attentive study' liberally to the asker with little or no inquiry," thus qualifying the person for admittance to the bar (Pound 1953: 230).

Standards remained lax in most states during the nineteenth century, and not at all uniform from state to state; government control of occupations remained weak. An open-ended bar attracted ambitious, if not talented, persons. By 1850, there were more than 20,000 lawyers in the United States, when the population was at 23 million, a ratio of 1 to 1,150. However, according to the Census Bureau, by 1880 there were more than 64,000 lawyers for a population of 50 million, a ratio of 1 to 781; by 1900, there were 108,000 lawyers for a population of 76 million, a ratio of 1 to 703; and by 1910, there were more than 115,000 lawyers for a population of almost 92 million, a ratio of 1 to 800. In some areas lawyers formed guilds (bar associations) to restrict the entry of new practitioners by holding down the number of apprentices, and this may have served to lessen the rate of increase.

The Growth of Bar Associations

Although a variety of bar associations existed by the early part of the nineteenth century, they failed to exert any real control over who was admitted to the practice of law. After 1870, bar associations became vigorous in their fight to limit entry into the practice of law, primarily by way of raising standards. This movement to limit entry into the practice of law coincided with Christopher Columbus Langdell at Harvard (discussed in Chapter 2) and the rise of the case method in legal education: "The two movements went hand in glove" (Friedman 1973: 536). The case method served to define the practice of law as a distinct and scientific discipline that required extensive education and training. There was now justification for a monopoly of practice.

In some cities, such as New York (where the Association of the Bar of the City of New York was founded in 1870), bar associations were "motivated in large part by the reformist intent of established patrician lawyers," a response to rampant judicial corruption (Powell 1988: 9). This reformist bent was tempered by self-interest—elite lawyers, in reforming the system, institutionalized the advantage of their most important clients: corporate America. Reform was also intertwined with **nativism**, striking a blow against the "blackguard Celtic tyrants," Irish machine politicians who dominated urban politics and thus the courts in metropolitan areas (Powell 1988).

For most of their existence, bar associations represented a distinct part of the legal profession—white, male, mostly Protestant, and devoid of the latest immigrant groups. Throughout the nineteenth century the organized bar fought "to keep the law in the hands of the profession and to keep the profession in the hands of the legal elite" (Hobson 1986: 57). Around the time of the Great Depression (1929 to the Second World War), in some urban areas this actually led to the formation of competing bar associations—one for lawyers who represented solo practitioners and small firms, often persons with strong ties to urban political machines, another for those who represented banks and corporate clients (Glick 1983).

The bar association movement was a characteristic feature of the turn of the century. Lawyers, in common with doctors, "flocked into professional associations whose growth—the number of bar associations jumped from 16 in 1880 to more than 600 by

---

Urban Machine Politics

Immigrants to urban America found employment in the most dangerous, monotonous, and poorly paid industries; women and children often labored as well. They were forced into slum housing reserved for their own ethnic group. Their culture, customs, and religious beliefs and practices were subjected to virulent attack by Americans of earlier stock. "Beset by hostility and discrimination on virtually all sides, the immigrant gradually found that he possessed at least one commodity that some native Americans coveted: his vote" (Buenker 1973: 3). A new breed of broker—the political boss—emerged to channel these votes into a powerful entity known as the "machine."

1916—expressed the impulse for professional cohesion in a fragmented society under-going rapid change" (Auerbach 1976: 62–63). As bar associations became more effec-tive, standards for practice were raised. By 1890, nearly half of the states required some preparation for practice, and after 1890, more and more states began requiring stringent levels of training and/or education. By 1928, every jurisdiction except Indi-ana had a compulsory bar examination, and there were training and/or educational requirements in order to qualify (Stevens 1983). However, as late as 1927, 32 of 49 jurisdictions had no prelegal educational requirement, and an additional 11 required only high school graduation (Abel 1989).

The Bar Examination

Some conflict occurred between bar associations and law schools over the **diploma privilege**. Beginning with Virginia in the 1840s, several states agreed to admit the graduates of leading law schools to the bar without further examination. By 1870, nine schools in seven states had this privilege. Diploma privilege made it possible for law schools to attract increasing numbers of students who desired to avoid the bar exami-nation. The bar leadership, however, "was not pleased with the diploma privilege, which it felt took control of entry into the profession away from practitioners and gave it to legal educators" (Stevens 1983: 26). Bar associations were successful in their efforts against the diploma privilege, and statewide boards of examiners slowly became the norm; by 1917, they existed in 37 jurisdictions (Stevens 1983). Standards for admission to the bar are still regulated by each state and differ accordingly.

All states except California require a college degree or at least three years of undergraduate education (Abel 1989).[1] Most states require a candidate to have gradu-ated from an accredited law school, show evidence of "sound character," and pass an examination testing his or her knowledge of the law and skill in legal reasoning.[2] Cal-ifornia, Vermont, Virginia, and Washington allow those who spend three or four years in a state-registered apprenticeship to take the bar exam, while New York, Maine, and Wyoming qualify those with a combination of apprenticeship and law school experi-ence (Associated Press 2005).

Although it varies from state to state, the typical bar examination requires the can-didate to analyze hypothetical cases and set forth proposed solutions and the applica-ble laws. It is heavily weighted toward business subjects (Smith 1997). Given in February and July, the exam takes about 12 hours over two days (except in California, three days, and Texas, two and a half days). The first is devoted to the National Con-ference of Bar Examiners (NCBE) multistate, a 200-question, multiple-choice exam that is computer graded, with questions on constitutional law, contracts, criminal law, evidence, real property, and torts. On the second day is a test of applicable state laws and practices that is typically a mix of multiple-choice and essay questions that focus on the law in that particular state. (The National Conference has also developed a

---

[1] Some law schools allow early entry—after completing three years of college—for students with outstanding grades and high LSAT scores.

[2] Under diploma privilege, graduates of the University of Wisconsin Law School and Marquette University Law School do not have to take the Wisconsin bar examination to practice law in the state as long as their schools certify their legal competence and the Board of Bar Examiners certifies their character and fitness for the practice of law.

multistate essay exam.) Forty-seven states and the District of Columbia require candidates to take the NCBE Multistate Professional Responsibility Examination, which consists of 50 multiple-choice questions.

New York University law professor Harry Subin states that "even the most competent law student in the country probably cannot pass [the bar exam] without taking a two-month cram bar review course" (1990: 10). Christopher Smith argues: "If you give any group of lawyers, including law professors, a bar exam as an unannounced 'pop quiz,' virtually all would fail," and "passing a bar exam does not mean that an attorney possesses lawyering skills or knows anything about various areas of law" (1997: 74).

Despite the trend toward standardization in testing, each state sets its own passing grade. Once admitted, a lawyer may practice only in the state where he or she is a member of the bar, although many states have reciprocal agreements and will admit lawyers from reciprocating states who have practiced law for a certain number of years. "The state-based system of bar admission is anachronistic. Ours is an era of multistate, even international, law firms. The practice of law is frequently multistate, but bar admission still occurs one state at a time" (Gerber 1989: 65–66). In 2012, 82,920 persons took bar examinations and 67 percent passed. States vary considerably in the number of persons taking the bar examination and the percentage who pass. For example, note the number of persons who took the exam and the percentage who passed in the following sample of states: California: 6,683—51%; New York: 9,680—61%; Texas: 3,002—75%; Wyoming: 80—53%. Ironically, California and Wyoming had similar percentages of persons who passed but a large difference in the number of persons who took the exam. The state with the highest passing percentage (91%) was Montana, where 200 persons took the exam (National Conference of Bar Examiners

Attorney's Oath of Admission

I do solemnly swear:

I will support the constitution of the United States and the Constitution of my State;

I will maintain the respect due to courts of justice and judicial officers;

I will not counsel or maintain any suit or proceeding which shall appear to me to be unjust, nor any defense except such as I believe to be honestly debatable under the law of the land;

I will employ for the purpose of maintaining the cause confided to me such means only as are consistent with truth and honor and will never seek to mislead the judges or jury by any artifice or false statement of fact or law;

I will maintain the confidence and preserve inviolate the secrets of my client, and will accept no compensation in connection with this business except from him or with his knowledge and approval; I will abstain from all offensive personality, and advance no fact prejudicial to the honor or reputation of a party or witness unless required by the justice of the cause with which I am charged;

I will never reject, from any considerations personal to myself, the cause of the defenseless or oppressed, or delay any man's cause for lucre or malice, so help me God.

Note: The American Bar Association commends this form of oath for adoption by the proper authorities in all the States and Territories.

2013). Interestingly, graduates of elite law schools generally do not do as well as those from less selective schools. The kind of knowledge required is often not learned in law school, so almost all graduates take a bar exam review course.

In 1913, Herbert Harley founded the American Judicature Society as a vehicle for judicial reform, including compulsory membership in bar associations. In labor-management relations this is referred to as the closed shop; Harley chose the more positive-sounding term **integrated bar** (McKean 1963). Thirty states have an integrated bar, which is mandated by the legislature or that state's highest court. Every lawyer must pay dues and subject him- or herself to its rules or forfeit the right to practice law in that state. Mandatory membership in the bar association has been upheld by the Supreme Court (*Lathrop v. Donohue* [1961]).

American Bar Association

The idea of a national association of lawyers originated in 1878 at a meeting of the Connecticut Bar Association, during which a motion was passed to have a committee consider the establishment of an association of American lawyers.[3] The committee of prominent members of the Connecticut bar subsequently reported in favor of the idea. A circular signed by prominent attorneys from throughout the United States issued a call for a meeting on August 21, 1878. The place was Saratoga Springs, a vacation spa just north of Albany, New York, famous for its mineral water and gambling. Although the invitation for the gathering had been circulated to 607 names drawn from 41 states, territories, and the District of Columbia, only 75 persons from 21 states and the District of Columbia were in attendance (Carson 1978). The South was well represented—many lawyers apparently saw the meeting as an opportunity to escape the southern heat. The American Bar Association (hereafter ABA) chose as its first president James O. Broadhead, a Virginian who had moved to Missouri, where he sided with the Union. The delegates met amidst the background of Reconstruction and the scandals of Ulysses S. Grant's second term as president.

Within a year, the ABA had 284 members in 21 states. From 1878 to 1889, the ABA met annually or in alternate years in Saratoga Springs. Until 1902, meetings alternated between Saratoga Springs and other cities. By 1909, the ABA had 3,716 members; by 1924 it had 22,024. The increase was the result of a reorganization that established a state director and 11 district directors to tie local associations closer to the national. In 1936, the ABA established a federalized system of governance; the ruling body is the House of Delegates whose membership is selected by state and local bar associations. The ABA now has more than 400,000 members and is headquartered in Chicago.

In its earlier days, the ABA supported conservative business values that were threatened by majoritarianism: "Irrational passion and ignorance might sweep through the majority, but if those committed to the rule of law could only prevail, social order could be reasserted through peaceful and institutional means" (Hobson 1986: 34). The association exhibited considerable nativism, racism, anti-Semitism, and

---

[3] Robert Stevens ascribes the founding of the ABA to meetings of the American Social Science Association in 1876 and 1877, during which the creation of a national lawyer's group was urged: "The creation of the American Bar Association (ABA) in 1878 was largely the result of these meetings" (1983: 27).

sexism—for the first 40 years, the ABA had no female members (Margolick 1994). In 1969, the ABA elected a Jewish president; in 1994, the association elected a woman president. Today the ABA commissions studies on a variety of matters important to the legal profession and recommends reforms on various issues such as uniform state laws, reciprocity for attorneys in one state to practice in others, maritime law, criminal law and procedure, patents, and trademarks.

In 1900, the ABA's Section on Legal Education organized a meeting of law school delegates in Saratoga Springs. At this meeting the American Association of Law Schools (AALS) was established to improve the legal profession through the improvement of legal education. To be eligible for membership in the AALS, law schools had to comply with admission and length of study requirements (not fewer than two years prior to 1905, and three years thereafter). Schools that failed to maintain the requirements were dropped from the AALS. There was friction between the teachers of law and the practitioners: "To generalize, teachers tended to view law as an instrument of social change; practitioners saw it as a means of social control" (Auerbach 1971: 570). In 1914, after the ABA shifted its annual meeting from August to October, an inconvenient time for teachers, the AALS ceased to have any organizational connection to the ABA.

The accreditation of law schools, however, is the responsibility of the Council of the Section of Legal Education and Admissions to the Bar of the ABA, and a few law schools that are not members of AALS are among the more than 175 law schools accredited by the ABA. Accredited law schools require three years of full-time study and passage of examinations in order to qualify for a *Juris Doctor* (JD) The stratification of legal education is reflected in the stratification of the legal profession.

The Stratification of the Legal Profession

The legal profession can be conceived of as having three strata. *Stratum I* attorneys are partners in the national law firms; in *Stratum II* are certain government and corporate attorneys; and *Stratum III* contains all other attorneys (see Figure 3.1). Stratum I law firms recruit and hire almost exclusively graduates of elite law schools. Although their education may be no better than graduates of less prestigious law schools, they are perceived as superior and perception creates its own reality.

Before the Civil War, the most prominent lawyers made their reputations in courtrooms and often went into politics—they were great litigators and orators. By the close of the nineteenth century, although most lawyers still went to court, "the Wall Street lawyer, who perhaps

| **Stratum I** |
| National Law Firms |

| **Stratum II** |
| Corporate Counsel for Leading Companies |
| Select Government Attorneys |

| **Stratum III** |
| Solo Practitioners |
| Small Law Firms |
| Attorneys for Small Corporations |
| Government Attorneys |

Figure 3.1   Stratification of the Legal Profession

never spoke to a judge except socially, made more money and had more prestige than any other lawyer" (Friedman 1973: 549). At the time of the founding of the ABA, the "legal profession was changing rapidly with the railroad lawyer and the business-man-lawyer emerging as the dominant type, keeping step with the emerging interpretation of the due process clause of the Fourteenth Amendment" in support of business "and the needs of the corporate form of organization in the new industrial age" (Carson 1978: 11–12). By the turn of the century, the ABA was headed by railroad and corporate attorneys, and a pattern of stratification was emerging, a situation strengthened by development of the large law firm, a response to the modern large corporation (Hobson 1986), and the advent of the Cravath system.

The Cravath System and Stratum I Attorneys

In 1906, Paul D. Cravath (1861–1940), a graduate of Columbia Law School (at the top of his class), became the head of a Wall Street law firm (now known as Cravath, Swaine, & Moore) that had been founded in 1819. He recruited associates right out of law school, thus avoiding experienced lawyers who had developed "bad habits." The ideal candidate was a Phi Beta Kappa and law review editor from Harvard, Columbia, or Yale. (The firm continues to recruit most of its lawyers from these three schools and New York University.) The **Cravath system** provided an internship for new recruits that was designed to supplement Ivy League law school study with a practical postgraduate induction into the world of corporate law and lawyering (Smigel 1964). Long hours and hard work were demanded; those unable to meet the Cravath standard were not retained. Other firms quickly followed the Cravath lead.

The "Cravath lawyer" is expected to be wholly devoted and loyal to a client. Each lawyer-intern does general work for several years, usually for a number of the firm's partners, before being placed in an area of specialization. Responsibilities increase with improved competence, and before the tenth year the question of partnership becomes relevant. An employee either becomes a partner or leaves the firm for other work. Partnership is a mark of success in legal practice: "It brings the lawyer into the ownership circle of the firm, enhances earnings, and opens further avenues for career advancement" (Kay and Hagan 1998: 728). According to Fiona Kay and John Hagan:

> The process begins with an intensive period of supervision. As associates enter the firm, they are assigned to work on specific matters by supervising senior partners. First assignments are typically in research, requiring work very similar to that already undertaken in law school; the partner wants a memorandum on a particular point of law or a particular fact situation. He outlines his problem and, in the process, points the associate in the direction of an answer. . . . Inevitably, of course, a certain number of mistakes will be made by younger attorneys. But even mistakes have their uses: they become opportunities for further teaching. Eventually, the associate will be producing satisfactory memoranda and will then go on to other tasks. (Kay and Hagan 1998: 728)

Eve Spangler outlines the additional pathways associates travel to become "partner":

> Once associates have passed through the apprenticeship stage, supervision is converted into consultation. Associates begin to work with increased autonomy. First they are encouraged to handle small matters on their own. Soon associates may

even be allowed their own less important clients. Then they join in the recruitment activities of the firm and in the training of younger associates. Eventually, they become members of the teams handling the largest and most sophisticated deals and cases in the office. When this happens in an orderly progression, associates can expect to be made partners. (Spangler 1986: 46)

Steven Kumble (with Lahart) provides a more stark description: "Top firms take a lot of lawyers out of law school, work them unmercifully, and over time, weed out those who are not going to make it" (1990: 23). "Making it" is in large part determined by hours billed (Kronman 1993); up to 2,500 billable hours for associates—50 hours a week, 50 weeks a year. Add to that nonbillable office hours and the total is a 65-hour workweek.

The growth of the large law firm (in excess of 200 lawyers) is a post-Second World War phenomenon "feeding on the ever-increasing intervention of government in what had once been private business—complicated tax codes, aggressive antitrust enforcement, antidiscrimination laws, environmental requirements, questions of corporate governance, and securities issues" (Linowitz and Mayer 1996: 100–101). However, the traditional Cravath-type tutelage system has given way to current economic realities: "Tutelage consumes valuable time of partners, as well as associates, that cannot be billed to clients. Thus it is hardly surprising that one-on-one sessions became shorter and formal continuing education programs were established in firms as competition for clients intensified in the 1980s. The mentoring system received another blow when starting salaries shot upward in 1986 as firms competed for top law graduates" (Glendon 1994: 27). Instead of the generalist training of the Cravath system, today's young associates are trained narrowly so they can be productive very quickly—specialization is the rule (Linowitz and Mayer 1996). If the attorney's specialty is no longer lucrative because of a change in market conditions, for example—he or she may face a career dilemma.

Into the 1960s, "most large firms ran with an egalitarian system of partner compensation that, except for a small bracket of 'name partners' or 'senior partners,' gave an equal share of annual profits to all those with the same seniority at the firm" (Linowitz and Mayer 1996: 102). Today, the field of corporate law is dominated by "rainmakers"—partners with client contacts. Rainmakers "are generally more heavily rewarded than those whose labors buttress the firm's reputation for quality" (1996: 32). Another pattern set by Cravath—attorneys totally dedicated to the interests of their wealthy clients expending an unlimited amount of time and effort on their behalf—has also changed; legal expenses have ballooned and cost-cutting has become a feature of the corporate practice of law. And the focus on profits has reportedly made firm loyalty a quaint practice of yesteryear: Successful partners (with their clients) are being lured away by competing firms offering greater rewards (Parsa 1999).

A Stratum I firm "is ordinarily divided into departments (corporate, banking, real estate, litigation, etc.) or working groups. Various specialists coordinate their efforts on the problems of the client" (Galanter and Palay 1991: 2). These law firms (often referred to as "Big Law") generally provide counseling, negotiation, and representation services, as opposed to trial advocacy. For these **national law firms** litigation generally represents failure—the firm practices preventive law and the goal is to avoid the uncertainty of trial courts. In fact, "much of what lawyers do involves planning a client's activities so that disputes are not likely to arise or can be settled advantageously if they do arise (dispute anticipating)" (Burton 1985: 19).

In the recent past, when litigation was inevitable, national law firms often recruited expert litigators from outside their traditional sources, from government service, for example (Hoffman 1982). This has changed. About one-third of Cravath, Swaine, and Moore's work now involves litigation: "The winds of change that have swirled through corporate America in recent years—the mega takeovers, the class-action suits, the rise of leveraged buy-outs and other complex financial transactions—have placed corporate litigators more and more in positions of power" (Reich 1986: 24). In fact, the Cravath reputation for handling litigation led to a contract from the Federal Deposit Insurance Corporation to help that agency recoup money from the savings and loan debacle (Margolick 1991a). More recently, the firm "represented AOL Time Warner in its antitrust suit against Microsoft, alleging that Microsoft's business practices had unfairly crushed AOL's Netscape Internet browser. Netscape got $750 million in the highly publicized 2003 settlement" (Ryan 2006). Even at the local level, prosecution of corporate defendants has increased dramatically (Benson, Cullen, and Maakestad 1993).

Many national law firm attorneys, however, are simply "paper litigators," taking depositions and exchanging motions: "Most have only a fraction of the courtroom experience of legal aid lawyers who are half their age and one-twentieth as well compensated" (former Federal Judge Harold R. Tyler, quoted in Margolick 1988a: 19). Such persons can be inadequate to the task of trying a case before a jury. "But agility in the courtroom is increasingly in demand as corporations and chief executives more often become targets for aggressive government prosecutors" (Thomas 2004: BU 1). As a result, many blue-chip firms recruit trial lawyers from the ranks of federal prosecutors whose caseload usually includes corporate crime, such as Dan Webb of Winston and Strawn, a former US attorney in Chicago who epitomizes the rise of a new breed of superlawyers "who are capable of securing a divorce settlement for a client, compiling an investigative corporate report or making a hard-hitting courtroom defense for a corporation, a chief executive or a politician" (Thomas 2004: BU 1). Ben Protess and Peter Lattman (2013: 1) point to a "quintessential Washington script: An influential government insider becoming a paid advocate for industries he once policed." Some white-collar criminal defense firms have merged with corporate firms that in the past shunned criminal defense work, and some elite firms are headed by former federal prosecutors (Lattman 2013a). In 2013, the former US attorney in Alexandria, Virginia, whose annual government salary was $155,000, became a partner in a stratum I law firm where he can expect to earn $2.5 million annually (Lattman 2013c).

The clients of such firms, of course, must be in a position to pay for dedication; accordingly, national law firms represent corporate America, not individuals. They recruit graduates with good grades from the elite law schools—highly competitive individuals eager to advance into partnership. Traditionally, qualifications included lineage—the "right social background," which had the effect of keeping out many Catholics and Jews, and virtually all blacks, few of whom graduated from prestigious law schools. In fact, when more Jews began qualifying for elite law schools, they were met with quotas that artificially restricted their numbers. "This exclusion began to break down after the Second World War. Jewish associates were hired and some moved up the ladder to partner. Cravath appointed its first Jewish partner in 1959" (Galanter and Palay 1991: 25).

Partners in law firms representing blue-chip corporations are overwhelmingly white males, and even in recent years the top firms have been slow in promoting minority lawyers to partner status (Glater 2001). When African Americans do become partners they find their social background a handicap in client development—finding firms capable of paying substantial billing rates requires networking of a type that traditionally has excluded persons of color (Keeva 1993).

Women are also underrepresented (compared to men) in the legal profession. A 2013 report by the ABA revealed that the legal profession employs 33% women compared to 67% men, and women's weekly salary as a percentage of men's weekly salary is 86.6 (in 2011) (American Bar Association 2013). According to The National Association of Women Lawyers (2012: 14), women constitute only 20 percent of the members of a typical firm's highest governing committee. One exception to the lack of women in leadership positions at top law firms is Kim Koopersmith who, in 2012, became chairperson of Akin Gump Strauss Hauer & Feld. She is the first woman to hold the top job at one of Washington DC's largest law and lobbying firms.

Women will continue to face a major hurdle, however, if they try to balance marriage and children with the long hours required of associates who are on a partnership track. Many settle for—or are forced into—the "mommy track," which allows them to remain with the firm without reaching partnership-or-out status. Gita Wilder (2007: 3) found that, in their early careers as lawyers: "Fewer women than men work in private law firms, where salaries tend to be higher than in other settings; women are less likely than men to be solo practitioners; women are considerably more likely than men to work in public interest, other nonprofit and legal service organizations, to serve as public defenders, and to work in educational institutions, where working conditions may be more flexible and salaries are generally lower; and the distribution of males and females varies by legal market as well as by work setting."

More recent reports indicate that for years while the nation's law schools have been graduating an equal number of men and women, and while law firms are hiring new associates who reflect that balance, partnerships continue to elude women, and family obligations do not appear to play a significant role. The "good-old-boy networks" are just that, as are golfing and football games. And it is more comfortable for a senior partner to have an after-work drink with a male associate than deal with the hypothetical implications of having one with a female (O'Brien 2006).

Although there is not a simple one-to-one relationship between size and prestige, the most prestigious law firms have more than 200 lawyers—Cravath has more than 450. About 50 firms in the United States have more than 200 lawyers, and about half

Anti-Semitism, Sexism, and Wall Street Law

In an interview, prominent defense attorney, author, and Harvard University law professor Alan Dershowitz recalled: "I was graduating from Yale law school. I was first in my class, editor of the *Law Journal*, but I was rejected when I applied for jobs with Wall Street firms" ("Q & A" 1991: 6). Ruth Bader Ginsburg, upon being nominated to the Supreme Court, recalled experiencing similar discrimination with respect to her gender.

qualify as "elite." The three largest firms have a total of more than 4,500 lawyers and thousands of support staff including paralegals, administrators, and librarians. Although most of these firms are in New York, several can be found in Chicago, Cleveland, Dallas, Houston, Los Angeles, Philadelphia, and San Francisco. Many New York law firms have offices in Washington, DC and Los Angeles—a gateway to Asia and in many respects the nation's second city in commerce and finance.

These law firms represent the corporate elite, companies found on the Fortune 500 list. For example, Skadden, Arps Slate, Meagher, & Flom, with about 1,800 lawyers in 24 offices in the United States and abroad, represents 175 of the Fortune 500 companies, 18 of the world's 25 biggest banks, and 23 of the 25 largest investment banks (Glater 2011; Lyon 1991). Exxon is represented by Baker and Botts of Houston; General Motors is represented by Well, Gotshal, and Manges of New York; Cravath represents IBM, Texaco, and CBS. "Only such clients can afford the elite corporate law firms and the kind of practice for which the firms pride themselves—one in which no stone is left unturned, no matter how seemingly insignificant, and with virtually no regard for time or money" (Stewart 1984: 14).

Washington law firms became particularly important during the New Deal era (1932–1941), when dramatic increases in government programs led to a corresponding increase in government attorneys.[4] This, in turn, led to a greater need for attorneys in Washington to represent business interests before Congress and regulatory bodies. These firms are often staffed by attorneys who previously worked for the government. Many Washington law firms practice influence rather than law. Thus, prestigious firms operating in the District of Columbia frequently have former members of Congress, cabinet officials, and White House staff as partners because of the access these persons presumably have to government decision makers. "Lawyer-lobbying" has proven very lucrative for about a dozen law firms who work for corporate interests: "They want a regulation changed, a law passed, amended or, more commonly, stopped. They thrive on contacts in government and the voracious appetite in Congress for campaign contributions" (Lewis 1989b: 26; McGuire 1993). The firms contribute to members of Congress through political action committees (PACs), and some have established their own PACs.

There are also "Washington lawyers" who specialize in the Supreme Court:

> They are former members of the solicitor general's staff who now utilize their enormous Supreme Court expertise in private practice. They are former clerks to the justices who have seen the Court from the inside. They are the well-educated, talented litigators who work in some of the nation's largest, most prestigious law firms and who represent a sophisticated clientele in the Court. They are counsel to any number of organized interests that have established offices throughout the neighboring streets of the capital community and that use appellate litigation to further their policy goals. These lawyers position cases in the lower courts for possible appeals. They file **briefs** at the agenda stage and argue cases on the merits. They strategize with amici curiae [friend of the court briefs] and consult with less experienced counsel. (McGuire 1993: 21–22; emphasis added)

An increasing number of major firms have expanded into global concerns with offices in major cities throughout the world. Baker and McKenzie of Chicago, for

---

[4] For an examination of the role of elite lawyers in the New Deal, see Shamir (1995).

example, has 74 offices in 46 countries, employing more than 4,100 lawyers; over 80 percent of its lawyers practice outside of the United States. About two dozen law firms have opened offices in Brussels, capital of the European Community.

Elite firms have been establishing new (for them) areas of specialization, for example, corporate crime. Ironically, the persons hired for this specialty are the ones responsible for creating the need—US attorneys who have been active prosecuting corporations and their executives. National law firms have also been establishing subsidiaries handling nonlegal business: real estate, banking, insurance, lobbying, health care and environmental consulting, and economic research. A number of firms—not necessarily "elite"—are providing "one-stop-shopping," diversifying into a broad array of nonlegal services that were once entirely independent: investigations and money management, for example. This raises two troubling concerns. First, clients utilizing the nonlegal services of a law firm may not be fully aware that they are not protected by attorney-client privilege. Second is a potential conflict of interest, the risk that lawyers will steer clients to their own business services rather than objectively laying out a range of options (Hines 2001a). The profusion of antitrust activities, leveraged buyouts, and mergers has also resulted in spin-offs from traditional law firms: firms managed by attorneys but that specialize in the economic analysis of legal issues (Margolick 1988b). Law firms faced with increasing technological complexity hire attorneys with science backgrounds, and there are nonlawyers with doctorates in scientific disciplines who work as in-house advisors.

At most big firms there are associates and partners. The former work for the latter; in fact, the partners earn profits largely on hourly billings of the salaried associates, and the more associates the greater the profits. The profits of the firm are typically shared by the partners in proportion to the amount of work brought in and their seniority. Most large firms have two or three associates per partner, and an associate should bring in three times his or her salary: one-third for the associate, one-third for overhead, and one-third for the firm (Lewin 1983). "Among larger firms it is common for name partners (the 'finders') to sign up the cases, then hand the actual work over to junior associates (the 'grinders')" (Grutman and Thomas 1990: 79). Because of increased competition, some firms base their billings on the size of the transaction and case success, rather than hours exerted (Freitag 1989; Slade 1993).

In competition for students from elite law schools, some New York firms have provided summer internships for third-year students at salaries of about $2,500 a week. Recruiters from elite firms such as Sullivan and Cromwell, founded in 1879, would visit about a dozen schools each year, primarily Columbia, Chicago, Harvard, Michigan, New York, Stanford, Virginia, and Yale (Jaschik and Lederman 2004). When the recession of 2008 hit, firms pulled back on the number of interns hired and the amount of money they paid. Although some law schools boast that their graduates will earn an annual starting salary of about $160,000 plus bonuses, this is not reality for many recent graduates. Indeed, the economic downturn caused firms to ask promising candidates to defer their starting dates, offering financial incentives and the opportunity to work for nonprofits such as public interest firms (Petak 2010). Moreover, by 2013, the economic downturn had significantly affected the elite firms—for the first time, there were lawyer layoffs. One New York-based firm with more than 1,000 attorneys dismissed 60 associates (Lattman 2013b).

Elite Lawyers

"These lawyers perform very significant work for very significant clients in every significant area of business and government activity" (Cherovsky 1991: 21).

Any number of firms have initiated two-tier hiring practices: "Service partners" on a nonpartnership (nonequity) track are drawn from less prestigious law schools and paid less than half of what associates typically earn. They are actually employees who provide low-cost legal help for the firm's more routine, but labor-intensive, work such as reviewing documents in a complicated commercial litigation case—a chore most lawyers disdain. They permit the firm to offer clients cheaper hourly rates. (Rampell 2011a).

Systemized recruitment patterns channel the legal talent flow into corporate law firms that provide comprehensive services to a restricted clientele whose common denominator is wealth (Auerbach 1976). Keenly aware of criticism leveled at them, these law firms typically provide **pro bono** (an abbreviation *for pro bono publico*—"for the public good") legal services. As part of their apprenticeship period, associates are often required to serve public interest groups such as those involved in civil liberties, civil rights, consumer, and environmental issues. During the politically volatile period of the 1960s, in order to recruit desirable law school graduates, prestigious law firms often found it necessary to promise prospective associates that they could work on public interest issues on company time. A number of prominent firms have established special counsel positions to oversee the pro bono work of associates (Donovan 2008).

Partners in national law firms are sometimes called on for government service, usually at the federal level. This represents a temporary financial loss—for a partner at Cravath, that would mean more than $2 million—that can frequently be more than offset by the contacts and exposure resulting from a highly visible federal position.

Stratum II Attorneys

The most prominent attorney categories in Stratum II are a select few employed by the federal government and those employed by large corporations. A relatively small number of government attorneys, for example, federal judges, US attorneys, cabinet officials such as the attorney general, legal advisor to the president, and the solicitor general, are in Stratum II. Numerically, most Stratum II attorneys are employed by corporations.

International Pro Bono

Lawyers Without Borders (LWB), www.lawyerswithoutborders.org, links private lawyers to work pro bono with nongovernmental organizations of the United Nations and others seeking a neutral, outside legal perspective. LWB have gone to Liberia to assess the legal system, make recommendations, and have worked to protect lawyers representing unpopular clients (Glater 2005b).

Prior to World War II, the general counsel of a company was likely to be its outside law firm, and in those cases where there was a full-time house general counsel, he was likely to be in charge of a small staff that did the repetitive scutwork. Not infrequently, such an inside general counsel would do double duty, serving as corporate secretary, a cognate activity, or in some more remote function such as personnel director.

As time passed, regulations proliferated, and the tax code grew, no single outside lawyer could answer the chief executives' questions about how some piece of law or regulation was going to affect the business. The lawyers who could answer the questions about regulations and specialized procedures at administrative agencies might well have the company's most feared competitors on their client roster. Many top executives were uncomfortable with the idea that they were getting advice on key decisions from the same people who were advising their rivals. (Linowitz 1996: 82–83)

Thus, in addition to retaining national law firms as outside counsel, large corporations employ salaried attorneys, often persons recruited from national law firms, as in-house counsel. Corporations prefer to hire experienced lawyers (Abel 1989). Since the 1970s, there has been a rapid growth in both the importance and size of corporate legal offices and the size of some corporate legal staffs exceeds that of many national law firms. They may train their own lawyers and compete with law firms in recruiting from elite law schools. This trend "is consistent with the general pattern of vertical integration—it is one more instance in which the corporation becomes an employer rather than a buyer of some element necessary to its production process, with all the enhanced control that such a move implies" (Spangler 1986: 72). The Association of Corporate Counsel (formerly the American Corporate Counsel Association), founded in 1982, now represents more than 30,000 members in over 75 countries and has chapters in the United States, Canada, Europe, Singapore, and Israel.

The legal division of major corporations is headed by the general counsel (a senior management official). Beneath the general counsel are deputy or associate administrators who supervise staff attorneys typically distributed throughout the ranking system established by corporate policy. Although they may be physically dispersed and work for different divisions within a corporation, staff attorneys are directly responsible to their superiors in the law department, which is a self-contained entity for purposes of evaluation and advancement. "This arrangement is designed to protect not only the autonomy of the law department but, more important, the corporation's long-term interests in having its executives' business practices adequately monitored" (Spangler 1986: 76). For **corporate counsel**, the corporation—not its officers and directors—is the client (Gillers 1996).

As a company employee, to avoid possible conflicts of interest, corporate counsel does not usually represent the employer. Rather, in-house counsel is involved with a myriad of legal concerns that are part of modern corporate activity. In-house counsel may:

- Assist with strategic planning whenever there are important legal implications, for example, providing a legal analysis to the board of directors and an evaluation of available options.

- Monitor business activities to ensure compliance with statutory and regulatory requirements, for example, securities, civil rights, and employee health and safety regulations.

- Provide continuing in-service education to ensure that corporate personnel understand compliance requirements.

- Serve as the corporation's liaison to the national law firm on **retainer** to the corporation.

Corporate counsel will review contracts and ensure that the firm's employment practices conform to relevant laws and regulations (Toedt, Robinson, and Segal 2005). They "pride themselves on doing preventive law by advising on the structure of a business deal as it evolves" (Spangler 1986: 78).

"While law departments formerly confined themselves to processing routine corporate legal matters and left major transactions and litigation work to outside counsel, they are now undertaking more work that once would have gone to outside lawyers (Galanter and Palay 1991). Omari Simmons and James Dinnage (2011: 88) describe in-house counsel as the "'Swiss army knife' of the legal profession." "In-house counsel decide what work should be performed in-house and which firms should be used for outsourced work. While most routine transactional work is kept in-house, specific types of matters tend to be outsourced. Litigation is the largest legal service for which corporations utilize outside counsel. Corporations typically outsource matters that are large, complex, or specialized" (Lipson, Engel, and Crespo 2012: 243).

Although corporate counsel does not enjoy the prestige or income of a partnership in a national law firm, the environment is more relaxed, hours are more limited, and the position has considerably more prestige than that enjoyed by most Stratum III attorneys.

Stratum III Attorneys

According to a study by J. Mark Ramseyer and Eric Rasmussen (2010), the United States ranked higher than Australia, Canada, France, Japan, and the United Kingdom in the number of lawyers per 100,000 people. Although the US topped these countries (with 391 lawyers per 100,000 people), it did not top Israel, which had 585 lawyers per 100,000 people (Zarchin 2011). The United States has more than 1.1 million attorneys— one for every 280 persons (The Harvard Law School 2011). In 2012 62,603 persons were admitted to the bar (*The Bar Examiner* 2013: 27). Supreme Court Justice Antonin Scalia has been critical that too many of the best minds have been devoted to the practice of law:

> "I mean lawyers, after all, don't produce anything. They enable other people to produce and to go on with their lives efficiently and in an atmosphere of freedom. That's important, but it doesn't put food on the table and there have to be other people who are doing that. And I worry that we are devoting too many of our very best minds to this enterprise." (quoted in Jones 2009)

Judge Scalia believes we graduate too many lawyers and not enough engineers and teachers. "'Society cannot afford to have such a huge proportion of its best minds going into the law,'" he said (Weiss 2012).

Over 70 percent of American lawyers are in private practice, and half of the attorneys who practice law are in solo practice or two-lawyer firms; about 30 percent of those who have been admitted to the bar have nonlaw-related jobs. Lawyers in firms of four to 10 lawyers account for about 20 percent of those in practice, and firms of 11 or more attorneys account for the remaining private practitioners. About 10 percent of

Inner Circle of Advocates

The Inner Circle is an invitation-only group, limited to 100 who have tried at least 50 personal injury jury cases and have won at least three verdicts in excess of $1 million or one verdict in excess of $10 million with the most recent verdict being no more than five years old.

all practicing attorneys are employed by government agencies on the federal, state, county, or municipal level.

Although the prestige of Stratum III attorneys is considerably less than that of their Strata I and II colleagues, income is not the decisive factor. In fact, there are Stratum III attorneys whose income surpasses that of most of those in Strata I and II. The nation's top litigator, Joseph Jamail of Houston, a billionaire known as "king of the torts," received a $335 million contingency fee in 1985 (the contingency discussed in Chapter 10) while ex-Marine Tony Buzbee of Galveston, Texas, made close to $100 million in contingency fees from one case against oil giant BP. They and a few other trial lawyers have incomes well in excess of that earned by most Stratum I attorneys. Indeed, there is an organization of attorneys, the Inner Circle of Advocates, whose members have all won at least one $1 million judgment. But millionaire trial lawyers are the rare exception among the tens of thousands found in Stratum III.

The solo attorney who predominates in Stratum III is typically identified by lack of a prestigious legal education and a social background that has kept him or her out of the circles of power and wealth that lawyers from the national law firms routinely frequent. The solo practitioner does not have the readily available research and investigative resources of a large law firm. By default, most solo lawyers end up doing the "dirty work" of the bar (Ladinsky 1963). Instead of depending on contacts with the world of big business, the solo practitioner depends on family, neighborhood, ethnic group, and local political contacts for clientele. He or she generally works for individuals, and the nature of the work may be distasteful. "Divorce work involves emotionally charged, embarrassing personal situations . . . personal injury work deals with grisly facts and with claimants who are badly maimed; and criminal work often requires the lawyer to associate with persons who are less than pleasant" (Heinz and Laumann 1982: 93). There is also the rural bar, strikingly homogeneous, whose practitioners work alone or with fewer than five partners, representing a broad range of clients (Landon 1990). Rural America is underserved by the legal profession. In 2013, South Dakota passed a law that offers lawyers an annual subsidy in return for living and working in rural counties.

Trial Lawyers

In 2006 "the Association of Trial Lawyers of America determined that the term 'trial lawyer' had become so toxic that it had to be jettisoned and voted to change its name to the American Association for Justice" (McCollam 2010: 48).

Whereas there is not a strong relationship between the prestige of a particular field of law and a lawyer's income, there is a high correlation with the prestige of clients: "Fields that serve corporate, wealthier, more 'establishment' clients are accorded more deference within the profession than are those that serve individual, poorer clients" (Heinz and Laumann 1982: 331). There are also types of law practice whose prestige ranking is somewhat ambivalent. "For example, the practice of labor law (for both unions and management) involves considerable financial stakes, but it also involves association with blue-collar workers or their representatives. Similarly, the lawyers who represent defendants in personal injury cases usually work for high status clients, since those defendants are typically insurance companies, but their work also involves unsavory fact situations" (Heinz and Laumann 1982: 331). In any event, "contrary to the impression that television drama gives, with its emphasis on courtroom battles, most lawyers generally practice 'preventive law.' They help people discover ways to reduce their taxes or write valid wills and contracts. They study complex insurance policies and bank loan agreements. Such efforts reduce the probability of conflict. Most lawyers usually play a planning role. They help people create their own 'private laws,' laws governing their personal affairs and no more" (Carter 1984: 4).

There is also the private practice of law as part of a franchise law firm that offers "no frills" or "discount" legal assistance. Some firms have more than a 100 such offices throughout the country; their services are promoted by heavy advertising. They are typically housed in storefronts in retail business districts or shopping malls. They earn their profits by handling a large volume of relatively uncomplicated cases such as uncontested divorces, simple wills, and bankruptcies or personal injury claims where the total dollar amount is relatively small. From the fees that are typically charged, these firms cannot easily engage in full-scale litigation and they have been criticized for "settling too quickly for too little" (Gould 1986: F15). There is a great deal of lawyer turnover in these firms, and this can affect continuity of service in more complex cases, such as contested divorces, which can take several years to complete (see Van Hoy 1997 for a discussion of these firms).

The difficulty experienced in securing affordable legal services has spawned a variety of self-help firms that provide the documents for *pro se* (for oneself) representation. Some are franchised "do-it-yourself" businesses operated by nonlawyers who serve a function similar to that long-performed by paralegals working for law firms—primarily filling out forms. Typical cases involve bankruptcy, uncontested divorce, living trusts, wills, and incorporation. These firms are prohibited from offering legal advice, but some have attorneys available—usually by telephone—to answer legal questions. Bar associations have been vociferous in their opposition to these establishments, argu-

A Matter of Status

The status of an attorney within the legal profession is dependent on who he or she represents. Those who represent corporate America receive the prominence their clients enjoy; those representing criminals . . .

"Between a Rock and a Hard Place"

Can a parent represent his or her disabled child in a legal action to get services under the federal Individuals with Disabilities Education Act if the parent is not an attorney? While federal courts have been divided on the issue, bar associations in Ohio answered "No." But if a parent with a disabled child is unable to afford the cost of hiring an attorney—there is no contingency fee—the child's needs may be ignored (Liptak 2006b).

ing that they are practicing law without a license and/or are misleading consumers into believing they can handle matters beyond their competence (Hines 2001b).

Now that we have examined legal education and the practice of law in the United States, in the next chapter we will examine the places most attorneys do their work—federal and state courts.

SUMMARY

- Throughout the colonial era, there was hostility toward lawyers.
- Despite hostility toward attorneys as a group, lawyers were elected to the highest levels of government.
- Efforts by bar association to limit the practice of law led to an increase in requirements and eventually bar examinations.
- Legal reform was frequently intertwined with nativism.
- Most states require lawyers to be members of that state's bar association, known as an "integrated bar."
- Accreditation of law schools is the responsibility of the American Bar Association.
- The legal profession is stratified into three levels.
- His/her clients determine the prestige of an attorney.
- The Cravath system involves recruiting associates right out of law school and an internship with for a number of the firm's partners.
- Elite law firms practice preventive law with the goal of avoiding the uncertainty of litigation.
- National law firms represent corporate America, not individuals.
- Prestigious law firms have in excess of 200 lawyers.
- At big firms associates work for the partners.
- National law firms typically provide pro bono legal services.
- Although the prestige of Stratum III attorneys is considerably less than that of their Strata I and II colleagues, income is not the decisive factor.
- The office of the general counsel does not usually represent the employer but is involved with a myriad of legal concerns that are part of modern corporate activity.
- While there is not a strong relationship between the prestige of a particular field of law and a lawyer's income, there is a high correlation with the prestige of clients.

KEY TERMS

brief
corporate counsel
Cravath system
diploma privilege

integrated bar
machine politics
national law firms

nativism
pro bono
retainer

REVIEW QUESTIONS

1. Why was there hostility toward lawyers throughout the colonial era?
2. What was the relationship between bar associations and limits placed on who could practice law?
3. What was the connection between legal reform and nativism?
4. What does the term "integrated bar" refer to?
5. Who is responsible for the accreditation of law schools?
6. How is the legal profession stratified?
7. What is the job of corporate counsel?
8. In the legal profession, what determines the prestige of an attorney?
9. What is the "Cravath system"?
10. Why do corporations employing many attorneys retain outside counsel?

INTERNET CONNECTIONS

American Bar Association: http://www.abanet.org
Inner Circle of Advocates: http://www/innercircle.org
Legal Research: http://www.ilrg.com
National Conference of Bar Examiners: http://ncbex.org

PART II
Courts

The Structure and Administration of the Courts

In the United States there are two parallel systems of courts: federal and state. Each system is divided into trial courts and appellate courts. There are more than 200 state-wide general and limited jurisdiction trial court systems in the United States, the District of Columbia, and Puerto Rico, as well as trial courts in each of the 94 federal districts, and more than 130 appellate courts on the state and federal levels. State appellate courts range in size from five to nine judges—most have a state court of last resort with seven members.

Law in Colonial America

Issues of survival dominated the primitive life of early American colonists. As time passed and life became more secure, the economy expanded and agriculture and commerce thrived. Important issues were not simply those of survival, but of more complex social and economic relationships. As the population increased, so did the complexity of relationships and the possibility of conflict. The shoemaker no longer dealt directly with the farmer, exchanging shoes for milk, meat, and vegetables. Now the farmer sold these items to a merchant, who in turn sold them to a variety of people, including the shoemaker. But what if there were defects or spoiled goods? Who was liable: the original producer? The merchant? Or was the ultimate buyer without recourse? The Puritans of New England could simply consult the Bible for guidance in matters of law and justice. But as Boston became a great seaport and commercial center, the greater complexity of society demanded a rationality greater than that offered by the Puritan Bible.

British colonization in America began in 1607 (during the reign of James I), a time when common law was quite formal and strict—equity and the Court of Chancery were still in a developmental stage. The common law of that period was heavily laced with Latin and French legal jargon developed in the Middle Ages and was unfit for a wilderness society that stressed individualism (Pound 1953). Some of the original colonies were corporations chartered by the Crown (e.g., Massachusetts Bay), and their legislative powers were limited to making bylaws and ordinances. Colonial charters required legislation to conform to the common law, and those deemed contrary could be reversed by an appeal to the Privy Council in England. Royal governors often inter-fered with the decisions of colonial courts, much as the Crown had done in England when judges ruled against its wishes or interests. Other colonies were royal colonies (e.g., Virginia), in theory controlled directly by the Crown, while still others were pro-prietary colonies (e.g., Maryland) in which a single owner exercised control (Hall 1989). "There could be little legal development under such a system" (Pound 1953: 134).

While colonial law was subordinate to English law, it was not clear which acts of Parliament and which court decisions were binding on the colonists. Although each group of settlers brought with them an English legal heritage, each colony was founded at a different time (Massachusetts was founded 100 years before Georgia), and they differed in geography, immigration, religion, and economic and political development. Within each colony were a commercial center, a seacoast, and a hinter-land. "The rugged independence which was born of the frontier brought about the scrapping of important common-law practices incompatible with life in the new agrarian communities" (Morris 1964: 20). Colonists were free of English supervision and tended to disregard the authority of the common law.

Although the Crown never intended that there be a legal culture in the colonies that differed from that in England, dramatically different conditions in the colonies led to that outcome. For example, land was scarce in England, where it was a symbol of power and social status; it was bound up in centuries of land law handed down from feudal times. In colonial America, however, there was a shortage of people, not land. In England land was important, but there were numerous landowners (Friedman 1973). Bradley Chapin notes that the labor supply influenced the law in England: "As a matter of policy it must have seemed that no great harm was done if the hangman thinned the horde of vagrant Englishmen.[1] In the colonies, the need for labor urged the use of penalties that might bring redemption" (1983: 9). Consequently, the use of capital punishment was severely restricted in the colonies. "Although the colonial law of crimes against persons remained basically English law," the colonial law of crimes against property was largely indigenous, and it virtually abolished the death penalty for property crimes, replacing it with branding, whipping, terms in the house of cor-rection, and restitution (Chapin 1983). There were, however, several notable and his-torical exceptions: the banning and hanging of Quakers by Puritans in the Massachusetts Bay Colony and the subsequent witchcraft trials and executions. The Quakers of Pennsylvania eliminated capital punishment for all crimes except murder; however, blacks convicted of burglary, buggery (sodomy), or rape could still be exe-cuted (Walker 1980). In New Amsterdam the system of law resembled that of Hol-land—a civil code; while the Puritans of New England and the Quakers of Pennsylvania sought to establish a society based on the Bible. And there was also a French influence.

"The Dutch and French influence in different colonies gradually disappeared, and other variations between colonies also diminished. By the time of the American Revo-

---

[1] In practice, however, mitigation was accomplished by the extensive use of pardons and the dismissal of indict-ments for technical reasons (Kelman 1987). Pardons typically required intercession by a powerful benefactor, gaining for local gentry the obligation and loyalty of the felon and his or her family (Turkel 1996). In England corruption, perjury, and jury tampering were widespread, mocking "the common law's reputation for fairness" (Bordenhamer 1992: 14).

lution, religious influence had declined noticeably" even in Massachusetts and Pennsylvania (Walker 1980: 12). As colonial conditions stabilized, commerce flourished and economic growth required an increasingly commercial America to turn toward economically advanced countries for guidance in law. The only country that could provide a supply of law without the need for translation was England—an ocean away in an era of sailing ships. As a consequence, "a distinctly American approach to law and justice emerged, based mainly on Anglo-Saxon legal heritage as modified by the colonial experience" (Walker 1980: 12).

Persons of power typically used common law in England—nobility, commercial classes, and wealthy clergy—while colonial law was substantially codified law, a response to frontier conditions. A newly settled colony cannot wait until a body of common law evolves before disputes are settled (Friedman 1973). Codes, on the other hand, can be reduced to knowable text in a single book or a short series of volumes. Common law is complex and unwieldy, whereas codes can be moved from one colony to another and adopted. Until the eighteenth century, some codes were borrowed in toto. The Inns of Court—English legal institutions—had their well-established method of study. The introduction of a new book, such as **Blackstone's Commentaries**, was not considered necessary in England, "but in the Colonies, where there were no schools of law, the Commentaries were hailed as absolutely essential to any legal education and as the only book in which extended legal knowledge could be easily acquired" (Zane 1998: 335).

The works of Sir William Blackstone (1723–1780) were widely cited in pre-Revolutionary American courts. While law books were quite scarce, Blackstone's four-volume work, based on his lectures at Oxford, *Commentaries on the Laws of England* (1765–1769), was generally available. This most influential writer on the common law undertook to demonstrate that England's legal system was not simply a confusion of rules justified only by their age. Blackstone organized the English common law into four areas: (1) the rights of persons, (2) the rights of property, (3) private wrongs (torts), and (4) public wrongs (criminal law). He provided the rules governing each legal topic and the logic behind them in an effort to gain support for the common law. Blackstone "tried to show that Englishmen had rationally, by trial and error through the centuries, worked out a system of social regulation which produced the greatest satisfaction for themselves, [and] the justest rule for their common existence" (Sutherland 1967: 23). He viewed the principles of common law as being derived from natural law or divine in origin. Blackstone's work was favored by the conservative Tory Party in England and gained the support of colonial lawyers, for whom it provided "an up-to-date shortcut to basic English law" (Friedman 1973: 88). Since there was a paucity of readily available alternatives, the influence of Blackstone was pervasive.

British equity, which had grown almost as complex as that of the common law, was not easily applied to colonial America. Some colonies established separate courts of equity; some merged equity with courts of common law; and in other colonies equity powers were the province of the legislature or the governor. Colonial equity procedures were simplified, relief more accessible and swifter, but less predictable than in the English Court of Chancery (Hoffer 1992). "With the eighteenth century, however, we reach the era of more sophisticated adoption of the common law and the emergence of a distinctive colonial equity law" (Katz 1971: 262).

The Legal System in Colonial, Revolutionary, and Post-Revolutionary America

Colonial courts assumed a wide range of responsibilities; they served as the legislative, executive, and judicial branches of county government—a reflection of the highly unspecialized nature of government during this time period (Walker 1980). For example, judges of the Superior Court of Massachusetts decided the validity of tax assessments and entertained damage suits against sheriffs, jailers, and customs officials (White 1976); the governor of colonial Maryland and his council sat as a chancery court (Katz 1971); and until the outbreak of the Revolution, the judges of Virginia's General Court were the governor and his council (Hoffer 1992). With significant economic and population growth, court structures moved from the simple to the more complex, from the undifferentiated to the hierarchical. Executive, legislative, and judicial powers that had not heretofore been clearly differentiated (e.g., legislatures heard appeals) became more distinct. English legal models, terms, and customs became more important and more frequently used (Friedman 1973). At the same time, the courts were increasingly seen as tools of the Crown and mistrusted by the common people, while legislatures generally supported popular sentiment against the king (Chroust 1965). Chancery courts were controversial because governors, in their capacity as chancellors, sought political ends rather than justice (Hall 1989).

On the eve of independence, the American colonies had a fully developed hierarchical court system, served by a professional bar operating under sophisticated procedural systems, although no two colonies had the same court structure. Colonial appellate courts were not necessarily composed of judges; most consisted of the governor and council (Wiecek 1988). A fully developed **separation of powers** had to await the Constitution as influenced by the writings of Charles-Louis de Secondat Montesquieu (1689–1755). In *The Spirit of Laws* (1748), Montesquieu advocated three branches of government, each confined to its proper sphere: "There is no liberty, if the judiciary power be not separated from the legislative and the executive" (1949: 152).[2]

Juries appeared in the colonies shortly after the founding of the Plymouth and Massachusetts Bay Colonies, but it was not until the revolutionary fervor of the eighteenth century that juries began to play an important role. They engaged in jury nullification by resisting unpopular decrees from England. People untrained in the law did much of the work of the courts, so juries were seen as every bit as competent as judges, and colonial systems tended to entrust juries with decisions as to law as well as facts. And they were viewed as important safeguards against official overreaching and incompetence. So much so, that when the proposed Constitution was drafted in 1787 without a guarantee of a right to civil jury trials, there was such an outcry that the guarantee was included in the Bill of Rights as the Seventh Amendment (Sward 2003).

The defeat of the British Army brought dramatic changes to the law and judicial process in America, though neither common law nor lawyers were any more popular in post-Revolutionary America than they had been in the colonial era. However, the

---

[2] England never adopted the concept of separation of powers: The prime minister is a member of parliament, and the lord chancellor, a member of the cabinet, is speaker of the House of Lords while also head of the judiciary (Abraham 1998).

courts, now with patriotic judges, continued to conduct business using the only law they knew—English law—and much of it was based on common law. While British statutes were put aside, the importance of common law remained. It was regarded as a source of protection for private rights and immunity from government oppression. "It would have been a political contradiction for the new states to jettison a legal system that they claimed [in the Declaration of Independence] as their birthright" (Hazard and Taruffo 1993: 6). Blackstone was frequently cited in American courts of this era, and popular British manuals of procedure were readily available and used in the United States.

There was a brief flirtation with France after the Revolution, and some even proposed basing the American legal system on that of the French codes. However, most Americans were unable or unwilling to read law books written in foreign tongues. The British common law prevailed, but not without vigorous opposition from those who favored codification. In general, the common law was favored by Federalists and, later, Whigs, who were aligned with commercial and business interests. They distrusted legislation that they feared might be used to promote the redistribution of wealth for egalitarian goals. They placed their faith in a judicial branch and common law. Codification or civil law was supported by Jacksonian Democrats. "The victory of common law in America was confirmed when [Judge James] Kent and [Justice Joseph] Story wrote their authoritative guides for judges and practitioners in the years between 1826 and 1845. After their texts were published, the cult of civil law virtually disappeared. They had restated the common law in American form. It was now so clearly presented that the energies of judges could be turned to applying common law principles to concrete cases" (Schwartz 1974: 29).

Except in Louisiana, the French and Spanish civil law of the West was eventually overwhelmed by the American settler invasion, although some of these traditions were incorporated into the common-law tradition. A civil code enacted in 1825 in Louisiana was drawn primarily from the Napoleonic Code, and the law of Louisiana is a blend of French, Spanish, and common-law traditions (Friedman 1973). However, most states added the part of the common law to their statutes that they found useful. This meant that each state had a different form of common law. Without recourse to a standard body of common law, judges and attorneys found themselves without authoritative sources for their arguments and decisions, and "there can hardly be a legal system until the decisions of the courts are regularly published and are available to bench and bar" (Gilmore 1977: 9).

Prior to the Civil War, "most lawyers and judges relied on treatise writers, who ascertained the state of the law and provided voluminous citations to state, federal, and English cases" (Hall, Wiecek, and Finkelman 1991: 114). At the turn of the nineteenth century, states began introducing the reporter system, which published the decisions of the state courts. By 1821, there were more than 150 volumes of such reports available (Chroust 1965). Decisions of federal courts were also being published, "as well as American republications (with added local annotations) of English books and case collections" (Gilmore 1977: 23). In 1879, the West Publishing Company established the *National Reporting System,* and an overwhelming number of decisions became readily available to every lawyer; ***stare decisis*** became a quantitative as well as a qualitative challenge.

Courts after the Revolution

In post-Revolutionary America, the concept of separation of powers developed slowly. Under the Articles of Confederation and Perpetual Union (1781), most functions of government were vested in a single-chamber legislature: Congress. Executive and legislative powers were not separated, and there was no national judiciary. State governments also reflected the absence of a clear separation of powers. Legislators and chief executives, often laypersons without legal training, served as justices of the states' highest courts (Friedman 1973). State legislatures began drafting detailed statutes setting out the structure and jurisdiction of the judiciary and the executive branches of government (Hurst 1950). But these were the years of legislative supremacy, and the legislatures frequently intervened in judicial activity, reversing decisions and passing special laws to the advantage of certain plaintiffs or defendants (Chroust 1965). State constitutions were viewed as inferior to legislative enactments, and the legislature had supremacy over the courts even when its enactments were contrary to the state constitution.

State court systems were characterized by decentralization, a Balkanization sometimes based on geographic jurisdiction, sometimes on the nature of the case, and sometimes on both. This was caused by the need to bring the courts closer to litigants in an expanding nation where transportation was primitive. Each court played an important political and social role in the life of its community. When court convened in the county seat, often only once a month, it was a major event. Large numbers of people came to town, conducted business, discussed politics, and socialized with one another (Walker 1980). These were the days before mass media, and people flocked to the courtrooms to hear the oratory of noted attorneys. Courtroom oratory and successful advocacy provided an attorney with a following and clients (Friedman 1973; Ferguson 1984).

Of particular importance in rural America was the justice of the peace (JP), who in colonial times had been appointed by the royal governor and served at the county level. Requirements were minimal; legal training was not one of them, but political connections were. The JP was the basis of the states' systems for handling everyday disputes (Hurst 1950). The JP was empowered to try minor cases; the more serious ones were reserved for the higher courts that met infrequently. As a result, justice suffered. The justice-of-the-peace court was an effort to bring the administration of justice close to a scattered population at a minimum of public expense, so the office was usually operated on a fee-for-service basis.

Following the Revolutionary War, there was a trend throughout the states toward establishment of a separate appellate branch. Over the decades, the appellate process improved as specialized courts developed that could review cases without recourse to a *trial de novo*, a retrial in a higher court (Hurst 1950). The trial courts, however, were neglected and became unwieldy, inefficient, and in many areas tied to corrupt political machines, a link that would remain a problem in many urban areas well into the twentieth century.

From the Revolution until 1832, most states provided for both elected and appointed (by the legislature or governor) judges. In that year, Mississippi initiated the popular election of all judges; in 1846, New York did the same. Within 10 years, 15 of the 29 states that then made up the Union had followed suit, and every state that entered the Union after 1846 stipulated the popular election of all or most of their judges (Hurst 1950). A number of the other states experimented with both electoral and appointment systems, sometimes, as Texas did, going back and forth (Friedman 1973).

Courts and Justice on the Frontier

With the westward expansion, judges in the newly settled territories borrowed from a variety of state sources, but primarily from those states with which they were most familiar. In many areas there was little law: Justice was decided in a rather crude fashion by persons having rather limited knowledge of law and legal processes and often acting on their own instincts. Lawyers and judges carried weapons, and duels often settled legal questions. There was a paucity of law books, and lawyers were often not law school graduates. Many had simply been law clerks, and others gained their knowledge of the law through experience—and often resorted to tricks or to the few technicalities with which they were familiar (Friedman 1973). Court sessions were usually held in makeshift courtrooms by judges who were ignorant of the law; some were even illiterate. Judges were chosen on the basis of personal qualities—Indian fighters (who often engaged in America's version of "ethnic cleansing") were popular—rather than legal knowledge. Justice was dispensed without resort to precedent or decorum, so administration varied widely from court to court. Courts were filled with rowdy, tobacco-chewing participants. "The backwoodsman was intolerant of men who split hairs, drew fine distinctions, or scrupled over methods of reaching the right solution" (Chroust 1965: 96). But frontier justice also had some outstanding lawyers who presided over quality justice (Stevens 1971).

Out of these frontier sentiments, writes Richard Maxwell Brown, **vigilantism** and lynch law "arose as a response to a typical American problem: the absence of effective law and order in a frontier region. It was a problem that occurred again and again beyond the Appalachian Mountains. It stimulated the formation of hundreds of frontier vigilante movements" (1971: 156). The **extralegal** violence that emerged in late nineteenth- and early twentieth-century America—southern lynch mobs, western vigilantes, and northern and eastern "whitecaps"—had the support of many leading members of the legal profession, whose "conception of law and order in regard to the problem of criminal and disorderly behavior did not stress the method of *due process* of law but the *aim* of crime repression. In the vast majority of their actions these attorneys, jurists, and legal writers were law abiding in deed and thought. However, when the disorder of late nineteenth century America confronted their devotion to the strict letter of the law, the latter gave way to their primary desire for order" (Brown 1971: 96).

Lynch law was an extreme manifestation of popular local democracy—government by the people or popular sovereignty—responding to community sentiments and needs. **Lynching** cuts through the complexities of procedural law that thwarted "popular justice" and avoided the costs of **jail** and trial (Brown 1971). Lynch law prevented the obviously guilty defendant from escaping justice; it also imposed the ultimate penalty on the innocent, often in collusion with local officials sworn to uphold law and order. And in some regions, particularly in the South, lynching served as an expression of racial hatred and intimidation.

Jurisdiction

As noted in Chapter 1, in the United States (as opposed to inquisitorial systems) trial courts differ rather markedly from their appellate counterparts. The trial court has criminal and civil (that is, noncriminal) parts, something rare at the appellate level except in Oklahoma and Texas, which split final **appellate review** between criminal and civil parts (Rottman and Strickland 2006). The trial court has responsibility for settling the issue at hand and need not interest itself in wider issues such as the precedential value of its decisions. Cases are disposed of in trial courts by negotiation, plea bargaining, bench trials, and (except in equity cases) jury trials. Whatever the outcome, trial court judges rarely draft elaborate explanations of their decisions. With the exception of the United States Supreme Court, courts—trial and appellate—are limited by their jurisdictions.

Jurisdiction is basic to understanding the organization of a court system. It is the geographic area, subject matter, or persons over which a court can exercise authority. The area of geographic jurisdiction is referred to as **venue**, and it can be limited to a particular district, city, or county. Venue in criminal cases is relatively simple—it is where the crime is alleged to have taken place. In civil cases, however, venue can be based on a number of factors, such as where the cause of the action arose, where the defendant resides or conducts business, or where the plaintiff resides.

A mistake in venue can result in a case being overturned on appeal. The issue of court jurisdiction—the authority to adjudicate a case—can be quite complex, since it has many dimensions:

1. *Venue* is the area of geographic jurisdiction of a court and can be limited to a particular district, city, or county.

2. *Subject jurisdiction* refers to the category of cases the court is authorized to consider, for example criminal (**misdemeanors** or felonies), civil, juvenile, or matters of equity.

3. *Personal (in personam) jurisdiction* refers to authority over the defendant; without it the court cannot proceed.

4. *In rem jurisdiction* is the result of the presence of tangible or intangible assets within the court's venue.

5. *Original jurisdiction* refers to the authority to hear or act on a case from its beginning to its conclusion.

6. *Appellate jurisdiction* refers to the authority to review decisions made by a lower court, to hear cases on appeal.

7. *Limited jurisdiction* means that the court has original jurisdiction in only a limited number of narrowly defined cases (e.g., only misdemeanors or civil cases where the money in dispute is below a specified sum, or only traffic cases).

8. *General jurisdiction* refers to the authority of a trial court to hear any type of case, civil or criminal, misdemeanor or felony, those involving small or unlimited amounts of money.

9. *Concurrent jurisdiction* occurs when two or more courts at the same time have the ability to hear and decide a particular case.

10. *Diversity jurisdiction* arises when litigants are from different states. (Diversity jurisdiction is discussed in more detail below.)

The jurisdiction of a state court never extends beyond that state's borders. However, various states have **long-arm statutes** providing jurisdiction over nonresident persons or corporations if they have ties to that state by virtue of business transactions such as the supplying of goods or services, or if the **cause of action** is local and affects local residents. These statutes are used, for example, to exercise jurisdiction over nonresident motorists involved in motor vehicle accidents. Paul Carrington (2011: 637) notes the need for long-arm statutes: "States seldom enact and enforce laws made to protect distant citizens of other states or nations at the expense of their local citizens or firms. Therefore, a state cannot rely on the law or the officers of a distant state to protect its citizens from risky or harmful decisions by business executives in that distant state." The issue of state court jurisdiction over out-of-state defendants is filled with controversy, particularly when it involves the liability of foreign corporations whose products are sold in a particular state as part of the "stream of commerce."

In only one case is the jurisdiction of a court established by the US Constitution; Article III, Section 2 states: "The judicial power of the United States shall be vested in one Supreme Court, and in such inferior Courts as the Congress may from time to time ordain and establish." Similarly, state courts derive their authority from state constitutions and legislative enactments. The jurisdiction of the unitary federal court system often overlaps that of state courts (**concurrent jurisdiction**). Because issues of jurisdiction are sometimes blurred, a litigant may have a choice of bringing a case to one or more state courts or to a federal court. However, the equitable doctrine of *forum non conveniens* allows a lawsuit to be dismissed, even when the court has jurisdiction, because it is inconvenient to the defendant(s) and/or witness(es) to try the case so far away, provided the plaintiff has an alternative forum available (Maag 2001). Some states, for example Texas, have abolished this doctrine, so if jurisdiction exists the judge is obligated to exercise it.

Diversity Jurisdiction

Because of our dual system of courts, a major question arises when litigants are from different states—**diversity jurisdiction**. In cases of diversity jurisdiction, based on Article III, Section 2 of the Constitution and the Judiciary Act of 1789, a plaintiff may choose either the state court or the federal court. If the action is brought in the plaintiff's state, the defendant has a right to remove the case from state court in favor of federal court. The federal court, however, must review the circumstances to determine if it will apply federal or state law. Federal courts must follow state law, including state case law, except where the Constitution, federal statutes, or treaties provide otherwise (*Erie R.R. v. Tompkins* [1938]). If the federal court is to defer to state law, however, it must determine which state law controls. Although these are typically complex legal issues, they often involve relatively small amounts of money. As a result, in 1958, Congress set $10,000 as the minimum amount being litigated before a federal court will assume jurisdiction in a diversity case; it has been raised to $75,000 in order to further reduce overburdened federal **dockets**. The court will usually take the plaintiff's word as to the amount being contested, unless it is obvious that the plaintiff could obtain only less than $75,000.

Diversity cases "often involve mortgage foreclosures, debt collections and commercial disputes far less rarified than the constitutional and Federal questions that judges prefer, and many Federal judges have long complained of being burdened by low-stakes cases that could more easily be decided in state courts" (Wiehl 1989a: 22). Federal courts will not consider domestic relations or probate cases even if there is diversity—lawyers sometimes attempted to get into federal court by appointing guardians or executors of **estates** from other states in order to satisfy the requirement for diversity jurisdiction. The Judicial Improvements and Access to Justice Act curtailed this practice in 1988.

Controversy exists over the reasons for diversity jurisdiction. Some scholars claim that its purpose is to protect commercial interests from hostile state legislatures that might pressure state courts. Others see it as a way of protecting out-of-state defendants against the possibility of prejudice by state courts ("home cookin'"). Although federal judges favor abolishing diversity jurisdiction, trial lawyers have been in opposition: The choice of courts provides an additional element in their legal strategy. The principal effect, noted former federal appellate Judge Frank Coffin,

> is to allow large nonresident corporations that are sued in state courts to remove their case to federal court. The results are to burden federal courts with one-fourth of their caseload and one-half of their jury trials, to require federal judges to engage in arcane efforts to guess what state law might be, to flout the basic idea of federalism, to foster the idea that state courts are second-rate, and to remove any incentive for the influential segment of the bar representing nonresident corporations to work for the improvement of state courts. (1994: 64–65)

Some crimes (e.g., bank robbery and drug trafficking) violate both federal and state laws. In such cases, providence (who arrests the defendant—federal or local officers) or agreements between state and federal authorities determine jurisdiction. The jurisdiction of the federal courts has been expanded by congressional enactments on such matters as organized crime, commerce, civil rights, and taxation. Thus, a black litigant could opt to bring a civil rights action based on the Civil Rights Act of 1964 in federal court rather than in a state court in the South. The Racketeer Influenced and Corrupt Organizations (RICO) section of the Organized Crime Control Act of 1970 authorizes prosecution in federal court for the violations of certain *state* laws if the violations were committed in a certain pattern defined as "racketeering" (see Abadinsky 2013). Thus, in Cook County, Illinois, beginning in 1985, a number of state (circuit) court judges were successfully prosecuted in federal court under RICO for accepting bribes (although most of these cases had nothing to do with organized crime).

Intersecting and Overlapping Court Systems

"The two realms of our dual court system are not entirely separate and independent; they intersect and overlap in a number of important ways—ways which require of the skilled practitioner a knowledge of the workings of both state and federal courts" (Coffin 1994: 46).

State Courts

Although there are systems of trial and appellate courts in each state, most are not at all systematic. The history that shaped our judicial systems has mitigated against uniformity. Consequently, it is difficult to generalize about state courts. Some states, such as New York, present a confusing system of courts, often with overlapping jurisdiction (Figure 4.1). Other states, such as Illinois, have created unitary court systems with relatively simple structures.

In 1964 Illinois was the first state court system to become unified. All trial courts in Illinois were consolidated into a unified circuit court with one chief judge overseeing the operations and procedures in each division. In 2004 Illinois' state court system included 1 court of last resort, 1 intermediate appellate court divided into 5 districts, and 1 court of general jurisdiction sectioned into 22 trial court divisions. From 1987 to 2004 most trial court expenses in Illinois were funded entirely at the state level. Counties were responsible for funding at least part of the operating and property expenses associated with the courthouse buildings in their jurisdictions.

In contrast New York's state court system in 2004 included 1 court of last resort, 2 intermediate appellate courts, 2 types of general jurisdiction trial courts divided into 69 divisions, and 8 types of limited jurisdiction trial courts separated into 1,695 divisions. In New York's numerous Town and Village Justice Courts most expenses, including salaries, travel, building, and property expenses, were funded at the county level.

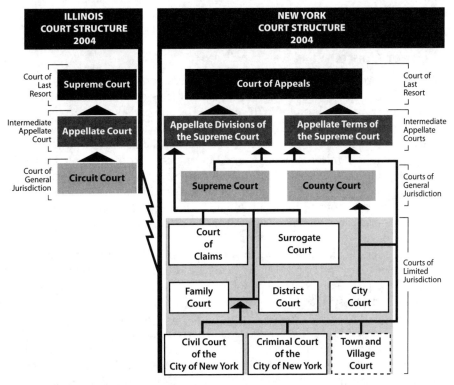

Source: Bureau of Justice Statistics (2007: 5).

Figure 4.1   Illinois and New York: Opposite Ends of Court Structure, Simplicity and Complexity

```
┌─────────────────────────────────┐
│        SUPREME COURT            │
│  Appeals/Court of Last Resort   │
└─────────────────────────────────┘
                ▲
┌─────────────────────────────────┐
│      INTERMEDIATE COURT         │
│          OF APPEALS             │
│            Appeals              │
└─────────────────────────────────┘
                ▲
┌─────────────────────────────────┐
│        SUPERIOR COURT           │
│   Trials/General Jurisdiction   │
└─────────────────────────────────┘
                ▲
┌─────────────────────────────────┐
│         LOWER COURT             │
│   Trials/Limited Jurisdiction   │
└─────────────────────────────────┘
```

**Figure 4.2   Structure of a
State Court System**

The 50 state-court systems present a complex array of structures: No two state-court systems are alike. There are two basic types of courts: those that try cases (trial courts) and those that consider cases only on appeal (appellate courts) from a trial court or a lower appellate court. In some states, a trial court of general jurisdiction may hear appeals from courts of limited jurisdiction. These courts are known by a confusing variety of names in different states, so generic titles will be used in this chapter (see Figure 4.2):

1. *Lower Courts:* limited jurisdiction (there are more than 13,500)

2. *Superior Courts:* general jurisdiction (there are more than 2,600)

3. *Intermediate Courts of Appeals:* appellate jurisdiction (not used in all states)

4. *Supreme Courts:* appellate jurisdiction of last resort

Lower Courts

Lower courts are composed of criminal and civil parts. (Lower courts are absent in six states, e.g., California and Illinois; see Figure 4.1.) Soon after the police arrest a person, he or she is usually brought to the criminal section of a lower court where the charges against the person are read, a determination is made about the appointment of an attorney (can he or she afford to hire one?) and, if the case is a felony, bail will be set. If the charge is a misdemeanor or less (an offense or violation), it can be dealt with immediately or at a later date (in which case bail will be set). Some jurisdictions may use a justice of the peace or, as in Connecticut, part-time magistrates for processing minor cases without a jury. After initial processing in a lower court, felony cases must be transferred to a superior court. Search warrants are also the responsibility of the lower court.

Depending on the state, the lower courts can include juvenile or family court (discussed in Chapter 11), probate or surrogate court, county or municipal court, traffic court, and justice-of-the-peace or police court. At this level there may also be other specialized courts, such as housing court (New York), tax court (Oregon), or water court (Colorado). Some observers point out that specialized courts are advantageous since "they have specific rather than general expertise over legal issues. A typical trial court whose caseload largely involves divorce matters will rarely have familiarity with the intricacies of the law in water rights disputes. The argument against most specialized courts is that they simply add another layer to the judicial bureaucracy and to the administrative problems that already plague the courts" (Stumpf and Culver 1992: 21).[3]

---

[3] There are also more than 450 justice forums among the 556 federally recognized tribes in the United States.

Courts of Limited Jurisdiction

Trial courts of limited jurisdiction are courts that deal only with specific types of cases. They are often located in/near the county courthouse and are usually presided over by a single judge. A judge sitting without a jury hears most of the cases heard by these courts.

- *Probate court.* This court handles matters concerning administering the estate of a person who has died (decedent). It sees that the provisions of a will are carried out or sees that a decedent's property is distributed according to state law if he/she died intestate (without a will).
- *Juvenile court.* This court usually handles cases involving delinquent children under a certain age, for example, 18 or 21.
- *Family court.* This court handles matters concerning adoption, annulments, divorce, alimony, custody, child support, etc. In some states, for example New York, juvenile and family court matters are handled by the same (called family) court
- *Traffic court.* This court usually handles minor violations of traffic laws.
- *Small-claims court.* This court usually handles suits between private persons of a relatively low dollar amount, for example, less than $5,000.
- *Municipal court.* This court usually handles cases involving offenses against city ordinances.

In civil matters, if the money at issue is less than a specific amount (e.g., $5,000), the case will be heard in the civil part of a lower court. Small-claims matters (discussed in Chapter 10), for example less than $1,000, will typically be heard in a court that bears that title or is sometimes known as *pro se* court. *Pro se*, or "for oneself," refers to a court in which litigants represent themselves rather than use lawyers. Matters involving disputes above a certain dollar amount are heard in the civil part of a superior court.

Superior Courts

Superior courts have criminal and civil parts. Although these courts are authorized to try any type of case, the criminal part typically deals only with felony cases and with civil cases above a certain threshold amount. In some instances they may hear cases appealed from a lower court, which can sometimes result in a trial *de novo* (a new trial) in a superior court. The civil part of the superior court can hear cases involving noncriminal disputes, but cases considered are usually limited to those involving a minimum dollar amount or issues of equity. There are more than 2,600 superior courts in the United States. They are called circuit courts in 16 states; 15 states call them district courts; 13 states and the District of Columbia call them superior courts; two states use other names; and four states use a combination of names.

Intermediate Courts of Appeals

The decision of a superior court in criminal and civil cases can be appealed (by the defendant in criminal cases; by either litigant in civil cases) to the appellate court. Most states divide this court into an **intermediate court of appeals** and a court of last resort or supreme court. Those states without an intermediate court of appeals have relatively small populations, such as Maine and Wyoming (Court Statistics Project 2013). States assign their intermediate courts of appeal to between five and 14 locations, and "some are limited to civil or criminal appeals" (Coffin 1994: 57). California, for example, has six appellate districts, and a decision made by one district appellate court is not binding on any other district. Intermediate courts of appeal are usually called the court of appeals, although in some states they may have other names.

In general, intermediate courts of appeals have mandatory jurisdiction—they must consider all appropriate cases—and cases are typically heard by panels of three judges (Flango and Flango 1997). But "there are wide variations in rules and patterns of practice" (Coffin 1994: 58). The intermediate court of appeals was designed to reduce the workload of the court of last resort, although in many instances the result appears otherwise; that is, it appears to encourage more appeals.

Supreme Courts

In states without an intermediate court of appeals, the supreme court, except in West Virginia, must consider virtually all appeals. (Most states refer to their court of last resort as the "supreme court.") The state of Texas has two courts of last resort: a supreme court and a court of criminal appeals. In other states, although rules vary from state to state, the supreme court usually has some discretion over the cases it will consider: "Almost everywhere the highest state court is not required to hear every appeal brought to it. The bigger the state and the higher the volume of litigation, the lower the likelihood that the state's highest court will decide any particular lawsuit" (Neely 1985: 34). Criminal cases involving the death sentence are automatically appealed to the supreme court and, in some states, so are those involving constitutional issues. "In courts having wide discretionary jurisdiction a major part of a judge's job is deciding which cases the court will hear. The litigant who lost below must apply for leave to appeal, or certiorari as it is called in some courts, and must file a brief [sometimes called a petition] supporting the application" (Marvell 1978: 17).

The supreme court generally sits in the state capital but may hear cases in other cities. Supreme courts hear cases *en banc*; that is, all of the justices—none has more than nine—of the court sit in judgment. The decision of a supreme court is binding throughout the state, and the line of appeal from a state supreme court is directly to the United States Supreme Court—*the* court of last resort. The decisions of appellate courts, particularly those of a supreme court, are often elaborate legal treatises that provide material for the case method and the rule of precedent, *stare decisis*.

Although the court system of every state approximates the pattern of organization just outlined, in states without a unitary system there is often a confusing maze of overlapping courts and jurisdictions, a situation that potential litigants may find quite dismaying but that knowledgeable lawyers may use to their advantage. Court organization has "demonstrated little logic or planning, because adding certain new courts serves various political goals" (Glick 1983: 41). (Efforts to simplify the structure of state court systems will be discussed later in this chapter.)

Federal Courts

The federal court system in the United States got off to a slow start. The Constitution provides federal jurisdiction for only two crimes: piracy and counterfeiting. The Supreme Court ruled early that there were no common-law crimes in the federal courts, and therefore no criminal prosecutions could be heard unless an act of Congress criminalized certain conduct. The federal trial courts had no "federal question" jurisdiction until 1875—if an individual wished to bring a lawsuit claiming that a right secured him or her by the federal constitution had been violated, that lawsuit had to be brought in state court. The Supreme Court of the United States could review a decision by the highest court of a state that decided a federal question, but the lower federal courts were not involved. Thus, for nearly the first century of their existence, the staple of the business of the lower federal courts were admiralty cases and cases in which jurisdiction was based on diversity of citizenship. This distribution of business between the state court systems and the federal courts changed dramatically after the so-called Civil War amendments to the Constitution were adopted. In particular, the Fourteenth Amendment has been a prolific source of federal judicial activity (Rehnquist 1996).

Until the Judiciary Act of 1875, federal courts had jurisdiction over only a few matters (Coffin 1994). That act gave federal district courts federal question jurisdiction. Furthermore, the increasing pace of the Industrial Revolution, the rapid spread of the railroad, and the increasing size of manufacturing enterprises all provoked calls for regulation of what was increasingly a commerce that went well beyond state borders. The general view that the federal government's role should be limited to providing for the common defense, coining money, carrying the mail, and paying for itself by collecting customs duties was changing.

Before the turn of the twentieth century, Congress had passed the Interstate Commerce Act (1887), giving a federal commission some control over railroad rates and practices, and the Sherman Anti-Trust Act (1890), forbidding conspiracies in restraint of trade. As we moved into the twentieth century, the coming of the automobile and the airplane continued the transportation revolution. The pace of increase in federal regulation also continued, driven partly by the interstate nature of so much of the country's business and partly by a number of reform movements seeking to ameliorate the plight of those who did not share in the generally rising tide of prosperity. The typical pattern was for reform movements to originate in the states, only to discover that the practices that they sought to prohibit or limit could not be prohibited or limited to their satisfaction without the intervention of the federal government (Rehnquist 1996).

First came concern about wages and hours worked in factories, and about child labor. States adopted maximum hour and minimum wage laws, and laws prohibiting child labor. But as often as not, the manufacturing plants, which would be affected by these laws, would pick up and move to a state that did not have such laws. Congress, viewing this phenomenon with dismay, finally enacted federal prohibitions against child labor and, later, a federal maximum hour and minimum wage law. This pattern has continued in various areas of law (Rehnquist 1996).

Today, federal courts enjoy rather extensive jurisdiction over five types of cases:

1. Those in which the United States is a party
2. Cases involving foreign officials

3. Those involving parties from different states if more than $75,000 is involved

4. Cases involving the US Constitution and federal laws

5. Those concerning specialty matters such as patent, copyright, customs, and **bankruptcy**

The state courts share jurisdiction with federal courts in categories 3 and 4, although the federal courts exercise exclusive jurisdiction in all other cases. "Only those state-court decisions involving the federal Constitution and laws may be appealed to the federal courts" (Wheeler and Levin 1979: 12). In the unitary federal system there are two basic classes into which courts may be classified: legislative and constitutional.

Federal Legislative Courts

The first two articles of the US Constitution deal with Congress (Article I) and the president (Article II). Article III states, "The judicial Power of the United States shall be vested in one supreme Court, and in such inferior Courts as the Congress may from time to time ordain and establish." Accordingly, courts created under Article III are known as **constitutional courts**, whereas those created by Congress under Article I are referred to as **legislative courts** because they may perform functions that are nonjudicial. As distinct from Constitutional (Article III) courts, legislative (Article I) courts have administrative and quasi-legislative as well as judicial duties. They are often created to help administer a specific congressional statute, while Constitutional courts are tribunals established to handle litigation (Carp, Stidham, and Manning 2014).

Legislative courts "focus on disputes between individuals and the federal government" (Smith 1997: 40). They include the Court of Military Appeals, Tax Court, Court of Veterans Appeals, and the Territorial Courts of Guam, Virgin Islands, Puerto Rico, and the Northern Mariana Islands. The Court of Military Appeals was established in 1950. Its three judges provide civilian review of military courts martial. The 19 members of the Tax Court hear appeals on Internal Revenue Service rulings; the court was originally an administrative (Article II—executive branch) court. The Court of Veterans Appeals, established in 1988, is the nation's newest federal court. Its seven judges review decisions of the Board of Veterans Appeals concerning veterans' claims against the government. All legislative court judges are nominated by the president, confirmed by the Senate, and (except those of Territorial Courts, who serve four to eight

---

Legislative (Article III) Courts (Created by Congress)

- *Magistrate judges.* These judges handle certain criminal and civil matters, often with the consent of the parties.
- *Bankruptcy courts.* These courts handle cases arising under the Bankruptcy Code.
- *US Court of Military Appeals.* This court is the final appellate court for cases arising under the Uniform Code of Military Justice.
- *US Tax Court.* This court handles cases arising over alleged tax deficiencies.
- *US Court of Veterans' Appeals.* This court handles certain cases arising from the denial of veterans' benefits.

> ### Legislative Court Example: United States Tax Court
>
> Congress created the Tax Court under Article I to provide a judicial forum in which affected persons could dispute tax deficiencies determined by the commissioner of Internal Revenue Service prior to payment of the disputed amounts. Composed of 19 presidentially appointed members who have expertise in the tax laws, the court is physically located in Washington, DC, but the judges travel nationwide to conduct trials in various designated cities. Trials are conducted before one judge, without a jury, and taxpayers are permitted to represent themselves if they desire. The vast majority of cases are settled by mutual agreement without the necessity of a trial. However, if a trial is conducted, in due course a report is ordinarily issued by the presiding judge setting forth findings of fact and an opinion.

years; or Puerto Rico's federal judges who enjoy lifetime tenure) serve terms of 15 years (instead of the lifetime appointments of all Article III judges).

To further complicate distinctions between these courts, Congress has redesignated some formerly legislative courts as constitutional courts. The Court of Claims was established by Congress in 1855 as a Constitutional (Article III) court but was declared a legislative (Article I) court by the Supreme Court in 1933, only to have it reestablished by Congress in 1953 as a constitutional court. In 1982, Congress created the Claims Court, replacing the Court of Claims as the "keeper of the nation's conscience," where citizens and corporations, foreign or domestic, can sue the government in those areas where Congress has waived sovereign immunity.

Federal Constitutional Courts

In addition to the US Supreme Court, there are five categories of courts established by Congress under Article III of the Constitution (see Figure 4.3 on the following page):

1. *Magistrates and Bankruptcy:* limited jurisdiction
2. *District Court:* general trial jurisdiction
3. *Specialized (constitutional) Courts:* specialized jurisdiction
4. *Court of Appeals:* intermediate appellate jurisdiction
5. *Supreme Court:* appellate jurisdiction of last resort established by the Constitution

Magistrates and Bankruptcy.   The Judiciary Act of 1789 created a system of federal trial courts, permitting federal criminal cases to be tried in the newly established circuit and district courts. But matters of arrest and bail were left to be governed by state law and handled by state judicial officers. It became apparent soon after passage of the Judiciary Act of 1789 that, because of resistance in some states to federal policies, federal criminal process could not rely solely on state judicial officers. In 1793, Congress authorized the federal circuit courts to appoint persons to take bail in federal criminal cases. In 1817, Congress officially named them commissioners of the circuit court and extended to them the authority to take depositions in civil cases. In 1842, Congress authorized circuit court commissioners to exercise general criminal process in federal cases by issuing arrest warrants and holding persons for trial (Foschio 1999).

```
┌─────────────────────────────────────┐
│    UNITED STATES SUPREME COURT       │
│     Appeals/Court of Last Resort     │
└─────────────────────────────────────┘
                  ▲
┌─────────────────────────────────────┐
│        13 COURTS OF APPEALS          │
│              Appeals                 │
└─────────────────────────────────────┘
                  ▲
┌─────────────────────────────────────┐
│         SPECIALIZED COURTS           │
│ Trial and Appellate Specialized Jurisdiction │
└─────────────────────────────────────┘
                  ▲
┌─────────────────────────────────────┐
│         94 DISTRICT COURTS           │
│        Trials/General Jurisdiction   │
└─────────────────────────────────────┘
                  ▲
┌─────────────────────────────────────┐
│  MAGISTRATE AND BANKRUPTCY COURT     │
│       Trials/Limited Jurisdiction    │
└─────────────────────────────────────┘
```

Figure 4.3   Structure of the Federal Court System

The jurisdiction and role of the commissioners was repeatedly expanded throughout the nineteenth century, reflecting the rapidly changing social and economic needs of the country. In 1896, Congress renamed the office of commissioner of the circuit court to "United States Commissioner" and established a four-year term, subject to removal by the district court at any time. There were no minimum qualifications, compensation was determined under a uniform fee schedule, and there was a prohibition against holding other federal, civil, or military offices (Foschio 1999).

In 1968, Congress authorized a system of magistrates to replace United States commissioners. **Magistrates** are appointed by majority vote of the active district judges of the district court to exercise jurisdiction over matters assigned by statute as well as those delegated by the district judges. Whereas commissioners did not need to be attorneys and worked part-time on a fee-for-service basis, the approximately 500 magistrates—whose title was changed to magistrate judge in 1990—must be members of the bar and are salaried employees appointed for eight-year (or four-year part-time) terms. The Judicial Conference of the United States determines the number of magistrate judge positions. The magistrate judge was granted authority to exercise all powers previously exercised by the commissioners, along with additional duties such as assisting district judges in the conduct of pretrial and discovery proceedings, review of *habeas corpus* petitions, and acting as special masters. The 1968 act also provided that magistrates could be given authority to perform other duties not contrary to law or the Constitution (Foschio 1999).

By statute, judges may assign a wide variety of pretrial work to magistrate judges. However, the Federal Judicial Center notes, "What is actually assigned to a magistrate depends upon a district's procedures for handling pretrial matters" (1985: xi). Typically, in criminal cases, magistrate judges conduct pretrial hearings—reading of the charges, bail, appointment of counsel—and, if both sides agree, try misdemeanors. In 1989, the Supreme Court ruled that magistrates do not have legal authority to preside over jury selection in felony cases without the defendant's consent (*Gomez v. United States*). If the charge is a felony, the case will be sent to the district court. Magistrate judges are authorized to consider civil matters when the amount in dispute is less than $10,000 or when both parties agree to have the magistrate decide the case with or without a jury.

In many districts, magistrate judges preside over pretrial case conferences and pretrial motions, although the final decision may be reserved for a district court judge based on a report and recommendation from the magistrate judge. Magistrate judges may deal with Social Security cases and *habeas corpus* petitions from prisoners, although this may involve only submitting a report and recommendation to the district court. Depending on local rules, the decisions of a magistrate judge can be appealed to the district court or directly to the court of appeals.

Federal courts have exclusive jurisdiction over bankruptcy cases. Bankruptcy judges, known as referees prior to 1973, although adjuncts of the district courts, are appointed by the courts of appeals for terms of 14 years. Congress determines the number of bankruptcy judges. As their title indicates, they handle the increasing number of bankruptcy cases entering the federal system (about one million a year). The decision of a bankruptcy judge can be appealed to the district court or a panel of bankruptcy judges, at the option of the district court or court of appeals.

District Courts.   In 1789, Congress divided the nation into 13 judicial districts, and in the early 1790s, some states were divided into multiple districts. The president was authorized to appoint a federal marshal and a US attorney for each district. As new states entered the union, Congress created additional districts. Today, there are 94 federal district courts with more than 650 judges plus senior judges.[4] The states, the Commonwealth of Puerto Rico, the District of Columbia, the Virgin Islands, Guam, and the Northern Mariana Islands each have at least one district, although three states (New York, California, and Texas) have four. With the exception of the District of Wyoming, which includes Idaho and Montana portions of Yellowstone National Park, no district cuts across a state line. Between one and 28 judges are assigned to each district, the largest being the Southern District of New York, headquartered at Foley Square in the Borough of Manhattan. The district court usually tries civil cases (more than $10,000) and criminal cases (misdemeanor trials and felonies) and deals with issues involving certain federal agencies. In the three territorial districts, the court also exercises local jurisdiction.

Although those who supported a strong national government favored *federal* district courts, there was the question of states' rights. The Supremacy Clause (Article VI of the Constitution) stipulates that "the Authority of the United States, shall be the supreme Law of the Land; and the Judges in every State shall be bound thereby, any Thing in the Constitution or Laws of any State to the Contrary notwithstanding." It was argued, since state judges are required to enforce the Constitution, federal courts would be redundant. Congress, however, established federal district courts in 1789, albeit with a great deal of ambivalence.

Early district courts served as the federal trial court for admiralty and maritime cases as well as for some minor civil and criminal cases. Gradually, over the nineteenth century, Congress expanded the jurisdiction of the district courts. However, it was not until the Judiciary Act of 1875 that district courts were empowered to hear civil suits involving at least $500 (if the dispute arose "under the Constitution, laws, or treaties of the United States"). In recent times, new statutes have expanded the jurisdiction of federal district courts, resulting in an increase in district court cases on such subjects as environmental

---

[4] The status of "senior judge" was established by Congress in 1919 and permits federal judges who meet the "Rule of 80" (reached the age of 65 and served as active judges for at least 15 years or reached the age of 70 and served for 10 years) to reduce their caseload, although still receiving full-time salaries. Among a variety of responsibilities, they may fill in for absent judges, deal with specialized issues, and provide judicial services in areas that have no permanent federal judge. Senior judges handle more than 15 percent of the federal courts' caseload.

protection, job discrimination, education of the handicapped, and (heretofore state) crime. About three-quarters of the civil cases, however, involve disputes between private individuals and businesses, and the United States is a party in the other 25 percent.

Appeals from a ruling by a district court go to the court of appeals, although in certain exceptional cases they may be appealed directly to the Supreme Court (e.g., injunctions against state laws).

Specialized (Constitutional) Courts.   Specialized courts include a three-judge panel consisting of two district court judges and one judge of the court of appeals. Since 1976, the use of the special three-judge tribunal has been limited to congressional and legislative apportionment cases and issues involving the Voting Rights Act of 1965 and the Civil Rights Act of 1964. Appeals from the decision of a special district court ruling go directly to the Supreme Court.

Other specialized (constitutional) courts include the Court of International Trade, which adjudicates tariff and related disputes, and the Court of Appeals for the Federal Circuit. The latter hears patent appeals from all district courts, appeals from the Court of International Trade and the US Claims Court, and appeals from various administrative bodies. Like all other constitutional (Article III) judges, the nine members of the Court of International Trade serve life terms. Unlike other federal constitutional courts, no more than five members may be from the same political party. Although these courts have constitutional status, "they nevertheless still occupy a special niche in the federal system" and "still perform, or at least may be viewed as performing, certain quasi-legislative and quasi-administrative functions" (Abraham 1998: 164–65).

Specialized courts (legislative or constitutional) provide several advantages: Judges with expertise in a technical field offer "the opportunity for a single court in a field to avoid legal conflicts that develop among courts or courts of appeals, and reducing the caseloads of generalist courts" (Baum 1994: 39). However, specialized courts may become unduly influenced by an interest group that the court deals with continuously— "repeat players." Support for the creation of a specialized court may reflect rather parochial interests: that the court would "rule more favorably toward them than would the district courts or courts of appeals" (Baum 1994: 39). The transfer of jurisdiction from generalist courts to specialized ones can produce fundamental changes in judicial policy.

Courts of Appeals.   The Judiciary Act of 1789 established a system of circuit courts—eastern, middle, and southern circuits—with both trial and **appellate jurisdiction**. Circuit courts served as trial courts for most federal criminal cases, for diversity cases, and for suits initiated by the United States; they also exercised appellate jurisdiction over civil cases originating in the district courts. The circuit had no judges of its own, but consisted of panels of two justices of the Supreme Court—reduced to one in 1793—and the local district court judge. The circuit is an English concept, transported to America in the colonial period. It allowed efficient use of judges by having them "ride circuit," traveling to several locations to hold court when no single location had enough judicial business to justify the appointment of a full-time judge for that court (Wheeler 1992).

As the country grew, the size of the Supreme Court was increased to provide a justice for each circuit. By 1869, faced with a sharp increase in federal litigation, Congress created a judgeship for each of the nine circuits then in existence. The circuit judge, the designated Supreme Court justice, the district judge, or some combination of two of them, presided over the circuit courts.

Until 1891, each Supreme Court justice would ride one of the federal circuits during recess and sit as a circuit court judge to hear appeals. This system, however, proved to be insufficient. After the Civil War, the phenomenal growth of the American economy led to an increase in government regulatory activity and, coupled with judicial activism on behalf of business and industry, produced a virtual breakdown in federal appeals by the 1880s (Howard 1981). In 1891, Congress created the circuit courts of appeals, although the position of circuit judge lingered on until 1911. The 1891 legislation (Evarts Act) gave the courts of appeals jurisdiction over the great majority of appeals from the federal courts and greatly limited the categories of cases that could routinely be appealed to the Supreme Court. The Judiciary Act of 1925 continued this trend, and by 1930, the courts of appeals also had jurisdiction over administrative appeals of decisions by federal regulatory agencies.

> *Judicial activism occurs when courts move beyond their assigned role, usurping the prerogative of the legislative branch.*

The name of the courts was officially changed to the United States Courts of Appeals in 1948, even though the judges are often referred to as circuit judges. Today, the 13 appellate courts have about 180 judges. Although the courts of appeals were designed "to help the Supreme Court enforce the supremacy and uniformity of federal law" (Howard 1981: 3), in a number of respects, this purpose remains to be accomplished.

Although in theory the federal judiciary is organized into a typical pyramidal structure, in practice federal judicial power is widely diffused among judges who "are insulated by deep traditions of independence, not only from the other branches of government but also from each other" (Howard 1981: 3). Local rules and customs distinguish one court of appeals from another. Some rely on oral argument in every case, although others allow it in only a small portion of the cases they consider; some provide long opinions with their decisions, although others, due to caseload pressures, frequently utilize summary dispositions—decisions without opinions or very brief orders. In only two circuits (District of Columbia and the Seventh in Illinois) do judges of the court of appeals work in the same courthouse. Geographic dispersion, coupled with "rotation of panel membership, large caseloads, and ideological differences, can contribute to inconsistency *within* a court of appeals, limiting the courts' ability to produce uniformity in national law and increasing the burden on the Supreme Court" (Wasby 1993: 57). Regionalism remains a source of disparity and conflict among the circuits, which can be resolved only by the Supreme Court (Howard 1981).[5] But the

---

[5] For example, in 1997 the Supreme Court agreed to hear a case (*Sacramento County v. Lewis*) involving a dispute over the rights of persons injured or killed in high-speed police chases—in this case the accidental death of a passenger on a motorcycle whose driver was fleeing the police. The Ninth Circuit in Sacramento (CA) had ruled that all that is required is proof of police conduct showing a "deliberate indifference" or "reckless disregard." Other federal circuits, however, adopted a higher standard: that the police action must also "shock the conscience."

Supreme Court reviews only about one out of every 200 cases decided by the courts of appeals, undermining the federal judicial system's capacity to promote uniformity in national law (Strauss 1990).

The defendant in a criminal case and the losing side in a civil case can appeal to the court of appeals in whose circuit the district court lies. There are 12 courts of appeals (if the Court of Appeals for the Federal Circuit, discussed above, is included, there are 13) in 11 numbered circuits and the District of Columbia, with between four and 28 judges. Each circuit, except the District of Columbia, encompasses at least three states. A court of appeals sits in three-judge panels, although in exceptional cases the court may sit *en banc*—most or all of the judges in the circuit hear the case. There are more than 200 appellate judges and senior judges assisting on circuit panels.

The jurisdiction of a court of appeals includes all of the cases decided by federal courts in its circuit and those of a number of federal administrative and regulatory agencies such as the Federal Communications Commission and the Environmental Protection Agency. An appeal from the decision of a court of appeals must be taken to the Supreme Court. Under certain conditions, a case can be appealed from a district court directly to the Supreme Court. This will occur, for example, when the case has been decided by a three-judge district court, or when a federal statute has been declared unconstitutional and the government is appealing, or when the issue is one of substantial national importance, such as the matter of the "Nixon tapes," White House recordings that played a crucial role in the resignation of President Richard Nixon.

Each circuit is assigned a Supreme Court justice, with the two most senior justices assigned to two circuits. This is a link to the earlier era before the appeals courts were established as separate intermediate-level courts (Goldman and Jahnige 1985). On occasion, Supreme Court justices are asked to act on emergency petitions from their circuits when the Supreme Court is not in session. These petitions often involve cases of capital punishment, and a justice can order a **stay** of execution until the Court convenes. The courts of appeals must consider all cases brought to them.

Some circuit courts, by virtue of law or their geographic location, become magnets for certain types of cases. Certain appeals involving federal agencies must be brought in the District of Columbia, the site of agency headquarters, whereas others have a choice; that is, the action may also be brought in the circuit where the controversy developed. Because of its location in the financial capital of the United States, the Second Circuit (New York) is the site of a great deal of commercial litigation.

The Supreme Court.   The Constitution, which provides for a Supreme Court, does not state how many members it is to have. The Judiciary Act of 1789 established a Supreme Court with one chief justice and five associate justices. As already noted, the size of the Court was increased to accommodate the establishment of new circuits to which each justice was attached; it reached nine in 1837. In 1863, a tenth justice was added, but in 1866, Congress reduced the number to seven. Legislation in 1869 provided for a justice for each of the nine circuits, and the number has since remained the same. The nine-member bench has become such a strong tradition that in 1937 even an overwhelmingly Democratic Congress refused to increase its membership at the request of Democratic President Franklin Roosevelt (discussed in Chapter 6).

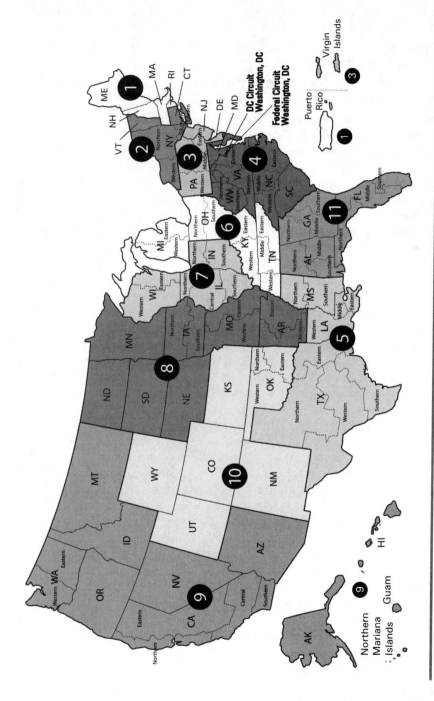

Figure 4.4 Geographical Boundaries of United States Courts of Appeals and United States District Courts

The Supreme Court has three fundamental responsibilities (Freund 1961):

1. To resolve disputes between states, which often involve boundaries or the apportionment of interstate waters.

2. To provide for the uniformity of federal law. The Court has ultimate authority in the event of conflicting decisions by lower courts.

3. To maintain the constitutional order. The Court determines if executive or legislative actions conform to the Constitution.

Once an institution of little consequence, the Supreme Court is now equal to the other branches of government. The decisions of the Court affect the lives of every person in the United States (and sometimes persons beyond its borders). Since the historic precedent in an otherwise unimportant case, *Marbury v. Madison* (discussed in Chapter 6), the Supreme Court has enjoyed the power to declare a statutory enactment (or executive action) void because it is unconstitutional. The Supreme Court became the interpreter of the law not because the delegates at the Constitutional Convention declared it so, but because things worked out that way. In 1907, three years before his appointment to the Supreme Court, Charles Evans Hughes, then governor of New York and later becoming chief justice, stated: "We are under a Constitution, but the Constitution is what the judges say it is" (Harrell and Anderson 1982: 11).

Each associate justice of the Court is entitled to employ up to four law clerks (the chief justice is entitled to more), who traditionally serve terms of one year. Recently, some justices have been keeping clerks on for a second year, and the Court has also hired some career law clerks to provide expertise and continuity. The selection of law clerks is up to each justice, and the position is quite prestigious. It usually goes to the top graduates of elite law schools, based on recommendations from law professors or former clerks. The Court has declared itself immune from charges of employment discrimination, and its law clerks, as the justices themselves, have been mostly white males. The **law clerks** examine and summarize petitions, review briefs, conduct research, and draft opinions. They often play a key role in selecting cases for certiorari consideration.

The importance of the role of clerks for members of the Supreme Court is not without controversy: "In a perfect legal world," notes Bernard Schwartz (1988: 16), "the law clerk would perform the functions of an associate in a law firm, that is, research for senior members and assistance generally in the firm's work. But the tasks assigned clerks at the Supreme Court depend solely on the view of the job held by the individual Justice for whom they are working." Indeed, "the scope of the clerk's responsibility expands in inverse ratio to the caliber of the Justice." Thus, "it may be doubted that the great Justices, such as Oliver W. Holmes or Louis Brandeis, used their clerks as more than research assistants. More run-of-the-mill Justices have given their clerks a larger share of responsibility, including (in some cases) the writing of opinions." Many Supreme Court justices were themselves clerks for Supreme Court justices. The Supreme Court is the subject of Chapter 6.

Judicial Administration and Reform

In the United States, the judicial branch is characterized by a lack of specialization. Judges are often confronted by case issues about which they have little knowledge or experience. A judge whose legal practice involved civil cases is found in criminal court, a criminal lawyer is found on the bench of juvenile court, and both may have to preside at a divorce hearing, an antitrust case, or a case involving highly technical scientific issues. Judges are also responsible for administrative duties for which they usually have no training. Judges prize independence, and traditions of civility and camaraderie associated with the legal profession mitigate against a chain of command and formal rules of interaction among judges. Judicial "independence explains the low interest many judges exhibit in the administrative affairs of the court and why they believe they have the 'right' to operate, administratively, with their own sense of what is best for them and their chambers" (Lefever 2010: 66).

Until the 1980s, judges typically avoided the advice of professional managers and proceeded without the benefit of modern techniques of careful research, planning, evaluation, and training (Cannon 1982). Instead, many judges relied on intuitions and predilections born of legal training and on a disposition to follow precedents.

Whereas operational agencies in the executive branch of government are organized bureaucratically, with day-to-day operations managed by a chain of command and carried out on the basis of a highly specialized division of labor, the judicial branch has resisted bureaucratization. What would be routine for an executive branch agency is often slow and inefficient in the judicial branch. Although executive-branch operations are under the control of administrators who are more or less trained and experienced in management, the judicial branch is under the control of judges who may have little or no experience, and even less interest, in such mundane matters as providing adequate lighting, heating and cooling, clean washrooms, and bulletin boards for posting the daily court calendars. There is also the pressing problem of case management, promulgating calendars, assigning judges, court security, and maintaining and safeguarding case files. Legal education provides no exposure to court administration.

The Administration of Federal Courts

At the beginning of this chapter, it was noted that no two state court systems are exactly alike, and the administration of each also varies. Although the federal system has some administrative responsibilities vested in the Supreme Court, there is no ministry of justice, a centralized system that exists in other democratic countries. A major difference between most state court governance structures and the federal system is the role of the jurisdiction's highest appellate court. Supreme courts dominate governance in most states. Other than the activities of the chief justice, however, the US Supreme Court's only significant role in federal judicial governance is in approving procedural rules developed by the Judicial Conference and sending them to Congress for review.

The Court has no other significant role in court governance, in part because of Chief Justice Charles Hughes' (1930–1941) reaction to executive–judicial conflicts in the 1930s, and the difficulties that federal court administration had caused the Justice Department. The chief justice wanted the Court free from contamination by bureaucratic infighting and inevitable charges of poor or even corrupt administration in faraway courts, about which the Supreme Court could know very little (Wheeler 1992). In 1938, Congress transferred the management of the federal judiciary from the Department of Justice to the federal judges themselves. However, because of Hughes' opposition, managerial control was not lodged in the Supreme Court. Instead, it is distributed throughout the federal judiciary (Howard 1981).

The Supreme Court promulgates rules for the lower courts, but its control over budgetary matters and policy making is minimal. Each federal circuit has a circuit judicial council, and in each of the federal districts there is a **chief judge** who has administrative responsibilities. But the chief judge's ability to carry out policies is based more on the level of cooperation in a district than on any real powers that he or she can exercise—each judge is independent and appointed for life. In 1971, Congress passed the Circuit Executive Act, establishing an executive for each federal circuit to provide managerial expertise in budgeting, information systems, personnel and training, facilities, furnishings, and supplies, research, and public relations.

A **Judicial Conference** serves as the chief administrative policy maker for the federal judiciary. Chaired by the chief justice of the Supreme Court, the conference has 26 members, including the chief judges of the courts of appeals, a district judge from each circuit except Washington, DC, and the chief judge of the Court of International Trade. The members meet twice a year, and the six-member executive committee acts for the conference between meetings. A variety of specialized committees conduct much of the work of the conference: rules of evidence and procedure, intercircuit transfers, need for additional judges to handle increasing caseloads, ethical standards for judges and other court personnel, qualifications for court personnel, and the budget for the federal judiciary. Lawyers serve on advisory committees, and lawyer representatives attend annual circuit judicial conferences. The Judicial Conference as a whole votes on committee recommendations and makes legislative recommendations for congressional action.

The Administrative Office of the United States Courts is headed by a director appointed by the chief justice in consultation with the Judicial Conference. The direc-

---

Judicial Conference of the United States

Congress created the Conference of Senior Circuit Judges in 1922 to serve as the principal policy-making body concerned with the administration of the United States courts. In 1948, Congress enacted Section 331 of Title 28, United States Code, changing the name to the Judicial Conference of the United States. District judges were formally added to the conference in 1957. Section 331 of Title 28 specifically provides that the Judicial Conference shall:

1. Make a comprehensive survey of the conditions of business in the courts of the United States;

2. Prepare plans for the assignment of judges to or from courts of appeals or district courts, where necessary;

3. Submit suggestions to the various courts in the interest of promoting uniformity of management procedures and the expeditious conduct of court business;

4. Exercise authority provided in Chapter 16 of Title 28 United States Code for the review of circuit council conduct and disability orders filed under that Chapter; and

5. Carry on a continuous study of the operation and effect of the general rules of practice and procedure in use within the federal courts, as prescribed by the Supreme Court pursuant to law.

tor serves as the chief administrative officer of the federal courts and is responsible for carrying out the policies of the Judicial Conference. The office provides staff support and counsel to the Judicial Conference and its committees, collects and reports judicial branch statistics, develops budgets, conducts surveys and assessments of judicial operations and programs, provides technical assistance to the courts, develops training programs, and fosters communication within the judiciary and with other branches of government and the public.

The Federal Judicial Center provides training and research for the federal judiciary in a wide range of areas including court administration, case management, budget and finance, human resources, and court technology. A board of directors consisting of the chief justice, the director of the Administrative Office, and seven judges chosen by the Judicial Conference oversees the center's operations. The center develops orientation and continuing education programs for judges and other court personnel. It conducts studies of judiciary operations and makes recommendations to the Judicial Conference for improvement of the administration and management of the federal courts.

The Administration of State Courts

Although court administration can affect the level of justice dispensed in a system, judicial management has typically been the most primitive of governmental services. David Saari points out that the courthouse has a natural aversion to change; the lawyers who dominate its operations

> are not interested in working in a typical executive type of bureaucratically dominated, centralized atmosphere, which they will resist by keeping courts locally controlled to suit their own professional interest. Thus the politically favorable, localized power and the professionalism trends [of the legal profession] join together to preserve that historical design concept of the judiciary from excessive bureaucratization that has overrun other institutions of society, especially executive-branch organizations and large businesses. This antibureaucratic strain of courts seems to explain many local examples and variations where the public and courts have rejected reform aimed toward centralized control. (1985: 32–33)

Moreover, the judicial branch was the last to take advantage of the Industrial Revolution in information management that resulted from the use of computers.

New York: Chief Judge and Chief Administrative Judge

The state constitution provides that the chief judge of the court of appeals is the state's chief judicial officer who, with the advice and consent of the administrative board—chief judge and the presiding justices of the four appellate divisions—appoints the chief administrative judge of the courts. The chief judge establishes statewide standards and administrative policies after consultation with the administrative board and promulgates these after approval by the court of appeals. The chief administrative judge is responsible for supervising the administration and operation of the trial courts and for directing the Office of Court Administration. The chief administrative judge appoints administrative judges in each jurisdiction who are given significant administrative latitude to carry out policy and address local issues.

At the top of a state court system is the chief judge of the court of last resort, who usually has certain statewide administrative responsibilities. There may also be a judicial conference or similar entity that promulgates rules for the entire state judiciary and helps to resolve disputes. The supreme court or the conference will have authority to remove judges for judicial misconduct. The day-to-day operations of a judicial district are the responsibility of the chief or presiding judge, who may gain the position by election (the judges in the district make the choice from among their colleagues) or by tradition (e.g., the judge with the most seniority who is not yet 65).

> His or her primary responsibilities are to keep the cases flowing in as efficient a manner as the administration of individual justice permits. [He or she will pressure judges to "move cases" whenever a backlog develops.] The other functions of this chief judicial officer vary depending upon local tradition and preferences but most perform the following tasks: (1) assign judges to various courts, (2) initiate disciplinary action against members of the bench, (3) act as spokespersons for bench to bar and general public, (4) preside over functions involving the bench, (5) serve as ex officio members of various committees within the court system, (6) decide administrative matters such as vacations and retirements of court members, and (7) plan and execute continuing education projects. (Wice 1985: 52–53)

Administrative Office of Pennsylvania Courts

Pennsylvania's constitution invests in the state's supreme court's general supervisory and administrative authority over all of the commonwealth's courts. The constitution also establishes the Office of Court Administrator of Pennsylvania, who is appointed by the supreme court. The court administrator heads the Administrative Office of Pennsylvania Courts (AOPC), whose supervisory, administrative, and long-range planning duties include:

- Reviewing practices, procedures and efficiency at all levels of the court system and in all related offices
- Developing recommendations to the supreme court regarding improvement of the system and related offices
- Representing the judicial system before legislative bodies
- Examining administrative and business methods used by offices in or related to the court system
- Collecting statistical data
- Examining the state of the dockets and making recommendations for expediting litigation
- Managing fiscal affairs, including budget preparation, disbursements approval, and goods and services procurement
- Supervising all administrative matters relating to offices engaged in clerical functions
- Administering human resource systems, including personnel and benefits counseling and management
- Conducting education programs for system personnel
- Receiving and responding to comments from the public

"While the bench often will view the chief judge as someone who needs to protect them from outside interference and the one responsible for garnishing important resources, they rarely view the chief judge as their 'boss'" (Lefever 2010: 69).

The size of the administrative office staff reflects both the degree to which there is centralized coordination of key functions and the allocation of some substantial responsibilities, such as juvenile probation, to the administrative office of the courts (Rottman and Strickland 2006). Important managerial aspects of any court system are the responsibility of the clerk of the court. In some systems, the chief or presiding trial court judge is assisted by a court manager, a professional who is responsible for many of the nonlegal aspects of the court system.

Clerk of the Court.   The duties and the title of clerk of the court vary from state to state. In about one-third of the states, there is a distinct elected office called county clerk. In other states, the functions of this official are performed by officers entitled clerk, circuit clerk, recorder of deeds, registrar of deeds, or even auditor. The clerk of the court may be elected or appointed and is responsible for maintaining the written records of the court and for supervising the work of the assistant clerks who attend all court sessions. According to the Dictionary of Criminal Justice Data Terminology (1981: 56), "The typical duties of the court clerk are receiving documents to be filed in the court record, assigning case numbers, scheduling cases on the court calendar [docketing], entering judgments and orders in the court record, preparing writs and warrants [for the judge's signature], and keeping the court records and seal," which must be affixed to all court documents if they are to be official. A clerk of the court typically has responsibility for docketing cases, collecting court fees, overseeing jury selection, and maintaining all court records (Rottman and Strickland 2006; Stout 1986).

Court Managers.   Court management is a relatively new profession, dating only from the 1960s, but it has expanded rapidly. In 1970, there were fewer than 50 persons in court administrative positions who had management training. By 1980, that number was over 500 (Solomon 1987). There are a few universities that provide graduate degrees in court management: The University of Denver offers a master of science in

---

Clerk of the Fulton County, Georgia, Superior Court

The clerk of the superior court is elected by the citizens of Fulton County to serve a four-year term. The clerk maintains a comprehensive record of all civil and criminal actions of the superior court and prepares and records accusations, indictments, and the disposition of cases. Records are prepared for the Georgia Court of Appeals and the Georgia Supreme Court. The clerk also provides each superior court judge, senior judge, and visiting judge with a calendar clerk to prepare the court calendar and otherwise assist the courts.

Additionally, the clerk is responsible for recording deeds related to the sale of real property, personal property liens, maintaining the chain of title to all property in the county, and collecting real estate transfer taxes. Other records include suits, pleadings, charters, contracts, professional licenses, trade-name registrations, and **notary public** appointments. All records maintained by this office are arranged to facilitate research and review by lawyers, real estate agents, and others.

legal administration (MSLA), which includes preparation for law office management and judicial administration; John Jay College of Criminal Justice (NY) and Jackson State University (MS) offer a master of public administration with a concentration in court administration; Michigan State University offers a master degree in criminal justice with a concentration in judicial administration.

Court managers oversee the administrative functions of the court under the general direction of the chief judge. In practice, the judges of the court play the role of members of a board of directors: The chief judge serves as chairman of the board, and the court manager is the administrator or executive officer. Under this system, the judges determine policy that is implemented by the court manager. Many of the functions performed by a court manager are traditionally the duties of the chief judge. Although the duties of court managers vary with the location and size of the court that employs them, their basic functions, according to the National Association for Court Management, include the following:

- *Personnel Management.* Administrating wage and salary systems; recruiting, selecting, training, developing, evaluating, counseling, and disciplining nonjudicial administrative staff; and facilitating personnel matters for judicial staff

- *Fiscal Management.* Preparing court budgets; administering accounting, purchasing, payroll, and financial control functions; guiding the budget through state and local government review processes

- *Caseflow Management.* Analyzing and evaluating pending caseloads; preparing and implementing recommendations for effective calendar management

- *Automated Office Management.* Analyzing, evaluating, and implementing management information systems to assist the court (computers, telecommunications equipment, microfilm and microfiche devices and techniques)

- *Jury Management.* Managing the jury system in the most efficient and cost-effective manner

- *Space and Equipment Management.* Planning for physical space needs; purchasing and managing equipment and supplies

- *Records Management.* Creating and managing uniform record-keeping systems

- *Information Management.* Collecting and providing management information for all departments and branches of government; publishing data on pending and completed judicial business and internal functions of the court system

- *Court Liaison.* Acting as a liaison to other courts, public and private agencies, governments, and attorneys to promote the work of the court

- *Public Relations.* Acting as a clearinghouse for the release of information to the media and the public; educating the public about the work of the court

- *Research and Advisory Services.* Identifying problems; recommending procedural and administrative changes to the court

The role of a court manager differs from the more conventional role of a business manager because the environment in which a court manager works is considerably different from that of a more routinized business organization. Clear hierarchical lines of authority are absent. Judges enjoy considerable autonomy, and they "share professional interests and values with lawyers, who, for the most part, function outside of traditional types of organizations" (Stott 1987: 22). The courts more closely resemble hospitals and universities, large partnerships, and professional groups than business organizations. This setting means that strain caused by role ambiguity is inherent in the position of court manager.

Administrative Reform

Suggestions for reform at the federal level include adding additional judges to handle the increasing federal calendars, geographic realignment to better effect a balancing of court caseloads, delegating court management to professional managers, diverting certain cases for arbitration, and transferring mandatory jurisdiction over certain cases, for example diversity of citizenship, to the state courts. There have also been proposals for the establishment of additional specialized federal courts (similar to the US Court of Tax Appeals) and pressure for the creation of another level of appeals courts in the federal system. But, in the assessment of J. Woodford Howard (1981), none of these proposals can respond to the problems created by the decentralized nature of the federal judiciary.

The three major administrative reforms for state court systems, advocated by such groups as the American Bar Association and the American Judicature Society, come under the heading of **court unification**: structural unification, administrative centralization, and unified budgeting.

Structural Unification

Structural unification includes consolidating and simplifying existing trial courts and forming a single superior court on a countywide basis; lower courts cease to exist. Although the consolidated superior court has specialized divisions, such as juvenile court, civil court, chancery court, **small-claims court**, misdemeanor court, and felony court, in exemplary unification all judges are equal and selected in the same manner—appointment, election, or merit (discussed in Chapter 7). Thus, the salary and authority of each trial judge is the same and, accordingly, judges can be allocated to whatever courts are in need during any particular period of time. With court unification, the

---

Court Unification

Court unification has three interrelated components

1. simplified state trial court structure

2. judicial system policy- and rule-making authority covering practice, procedure, and administration vested in the supreme court or judicial council with system governance authority vested in the chief justice of the supreme court

3. funding of all or a substantial portion of the judicial system, with a unified judicial system budget prepared by the administrative office of the courts

Source: Bureau of Justice Assistance (1988).

neglect of the lower courts caused by judges aspiring to a superior-court bench would no longer be relevant.[6] In 1964, Illinois became the first state in the nation to adopt a unified court system.

Administrative Centralization

Administrative centralization places statewide authority for court policy and administration in the supreme court or judicial council. Governance responsibility is vested in the chief justice of the highest court or the position of chief administrative judge is established. "Centralized management provides the state's highest court with the power to make rules, appoint managerial personnel, assign judges and nonjudicial staff, and prepare and execute a centralized, state-financed yearly budget" (Stout 1986: 206). Under this system, there is a degree of uniformity rarely reached in more decentralized systems, and judges can be moved across counties on temporary assignments to reduce case backlogs. For example, in Illinois, which has unification and centralization, judges from downstate counties, which have a reduction in their court calendars during the summer months, are transferred to Cook County (Chicago) to help reduce calendar backlog there.

In New York, the court system is centralized under the state's chief judge who appoints a chief administrator for the courts; the administrator operates under policy and standards approved by the court of appeals, the state's highest court. The chief administrator is responsible for the day-to-day operations of the state's more than 3,500 judges and 9,000 support personnel. He or she estimates the financial needs of the courts, designates administrative judges for the trial courts, transfers judges to balance workloads, hires nonjudicial personnel, prepares reports of the activities of the courts, and makes recommendations for legislation affecting the courts.

Thomas Henderson and his colleagues summarize the arguments for and against court unification and centralization: "A simplified court structure and strong central direction . . . will increase uniformity of justice and enhance the managerial capability of the courts. Opponents of unification have countered that such changes will lead to a large central bureaucracy that will be insensitive to local concerns. In their view, rigidity will be substituted for individualized justice" (1984: 5).

Unified Budgeting

Unified budgeting "means that the budget for the court system is prepared at the state level, regardless of the source of funds, and that the executive branch does not have the authority to modify the budget request," since this would encroach on the separation of powers. There are 27 states in which the primary responsibility for funding the trial courts is unified (Stout 1986: 206). Since the ability to prepare and implement the budget is a prime feature of the exercise of power, unified budgeting and court centralization are closely related, if not necessarily intertwined.

---

[6] "One-tier court systems," however, "tend to re-create a limited jurisdiction court by establishing an unofficial lower level of judges and staff who process routine, high-volume cases" (Rottman and Hewitt 1996: 83). In some jurisdictions these judges are part-time; in Illinois, they are associate judges appointed by the elected trial judges.

Obstacles to Reform

The options for restructuring a court system are limited by the constitutional requirements of separation of powers and the judicial norms of the adversary system. Simplification and centralization available to other organizations may be inappropriate for
the courts. Furthermore, many court-related functions have been relegated by law to
other organizations such as the prosecutor, public defender, sheriff, corrections
department, county commission, and clerks (Henderson et al. 1984). Lawyers and
court personnel, ranging from bailiffs to judges, are socialized into a particular system, and the familiar is often the most comfortable setting in which to spend one's
working days. Private attorneys who have learned to negotiate the system enjoy certain advantages, and they are loath to give them up in the name of reform or efficiency—"If it ain't broke, why fix it?"

Those who have the most to gain from greater efficiency, the public, are rarely
exposed to the judicial system on any regular basis. Litigants and defendants are only
peripheral players, whose time-limited participation in the judicial system has little or
no impact. The very inefficiency of the system is often a basis for additional personnel
needs that provide patronage for the politicized judiciary. Court reform is usually
opposed by Stratum III attorneys

> who deal almost daily with local courts [and] become accustomed to and depen-
> dent on existing court organization, procedures, and personnel. Their intimate
> knowledge of how local courts operate is an important key to their legal success.
> Changes in court structure disrupt their routine and create new uncertainties about
> how courts will behave. Justice delayed is not necessarily justice denied, since
> delay may be part of a legal strategy to reach a negotiated settlement, to prepare a
> case more carefully, or to permit a lawyer to take on a larger volume of business
> than he or she can handle at one time. (Glick 1982: 23)

Trial lawyers frequently form associations to protect their legislative interests. Rural
and small-town lawyers also oppose court reform, particularly the streamlining of state
courts, if it means that the local judges will be transferred to a larger city (Glick 1982).

As we might expect, lawyers usually found in the forefront of efforts at court
reform are from Stratum I, attorneys seldom found in court, particularly the state
courts. In general, like the clients they represent, Stratum I attorneys are Republicans
working in urban areas dominated by Democrats, and the clash over court reform
often becomes embroiled in highly partisan politics. The most significant impetus for
a major reform, improving case management in criminal court, has been the Fifth
Amendment's guarantee of a speedy trial and legislation based on court interpretations of this amendment.

In jurisdictions that have a strict speedy trial rule (i.e., the required dismissal of
the charges against any defendant whose trial and dispositions had been unreasonably delayed beyond a fixed time period, such as 90, 120, or 170 days) and where there
is public pressure on the judiciary to avoid any such dismissals, the various court
organizations work together to expedite the flow of cases. The incentive in such courts
apparently is not the goal of general improvement in the administration of justice, but
the avoidance of the very visible public outcry seen in jurisdictions where a defendant
is released and his or her case is dismissed, not because he or she was found not guilty,

but because of delays in the processing of the case through the court. This incentive is particularly effective in those jurisdictions where the judiciary faces periodic elections (Kreindel et al. 1977: 35).

Some are also concerned that speedy trial legislation may serve to force criminal defendants to trial before they are fully prepared. Although the government may have been gathering evidence and preparing a case for a long period of time, particularly on the federal level, defendants can be forced to go to trial 70 days after indictment.

In the next chapter, we will examine the appellate process and judicial review.

SUMMARY

- In the United States there are two parallel systems of courts: federal and state. Each is divided into trial courts and appellate courts.

- Increased social and economic complexity led to the need for a more complex court system.

- An American approach to law, courts, and justice emerged, based mainly on Anglo-Saxon legal heritage as modified by the colonial experience.

- Different conditions in England and the colonies resulted in differing needs and thus differing laws.

- British equity, which had grown almost as complex as that of the common law, was not easily applied to colonial America.

- Some colonies established separate courts of equity; some merged equity with courts of common law; and in other colonies equity powers were the province of the legislature or the governor.

- There were no schools of law, so Blackstone's Commentaries were essential to any legal education.

- Commercial and business interests favored courts and common law; legislation they feared might be used to promote the redistribution of wealth.

- State court systems were characterized by decentralization.

- Courts convened in the county seat usually once a month, and large numbers of people came to town, conducted business, discussed politics, socialized, and flocked to the courtrooms to hear the oratory of noted attorneys. Courtroom oratory and successful advocacy gained an attorney a following and clients.

- Most states provided for both elected and appointed (by the legislature or governor) judges.

- On the frontier, there was an absence of law books and trained lawyers, and often disregard for due process and a preponderance of lynching.

- Trial courts have responsibility for settling the issue at hand and need not interest themselves in wider issues such as the precedential value of their decisions.

- Jurisdiction is the geographic area, subject matter, or persons over which a court can exercise authority.

- Jurisdiction is relatively simple in criminal cases, but in civil cases jurisdiction can be complex, particularly when litigants are from different states.

- In only one case does the US Constitution establish the jurisdiction of a court.
- The jurisdiction of federal courts often overlaps with that of state courts (*concurrent jurisdiction*).
- A lower court handles misdemeanors, early stages of felony cases, and civil cases in amounts below a certain threshold.
- Superior courts have criminal and civil parts and are authorized to try any type of case.
- Most states have an intermediate court of appeals and a court of last resort or supreme court.
- The highest state court is usually not required to hear every appeal brought to it.
- Decisions of appellate courts provide material for the case method and the rule of precedent, *stare decisis*.
- The Constitution provides federal jurisdiction for only two crimes: piracy and counterfeiting.
- In the unitary federal system there are two basic classes into which courts may be classified: legislative and constitutional.
- Federal magistrates are appointed by judges of the district court to exercise jurisdiction over matters assigned by statute as well as those delegated by the district judges.
- Federal district courts are created by Congress.
- The Constitution, which provides for a Supreme Court, does not state how many members it is to have.
- Supreme Court law clerks examine and summarize petitions, review briefs, conduct research, and draft opinions. They often play a key role in selecting cases for certiorari consideration.
- Judges are responsible for administrative duties for which they usually have no training and judicial independence mitigates against a chain of command.
- What would be routine for an executive branch agency is often slow and inefficient in the judicial branch.
- Court managers oversee the administrative functions of the court under the general direction of the chief judge.
- Three major administrative reforms for state court systems come under the heading of court unification: structural unification; administrative centralization; and unified budgeting.
- The options for restructuring a court system are limited by the constitutional requirements of separation of powers and the judicial norms of the adversary system.
- Court restructuring is often opposed by those who are comfortable with the status quo and by lawyers who may benefit from inefficiency.

KEY TERMS

appellate jurisdiction
appellate review
bankruptcy
Blackstone's Commentaries
cause of action
chief judge
concurrent jurisdiction
constitutional courts
court manager
court unification
diversity jurisdiction
docket
en banc

estate
extralegal
forum non conveniens
habeas corpus
immunity
intermediate court of appeals
jail
Judicial Conference
jurisdiction
law clerks
legislative courts
long-arm statutes

lynching
magistrates
misdemeanor
notary public
probate court
reporter system
separation of powers
small-claims court
stare decisis
stay
venue
vigilantism

REVIEW QUESTIONS

1. What led to greater complexity of the court system?

2. How did different conditions in England and the colonies affect law?

3. Why were Blackstone's Commentaries so important in America?

4. What was the basis for the disagreement between those favoring common law and those who preferred codes?

5. How did the *reporter system* affect the use of common law?

6. How could law and justice on the frontier be characterized?

7. Why is jurisdiction in a civil case more complex than that in a criminal case.

8. What is diversity jurisdiction?

9. What are the responsibilities of a lower court?

10. What state courts provide the basis for *stare decisis*?

11. In the federal system, how do legislative courts differ from constitutional courts?

12. What are the responsibilities of a federal magistrate?

13. What does the Constitution say about the Supreme Court?

14. What are various duties of a US Supreme Court law clerk?

15. What accounts for the inefficiency of the judicial branch?

16. What reforms are recommended for improving judicial branch efficiency?

17. What is the role of a court manager?

18. What are the three major administrative reforms for state court systems under the heading of court unification?

19. Why would lawyers oppose efforts to improve court efficiency?

INTERNET CONNECTIONS

Administrative Office of the U.S. Courts: http://www.uscourts.gov/Home.aspx

Association of Legal Administrators: http://www.alanet.org

Conference of Chief Justices: http://ccj.ncsc.dni.us

Conference of State Court Administrators: http://cosca.ncsc.dni.us

Council for Court Excellence: http://courtexcellence.org

Federal Judicial Center: http://www.fjc.gov

Judicial Conference of the United States: http://www.uscourts.gov/FederalCourts/JudicialConference.aspx

National Association for Court Management: https://nacmnet.org

National Center for State Courts: http://www.ncsc.org

State Courts, Court Statistics Project: http://www.courtstatistics.org

U.S. Supreme Court: http://www.supremecourt.gov

The Appellate Process and the Role of the Judiciary

In this chapter we will review the appellate process and examine the role of judicial review. In addition, we will examine the related issues of legitimacy, and implementing judicial decisions, and other issues relating to courts' roles and functions.

The Appellate Process

While trial courts determine issues of fact, such as determining guilt or liability, appellate courts correct procedural errors and ensure that law is interpreted correctly and consistently. Their decisions and explanations—*stare decisis*—provide **precedent**. Appellate courts resolve conflict of laws, create new principles of law, and clearly articulate principles to guide lower-court decisions (Flango 2010).

A few states with smaller populations have only one appellate court. Most states have two levels, and the intermediate appellate court is often assigned the error-correcting role, while the court of last resort, most often called the supreme court, "is primarily concerned with the development and declaration of law. Indeed, a primary rationale for the creation of intermediate appellate courts is to dispose of the bulk of appeals so that supreme courts can focus on cases with significant policy implications or cases of high salience to the public" (Flango 2010: 142).

"The appellate process requires that courts provide the reasons behind their decisions" (Flango 2010: 142). In trial courts, outcomes are based on witness testimony, whereas in appellate courts, case decisions are based on:

- *Petition*: appellant's request or "prayer" for a certain action
- *Briefs*: written explanations and versions of the case prepared by opposing attorneys
- *Case records*: written documents, including the **transcript**, from the court whose decision is being appealed
- *Oral arguments*: presented from both sides (but are not presented in every case)

New evidence, which was not presented at trial, is not permitted: "The appellate court cannot stray outside the 'record' (the pleadings, exhibits, and transcript of the proceedings in the court below)" and these "are wholly the product of the parties'

Elements of the Appellate Process
• Reliance on a closed lower court record
• Deferential review of a prior heat-tested—via the adversarial method—decision
• Graduated, sequential decision making, carefully applying precedent
• Collegial decisions
• Substantial (though not complete) reliance on the oral and written presentations of adversaries
• The restraint of professional legal conventions and rules
• The discipline of justifying a decision in writing

Source: Coffin (1994).

lawyers working in a strongly adversarial manner" (Hughes 1996: 22). (For a discussion of this issue and exceptions to "no new evidence," see Dobbins [2012].)

During oral arguments appellate court judges often assume an inquisitorial role, asking the attorneys probing questions. There may also be *amicus curiae* ("friend of the court") briefs with or without oral arguments. *"Amici curiae* are organizations or, rarely, individuals not a party to the appeal but likely to be affected by the precedent created. They are then, interested in the lawmaking aspects of deciding appeals, and not the case-deciding aspects" (Marvell 1978: 80).

Appellate court justices and their law clerks read the briefs submitted by each side, *amicus curiae*, and research previous decisions that can have a bearing on the case at issue. Appellate court judges (as well as all federal and many state trial judges) are assisted by law clerks and staff attorneys. The clerks are usually recent law school graduates who perform research and may even draft initial, if not final, opinions. They bring with them their recent exposure to outstanding law professors (Coffin 1994) and typically serve for one or two years. Cynics sometimes remark that the literary style of some judges appears to change with the same frequency as their law clerks. According to federal appeals judge Richard Posner, "Law clerks, being selected by judges rather than, as judges are, by politicians, are often abler legal analysts and legal writers than their judge" (2013: 21). A great deal of competition takes place among federal judges seeking to secure the brightest candidates from among third-year law students and recent law school graduates (Margolick 1989a). "The judges compete aggressively each year to recruit the best law students to work for them as clerks, prestigious positions that involve research, counsel and ghostwriting" (Rampell 2011b: B1, 7).

Anthony Kronman is critical of a "growing tendency of appellate judges to work by editing draft opinions prepared for them by their clerks instead of writing opinions themselves." Editing, he states, "does not in general make as strong a demand on the imagination as original composition," and editors tend to feel a diminished responsibility for the writings they produce even when it is their name the writings bear. There is also the "increased tendency to defer to the judgment of the original author; and the temptation, to which every editor is liable, to view his primary task as one of stylistic improvement only" (1993: 331). This trend, he notes, has led to increasing both the length of decisions and the number of footnotes they contain, an indication of clerks' insecurity, a feature of their relative inexperience. Kronman argues there is a vicious circle at work: "The opinions that law students read have been written by law clerks, that is, by other beginners like themselves" (1993: 351).

A Rational Appellate Court

In his classic, *The Common Law Tradition,* Karl Llewellyn (1960) provides 14 points against which to measure an appellate court:

1. *Law-conditioned officials.* The personnel must be trained and experienced lawyers who come to the appellate bench with years of active legal work.

2. *Legal doctrine.* There must be an accepted body of legal doctrines that are to be used in deciding specific cases. These doctrines serve to restrain appellate decisions.

3. *Known doctrinal techniques.* The legal doctrines must be used in a standard and generally accepted fashion.

4. *Responsibility for justice.* The justices must have an ingrained sense of duty to bring about a just result.

5. *One single right answer.* Although there can often be in fact several answers, justices must act with an urge to find one answer alone that is the right one.

6. *An opinion of the court.* The decision must be made with a published opinion that "reaches far beyond the case in hand; the opinion has as one if not its major office, to show how like cases are properly to be decided in the future" (1960: 26).

7. *A frozen record from below.* The facts that the appellate court must consider should be largely the immutable record of the trial court.

8. *Issues limited, sharpened, and phrased in advance.* Lawyers must submit briefs that provide the justices with a basis for a decision.

9. *Adversary argument by counsel.* An appellate decision must be rendered only after written and oral arguments are presented by trained counsel. This assists in the predictability of outcome.

10. *Group decision.* "A group all of whom take full part is likely to produce a net view with wider perspective and fewer extremes than an individual . . . and continuity is likely to be greater with a group" (1960: 31).

11. *Judicial security and honesty.* The justices must be immune from personal or political retribution for their decisions.

12. *A known bench.* The appellate court establishes a way of looking at things that can be known to those who follow the court's decisions. This forms a tradition to which new justices are socialized.

13. *The general period-style and its promise.* A way of thought and writing must be closely associated with the court during particular periods. This enhances predictability—an inarticulate court produces excessive appeals by a confused or speculative bar.

14. *Professional judicial office.* The justices are full-time officeholders who must not allow personal predilections to keep them from their responsibilities to the court.

The "Without Comment" Disposition

In cases without obvious precedential value, an appellate court can render a "disposition without comment," a terse, not-for-publication opinion or a disposition without any comment whatsoever. While rendering a decision on the merits of the case, these dispositions do not make law—they have no precedential value. This approach is similar to the civil/code systems (discussed in Chapter 1) in which case law does not play a central role (Gulati and McCauliff 1998).

A typical appellate decision contains (Re 1975b: 11–13):

1. An introductory statement or paragraph setting forth the nature of the case and the appeal
2. The question presented in the appeal: What is the court being asked to decide?
3. The essential or salient facts
4. The judicial discussion of the pertinent authority (precedent) that resolves or decides the question or issues presented (*ratio decedendi*)
5. The precise disposition of the appeal

The decision-making process of appellate courts is shrouded in secrecy; during deliberations, even clerks are rarely if ever present. "All internal communications about the cases (draft opinions, talk, and memoranda) are confidential. Until the decision is announced, no outsider is supposed to know which judge is writing on a case or how a case will be decided" (Marvell 1978: 7–8). Secrecy encourages the free flow of information between judges and allows for a change of mind without being subjected to question or criticism. Knowledge of the outcome of a case might also provide someone with a financial advantage (Marvell 1978).

Judicial Review by the US Supreme Court

According to the Constitution, the Supreme Court has original jurisdiction "in all Cases affecting Ambassadors, other public Ministers and Consuls . . . [and] to Controversies to which the United States shall be a Party" (Article III, Section 2). In theory, the Court will also consider disputes between states, or between a state and the federal government, but in practice, it rarely does. Original jurisdiction is seldom exercised; by 1984 the Supreme Court had issued full opinions in only 164 such cases (Goldman and Jahnige 1985). In cases of original jurisdiction where the Court cannot reach a decision on the pleadings of the litigants, a senior district judge is usually appointed to hear testimony and make a finding and recommendation upon which the Court can act.

The Constitution is not explicit in stating the jurisdiction of the Supreme Court other than making it "appellate." Therefore, except when the Court interprets the Constitution, its jurisdiction is subject to congressional modification. Originally, the Court was required to hear all cases that came before it on a writ of error: under common law, an order from an appellate court directing a trial court to send up its record

Congress v. Supreme Court

"Congress may not legislatively supercede our decisions interpreting and applying the Constitution" (*Dickerson v. United States* 530 U.S. 428 [2000]).

of a case for review. In 1914, the Court was granted **certiorari** jurisdiction, according to which it could deny consideration to any petition that is not supported by four (that number is tradition not law) justices. This discretion was at first limited to certain state decisions—those favoring rights claimed under federal law—but in 1916, all cases involving alleged denials of federal rights were shifted to the Supreme Court's certiorari jurisdiction.

The so-called Judges' Bill, the Judiciary Act of 1925, was drafted and promoted by members of the Supreme Court at the request of Congress to deal with the Court's growing caseload. It fundamentally redefined the Supreme Court's role by repealing much of the mandatory jurisdiction of the Court. According to the act, which finalized the Court's power to pick the cases it will consider, some cases are technically *outside* the Court's certiorari jurisdiction. These include:

- A case coming from a state supreme court when a federal law or treaty has been declared unconstitutional or when a state law or provision of a state constitution has been upheld against a challenge that it is in conflict with a federal law, treaty, or the Constitution

- Cases from a US court of appeals when a state law or provision of a state constitution has been ruled unconstitutional

- Cases from any federal court when a federal law has been held unconstitutional and the United States—officers or agencies—is a party

- Cases required to be considered by a three-judge special district court which has granted or denied an injunction

In practice, however, the Court has exercised considerable discretion over "mandated" cases, frequently dismissing them for "lack of a substantial federal question" or "want of jurisdiction." Even when an appeal is accepted for review, the Court frequently disposes of it without any oral arguments, simply affirming the decision of the court below (Goldman and Jahnige 1985). Instead of overruling decisions originating in state courts, as a matter of policy, the Court typically remands the case to the state supreme court for "further proceedings not inconsistent" with their opinion (Spaeth 1979). In 1988, Congress eliminated all mandatory appeals except those few cases involving the special categories decided by three-judge federal district courts (Baum 2013).

The Supreme Court is also empowered to receive cases for *certification*. In this instance, a lower court—federal district court or court of appeals—requests (certifies) that the Court rule on a legal question in a pending case that it cannot resolve. If the Court accepts the certificate, the justices answer the question, which is then applied by the lower court in deciding the case. The procedure is rarely utilized. Even more rare is the use of Court authority to intervene in the activities of a trial court with an extraordinary writ ordering the judge to perform some act (*writ of mandamus*) or forbidding him or her from doing so (*writ of prohibition*).

Petition for a Writ of Certiorari

According to Supreme Court rules, a petition for a **writ of certiorari** should be no longer than 30 pages and should contain a copy of the lower-court decision that the defendant wants reviewed, as well as a statement of the legal question(s) the case presents. Since 1980, Court rules have required that petitions list the questions presented by the case on the first page and a statement of the reasons why the Court should consider the case. The page limitation does not include appendices, which can run hundreds of pages and may be more important than the actual petition (Baum 2013; Perry 1991). Many petitions come to the Court from prison inmates who do not have attorneys to see to it that legal papers are submitted in proper form. Often only a page or two, they rarely conform to any legal specifications and are placed in a special group (*in forma pauperis*—brought by paupers) and examined by the chief justice's law clerks. In other courts, these papers would typically be rejected for lack of proper form. Since the Court grants certiorari in relatively few of the cases that are appealed, a lawyer who declares that he or she will take a case all the way to the Supreme Court is usually engaging in rhetorical excess. The Court does not give reasons for turning down a case (nor, for that matter, why a case is accepted for review). Most cases heard by the Court, however, result in reversals of the lower-court decision.

For about a decade, the Court decided about 150 cases each term with full opinions, fewer than 4 percent of all petitions filed, with about half granted a hearing, that is, oral arguments by attorneys for both sides of the question. By 1993, that number

---

Supreme Court Rule 10: Considerations Governing Review on Writ of Certiorari

"Review on a writ of certiorari is not a matter of right, but of judicial discretion. A petition for a writ of certiorari will be granted only for compelling reasons. The following, although neither controlling nor fully measuring the Court's discretion, indicate the character of the reasons the Court considers:

(a) A United States court of appeals has entered a decision in conflict with the decision of another United States court of appeals on the same important matter; has decided an important federal question in a way that conflicts with a decision by a state court of last resort; or has so far departed from the accepted and usual course of judicial proceedings, or sanctioned such a departure by a lower court, as to call for an exercise of this Court's supervisory power;

(b) A state court of last resort has decided an important federal question in a way that conflicts with the decision of another state court of last resort or of a United States court of appeals;

(c) A state court or a United States court of appeals has decided an important question of federal law that has not been, but should be, settled by this Court, or has decided an important federal question in a way that conflicts with relevant decisions of this Court.

A petition for a writ of certiorari is rarely granted when the asserted error consists of erroneous factual findings or the misapplication of a properly stated rule of law."

had fallen to little more than 100 cases, with two one-hour oral arguments a day instead of the usual four (Greenhouse 1993b). When the Court opened its 1994–1995 term, it granted certiorari to none of the more than 1,600 cases that had been submitted over the three-month summer recess (Greenhouse 1994). In its 1999–2000 term, the Court decided 73 cases, the fewest of any term since the 1950s (Greenhouse 2000). In 2004, the Court decided 73 cases with full opinions.

Of those receiving a full hearing, about 85 percent are subjected to a detailed opinion written by one of the justices voting in the majority, to which **dissents** and concurring—agreeing with the outcome but not the reasoning—opinions can be attached. The remaining cases and those for which no oral arguments were conducted are typically disposed of by a *per curiam* opinion (in which the Court states its opinion, but the author is not revealed), or by a brief memorandum order such as "dismissed," "vacated" (rendered void), or "**reversed** and **remanded**" (overturned the decision and sent the case back to the lower court for further consideration). The Court can also choose to **affirm** the judgment of the court below, which means the lower court decision stands, although this type of decision does not serve as a precedent. A full opinion is one in which there is an extensive discussion of the merits of the case and/or the defect or procedural error on which the appeal is based.

In contrast, a memorandum opinion—or *per curiam affirmanace* (PCA)—has only a "limited discussion of the merits of the case or the procedural determination," and the summary/dispositional order has very little discussion or comment on the case (Flango 2010: 143). PCA decisions terminate an appellate case with one word, "affirmed." The PCA is justified when the application of legal precedent to the facts of the case seems straightforward to the appellate court. The PCA saves resources by dispensing with the preparation of an appellate opinion. Because the "case makes no new law, further savings can be accomplished by dispensing with the publication of a full decision, which would further clutter the already voluminous official report of decisions and risk both lawyer and judicial confusion" (Ronner and Winick 2000: 500).

US Supreme Court Rules

Although some rules of the Supreme Court are published, "most of the internal procedures are by consensus, are unpublished, and are frequently unknown" (Perry 1991: 17). Justice Louis D. Brandeis outlined several rules in a concurring decision (*Ashwander v. Tennessee Valley Authority* [1936]):

1. Cases must not be presented in a friendly, nonadversarial proceeding (to get an advisory opinion, for example); the dispute must be a real one.[1]

2. The Court will not anticipate a question of constitutional law in advance of the necessity of deciding it.

3. The Court will not formulate a rule of constitutional law broader than is required by the precise facts to which it is to be applied.

4. If a case can be decided on constitutional grounds or on the grounds of statutory construction or general law, the Court will rule only on the latter.

---

[1] Some state constitutions provide for advisory opinions at the request of the governor or legislature.

Act of Congress

"When the validity of an act of Congress is drawn into question, and even if a serious doubt of constitutionality is raised, it is a cardinal principle that this Court will first ascertain whether a construction of the statute is fairly possible by which the question may be avoided" (Charles Evans Hughes, *Crowell v. Benson* [1932]).

5. The Court will not decide the validity of a statute upon the complaint of a person who fails to show that he or she is injured by its operation [has standing].

6. The Court will not pass upon the constitutionality of a statute at the request of a person who has benefited from it.

7. Whenever possible, the Court will avoid making a determination of the validity of an act of Congress.

Despite requiring that a case be presented in an adversarial manner, the Supreme Court has a procedure for dealing with the occasional "orphan," a case that presents an important issue but which the government does not wants to defend. The Court will ask a prominent attorney to argue the case, for which he or she receives no financial compensation but significant prestige (Liptak 2010b).

US Supreme Court Procedures

The annual term of the Supreme Court begins on the first Monday in October and is known by the year in which it starts; the term ends toward the end of June. More than 4,000 petitions are received each year; most are reviewed and summarized by clerks for the justices, and the Court has used a "cert pool" of clerks from various justices who collectively divide up the petitions for review and summary; some justices have opted out. The petition format is quite formal so, for example, the paper on which it is written must be 6-1/8 by 9-1/4 and not less than 60 pounds in weight and it must be typed in 11-point Roman and double-spaced. There are numerous other format requirements that if not met will result in the petition not being considered. Petitions are voted on by the justices at weekly conferences closed to the public.

Certain "cues" make a case stand out, thereby improving its chances for review: the reputation of the lower appellate judges; written dissents in the lower courts indi-

A Supreme Court Clerkship

The most coveted credential in American law is a Supreme Court clerkship: "Clerking for a justice is a glittering capstone on a résumé that almost always includes outstanding grades at a top law school, service on a law review and a prestigious clerkship with a federal appeals court judge" (Liptak 2010a: 1). In recent years, liberal justices have tended to choose candidates who have clerked for liberal appellate judges, and conservative justices have selected those who have clerked for conservative appellate judges.

cating controversy; the US government being a party to the case and seeking review; and the presence of race relations, civil liberties, or a variety of economic issues. Other elements being equal, the more cues, the greater the likelihood of review (Glick 1983; see Perry 1991 for an examination of agenda setting in the Supreme Court). When a case is rejected for review, the decision of the lower court stands.

In some cases, usually those involving important public issues, oral arguments will be scheduled and opposing attorneys will be given an opportunity to appear before the Court, which meets *en banc*. Between the granting of certiorari and oral arguments, briefs must be filed by the parties according to particular specifications as to size of print, size of pages, and cover color: Petitioners must use a blue cover; respondents must use red; *amici curiae* briefs must have a green cover. These colors make it easier for justices to find particular briefs. An index of cases or authorities cited must be included, and briefs cannot exceed 50 pages; *amici curiae* briefs cannot exceed 30 pages (Rehnquist 1987).

At the oral sessions, the Court has a record of prior proceedings and briefs containing the arguments of each side. Each attorney is usually permitted half an hour to present his or her case[2] and must be prepared to answer the often-probing questions of the justices, some of whom may pepper the attorney with queries. The justices do not wait until the attorney is finished but often interrupt with questions.[3] Attorneys are advised: "Under no circumstances should you read your argument from a prepared script," although a lawyer may use notes. "Showmanship is disfavored; when an inexperienced lawyer makes a florid presentation, a chill almost visibly settles on the bench" (Greenhouse 1993a: 84). Not only do the justices ask questions, they also make statements and suggest positions not raised by the lawyers and they may be in the form of hypotheticals: The Court's *Guide for Counsel* (Part II: 4) advises: "Be careful when you answer a hypothetical question posed by a Justice. A 'yes' or 'no' answer might be suitable for a narrow question. Nevertheless, your answer should be carefully tailored to fit the question. A simple 'yes' or 'no' in response to a broad question might unintentionally concede something and produce a follow-on question the answer to which is damaging to your position."

When seeking to establish a new precedent, a justice will usually ask if any Supreme Court cases support that argument, and attorneys are advised (*Guide for Counsel* Part II: 7): "Be ready for the question, but be careful to cite only those cases that truly support your position" and be careful not to distort the meaning of a precedent since "the author of the opinion is likely to be a member of the Court and to have a remarkable memory of exactly what the opinion says."

The purpose of a justice's questions and statements is often to influence his or her colleagues. There is some doubt as to the effect of oral arguments: "The arguments

---

[2] Chief Justice Rehnquist writes: "In the fifteen years that I have been on the Court, the presentation of each side of a case has been limited to one half hour except in cases of extraordinary public importance and difficulty. Three hours were allowed in *United States v. Nixon* in 1974" (1987: 274). In this case, President Richard M. Nixon argued that he did not have to release the "Watergate tapes" based on a claim of executive privilege—the Court ruled otherwise, and the president subsequently resigned.

[3] Justice William J. Brennan, Jr., states that he prepared for oral arguments by using his law clerks to help pick "to pieces every single case, the record, and briefs" (quoted in Taylor 1986c: 10). A Bench Memo submitted by law clerk Harlan Stone to Justice Oliver Wendell Holmes appears later in the chapter (Stone would later become a justice of the Supreme Court).

come after the opposing sides have filed long written briefs that state their cases in far more detail than can be done in 30 minutes of oral advocacy amid frequent interruptions from the bench." However, in close cases, where one or more justices may not have made a definite decision, "an especially good oral argument or an especially bad one may make a difference. A justice who is on the fence may be swayed" (Taylor 1986a: 12). In some cases someone who is not a party to the case—interest groups or the US government represented by the solicitor general (Chapter 7)—may, with the permission of the Court or the litigants, file an *amicus curiae* brief advocating a particular outcome. (Such briefs may also be submitted when the Court is considering certiorari.) Stephen Wasby notes that although the *amicus curiae* may at first have been thought to serve the Court as neutral participants, "over time, there has been a shift in *amicus* participation from neutrality, actually being a friend of the court, to advocacy, being a friend of one of the parties" (1993: 153).

In order to appear before the Court, attorneys must be members of the bar of the Supreme Court, although temporary admission (*pro hac vice*) is usually granted if

---

Supreme Court Rule 28: Oral Argument

1. Oral argument should emphasize and clarify the written arguments in the briefs on the merits. Counsel should assume that all Justices have read the briefs before oral argument. Oral argument read from a prepared text is not favored.

2. The petitioner or appellant shall open and may conclude the argument. A cross writ of certiorari or cross-appeal will be argued with the initial writ of certiorari or appeal as one case in the time allowed for that one case, and the Court will advise the parties who shall open and close.

3. Unless the Court directs otherwise, each side is allowed one-half hour for argument. Counsel is not required to use all the allotted time. Any request for additional time to argue shall be presented by motion under Rule 21 no more than 15 days after the petitioner's or appellant's brief on the merits is filed, and shall set out specifically and concisely why the case cannot be presented within the half-hour limitation. Additional time is rarely accorded.

4. Only one attorney will be heard for each side, except by leave of the Court on motion filed no more than 15 days after the respondent's or appellee's brief on the merits is filed. Any request for divided argument shall be presented by motion under Rule 21 and shall set out specifically and concisely why more than one attorney should be allowed to argue. Divided argument is not favored.

5. Regardless of the number of counsel participating in oral argument, counsel making the opening argument shall present the case fairly and completely and not reserve points of substance for rebuttal.

6. Oral argument will not be allowed on behalf of any party for whom a brief has not been filed.

7. By leave of the Court, and subject to paragraph 4 of this Rule, counsel for an *amicus curiae* whose brief has been filed as provided in Rule 37 may argue orally on the side of a party, with the consent of that party. In the absence of consent, counsel for an *amicus curiae* may seek leave of the Court to argue orally by a motion setting out specifically and concisely why oral argument would provide assistance to the Court not otherwise available. Such a motion will be granted only in the most extraordinary circumstances.

Conference Handshakes

Since the days of Chief Justice Melville W. Fuller (1888–1910), at the beginning of the private conferences each justice shakes hands with each of the other eight, a tradition meant to symbolize that individual differences do not preclude overall harmony of purpose.

requested by another lawyer or agency employing the attorney. Membership requires the lawyer to have been a member of the bar in his or her home state for at least three years, to have two sponsors, and to pay a small fee. Very few applications are rejected, and the rejections are usually based on disciplinary violations back home. Lawyers who have no intention of practicing before the Supreme Court may request admission for status reasons. Every attorney who does practice before the Court receives a souvenir—two white handcrafted quills that are placed on counsel tables each day that the Court sits. Admissions may be revoked, which was the fate of several Watergate defendants in the 1970s.

After the *en banc* session, the justices go over the cases with their law clerks and tentatively decide on which way to vote. Prior to a final vote, justices may distribute memos indicating their thinking and to influence their colleagues. They meet in conference—with only justices present—to discuss the cases under consideration. The chief justice speaks first, and the discussion continues according to seniority. No one speaks twice until everybody has spoken once. Justices usually do not participate (that is, they *recuse* themselves) in a case when they know the parties, in cases in which they were involved prior to their appointment to the Court, or when they have even a small, indirect financial interest, usually stock ownership.[4] When a consensus develops, a vote is taken. In the Rehnquist Court, at the end of the discussion, the chief justice announced how he is recording the vote, and members then had an opportunity to dispute the count if they believe he was mistaken. According to Chief Justice Rehnquist:

> If a case is a relatively simple one, with only one real legal issue in it, it will generally be very clear where each member of the Court stands on that issue. But many cases that we decide are complex ones, with several interrelated issues, and it is simply not possible in the format of the conference to have nine people answering either yes or no to a series of difficult questions about constitutional law. One justice may quite logically believe that a negative answer to the very first of several questions makes it unnecessary to decide the subsequent ones. . . . But if a majority answers the first question in the affirmative, then the Court's opinion will have to go on and discuss the other questions. (1987: 293)

The chief justice, if part of the majority, may write the decision him or herself or choose an associate justice from the majority side to write the opinion of the Court;

---

[4] A 1974 statute requires all federal judges to disqualify themselves in any case in which their "impartiality might be reasonably questioned." Custom requires recusal whenever a judge has a financial interest in the case, personal knowledge of the dispute, or a blood relationship with a lawyer representing any party. There is some concern that Supreme Court justices, who typically do not explain their recusals, may be withdrawing from cases unnecessarily, and this could place a burden on the Court and its ability to render meaningful decisions (Greenhouse 1989).

otherwise, the opinion is written by the senior justice in the majority or his or her designate. The chief justice assigns opinions when the decision is unanimous. The only exception is a tradition of allowing a new member of the Court to choose the first opinion he or she will write (Abraham 1998). A draft of the opinion is circulated to the other justices so they can offer changes that, if accepted, require a redraft and recirculation. Members may add their dissenting opinions, and sometimes a member of the majority will also provide a separate but **concurring opinion** in the case, agreeing with the outcome but, for example, not the reasoning behind it. If five or more justices agree on the outcome but several submit concurring opinions, it may be difficult or impossible to ascertain the *ratio decedendi*. Some memorable dissents subsequently became majority decisions, such as that of Justice John M. Harlan in *Plessy v. Ferguson*. His arguments against "separate but equal" in 1896 would become a unanimous decision in *Brown v. Board of Education* in 1954 (Abraham 1998).

The written opinion is often as important as the actual vote, since it provides the material for case law. Sometimes members use footnotes as a way of "dissenting" while casting a concurring vote (Toch 1982). The opinion of the Court is a closely guarded secret until it is announced and copies of the judgment are sent to the lawyers and the printer—leaks are rare. The Court has the final word if it affirms the decision of the lower court; otherwise, the case may be sent back for further judicial action, often a retrial.

When decisions are announced, justices usually rely on a standard formula, briefly describing the facts and the holding and concluding that "for reasons stated at greater length in an opinion filed with the clerk this morning," the judgment of the lower court has been either affirmed or reversed (Greenhouse 2005b).

Bench Memo on *Meyer V. Nebraska* to be Argued February 23, 1923

From Harlan Stone, Law Clerk, to Justice Oliver Wendell Holmes

QUESTION PRESENTED

Does Nebraska's Siman Law, which prohibits the teaching of foreign languages to children in the primary grades, violate the 14th Amendment due process clause rights of parents, teachers and students?

LOWER COURT HOLDING

The Supreme Court of Nebraska held that the Siman Law does not violate students', teachers' or parents' 14th Amendment rights because it is not arbitrary but is rationally related to the state's purpose of educating children to become good citizens in a democracy.

STATUTES, CASES, AND AUTHORITIES

— Amendment XIV: "Nor shall any state deprive any person of life, liberty, or property, without due process of law."

— The Siman Law, Nebraska Code 2567 (1919) (prohibiting teaching of foreign languages, with the exception of Greek and Latin, to children below eighth grade in private and public schools).

— *Adams v. Tanner*, 244 U.S. 590 (1917) (striking down law prohibiting employment agencies from charging fees).

(continued)

— *Muller v. Oregon*, 208 U.S. 412 (1908) (upholding law limiting hours of work for women).

— *Lochner v. New York*, 198 U.S. 45 (1905) (striking down law regulating hours and working conditions of bakers as violating 14th amendment liberty of contract).

— Puffendorf, *Le Droit* (European philosopher, explicating a theory of natural law).

FACTS

Nebraska, following World War I and during a period of "Americanization," passed a statute prohibiting the teaching of any modern foreign languages to students who had not completed the eighth grade. Meyer, a schoolteacher in a rural Lutheran church school, was charged with violating that law. He appealed his conviction to the Supreme Court of Nebraska and lost. He is joined by parents and teachers alleging the law infringes their constitutional rights as well.

DISCUSSION

The petitioners argue that the law infringes the 14th Amendment liberty of (1) teachers to pursue a lawful occupation (teaching languages); (2) parents to control the education of their children and; (3) pupils to learn. They contend that the legislation is based on anti-German sentiments and that no legitimate purpose is served by the law since the study of languages is harmless. The law serves not to Americanize but to standardize children.

Nebraska counters that the law is a rational way of accomplishing a legitimate state purpose. The purpose is to promote civic unity and make English the mother tongue of all citizens. This purpose is no less legitimate than bringing light into dark tenements and is comparable to compulsory education and vaccination, provisions which the Court has upheld in the past. They point out that all kinds of supposedly private activities may properly be subjected to regulation by the states under their **police powers** without infringing federal constitutional rights.

Aside from cases about economic liberties, there is very little precedent in this area. The Court has not yet stated what, if any, family liberties are protected under the 14th Amendment Due Process Clause. Petitioners suggest that the rights to marry and raise a family and to acquire useful knowledge are within the liberties protected by the 14th Amendment. These claims are really substantive due process arguments, similar to those made in cases like *Adams v. Tanner*, and *Lochner v. New York*. These cases might provide precedent for striking down the state law, at least if we equate the freedom to raise one's children with the freedom to enter into a lawful profession and conclude that states may not infringe such liberties without some very weighty justification.

However, there are also conflicting precedents, such as *Muller v. Oregon*, holding that the state has broad "police powers" to pass legislation for the public good, including wage, education and labor laws. In *Muller*, the state's interest in protecting women from the rigors of long hours and heavy labor outweighed the freedom of employers to contract and of women workers to exploit their property rights in their own labor.

The crux of the case presented here is whether the Constitution should constrain states from making decisions regarding local matters such as education, absent some specific textual hook which explicitly limits state and local powers. Arguments can be made on both sides. Puffendorf is often cited for the proposition that parents possess natural rights to control and custody of their children which the framers never imagined could be invaded by man-made laws. Your dissent in *Lochner*, however, illustrates the danger that the judiciary may misuse the Constitution to displace democratically enacted legislative judgments with their own personal value judgments.

RECOMMENDATION

Affirm. This is the thin edge of the wedge of federal courts' veto power over virtually any kind of local activities under the guise of protecting 14th Amendment liberties. If the Court recognizes this expansive version of the 14th Amendment, no legislation about families or education will be safe. Laws about marriage, about child labor, about health, and so on, will be challenged as impinging on 14th Amendment rights. Parents will be free to control their children's lives (preventing them from learning English, for example) even if it is not in the best interest of the child. The idea that parents' liberties include the freedom to control another person seems antithetical to the notion of liberty and evokes the shades of Dred Scott.

If you decide to reverse and strike down the Siman Law, consider basing your vote on the antidiscrimination principles of the Equal Protection clause or perhaps on the children's intellectual liberty, as opposed to the parents' rights of custody and control. Why not use this as the opportunity to interpret the 14th Amendment as incorporating freedom of religion as well as freedom of speech?

SUGGESTED QUESTIONS

For Meyer:

The state says that keeping children from exposure to English is as dangerous to their future development as keeping them in dark and unsanitary houses. How will the children in Zion church make their way in the world? Don't the children have any rights to a useful education?

For Nebraska:

If the purpose of your Law is to insure children learn English without any other linguistic distractions, can you explain why only modern languages are banned by Nebraska? Why not Latin and Greek? Isn't the Law simply an excuse to go on harassing German Americans and their religious practices by prohibiting the language they use in their homes and church schools?

The Legitimacy of Courts

It is important to recall that the judiciary is the "least dangerous branch of government," having no powers of enforcement beyond that offered by the other branches. The precedential effect of most court decisions can be nullified by subsequent legislation. Even decisions based on the Constitution can be nullified, albeit with great difficulty, by constitutional amendment (Burton 2007). The judicial branch is dependent on a perception of **legitimacy** surrounding its decisions, and it uses a variety of symbols to perpetuate the myth that judicial decision making is neutral and objective: black robes[5] and elevated benches alongside a formal, solemn courtroom environment "more akin to religious institutions and ceremonies than any other setting in American society" (Smith 1993a: 14).

Under our system of case law, the courts are not free to impose their own version of social arrangements; instead, they are constrained by four fundamental principles (Eisenberg 1988):

1. *Objectivity.* The courts derive their legitimacy in large measure from a perceived adherence to objectivity. That is, judges will be impartial and devoid of

---

[5] Black robes are a tradition. The US Supreme Court has no rules on attire.

ties to disputants. Objectivity also requires the court to avoid ad hoc justice, that disputes be resolved not through the application of rules that are peculiar to the case at hand but according to universal rules applicable to all similarly situated cases. (*Rational law*, as discussed in Chapter 1.)

2. *Support.* The universal rules applied by a court must be supported by general societal standards or the particular standards of the legal system. This is necessary so that claimants can utilize the courts to uphold a claim of a right based on existing standards. Changes in existing standards are the province of legislative bodies whose enactments govern the future and may be deliberately designed to alter existing standards. This approach, Melvin Eisenberg points out, presents a fairness dilemma: "How can it be fair to resolve a dispute concerning a past transaction by applying a legal rule that is articulated after the transaction occurred?" (1988: 10). Requiring judges to reach decisions based on existing standards helps to alleviate this problem; it is reasoned that the disputants knew or had reason to know at the time of their transaction that standards not previously officially recognized were applicable.

3. *Replicability.* In a complex society, it is desirable that lawyers be able to apply their skills of judicial reasoning in order to predict the likely outcome of a particular dispute. This enables legal advice to substitute for litigation. When the outcome is clear, disputes can be settled without recourse to formal judicial proceedings and the costs they can incur. This facilitates transactions since the parties involved, acting on "sound legal advice," can anticipate the likely outcome of any disputes arising out of the transaction. Furthermore, replicability ensures that the parties in dispute will be able to be pursue the case with knowledge of the types of proofs and arguments that the courts will attend in reaching a decision.

4. *Responsiveness.* The courts are obligated to be responsive not to the citizenry at large but to the legal profession. As such, they are responsive to, but not obliged to follow, the briefs and oral arguments, material in law reviews, treatises and monographs, the decisions of sister courts, and addresses by legal scholars and practicing lawyers at bar associations or other professional conferences.

To the extent that courts do not adhere to these principles, they undermine a rational system of law and move in the direction of what Max Weber (1967) refers to as *kadi* justice (justice not based on a legal standard but on an individual's sense of fairness) and they erode the legitimacy of the judicial decision. "It is far-fetched," states Steven Burton (1985: 189), "to think that the American people in any sense have consented or would consent to be governed in significant measure by the personal value preferences of judges, rather than by law." In a democratic society, it is hard to imagine why "the people should consent to such unbridled power in any office that is not politically responsible to the electorate at frequent intervals. If judicial decisions were a matter of personal value preferences, there would seem to be no good reason why the preferences of judges should prevail over the preferences of elected representatives of the people or, in the absence of a clear political expression of majoritarian preferences, the autonomous decisions of individuals."

This is why judges exercising the power to invalidate legislation as unconstitutional insist that their rulings simply give effect to the law set forth in the Constitution—they are not empowered to substitute their own policy judgments for those of democratically elected legislators (George 2000). A sound, "legitimate," judicial decision is supported by accepted legal reasoning and consideration of legislative prerogatives.

Judicial Restraint

As we saw in Chapter 1, in civil law countries there is legislative supremacy and therefore the judiciary defers to the legislative branch. In contrast, the United States is characterized by a system of checks and balances effected by a separation of power, three branches of government that are, at least in theory, equal. So, whenever the Supreme Court overturns a law, unelected judges are exercising authority over another branch of government. Critics argue judges can effectively deprive the people of the right to resolve disputed issues in accordance with the normal procedures of democratic self-government, that is, in the political as opposed to the judicial arena (George 2000). "Little did the Framers dream that the judicial power would be construed as a license to supersede the exercise of power by the other branches." Thus, according to Raoul Berger (1977: 249–50), the Supreme Court "has invaded the exclusive jurisdiction of a sister branch; it has violated the injunction of the separation of powers." It has done this in the name of a self-created doctrine—*substantive due process*, under which courts examine the reasonableness of government policy[6]—based on a concept as vague and self-serving as natural law." Judges "were not authorized to revise the Constitution in the interests of 'justice'" (1977: 299), to usurp the policy-making authority of the legislative branch.

At the investiture of William H. Rehnquist as chief justice and Antonin Scalia as associate justice (September 26, 1986), President Ronald Reagan stated that he had appointed these men to the Supreme Court because their opinions had demonstrated that they adhered to the concept of "judicial restraint." But, as examined in Chapter 6, "judicial activism has characterized the Supreme Court from its early history" (Levy 1988: 56). There was a period of negative activism from 1898 to 1938, when "it seemed as though no progressive social or economic legislation was constitutionally permissible." During this period, the Court invalidated some 50 acts of Congress and about 400 state laws, as compared to 12 and 125, respectively, from the period 1874 to 1898 (McDowell 1988: 3). In contemporary times, it is common to portray those who argue for judicial restraint as "conservatives," and those who support judicial activism as "liberals," but American history does not support this view: During the later decades of the nineteenth century, *judicial activism* protected property rights while *judicial restraint* ignored the civil rights of African Americans (discussed in Chapter 6).

Since 1954, states McDowell (1988), judicial activism has been far more positive in its assertions, as the federal judiciary, with the Supreme Court leading the way, has undertaken to achieve what the Court majority holds to be fair, decent, and humane, regardless of constitutional text, **original intent**, or judicial precedent, thereby *acting more like legislators than judges*. For example, in *Griswold v. Connecticut* (1965), rather

---

[6] The conventional interpretation of the due process clause is that government must follow certain procedures before taking a person's life, liberty, or property.

than leave its resolution to the legislature and the political arena, the Court majority overturned an objectionable statute (prohibiting physicians from providing birth control information to married persons) by invoking the "right to privacy," an allusion to natural law that is not mentioned in the Constitution.

In recent decades conservatives have leveled the charge of usurpation by the judicial branch, although in the decades before the Great Depression, activist courts effectively restrained organized labor and legislative efforts designed to aid workers. And, during the administration of Franklin Roosevelt, when it was the liberals whose programs were found unconstitutional, conservatives defended the Supreme Court's activism (George 2000). In a March 9, 1937, fireside chat, President Roosevelt argued in favor of "a Supreme Court that will enforce the Constitution as written—that will refuse to amend the Constitution by the arbitrary exercise of judicial power—amendment by judicial say-so." Roosevelt argued that the Court had usurped the legislative function by "reading into the Constitution words and implications which are not there, and which were never intended to be there." The president promised to appoint justices "who will act as justices and not as legislators." During his first campaign for the presidency, Texas Governor George W. Bush made a similar assertion: "I don't believe in liberal activist judges; I believe in strict constructionists, and those are the kind I will appoint" (quote from the presidential debate of October 3, 2000).

The judiciary, particularly at the federal level, is insulated from the political pressures that typically affect legislators; thus, the courts are often in a better position to attend to the problems of persons who do not represent an important political constituency, a source of votes, or campaign funds. Of course, judges rendering policy decisions can also be viewed as undemocratic legislators, a position expressed by Gary McDowell (1988).

McDowell (1982) decries the expansive use of **equity** (discussed in Chapter 1), with its inherent discretionary prerogatives, arguing that judicial activism under the guise of equity has been ignoring its history and distorting its purpose—**equitable** remedial powers have been used to impose a particular brand of liberal policy on society. The courts have done this, he argues, by denying or ignoring the great tradition of equitable principles and precedents that have always been viewed as the inherent source of restraint in rendering equitable dispensations. "When the framers of the Constitution assigned the authority to decide legal 'cases in law and equity,'" states Jeremy Rabkin, "they understood themselves to be entrusting a rather more modest power to the courts because they took for granted much more modest notions about the proper ends of law" (1989: 118). Indeed, according to Christopher Wolfe, "equity is not the correction of mistakes made by the lawgiver in enacting the law in question, but rather corrections of the law that the legislator would have wanted had he been able to foresee the defects that would necessarily result from its generality. The purpose of equity is not to frustrate the will of the legislator but to effect it" (1986: 19).

Whereas the legislative branch "can make a thousand detailed trade-offs and produce a complex code that articulates no general principle but reflects moral intuitions, political pressures, and compromises," it is not the function of the judicial branch to decide what is good for us (Bork 1989: 81). Raoul Berger (1987) concludes that many of the Supreme Court's decisions represent an ongoing revision of the Constitution and, thus, a usurpation of the amendatory function that is reserved to the people by Article V.

> **Judicial Restraint**
>
> Except when there is a clear violation of the Constitution or well-established precedent, do not overturn an act of federal or state legislative or executive branches.
>
> **Judicial Activism**
>
> When appellate courts disregard precedent in an effort to achieve some public benefit, they are usurping the legislative function.

Conservative appointees selected by Presidents Reagan and Bush, however, proved to be just as "active" as their liberal counterparts in distinguishing away, overturning precedent, and reaching for new legal doctrines.

The Courts headed by Chief Justice Warren Burger and Chief Justice William Rehnquist, "while perhaps less relentlessly adventurous than the Warren Court, displayed a strong affinity for legislating policy in the name of the Constitution" (Bork 1989: 101). For example, in a 5–4 decision (*Wards Cove Packing Co. v. Atonio* [1989]) the Court ruled against its own precedents in cases brought under the Civil Rights Act of 1964. In 1971, the statute had been interpreted as placing the **burden of proof** on employers to prove that they had not deliberately engaged in unlawful discrimination whenever statistical evidence revealed a discriminatory impact on women or minorities (*Griggs v. Duke Power*). In *Wards Cove* the Court reinterpreted the statute and reversed the burden of proof. The Court majority in *Rust v. Sullivan* (1991) was taken to task by Associate Justice Sandra Day O'Connor, a Reagan appointee, for judicial activism: "It is a fundamental rule of judicial restraint," she noted, "that this Court will not reach constitutional questions in advance of the necessity of deciding them." The 5–4 decision upheld administrative restrictions on abortion counseling for agencies receiving federal funding. Justice O'Connor argued that this decision needlessly addressed constitutional issues when an interpretation of legislation would have been sufficient.

In its 1991 term, the Court overturned five of its own precedents, leading the editorial board of the *New York Times* (June 30, 1991) to decry the easy manner in which the new "conservative" majority was "recklessly reversing precedents." Their editorial argued "that it is not the role assigned to the Supreme Court." During the term of Chief Justice Earl Warren (1953–1969), the liberal Court overruled precedent in 63 cases. During Warren E. Burger's tenure (1969–1986), precedent was overruled 61 times (Greenhouse 1991b). The Court headed by William Rehnquist did not hesitate to overturn precedent in support of the government's position. For example, in a 1997 decision (*Agostini v. Felton*), the Court overturned a 1985 ruling that prohibited public employees from providing services in religious schools. And in what probably will be the Court's most controversial decision, a five-member majority determined the outcome of the 2000 election for president using the favored tool of judicial activists—the Fourteenth Amendment. The title of an article by Linda Greenhouse (1991c) noted: "Conservatively Speaking, It's an Activist Supreme Court." A long-time Court observer, journalist Stuart Taylor, Jr. (2000: 50), pointed out that all nine justices, despite their liberal or conservative labels, are "activists who boldly use federal judi-

The Reality of Judicial Activism

"Criticizing a decision as judicial activism, whether liberal or conservative, often conveys little of substance beyond the fact that the decision has produced a result with which the critic disagrees" (Liu, Karlan, and Schroeder 2009: 41).

cial power to displace decisions by elected officials and state courts that offend their personal, philosophical or political values."

Cass Sunstein (2002: 29) points out that in the 1960s and 1970s, judicial restraint was the mantra of political conservatives. The Supreme Court, they argued, "should not use vague provisions of the Constitution to strike down laws enacted by elected officials." But their views changed in the 1980s when conservatives began advocating an aggressive role for the Supreme Court: "Once conservatives began to occupy the federal courts, the argument for judicial restraint suddenly seemed less appealing." A study of decisions of 2005 Supreme Court revealed that the five most conservative Supreme Court justices (Thomas, Kennedy, Scalia, Rehnquist, O'Connor) had a marked pattern of voting to invalidate acts of Congress; in other words, they were *activists*. Conservative icon Justice Clarence Thomas, appointed by George H. W. Bush, voted to overturn Congressional actions in more than 65 percent of the cases, while Justice Stephen Breyer appointed by Bill Clinton, did so in fewer than 29 percent of the cases (Gerwitz and Golder 2005). As the title of an article by Stuart Taylor, Jr., indicates: "The 'Judicial Activists' Are Always on the Other Side" (1988: E5).

"At the beginning of the 20th century, liberals argued that the courts were activist in opposing the rights of workers and unions when they overturned legislation regarding such matters as minimum wage and overtime restrictions. At the beginning of the 21st century, however, it is now conservatives arguing that the courts are activist—creating a right of privacy and opposing religious expression in public" (Neubauer and Meinhold 2006: 9). As Noah Feldman (2010: 41) points out: "The ideal of judicial restraint has been undercut by the selective and opportunistic way in which liberals and conservatives alike have invoked it." Federal Appellate Court Judge J. Harvie Wilkinson III (2012: 4), a Reagan appointee, points to competing schools of liberal and conservative activism, "schools that have little in common other than a desire to seek rhetorical cover for prescribed and often partisan results"—both sides violating the "ideal of restraint that the greatest judges in our country once embraced."

Interpreting the Constitution

The Constitution does not prescribe a specific method of interpretation, so how are judges interpret a document whose language and grammar reflect that of its time— late eighteenth century—drafted by a group of white Englishmen, revolutionaries all? Supreme Court Justice Stephen Breyer notes the basic tools justices use when making statutory or constitutional interpretations. First, "they read the text's language along with related language in other parts of the document." Then they review its history, "including history that shows what the language likely meant to those who wrote it. They look to tradition indicating how the relevant language was, and is, used in the law." Next, they examine precedents suggesting how a phrase has been applied in past cases. Finally, "they consider the likely consequences of the interpretative alternatives, valued in terms of the phrase's purposes" (2005: 7–8). Although judges may use the same approach, they can arrive at different interpretations because some "emphasize the use of language, history, and tradition," while "others emphasize purpose and consequences" (2005: 8). Cass Sunstein (2005) notes that although it is customary to characterize disagreements over interpreting the Constitution as *liberals versus conservatives*, that description is inadequate because, while ideology matters, judges follow different approaches to constitutional law that go well beyond ideology.

The first major dispute over an interpretation of the Constitution occurred shortly after its ratification when Alexander Hamilton proposed a national bank that was opposed by Thomas Jefferson. At issue was Article I, Section 8 authorizing Congress "to make all laws which shall be necessary and proper for carrying into execution the foregoing Powers." Hamilton argued that Article I *implied* powers necessary for the proper implementation of the constitutional mandate, while Jefferson cited the Tenth Amendment reserving powers not delegated to the federal government to the states. The bank was established and, as noted in Chapter 6, Hamilton's position was eventually upheld by the Supreme Court (*McCulloch v. Maryland* [1819]).

Another dispute arose over the purchase of the Louisiana Territory, and this time positions were reversed. The Federalists adopted the strict constructionist argument that the Constitution did not authorize the president to purchase territory. President Jefferson argued that this power is implied by Article II, Section 2, which provides that the president "shall have Power, by and with the Advice and Consent of the Senate, to make Treaties." Jefferson's position triumphed, and on April 30, 1803, the United States purchased from France the Louisiana Territory, more than 800,000 square miles of land extending from the Mississippi River to the Rocky Mountains.

The founders were not saints writing a sacred text; they were, in the final analysis, politicians (Shaman 1992). Of the 55 convention delegates meeting in Philadelphia in 1787, only 39 signed the Constitution, and any number of them may have been casual in their attendance. We also know that the final document is the result of many compromises. "Moreover, many delegates (and still more state legislators, and even voters) clearly intended nothing at all about particular provisions but rather simply preferred the whole constitutional package to what they must have viewed as the likely alternative" (Kelman 1987: 216). The Constitution was drafted and ratified by persons who were certainly not representative of the people as a whole, given that a majority of Americans were ineligible to vote: blacks, women, Native Americans, and the poor who lacked real property. "Nor was democracy sufficiently advanced, even by the time of the post-Civil War amendments, to provide a democratic argument of fairness for taking the legislators' concrete opinions as good evidence of public opinion at the time" (Dworkin 1986: 364). The homogeneity of the founders certainly does not reflect the diversity of contemporary America. With every passing year, the Constitution becomes more remote (Posner 1990).

In addition, since the Constitution required ratification by the state legislatures, does their intent also need to be considered? In fact, argues Judge Irving Kaufman,

Intent?

The intentions of the framers of the Constitution "were indissolubly connected with the philosophy of natural rights and natural law expressed in the Declaration of Independence." Accordingly, any attempt to find original intent *only* in the Constitution is misguided (Jaffa 1988: 40).

many provisions in the Constitution were left deliberately vague; when the framers had a clear intent, they were explicit: "Article II, for example, specifies a minimum Presidential age of 35 years instead of merely requiring 'maturity' or 'adequate age'" (1986: 59). Former Attorney General Edwin Meese (1986) responds that the period of the creation of the Constitution was alive with pamphlets, newspapers, and books on the great issues of the day. Furthermore, the disputes and compromises of the Constitutional Convention were carefully recorded, and the minutes of the convention are a matter of public record. Edward Levi, also a former Republican US attorney general, states that when it comes to a constitution, a change of mind from time to time is inevitable: "There can be no authoritative interpretation of the Constitution. The Constitution in its general provisions embodies the conflicting ideals of the community" (2013: 58). And what about equity: Should people be governed "by the detailed political convictions of officials elected long ago, when popular morality, economic circumstances, and almost everything else was very different?" (Dworkin 1986: 364). Punishment prohibited by the Eighth Amendment, for example, has obviously changed with modern definitions of what is "cruel and unusual"—we no longer accept flogging and branding. And the original Constitution recognized and permitted slavery—many delegates owned slaves.

Strict constructionists argue, justices "must take the Constitution as they find it, and not make things up as they go along. Even if the Justices are appalled by the results this method produces, or believe that the Constitution's literal commands are severely out of step with the times, it is not their job to rewrite it. That prerogative belongs to the Congress and the President—and ultimately to the people, who retain the power to *amend* the Constitution" (Tribe 1985: 42; see also Tribe and Dorf 1991.

Many of the Constitution's limitations on government are couched in obscure language so that the judicial branch, sooner or later, must deal with potentially explosive

Originalism

"The advocates of *originalism* argue that the meaning of the Constitution (or of its individual clauses) was fixed at the moment of its adoption, and that the task of interpretation is accordingly to ascertain that meaning and apply it to the issue at hand. The critics of originalism hold that it is no easy task to discover the original meaning of a clause, and that even if it were, a rigid adherence to the ideas of the framers and ratifiers would convert the Constitution into a brittle shell incapable of adaptation to all of the changes that distinguish the present from the past" (Rakove 1996: xiii).

cases on important social issues, such as those involving schools or prisons (Lieberman 1989). "The equal protection clause mandates equal treatment under law but provides no specific definition of equality. And the privileges or immunities clause says that its namesake may not be denied but leaves their definition open" (Wilkinson 2012: 36).

Should a judge's personal preferences influence his or her decision? Should a judge uphold a legislative enactment that he or she finds personally objectionable, such as requiring students to salute the flag or face expulsion? This question was central to the historic confrontation between two giants of the Supreme Court: Hugo Black and Felix Frankfurter. Frankfurter answered in the negative—judicial restraint requires that a judge's personal preferences not influence his or her decision (see Simon 1989). Should a judge—using the power of equity—vote according to conscience or support an offensive outcome that is, nevertheless, constitutional?

Robert Bork refers to this dilemma as a moment of temptation "when a judge realizes that in the case before him his strongly held view of justice, his political and moral imperative, is not embodied in a statute or in any provision of the Constitution. He must then choose between his version of justice and abiding by the American form of government" (1989: 1). For a judge to give in to "temptation," Bork argues, is to usurp the legislative prerogative (1989: 1), a position that is an anathema to judicial positivists such as Bork, persons who believe that a judge should not stray beyond the written word of a statute or precedent. But liberals express similar views. In discussing several of his own majority opinions, Supreme Court Justice John Paul Stevens said he considered the outcomes "unwise," but nevertheless "in each I was convinced that the law compelled a result that I would have opposed if I were a legislator" (Greenhouse 2005b).

The view expressed by Judge Bork can be found in the work of Blackstone, who cautioned:

> "The liberty of considering all cases in an equitable light must not be indulged too far, lest we destroy all law, and leave the decision of every question entirely in the breast of the judge [*kadi law*]. And law, without equity, though hard and disagreeable, is much more desirable for the public good than equity without law; which would make every judge a legislator, and introduce most infinite confusion; as there would then be almost as many different rules of action laid down in our courts, as there are differences of capacity and sentiment in the human mind." (quoted in Wolfe 1986: 19)

In practice, a judge "can have his cake and eat it too," because words often lack clarity and can be given more than one interpretation, and nearly all of the Constitution's most important phrases—such as "unreasonable searches" and "due process of

Superprecedent

During the Supreme Court confirmation hearings in 2005, a new term surfaced, *superprecedent*, referring to case precedents so deeply engrained in the fabric of law they should be especially hard to overturn (Rosen 2008).

Text v. Context

For Linda Greenhouse (2002) of the *New York Times*, it is a debate of *text versus context*, and she refers to the conflicting visions of Justice Stephen G. Breyer, a former Harvard law professor appointed by President Bill Clinton, and Justice Antonin Scalia, a former University of Chicago law professor appointed by President Ronald Reagan. "For Justice Scalia, who focuses on text, language is supreme and the court's job is to derive and apply rules from the words chosen by the Constitution's framers or a statute's drafters. For Justice Breyer, who looks to context, language is only a starting point to an inquiry in which a law's purpose and a decision's likely consequence are the more important elements" (2002: 3). For Breyer (2005), the critical test is whether or not the outcome promotes democratic principles.

law"—"are deliberate models of ambiguity" (Tribe 1985: 42; see also Tribe and Dorf 1991). The document fails to define such key terms as "necessary and proper" or "an establishment of religion." Thus, "the text does not always provide a definitive answer to a question(s) before the judge. The due process, equal protection, free speech, and antiestablishment clauses are scarcely self-defining in the same way that the clause giving each state two senators is" (Bond 1987: 10).

The ambiguity in the Constitution provides opportunity "for judicial officers from both ends of the ideological spectrum to assert their authority and shape public policy" (Smith 1993b: 6). Take, for example, the emotionally laden debate over the meaning of the Second Amendment (1791): "A well regulated Militia, being necessary to the security of a free state, the right of the people to keep and bear arms shall not be infringed." Does "the right of the people to keep and bear arms" provide authority for individuals to possess firearms, or does this right apply only to a "well regulated Militia"? While most modern court decisions have held that the Second Amendment refers to a state militia—the National Guard—this interpretation has been vigorously contested in and out of legal circles (Glaberson 2000d). In 2008, the Court determined (5–4) that the Second Amendment refers to an individual's right to possess firearms (*District of Columbia v. Heller*), and in 2010 the Court imposed this view on the states (*McDonald v. City of Chicago*).

Should nine unelected lawyers determine policy on important public issues?

When there is ambiguity in applying a constitutional provision to specific cases, strict constructionists argue that judges should utilize the concept of *original intent* (Polin 1986). Only through a search for original intent can the courts be faithful to the

Toward *Kadi* Justice?

"As more judges began to taste and enjoy the once-forbidden fruits of emancipation from the constraints of statute, precedent, Constitution, or tradition, the classical ideal associated with modesty, impartiality, restraint, and interpretive skill has been rivaled by an image of the good judge as bold, creative, compassionate, result-oriented, and liberated from legal technicalities" (Glendon 1994: 152).

central tenet of our democratic system, the rule of law (Berger 1987). Ronald Dworkin describes two basic schools of thought on this issue:

> One side argues that in spite of the difficulties every effort must be made, with the resources of history and analysis, to discover what the collective intention of the constitutional Framers was on disputed matters of interpretation. They believe that dogged historical study will reveal important and relevant original intentions. . . . The other side argues that any effort to discover the original collective intention of the Framers will turn out to be fruitless, or even perverse. It will end in the discovery that there are no, or very few, relevant collective intentions, or perhaps only collective intentions that are indeterminate rather than decisive one way or another, or perhaps intentions so contrary to our present sense of justice that they must in the end be rejected as a guide to the present Constitution. (1985: 38–39)[7]

If historical analysis is critical, should it be left to amateurs or should Court membership require training in the discipline?

Edwin Meese (1986: 38) states that it was Ronald Reagan's intention during his presidency to appoint to the federal courts persons who had a traditional approach to the judiciary—persons whose deliberations and decisions would be in accord with what was intended by the framers of the Constitution: "Where the language of the Constitution is specific, it must be obeyed. Where there is a demonstrable consensus among the framers and ratifiers as to a principle stated or implied by the Constitution, it should be followed. Where there is ambiguity as to the precise meaning or reach of a constitutional provision, it should be interpreted and applied in a manner so as to at least not contradict the test of the Constitution itself." However, in the easier-said-than-done vein, "there are multiple strands of originalism, some quite dramatically different from others in both their theoretical tenets and their practical implications" (Fallon 2011: 27–28).

The delegates included two future presidents (including George Washington, the convention's president) and one vice president, two future chief justices of the Supreme Court, and 16 who became state governors. Thomas Jefferson, a delegate from Virginia, did not attend the convention (Maggs 2011). Rakove (1996: 7) argues, "Not only do Madison's notes[8] and other sources allow us to track the daily progress of the deliberations at Philadelphia, but the records of the ensuing ratification debate reveal the range of meanings that the American political nation first attached to the proposed Constitution." But delegates who took notes did not make verbatim transcripts of what was said, and disagreements over particular provisions led Benjamin Franklin to urge fellow delegates to put aside their differences and ratify the document in toto—38 of the 55 delegates signed (Maggs 2011).

But, Judge Kaufman (1986) states that there is a paucity of material on which to make a determination of original intent. The minutes of the Constitutional Convention

---

[7] For a history of the issues surrounding ratification of the Constitution and the issue of *originalism*, see Rakove (1996).

[8] There is evidence that in his notes Madison "cleaned up" or elaborated on the remarks he made at the Convention (Maggs 2011).

and James Madison's notes of the proceedings, edited by Madison 20 years after the convention and first published in 1840 (Farrand 1967), are cursory, particularly with respect to the role of the judicial branch. There was a ban on note taking (that Madison and a few other delegates violated), and convention rules required that proceedings be kept secret. While there was a convention secretary, he made some mistakes, omitted various important details, and intentionally destroyed some records because he did not deem them worth saving or he wanted to preserve secrecy (Maggs 2011). The preferred source of convention records for scholars and courts is a four-volume 1937 publication by Max Farrand—the Library of Congress' website includes a copy of the 1911 three-volume edition of Farrand's work.

Madison himself rejected the doctrine of original intent: "As a guide in expounding and applying the provisions of the Constitution, the debates and incidental decisions of the Convention have no authoritative character" (quoted in Levy 1988: 1). "If the Framers, who met in executive sessions every day of their nearly four months of work, had wanted their country and posterity to construe the Constitution in the light of their deliberations," states Leonard Levy, "they would have had a stenographer present to keep an official record, and they would have published it" (1988: 2). In fact, he argues, the "Founders of the national government and its early officers simply did not think in terms of the original intent at Philadelphia" (1988: 6–7). Several years after it was ratified, Hamilton, Madison, and Jefferson were already clashing over the meaning of the Constitution on the issue of a national bank (Wolfe 1986).

Robert Post (1995: 33–34) notes:

> It is hard enough to ascertain the intention of a living individual. It is harder still to determine the intention of a group of living individuals like a legislature or a Congress. The difficulty is compounded when the group of individuals is two centuries removed in time and the evidence of their thoughts and purposes is scattered, fragmentary, ambiguous, and conflicting. And the task is made almost impossible when the relevant intention pertains to questions which in all probability never occurred to that group of individuals and which are meaningful only in light of circumstances that would to them be inconceivable.

Sunstein (2005) argues that even if such determinations were possible, why should the living be governed by the ideas of those who died hundreds of years ago, all of whom

---

Soft and Hard Originalism

"For the hard originalist, the meaning of the Constitution is settled by asking how those who ratified the relevant provision would have answered very specific questions. Does the free speech principle include commercial advertising, a particular kind of libelous statement, or sexually explicit movies? . . . For soft originalists, things are different. For them, the historical inquiry is necessary not to obtain specific answers to specific questions, but instead to get a more general sense of goals and purposes; it is these more general goals and purposes that matter in constitutional interpretations. For the hard originalist, the goal of originalism is to discover rules; for the soft originalist, the goal is to discover constraining but nonetheless flexible standards" (Sunstein 1996: 173).

were white men whose views on race, gender, and voting rights would never be accepted in today's society?

In a 1996 speech Antonin Scalia, who apparently relishes the role of legal scholar/ iconoclast, makes it clear that he supports a **plain meaning** approach to interpreting the Constitution and statutes; he is critical of those who revert to "intentions," either of the Constitution's framers or legislators, as the basis for interpretation:

> I belong to a school, a small but hardy school, called "**textualists**" or "originalists." That used to be "constitutional orthodoxy" in the United States. The theory of origi- nalism treats a constitution like a statute, and gives it the meaning that its words were understood to bear at the time they were promulgated. You will sometimes hear it described as the theory of original intent. You will never hear me refer to orig- inal intent, because as I say I am first of all a textualist, and secondly an originalist. If you are a textualist, you don't care about the intent, and I don't care if the framers of the Constitution had some secret meaning in mind when they adopted its words. I take the words as they were promulgated to the people of the United States, and what is the fairly understood meaning of those words. (Scalia 1996; emphasis added)

Judges often rely on period dictionaries to ascertain the meaning of words (Maggs 2011; for problems in using dictionaries in legal deliberations, see P. Rubin [2011]). There is also the matter of framing-era grammar (Yellin 2011). According to Thomas Jefferson, however, "the true key for the construction of everything doubtful in a law is the intention of the law-makers. This is most safely gathered from the words, but may be sought also in extraneous circumstances provided they do not contradict the express words of the law" (Taylor 2008; University of Virginia Online Resources). Stan- ley Fish states that what the author(s) intended gives meaning to text, and without understanding intention, there is nothing to which a textualist could be faithful (2005).

Interpreting Statutes

Interpreting a statute is prima facie less controversial than interpreting the Constitu- tion; the legislative branch can change a law viewed as incorrectly interpreted, while the Constitution can be altered only via the difficult amendment process. The interpre- tation of a statute does not typically involve controversial notions of judicial activism versus judicial restraint, although reversing a precedent is, arguably, activism.

Legislative Intent

Interestingly, the Constitution does not have much to say about statutory interpreta- tion and what it does say is minimal and abstract. The Constitution does not provide explicit instructions to judges about the method(s) to use when interpreting statutes (Vermeule 2000). Therein lies a problem: "Words have no inherent significance; they are supplied with meaning by those who use them, and the problem before the judge is to determine meaning when it is not clear what the legislator meant when he used the words" (Merryman 1985: 44). In 2001, for example, the Supreme Court (*Toyota Motor Manufacturing v. Williams*) agreed to determine the meaning of "disability" in an effort to provide guidance for interpreting an 11-year-old statute. The Americans with Disabilities Act uses phrases such as "substantially limits" and "major life activities" that courts have struggled to understand and apply (Greenhouse 2001a).

Legislation may fail to define key terms. For example, there is no statutory definition of "restraint of trade" or "monopolization," although both are prohibited by federal statute. These terms have been given meaning through judicial interpretation—case law (Berman and Saliba 2009). The Organized Crime Control Act of 1970 fails to define "organized crime," a term whose definition is the subject of debate in academic and law enforcement circles (Abadinsky 2013).

At the time of its enactment, a statute usually resolves the most pressing legal questions that gave rise to it, and there is little need for interpretation because the statute is clear. "Interpretation is required for those issues that were either not anticipated or politically sidestepped" (Eskridge 1994: 9). "It is the function of the legislative organ to make laws," states Roscoe Pound, "but from the nature of the case it cannot make laws so complete and all embracing that the judicial organ will not be obliged to exercise a certain lawmaking function also" (1975: 51). In other words, the concept of a separation of powers is in reality tenuous.

Legislative enactments are the result of political compromise, and controversial laws may be deliberately ambiguous to protect legislators voting for them (Levi 2013). Legislators tend to avoid controversial issues since they generate negative publicity and may antagonize the media and turn off campaign contributions (Neely 1981). Legislators "are the world's only entrepreneurs devoted to shunning risk" (Alter 1989: 28). Lobbyists exert an influence that is usually opaque, and legislators often vote for bills about which they know little or nothing following the party leadership, so bills are often the result of political compromise, not rational lawmaking (Rembar 1980). Complex statutes are the result of an "intricate game of give-and-take in which legislators, nudged constantly at the elbow by constituents, play power poker with each other" (Friedman 1984: 106). At the federal level, a single issue may require compromise among dozens of committees that have authority over some part of any legislation; controlled substances (drugs), for example, fall under the aegis of no fewer than 80 congressional panels (Alter 1989).

Much, if not most, of a legislator's energy is expended on getting elected and reelected. As a result of these realities, legislation is often ambiguous, confused, contradictory, or unconstitutional. Legislators, with an eye toward satisfying constituents and winning reelection, typically disregard issues of constitutionality (Parsons 1997). Congress has devised its own language to obscure and confound, rather than anger, constituents; for example, budget-talk: "baseline," "outyears," "off-budget," "outlays," and "budget authority" (Alter 1989). "Some statutes are little else but back-

---

Legislative Intent: Business as Usual

Late in the evening and early morning in 2002, the New York State legislature passed a health care bill—61 densely-worded pages still hot from the copying machine—that few legislators had any an opportunity to read (Pérez-Peña 2002).

The Patient Protection and Affordable Care Act, "Obamacare," has more the 900 pages of complex material overhauling the American health care system. Did your member of Congress or your Senators read this bill in its entirety before voting on it?

room deals which distribute public benefits to groups that legislators want to help. This suggests that identifying the actual or even conventional purpose of a statute is just as difficult as identifying the actual or conventional intent of the legislature, perhaps even more so, since legislators may have incentives to obscure the real purposes of the statute" (Eskridge 1994: 27). And legislators engage in a great amount of symbolic politics: "At one extreme, symbolic politics consists of speech making and public position-taking in the absence of any real action or intention of taking action; casting the right vote is more important than achieving the right outcome. At the other extreme, symbolic politics consists of whole government programs that are ostensibly designed to achieve one set of objectives but are actually designed to achieve other objectives (in some cases simply the reelection of the politicians who can claim credit for them)" (King 1997: 48). Lobbying, the "pork barrel," and "logrolling," which are synonymous with the legislative endeavor, are anathema to the judiciary.

In order for a statute to be applied, it requires interpretation. Application also requires that the constitutional significance, if any, be determined. Statutory ambiguity is inevitable. No statute, writes Edward Levi, no matter how clearly written and intended, "can be completely unambiguous and applied as intended to a specific case" (2013: 6). On what basis is the judicial branch to interpret—for the purpose of application—the actions of the legislative branch? One approach is to determine **legislative intent** with respect to each specific case; another entails using the *plain meaning* of the statutory words, no matter how absurd the outcome, "We are governed by what legislators enacted, not by the purposes they had in mind"; say what you mean and mean what you say (Scalia and Manning 2012: 1612).

When a statute is clear, it is a rule of statutory interpretation that no further examination is necessary (Scalia 1997). When a statute is unclear with respect to a particular question, lawyers and courts generally commence their search for statutory meaning by asking the question: Did the legislature intend this particular statutory provision to cover this particular fact pattern? (Lane 1999). "The resort to legislative intent may be helpful in some cases, but reconstruction of the historical process of framing and expressing intent in a forum as complex as a representative legislature is a very risky enterprise. In a surprising number of cases, the legislative history will show that the legislature did not foresee the problem facing the judge and consequently had no intent concerning it" (Merryman 1985: 44).

Adrian Vermeule (2000) presents the choices with respect to using legislative history:

- Judges should not consider legislative history.
- Judges may consider legislative history as a "persuasive," but not "authoritative," source.
- Judges should consider legislative history only if the statute is so ambiguous as to lack a plain meaning.
- Judges may always consult legislative history according to a hierarchy of relevance: committee reports, sponsors' statements, floor debate.

Determining legislative intent may entail a review of the committee reports, debates, or earlier drafts of the final bill. On the federal level, deciding on legislative intent may be quite difficult because the *Congressional Record* often contains remarks never made on the floor of either house, while omitting remarks that are made but

Conflicting Interpretations

It is a principle of legal interpretation that if a later law means to override or amend an earlier one, it should state so specifically. The 1978 Foreign Intelligence Surveillance Act (FISA) forbids domestic electronic surveillance without court authorization and created a Foreign Intelligence Surveillance Court to promptly and secretly consider electronic surveillance applications. In 2001, in the wake of 9/11, Congress passed a resolution giving the president authority to use force to combat terrorism. The 2001 resolution does not mention FISA, but the attorney general maintains that by inference it authorizes the executive branch to spy on communications between people in the United States and abroad without court authorization. Alberto Gonzales, attorney general at the time, acknowledged that at least some members of Congress did not realize they were voting to approve a surveillance program, but argued "we are a nation governed by written laws, not the unwritten intentions of individuals" (Liptak 2006a).

which the speaker wants deleted (Spaeth 1979). Furthermore, when attempting to determine the legislative intent of an act of Congress, there are several difficult questions, including how much weight, if any, should be given to different participants: "Are the thoughts of some—for example, those who spoke, or spoke most often, in the debates—more important than the thoughts of others? What about the executive officials and assistants who prepared the initial drafts? What about the president who signed the bill and made it law? Should his intentions not count more than any single senator's?" (Dworkin 1986: 318).

Historically, reference by the courts to legislative intent has been the subject of intense critical analysis. Such criticism argues that judges frequently use legislative intent to trump statutory language disfavored by the judges. In other words, if they do not like the outcome affected by the statutory language, they declare that a favored outcome was required by legislative intent (Lane 1999). Justice Scalia (1997: 17) argues that to have the meaning of a law determined by what the lawgiver meant rather than by what the lawgiver promulgated is contrary to democratic government and the requirement for accountability. "It is the law that governs, not the intent of the lawgiver," which is fundamental to the ideal of "a government of laws, not of men." Scalia argues that legislative intent" is a handy cover for *judicial* intent. "It is the last surviving legal fiction in American law that legislative history reflects the purpose of the Congress. It does not." And, even if it did, "I [Justice Scalia], frankly, don't care what the legislators' purpose is beyond that which is embodied in the duly enacted text" (Scalia and Manning 2012: 1612).

Twentieth-century theories of statutory interpretation in the United States have emphasized the *original* meaning of statutes (Eskridge 1994). However, a legislator originally voting for a statute might have a different interpretation than contemporary lawmakers. "Over time, the gaps and ambiguities proliferate as society changes, adapts to the statute, and generates new variations on the problem initially targeted by the statute. The original meaning of the statute or the original intent of the legislature has less relevance for figuring out how the statute should apply to unforeseen circumstances" (Eskridge 1994: 9–10). In fact, the "Supreme Court often interprets

statutes in ways that reflect statutory purpose or current values instead of original legislative intent" (1994: 15). Judge Posner is critical of the Scalia/plain meaning
approach because the "legislature is thwarted when a judge refuses to apply its hand-
iwork to an unforeseen situation that is encompassed by the statute's aim but does not
make a smooth fit with its text" (2013: 182).

Plain Meaning v. Legislative Intent

In addition to the difficulties inherent in determining legislative intent, some oppose
the practice on ideological grounds. They argue for the supremacy of plain meaning,
noting "ours is a government of laws, not persons, so law should be based on the
objective import of statutory language rather than the unenacted intent of legislators."
Once enacted, they argue, "a statute becomes the domain of the executive officers and
judges charged with its enforcement and application, rather than remaining somehow
tethered to the unenacted intentions of legislators" (Farber and Frickey 1991: 90). But
the plain meaning may be unclear—as a result of printing errors or careless drafting,
statutes sometimes contain grammatical errors and words are omitted (Ohlendorf
2011). The courts are "reluctant to follow statutory language when the result would be
absurd or contrary to the statute's obvious purpose" (Farber and Frickey 1991: 91).
The state of Illinois enacted a law to benefit a firm that was licensed to manufacture
machine guns. The intent was clearly to make it easier to move the weapons for ship-
ping. Instead, because of careless drafting, the final statute legalized the possession of
such weapons by state residents—how should the courts rule? Some recommend
invoking the "absurdity rule" in such instances (Ohlendorf 2011).

In Illinois, for the first time in more than 25 years, the legislature and the governor's office were in Republican hands, and they sought to repeal a law that business
interests called an expensive relic. That law permitted injured construction workers to
sue for job-related injuries in addition to collecting workmen's compensation. In 1996,
the legislature passed and the governor signed a bill halting the practice. The bill's *preamble* clearly stated that it was the intent of the legislature that all pending suits continue until resolved—only new suits were barred. Case law in Illinois holds that if a
statute is repealed without a clause exempting pending lawsuits, then the repeal
applies to all lawsuits that have not reached final judgment, and a preamble is to be
considered *only* when the law is ambiguous. Four thousand cases involving millions
of dollars hinged on the judicial interpretation of this law. In 1997, the Illinois Supreme
Court, using the concept of legislative intent, "saved the lawmakers from further
embarrassment" by exempting pending lawsuits (Armstrong and Fegelman 1996;
Armstrong 1997: Sec. 2, 6). In 1994, the Supreme Court was faced with ruling on a statute so carelessly written that its plain meaning rendered it unconstitutional. A misplaced word—"knowingly"—in the Protection of Children against Sexual Exploitation
Act left the Court with a dilemma: Interpret the law in the way Congress intended—in
effect, rewrite the statute—or respond to it as written, the plain meaning? By a vote of
7–2 the Court voted to "rewrite" the law (*United States v. X-Citement Video*). But should
the courts be responsible for cleaning up the legislative act?

In 2005, the Supreme Court accepted a case in which the issue concerned the interpretation of a single phrase. The Federal Tort Claims Act provides immunity from liability for "any claim arising out of the loss, miscarriage, or negligent transmission of

letters or postal matters." In the case of *Dolan v. United States Postal Service* (2006), the plaintiff injured her back when she tripped over packages that a letter carrier had left on her porch. A federal district court in Philadelphia, in a decision affirmed by the Court of Appeals for the Third Circuit, dismissed the suit on the grounds that "transmission" includes the actual delivery of the mail. However, in a similar case, the Court of Appeals for the Second Circuit in New York ruled that "negligent transmission" is limited to loss or damage to the mail while in actual transit. In 2006, the Supreme Court ruled 7–1 that the *intent* of Congress was to immunize the Postal Service from liability *only* for injuries caused by late or failed delivery, and damaged mail. Thus, the Postal Service could be held liable (sued) by people injured as a result of letter carriers carelessly leaving packages in their way.

The courts have an advantage over the legislature—access to information generated by parties to a dispute: "The legislature passes a rule, thinking it knows what the effects will be, but cannot have a precise understanding of them in advance of the actual application of the rule. The judge has the advantage of seeing the rule in operation, and he can deal with problems of application that the legislature did not foresee" (Posner 1985: 5). "Case law rules can be more readily modified at the point of application (if judges so wish) so as to minimize the gap between rules themselves and substantive rationales and purposes" (Atiyah and Summers 1987: 97). Whereas statutes are devoid of facts, judges make their determinations in light of the facts before them (and, it is hoped, without the untoward influence of lobbying and politics).

Obsolete, outdated, or anachronistic statutes that legislative bodies have simply failed to amend or repeal—legislative inertia—are another problem. In such cases it may be left to the courts to interpret them into harmlessness or strike them down on constitutional grounds (Atiyah and Summers 1987; see Calabresi 1982 for a discussion of this issue).[9] Or, as time passes and a statute must be applied in changed circumstances, judges may be confronted with having to enforce the original statute with the meaning it has always had or covertly amending the statute to make it current. In complex societies, "many issues will arise in cases that do not attract the substantial public or political attention needed to move a legislature to act. The avenues to legal change by the more democratic branches of government may be too broad to notice, in

---

Judicial "Legislating"

When a legislature enacts a statute, "it necessarily does so without full knowledge of the circumstances in which the rule might be invoked in the future. When the unforeseen circumstance arises—it might be the advent of the motor vehicle or of electronic surveillance, or a change in attitudes toward religion, race, or sexual propriety—a court asked to apply the rule must decide, in light of information not available to the promulgators of the rule, what the rule should mean in its new setting. Realistically, it is being asked to make a new rule; in short to legislate" (Posner 1995: 231).

---

[9] At times, legislative and administrative bodies include "sunset" provisions—expiration dates—in their statutes and rules.

a timely way, small matters of significance in their cumulative effect. Incremental change by judicial decision keeps the law up to date on a case-by-case basis in a way that augments the more democratic avenues of legal change" (Burton 1985: 231). Thus, while there is a clear separation of powers in theory, in practice there is an overlap and dynamic tension between the legislative and judicial branches, with the courts often involved in policy making.

Policy Making

Policy can be conceived of as deciding among alternative choices of action, particularly in the allocation of resources, "where the chosen action affects the behavior and well-being of others who are subject to the policy maker's authority" (Spaeth 1979: 19). As noted in Chapter 1, courts in civil law systems are distinguished from those in the United States by their lack of involvement in government policy. In the United States, it is the responsibility of the judicial branch to interpret the law and to provide a public forum—courts—for resolving legal disputes. In every case the court must determine the facts and their legal significance. If the court determines their legal significance by applying an existing rule of law unchanged (finding law), it is engaged in pure dispute resolution. "But if to resolve the dispute the court must create a new rule or modify an old one, that is law creation" (Posner 1985: 3) or lawmaking: "lawmaking aspects create precedent that can be applied to other disputes" (Marvell 1978: 216). This constitutes the policy-making function of the judicial branch.

The policy decisions of the judicial branch of government affect virtually all areas of life in the United States. Our complex system of government, with overlapping branches and territories, "ensures that disputes will arise among the branches and between the states and the central government" (Lieberman 1989: 20). The American "proclivity to think of social problems in legal terms and to judicialize everything from wage claims to community conflicts and the allocation of airline routes makes it only natural to accord judges a major share in the making of social policy" (D. Horowitz 1977: 12). "In spelling out limitations on the power of government, the Constitution preordained that issues which in other countries would be labeled political would in America be resolved in court" (Lieberman 1989: 20).

In the decades following the Second World War, the courts have been called on to deal with a variety of issues that heretofore were the province (intended or unintended) of the legislative and executive branches (D. Horowitz 1977). Susan Lawrence (1990) points out that while courts in general, and the Supreme Court in particular, will not consider questions of policy, skillful attorneys can transform almost any policy issue into at least an arguably relevant judicial issue Thus, "we have a two-track system where issues stuck in Congress can now jump off that track into the courts." But the attorneys who promote this legal activism are not answerable to the public (Meier 2000: WK 3).

The Supreme Court has revolutionized race relations, altered forever the manner in which legislative districts are drawn, overhauled the procedures of the juvenile court, dramatically increased the rights of accused criminals, prohibited prayer in public schools, overturned laws prohibiting abortion and the destruction of the American flag, and provided due process rights to welfare recipients. State and federal courts have overturned minimum-residency requirement laws for welfare recipients and expanded welfare eligibility, causing states to increase their welfare budgets. They have established elaborate standards for all aspects of prison life and have ordered some prisons closed, and they have done the same for mental institutions. The courts have ordered the equalization of school expenditures and established procedures for the handling of school discipline. Using the powers of equity, they have enjoined the construction of roads and bridges as damaging to the environment and have ordered the Forest Service to stop the clearing of timber. They have ordered the US Army Corps of Engineers to maintain America's nonnavigable waterways and have eliminated the requirement of a high school diploma for a firefighter's job. Judges have taken over the operation of the entire state prison system in Alabama to end unconstitutional conditions (*Pugh v. Locke* [1976]) and public schools in Boston (*Morgan v. Hennigan* [1974]) to achieve desegregation. They have ordered sharp increases in property taxes in order to pay for school desegregation in the Kansas City school district (upheld by the Supreme Court in *Missouri v. Jenkins* [1990]), and more recently the Court has become enmeshed in foreign affairs (Feldman 2008).

Cases in which courts make policy determinations usually involve government, the Fourteenth Amendment, and the use of equity (discussed in Chapter 1), although "we have seen an increase in recent decades of policy-oriented suits in private law cases" (Cooper 1988: 13). For example, **product liability** "suits and personal injury litigation have been used not merely to recompense persons hurt by industrial practices, but also in an attempt to change the business policy of these private firms." Even when the plaintiff's goal is compensatory, a significant damage award can shock private firms or government agencies into developing new policies (Smith 1997). Since units of government and their officials generally enjoy immunity from damage claims (states are immune from damage suits under the Eleventh Amendment), and monetary awards in some cases may not be relevant (e.g., protecting mental patients or prison inmates), equity is the remedy most often used against governmental violations of law. Relief through equity can be negative and/or affirmative: "The plea for negative relief is generally a request that the judge declare past actions illegal and enjoin the government from any further practices. . . . The affirmative relief requested is for a decree with provisions which attempt, by directing changes in structure or practice, to undo the damage done to the plaintiffs and others similarly situated" (Cooper 1988: 14). In public law policy cases, both negative and affirmative relief are often requested.

In some cases, the legislative branch fails to act, leaving important areas of law in a void for varying periods of time: "During the interim, the courts may have no realistic choice but to make law in the political vacuum or allow disorder or injustice to prevail," such as the area of copyrights. In 1909, Congress enacted a copyright act that was not revised until 1978. For almost 70 years the courts had to deal with an outdated copyright law as it applied to changing audio and visual technology (Burton 1985: 232). The Internet has added a complicated mix to the issue of intellectual property rights.

However, judges cannot impose their views until someone brings a case to court, often as a last resort after complaining to unresponsive legislators and executives (Wasby 1993). Plaintiffs must be truly aggrieved, or have *standing* (mentioned above and discussed in detail in Chapter 10). The judicial response is focused sharply on the questions presented and "not [on] related matters that a legislator might take up" (Lieberman

1989: 29): specific acts of discrimination perpetrated by particular actors, as opposed to remote but related issues, such as the causes of sexism or racism. The independence of the judicial branch, particularly at the federal level where judges are appointed for life, permits the courts to act as champions on behalf of those who do not command financial resources, large amounts of votes, or a positive public profile—that is, those who would otherwise receive no (or negative) attention from other branches of government. (Of course, a lifetime appointment can also lead to arrogance and petty tyranny.) The ability of appellate courts in general and the Supreme Court in particular to choose the cases it will decide strengthens the judicial branch's ability to enter policy areas.

Administrative Agencies and Judicial Policy Making

A great deal of the judicial branch's policy-oriented decisions have been based not on the Constitution but on federal statutes concerning the rights of the disadvantaged, consumers, and the environment: "Such litigation results from the need to have judges interpret and enforce vague and ambiguous statutory provisions and the regulations developed to implement the statutes" (Wasby 1993: 5).[10] Congress has been accused of creating administrative agencies with vague mandates in areas of controversial public policy (e.g., environmental protection) so as to avoid taking the political heat that more specific legislation can generate (Lieberman 1981).

Prior to the 1960s, the courts were reluctant to consider suits that called for more vigorous or extensive enforcement by regulatory agencies. The courts typically deferred to administrative discretion except when litigants were entitled to an application of the law in their own personal cases. Since administrative agencies, by definition, are composed of experts, judges typically deferred to their expertise. Beginning in the 1950s, however, there was concern that any number of these agencies had been "captured" by the very industries they were supposed to regulate (Shapiro 1988). Furthermore, when the appointees of more conservative executives, particularly President Richard Nixon and Ronald Reagan (both when he was governor of California and president of the United States), began to wield this discretionary power, liberal policy activists and public interest law firms (discussed in Chapters 3 and 10) initiated litigation to force agencies to comply with regulatory duties as seen by the plaintiffs. The courts granted standing to interest groups whose claims were general, rather than the individual and personal claims typically required of plaintiffs (Rabkin 1989). These efforts were furthered by Congress, which enacted legislation allowing citizen lawsuits when certain federal regulatory agencies, such as the Environmental Protection Agency (EPA), fail to perform a specific act or duty as required by statute. Thus, under the Clean Air Act, the Sierra Club was allowed to sue the EPA.

Entry of the judicial branch into the arena of administrative policy, in response to public interest group litigation, is not without controversy, as the title of a book by Jeremy Rabkin implies: *Judicial Compulsions: How Public Law Distorts Public Policy* (1989). Rabkin decries the courts' assumption of an oversight role for which they are not prepared: "Courts are entirely unequipped to act as ongoing, freestanding guardians of administrative performance. Our entire judicial system has developed on the assump-

---

[10] Administrative law is discussed in Chapter 1.

tion that courts will simply be deciding cases about property rights or personal rights, in the traditional sense" (1989: 20). Why should the judiciary recognize the policy preferences of plaintiffs purporting to represent the interests of the general public? Why should "factional interests be allowed to make preemptive claims on public policy?" (1989: 73) Furthermore, in the criminal sphere, private parties cannot compel the initiation of a prosecution; yet the courts have allowed parallel action when it involves regulatory agencies. Advocates of public interest law state that judicial intervention was necessary to keep appointees of the Reagan administration from subverting the historical mission of their agencies: "Much of public interest litigation," they argue, "aims simply to enforce existing laws" (Aron 1989: 100).

The Implementation of Judicial Decisions

Judicial decisions are not self-implementing. Whereas lower-court responses to most controversial decisions have been immediate and implementation by other government agencies almost complete, such as the 1973 abortion decision in *Roe v. Wade*, compliance was not forthcoming in the 1954 desegregation decision of *Brown v. Board of Education*— several federal court judges in the South, in fact, refused to implement the decision (Abraham 1998). And the 1963 decision prohibiting prayer in public schools (*Abington School District v. Schempp*) was implemented to varying degrees across the country. In 1986, segregation was again litigated in Topeka, Kansas, to force greater compliance with *Brown*, and in 1989, a federal appeals court ruled that while the Topeka school board was not resisting desegregation, it still had not fully carried out the Supreme Court mandate ("Court Allows Challenge to Bias Ruling to Continue" 1989). And, of course, the issue of school prayer is still being subjected to litigation in various parts of the country.

In some cases, it is necessary for judges to retain jurisdiction after immediate legal issues have been settled in order to monitor the implementation of a court decree (Lieberman 1981). For example, in 1987 the federal district judge monitoring the 1981 settlement of a lawsuit against the Texas prison system held the state in contempt of court for failing to carry out court-ordered reforms. The same day, a judge of the Massachusetts Superior Court ruled that the state welfare department had ignored his order to provide a standard of assistance that would allow welfare recipients to rear their children at home. Accordingly, he ordered a 30 percent increase in welfare benefits (*New York Times*, Jan. 6, 1987, p. 7). In 1976, a federal judge took control of the Cleveland, Ohio, public schools for failing to end segregation. In 1998, a federal judge agreed to free the school district from court supervision because he said the district had done as much as it could to meet the court-imposed standards for integration.

Whereas some judicial decisions lack the clarity necessary for easy implementation (as attempts to define pornography have proven), others have been subjected to one of three forms of opposition: defiance, avoidance, and **limited application** (Canon and Johnson 1999):

1. *Defiance.* Overt defiance is a relatively rare and highly unprofessional response in which a lower-court judge refuses to follow the decisions of a higher court. Examples of defiance were seen in the South when some judges refused to uphold and implement the decision in *Brown*. Defiance may also take the form of simply ignoring the higher court's policy. This is more easily

done in cases decided by trial courts, since appellate tribunals promulgate written decisions that are available to the public.

2. *Avoidance.* Procedural or technical considerations can be used in to avoid having to implement unacceptable higher-court policy. A judge may also separate out the repugnant language of a decision as *dicta*, or commentary outside of the *ratio decedendi*. Such tactics serve merely to delay implementing judicial policy.

3. *Limited application.* Because this is a normal response to many judicial decisions, a judge can distinguish away the precedent from the case at issue.

Edward Hartnett (1999: 127) points to differences between an *opinion* and a *judgment*: The latter is a judicial order applied to a specific case, whereas an opinion is the explanation for the judgment. "It is the judgment," he contends, "not the opinion, that settles authoritatively what is to be done." Indeed, a court can issue a judgment without providing an opinion, whereas judicial opinions may lack the degree of clarity and specificity necessary to implement them. Vague decisions, such as those concerning obscenity or *de facto* segregation, often result in numerous interpretations, which may encourage lower-court judges who oppose the decisions to resort to avoidance or limited application. Confusion over what is required by a decision may also result in multiple interpretations throughout a state, a federal circuit, or, in the case of the Supreme Court, the entire country. With respect to state courts, the US Supreme Court

> has no power to make a *final determination* in any case in which it reviews state court judgments. All it can do in these instances is to decide the federal issue and remand it to the state court below for final judgment "not inconsistent with this opinion." Because the state courts possess the power to raise new issues—issues based on "independent and adequate state grounds"—after they receive the case back from above, they are provided with an opportunity to evade the substantive effects of the reversal by the Supreme Court in a number of ways. (Abraham 1998: 252)

Summary

- Trial courts determine issues of fact, while appellate courts correct errors and ensure that law is interpreted correctly and consistently.

- Appellate court decisions and explanations of decisions provide precedent.

- Appellate courts do not use witness testimony.

- During oral arguments appellate court judges often assume an inquisitorial role.

- Persons without standing may be permitted to submit *amicus curiae* briefs.

- Law clerks are usually recent law school graduates who perform research and may even draft initial, if not final, opinions.

- The decision-making process of appellate courts is shrouded in secrecy.

- The Supreme Court has the final word when interpreting the Constitution.

- The Supreme Court enjoys power of certiorari.

- The Supreme Court grants certiorari in relatively few of the cases that are appealed,

- The Supreme Court does not give reasons for turning down a case or why a case is accepted for review.

- The Supreme Court will not decide the validity of a statute on the complaint of a person who fails to show that he or she has standing.
- The rules for submitting a petition to the Supreme Court are formal, and a failure to adhere to them will result in the petition not being considered.
- Certain "cues" make a case stand out, thereby improving its chances for review.
- The chief justice, if part of the majority, may write the decision him or herself, or choose an associate justice from the majority side to write the opinion of the Court; otherwise, the opinion is written by the senior justice in the majority or his or her designate. The chief justice assigns opinions when the decision is unanimous.
- Having neither the "power of the purse, nor the power of the sword," the judicial branch is dependent on a perception of legitimacy surrounding its decisions.
- Being unelected, Supreme Court justices should exercise "judicial restraint": Except when there is a clear violation of the Constitution or well-established precedent, do not overturn an act of federal or state legislative or executive branches.
- Various methods are used for interpreting the Constitution and different justices give greater emphasis to one over the other: text, history, and precedent.
- Some argue for original intent while others claim that the intent of the author cannot reasonably be determined.
- Some argue that original intent is irrelevant.
- Interpreting a statute is less controversial than interpreting the Constitution; the legislative branch can change a law viewed as incorrectly interpreted.
- Because of the manner in which the legislative branch drafts statutes, they frequently lack clarity.
- In addition to the difficulties inherent in determining legislative intent, some oppose the practice on ideological grounds. They argue for the supremacy of plain meaning.
- While in theory there is a separation of powers, in practice there is overlap between the legislative and judicial branches.
- When the court resolves a dispute by creating a new rule or modifying an old one, that is policy making.
- Opposition by lower courts to carrying out an appellate decision includes: defiance, avoidance, and limited application.

KEY TERMS

affirm	*in forma pauperis*	precedent
amicus curiae	judicial activism	product liability
burden of proof	judicial restraint	*ratio decedendi*
certiorari	legislative intent	remand
concurring opinion	legitimacy	reverse
de facto	limited application	textualist
dissent	original intent	transcript
equitable	plain meaning	writ of prohibition
equity	police powers	

REVIEW QUESTIONS

1. What distinguishes the role of trial courts from that of appellate courts?
2. On what do appellate courts base decisions?
3. What is an *amicus curiae* brief?
4. How does the appellate process resemble the inquisitorial model?
5. What is the role of law clerks in the appellate process?
6. What criticism is leveled at the role of law clerks in the appellate process?
7. What are the typical contents of an appellate court decision?
8. Why is the decision-making process of appellate courts shrouded in secrecy?
9. What is meant by the power of *certiorari*?
10. What are the reasons the Supreme Court usually gives for turning down a case for review?
11. What does standing require?
12. What are the "cues" that improve chances for Supreme Court review?
13. How is it decided which justice will write a Supreme Court decision?
14. Why is the judicial branch dependent on a perception of legitimacy surrounding its decisions?
15. What is meant by judicial restraint?
16. Why is "judicial activism" an irrelevant issue?
17. What are three methods for interpreting the Constitution?
18. Why is original intent difficult to determine?
19. What are the arguments of those who believe original intent to be irrelevant when interpreting the Constitution?
20. Why is interpreting a statute less controversial than interpreting the Constitution?
21. Why is it necessary for the judicial branch to interpret statutes?
22. Why is it difficult to determine legislative intent?
23. What is the disagreement between those who support legislative intent and those argue for the supremacy of plain meaning?
24. What is the "limited application" technique by which a lower court can try to avoid carrying out the mandate of an appellate decision?
25. What is the *textualist* view of statutory interpretation?

INTERNET CONNECTIONS

Legal Information Institute (Cornell University): http://www.law.cornell.edu
Legal Resource Center: http://crimelynx.com/research.html
Legal Sites on the Web: http://ih2000.net/ira/legal.htm
Meta-Index for Legal Research: https://gsulaw.gsu.edu/metaindex
US Supreme Court: http://www.supremecourt.gov

The Supreme Court

Shortly after the **Articles of Confederation** were adopted by the 13 sovereign states (1781), it became obvious that they were not a viable basis for governing the United States—federal authority was concentrated in a unicameral legislative body; there was no separate executive branch. The people were divided geographically—the journey from Boston to New York took a week, while Boston to Savannah was a trip of several months—and "by differences of religion, environment, and custom that bred fierce jealousy and local pride." Thus, "a man thought of himself as a Georgian, a Virginian, or a New Yorker but hardly ever as an American" (Cox 1987: 32).

Shay's rebellion (1787), in which destitute farmers in western Massachusetts, led by a Revolutionary War veteran, rebelled against onerous taxes, had revealed the inadequacies of executive power; the national currency was practically worthless, and there was real fear that European nations would take advantage of governmental anarchy as states squabbled over interstate trade. This commercial warfare led to the Philadelphia Convention:

> The taxes levied upon goods moving through the Ports of New York and Philadelphia were bleeding portless New Jersey white. Virginia and South Carolina were bleeding North Carolina. Baltimore was fattening on the people of the interior valleys. When Virginia passed a law declaring that vessels failing to pay duty in her ports were subject to seizure, she was aiming at cargoes from Massachusetts, New York, and Pennsylvania. In 1786 delegates from the States bordering on Chesapeake Bay met at Annapolis in an effort to stop the commercial warfare on the bay. The Annapolis Convention led to the broader summons to Philadelphia. (Cox 1987: 34)

As criticism grew, Congress reluctantly called for a convention to meet in Philadelphia in 1787 to revise the Articles of Confederation.

Articles of Confederation, Article 2

"Each state retains its sovereignty, freedom, and independence, and every power, jurisdiction, and right, which is not by this confederation expressly delegated to the United States, in Congress assembled."

Even though the delegates were not authorized to create an entirely new instrument of government, they did so. James Madison wrote (*Federalist* No. 40) that the convention had not exceeded its authority; but even if it had, he argued, it was justified by the need to protect the welfare of the nation. Out of this Constitutional Convention emerged the cornerstone of American government, separation of powers, which sought to answer one of the oldest problems of democratic government: how to provide for efficiency without tyranny.

The Separation of Powers and the Birth of a National Judiciary

A bicameral legislature (Article I) and a chief executive (Article II) were agreed on after long and often acrimonious debate. The idea of a national judiciary was widely accepted, but delegates could not agree on the details. While there was general agreement on the need for a supreme court, the advocates of **states' rights** opposed the creation of a system of inferior federal courts. They argued that state courts were sufficient, and a single federal appellate court was adequate to protect national rights and promote uniformity of judgments. In a compromise, delegates approved **Article III**, which says in part, "The judicial power of the United States, shall be vested in one Supreme Court, and in such inferior Courts as the Congress may from time to time ordain and establish." They left it up to Congress to establish inferior courts and to set the size of the membership of the Supreme Court (Schwartz 1993).

The new Constitution needed to be ratified by nine of the original 13 states, and the outcome was in doubt. A war of words broke out, and the press of the day was deluged with contributions from anonymous citizens writing under various *noms de plume* (Earle 1937). "Publius"—the pen name chosen for the joint writings of Federalists Alexander Hamilton, John Jay, and James Madison—wrote a series of 85 essays between October 1787 and May 1788 in support of the Constitution. These essays have become known as *The Federalist Papers* (1937). Designed primarily to support ratification of the Constitution in New York, *The Federalist Papers* were known throughout the states. Although it is doubtful whether they had much influence in determining ratification, they provide an illuminating discussion of intent and a basis for interpreting the Constitution (Earle 1937).

The role of the judiciary was clear: "The courts were designed to be an intermediate body between the people and the legislature, in order, among other things, to keep the latter within the limits assigned to their authority. The interpretation of the law is the proper and peculiar province of the courts. A constitution is, in fact, and must be regarded by the judges, as a fundamental law. It therefore belongs to them to ascertain its meaning, as well as the meaning of any particular act proceeding from the legislative body" (*Federalist* No. 78: 506). Publius argued that "limitations of this kind can be preserved in practice no other way than through the medium of courts of justice, whose duty it must be to declare all acts contrary to the manifest tenor of the Constitution void. Without this, all the reservations of particular rights or privileges would amount to nothing" (*Federalist* No. 78: 505).

In his assessment of *Democracy in America*, Alexis de Tocqueville, a French aristocrat studying the American prison system and writing in the 1830s, stated that "the power vested in the American courts of justice, of pronouncing a statute to be unconstitutional, forms one of the most powerful barriers which has ever been devised against tyranny of political assemblies" (1956: 76) and is a methodological expression of the supremacy of *natural law*: ensuring majority rule without trampling on minority rights.

The courts have neither the power of the purse nor the power of the sword.

The Federalist Papers noted the relative weakness of the judicial branch and its dependency on the executive branch to carry out its decisions:

> The Executive not only dispenses the honors, but holds the sword of the community. The legislature not only commands the purse, but prescribes the rules by which the duties and rights of every citizen are to be regulated. The judiciary, on the contrary, has no influence over either sword or purse; no direction either of the strength or of the wealth of the society; and can take no active resolution whatever. It may truly be said to have neither *force* nor *will*, but merely judgment; and must ultimately depend upon the aid of the executive arm even for the efficacy of its judgments. (*Federalist* No. 78: 504)

They also stressed the need for judicial independence, a principle that has become a cornerstone of the federal courts: "That inflexible and uniform adherence to the rights of the Constitution, and of individuals, which we perceive to be indispensable in the courts of justice, can certainly not be expected from judges who hold their offices by a temporary commission. Periodical appointments, however regulated, or by whomsoever made, would, in some way or other, be fatal to their necessary independence" (*Federalist* No. 78: 510). This warning was heeded—all federal judges are appointed to lifetime terms.

The Constitution was ratified by the ninth state, New Hampshire, on June 21, 1788, but the size of the Supreme Court was not determined until the Judiciary Act of 1789, which set membership at six: a chief justice and five associate justices. The act also created three circuit courts, each made up of two justices of the Supreme Court and a district court judge, and 13 district courts, each presided over by a district judge (Carp, Stidham, and Manning 2014).

After his inauguration, President Washington appointed six justices, loyal Federalists, three from the South three from the North—he established the traditions of appointing the party faithful and of geographic balance. The Court began operations in the Wall Street area of New York City on February 1, 1790, and the most immediate controversy concerned attire—the English wig was rejected, but robes were accepted (Schwartz 1993). The first Supreme Court was weak, ineffective, and relegated to a room in the basement beneath the Senate chamber. Only two justices and John Jay

Article III, Sec. 1

"The judicial power of the United States shall be vested in one supreme court, and in such inferior Courts as the Congress may from time to time establish."

were present on opening day. When war raged between England and France, President Washington, hoping to keep America neutral, asked the Court for advice on 29 questions on international law and treaties. In a precedent-setting response, Chief Justice John Jay politely declined to provide advisory decisions, pointing out that each branch is responsible for acting as a check on the other and that such responsibility could not be fulfilled if the Court served as a presidential advisor. "However, as did many subsequent members of the Court, Jay acted extensively as a presidential advisor in an informal, behind-the-scenes capacity" (Wiecek 1988: 25).

When the chief justice, John Jay, was elected governor of New York he resigned from the Court, because the judiciary was still the least important branch of government.[1] Several individuals declined appointments to the Court, and one, Robert H. Harrison, refused the appointment even after the Senate confirmed him; he chose, instead, to become chancellor of Maryland (Cox 1987). Alexander Hamilton and Patrick Henry refused appointments. Particularly onerous was the requirement that members of the Court personally sit on circuit courts, trial courts that had been set up by the 1789 Judiciary Act. This required a great deal of travel at a time when transportation was quite primitive (Schwartz 1993). "Required by law to sit twice a year, the Court began its first term with a crowded courtroom and an empty docket. Appeals from lower tribunals came slowly; for its first three years the Court had almost no business at all" (Harrell and Anderson 1982: 15). For this reason Congress was reluctant to relieve the justices of the circuit riding responsibilities (Schwartz 1993). In 1800, the federal capital moved to Washington, DC, a federal bar began to develop, and a number of more prominent attorneys settled in Washington to argue cases before the Court (Chroust 1965).

During the Constitutional Convention, debates arose over the exercise of judicial review—the power to determine the constitutionality of an action by the legislative or executive branch—and they were inconclusive.

> The convention delegates agreed to the establishment of a Supreme Court only after they had rejected proposals for a Council of Revision to scrutinize congressional legislation and another to allow Congress to veto state legislation. That the delegates debated these methods of constitutional oversight in the context of the judicial power indicates that they assumed the Supreme Court would oversee the constitutionality of acts of Congress and state legislatures. (Hall 1989: 73)

Although it seems clear that the delegates intended some type of judicial review, its content and scope were not defined, and the Constitution remained silent about the issue. Leonard Levy concludes that "the evidence seems to indicate that the Framers did not mean for the Supreme Court to have authority to void acts of Congress" (1988: 100). While in state systems the practice of judicial review was beginning to emerge (Wiecek 1988), the Supreme Court did not assert this authority until its most important historical decision, *Marbury v. Madison* (1803), for which only three of the Court's six justices showed up to hear arguments.

---

[1] Jay's view of the Court is highlighted by the appointment he accepted in 1794 as special ambassador to England where he negotiated the treaty that bears his name—without resigning as chief justice (Schwartz 1993).

The Marshall Court

The Court moved to a site on the Potomac in 1800. In that year the Federalists were defeated. Chief Justice Oliver Ellsworth became ill and resigned, and Jay refused to serve again. In 1801, in an effort to "save" the Constitution from the "radical" Democratic Republicans led by Thomas Jefferson, lame-duck President John Adams appointed his secretary of state, the Virginia Federalist and Jefferson's cousin, John Marshall, as the Court's fourth chief justice. As a young man on Washington's staff, Marshall had experienced the horrors of Valley Forge, caused largely by selfishness and rivalry between states. He appreciated the need for national unity and had taken an active role in winning Virginia's ratification of the Constitution (Cox 1987; Maier 2010).

Marbury v. Madison

In his last act before leaving office, President Adams appointed 42 justices of the peace for the District of Columbia, which the lame-duck Senate quickly confirmed. Although he had affixed the great seal of the United States, in the haste surrounding the appointments, John Marshall, the secretary of state, failed to deliver the commission for William Marbury. When he took office, President Jefferson ordered that the commission not be delivered. In December of 1801, Marbury applied to the Supreme Court for a *writ of mandamus* (an extraordinary court order compelling a public official to perform his or her duty) ordering James Madison, the secretary of state at that time, to give him his commission as justice of the peace. Although the Supreme Court agreed to hear the controversial case, Congress enacted a law that stopped the Court from convening for 14 months. In 1803, the Court finally heard the case of *Marbury v. Madison*.

Marry Ann Harrell and Burnett Anderson describe the quandary of the Court headed by Marshall:

> If the Court ordered Madison to produce that commission, he could simply ignore the order; President Jefferson would defend him. If the Court denied Marbury's right to his commission, Jefferson could claim a party victory. [Either decision would mean a significant loss of prestige for the Court.] Marshall found an escape from this dilemma. Point by point he analyzed the case. Did Marbury have a legal right to his commission? *Yes.* Would a writ of mandamus enforce his right? *Yes.* Could the Court issue the writ? *No.* Congress had said it could, in the Judiciary Act of 1789. It had given the Court original jurisdiction in such cases—power to try them for the first time. But, said Marshall, the Constitution defined the Court's original jurisdiction and Congress could not change it by law. Therefore that section of the law was void. (1982: 25–26; edited)

The Court could do nothing to help Marbury.

Marbury v. Madison (1803)

"Certainly, all those who have framed written constitutions contemplate them as forming the fundamental and paramount law of the nation, and consequently the theory of every such government must be, that an act of the legislature, repugnant to the Constitution, is void."

While Marbury never did get his commission, he was saved from historical obscurity "by the fact that he was the plaintiff in the most famous case ever decided by the United States Supreme Court" (Rehnquist 1987: 114). With this decision, John Marshall—whose oversight was the reason for this case—asserted the principle of *judicial review,* the power of the Supreme Court to determine the constitutionality of acts of Congress and actions of the president.[2] Although such power is inherent in the very idea of a written constitution (Tushnet 2000), "had Marshall not confirmed review power at the outset in his original magisterial manner, it is entirely possible it would never have been insisted upon, for it was not until 1857 that the authority to invalidate a federal statute was next exercised by the Supreme Court" (Schwartz 1974: 32–33).

Marbury left unresolved the question of the scope of the power of judicial review (George 2000), but once the decision was made, the Court also claimed the right of judicial review over state legislation (*Fletcher v. Peck* [1810]), and the Marshall court (1801–1835) overturned more than a dozen state laws on constitutional grounds (Carp, Stidham, and Manning 2014). "Once Chief Justice Marshall had established the prerogative of the Supreme Court to declare statutes unconstitutional, the Court employed natural law thinking to protect vested property rights against legislative incursions" (Levy 1988: 13). However, it was not until 1857, in *Dred Scott v Sandford,* that the Court overturned another in federal statute, a decision that helped fuel the movement toward Civil War.

Marshall initiated a major change in the way decisions were presented by encouraging collective opinions in place of the usual *seriatim* (separate) opinions authored by each justice. He was responsible for the Supreme Court being the only one of our three branches of government that provides a written statement of its reasons when it renders a decision (Tribe 1985). "He created the judicial tradition," notes William Wiecek, "out of the scant and unpromising prospects he found when he took office in 1801" (1988: 55). G. Edward White sums up Marshall's contribution: "Appointed to a court that could easily have become and nearly did become a resting place for minor political officials, Marshall gave to succeeding judges a national judiciary able to stand equal alongside the other two branches of government" (1976: 35).

Judicial Review

"Judicial review is the practice by which the Supreme Court scrutinizes state and federal legislation and the acts of state and federal executive officers and courts in order to determine whether they are in conflict with the Constitution" (Hall 1989: 1). However, "neither the words of the Constitution nor the provable intent of those who framed and ratified it justified in 1790 any certitude about the scope or finality of the Court's power to superintend either the states or Congress" (McClosky 2010: 5).

---

[2] For a revisionist view of *Marbury,* see Whittington and Rinderle (2012).

McCulloch v. Maryland and Implied Powers

In 1819, the Court extended the power of the federal government when it found that among those powers specifically enumerated in Article I, Section 8, of the Constitution, were "implied powers" necessary for the proper implementation of the constitutional mandate. Accordingly, in *McCulloch v. Maryland* (1819), the Court upheld the power of the federal government to establish the Bank of the United States and ruled that a state could not tax that bank. Although President Andrew Jackson thwarted *McCulloch* in 1832 by vetoing legislation to extend the charter of the bank, the impact of Marshall's finding of implied powers "was the basis for the expansion of federal power and the rise of the welfare state that began during the depression of the 1930s" (Spaeth 1979: 200).

The Supremacy Clause

The Court also transformed Article VI, the **Supremacy Clause**, into an operating reality, and this was not a simple task. At times, sectionalism was rife in New England, the West, and finally the South, threatening to tear the union apart (Wiecek 1988). Although state court decisions had to conform to the Constitution, that document left enough room for diverse interpretations. Various states' courts might interpret the Constitution differently, while others might claim state sovereignty in certain cases. This issue came to the fore in a case that involved land in northern Virginia that had been part of the same tract as the John Marshall homestead; accordingly, in *Martin v. Hunter's Lessee* (1816) Marshall recused (disqualified) himself. In his place, Justice Joseph Story upheld the appellate jurisdiction of the Supreme Court as the "final word" over all federal *and* state courts. The issue emerged again in 1821 in a case involving the sale of lottery tickets authorized by Congress but outlawed by Virginia (*Cohens v. Virginia*). Marshall wrote the opinion, again upholding both the power of the Supreme Court and federal supremacy. The Supremacy Clause specifically obligates state courts to recognize the superiority of federal law and to apply the latter when state law has been superseded (Schwartz 1993).

Gibbons v. Ogden and Interstate Commerce

In 1824, the Supreme Court handed down a decision that proved crucial for economic development in the United States. It was also one of the more popular decisions

---

McCulloch v. Maryland (1819)

"A constitution, to contain an accurate detail of all the subdivisions of which its great powers will admit, and of all the means by which they may be carried into execution, would partake of the prolixity [tediousness] of a legal code, and could scarcely be embraced by the human mind. It would probably never be understood by the public. Its nature, therefore, requires that only its great outlines should be marked, its important objects designated, and the minor ingredients which compose those objects be deduced from the nature of the objects themselves. That this idea was entertained by the framers of the American constitution, is not only to be inferred from the nature of the instrument, but from the language."

Article VI (Supremacy Clause)

"This Constitution, and the Laws of the United States which shall be made in Pursuance thereof; and all Treaties made, or which shall be made, under the authority of the United States, shall be the supreme Law of the Land; and all the Judges in every State shall be bound thereby, any Thing in the Constitution or Laws of any State to the Contrary notwithstanding."

handed down by the Marshall Court. In 1803, Robert Fulton demonstrated his steam-powered ship on the Seine in Paris. Subsequently, the New York State legislature granted Fulton and his partner exclusive rights to issue licenses to run steamships on the Hudson River. In 1811, the territorial legislature in New Orleans granted them a similar monopoly; they controlled the two most lucrative ports in the country. Other states enacted similar legislation.

One of the licensees of the New York monopoly, ex-New Jersey Governor Aaron Ogden, sued his former partner, Thomas Gibbons, for navigating in New York waters without a state license. The New York courts found for Ogden and forbade Gibbons to operate in New York ports or to interfere with Ogden's monopoly. Gibbons appealed to the Supreme Court, arguing that his (federal) license under the Federal Coasting Act entitled him to trade between the ports of different states. The overriding legal issue concerned state and federal powers under the commerce clause, Article I, Section 8, Clause 3: regulation of intra- and interstate commerce. In his decision, Marshall asserted the federal government's supreme authority over the regulation of interstate commerce, while leaving the regulation of intrastate commerce to the states. The decision did not attend to the area of overlap between state and federal regulation, although subsequent cases for more than 150 years have clarified the issue.

Gibbons had an immediate and important economic impact—the destruction of state trade monopolies that stimulated business in their states, while other states retaliated against these protectionist measures. The decision facilitated the creation of the unified market essential for economic development in the United States and, later in the century, encouraged Congress to appropriate funds for improving interstate trade routes, interstate highways, and the transcontinental railroad. "The modern free flow of commerce in the American economy's enormous national market is the legacy of *Gibbons v. Ogden*" (Richert 1987: 15).

The Eleventh Amendment and Sovereign Immunity

While the Supreme Court dominated constitutional issues, it was the state courts' decisions that affected the day-to-day activities of most citizens. From the time of the ratification of the Constitution until the Civil War, the primacy of the state courts was not seriously questioned. The Judiciary Act of 1789 affirmed the primary role of the state courts and narrowly confined the jurisdiction of the federal trial courts. In 1793, however, the pre-Marshall Supreme Court, in its first constitutional decision, ruled in *Chisholm v. Georgia* that a state is not a sovereign entity and therefore a citizen in one state could sue the government of another state in federal court, in this case to recover a debt. States "feared ruinous suits on Revolutionary War debts that they had not paid on Tory property that they had confiscated" (Tribe 1985: 55). Congress responded with the Eleventh Amendment, ratified in 1795 (although the presidential proclamation was delayed until 1798) barring suits in federal court similar to the one sustained in *Chisholm*: "The Court's first constitutional decision conflicted with statements of Framers in 1788 and provoked an amendment to the Constitution to make it conform to a general understanding throughout the nation" (Levy 1988: 59).

In order to protect the independence of state courts—a practice known as **judicial comity**—the Eleventh Amendment provides that "the Judicial Power of the United States shall not be construed to extend to any suit in law or equity, commenced or prosecuted against one of the United States by Citizens of another State, or by Citizens or Subjects of any Foreign State." The Marshall Supreme Court, however, limited the impact of the Eleventh Amendment by holding that a suit against a state *officer* is not a suit against a *state*, if the officer was acting pursuant to an unconstitutional state law (*United States v. Peters* [1809]; *Osborn v. Bank of the United States* [1824]). This interpretation would hold until the Reconstruction era, when the Supreme Court extended the protections afforded states—**sovereign immunity**—by the Eleventh Amendment, thus protecting state officers from lawsuits by nonresidents (Orth 1987). In 1890, the Court further extended sovereign immunity, prohibiting suits by citizens against their own states (*Hans v. Louisiana*), although a state may waive this immunity. People can still sue states on "equal protection" grounds, alleging a violation of the Fourteenth Amendment. Local governments lost their sovereign immunity defense in 1978, the result of a Supreme Court decision (*Monell v. New York City Department of Social Services*) reaffirmed in 2006 (*Northern Insurance Company of New York v. Chatham County*).

In 1946, Congress enacted the Federal Tort Claims Act, which provides the legal mechanism for compensating persons injured by the negligent or wrongful acts of federal employees committed within the scope of their employment. The injured party must first file an administrative claim with the appropriate federal agency. Only if the claim is denied or not acted on within six months can the claimant file a suit in federal district court. Under the act, these lawsuits can only be tried by a bench (no jury) trial. States soon followed the federal lead and enacted legislation allowing citizens to seek redress against state actions in state court.

A person cannot sue a *state* government by invoking *federal* law, unless Congress specifically provided for an exception to sovereign immunity. State *officials*, however, can be held liable under federal law, 42 U.S.C. Sec. 1983: "Every person who, under color of any statute, ordinance, regulation, custom, or usage, of any State or Territory, subjects or causes to be subjected, any citizen of the United States or other persons within the jurisdiction thereof to the deprivation of any rights, privileges, or immunities secured by the Constitution and laws, shall be liable to the party injured in any action at law, suit in equity, or other proper proceeding for redress." Public officials may also be subject to an action in equity seeking an injunction to prevent them from acting **ultra vires** (beyond their power); or a tort action may ask for damages as a result of injury for behavior that was *ultra vires*.

The application of the Eleventh Amendment is still unclear. In 1989, for example, the Court held that while municipal (and county) governments are not protected by the Eleventh Amendment, states are immune from lawsuits growing out of constitutional violations committed by state agencies or their officials even when those lawsuits were brought in *state* courts (*Will v. Michigan*). During the same session, however, the Court ruled that Congress had the authority to authorize persons to sue their states in federal court to recover damages for cleaning up toxic waste for which the state was allegedly responsible (*Pennsylvania v. Union Gas*). In 1999, in three cases, all decided 5–4, the Court expanded the reach of the Eleventh Amendment when it ruled that states are immune from suits by state employees for violations of federal labor law (*Alden v. Maine*); by patent owners for infringement of their patents by state government (*Florida v. College Saving Bank*); and by people bringing unfair-competition suits over states' activities in the marketplace (Greenhouse 1999).[3] In 2002, the Court ruled 5–4 that sovereign immunity bars private citizens from suing a state before a federal regulatory agency—the Maritime Commission—for injuries resulting from a violation of federal law (*Federal Maritime Commission v. South Carolina Ports Authority*).

Slavery

The Constitution makes no direct mention of slavery, but as the result of a compromise to gain support of Southern states, the document clearly recognizes that there could be *property in people*: Article I, Section 2, refers to "free persons" and "three fifths of all other persons," and Article IV, Section 2, refers to the escape of a "person held to service or labour," a clause essential for gaining Southern support for the ratification of the Constitution. In the years preceding the Civil War, issues of states' rights and slavery were paramount. In 1857, for the first time since *Marbury v. Madison*, the Court exercised the power of judicial review over a federal statute: the case of *Scott v. Sandford*.

The case involved the status of a black man, Dred Scott, who had filed a suit for his freedom in a Missouri court in 1846. As a slave, Scott had been taken to a frontier US Army post where slavery was forbidden (Illinois) and later to territory in which the Missouri Compromise banned slavery (Minnesota). He was subsequently taken back to Missouri, a slave state, where his master died. Scott, claiming that his sojourn on free soil released him from slavery, brought suit, and in 1850 a state trial court declared him free. The widow of Scott's master appealed, and the state's highest court ruled that, free on free soil or not, when Scott returned to Missouri he became a slave again. In an effort to make this a test case, Scott's lawyers arranged to have the widow pass title to her brother, John F. Sanford (misspelled in the records) of New York. This provided for the **diversity of citizenship**—Missouri and New York—necessary for bringing a federal appeal. Claiming Missouri citizenship, Scott sued for his freedom in St. Louis.

In 1854, the Circuit Court of Appeals ruled that Scott could not be a citizen because he was a Negro. The case was certified to the Supreme Court that same year. Abolitionist feelings were running quite high; that year Congress passed the Kansas-Nebraska Act (which repealed the Missouri Compromise),[4] opening up areas of the

---

[3] It should be noted that while the Eleventh Amendment bars suits for damages, it does not bar equity lawsuits: for example, an injunction against a state official to enjoin the official from taking an action(s) that would violate the plaintiff's rights under the Constitution or federal law (Emanuel 2014).

[4] The Missouri Compromise involved statutes passed by Congress in 1820 and 1821 to deal with the issue of extending slavery. Under the compromise, Maine was admitted as a free state and Missouri as a slave state, and slavery was banned in much of the Louisiana Purchase. By the time of the *Scott* case, Congress had already repealed the compromise (Hall 1989).

West to slavery, and fighting broke out in what became known as "Bloody Kansas." In 1856, the Supreme Court heard the case of *Scott v. Sandford*, and early the following year a majority of the justices, each of whom rendered a separate opinion, determined that Scott would remain a slave. Although a state could confer citizenship on a Negro, this would not affect his status in another state, nor would it give rise to a claim of constitutional protections even within the granting state.

While the case before the Court did not require consideration of the wider issue of slavery, Chief Justice Roger Taney, a Marylander from a wealthy slave-owning family, appointed by President Andrew Jackson, argued that according to the original intent of the framer's Constitution, members of the black race were "altogether unfit to associate with the white race either in social or political relations; and so far inferior, that they had no rights which the white man was bound to respect."[5] "The right of slavery," he declared, "is distinctly and expressly affirmed in the Constitution." Slaves or free, blacks could never be citizens. According to Taney, the Declaration of Independence's phrase "all men are created equal," was not intended to include blacks, despite the fact that in 1776, in five of the original states, African Americans had full citizen voting rights. During his lifetime, Virginian Thomas Jefferson, the Declaration's primary author, owned hundreds of slaves (Wiencek 2012).

Justice Peter Vivian Daniel, a Virginian, added that slaves were *"property,* in the strictest sense of the term." The Court would not invoke *natural law*: when natural rights (liberty) conflicted with property rights (slaves), property rights were supreme. Furthermore, the Court ruled, the Missouri Compromise was unconstitutional; Congress had no right to limit the expansion of slavery. Rather than minimizing the role of judges and limiting its decision only to those issues necessary for resolving the case—a concept known as *judicial restraint*—the Court decided *every* issue raised by the case (Sunstein 2000a). The scene was set for the most devastating war in American history.

Reconstruction and the Expansion of Federal Authority

Prior to the Civil War, the Supreme Court "had been perennially haunted by the danger that centrifugal forces would tear the nation apart, and their jurisprudence had

---

Scott v. Sandford (1857)

"A . . . Negro of the African race was regarded by them [English colonists] as an article of property, and held, and bought and sold as such, in every one of the thirteen Colonies which united in the Declaration of Independence, and afterward formed the Constitution of the United States. . . . Therefore, it is the judgment of this court, that it appears by the record before us that the plaintiff in error is not a citizen of Missouri, in the sense used in the Constitution."

---

[5] Chief Justice Roger Taney (1836–1864) tolerated dissenting and concurring separate opinions that, in slavery cases, gave rise to extreme positions, "which encouraged others on the Court to write their own extreme concurrences or dissents and, in turn, contributed to a widening spiral of polarization" (Wiecek 1988: 73).

been shaped by that terrible threat always in mind" (McClosky 2010: 67). Union victory changed the atmosphere in which the Court operated.

In the postwar era, African Americans found themselves caught between two differing interpretations of emancipation: "Northerners assumed that once slavery was abolished the ex-slaves immediately and automatically ascended to all the rights and privileges and responsibilities of full citizenship, impeded by some racially based disabilities, to be sure, but nevertheless in possession of all civil rights whites enjoyed" (Wiecek 1988: 93). But Southerners knew better—to them emancipation simply freed blacks from the authority of a master. Following the Civil War, Southern states enacted **Black Codes**, denying to blacks many basic rights secured to whites: freedom to move, to contract, to own property, to sue in courts, to assemble, to bear arms, and to be witnesses against whites (Curtis 1986; Wolfe 1986).

Blacks received no sympathy from President Andrew Johnson of Tennessee, a supporter of states' rights, but the Republican-controlled Congress reacted with passage of the Civil Rights Act of 1866 and the Fourteenth Amendment, ratified in 1868. It reads in part: "No State shall make or enforce any law which shall abridge the privileges or immunities of citizens of the United States; nor shall any State deprive any person of life, liberty, or property, without due process of law; nor deny to any person within its jurisdiction the equal protection of the laws." But Republicans had a particularly partisan concern. Instead of being counted as "three-fifths" for purposes of representation, black males in the South now constituted full persons who could strengthen the Democratic Party in Congress and the Electoral College, while that same party was denying blacks the right to vote (Berger 1977). Instead of granting suffrage as part of the privileges of citizenship, the Fourteenth Amendment reduced representation in proportion to the number of males over 21 who's right to vote was in any way abridged. This also affected Northern states that denied blacks suffrage, but there were not enough blacks in those states to matter. "As a matter of law and as a matter of political objectives, most contemporaries distinguished between civil rights and voting rights" (Kaczorowski 1987: 49). In 1870, the Fifteenth Amendment was passed to prohibit the denial of suffrage based on race, and the Civil Rights Law of 1871 provided federal courts with jurisdiction in equity to remedy state encroachments on individual civil rights.

While Congress sought to protect and expand some of the rights of African Americans in the South, Southern officials were aided by the Supreme Court in efforts to deprive them of these same rights. The Court aided Southern Democrats by supporting an antebellum view of federalism based on *states' rights* and **dual federalism**—"that state and nation were rival sovereignties that operated beyond the complete

Civil Rights Act of 1866

"All persons born in the United States ... are hereby declared to be citizens of the United States; and such citizens, of every race and color ... shall have the same right ... to full and equal benefit of all laws and proceedings for the security of person and property, as is enjoyed by white citizens, and shall be subject to like punishment, pains, and penalties, and to none other."

grasp of each other," with the "no-man's land" between them patrolled by an impartial Supreme Court (Hall 1989: 18). Thus, states continued to enjoy those aspects of sovereignty that had not been explicitly conveyed to the federal government by the Constitution, and states were the equal of the national government in the federal system, each with an independent structure and power to exercise sovereignty. According to this view, there are two sets of rights and privileges, state and federal, and only the latter could be secured by federal action (*Slaughter-House Cases* [1873]). The Supreme Court thereby left the protection of the rights of African Americans to legislatures and courts that were quickly becoming filled with ex-Confederates, ex-successionists, and racists. "In the late nineteenth century, the Court devised several doctrines and attitudes that resulted in a further erosion of the constitutional status of black people. This erosion occurred especially in three areas: voting, jury service, and public accommodations" (Wiecek 1988: 101). To provide African Americans with equal access to public accommodations, Congress passed the Civil Rights Act of 1875, which was ruled unconstitutional in the *Civil Rights Cases* of 1883. Despite its infamous past, the *Civil Rights Cases* would be cited by the Supreme Court majority in 2000 as a precedent for overturning the federal Violence against Women Act (*United States v. Morrison*).

The Reconstruction era ended with the presidential election of 1876, when the last of the Radical Republican regimes in the Old Confederacy were ousted along with the hopes of black Americans in the South (Orth 1987). By 1900, the Fourteenth Amendment "had virtually ceased to shield blacks against discriminatory action" (Gerber 1981: 144).

Business, Unions, and Civil Liberties

It is of historical importance to note that the Bill of Rights (the first ten amendments to the Constitution) was intended to apply only to the federal government (although many states had similar clauses in their constitutions, none were as extensive as those of the Constitution).

From the decision in *Barron v. Baltimore* (1833) until the ratification of the Fourteenth Amendment (1868), the Supreme Court held that none of the rights in the Bill of Rights limited the states, and there is continuing controversy over whether or not the Fourteenth Amendment was meant to apply the Bill of Rights to the states (see, for example, Berger 1977; Abraham and Perry 2003). From 1868 to 1925 the Court "found very few of these liberties protected from state action. Those liberties the states were free to flout (so far as federal limitations were concerned) seemed to include free speech, press, and religion; the right to jury trial; freedom from self-incrimination, from infliction of cruel and unusual punishment, and more. State constitutions, with

Barron v. Baltimore (1833)

"These Amendments [Bill of Rights] contain no expression indicating an intention to apply them to the state governments. This court cannot so apply them."

their own bills of rights, were available to protect the individual, but too often proved to be paper barriers" (Curtis 1986: 1). The *Slaughter-House Cases* exemplified this.

Like many phrases in the Constitution, the wording of the Fourteenth Amendment allows for a variety of interpretations, and what is meant by "privileges or immunities of citizens of the United States" has been subject to vigorous debate. In a case alleging the unconstitutional nature of the granting of a slaughter-house monopoly by the Reconstructionist government of Louisiana, in 1873 the Supreme Court ruled:

> Beyond the very few express limitations which the Federal Constitution imposed upon the states—such, for instance, as the prohibition against ex post facto laws [punishment for an action that was not prohibited when the behavior occurred] bills of attainder [legislative act that singled out one or more persons and imposed punishment on them, without benefit of trial], and laws impairing the obligation of contracts . . . and a few other restrictions, the entire domain of the privileges and immunities of citizens of the states . . . lay within the constitutional and legislative power of the states.

Slowly, and over a long period of time, the Court began to apply these rights to the states. Ironically, they served to protect conservative business interests against legislative enactments designed to improve the conditions of workers. In an era swimming with legislative reforms, the judiciary remained a bastion of conservatives from the prosperous stratum of society. And it was to them that the owners of property turned for aid and protection. For these wealthy businessmen, the Fourteenth Amendment would prove to be a form of deliverance: "nor shall any State deprive any person of life, liberty, or property without due process of law." "Due process of law after the Civil War had two meanings—one procedural, the other substantive. The second stirred controversy. The phrase *substantive due process* meant that there existed an irreducible sum of rights that vested in the individual and could not be unreasonably or arbitrarily interfered with; this meant there were substantive limits on what legislatures could do" (Hall 1989: 26).

The Court decided it had the power to address the reasonableness of legislative interference with these rights, to determine if the rather vague doctrine of *substantive due process* had been improperly abridged—a judgment call with important policy implications.

> The Fourteenth Amendment had been adopted after the Civil War to assure the rights of the liberated slaves. But in a series of decisions from the Seventies on, the courts spelled out the doctrine that *any person* might also mean any corporate body, company, or association; and *property* might mean business or the profits of business. The courts, by interpreting the Fourteenth Amendment this way, opened the door to a long line of attacks on state laws that governed wages, hours, safety provisions, and the like—because such laws increased the cost of doing business and thus ate into the employer's "property." (Todd 1968: 9)

The Supreme Court determined that a business entity has
all of the due process rights granted to persons.
Thus, for purposes of law, a corporation is a person.

The "corporation as person" will arise later in a discussion of the Supreme Court's ruling in the 2009 landmark case known as *Citizens United*.

"Substantive due process became the Court's single most important doctrinal base for exercising the power of judicial review" (Hall 1989: 27). The Court's narrow construction of the Fourteenth Amendment when the case involved the civil rights of African Americans must be contrasted with the Court's extension of the Fourteenth Amendment to protect corporate America (Schwartz 1993). A "constitutional amendment designed to protect the rights of liberated Negro slaves, became an instrument for the exploitation of industrial wage slaves" (Todd 1968: 9). Justice Stephen J. Field who promoted the concept of "substantive due process," served on the Supreme Court from 1863 to 1897 during which time he voted against protecting the rights African and Chinese Americans. (He was the brother of David D. Field, author of the "Field Code" discussed in Chapter 1. Another brother, millionaire Cyrus Field, is responsible for the laying of the first Atlantic cable.)

Congress enacted legislation expanding the power of the federal judiciary with respect to federal laws in general and civil rights in particular. However, despite Court rulings under Marshall, during Reconstruction the federal courts refused to sustain an action against a state official administering an unconstitutional law, on the grounds that the Eleventh Amendment prohibited such suits. "In a break with tradition, the Court held that it was without jurisdiction over a wide variety of suits against states" (Orth 1987: 58). Between 1875 and 1885, state governments, particularly in the South, used this shield and passed unconstitutional legislation to nullify debt obligations, "which profoundly disturbed the conservative elements of the community" (Warren 1966: 942). The Supreme Court, conservatives argued, should be able to compel a state to pay its debts.

This wide interpretation of the Eleventh Amendment would prove disastrous to the credit ratings of Southern states, many of which repudiated debts during the Reconstruction era. Bondholders were unable to sue in state courts, and their claims were barred in federal court. "It is one of the neglected ironies of history that federal judges firmly committed to the protection of property countenanced the repudiation of millions of dollars' worth of Southern bonds. Still more ironic, Southern courtroom victories were won by arguing the cause of state sovereignty within a generation of the military defeat of that principle in the Civil War" (Orth 1987: 8–9). While the rest of the country was undergoing industrialization and urbanization, the South was unable to finance industry by borrowing and reverted to an antebellum cash-crop economy.

As state governments fell under the sway of Populists and (later) Progressives who favored farmers and workers over banking and business interests, the Supreme Court reacted. In 1885, in *Poindexter v. Greenhow*, the Court "made a clear distinction between a suit against a State or a State official to compel it or him to perform an obligation of the State, and a suit against a State official to recover damages for an act performed in carrying out an unconstitutional State law." The Court, as it had under Marshall, ruled "no official could claim an exemption from personal responsibility for acts committed under such an invalid law" (Warren 1966: 943). In an extension of *Poindexter*, the Court ruled in 1908 (*Ex parte Young*) that the Eleventh Amendment does not bar a suit against a state official where a violation of constitutional rights is alleged and that the sovereign immunity enjoyed by state officials is nullified when, under

color of law, they violate civil rights. When a state officer acts in violation of the Constitution, the official thereby loses "official capacity," making him or her, and not the state, liable for the official's actions. Since the state is not a defendant, the claim can be heard in federal court. These precedents have provided the basis for contemporary federal equity suits against public officials, operating prisons in a manner that violates the Eighth Amendment, for example.

> *Sovereign immunity enjoyed by state officials is nullified*
> *when, under "color of law," they violate civil rights.*

The increase in commerce and industry following the Civil War, and fears of state-court parochialism ("hometown decisions"), lent support to increasing the role of the federal judiciary at the expense of state courts. During the immediate postwar years there were important cases concerning currency laws and disputes between the states and the railroads. In what became a trend, the Court ruled in favor of business and against organized labor. There are observers who argue the contemporary Supreme Court is repeating this pattern (Liptak 2010a; Rosen 2008).

English common law, the "Tudor Industrial Code," considered any combination of workers to improve wages or conditions of employment as a criminal conspiracy, and this usage entered American law as a prohibition against any restraint of trade by workers acting in concert (Woodiwiss 1990). During the nineteenth century, until the time of the Civil War, the criminal conspiracy doctrine was used against labor organizations. This approach was subsequently replaced by the use of equity in the form of an injunction restraining the civil, rather than the criminal, aspects of organized labor (Blumrosen 1962). Injunctions deprived workers of their First, Sixth, and Eighth Amendment protections. Wiecek explains how the process worked: "A United States attorney hostile to unions and seeking to break a strike would find a sympathetic federal judge and persuade him to issue an injunction, often in an ex parte [only the plaintiff present] hearing. The injunction would restrain not only violence and concerted refusal to work, but also rights of speech, press, and assembly" (1988: 122). A failure to abide by the injunction would result in the union members being summarily imprisoned for contempt. This equity procedure permitted the plaintiff to avoid a trial by jury whose members might prove sympathetic to the strikers.

"Nineteenth and early-twentieth-century lawyers," Archibald Cox points out, "lived almost entirely in the world of business, finance, and property. It is unlikely that many of them could as judges wholly slough off the premises of their earlier years of private practice, whatever their effort to achieve detachment" (1987: 135). "The professional lives of the bar elite increasingly isolated them from other classes to the extent that they were able to create unreal images of the dangerous tendencies lurking outside their select social circle" (Hobson 1986: 68). Supreme Court Justice Stephen Breyer (2005: 10) notes that the nineteenth and early twentieth centuries were a period "during which the Court overly emphasized the Constitution's protection of private property." Thus, in 1909, when the Populist government of Kansas enacted a law prohibiting "yellow dog" contracts that required a prospective employee to agree to not

> **Taking Sides**
>
> "A Court committed by its tradition to the cause of property rights, composed of judges who were inevitably drawn largely from the ranks of the 'haves' and who were of course by definition lawyers and thus imbued with the conservative bias that has always characterized the American legal fraternity—such a Court was almost certain to throw its weight against the regulatory movement and on the side of the business community" (McClosky 2010: 69).

join a labor union, the Supreme Court found the legislation unconstitutional because the worker was not coerced—he could forgo employment (*Coppage v. Kansas* [1914]).

In the decades following the Civil War, when the powerless attempted to make the Constitution and the law work for them,

> they found the constitutional high ground already occupied by powerful business interests, which were supported by the middle class and both political parties and backed by the military authority of the state. Buttressing the conservative legal structure was the Supreme Court under Chief Justices Morrison Waite [1874–1888] and Melville Fuller [1888–1910], which moved boldly to make the Fourteenth Amendment serve business but refused to make it work for the black Americans for whom it was intended. Business consolidated with the blessings of the law; labor's attempt to organize and bargain was opposed by an impressive array of legal stratagems. (Newmyer 1987: 814)

The Supreme Court transformed judicial review into a defense not so much of the Constitution but of a particular version of natural law: that is, natural rights, particularly property rights. With support from the legal profession, the Court "adopted a particular understanding of the property rights guaranteed by natural law, that of '*laissez-faire*' **capitalism**. On the basis of that political philosophy, it struck down many attempts to regulate economic affairs in the period from 1890 to 1937" (Wolfe 1986: 4; emphasis added). The Supreme Court used the Fourteenth Amendment to create a national citizenship, "fitted it out with 'privileges and immunities,' and placed this heritage from times of old beyond the power of the state government." According to the Court, "these privileges and immunities are nothing other than the natural rights of man" (Hamilton 1999: 7). From 1898 to 1937, the Court handed down 401 rulings invalidating state legislation; more than half relied on the Fourteenth Amendment. As Charles Hoffer points out: "The Supreme Court's decisions in labor, taxation, hours and safety regulation, and a host of other cases demonstrated antipathy to the claims of workers, reformers, and the local governments they had captured. Powerful minds on the bench made very creative use of law to defend corporate accumulation of wealth and power" (1990: 159). "It furnished the legal tools to further the period's galloping industrialism and ensure that public power would give free play to the unrestrained capitalism of the era" (Schwartz 1993: 174).

Organized labor sought relief from Congress, but the Supreme Court (*Adair v. United States* [1908]) declared that Congress had no power with respect to union activities. It was not until 1932 and the Great Depression that Congress stripped the federal courts of their power to issue injunctions in labor disputes (Norris-La Guardia Act). In

NLRB v. Jones and Laughlin Steel Corporation (1937)

"Although activities may be intrastate in character when separately considered, if they have such a close and substantial relation to interstate commerce that their control is essential or appropriate to protect that commerce from burdens and obstructions, Congress cannot be denied the power to exercise that control."

1935, the Wagner (National Labor Relations) Act provided explicit protection to the rights of workers to organize and created an affirmative duty on the part of employers to engage in collective bargaining. In 1937, The Supreme Court, which offered a more expansive view of the commerce clause than heretofore, declared the statute constitutional (*National Labor Relations Board [NLRB] v. Jones and Laughlin Steel Corporation*). Article I, Section 8 of the Constitution provides the federal government with power "To regulate Commerce." Those taking a conservative "original intent" view argue that this applies only to economic interactions. But the term "commerce" is read by liberals to include a wider range of social interactions since that is how the term was used in 1787 (Amar 2005).

Congress voted to impose a federal income tax, but the Court ruled it unconstitutional (*Pollock v. Farmer's Loan and Trust Co.* [1895]); this brought about the Sixteenth Amendment, which became part of the Constitution in 1913. In 1883, the Court again upheld the sanctity of property rights when it ruled that Congress did not have the power to outlaw racial discrimination in private accommodations. An 1875 statute that granted blacks equal access with whites to inns, theaters, and public transportation was declared unconstitutional (*Civil Rights Cases* [1883]). As a result, eight states enacted legislation requiring railroads to maintain separate facilities for whites and blacks. In 1896, a seven-judge majority (*Plessy v. Ferguson*) ensured that the Fourteenth Amendment would be of little value to African Americans when it ruled that a Louisiana law that mandated "equal but separate accommodations for the white and colored races" on all railroad cars was reasonable. One justice did not vote, and John Marshall Harlan, ironically a former Kentucky slave owner, offered a powerful dissent: "Our Constitution is color blind, and neither knows nor tolerates classes among citizens."[6] Nevertheless, the doctrine of "separate but equal" received the blessing of the Supreme Court and remained the controlling decision in race relations until 1954. (For a full discussion of this case and its implications, see Lofgren 1987.) Thus, while it overemphasized protection of private property, the Court "wrongly underemphasized the basic objectives of the Civil War amendments" (Breyer 2005: 10).

During this period, state and federal judges routinely involved themselves in the formulation of public policy, substituting their policy choices for those of legislators. And these efforts were supported by bar association leaders allied with corporate America: "In the 1890s lawyers looked to the courts to act for the party of reason, order, and property and to restrain the parties of passion, ignorance, democracy, and socialism" (Hobson 1986: 34). In 1895 the Supreme Court refused to let stand a crimi-

---

[6] For a biography of this "judicial enigma," see Yarbrough (1995).

> **Sherman Antitrust Act (1890)**
>
> "Every person who shall monopolize, or attempt to monopolize, or combine or conspire with any person or persons to monopolize any part of the trade or commerce among the several States, or with foreign nations, shall be deemed guilty of a misdemeanor." The act does not define key terms such as "attempt to monopolize," leaving interpretation to the courts.

nal prosecution of the American Refining Company for Sherman Act antitrust law violations, despite the fact that this Sugar Trust controlled almost all of the sugar refining in the country (*United States v. E. C. Knight & Co.*). During that same term, the Court unanimously upheld the issuance of an injunction against the American Railway Union under the Sherman Act (*In Re Debs*). This, despite assurances by the statute's sponsor, Senator John Sherman (R-OH), that it would have no effect on workers (Eskridge 1994). However, "while the courts trimmed many regulatory efforts, they left in place major pieces of federal legislation and retained for the state legislatures important, if somewhat hollow, authority to deal with economic matters" (Hall 1989: 238). (For an examination of nineteenth-century state and local government regulation in the economy, public safety, and public health, see Novak 1996.)

A Policy-Making Judiciary

After the turn of the century, Supreme Court rulings began to support the efforts of government in dealing with the giant trusts, such as Rockefeller's Standard Oil (*Standard Oil of New Jersey v. United States* [1911]), whose restraint of trade was undermining capitalism, "and in this era the Court also handed down numerous decisions supporting state and federal efforts to protect workers" (Wiecek 1988: 126). The basic probusiness thrust of the Court continued, however, and in 1905 five of the nine justices of the Supreme Court, contrary to the Court's decision in the *Slaughter-House Cases*, held that an 1897 New York statute providing maximum hours for bakers was unconstitutional. The law violated the Fourteenth Amendment and interfered with the baker's right to "liberty of contract" because the baker might want to work more than 60 hours a week (*Lochner v. New York*, [1905]).[7] In his famous dissent, Justice Oliver Wendell Holmes, Jr., argued that "liberty of contract" is not found in the Constitution, but was a concept created by judges. He accused his colleagues of embracing the social Darwinist philosophy of Herbert Spencer. The Constitution, he wrote, "is not intended to embody a particular economic theory, whether of paternalism and the organic relation of the citizen to the State or of *laissez-faire*." While Holmes himself was a supporter of free market economics and expressed support for the social Darwinist view (Novick 1989; Alschuler 2000; *Buck v. Bell* [1927]), he favored a system that allowed labor and capital to compete without judicial intervention that typically favored business (Wall 1981; Cosgrove 1987). Southern conservatives criticized *Lochner* on the basis of "states' rights" (Wall 1981).

---

[7] In 1917, *Lochner* was overturned and the constitutionality of the ten-hour law upheld in *Bunting v. Oregon*. For a discussion of *Lochner*, see Kens (1990).

Social Darwinism

"Darwin's theory of natural selection supplied the conceptual ammunition for an ideology (later labeled as social Darwinism) which allayed the qualms of the rich about not helping the poor by telling them that the latter's sufferings were an inevitable price which could occur only through the struggle for existence ending in the survival of the fittest and the elimination of the unfit" (Andreski 1971: 26).

While Charles Darwin's (1809–1882) first book (*Origin of Species* 1859) was concerned exclusively with nonhuman organisms, his second (*Descent of Man* 1871) included humanity as being shaped by the forces of *natural selection*. According to Yale professor William Graham Sumner (1840–1910) "the truth is that the social order is fixed by laws of nature precisely analogous to those of the physical order" (1992: 172). Along with the English philosopher Herbert Spencer (1820–1903), Sumner applied Darwin to social evolution, a progressive phenomenon based on the "survival of the fittest" (Spencer 2002[1864]). This mitigates against activities on behalf of those who are "inferior," thereby providing a doctrine for persons who opposed governmental intervention on behalf of the downtrodden. "Whatever you do for any of the petted [poverty] classes wastes capital" (Sumner 1992: 222), while "the quality of a society is lowered morally and intellectually, by the artificial preservation of those who are least able to take care of themselves" (Spencer 1961[1871]: 313). For a discussion of social Darwinism, see Degler (1991).

In 1918 and again in 1922, the Court ruled that federal laws prohibiting child labor were unconstitutional—the right of young boys to work in coal mines and young girls in textile mills was upheld (*Hammer v. Dagenhart*; *Bailey v. Drexel Furniture Co.*). "If a ten-year-old child wants to work twelve hours a day in a textile mill, by what warrant is the legislature empowered to deprive the child's parents of their right to enter into such a contract on his behalf?" (Gilmore 1977: 63). In 1924, a frustrated Congress countered by attempting to amend the Constitution, a failed effort that was ratified by 28 states (Hall, Wiecek, and Finkelman 1996). It was not until 1941 that the Court reversed these child labor decisions (*United States v. Darby Lumber Co.*).

The Court's willingness to support *laissez-faire* economic rights, states Rogers Smith, stemmed from a variety of political, legal, and intellectual influences of the late nineteenth century. "Common law traditions, the legacy of Adam Smith's [1723–1790] economic liberalism, and the social Darwinism of Herbert Spencer [1820–1903] and William Graham Sumner [1840–1910] were combined into a legal ideology that justified opposition to the extensive reform legislation of the Populist and Progressive eras on higher law grounds." This involved "significant revisions in the natural law theories of the early liberals, but they appealed to those theories to justify their reading of the Constitution as intended to protect economic liberties" (1985: 75–76). Social Darwinism also played a role in legal decisions that supported segregation (Lofgren 1987), and the Court was criticized for using the Fourteenth Amendment to invalidate a state law protecting workers while restricting that same amendment so as to uphold a Kentucky statute requiring segregation even in private colleges (Wall 1981).

Kermit Hall argues that although the courts during these years are often portrayed as reactionary supporters of *laissez-faire*, their behavior was more complex than the stereotype suggests: "Appellate judges did invoke *laissez-faire* principles in a few celebrated cases, but in most instances state and federal courts 'moved consistently toward approval of a wide range of reform legislation' which although occasionally delayed in the courts, [was] not blocked there" (1989: 226; see also Wolfe 1986). And Joseph Wall (1981) denies that the *Lochner* Court was acting out of a philosophy of social Darwinism, as opposed to older concepts of *laissez-faire* and property rights (see also Schwartz 1993).

Political Dissent

While the Court continued to provide protection for economic liberties, it had no difficulty denying other forms of liberty. "Beginning in 1895 the Court set itself as a bulwark against disorder from any source," particularly unions and political radicals (Gerber 1981: 181). In a unanimous decision the Court upheld the conviction of Eugene V. Debs and members of the Socialist Party who, during World War I, campaigned against the draft, and it supported convictions in similar anti-free speech cases tried under the Sedition Act of 1918. In a decision written for one of these cases (*Schenck v. United States* [1919]), Justice Holmes elaborated on the limitations of free speech: "The most stringent protection of free speech would not protect a man falsely shouting fire in a theater and causing a panic." Thus, "the question in every [First Amendment] case is whether the words used are in such circumstances as to create a clear and present danger that they will bring about the substantive evils that Congress has a right to prevent." In this case, "when a nation is at war many things that might be said in time of peace are such a hindrance to its effort that their utterance will not be endured." As a result "little constitutional protection was left for wartime critics of government policies" (Cox 1987: 219). Later that year, Holmes began to alter his opinion on free speech in favor of more liberal interpretations (*Abrams v. United States* [1919]; also *Gitlow v. New York* [1925], applied First Amendment protection to the states via the Fourteenth Amendment).[8]

During the 1920s, the attack on political dissidents shifted from Socialists to Communists, and the Supreme Court upheld the convictions of members of the Communist Labor Party because their platform advocated syndicalism—a worker takeover and control of the means of production (Cox 1987). While the Court reined in on the rights of political "offenders," it began to expand the due process protections of criminal defendants. In cases that involved black sharecroppers who, in 1919, believing they had been cheated, rioted in Arkansas, the Court ruled for the defendants, declaring an obligation to ensure that criminal defendants received a fair trial in state courts. And in 1932, the Court decided the famous case of the "Scottsboro Boys." In 1931, nine black youths were arrested in Scottsboro, Alabama, and charged with raping two white girls on a freight train. They were found guilty in three trials that received international attention, and their convictions were twice reversed by the Supreme Court, which ruled that if a defendant in a capital case lacks an attorney and a fairly chosen jury, he or she cannot be convicted under law (*Powell v. Alabama* [1932]; see Goodman 1994 for a historical examination of this case). The issue of legal representation was

---

[8] For a discussion of the "clear and present danger" issue, see Kessler (1993).

raised again in 1942, when the Court ruled (*Betts v. Brody*) that the Sixth Amendment's right to an attorney only applied to the federal courts and that the Fourteenth Amendment did not require states to provide counsel to **indigents** except in special circumstances—when the defendant clearly is unable to defend him- or herself.

The Depression

In 1929, the stock market collapsed and the Great Depression quickly ensued. Millions of Americans were unemployed, farmers were forced off their land, and the economy was in ruins. In 1932, Franklin D. Roosevelt was elected president and enjoyed an overwhelmingly Democratic Congress. With New Deal inspiration, Congress enacted a series of laws designed to provide emergency relief for farmers, coal miners, and the unemployed. In a series of decisions denounced as "judicial activism" (an issue first discussed in Chapter 4), the Supreme Court, seven of whose members had been appointed by Republican presidents, ruled these statutes unconstitutional.

While Roosevelt was reelected by a landslide in 1936—Republican Alfred Landon won only Maine and Vermont—and Democrats took more than 75 percent of the seats in Congress, the Supreme Court remained a bulwark against legislative efforts to respond to the Depression. "Nine old men," appealing to the principles of natural law, were supporting the status quo. Between January 1935 and May 1936, 12 major pieces of New Deal legislation were ruled unconstitutional (Murphy and Pritchett 1986).[9]

Judicial/legal realists attacked the Court,[10] dismissing "notions of natural law limits on governmental policies and methods as 'transcendental nonsense'" (Smith 1985: 78). Generally, the realists argued for a more utilitarian version of judicial lawmaking, although there was some disagreement over limitations that could be placed on government activity by the judiciary. It took a dramatic confrontation between the president and the Court to produce agreement that the rights of property and contract were not absolute.

Since 1789, Congress had changed the number of justices several times: from nine to seven in 1807, nine in 1837, ten in 1864, and back to nine in 1867. On February 5, 1937, the president asked Congress for the power to appoint an additional justice whenever a sitting member of the Court reached the age of 70 and did not resign, with the upper limit being 15 members. In 1937, six justices were over 70. Roosevelt at first based his legislation on the need to help senior justices carry out their responsibilities. In a radio speech ("Fireside Chat") on March 9, 1937, the president took a different approach, criticizing the Court for obstructionism: "I want—as all Americans want— an independent judiciary as proposed by the framers of the Constitution. That means a Supreme Court that will enforce the Constitution as written—that will refuse to amend the Constitution by the arbitrary exercise of judicial power—amendment by judicial say-so. It does not mean a judiciary so independent that it can deny the existence of facts universally recognized." As discussed in Chapter 5, Roosevelt was attempting to impede judicial activism.

---

[9] New Deal lawyers were aware that much of their legislation was probably unconstitutional. They went ahead anyway, "based on a tacit understanding that in order to enhance recovery one had to operate, at least to some extent, outside the established boundaries of constitutional discourse" (Shamir 1995: 16; see also White 2000).

[10] Judicial and legal realism are discussed in Chapter 2.

The reaction to Roosevelt's "Court-packing" plan was overwhelmingly negative. Even congressional opponents of the Court did not want to tinker with tradition. As it turned out, there was no need to tinker with tradition. On April 12, 1937, as a result of a change in voting by one justice, Owen Roberts, the Court reversed a previous position and ruled an important piece of New Deal legislation (the Wagner Labor Relations Act) constitutional, and it backed away from a previous position on the constitutionality of minimum-wage legislation.[11] Shortly thereafter, a New Deal opponent announced that he was resigning from the Court, apparently in an attempt to influence the congressional vote (Rehnquist 1987). Later that same day, the Senate Judiciary Committee voted against the Court-packing legislation, and with Senate support waning, the bill was withdrawn by the administration. "In March 1937, with startling speed, the Court virtually adopted a whole new set of constitutional precedents" (Murphy and Pritchett 1986: 14). Without a change in the total number of justices, the president soon enjoyed a Supreme Court majority that upheld the constitutionality of his legislation. Within four years, he was able to name six new justices. (Jeff Shesol [2010] presents a detailed examination of the Court-packing effort.) "By the end of the 1930s, federal authority had reached a new height. New grounds for executive power had been sanctioned. Previously limiting concepts like liberty of contract, economic due process, and strict commerce and taxing limitations had been rejected. The Court endorsed government regulation of the economy and approved changes in federal-state relations that increased government power and extended it into a variety of new areas" (Murphy and Pritchett 1986: 15).

In 1939, Roosevelt's Senate opponents saw an opportunity to strike back: Felix Frankfurter, the president's choice to succeed retiring justice Louis Brandeis, was required to appear in person at his confirmation hearings—the first time this was ever done. Frankfurter, a professor at Harvard Law School and presidential advisor, established what has now become routine for Court nominees: He refused to discuss how he might decide specific matters that might come before the Court (Zobel 1991). Frankfurter served until his retirement in 1962 and, despite his pre-appointment political liberalism, came to support judicial restraint: In his view, when exercising the power of judicial review, Supreme Court justices act as legislators and, as unelected officials, should therefore act with restraint (Wolfe 1986). This view enabled New Deal legislation to remain largely intact.

In the years leading up to America's entry into Second World War, Democratic leaders were unwilling to advance the cause of black Americans for fear of alienating the Southern wing of the party. The Supreme Court, however, handed down a series of rulings in favor of African Americans, particularly in the area of education (Murphy and Pritchett 1986).

America at War

As war raged in Europe and US involvement was debated (it wasn't until the Japanese attacked the US naval base at Pearl Harbor in 1941 that the United States decided to

---

[11] In *West Coast Hotel v. Parrish* (1937) the Court upheld a Washington State minimum wage law for women and, "in doing so, announced their intention to disengage from further scrutiny of economic regulatory legislation on substantive due process grounds" (Hall 1989: 29).

enter the war), the Supreme Court ruled 8–1 that public school students (Jehovah's Witnesses) who refused to salute the flag or participate in the pledge of allegiance (which they considered a violation of the Second Commandment) could be expelled (*Minersville School District v. Gobitis* [1940]). In the wake of this decision, Witnesses were subjected to brutal mob attacks and police harassment. In the midst of the Second World War, the Court repudiated the *Gobitis* decision (*West Virginia Board of Education v. Barnette* [1943]) with a telling comment: "If there is any fixed star in our constitutional constellation, it is that no official, high or petty, can prescribe what shall be orthodox in politics, nationalism, or religion, or other matters of opinion or force citizens to confess by word or act their faith therein." (In 1989, in a 5–4 decision [*Texas v. Johnson*] that cut across the Court's usual ideological lines, Justice William J. Brennan, Jr., cited *Barnette* in ruling that burning the American flag as part of a protest demonstration was protected by the First Amendment.)

In 1944, in a 6–3 decision, the Court upheld a relocation order for Americans of Japanese ancestry (*Korematsu v. United States* [1944]), although no similar action had been taken against German Americans or Italian Americans. In his biting dissent, Justice Robert Jackson noted that being in a locality "was made a crime only if his parents were of Japanese birth. Had Korematsu been one of four—the others being, say, a German alien enemy, and Italian alien enemy, and a citizen of American-born ancestors, convicted of treason but out on parole—only Korematsu's presence would have violated the order."[12]

In 1951, the United Steel Workers Union demanded a raise, which the steel companies were unwilling to grant because they had been prohibited from raising prices by the Office of Price Stabilization; it was the era of the Korean War and there was fear of inflation. A strike that would impact on the war effort was set for April 9, 1952, and President Harry S. Truman reacted. By executive order, on April 8 he had the secretary of commerce seize the steel mills. In response to a legal action by the steel owners, a federal district court ruled against the government. The rules of the Supreme Court permit a losing litigant to petition the Supreme Court for an immediate hearing that is granted "only upon a showing that the case is of such imperative public importance as to justify deviation from normal appellate processes and to require immediate settle-

---

Youngstown Sheet and Tube Co. et al. v. Sawyer (1952)

"The President's power, if any, to issue the order must stem either from an act of Congress or from the Constitution itself. There is no statute that expressly authorizes the President to take possession of property as he did here.... In the framework of our Constitution, the President's power to see that the laws are faithfully executed refutes the idea that he is to be a lawmaker. The Constitution limits his functions in the lawmaking process to the recommending of laws he thinks wise and the vetoing of laws he thinks bad. And the Constitution is neither silent nor equivocal about who shall make laws which the President is to execute."

---

[12] For an analysis (and defense) of *Korematsu* by the Chief Justice of the United States, see Rehnquist (1999).

ment in this Court" (Rehnquist 1987: 55). This extraordinary case received such a grant—**certiorari before judgment**.[13] In a 6–3 decision (*Youngstown Sheet and Tube Co., et al. v. Sawyer* [1952]), the Court ruled that the president had acted beyond his constitutional authority, and Truman immediately ordered the Secretary of Commerce to return control of the mills to their owners. (For a detailed look at this case, see Westin 1990.)

In his very personal history of the Supreme Court, William H. Rehnquist argues that justices cannot isolate themselves from public opinion:

> We read newspapers and magazines, we watch news on television, we talk to our friends about current events. No judge worthy of his salt would ever cast his vote in a particular case because he thought the majority of the public wanted him to vote that way, but that is quite a different thing from saying that no judge is ever influenced by the great tides of public opinion that run in a country such as ours. Judges are influenced by them, and I think that such influence played an appreciable part in causing the Steel Seizure Case to be decided the way it was. (1987: 98)

Warren Court Decisions: 1953–1962

Political Dissent

In the post-World War II/Korean War era there was a renewed attack on political dissidents by the House Un-American Activities Committee (whose first chairman, Martin Dies, sought to rid the government of communists, radicals, fascists, crackpots, and internationalists) and by Senator Joseph McCarthy of Wisconsin. "Loyalty oaths" and being "soft on communism" were the buzz words. At first the Court came down on the side of the anticommunist orthodoxy, but by the late 1950s and early 1960s there was a shift toward protecting the rights of dissidents (Cox 1987), which became intertwined with the civil rights movement.

The Civil Rights Movement

Linda Carol Brown, eight years old, had to cross a railroad yard in Topeka, Kansas, to reach a bus that would take her to a school 21 blocks away. There was another school five blocks away from her home, but it admitted only white children. Her father appealed to the federal courts that, in accord with *stare decisis*, ruled against him; the doctrine of separate but equal had been upheld by the Supreme Court in *Plessy v. Ferguson*. When the case (and three others from Delaware, South Carolina, and Virginia) reached the Supreme Court, a unanimous decision resulted (*Brown v. Board of Education of Topeka, Kansas* [1954]). The Court found that equity required the abrogation of school segregation: "*Brown* was and remains the greatest 'equity' suit in our country's history" (Hoffer 1990: 4).

In equity cases, Hoffer points out, "the petitioner seeks fair play. The court probes deeply into the reality of social harms and tries to make the world whole. Defendants are given time and assistance to act in good faith, for the object is not to punish or

---

[13] During a period of less than one year, some 300 federal district court judges had to address a major constitutional issue with respect to the federal Sentencing Reform Act. In response, the Supreme Court granted certiorari before judgment in the case of *Mistretta v. United States* (1989).

deprive wrongdoers but to promote mutual justice" (1990: 180). Without rejecting the precedent of "separate but equal" established in *Plessy*, the Court, using controversial sociological and psychological evidence, held that "separate educational facilities are inherently unequal"[14] (see Patterson 2001). Instead of ordering immediate desegregation of all public schools, the Court used the phrase "with all deliberate speed," which served to encourage the South to respond with resistance and delay. In the years that followed, however, the Court summarily invalidated a host of other laws requiring segregation in public facilities and interstate commerce. The Warren Court "interpreted the Civil War amendments in light of their basic purposes thereby directly helping African Americans become full members of the nation's community of self-governing citizens" (Breyer 2005: 10). But, notes Cass Sunstein (2005: 248), "real desegregation began only after the Department of Justice, empowered by the Civil Rights Act of 1964, started to bring pressure on segregated schools."

The Supreme Court, as the least democratic of our branches of government, is able to render unpopular decisions to support the interests of white people against the "natural rights" of persons of color, or the rights of employers against the interests of children, or in support of business against the overwhelming wishes of Congress and the president. It can also insist that, no matter how strong the opposition, black persons have *all* of the rights of white persons. But the Court has no powers of enforcement. As Alexander Hamilton wrote (*Federalist* No. 78), the Supreme Court is *the least dangerous branch*, having neither the "power of the purse nor the sword." The judicial branch is totally dependent on the other branches, particularly the executive, to carry out its mandates. The president even appoints the US marshals who are responsible for enforcing orders of federal courts. This has been a problem on a number of occasions.

President Andrew Jackson refused to enforce an order of the Court designed to protect the federal treaty rights of the Cherokee Nation against their violation by the state of Georgia. Jackson's attitude toward the Court had been expressed in 1832, when he granted the Court "only such influence as the force of their reasoning may deserve." In a Maryland case (*Ex parte Merryman* [1861]), on the eve of the Civil War, a writ of *habeas corpus* issued by (proslavery) Chief Justice Taney was defied by military authorities acting under an executive order from President Lincoln. "The lack of any

---

Jefferson in Opposition

"The opinion which gives to the judges the right to decide what laws are constitutional and what not, not only for themselves in their own sphere of action but for the Legislature and Executive also in their spheres, would make the Judiciary a despotic branch."

Source: Thomas Jefferson to Abigail Adams, 1804 (University of Virginia Online Resources).

---

[14] It was obvious that segregation was designed to keep blacks in a subservient position, but the Court chose not to focus on this "political" reality (Posner 1995). Indeed, the average per student investment in Atlanta, which was typical across the South, was $570 for white children and $228 for black children (Menand 2001).

> ### *Brown v. Board of Education* (1954)
>
> "Does segregation of children in public schools solely on the basis of race, even though the physical facilities and other 'tangible' factors may be equal, deprive the children of the minority group of equal education opportunities? We believe that it does. . . . To separate from others of similar age and qualifications solely because of their race generates a feeling of inferiority as to their status in the community that may affect their hearts and minds in a way unlikely ever to be undone."

formal connection to the electorate and its rather demonstrable vulnerability before the president and Congress mean that the United States Supreme Court must depend to an extraordinary extent on the confidence, or at least the acquiescence, of the public" (Caldeira 1986: 1209).

In 1957, Governor Orval Faubus of Arkansas defied a federal district court order based on *Brown* and called out the National Guard to prevent nine black students from entering Little Rock High School. An angry mob of whites surrounded the school. After several weeks of indecision, the National Guard was put under federal command and President Eisenhower ordered the US Army's 101st ("Screaming Eagles") Airborne Division into Little Rock—however reluctantly, the decisions of the Supreme Court would be upheld. (Many of the briefs and case records for *Brown* can be found in Whitman 1993.)

The Due Process Revolution

During the 1960s, the Court handed down a series of landmark (and highly controversial) due process decisions. In 1914, the Court (in *Weeks v. United States*) had ruled that evidence obtained in violation of the Fourth Amendment's prohibition against illegal search and seizure was not admissible in federal criminal cases. This decision established the **exclusionary rule**, and in 1961 (*Mapp v. Ohio*), the Court, citing the Fourteenth Amendment, extended the rule to state criminal cases. The Court recognized that the exclusionary rule (discussed in Chapter 8) would sometimes have the effect, as Supreme Court Justice Benjamin Cardozo had noted generations earlier, of permitting the criminal to go free because the constable had blundered. However, the Court also recognized the potential for a greater evil: unbridled police powers. In the *Mapp* decision the justices said, "We can no longer permit it [the due process clause] to be revocable at the whim of any police officer who, in the name of law enforcement chooses to suspend its enjoyment." In 1963, overturning the 1942 precedent established in *Betts* (discussed earlier), the Court ruled in *Gideon v. Wainwright* that the states must provide counsel for all indigents in felony cases, and in 1966 the Court determined (*Miranda v. Arizona*) that prior to questioning, the police must warn a suspect of the right to remain silent. (Due process is discussed at length in Chapter 8.)

Other Warren Court Decisions

Even as the populations of many states shifted from rural to urban, state legislatures remained dominated by rural voters because of a practice known as *gerrymandering*:[15] legislative districts were drawn in such a fashion that less populated rural areas had more legislators than heavily populated urban areas. In 1962, 1963, and 1964, the Court initiated a legislative revolution in the United States when it determined that legislative and congressional districts had to have populations that are roughly equal: "one person, one vote" (*Baker v. Carr*; *Gray v. Sanders*; *Wesberry v. Sanders*; *Reynolds v. Sims*). Rural domination ceased and Democrats took control of many legislatures in populous states that had heretofore been Republican.

In 1962 and 1963, the Court found prescribed religious ceremonies in public schools unconstitutional (*Engle v. Vitale*; *Abington School District v. Schempp*). In 1964, the Court ruled that in order for public officials to collect damages for libel, they need to prove actual malice. This decision (*New York Times v. Sullivan*) provides important protection for reporters and others writing on public affairs. In 1965, a Connecticut statute prohibiting birth control devices or the providing of information on contraception was ruled unconstitutional. The Court admitted that the statute did not violate any specific guarantee contained in the Bill of Rights. It was, however, contrary to the *right of privacy*, which the Court ruled is *implied* in the Constitution, insofar as it involved an intolerable intrusion into the bedroom of married persons (*Griswold v. Connecticut*). *Griswold* provided the precedent for *Roe v. Wade* (1973), the case that struck down laws prohibiting abortion.[16]

The Post–Warren Court

The chief justice stepped down, and the era of the Warren Court was over. President Richard M. Nixon chose Warren Burger as chief justice. Nixon was overwhelmingly

---

The Right to Privacy and Abortion

Supporters of *Roe v. Wade* (1973) claim that the "right to privacy" is implicit in our constitutional tradition and, therefore, the logical implications of that principle regarding free choice are sufficiently clear to justify judicial support of abortion. Critics argue that the abortion issue is not properly subject to judicial authority because the Constitution does not explicitly endorse a "right to privacy" or "freedom of choice" or any other generalized principle that unambiguously provides support for abortion (Burt 1995).

---

[15] Elbridge Gerry (1744–1814) was a signer of the Declaration of Independence, a member of the Constitutional Convention, and vice president of the United States under James Madison. During his term as governor of Massachusetts, a law was enacted that redrew Senate boundaries in such a way as to ensure domination by Democratic Republicans. One district resembled a salamander, which gave rise to the term "gerrymander."

[16] In 1989, a bitterly divided Court ruled 5–4 to limit the application of *Roe*. In *Webster v. Reproductive Health Services* the Court upheld a Missouri law that prohibited the use of public funds, facilities, or state medical personnel to perform abortions except to save the life of the mother. The decision also upheld a requirement that doctors determine if a fetus is viable or capable of living outside of the womb: Missouri law prohibits abortions of a viable fetus.

reelected in 1972, and one year later there was a confrontation between the executive and judicial branches. The president claimed **executive privilege** in response to a **subpoena** *duces tecem*, an order to produce physical evidence, in this case the famous "White House tapes." In 1974, the Supreme Court, three of whose members and the chief justice had been appointed by Nixon, upheld the rulings of the lower courts requiring the president to submit to subpoenas issued by Watergate special prosecutors (*United States v. Nixon* [1974]). Later that year Nixon resigned.

Although judicial restraint—that judges should generally defer to legislators who are democratically accountable—was to be the cornerstone of the Burger Court, Stephen Wasby comments that the Court's overall record of invalidating federal and state legislative acts provides evidence of an *activist* Court, albeit in a more conservative direction (1993). In 1972, the Burger Court found that the then-current capital punishment laws violated the Eighth Amendment's guarantee against "cruel and unusual punishment"—"evolving standards of decency" can render once constitutional behavior unconstitutional (Tushnet 2000). The decision in *Furman v. Georgia* stopped executions until 1976, when the Court ruled that statutes imposing capital punishment, if drafted in a certain manner, were constitutional (*Gregg v. Georgia*). In 1973, the Court decided (*Roe v. Wade*) that state laws prohibiting abortion—several states, e.g., New York, already permitted abortion—unconstitutionally restricted personal liberty and the right to privacy guaranteed by the Fourteenth Amendment. (In 1986, however, the Court refused to extend the right of privacy to adults engaging in consensual homosexual acts when it ruled that laws banning such activities were fully within the police powers of the state, *Bowers v. Hardwick*). In 1978, by a vote of 5–4, with six separate opinions, the Court ruled that the quota system used by the University of California at Davis medical school, which reserved 16 positions for black, Chicano, and Asian applicants, had unlawfully denied admission to an otherwise qualified applicant, Allan Bakke (*University of California Regents v. Bakke*).

The Court also began trimming some of the decisions of the Warren Court that provided extensive due process rights to criminal suspects and prison inmates (see Chapter 8). Associate Justice William J. Brennan, Jr. (1986) recalled that in 1963 the Warren Court sustained 86 percent of the cases involving constitutional issues, whereas in 1983, the Burger Court sustained only 19 percent of the cases. This led Christopher Wolfe (1986: 297) to conclude: "Fidelity to the original intention of the Constitution and even the coherence of constitutional doctrine (whether or not closely tied to the Constitution) do not seem to be the guiding lights of the Burger Court." In 1986, the Chief Justice stepped down, and President Reagan appointed Associate Justice William Rehnquist, a legal scholar—first in his class at Stanford—guided by issues

***Bowers v. Hardwick* (1968)**

"[Sodomy was a criminal offense at common law and when the Fourteenth Amendment was ratified in 1868, sodomy was illegal in 32 of the 36 states]: Against this background, to claim that a right to engage in such conduct is 'deeply rooted in the Nation's history and tradition' or 'implicit in the concept of ordered liberty,' is, at best, facetious."

of strict constructionism, original intent, and judicial restraint (discussed in Chapter 5), to be the Court's 16th chief justice.

As a result of the appointment of Rehnquist and associate justices by Presidents Reagan and George H. W. Bush, the Court took a clear turn toward the right, but without upsetting any significant precedents established by previous Courts. (From 1991 to 1994, there was only one justice who had been appointed by a Democratic president.) For example, in 2000, the Court affirmed the *Miranda* decision by a vote of 7–2 (*Dickerson v. United States*).[17] The business community, which supported Republican efforts to move the Court in a more conservative direction, was disappointed: Instead of *probusiness*, the conservatism of the Rehnquist Court has been *progovernment* (Savage 1991). This was exemplified by a unanimous decision (*Whitman v. American Trucking Associations* [2001]) written by Justice Antonin Scalia in which the Court rejected arguments from industry lawyers attacking enforcement of the Clean Air Act by the Environmental Protection Agency.

With the election of Bill Clinton, appointments to the Supreme Court became decidedly more liberal, and for the first time in history, two women were serving as justices. Nevertheless, a conservative five-member majority had an impact on such areas as affirmative action. In *Adarand Construction v. Peña* (1995), the Court raised the legal standard required to invoke race-based criteria: "We hold today that all racial classifications imposed by whatever Federal, state, or local actor, must be analyzed by a reviewing court under strict scrutiny. In other words, such classifications are constitutional only if they are narrowly tailored measures that further **compelling government interests**" (emphasis added). In support of the chief justice's views of (dual?) federalism, the Court has modified the influence of federal courts and the power of Congress to expand federal authority. This was highlighted by several cases.

Although conservative jurisprudence stresses deference to the legislative branch, in 1995 the Supreme Court ruled (*United States v. Lopez*) that Congress exceeded its authority when it enacted a law—the Gun-Free School Zones Act—making it a *federal* crime to possess a firearm in proximity to a school. In his 1999 annual message on the judiciary, Chief Justice Rehnquist appealed to Congress to refrain from creating federal laws that are redundant with existing state laws. He reprimanded the lawmakers for transforming highly publicized crimes into federal law, reminding Congress that crime and law enforcement fall within the jurisdiction of the state governments.

The Twenty-First Century

Two decisions in 2000 continued the same theme: Congress exceeded its authority when it passed a law making federal statutes against age discrimination binding on state governments, an Eleventh Amendment issue (*Kimel v. Florida*), and in *United States v. Morrison* the Court ruled that Congress had overstepped its bounds by enacting a statute (Violence Against Women Act) permitting rape victims to sue their attackers in *federal* court. The trend continued in 2001, when the Court ruled 5–4 (*Board of Trustees of the University of Alabama v. Garrett*) that state employees cannot sue for

---

[17] The Court held that *Miranda* was a *constitutional* ruling and, therefore, Congress could not supersede *Miranda* by legislative enactment—only a constitutional amendment can undo a constitutional ruling.

damages for violations of the Americans with Disabilities Act: Congress does not have authority to permit such suits. In a historically familiar reframe, liberal critics accused the Court of disregarding judicial restraint in favor of (a conservative-oriented) political activism (Greenhouse 2001a). In 2006, however, the Court ruled 5–4 against states' rights/sovereignty when it found that states are not immune from private lawsuits brought under the federal bankruptcy law (*Central Virginia College v. Katz*).

The Court's most controversial opinion concerned the presidential contest of 2000, in which election results were so close in some Florida counties that the Florida Supreme Court allowed a manual recount in those counties. George Bush appealed the decision to the US Supreme Court. In *Bush v. Gore* (2000), the five-member majority overruled the Florida Supreme Court and refused to permit any further counting of disputed ballots, many, if not most, of which were from primarily African American election districts. The Court based its decision on the "equal protection" clause of the Fourteenth Amendment that, as noted earlier, was enacted to aid blacks in the post–Civil War South. Ironically, the use of the Fourteenth Amendment by the Warren Court in the 1960s had been criticized by political conservatives as an all-purpose tool for judicial activism (Dershowitz 2001; Posner 2001).

In the wake of 9/11, Congress passed the Patriot Act, and in 2004, there were decisions challenging parts of the act in which the executive branch argued for the indefinite detainment (without a hearing) of people suspected of being complicit in subversive acts against the United States. In *Rasul v. Bush* (2004) the Court held that United States courts have jurisdiction to consider challenges to the legality of the detention of foreign nationals captured abroad in connection with hostilities and incarcerated at Cuba's Guantanamo Bay. In *Hamdi v. Rumsfeld* (2004), the Court noted that although Congress authorized the detention of combatants in narrow circumstances, due process demands that a citizen held in the United States as an enemy combatant be given a meaningful opportunity to contest the factual basis for that detention before a neutral decision maker.

The following year, in a controversial 5–4 decision, the Court upheld the use of the government's power of **eminent domain** in support of a New London, Connecticut, plan to displace an old residential neighborhood with commercial enterprises (*Kelo v. City of New London* [2005]). In its decision, the Court made it clear that states could set different standards for property rights, and in response, state lawmakers throughout the country began introducing bills and constitutional amendments designed to limit the power of government to seize private property for commercial

---

Bush v. Gore (2000)

"None are more conscious of the vital limits on judicial authority than are the members of this Court, and none stand more in admiration of the Constitution's design to leave the selection of the President to the people, through their legislatures, and to the political sphere. When contending parties invoke the process of the courts, however, it becomes our unsought responsibility to resolve the federal and constitutional issues the judicial system has been forced to confront."

Legacy

"[William H. Rehnquist] helped lead a conservative revolution on the Supreme Court during 19 years as chief justice of the United States" (Greenhouse 2005a: 38).

use (Broder 2006). State legislatures have since passed new protections against eminent domain, and in 2006, the Ohio Supreme Court ruled that a Cincinnati suburb could not take private property for a redevelopment project (Urbina 2006).

By 2005, acrimony between the Republican-led Congress and the federal judiciary reached a fever pitch with leaders threatening to curb judicial power. Legislation to accomplish this passed the House but was stalled in the Senate. Hot button topics such as late-term abortion, gay marriage, "under God" in the pledge of allegiance, displaying the Ten Commandments on public property, prayer in public school, and eminent domain continue to embroil the Court in political and policy issues.

In 2005, Chief Justice Rehnquist, who had headed the Court for almost 20 years, died. During his tenure the Court provided an enhanced role for the states "by overturning dozens of federal laws that sought to project federal authority into what the Supreme Court viewed as the domain of the states" (Greenhouse 2005a: 38). He was replaced by John G. Roberts, Jr., a US Court of Appeals judge and former assistant **solicitor general** who had argued 39 cases before the Supreme Court—at 50, he was the youngest chief justice since John Marshall—who was confirmed by a Senate vote of 78–22. Shortly afterward, Associate Justice Sandra O'Connor announced her retirement, and President George W. Bush nominated White House counsel Harriet Miers whose primary qualifications appeared to be loyalty to the president and, as she was not a judge, and had no paper trial that could provoke criticism. While Roberts enjoyed wide support among political conservatives, Miers' lack of a public record caused widespread criticism, and she subsequently withdrew her nomination. In her place, the president nominated Samuel A. Alito, Jr., who was a graduate of Yale Law School and a US Court of Appeals judge for more than 15 years. Known for his conservative rulings, Judge Alito generated considerable opposition in the liberal community and almost unanimous opposition by Senate Democrats. Nevertheless, in 2006, he became the 110th justice by a confirmation vote of 58–42, the first time in history that every member of the Court was a former federal appeals judge. That year, in a 5–3 decision, with the chief justice abstaining (he had been involved with the case as an appellate court judge), the Court found that the driver for Osama bin Laden, who had been captured in Afghanistan and held at the Guantánamo Bay Naval Base detention center in Cuba, could not be tried by a military court because such action had not been authorized by Congress and also violated the Geneva Convention.

In 2008, a nonprofit corporation, Citizens United, wanted to run an unflattering documentary on Hillary Clinton—*Hillary: The Movie*—as a cable TV documentary during the 2008 presidential primary season. The broadcast was barred by the Federal Communications Corporation (FCC) based on a provision of the McCain-Feingold Act (Bipartisan Campaign Reform Act of 2002) prohibiting unions, corporations, and not-for-profit organizations from broadcasting electioneering communications that refer to a candidate within 60 days of a general election or 30 days of a primary election. Citizens United appealed and a three-judge federal district court panel upheld the FCC ruling. On appeal, instead of a narrowly focused decision about the application of a single provision of the McCain-Feingold Act, and despite a century of precedent, in a 5–4 decision (*Citizens United v. Federal Election Commission* [2010]), the Court lifted restrictions on corporate (and union) spending on candidate elections. The Court ruled that as a "person," a corporation's free speech is protected by the First Amendment (Toobin 2012). Adam Cohen (2007) and Geoffrey Stone (2012) point to this decision as an indication of the Court's activism, albeit in a politically conservative direction. Similarly, in 2008, the Supreme Court intervened in the contentious issue of gun control (*District of Columbia v. Heller* and *McDonald v. City of Chicago*), which in the view of Federal Appellate Judge J. Harvie Wilkinson, (2012: 58), an appointee of President Ronald Reagan, "disenfranchised democratic majorities across the nation" (Wilkinson's views on judicial activism are mentioned in Chapter 5). In fact, "if judicial activism is defined as the tendency to strike down laws, the court led by Chief Justice John G. Roberts, Jr. is less activist than any court in the last 60 years" (Liptak 2013b: SR 4).

Summary

- Under the Articles of Confederation there was no executive branch at the national level, a dilemma that resulted in a constitutional convention in 1787.

- Out of the Constitutional Convention emerged the cornerstone of American government—separation of powers.

- In a compromise over the issue of a federal judiciary, Article III of the Constitution established a Supreme Court and delegated power for establishing other federal courts to Congress.

- The essays of Alexander Hamilton, John Jay, and James Madison are known as *The Federalist Papers* and provide insight into the intent of the authors of the Constitution.

- *The Federalist Papers* note that the judicial branch has neither the power of the purse (Congress) nor the power of the sword (President).

- In a precedent-setting response, Chief Justice John Jay declined to provide advisory decisions, pointing out that each branch is responsible for acting as a check on the other and that such responsibility could not be fulfilled if the Court served as a presidential advisor.

- Chief Justice John Marshall converted a case involving a trivial issue into one of the most significant cases ever decided by the Supreme Court by asserting the power of judicial review.

- The Supremacy Clause (Article VI) obligates state courts to recognize the superiority of federal law.

- *Gibbons v. Ogden* provides the federal government with supreme authority over the regulation of interstate commerce.

- The issue of sovereign immunity and the Eleventh Amendment remain unclear.

- Sovereign immunity enjoyed by state officials is nullified when, under "color of law," they violate civil rights.

- The inflammatory language in *Scott v. Sandford* helped propel the country toward a civil war.

- The Fourteenth Amendment was enacted to protect former slaves in the South.

- The Court failed to protect blacks in the South by supporting states' rights and dual federalism.

- The Court interpreted the Fourteenth Amendment in a manner that protected business from state laws designed to protect workers.

- The Court determined that a business entity has all of the due process rights granted to a person.

- During the nineteenth century, until the time of the Civil War, the criminal conspiracy doctrine was used against labor organizations. This approach was subsequently replaced by the use of equity in the form of an injunction restraining the civil, rather than the criminal, aspects of organized labor.

- In 1932 Congress stripped the federal courts of their power to issue injunctions in labor disputes.

- In 1935, the Wagner (National Labor Relations) Act provided explicit protection to the rights of workers to organize and created an affirmative duty on the part of employers to engage in collective bargaining.

- In 1896, the Court held (*Plessy v. Ferguson*) a Louisiana law that mandated "equal but separate accommodations for the white and colored races" on all railroad cars was reasonable.

- In the first decades of the twentieth century, the Court continued to protect business against state efforts to improve working conditions of employees and children, while ruling in favor of state laws promoting segregation.

- In the first three decades of the twentieth century the Court rulings limited the free speech rights of political dissidents.

- During the Great Depression, Congress enacted a series of laws designed to provide emergency relief for farmers, coal miners, and the unemployed, which the Supreme Court ruled unconstitutional.

- President Franklin Roosevelt attacked the Court for its "activism" and responded with a "Court-packing plan" that failed to garner congressional support.

- In 1940, the Court upheld the expulsion of students who refused to participate in the pledge of allegiance, a decision that was repudiated by the Court in 1943.

- In 1952, President Harry Truman seized the country's steel mills to prevent a strike that could impact the (Korean) war effort. The president complied with a Court ruling that the seizure was unconstitutional.

- In 1954, the Court ruled that equity requires an end to school segregation and subsequently banned segregation in all public facilities and interstate commerce.

- Southern states reacted with "massive resistance," requiring the president to use federal marshals and troops to enforce court orders, the judicial branch having no "power of the purse or the sword."

- During the 1960s, the Court handed down a series of due process decisions involving the Fifth Amendment (*Miranda*) and the Fourth Amendment (*Mapp*) extending the exclusionary rule to the states.

- In the first half of the 1960s, Court decisions against the practice of gerrymandering changed the political landscape by establishing a "one man [or woman], one vote" requirement.

- In 1965, the Court found that the *right of privacy* is *implied* in the Constitution, setting a precedent for the *Roe v. Wade* decision affecting abortion.

- In 1974, the Court rejected President Nixon's claim of executive privilege in response to a congressional subpoena, leading to his resignation.

- In 2008, the Court continued its political activism by lifting restrictions on corporate spending on candidate elections: as a "person," a corporation's free speech is protected by the First Amendment

- That same year, the Court overturned local gun control laws on grounds they violated the Second Amendment.

KEY TERMS

Article III	dual federalism	solicitor general
Articles of Confederation	eminent domain	sovereign immunity
Black Codes	exclusionary rule	states' rights
certiorari before judgment	executive privilege	subpoena *duces tecem*
color of law	indigent	Supremacy Clause
compelling government interest	judicial comity	*ultra vires*
diversity of citizenship	*laissez-faire* capitalism	writ of mandamus

REVIEW QUESTIONS

1. Why was it necessary to replace the Articles of Confederation?
2. How does the Constitution provide for efficiency without tyranny?
3. What was the controversy over a federal judiciary?
4. What was the compromise that emerged from the controversy of a federal judiciary?
5. What are *The Federalist Papers*?
6. Why are *The Federalist Papers* important?
7. How did *The Federalist Papers* attempt to allay the fear of a too powerful federal judiciary?
8. Why did Chief Justice John Jay politely decline to provide advisory decisions?
9. Why is the case of *Marbury v. Madison* so important?
10. What is the Supremacy Clause?

11. What crucial issue was decided in the case of *Gibbons v. Ogden*?

12. What is sovereign immunity?

13. What are the limitations of sovereign immunity?

14. What does the Constitution say about slavery?

15. What was the significance of *Scott v. Sandford*?

16. What was the purpose of the Fourteenth Amendment?

17. How did the Court thwart this purpose?

18. How did Court decisions protect business interests?

19. What was the purpose of President Roosevelt's Court-packing plan?

20. How did the Court's position on students being required to recite the pledge of allegiance change?

21. What was the outcome of President Truman's seizure of the country's steel mills to prevent a strike that could impact the (Korean) war effort?

22. Why was it necessary for the president to use federal troops to enforce Court desegregation orders?

23. How did Court decisions against gerrymandering cause a legislative revolution?

24. How did the 1965 Court's finding that the *right of privacy* is *implied* in the Constitution affect the *Roe v. Wade* decision concerning abortion?

25. What action of the Court led to the resignation of President Nixon?

26. In 2008, what did the Court rule (*Citizen's United*) with respect to corporate spending on candidate elections?

INTERNET CONNECTIONS

American Constitution Society: http://www.acslaw.org
Avalon Project: http://avalon.law.yale.edu/default.asp
Constitution Project: http://www.constitutionproject.org
Legal History: http://jurist.law.pitt.edu/sg_hist.htm
Legal Information Institute (Cornell University): http://www.law.cornell.edu
Supreme Court (Chicago Kent College of Law: http://www.oyez.org
U.S. Supreme Court: http://www.supremecourt.gov

7

Judges, Prosecutors, and Criminal Defense Attorneys

At the center of our adversarial system of justice are the lawyers—judges, prosecutors, and attorneys who represent criminal and civil (noncriminal) defendants and plaintiffs. (Defense attorneys in civil cases are discussed in Chapter 10.) Judges, prosecutors, and attorneys share a common education—law school—and, given the nature of the practice of law in the United States, their roles can be interchangeable; that is, many judges were at one time prosecutors and/or defense attorneys. Private defense attorneys, particularly those in criminal practice, have often served as prosecutors or **public defenders**. The ranks of these key actors, particularly those who practice in state courts, usually do not include lawyers who graduate from the elite law schools. One reason is the salaries, which are not competitive with those of partners in national law firms. Another is the need for political connections of a type normally shunned by those practicing in large law firms. Furthermore, lawyers working for the government (e.g., judges or prosecutors) are quite limited in the type of additional remunerative work they may perform, with teaching and lecturing offering the least risk of a conflict of interest.

Judges

Reflective of our system of courts, there are two basic types of judges: the appellate judge who determines issues of law on appeal and the trial judge who, under our adversarial system of justice, is a referee responsible for enforcing rules that govern criminal and civil cases. When carrying out these responsibilities, the judge has total immunity from any legal action arising out of his or her decisions (*Mireles v. Waco* [1991]). The judge has no interest in the outcome of a case before him or her but must ensure that it has been conducted fairly—according to codes of procedure, applicable statutes, and case law. In a trial court when a jury is used, the judge determines issues of law and the jury determines issues of fact (the truthfulness and relevance of evidence). When there is no jury, the judge determines both issues of law and issues of fact. Because judges commonly come to the bench after years of litigation practice, it is vital that they can quickly change hats—make the transition from advocacy to neutrality. In contrast to judges in Continental Europe (civil-law countries) such as France and Germany, discussed in Chapter 1, judges in the United States receive no formal training before they assume their positions (although there is training available at state and national institutes). Their training is primarily "on the job."

Judges in the United States are generalists whose education and experience in nonlegal areas are typically quite limited. This led to the establishment of specialized courts—for such matters as patents and taxes—and agency tribunals for particular technocratic concerns, such as the environment and communications. Nevertheless, judges are frequently required to deal with scientific or technical issues for which they have little or no background, such as those of molecular biology, genetics, and computer technology. "To do their jobs well, modern judges must know the difference between DNA and RNA, and be able to evaluate the predictive value of a genetic test" (Blakeslee 1996: B7). And rapid changes in computer technology require judges to make determinations on matters they do not fully comprehend. They typically have "limited understanding of the economics and technology of innovation" (Posner 2013: 75). (No member of the Supreme Court in 2014 has an undergraduate or graduate degree in science or technology, or a background in statistics.) In response, some jurisdictions provide science and technology seminars to educate judges on matters they are likely to encounter in the courtroom.

A judge's behavior on the bench is subject to few controls, the most important being the possibility of a reversal of a case outcome by an appellate court—a blow to the professional standing of any trial judge. In states using some form of election, a judge can also suffer at the hands of the electorate. Trial judges actually preside over few trials—most criminal and civil cases are settled without a trial. The role of the judge when bringing about these settlements varies from jurisdiction to jurisdiction, but mediation and conciliation skills are often as important, if not more so, than trial skills for the average judge (discussed in Chapter 12). A judge's action in chambers, the judge's private office where he or she meets with parties to actions, may be more important than what he or she does in the courtroom. A trial judge also has courtroom administrative responsibilities and, in criminal courts, may issue search warrants, impose sentences on defendants, and conduct probation revocation hearings. How are persons with all the talents required of a judge selected for their positions?

Selecting Judges

The qualities generally voiced as necessary for a "good" judge (e.g., being fair minded, having personal integrity and judicial temperament) are so vague and devoid of objective measurement as to be irrelevant. Even judicial experience may be of questionable value—many outstanding justices of the Supreme Court never held a judicial office. Most important is the recognition of the judicial system as a rich source of political patronage. Accordingly, there are important political implications in any method used to select judges, of which there are four, with a number of variations in each: (1) appointment by a chief executive; (2) election; (3) merit system; and (4) selection by the legislature[1] (not discussed in this text). General jurisdiction trial court judges are

---

[1] In Virginia, for example, judges are elected by a joint vote of both houses of the General Assembly and are commissioned by the governor for a term of six years (district court), eight years (circuit courts and court of appeals), or 12 years (supreme court). The governor can make interim appointments when the General Assembly is in recess. There are also magistrates appointed by the chief judge of the circuit court for terms of four years.

selected through nonpartisan elections in about 18 states and through partisan elections in about 10 states; in 15 states, the governor selects them; and they are appointed by the state legislature in three states. Fewer than half the states select their appellate judges by gubernatorial appointment. Fourteen states use nonpartisan elections and eight use partisan elections (Rottman and Strickland 2006).

Many states use a mixed system, with different judges selected through different systems. In New York, for example, all judges are elected except those serving on the court of appeals (court of last resort), who are appointed by the governor for terms of 14 years, and some serving in courts of limited jurisdiction, such as the New York City Criminal Courts, who are appointed by the mayor. In Illinois, all judges are elected, but the judges of the circuit court (general jurisdiction) appoint associate judges, who enjoy the same authority as (but less salary than) their elected colleagues (and serve for only four years instead of six). The Constitution provides for the presidential nomination of Supreme Court justices but does not provide a method for selecting other federal judges.

Appointment by a Chief Executive

Appointment by a chief executive—a mayor, governor, or the president—is used in some states and is the method by which all federal judges are selected. In the federal system, all (constitutional) judges are appointed by the president for life terms (for legislative judges, see Chapter 4). Whenever there is a vacancy on a district (trial) court bench, the president (actually officials in the Department of Justice) consults the senior US senator from the state involved if he or she is a member of the president's party. Otherwise, there is consultation with the junior senator. If neither senator is of the same party as the president, consultation involves the senior member of the House of Representatives from that state who is a member of the president's party, or the chair of the president's political party in the particular state, or even the governor. The official(s) consulted is asked to submit a list of candidates to the Department of Justice. Each candidate fills out an extensive questionnaire that is used as the basis of a background investigation conducted by the Federal Bureau of Investigation.

At some point the final list of prospective candidates is reviewed by the Standing Committee on the Federal Judiciary of the American Bar Association (ABA). It was not until after the Second World War that the ABA became a major influence on the selection of federal judges. Almost immediately on its establishment, the ABA committee was invited by the chairman of the Senate Judiciary Committee to make recommendations on each nomination. The ebb and flow of ABA influence coincided with different administrations, reaching something of a crest in 1958. Under Dwight D. Eisenhower (1952–1960), the attorney general agreed to refer to the ABA committee, for an informal evaluation, the name of every potential candidate for a federal judgeship, followed by a formal submission of potential nominees for official evaluation and recommendation (Grossman 1965). This procedure has generally been followed by succeeding administrations.

The 15 members of the committee are chosen by the ABA president and serve for three years, an appointment that is considered to be quite prestigious within the legal community. For each judicial nomination, members of the committee conduct confidential interviews with dozens of lawyers and judges who are familiar with the candidate.

The first step is to submit a detailed questionnaire, often running 15 to 20 pages and covering

> some 30 points of inquiry. One of the questions asks the candidate's judgment and evaluation of the ten "most significant" cases at constitutional law the candidate has litigated. A candidate is interviewed at length by a Committee member, normally one from the candidate's own judicial circuit base. Through interviews with lay and professional individuals—including all pertinent federal judges in the candidate's area, top state judges, local law school deans, lawyers, and certain non-lawyers—the Committee member presumably becomes generally familiar with the candidate's qualifications and character, rendering a useful and reliable appraisal of his ability. (Abraham 1990: 63)

The committee votes, using a rating system: (1) exceptionally well qualified, (2) well qualified, (3) qualified, or (4) not qualified. A rating may also note that a majority of the committee found the candidate minimally qualified, while a minority found him or her unqualified; this rating is "qualified/unqualified." The committee chair receives the information and submits a report to the full committee and the attorney general, who must decide if he or she wishes the ABA to present a full report. The ABA committee considers how long the candidate has been a member of the bar (not fewer than 15 years); the amount of trial experience (particularly for a district court appointment); reputation among the bar; scholarship (particularly for a court of appeals position, for example, publication of law journal articles and quality of any appellate decisions drafted by the candidate); and a rather vague quality known as "judicial temperament." Although the nominee's ideology is not part of the evaluation process, as stated in its literature, the committee considers "extreme views" that "might bear on judicial temperament or integrity." The ABA committee's Supreme Court procedures are somewhat different, including the use of teams of law school professors, practicing lawyers, and former Court clerks who examine the candidate's writings.

The president is under no compulsion to accept an ABA rating, but it can carry a lot of weight with the news media and with US senators who must act on any judicial nomination. Very few candidates are publicly declared "unqualified" by the ABA, but such a rating can kill an appointment. Richard Nixon, until the last days of his presidency (1968–1974), would not nominate any person rated "not qualified" by the ABA committee. However, during his last full day in office, he nominated Thomas Meskil, governor of Connecticut, to the Court of Appeals, despite an ABA rating of "not qualified," and Meskil was confirmed by the Senate.

The importance of the ABA in the selection process has at various times come under attack from liberals and conservatives. Liberals were critical when the committee supported Nixon Supreme Court nominees who failed to receive Senate ratification. Conservatives reacted when, in 1987, the committee gave Reagan Supreme Court nominee Robert H. Bork (a distinguished, albeit "original intent" conservative, federal judge and former solicitor general) a split decision in favor of his confirmation, which helped deny him ultimate Senate approval. At the beginning of his term, President George H. W. Bush, for the first time since the administration of Dwight D. Eisenhower (1952–1960), refused to send prospective judicial nominees to the ABA for evaluation because of the ABA's handling of the Bork nomination. In testimony before the House Judiciary Committee, Attorney General Dick Thornburgh stated, "The [ABA] committee has extended its inquiry into areas which I believe are more properly left to the administration and the legislative branch. That is, into the ideological or political views of prospective nominees for the Federal bench" (Johnston 1989: 7).

In response, the ABA agreed to drop from its list of criteria references to political or ideological philosophy "except to the extent they may bear upon the other factors" such as temperament, integrity, or competence, and the administration agreed to resume submitting judicial candidates to the ABA for evaluation (Johnston 1989). Later that year, in the face of conservative opposition, Robert Fiske, a former US attorney in Manhattan, had to withdraw his candidacy for the number two position in the Department of Justice. Fiske had served as chairman of the ABA Standing Committee on the Federal Judiciary from 1984 to 1987, a time when the committee had criticized some Reagan judicial nominees (Wines 1989). In 1989, the Supreme Court ruled 8–0 that the ABA committee did not have to comply with the Federal Advisory Committee Act requiring open public meetings and records (*Public Citizen v. United States Department of Justice*).

Shortly after he took office in 2001, President George W. Bush ended the ABA role in the judicial selection process (Lewis 2001). Later in the year, when the Democrats took control of the Senate, they began submitting the names of nominees to the ABA and agreed to wait for the group's rating before acting on a candidate. In 2009, President Barack Obama restored the importance of the ABA committee, sending names of potential candidates prior to their nomination.

The practice of **senatorial courtesy** requires the president to solicit nominations from the senior senator of the president's party in the state where a district court vacancy exists. According to the unofficial, yet binding, rules of the Senate, which in many ways is a "gentlemen's club," failure to follow this tradition will be viewed as "personally obnoxious," and Senate colleagues will not vote to confirm. A senator from either party can use the "blue slip blackball": A senator who opposes a nominee from his or her state deliberately fails to return the blue—the color of the—slip of approval to the chairperson of the Senate Judiciary Committee. This can effectively kill a nomination.[2] Thus, in practice, although the president makes the nomination, the president does not dominate the appointment process. A number of senators utilize advisory commissions to aid their judicial recommendations. During the administration of Bill Clinton (1992–2000), the Senate was controlled by Republicans who made it a practice of stalling the confirmation process whenever the president nominated judicial candidates whom they considered "too liberal" or "too activist." As a result many federal judicial vacancies went unfilled, some for several years. Unless the president's party has a filibuster-proof majority (60 senators), a nomination is always in jeopardy of being blocked by the opposition. In 2011, for example, a Republican filibuster succeeded in blocking President Barack Obama's nominee (Goodwin Liu) for a federal appeals court opening, despite a bipartisan agreement in 2005 to oppose filibusters against judicial nominees except in extraordinary circumstances.

---

[2] Thus, the appointment of Federal District Court Judge J. Skelly Wright of New Orleans to the Fifth Circuit Court of Appeals was vetoed by Louisiana's senators using senatorial courtesy. Judge Wright's firm stand in desegregation cases had made him quite unpopular among Southern politicians. He was eventually appointed to the Court of Appeals for the District of Columbia, a circuit outside the power of Southern senators.

Courts in Crisis

There is an ongoing vacancy crisis in federal district courts that is unprecedented, the result of acrimony between a Democratic president and Senate Republicans (Bannon 2013).

There are 12 federal appellate regional circuits (not including the District of Columbia and territorial circuits); each circuit includes several states. Courts of appeals judgeships are informally allocated among the states of a particular circuit in rough proportion to the number of court of appeals cases that arise in each state. In this case, power over the appointment process is reserved for officials of the state to which the judgeship in question has been allocated (Posner 1985). A presidential nomination is referred to the Judiciary Committee, which conducts its own investigation and holds public hearings on all nominees. The committee then votes on whether to send the nomination to the full Senate for confirmation. In most instances, both the Judiciary Committee and the Senate routinely approve judges. For appointments to the Supreme Court, the process is the same, but no senator enjoys senatorial courtesy. For appointments to a state bench, it is the governor who makes the nomination and senatorial courtesy is customary in only six states. In New Jersey, for example, the practice allows senators to block judicial (and other) appointments from their county without giving a reason (Gray 1993).

Because the only formal qualification for federal judicial positions is that a district court appointee must live in the state where the vacancy exists, presidential nominees have only infrequently been voted down by the Senate. In 1986, the Republican-controlled Judiciary Committee refused to vote out—submit to the full Senate for a confirmation vote—the nomination of a candidate for a district court judgeship in Alabama—the second judicial nominee in nearly half a century to suffer such a fate. The first rejection of a candidate in 43 years, nominated by President Jimmy Carter for a North Carolina district court, occurred in 1980 (when the Judiciary Committee went against the wishes of the Democratic senator from North Carolina, whose candidate had been found "qualified" by the ABA).

In addition to passing investigative screening and securing an ABA rating of "qualified," becoming a candidate requires political connections and often ideological compatibility with the appointing authority. Although it is somewhat less important on a state level, ideological compatibility can be crucial in the case of federal judgeships. Democratic presidents tend to nominate liberals, and Republicans nominate conservatives. Presidents Nixon and Reagan ran on pledges to appoint only conservatives—"traditionalists"—to the federal courts. During the Reagan years (1980–1988), the issue of judicial selection and the responsibility of the Senate regarding confirmation of presidential nominees received considerable attention. Liberals argued that Ronald Reagan was out to remake the federal judiciary generally, and the Supreme Court in particular, in his own image and that his Justice Department

> used an ideological 'litmus test' in screening candidates for judicial appointments. Conservatives, on the other hand, argued that those who opposed Reagan's nomi-

nees were injecting partisan politics into the confirmation process and guilty of distorting the degree to which this president, like all of those who preceded him, was merely attempting to appoint men and women to the federal courts who espoused a judicial philosophy similar to his own. (McDowell 1990: xiii–xiv)

In his campaign, Bill Clinton pledged to appoint judges whose views were similar to his own, particularly concerning the issue of abortion.

Geographic balance can also play a role in a federal district or circuit court nomination: At the district level there is pressure on senators to "balance" the judicial process geographically. Accordingly, a senator may feel obligated to allocate a judicial vacancy to a particular congressional district, especially where that position had traditionally "belonged" to a particular district. There is also the need to balance rural and urban areas, eastern and western or northern and southern parts of a state. One arcane kind of turf fighting among states and senators that occurs only at the court of appeals level is the allocation of circuit court judgeships among the states of a given circuit. Some try to allocate judgeships among the states in a given circuit by looking at the percentages of caseloads originating from each state compared to the total number of caseloads of the circuit; judgeship allocations can also be based on a state's percentage share of population within the circuit (Friend of the Constitution 1990).

As with other federal judicial posts, Supreme Court nominations tend to involve religious, racial, gender, and ethnic considerations. Geographic considerations have also played a role; presidents attempt to have all regions of the country represented on the Court. Because of the importance of the Supreme Court, nominees are subjected to greater scrutiny, although there have been infrequent vetoes by the Senate—two when Richard Nixon was president. In 1969 the Senate rejected, 55–45, Clement E. Haynsworth, a federal appellate court judge from South Carolina, over questions of judicial ethics (he had participated in a case involving a company in which he had a one-seventh interest) and strong opposition from labor and civil rights groups. In the 1970 vote on G. Harold Carswell, a little-known federal judge, the Senate floor manager for his nomination, Roman Hruska (R-NE), responded to critics who accused Carswell of having mediocre legal qualifications. "Even if he is mediocre," the senator argued, "there are a lot of mediocre judges and people and lawyers. They are entitled to a little representation, aren't they, and a little chance? We can't have all Brandeises, Cardozos, and Frankfurters [Louis Brandeis, Benjamin Cardozo, and Felix Frankfurter, notable Court members], and stuff like that there." His argument was not persuasive; the nomination was defeated by the rather slim margin of 51–45 (Lewis and Peoples 1978). It was only the third time in the twentieth century that a nominee had been rejected. In 1987, the Senate rejected Judge Bork by the largest margin ever cast against a Supreme Court nominee—58–42. (For opposing views of this case, see Bork 1989; Pertschuk and Schaetzel 1989; and Bronner 1989.)

One of the more recent and controversial elements in the Senate confirmation process involves Judiciary Committee scrutiny. The practice of questioning nominees dates back to the 1930s, but the questioning was usually perfunctory. Now hearings are televised and receive widespread media attention. Nominees are asked about specific political issues and cases, often raising serious questions about judicial integrity. Robert Bork (1993: 11) refers to the proceedings as "televised inquisitions concerning every thought a nominee ever had about the minutiae of constitutional law." The purpose, Bork argues, is to use the answers against the nominee or, perhaps worse, to elicit commitments on future votes.

The appointment of judges by a chief executive places the decision in the hands of a highly visible public official. This system provides the greatest level of accountability. A president or governor will be praised or criticized for his or her judicial appointments, a factor that can encourage the appointment of qualified candidates. On the other hand, governors and presidents have at times shown a willingness to appoint persons of dubious ability or questionable background, public criticism notwithstanding. The appointment process removes the public from any direct participation in the judicial selection process, weakening the quest for legitimacy (discussed in Chapter 5).

Elections

Prior to the Jacksonian era (1829–1837), the governor or the state legislature appointed most judges. Jacksonian democracy led to the popular election of judges. Today, judges are elected in 42 states at some level, and more than 80 percent of appellate judges face election (Glaberson 2000a). This raises the question of judicial accountability—to whom and for what should a judge be accountable? Elected officials should be held accountable for their decisions: This furthers the ends of a democratic society. But does holding judges accountable to the electorate for their decisions further the ends of justice? Indeed, the legal profession values judicial independence and abhors judicial partisanship and pandering to a (legally) unsophisticated electorate.

State judges may be elected in a partisan election, in which there is a party primary and the candidates are listed as Democrats or Republicans (or with some local party affiliation) in the general election, or in a nonpartisan election where candidates are not listed by any political affiliation. The nonpartisan election was largely an unsuccessful effort to remove judicial selection from the control of often-corrupt political organizations. In theory, the electoral system for selecting judges is clearly the most democratic, and it is the way we select most important public officials in the other branches of government. But the nature of judicial office makes the electoral process controversial.

The attorney-as-advocate must leave that role behind when becoming a judge. As a candidate for judicial office, an attorney is restrained by a canon of ethics from taking positions on partisan issues (see Figure 7.1 on the following page). Whereas a candidate for legislative office is free to state a position on a host of controversial issues ranging from taxes to abortion, until 2002 a candidate for judicial office was constrained from taking positions on such issues by state laws or state high-court decrees based on an ABA code of judicial conduct. In California, for example, Canon 5 of the *Code of Judicial Ethics* warns: "A candidate for election or appointment to judicial office shall not make statements to the electorate or the appointing authority that commit or appear to commit the candidate with respect to cases, controversies, or issues that could come before the courts." The *Indiana Code of Judicial Conduct* [Sec. 5A(3)(d)] has similar cautions: Judicial candidates "shall not make pledges or promises of conduct in office other than the faithful and impartial performance of the duties of office; make statements that commit or appear to commit the candidate with respect to cases, controversies or issues that are likely to come before the court." In 2002, the Supreme Court ruled 5–4 (*Republican Party of Minnesota v. White*) that such restrictions violate the free speech rights of judicial candidates.

A Judge Should Refrain from Political Activity Inappropriate to His Judicial Office

A. Political Conduct in General

(1) A judge or a candidate for election to judicial office should not:

    (a) act as a leader or hold any office in a political organization;

    (b) make speeches for a political organization or candidate or publicly endorse a candidate for public office;

    (c) solicit funds or pay an assessment or make a contribution to a political organization or candidate, attend political gatherings, or purchase tickets for political party dinners, or other functions, except as authorized in subsection A(2).

(2) A judge holding an office filled by public election between competing candidates, or a candidate for such office, may, only insofar as permitted by law, attend political gatherings, speak to such gatherings on his own behalf when he is a candidate for election or reelection, identify himself as a member of a political party, and contribute to a political party or organization.

(3) A judge should resign his office when he becomes a candidate either in a party primary or in a general election for a nonjudicial office, except that he may continue to hold his judicial office while being a candidate for election to or serving as a delegate in a state constitutional convention, if he is otherwise permitted by law to do so.

(4) A judge should not engage in any other political activity except on behalf of measures to improve the law, the legal system, or the administration of justice.

B. Campaign Conduct

(1) A candidate, including an incumbent judge, for a judicial office that is filled either by public election between competing candidates or on the basis of a merit system election:

    (a) should maintain the dignity appropriate to judicial office, and should encourage members of his family to adhere to the same standards of political conduct that apply to him;

    (b) should prohibit officials or employees subject to his direction or control from doing for him what he is prohibited from doing under this Canon; and except to the extent authorized under subsection B(2) or B(3), he should not allow any other person to do for him what he is prohibited from doing under this Canon;

    (c) should not make pledges or promises of conduct in office other than the faithful and impartial performance of the duties of the office; announce his views on disputed legal or political issues; or misrepresent his identity, qualifications, present position, or other fact.

(2) A candidate, including an incumbent judge, for a judicial office that is filled by public election between competing candidates should not himself solicit or accept campaign funds, or solicit publicly stated support, but he may establish committees of responsible persons to secure and manage the expenditure of funds for his campaign and to obtain public support from lawyers. A candidate's committees may solicit funds for his campaign no earlier than [90] days before a primary election and no later than [90] days after the last election in which he participates during the election year. A candidate should not use or permit the use of campaign contributions for the private benefit of himself or members of his family.

(3) An incumbent judge who is a candidate for retention in or reelection to office without a competing candidate, and whose candidacy has drawn active opposition, may campaign in response thereto and may obtain publicly stated support and campaign funds in the manner provided in subsection B(2).

Figure 7.1 Canon 7 of the American Bar Association Code of Judicial Conduct

***Republican Party of Minnesota v. White* (2002)**

Justice Sandra Day O'Connor concurring:

> Minnesota has chosen to select its judges through contested popular elections instead of through an appointment system or a combined appointment and retention election system. . . . In doing so the State has voluntarily taken on the risks to judicial bias. . . . As a result, the State's claim that it needs to significantly restrict judges' speech in order to protect judicial impartiality is particularly troubling. If the State has a problem with judicial impartiality, it is largely one the State brought upon itself by continuing the practice of popularly electing judges.

The electorate is typically faced with judicial candidates about whom little is known, and what is known usually has little or no bearing on the candidate's qualifications for judicial office (e.g., ethnic background, race, religion, and, in partisan elections, party affiliation). The outcome of a judicial election, particularly for the appellate bench, may depend on the ability of a candidate to promote his or her candidacy through advertising. The source of campaign funds raises questions of judicial independence. Trial lawyers, insurance companies, the gambling and medical care industries, unions, and energy and natural resources companies have all been substantial contributors to judicial candidates. In 2000, the United States Chamber of Commerce announced their intent of spending more than $1 million for advertising in state supreme court races. In West Virginia, a coal company executive contributed more than $3 million to the successful campaign of a judge who would sit on a state appeals court considering a case in which the executive had an interest. In 2009, the US Supreme Court (*Caperton v. Massey*) ruled that the failure of the judge to recuse himself was improper. Michael Kang and Joanna Sherherd (2011: 69) found over a four-year period that in all 50 states elected judges "are more likely to decide in favor of business interests as the amount of campaign contributions received from those interests increases. In other words, every dollar of direct contributions from business groups is associated with an increase in the probability that the judge in question will vote for business litigants." They report this does not occur in nonpartisan elections.

A study by Billy Corriher (2013) found that as campaign funding increased, appellate courts more frequently began to rule in favor of prosecutors and against defendants. The growing use of attack ads criticizing judges for being "soft on criminals" had the same effect and became acute with the approach of elections. "Most of these attack ads allege that a certain judge is soft on crime, telling voters that he or she ruled in favor of a violent criminal without any context or discussion of the legal issue

Electing Judges

"Elections turn judges into politicians, and the need to raise money to finance ever more expensive campaigns makes the judiciary more vulnerable to improper influence by donors" (*New York Times* editorial, August 20, 2012: 18).

at stake. A single ruling in a case, replete with gruesome facts, can provide fodder for an attack ad" (2013: 3).

By 2004, campaign spending for elected judges had skyrocketed, and in 2009 and 2010, contributions in appellate court races exceeded $45 million (Casey 2012). Most state high courts have five or seven judges "and they are often closely divided, meaning that a shift in a single seat can have enormous significance." As a result, the "sums of money being spent to capture these seats is growing exponentially" (Liptak 2004: 30).

In addition to money, three often overlapping variables control an election for judicial office: (1) political party support, (2) ethnicity, race, and religion, and (3) position on the ballot. Let us look at these in reverse order of importance.

- *Position on the Ballot.* The position of a candidate on the election ballot is governed by election law and can be determined in several ways. In some states, the position of all candidates is determined by a lottery drawing, at least in the party primary. In the general election, it may depend on the number of votes for governor cast at the last general election; the party receiving the highest number of votes gets the first position on the ballot. This position is preferred, because in jurisdictions that have a long ballot with dozens of usually unknown candidates running for a wide array of offices, many voters have a tendency to vote only for the first few candidates. In some states, the names of candidates are randomly rotated from election district to election district—obviously the fairest method.

- *Ethnicity, Race, and Religion.* In judicial elections, voters are usually faced with a list of names of persons about whom they know little or nothing. Under such circumstances (as every politician recognizes), the voter is likely to vote for names with which he or she identifies on the basis of ethnicity, race, or religion, if these characteristics can be determined. Thus, Irish voters may vote for Irish-sounding names, and the same would hold for Italian, Jewish, German, Polish, Bohemian, and other identifiable groups. Judges are often nominated and elected on the strength of their ethnic surnames. In some jurisdictions, candi-

Electing Judges in Cook County, Illinois

In the 1994 Cook County (Chicago) Democratic primary, voters were faced with a ballot that, in addition to statewide candidates for the appellate court, listed 85 candidates vying for 14 countywide vacancies, and 166 candidates running for election to one of the 15 subcircuits into which the county is divided. Voters chose 16 candidates who were considered unqualified by the four local lawyers' groups who evaluate judicial candidates. In 1996, Cook County voters elected six judges who had not submitted information about their backgrounds to any of the local bar groups. One had been licensed to practice law in Illinois for less than two years—beyond that, nothing was known about her background. In 1998, in Cook County there were 178 candidates running for election to the appellate and circuit courts. In the 2000 general election, there were 77 judges seeking retention in office that requires a "yes" vote of 60 percent—all were retained. In the same election, all of the Democratic candidates for the circuit court (a trial court) had no opponents.

dates utilize middle and/or (hyphenated) maiden names to increase voter ethnic appeal. In Cook County, for example, L. Michael Getty (Getty being a Scottish name) was defeated in the 1984 Democratic Party for the circuit court; he changed his name to Michael Brennan (Brennan being an Irish name) Getty and was elected in 1988.

- *Political Party Support.* A circuit court judge in Chicago, "who had spent more time with a bottle of blended whiskey than with a volume of revised statutes," says political reporter David Axelrod, "offered a surprisingly candid self analysis: 'You know, I may not be much of a judge, but I'm one hell of a precinct captain'" (1983: 4). In order for an aspiring candidate for judicial office to appear on the election ballot, he or she must secure the signatures of hundreds, sometimes thousands, of voters on nominating petitions. The precinct captains of a political party usually accomplish circulating petitions. These persons also have responsibility for getting out the vote for the party ticket. More organized political groups, those with active precinct captains, usually dominate judicial elections.

  In partisan systems, a primary election is required to determine who will have the right to appear on the ballot in the general election with a particular party affiliation. In most areas, the primary election is controlled by a particular dominant political organization, Republican or Democrat. The leaders ("bosses") of such organizations select party candidates who, particularly for judicial office, are usually successful in the primary election. Since only a minority of eligible voters usually votes in any primary and still fewer actually cast votes for judicial offices, party leaders are able to dominate the election of judges by the discipline they can exert on party loyalists. In practice, it is the party leadership that typically determines who is elected to judicial office.

In some areas, the election of judges does not provide the electorate with a choice, because the elections are uncontested. In general elections, it is not unusual for candidates, judicial and otherwise, to be unopposed in districts where there is an absence of a viable two-party system. Thus, for example, judicial candidates in Chicago on the Democratic ticket usually run unopposed in the general election, while the same is true of Republican candidates in suburban and more rural downstate areas. From 1974 to 1984, for example, 71 percent of circuit court judgeships in Chicago were filled by candidates who ran unopposed in both the primary and general elections (Aspen 1987).

In New York City, Democratic candidates for judicial office frequently run unopposed, while in some suburban and upstate areas the same is true of Republican candidates. A study in New York found that in six consecutive elections for supreme

---

The Peculiar Americans

"Of all those parts of the world entitled to be called civilized, the States of our Union . . . are the only places where judges are elected" (Zane 1998: 284). As we saw in Chapter 1, in civil-law countries judges are career civil servants and judges in England are chosen by, or on the recommendation of, the Lord Chancellor, a member of the prime minister's cabinet.

court (a trial court) judges, 87 percent were either uncontested or noncompetitive. Either an opposition candidate did not appear on the ballot or the leaders of the Democratic and Republican parties made a deal to cross-endorse the same candidates (a frequent occurrence in New York City) rather than leave it up to the electorate. In 2002, for example, the 10 candidates for the 10 supreme court openings in Manhattan were endorsed by both the Democratic and Republican Parties. Another study found the identical situation with respect to the election of civil-court (lower court) judges in New York City (Fund for Modern Courts 1986). An editorial in the *New York Times* (October 25, 1986: 14) referred to this system as a "form of election fraud" that "is perpetrated every time New Yorkers cast votes for judges." An editorial in the New *York Daily News* (November 3, 2002: 40) refers to it as "a coronation" by political bosses.

Although it may not be extraordinary, political influence in the judiciary of New York City is extensive. When Assemblyman George Friedman, Democratic leader of the Bronx, decided to become a judge, he sponsored a bill creating an additional judgeship to which he was nominated by his party and ran unopposed in the general election. In return, he awarded hundreds of thousands of dollars in court work to party officials, and when he retired, Judge Friedman was appointed to serve on a commission charged with reforming the state judiciary (Levy et al. 2004).

In most states, no matter how the judge is initially selected, he or she must submit either to reelection or to a nonpartisan retention or confirmation ballot after a certain amount of time on the bench. In Illinois, for example, after a circuit court judge serves for six years and a supreme court judge has served for 10 years, the judge's name will appear on the ballot of a general election, providing voters with an opportunity to vote for or against retention.

California, which has the largest judicial system in the country (about 1,500 judgeships), uses a nonpartisan election system for trial court judges and executive appointment for appellate court justices. The governor submits nominees for the supreme court and courts of appeal to the Commission on Judicial Appointments consisting of the chief justice of the supreme court, the attorney general, and the senior presiding judge on the court of appeals. The commission holds public hearings to receive comments on the nominee's qualifications before voting on whether to confirm the governor's choice. If they approve of the nominee—and they almost always do—the person serves until the next election, but not less than one year, at which time the judge's name appears on a retention ballot for a full 12-year term. At the end of their 12-year terms, justices are again subjected to a retention ballot.

Financing Judicial Elections

Concerned with the specter of judges taking campaign contributions from lawyers, businesses, and others who have a financial stake in the outcome of cases, a committee of the ABA recommended public financing of judicial elections (Bendavid 2001). For example, in 2003, a Bronx Supreme Court judge up for reelection sent solicitation letters to and received donations from 150 lawyers who had some 300 current cases before him. He was reelected (Levy et al. 2004).

In 1986, a successful campaign effort was launched by two political consulting firms against the retention of Rose Bird, chief justice of the California Supreme Court, and two associate justices, based on claims that they had refused to uphold the death sentence against scores of convicted murderers. "For the first time since retention elections were adopted for the state's appellate justices in 1934, the public not only rejected a chief justice but defeated two other justices" (Wold and Culver 1989: 323). In 2010, three Iowa supreme court justices lost their seats in a retention election because of votes to allow same-sex couples to marry.

Noted legal scholar Karl Llewellyn (1960) expressed disapproval of the retention vote, arguing that appellate court justices must be immune from personal or political retribution for their decisions. (It is the reason federal judges enjoy life terms.) In 2000 a trial court judge who campaigned on the issue of evolution defeated a member of the Idaho Supreme Court: Evolution "could not possibly be true," the victor argued. Less idiosyncratic issues such as school financing, abortion, health care, and liability laws with caps on torts have led to increased contributions to judicial campaigns from interest groups whose involvement threatens judicial independence. Judicial elections have become bitter, with attack ads and thinly veiled advertising by which candidates express opinions about issues that, as judges, on which they may have to rule (Glaberson 2000a). And "across the country, judges are being fined, censored and even threatened with removal for practicing that venerable political art: exaggerating or outright lying during a campaign" (Glaberson 2000c: 1).

The electoral method receives support from political party leaders with whom the power of judicial selection is largely vested. They argue that it is "democratic," that all other important public officials are elected by the people. However, the electoral method of selecting judges receives little support from political scientists, bar associations, and newspaper editorial boards, because it places too much power in the hands of party officials. Furthermore, these party officials, who in reality select the candidates, are able to avoid accountability because the electorate officially puts judges into office.

Judicial candidates in contested elections (or those facing retention elections) must raise funds for their campaigns and attempt to win over blocks of voters, actions that can compromise judicial independence. Most of those who contribute to judicial campaigns are attorneys (who else would be interested enough to contribute their money?) whose practice will bring them into the courts of the very judges they help to elect.

The *Journal of the American Judicature Society* ("Editorial" 1964: 124–25) referred to the nonpartisan election of judges "as the worst of all the traditional methods." Under this system, "having the same name as a well-known public figure, a large campaign fund, a pleasing TV image, or the proper place on the ballot are far more influential in selecting judges than character, legal ability, judicial temperament or distinguished experience on the bench."

In the 1973 election for chief justice of the New York Court of Appeals (court of last resort), the successful candidate spent more than $1.2 million and defeated a highly respected appellate judge. As a result, the legislature passed a **merit system** law for the state's highest court. Now a commission of lawyers and laypeople draws up a list of candidates, and the governor makes the final selection.

A Political Judiciary

"The courts are often thought to be less 'political' than the other branches of government. This popular view is probably too much influenced by the workings of the Supreme Court. The justices of Supreme Court, cloistered, unelected, and appointed for life, are free to ponder and ruminate on the grand issues of jurisprudence. The judges in a state court are more constrained. Elected judges know they rule at the discretion of the voters, and, like politicians, they rule accordingly" (Tabarrok and Helland 1999: 187). "Since most plaintiffs are in-state voters and many defendants are out-of-state nonvoters, elected judges have an incentive to service their constituency by aiding plaintiffs. A particularly low-cost method of aiding plaintiffs is to transfer wealth from out-of-state business defendants to in-state plaintiffs. Campaign contributions from trial lawyers are also likely to increase the proportion of 'high aware' judges in elected states" (1999: 186).

Merit System

Efforts to reform the way judges are chosen have taken a number of forms. The most notable is **The Missouri Plan**, adopted in Missouri in 1940 as a way to eliminate corruption from the selection of judges by popular election. For many years, the politics of Missouri were influenced by the often-corrupt activities associated with Tom Pendergast (1873–1945), a political boss who, often in collusion with the local Mafia, helped elect politicians. The Pendergast machine of Kansas City (see Dorsett 1968) negatively impacted the selection of judges, but the leadership of the Missouri bar, with the support of the press, was successful in instituting a unique way of selecting some judges (originally proposed by Albert Kales of the American Judicature Society in 1914 [Stumpf and Culver 1992]). The system, called The Missouri Plan, or The Missouri Non-Partisan Court Plan, has three basic features:

1. *Nominating commission.* There is a nominating commission for each level of courts to which the plan applies (some local courts continue to use popular election), made up of lawyers (elected by the attorneys residing in each jurisdiction); laypersons whose only legal qualification is residency in the jurisdiction and who are appointed by the governor; and the chief justice of the supreme court, who is the ex officio chairman.

2. *Governor's selection.* When there is a judicial vacancy in any applicable court, the nominating commission sends a list of three candidates to the governor, who is required to pick one of the three.

3. *Retention ballot.* After one year of service, each judge appointed under the system appears on a retention ballot: "Shall Judge _____ be retained in office?" If a majority of those casting votes on the question say yes, the judge remains in office for the full term (either six or 12 years, depending on the court). If the judge does not receive a majority of yes votes, the office is declared vacant, and the nominating commission drafts a new list for the governor.

Currently there is a national trend toward using some form of merit system. In 1960, only four states utilized merit systems based, in whole or in part, on The Mis-

Lawyers Evaluating Judicial Candidates

Lawyers are in a better position to evaluate the merits of judicial candidates than the public because they are less likely to be swayed by single-issue politics or irrelevant matters, and a lawyer is in a better position to identify judicial incompetence than the public (Failinger 2005).

souri Plan; by 1997 almost one-half of the states had done so (Abraham 1998). Most use a modified form of the Missouri system, the salient feature being a nominating commission of lawyers and laypeople. More than half the states have established judicial nominating commissions that review candidates for all of the courts. Some have different nominating commissions for each court level, and in a few, a commission reviews candidates only for certain courts—such as the court of last resort in New York and the general and limited jurisdiction courts in North Carolina. All of these states permit laypersons to serve on the commissions. In Connecticut, the commission provides a list of nominees to the legislature, not the governor, which makes the appointment.

The merit/Missouri system has many supporters among editorial writers, the ABA, and the American Judicature Society, who favor taking the courts "out of politics." "At the very least," states US District Court Judge Marvin Aspen, "merit selection will broaden the pool of potential judicial applicants to include many fine lawyers who have little hope of serving on the bench under present election procedures" (1987: 17). However, under this system accountability is almost completely absent because the selection process is diffused among a commission, the governor, and, finally, the electorate (and there is a great lack of voter interest in retention elections).

The laypeople appointed to commissions are usually closely aligned with the governor and support the governor's preferences. And governors often covertly influence commission deliberations by conveying their preferences for a judicial vacancy. "As a result," states Alan Tarr (1999: 70), "under merit selection governors may exercise as much control [with a great deal less accountability] as they do under a system of gubernatorial appointment." Furthermore, in the appointed and electoral systems, political leaders are concerned with fulfilling political commitments—patronage. In the lawyer-dominated merit system, the focus is on the expected judicial attitudes and policies of potential candidates, a more personal, and perhaps compromising, concern.

Marie Failinger (2005: 514) states: "There is no guarantee that appointed merit selection commissions are going to obviate the problems of partisanship or elitism. Gubernatorial commissions are likely to reflect either the political or the community connections of the governor and his staff. As such, in the worst cases, such commissions may be highly politicized and select judicial appointees who have been active in the party, raised funds for candidates, or otherwise reflect party values." Henry Glick notes that all of the research on the selection of state judges reveals that "while there are some differences among state judges, differences do not result from the particular selection system used and the Missouri plan does not produce judges with superior formal credentials for office" (1983: 89; see also Stumpf 1998). And retention elections can easily become focused on the decisions of judges, something the Founding Fathers wanted to keep out of the political arena.

Removing Judges

Russell Wheeler and A. Leo Levin point out the issues and delicate balance involved in dealing with judicial discipline. There is a "need to preserve judicial independence and need to deal with the judge who cannot or will not properly discharge the functions of office. Moreover, the problems of defining unfitness are subtle and complicated: what some may perceive as judicial incompetence—such as comments to witnesses and attorneys that are seen as rude or insensitive—others may perceive as conduct well within the bounds of discretion that judges must have for the effective movement of cases" (1979: 3).

Four basic methods are used to impose judicial discipline and removal, although concern over age-related impairment has led some states to impose a mandatory retirement age, usually 70. Of the four methods listed below, the first is the only one used in the federal system.

1. *Impeachment and conviction.* Removing a federal judge involves the cumbersome and infrequently invoked impeachment process. Impeachment refers to the bringing of charges; it is analogous to an indictment in the criminal process. Even federal judges who are convicted of crimes can be removed from office only by impeachment. Thirteen federal judges have been impeached: eight were convicted and removed and one resigned. A federal judge impeached and removed from office in 1989 was subsequently elected to Congress.

   The process begins in the House of Representatives, whose members vote on articles of impeachment. The articles are prosecuted in the Senate by members of the lower house chosen by their peers; they act as prosecutors before the Senate, which serves as judge and jury. According to the Constitution (Article I), "The Senate shall have the sole Power to try all Impeachments." In order to avoid tying up the entire Senate, a panel chosen by the Senate leadership usually handles this. The panel hears the evidence and makes a recommendation to the full body. The Constitution (Article I) provides that "no person shall be convicted without Concurrence of two thirds of the Members present." All states have provisions for the impeachment of public officials, and the procedures generally follow the federal model.[3]

   In 1980, Congress enacted the Judicial Councils Reform and Conduct and Disability Act, which provides for the judicial council in each of the 13 appellate circuits to consider allegations about the personal conduct, and mental and physical condition of federal district court judges. If the council finds that a judge has engaged in conduct that is grounds for impeachment, it can request that the Judicial Conference[4] refer the matter to the House of Representatives for impeachment proceedings. Short of that, the council can censure or reprimand an offending judge, publicly or privately. Before such sanctions can be imposed, however, the judge has the right to appeal to a three-member panel of the Judicial Conference. The procedure has been closed to outside scrutiny, and judges rarely, if ever, receive public reprimands (Margolick 1989b).

---

[3] For a cross-national comparison of procedures for judicial misconduct, see Volcansek (1996).

[4] The Judicial Conference is discussed in Chapter 4.

2. *Legislative resolution.* More than half the states permit the removal of a judge by a concurrent two-thirds vote of both houses or by the governor with the concurrence of a majority vote of both houses.

3. *Recall.* Seven states, mostly in the West, have constitutional provisions for the recall of elected officials, including state judges. Recall requires circulating a petition. If enough valid signatures are secured, the name of the official appears on the ballot at the next general election; the electorate votes *yea* or *nay* with respect to continuing the official in office.

4. *Commission system.* In 1960, California became the first state to establish a permanent commission charged with the regulation of judges' conduct. By 1981, all states had established—by constitutional amendment, by statute, or by court rule—commissions on judicial conduct empowered to investigate, prosecute, and adjudicate allegations of judicial misbehavior. Though the commissions vary widely in structure, composition, and procedure, they are typically authorized either to recommend or to impose sanctions on a continuum that extends from private reprimand to removal from office. Most are composed of about five to 15 members and include judges, lawyers, and laypersons (Rottman and Strickland 2006). Moreover, nearly every state has also adopted a version of the Model Code of Judicial Conduct, which sets mandatory standards for both official and off-the-bench conduct.

Removing Judges

Illinois

The two-tiered discipline process provided for by the Illinois Constitution began in 1971 and is typical of many states: There is a Judicial Inquiry Board with nine members; two are circuit (superior) court judges selected by the supreme court and seven are appointed by the governor—three lawyers and four nonlawyers. The board has authority to receive or initiate complaints concerning judges and file them with the Court Commission. "The Board shall not file a complaint unless five members believe that a reasonable basis exists (1) to charge the Judge or Associate Judge with willful misconduct in office, persistent failure to perform his duties, or other conduct that is prejudicial to the administration of justice or that brings the judicial office into disrepute, or (2) to charge that the Judge or Associate Judge is physically or mentally unable to perform his duties."

The Judicial Inquiry Board prosecutes the complaint before the Court Commission: one supreme court judge, two appellate court judges, and two superior court judges. With the concurrence of three members, the commission has the final authority to remove the judge from office, suspend without pay, or censure.

New York

The New York State Commission on Judicial Conduct consists of 11 members—four appointed by the governor, three by the chief judge of the court of appeals, and one each by the speaker of the assembly, the majority leader of the senate, and the two legislative minority leaders. At least two of its members must be nonlawyers and four must be judges. Members serve staggered four-year terms, and they appoint an administrator who is charged with the day-to-day operations of the commission.

(continued)

The commission receives or initiates complaints about the conduct, qualifications, fitness to perform, or performance of official duties of any judge in the state and conducts an investigation and a hearing, both of which are confidential until complete. If the commission finds cause for disciplinary action against a judge, its findings are made available to the public through the clerk of the court of appeals; the commission publishes an annual report of its activities. The commission has the power to admonish, censure, remove, or retire a judge based on its findings.

California

The Commission on Judicial Performance, a constitutionally created independent agency, was the first in the United States established to monitor judicial conduct and has served as a model for most other states. The commission is composed of 11 members: one justice of a court of appeals and two judges of superior courts appointed by the supreme court; two attorneys appointed by the governor; and six lay citizens—two appointed by the governor, two appointed by the Senate Committee on Rules, and two appointed by the speaker of the assembly. Members are appointed to four-year terms.

The commission receives and investigates all complaints of judicial misconduct. In the most serious cases, the commission may determine—following a hearing—to remove a judge from office. Typically, these cases involve persistent and pervasive misconduct. In cases in which a judge is no longer capable of performing judicial duties, the commission may determine—again, following a hearing—to involuntarily retire the judge from office.

Virginia

The Judicial Inquiry and Review Commission has seven members consisting of three judges, two lawyers, and two citizen members who are not lawyers. The Virginia General Assembly elects the members for four-year terms. The commission employs a staff to assist in the investigation of complaints of misconduct against all state court judges.

Following the investigation, the commission may consider the complaint informally or it may conduct a formal hearing. If the commission determines there has not been an ethical violation, the complaint will be dismissed. If there has been a violation, the commission may summon the judge and advise the judge of its findings. The commission in the Supreme Court of Virginia may file charges that are sufficient to require the retirement, censure, or removal of the judge. The commission may conclude the complaint after counseling with the judge. It may reprimand the judge privately, or place the judge on a period of supervision subject to terms and conditions, or refer the matter to the Virginia Supreme Court. The supreme court may dismiss the complaint or it may retire, censure, or remove the judge.

Prosecutors

In British common law, a crime was viewed not as an act against the state but as a wrong inflicted on the victim, who was responsible for the arrest and prosecution of the offender. The common-law courts would adjudicate the matter "much as they would a contract dispute or a tortuous injury" (Kress 1976: 10). The origins of the public prosecutor in the United States is in doubt. Some trace it to the Dutch experience in New York, where the sheriff acted as a prosecutor; some see its roots in the French *procureur publique*, who operated under an inquisitorial system; others see its origin in the English post of the king's attorney (Kress 1976). In colonial America, the prosecution of cases was the responsibility of a district attorney (the title varied), usually appointed by the governor and assigned to a particular county or region. "In this respect colonial practice diverged from the custom in England, where private prosecutors handled all but the most important cases" (Walker 1980: 22). By the end of the American Revolution, all states had enacted legislation establishing the office of public prosecutor, who was usually an elected county official. In the federal system, the Judiciary Act of 1789 provided for a United States attorney to be appointed by the president in each court district.

Before the twentieth century the prosecutor was a secondary figure in American criminal justice. "The office of the public prosecutor first appeared in the executive articles of state constitutions in the 1850s" (Steinberg 2003: 752), but prosecutors were little more than clerks: Only in serious felony cases, such as murder, did they actively prosecute a case, and even then, they hired private attorneys to represent them. In the decades following the Civil War, when the police replaced private citizens as typical complainants in criminal cases, "decisions about whether to pursue a case and to what end remained in the hands of the parties: usually the police and the people they arrested, overseen by a magistrate" (Steinberg 2003: 755).

The "prosecutor's virtually unreviewable discretion to decide whether to prosecute, began to appear in the mid-1880s, around the same time that state courts first explained to public prosecutors that they were not the 'plaintiff's attorney' and should not prosecute a person they believed to be innocent" (Steinberg 2003: 753). Since then, the prosecutor has become the most powerful figure in the criminal justice system, exercising enormous discretion, the decision to prosecute being "one of the most solitary and unfettered exercises of power in the American political system"[5] (Stewart 1987: 10). Indeed "the prosecutor's decision to institute criminal charges is the broadest and least regulated power in American criminal law" (Gershman 2002: 57).

The prosecutor is the most powerful official in the criminal justice system.

Federal Prosecutors

Since the Senate must confirm the 93 US attorneys, a senator's influence over the appointment of a US attorney (USA) is similar to his or her influence in the appointment of a district court judge. In 1870 Congress created the Department of Justice (DOJ) with the attorney general as its head. The attorney general supervises USAs and their assistants (who are generally not political appointees) and investigative agencies, such as the Federal Bureau of Investigation and the Drug Enforcement Administration.

The position of US attorney holds a great deal of prestige and public visibility; the names of USAs are frequently mentioned in the local news media. Service as a USA can lead to a position in a higher office (e.g., a federal judgeship) or can be a springboard for an elected office. Although part of the DOJ, a USA enjoys considerable

---

[5] For a discussion of prosecutorial immunity, see Chemerinsky (1998).

Primary Federal Law Enforcement Agencies

Department of Justice
Bureau of Alcohol, Tobacco and Firearms
Drug Enforcement Administration
Federal Bureau of Investigation
Marshals Service

Department of the Treasury
Internal Revenue Service

Department of Homeland Security
Coast Guard
Customs and Border Protection
Immigration and Customs Enforcement
Secret Service

autonomy and a great deal of discretionary authority. Subject only to being overruled by the attorney general (an infrequent occurrence), the USA decides which cases will be investigated and prosecuted. Observers have noted that a US attorney's relationship with the judges of the district is actually more important than the USA's relationship with the DOJ (Wasby 1993; Goldman and Jahnige 1985). The ability of the attorney general to hire and fire a USA depends on his or her influence with the president—the president appoints USAs, and only the president can fire a USA (Eisenstein 1978). When a new president takes office, incumbent USAs (but not assistant USAs) usually submit their resignations. In a few cases, USAs may serve several administrations.

The US attorney receives cases for prosecution from a variety of federal law enforcement agencies in several departments, primarily Justice and Treasury, but also Homeland Security, Transportation, Interior, Agriculture, Defense, Education, and the Postal Service. (For an interesting look at the work of Justice Department attorneys, see McGee and Duffy 1996.) A solicitor general in the DOJ handles cases to be taken before the Supreme Court.

Solicitor General

Prior to 1870, every major department in the executive branch had its own solicitor. The Office of Solicitor the General was created by the Judiciary Act of 1870—"There shall be an officer, learned in the law, to assist the Attorney General"—in an effort to centralize this function.

The solicitor general is nominated by the president and confirmed by the Senate. As an officer of the Department of Justice, with a staff of about five deputies and 20 assistant solicitors, the solicitor general decides what cases the government should ask the Supreme Court to review and represents the United States in all cases before the Court. The federal government is involved in about two-thirds of the cases decided by the US Supreme Court. The Office of the Solicitor General also reviews all cases decided adversely to the government in the lower courts to determine whether they should be appealed and, if so, what position should be taken. The solicitor general determines whether the government will participate as *amicus curiae*, or intervene, in cases in any appellate court.

Although the solicitor general's primary office is in the building of the Department of Justice, there are also permanent chambers in the Supreme Court Building. The Office of the Solicitor General reviews every case in which the government was a losing litigant and determines whether or not to appeal. When the solicitor general appears before the Supreme Court, he or she has a distinct advantage over other attorneys: "Partly because his client is the Government, partly because his office has a reputation for professional excellence and a measure of independence, his arguments have usually carried special weight with the Court" (Taylor 1986b: 8). Whereas the Court hears fewer than 4 percent of all petitions, more than 70 percent of those filed by the solicitor general receive hearings, and of those, the office has won a comfortable majority in every term since 1935–1936 (Chandler 2011). Although most lawyers appear in business suits, tradition requires the solicitor general to be attired in a morning coat and striped pants (Taylor 1986b).

> *"The Solicitor General is the federal government's chief appellate lawyer, as well as the country's most influential litigator" (Chandler 2011: 725).*

The justices of the Supreme Court "turn to the SG for help on legal problems that appear especially vexing, and two or three dozen times a year they invite him and his office to submit briefs in cases where the government is not a party. In these cases especially, the justices regard him as a counselor to the Court" (Caplan 1987: 7). The Court provides the solicitor general with a special dispensation to file a brief as a friend of the Court without the permission of the parties to the suit. Consistent with this special role, the solicitor general "confesses to errors." That is, when the government wins on grounds that appear to the solicitor general to be unjust, he or she recommends to the Supreme Court that the decision be overturned.

In 2002, President Barack Obama appointed Elena Kagan, who at the time was dean of the Harvard Law School, to be solicitor general—the first woman to serve in this position. She was subsequently appointed to the Supreme Court.

State Prosecutors

Like his or her federal counterpart, the prosecutor in a state system (sometimes called district attorney, county attorney, commonwealth attorney, solicitor, or state's attorney) receives a great deal of media attention and, in most states, enjoys complete autonomy. By the Civil War, 25 of 34 states elected prosecutors, and all but four states would soon follow; every state admitted to the Union after the Civil War elected prosecutors. The United States is the only country where voters elect prosecutors (Ellis 2012). In Alaska, Connecticut, Delaware, and Rhode Island criminal prosecution is the responsibility of the state's elected attorney general, and in New Jersey the governor appoints a prosecutor for each county (Dawson 1992). In most states, the primary responsibility of the attorney general is to provide legal advice to state agencies and represent the state in any legal action in which the state is a defendant or plaintiff. Attorneys general may have an office to deal with consumer **complaints**, and in a high-profile action, attorneys general in several dozen states brought suits against the tobacco industry. The office may also have responsibility in certain criminal actions such as stock fraud.

In many states, city ordinances duplicate state criminal statutes, and therefore minor offenses can be prosecuted under state law or local ordinances (Kamisar et al. 2012). A city attorney who often has the title of corporation counsel, for example, typically prosecutes traffic violations. They may also represent the government in lower courts where they handle the early stages of felony cases.

> *In most states, the primary responsibility of the attorney general is to provide legal advice to state agencies and represent the state in any legal action in which the state is a defendant or plaintiff.*

In states that elect prosecutors, the aspiring candidate, if he or she is to be successful, obviously needs the support of a political organization and campaign contributors. The office of prosecutor has served as an important source of political patronage, and it can investigate political enemies while protecting political friends. Being a prosecutor has often been seen as a stepping-stone to higher public office. Most prosecutors aspire to higher office, and many important public officials were at one time prosecutors.

A prosecutor's office decides which cases are to be prosecuted, and for what criminal charges. Although a prosecutor's office cannot control intake—it is dependent on the police to bring cases—prosecutors can decide not to prosecute and legally need not provide any reason, although politically it might be a necessity in highly publicized cases. The prosecutor's office can decline to prosecute a case, dismiss it, accept a plea of guilty to a reduced charge, or prosecute it to the fullest extent allowable by law. The enormous discretion enjoyed by the prosecutor provides the basis for much of the plea bargaining in criminal courts (which will be discussed in Chapter 9).

Like a US attorney, a prosecutor employs assistants who do most of the actual trial work (in large counties they do it all). In practice, as we shall see in later chapters, there are relatively few trials in either the criminal or civil courts. Most assistant prosecutors are recent law school graduates who use the prosecutor's office as an opportunity to gain trial experience. Because law school provides little on criminal law and procedure, and the prosecutor's office provides little or no training, assistants typically learn on the job through observation and questions to their experienced colleagues and other court actors, such as clerks and court officers. A typical assistant prosecutor works for three or four years and then enters private practice, often to do criminal defense work. The prosecutor's office, then, is characterized by a great deal of turnover, sometimes due to electoral politics, but often as a result of assistants leaving to seek more lucrative opportunities in private legal practice.

As noted in Chapter 3, the legal profession is highly stratified with only limited mobility. "One's final position in the status hierarchy of the profession is heavily determined by the status position of one's first job as a lawyer. That, in turn, is influenced by the prestige of one's law school, which, in turn, is influenced by the prestige of one's college, which, in turn, is influenced by one's family socioeconomic background. Being an assistant prosecutor as the first job in one's legal career does little to enhance one's occupational mobility" (Fishman 1979: 252). Most assistants are not graduates of prestigious law schools, although there are some exceptions. The New York (Manhattan) County District Attorney's Office has had an outstanding reputation ever since Thomas E. Dewey was elected to the position in 1937. Dewey, a Republican, became governor and was succeeded by his first assistant, Frank S. Hogan, a Democrat who remained district attorney until he retired 34 years later. The nonpolitical nature of the office, its reputation for excellence, and its jurisdiction attract many law school students who might otherwise enter corporate practice after graduation. The office receives more than 1,500 applications for the approximately 50 annual vacancies.

In some jurisdictions, the decision to charge a suspect is left to the police (usually detectives), and the prosecutor's office receives the case only after charges against the subject have already been filed. In other jurisdictions, the charging decision is controlled by the prosecutor from the beginning: An assistant prosecutor decides what, if any, charges should be filed. In still other jurisdictions, if a felony is to be charged by the police, the prosecutor must first give permission; the police can usually charge misdemeanors without any consultation.

Early screening keeps weak and petty cases from overburdening the system (see Figure 7.2 on the following page). For example, the Los Angeles County District Attorney's Office, which has about 1,000 prosecutors, handles approximately one million cases annually. However, early screening can also result in faulty decisions since there may not be a great deal of information available about the case and/or the suspect so early in the process.

The prosecutor's office may be organized to handle cases horizontally, vertically, or in a combination of the two methods.

1. *Horizontal prosecution.* This is the predominant mode of handling cases in more populous jurisdictions—each assistant prosecutor is assigned to handle a different step in the judicial process (See Chapter 8 for these steps) and/or a specific courtroom. For example, the Cook County, Illinois, State's Attorney's Office, the country's second largest, employs nearly 900 assistant prosecutors assigned to seven bureaus. In every prosecutor's office, assistants are assigned to receive and screen cases as they enter the system; some will be assigned to the lower courts to deal with **bond hearings**, probable-cause hearings, and misdemeanor cases. If a felony case is sent to the **grand jury** or superior court, assistants assigned to those bodies will manage it. If a case is appealed, assistants who specialize in appeals will handle it. (Those who are familiar with basketball will recognize this method as the *zone defense*.) **Horizontal prosecution** in felony cases means that a victim or complainant may have to deal with a different assistant prosecutor at each stage of the judicial process. The victim may feel tossed about, receiving little personal attention, and this can be costly in terms of cooperation.

2. *Vertical prosecution.* This system is used in smaller jurisdictions where the prosecutor's office is not overburdened by the mass of cases that characterize

Figure 7.2   Differences in How Prosecutors Handle Felony Cases

most metropolitan areas. Each assistant prosecutor is assigned a caseload (a number of specific cases) for which he or she has total responsibility. The assistant picks up the case after the decision to charge has been made and stays with it until the final disposition. (Those familiar with basketball will recognize this method as the *man-to-man defense*.) The victim has the comfort of one assistant throughout the entire judicial process; he or she does not have to discuss the case anew with each new assistant. The **vertical prosecution** method can be quite costly in terms of personnel. It is often difficult to gather all of the primary and secondary actors in court at the same time, with the necessary files and exhibits needed for the case to move forward. Quite often, an assistant prosecutor will find that he or she is prepared for trial but other actors or records are either missing or not prepared, and the case will be rescheduled for another date. With horizontal prosecution, the clerk will call the next case and the prosecutor will deal with that one; with vertical prosecution, the entire day may be wasted.

3. *Mixed prosecution.* This system takes advantage of the strengths inherent in horizontal and vertical prosecution. Most routine cases will be handled in a horizontal (cost-effective) manner, while certain targeted cases (e.g., murder, those involving organized crime, or serious repeat offenders) will be subject to vertical prosecution. When using the **mixed prosecution** method the prosecutor may set up special bureaus such as a homicide bureau, a rackets bureau, or a serious repeat offender bureau with assistants and investigators who have special training or experience in dealing with these types of cases.

Like the police, a prosecutor is responsible for enforcing the law, and as such acts in the name of "the people" (actually, in the name of the United States of America or the State of _____). Unlike the police, however, a prosecutor has an additional responsibility: *justice*. A police officer who has the minimum level of evidence necessary to effect a lawful arrest (probable cause) must, in the case of a felony, arrest the suspect. The prosecutor needs a much higher level of evidence—**beyond a reasonable doubt**. (Differing levels of proof play an important role in plea bargaining, which will be discussed in Chapter 9.) As a public official representing "the people," a prosecutor must be concerned with the possibility of prosecuting a person who is innocent or a person against whom the evidence is not sufficient to justify a verdict of guilty; to prosecute under such circumstances would be unjust. This explains why prosecutors will often dismiss cases or declare *nolle prosequi* (or simply "nol pros"), a formal entry on the record by the prosecutor that he or she will not prosecute the case any further. According to legal ethics scholar Monroe Freedman, a prosecutor cannot properly go forward with a case unless satisfied beyond a reasonable doubt that the accused is guilty. "A prosecutor should be professionally disciplined for proceeding with a prosecution if a fair-minded person could not reasonably conclude, on the facts known to the prosecutor, that the accused is guilty beyond a reasonable doubt" (1975: 88). (For a fascinating examination of the issue of prosecutorial ethics, see Luban 2010.)

Whereas the police are sensitive to immediate demands for crime control, prosecutors must be sensitive to the legal constraints on governmental action (McDonald et al. 1982). In addition to having different evidentiary concerns, there are social and

Prosecution Standards

American Bar Association General Standards for Prosecutors

1. The duty of the prosecutor is to seek justice, not merely to convict.

2. A prosecutor should not institute, cause to be instituted, or permit the continued pendency of criminal charges in the absence of sufficient admissible evidence to support a conviction.

Reality According to the *Chicago Tribune*

"With impunity prosecutors across the country have violated their oaths and the law, committing the worst kinds of deception in the most serious of cases. They have prosecuted black men, hiding evidence that the real killers were white. They have prosecuted a wife, hiding evidence that her husband committed suicide. They have prosecuted parents, hiding evidence their daughter was killed by wild dogs. They do it to win. . . . They have done it to defendants who came within hours of being executed only to be exonerated" (Armstrong and Possley 1999: 1).

educational differences between police officers and prosecutors. Although a number of jurisdictions have increased educational standards, qualifications for the position of police officer do not go beyond a bachelor's degree. Whereas prosecutors conceive of their positions as a point of entry to private practice or some other public service, police are likely to see their job as a career. In order to reduce some of the distance between police officers and prosecutors that can hinder effective prosecution, several jurisdictions have established special cooperative programs to have prosecutors work directly with the police on specialized (e.g., drug or gang crime) investigations.

Criminal Defense Attorneys

In civil matters (discussed in Chapter 10), neither plaintiff nor defendant is constitutionally entitled to an attorney. However, in criminal cases a government attorney—the prosecutor—represents the complainant and the defendant has a constitutional right to be represented by "competent" counsel. Criminal justice in the United States is based on an adversarial model (Chapter 1), and the defense counsel is one of its cornerstones. Within this adversarial system of justice, the attorney for the accused has a singular purpose: As an advocate, he or she must use every lawful means to exonerate the accused or, failing that, to mitigate punishment. Questions of justice, of guilt or innocence, which should concern the prosecutor, are not the responsibility of defense counsel—at least not in the United States. Monroe Freedman (1975) notes that in some totalitarian countries, such as China or Cuba, it is the responsibility of the lawyer not to argue that his or her client is innocent but to determine if the client is guilty, and if so, to seek the sanction necessary to best provide rehabilitation—even if that means execution. In China, lawyers may be aided in this endeavor by judges who, under communism, are considered agents of the state and who frequently lack legal training; there is little judicial autonomy (Kynge 2001; Yardley 2005). At least three attorneys who defended protesters involved in the 1989 Tiananmen Square incident (a massive protest against the Chinese government) were suspended by the People's Republic for trying too hard on behalf of their clients (Schmetzer 1991). And in 2008, two lawyers had their licenses suspended after volunteering to defend Tibetans accused of partici- pating in anti-China protests (Yardley 2008). Justice in China is swift. Criminal investi- gations nearly always end in guilty pleas—forced confessions are endemic—and prosecutors almost never lose cases brought to trial (Kahn 2005). In contrast, Lon Fuller argues that under our adversarial system, an attorney who refuses to defend a client because the attorney thinks he or she is guilty "is wrongfully usurping the office of judge and jury" (1961: 34).

In the United States, only agents of government must be dedicated to truth find- ing. Defense counsel is under no comparable obligation; his or her role is to defend the client whether innocent or guilty. In fact, defense counsel is required to throw up road- blocks in the face of the truth, to prevent admission of evidence that may be wholly reliable, such as a murder weapon seized in violation of the Fourth Amendment or a truthful but involuntary confession. "Our interest in not convicting the innocent," notes Justice Byron R. White, permits counsel "to put the State's case in the worst pos- sible light, regardless of what he thinks or knows to be the truth" (*United States v. Wade* [1967]). Freedman says that in the adversary system, "it is not the role or function of the advocate to act upon conclusions of ultimate facts such as guilt or innocence. That function is assigned to the judge or jury, which bases its decision on the adversaries' presentation of their clients' cases. Thus, the fact of guilt or innocence is irrelevant to the role that has been assigned to the advocate" (1975: 57).

A public defender writes: "It is an axiom of criminal defense practice that you rep- resent your guilty clients as zealously as you do your innocent ones (not that you can always tell the difference). A client who you really believe is innocent . . . does not happen very often. In fact, it happens rarely enough to be considered remarkable. One of the awkward truths about being a public defender is that you are in the practice of representing people who are, indeed, guilty as charged" (Bellows 1983: 8).

The right to counsel existed in colonial America, although often in practice rather than by law. In Connecticut it has been the custom since 1750 to appoint counsel for defendants who requested attorneys, although there was not a statutory provision until 1818. As early as 1701, Pennsylvania and Delaware provided all criminal defen- dants with the same privilege of counsel as their prosecutors, and South Carolina did the same in 1731. Most states made the provision regarding the right to counsel in their post-Revolutionary constitutions (McDonald 1983). The Sixth Amendment pro- vides that "in all criminal prosecutions, the accused shall enjoy the right . . . to have the assistance of counsel for his defense." In 1932, the Supreme Court ruled (*Powell v. Alabama*) that an indigent defendant accused of a capital offense in a state court is enti-

American Bar Association General Standards for Defense Counsel

"The basic duty the defense counsel for the accused owes to the administration of justice is to serve as the accused's counselor and advocate with courage, devotion, and to render effective, quality representation."

tled to counsel at public expense. In 1928 the Court (*Johnson v. Zerbst*) ruled that an indigent defendant is entitled to counsel in a federal criminal prosecution. In 1963 the Court ruled (*Gideon v. Wainwright*) that all indigent defendants accused of felonies are entitled to counsel at state expense, and in 1972 the Court (*Argersinger v. Hamlin*) extended the right to counsel for indigent defendants accused of misdemeanors for which the penalty includes possible imprisonment. These decisions established lawyers as a cornerstone for criminal justice. They asserted the value of the legal profession for ensuring equality in the midst of gross inequalities (McDonald 1983). However, in certain civil cases where incarceration is possible, such as child support, a defendant is not entitled to an attorney.

In the United States today, there are three ways to accomplish the right to counsel: (1) engaging a private attorney, (2) public defender systems, and (3) assigned counsel.

Private Defense Attorneys

Relatively few lawyers in private practice handle criminal cases on a regular basis, and most of them are solo practitioners or work within law firms of fewer than four partners or associates. The professional and private lifestyle of the criminal attorney usually falls far short of the glamorous portrayals in books, in movies, and on television. Paul Wice (1978) presents a portrait of the private criminal attorney that is rather depressing. He (very few are women[6]) must be concerned about continually securing clients, and in some jurisdictions this requires unlawful kickbacks to other attorneys or persons working in criminal justice (such as clerks, police officers, or bailiffs) for referrals (often by providing an attorney's business card to defendants). He must worry about being paid, because criminal defendants usually are poor and may refuse to pay when a case is over. The hours are long, and a great deal of time is spent simply waiting in, or traveling to, courthouses. Private criminal lawyers are usually at the office for an hour or two prior to their morning court appearance and will return there in the late afternoon for a few additional hours. They may also be found in their office on weekends and on those rare days when no court appearances are required. For the bulk of the day, however, criminal lawyers will be in the courthouse, roaming hallways, waiting for appointments, chatting with other practitioners over rancid coffee, and occasionally carrying out professional responsibilities before a judge (Wice 1978). The daily routine of famed Bronx, New York, criminal defense attorney Murray Richman is typical: "Despite the frenetic pace of his daily calendar, a great part of Richman's working life is spent idling, waiting out the inevitable delays in court, or in jail, for something that's supposed to happen, or someone who's supposed to appear" (Gourevitch 2001: 163).

The private practice of criminal law not only is physically demanding, but it also has significant social and psychological costs. Attorney Murray Richman states that people ask him "How can you represent people like this?" (Gourevitch 2001: 164). "The private criminal lawyer obviously suffers from guilt by association. The public reflexively links the client with his attorney and fails to appreciate the professional and constitutional responsibility that the latter must exercise. The public seems to rea-

---

[6] A noted exception is Leslie Abrahamson who has been the defense attorney in a number of high-profile cases. She has written about her experiences (Abrahamson with Flaste 1997).

son that if a lawyer chooses to defend a guilty man, then the lawyer must himself also be tainted with some guilt" (Wice 1978: 91).

Because their clients are poor financial risks, private criminal attorneys usually require at least part of their fee in advance—"upfront money." In many cases this is the only fee they can expect to receive. Since the fee any single client can afford to pay is relatively low, criminal attorneys must substitute quantity for quality. That is, they must have numerous clients to maintain a profitable criminal practice, and they cannot spend too much time on any single case since the fee is inelastic, and extra time will not necessarily result in additional payment. Federal court of appeals judge Frank Easterbrook suggests that defendants who prevail at or before trial be reimbursed for the market cost of legal assistance. "Just as the promise of compensation attracts able counsel to antitrust and civil rights litigation, so it would attract counsel to criminal litigation" (1992: 1974). For cynical defense attorney Richman, "reasonable doubt begins with the payment of a reasonable fee" (Gourevitch 2001: 160).

It is not unusual for attorneys to find themselves prepared for a hearing that fails to take place, because, for example, the defendant, complainant, or other principal fails to appear or records have been misplaced. Because of the likelihood that any one case scheduled for a court hearing on a particular day will result in a continuance, private attorneys, like airlines, usually **overbook** (airlines may book more passengers for a flight than the plane has seats, under the assumption that not everyone will actually show up for the flight, and every empty seat represents lost income).[7] Case management becomes a preoccupation as attorneys rush from courtroom to courtroom juggling their cases, frequently requesting continuances. In New York City, for example, one study found that 43 percent of the criminal cases were adjourned at least once because of defense counsel trial-scheduling conflicts (Jacobs and Chayet 1986). Since the prosecutor can object to a continuance, and a judge need not grant one, the attorney needs to maintain good relations with the other key actors. This has implications for plea bargaining (Chapter 9).

Public Defenders

The public defender is a counterpart of the prosecutor; that is, he or she is a government official. Instead of representing "the people," however, the public defender represents the interests of indigent defendants. The public defender is an anomaly, "paid by the state to befriend those whom the state believes are its enemies and to question—and, whenever possible, to thwart—the prosecution of those whom the state suspects are criminals" (McIntyre 1987: 1). Unlike most prosecutors, public defenders typically are not elected officials but are usually appointed by the judiciary or county board. The reason for using an appointment system is quite simple: On what would an aspiring candidate for public defender base his or her campaign: "If I am elected, more criminal defendants will go free, and others will serve less time in prison"? Whereas a candidate for prosecutor can engage in a great deal of law-and-order rhetoric and posturing, promising to be "tough on criminals," the aspiring public defender is limited in what he or she could possibly do to attract votes. "A few jurisdictions

---

[7] Barry Mahoney points out that courts also overbook: "Almost always, courts 'overset' their trial calendars, scheduling more cases for trial on a given day or week than they could possibly try if some did not settle" (1988: 81).

Losing Cases

"Given the abundance of difficult, even unwinnable, cases that public defenders are obligated to defend, experienced attorneys advise recent additions to the office (also possibly trying to convince themselves) that good lawyers should not worry about the results of individual cases. Working as a public defender means a career filled with 'loser cases,' and, conversely, very few winning cases" (Wice 2005: 116).

---

actually do elect their public defenders: Florida, Tennessee, and a few places in California and Nebraska" (Wright 2010: 803). In these jurisdictions, incumbent public defenders win as often as do prosecutors.

A victorious public defender raises the specter of unfairness or incompetence since the victory can only mean that "(1) the defendant was actually innocent and ought not have been arrested in the first place and prosecuted in the second, or (2) the police and/or prosecutor failed to properly handle the case such that a conviction could be won" (McIntyre 1987: 72). Conventional wisdom in criminal justice holds that if everyone is doing his or her job properly, the public defender does not win cases. For this reason, public defenders do not usually broadcast their successes for public consumption.

Nationally, in urban areas public defenders represent three-fourths of the defendants facing felony charges (Wice 2005). Although public defenders are the primary providers of criminal defense services in only about 35 percent of all counties in the United States, they serve almost 70 percent of the nation's population. More than 40 percent of the largest 50 counties in the nation are served predominantly by a public defender program (*Criminal Defense Systems* 1984; DeFrances and Litras 2000). There are statewide and local public defender systems:

> Under statewide public defender systems [used in 24 states], an individual is designated by statute as the State public defender and is charged with developing and maintaining a system of representation for each of the counties in the State. In such systems, there is usually a governing board that shares responsibility with the State public defender for the operation of the program. Most statewide systems are part of the executive branch, but others may operate as part of the judicial branch, as independent State agencies, or as independent nonprofit organizations. (*Criminal Defense Systems* 1984: 3; for a discussion of the statewide system used in New Jersey, see Wice 2005)

Local public defenders are usually part of county government and are often appointed by the county legislature on a recommendation from the judiciary. An independent nonprofit organization is used in New York City, where the Legal Aid Society represents all indigent criminal defendants except those accused of murder. A board of directors governs the society "that's a *Who's Who* of prominent lawyers, businessmen, and educators" (Pileggi 1982: 30). It was founded in New York City in 1876 as *Der Deutscher Rechts-Schutz Verein*, an association to help German immigrants. This limitation and the German name were soon dropped in favor of helping the poor of all nationalities (Brownell 1951). As opposed to public defender offices, which handle only criminal matters, the Legal Aid Society has a civil division. Like the prosecutor's office, a public defender's office may be organized horizontally ("zone defense"), vertically ("man-to-man defense"), or a combination of the two ("mixed system"). Like the prosecutor, the public defender employs assistant or deputy defenders, who may be full- or part-time, and investigative personnel. Like the prosecutor's office, that of the public defender suffers from a high personnel turnover rate. The position of an assistant is attractive to lawyers who are interested in gaining a great deal of criminal trial experience in a relatively short period of time. However, the public defender suffers from a lack of "respect" in the legal community and the community at large, a failure to acknowledge the individual public defender's legitimacy as a "real" lawyer (McIntyre 1987).

Like providers of other forms of welfare, the public defender may be resented by the recipients of his or her services. In addition to this attitude toward receiving a necessary beneficence, there is the common folk wisdom that "you only get what you pay for!" Jonathan Casper points out:

> What attracts defendants to private lawyers is, for a large number of them at least, the notion that, because of the financial exchange between lawyer and client, the lawyer will be more committed to the defendant's interests. It is money that provides a sense of control, the leverage to insure that lawyers will listen to their clients, take instructions from their clients, and generally exert themselves on their clients' behalf. Moreover, not only does the client fail to pay, and thus lack this leverage over public defenders, but someone else does. And that someone else is "the state"—the very same institution that is proceeding against the defendant. Thus, the public defenders suffer not only from the fact that they are imposed upon defendants rather than being selected, and from the absence of financial exchange, but they are employed by the enemy. (1978: 4)

For that reason, public defender offices are usually located outside of the courthouse that houses the prosecutor's office, "seeking to establish the appearance of their independence" (Wice 2005: 24). There does not appear to be any significant difference in the conviction rates of defendants represented by private or publicly financed attorneys. However, of those found guilty, "higher percentages of defendants with publicly financed counsel were sentenced to incarceration" (Harlow 2000: 1).

Wice contrasts the public defender with the private criminal attorney. He notes that, by developing a reputation as a successful advocate, a private criminal attorney can improve his or her economic condition. "Public defenders," he writes, "will receive their salaries regardless of the outcome of the case, but private attorneys know that their economic worth is directly related to how well they satisfy their clients." Private attorneys "are motivated to offer several benefits usually unavailable at the public defender's office. Although these advantages may not be related to the ultimate

Adversarial Justice: The Reality

Public defenders, often inexperienced and just commencing their legal career, are handicapped by staggering caseloads and inadequate resources (Wice 2005).

disposition of the case, they nevertheless do heighten the prestige of private criminal lawyers in the eyes of their clientele" (Wice 1983: 41). There are two major advantages of private lawyers:

1. *They can provide personalized attention, sometimes referred to as "hand-holding."* The large caseloads typical of a public defender's office result in cases being handled horizontally—clients are represented by different attorneys at various stages of the judicial process. Clients do not have their own attorney and cannot drop in for a review of their case in a secluded office. In addition, among criminal clientele, there is prestige in having one's own attorney.

2. *Private lawyers are more willing to take an aggressive stance toward both the judge and the prosecutor on behalf of the client.* Private criminal attorneys have been found to be much more willing to risk contempt citations and other forms of judicial anger than public defenders, who are often assigned to a specific judge for a length of time; confrontations with the judge could make things quite difficult for the public defender. Some observers, however, have found the opposite—that private attorneys are more willing to compromise, and public defenders are more aggressive. This issue will be looked at again when plea bargaining is discussed in Chapter 9.

But public defenders have advantages, too. As opposed to most attorneys in private practice who handle criminal cases, they have access to their own law libraries and at least limited use of investigators. "Additionally, the public defender is clearly a criminal specialist" and, "because of his continued involvement with the prosecutors and judiciary, the public defender can frequently develop a working relationship in which the exchange of favors, so necessary to greasing the squeaky wheel of justice, can directly benefit the indigent defendant" (Wice 1985: 65). Since most cases are resolved not by trial but by negotiation, public defenders can accumulate favors as well as develop a mutual respect with prosecutors and judges to their client's advantage. "At the very least, indigent defendants can be reassured that their attorney is not only knowledgeable in terms of the law but knows his or her way around the local criminal justice system" (Wice 2005: 11).

Lisa McIntyre is more cynical; to her, the public defender merely serves to provide legitimacy for the criminal justice system: "The role of the public defender is not justice, but is to strengthen the perception that justice is being done, to make the system appear more legitimate" (1987: 52). Since all indigent criminal defendants are entitled to legal representation, without public defender systems large urban jurisdictions would be unable to process their enormous criminal caseloads. One study found that private attorneys, as opposed to public defenders, received more favorable plea bargain offers for their clients. Thus, "persons unable to afford the services of a private attorney must face more punitive or severe conditions as part of their plea bargain agreements" (Champion 1989: 262).

Assigned Counsel

One study (Smith and DeFrances 1996) revealed that about three-fourths of the inmates in state prisons and about half in federal prisons received a public defender or assigned counsel for the offense for which they were serving. About 60 percent of the counties in the United States use court-appointed private attorneys as the primary method for providing legal representation for indigent criminal defendants. These are primarily rural counties with small populations; their limited number of cases do not justify a salaried public defender system. Even in counties that use a public defender system, many defendants are represented by private attorneys assigned by the trial judge.

There are two reasons for this. First, when public defenders are unable to handle their caseloads adequately, especially during certain peak seasons, judges supplement them by appointing private counsel. Second, the court will appoint attorneys when there is a conflict of interest because one attorney or a single law firm (the public defender's office fits this definition) would be representing codefendants. There is always a potential conflict of interest between codefendants, because one may testify against the other(s) in return for leniency or to exculpate him- or herself.

Private attorneys in most jurisdictions are assigned by individual judges on an ad hoc, case-by-case basis. In some areas, however, the assignment of private counsel is more systematic and involves an administrator who oversees the program and develops standards and guidelines. In a few jurisdictions, responsibility for appointment is given to the public defender or clerk of the court. In a growing number of jurisdictions, there are contracts with private attorneys or a law firm to provide legal services for indigent criminal defendants. This system has been criticized (much like HMOs—health maintenance organizations) for placing cost containment ahead of quality representation and creating incentives to plead cases rather than go to trial (Spangenberg et al. 2000). Most criminal defendants in the United States cannot afford to hire an attorney, and thus, their lawyers are government funded. "Unfortunately, some state and local governments drastically under-fund indigent defense services. Criminal defense lawyers serving in these jurisdictions typically carry grossly excessive caseloads and are therefore severely restricted in how much time they can devote to individual clients" (Green 2003: 1169).

> *"Those defendants who cannot afford a lawyer have the right*
> *to have counsel appointed free of charge. A considerable majority of*
> *criminal defendants in the United States fall into this category; yet, there*
> *are insufficient resources to meet their legal needs" (McGough 2011: 36).*

In most jurisdictions, a list of attorneys who have requested to be considered for appointment provides the basis for assigning private counsel. Compensation for assigned counsel is usually based on a fee schedule for in-court and out-of-court hours spent on a case. The hourly fee varies with the jurisdiction and sometimes with the complexity of the case. Hourly fees are considerably less than what an attorney would normally expect for representing a private client—but payment is guaranteed. Accepting indigent assignments ensures that an attorney will be able to pay his or her "nut," fixed expenses such as office rent and secretarial services.

Because of inadequate compensation, some jurisdictions have a difficult time finding attorneys who will accept assignments to represent indigent defendants. In

New York City, "underpaid, ill-prepared, virtually unsupervised private attorneys sometimes represent hundreds of defendants per year, leaving little time or incentive for them to master the facts, prepare and argue the cases or file appeals of dubious convictions" ("Drive-by Legal Defense" 2001: 26).

Until 2003, they were paid $40 per hour for work performed in-court and $25 per hour for work performed out of court. As a result, trials in serious cases—murder, rape, and robbery—were repeatedly delayed because overloaded assigned counsel were often on trial in other cases on virtually a continual basis. When criminal cases are delayed this long, prosecutors often have great difficulty securing their witnesses for trial, and criminal defendants are denied a speedy resolution of the charges against them. In 2001, lawyers in New York City refused to take Family Court assignments, causing a due process crisis in that court. Meanwhile, criminal cases continued to back up because of a shortage of attorneys for indigent defendants. In 2003, as the result of a lawsuit, the City of New York agreed to raise the fees paid to assigned counsel to $75 an hour for felonies and $60 an hour for misdemeanors. Referred to as 18-B attorneys, in better economic times assigned counsel could count on wealthier clients to supplement their indigent employment. Such persons have become harder to find and more reluctant to pay or afford substantial rates (Feuer 2011).

A study in Philadelphia compared outcomes for homicide cases in which indigent defendants were represented either by appointed counsel or a public defender. In that city, every fifth homicide case is assigned to the public defender's office while the other four are assigned to appointed counsel. The research disclosed that defendants represented by a public defender had significantly better outcomes, the disparity related to the failure of appointed counsel to prepare cases as thoroughly as the public defenders due to their inadequate pay scale (Anderson and Heaton 2012).

Assigned private attorneys suffer from much the same negative client perception as do public defenders. One study found that "attorneys with public clients labor in the shadow of the 'public defender' stereotype. Whether they actually work as public defenders makes no difference, their clients give them little respect and distrust them" (Flemming 1988: 230). In her research, Jennifer Shinall (2010) found that while a skillful prosecutor can drastically increase the defendant's chances of being convicted and an unskilled prosecutor can increase the likelihood of a hung jury or acquittal—no matter how strong the case is against the defendant—a skillful defense attorney has no such effect.

In Part III we will examine "justice," beginning with the chapter on criminal justice.

SUMMARY

- When there is no jury, the judge determines both issues of law and issues of fact.
- Judges in the United States receive no formal training before they assume their positions.
- Judges in the United States are generalists whose education and experience in non-legal areas are typically quite limited, requiring specialized courts.
- Trial judges preside over few trials because most criminal and civil cases are settled without a trial.

- There are four methods commonly used to select judges and some states use more than one: (1) appointment by a chief executive; (2) election; (3) merit system; and (4) selection by the legislature.

- The Constitution provides for the presidential nomination of Supreme Court justices but does not provide a method for selecting other federal judges.

- Candidates for federal judgeships are commonly submitted to the American Bar Association for an evaluation and rating. There has been controversy over this role.

- While the president nominates candidates for federal judgeships, except for the Supreme Court, members of the Senate dominate the process.

- There are four methods used for removing judges: (1) impeachment and conviction, (2) legislative resolution, (3) recall, and (4) commission system. Federal judges can be removed only by impeachment and conviction.

- Because a prosecutor has virtually unlimited discretion to determine who to charge and what to charge, he or she is the most powerful person in criminal justice.

- The solicitor general represents the United States in cases before the Supreme Court.

- In most states, the primary responsibility of the attorney general is to provide legal advice to state agencies and represent the state in any legal action in which the state is a defendant or plaintiff.

- In most states, the prosecutor is an elected county official.

- A prosecutor may organize his or her office to handle cases horizontally, vertically, or mixed.

- As a public official representing "the people," a prosecutor has an obligation to be concerned with justice; defense counsel has no parallel obligation.

- Agents of government must be dedicated to truth finding. Defense counsel is under no comparable obligation; his or her role is to defend the client whether innocent or guilty.

- There are three ways to accomplish the right to counsel: (1) engaging a private attorney, (2) public defender systems, and (3) assigned counsel.

- Relatively few lawyers in private practice handle criminal cases on a regular basis.

- The difficulties of being a criminal attorney include clients with limited funds.

- The private practice of criminal law is physically demanding and has significant social costs associated with defending criminals.

- The public defender, a government official who represents the interests of indigent defendants, is the counterpart of the prosecutor.

- Distinct from the prosecutor, the public defender is usually appointed by the judiciary or country board.

- The public defender may be resented by the recipients of his or her services due to wisdom that "you only get what you pay for!" And the public defender is being paid for by the same source that pays the prosecutor.

- Public defenders have access to their own law libraries and at least limited use of investigators. The public defender is clearly a criminal specialist and has continued involvement with the prosecutors and judiciary, a working relationship that can directly benefit the indigent defendant.

- Assigned counsel is used when public defenders are unable to handle their caseloads adequately and when there is a conflict of interest because one attorney or a single law firm would be representing codefendants.
- Hourly fees for assigned counsel are considerably less than what an attorney would normally expect for representing a private client, but payment is guaranteed.

KEY TERMS

beyond reasonable doubt	grand jury	overbook
bond hearing	horizontal prosecution	public defender
chambers	merit system	senatorial courtesy
complaint	Missouri Plan, The	vertical prosecution
continuance	mixed prosecution	

REVIEW QUESTIONS

1. What are the three methods commonly used to select judges?
2. What are the advantages and disadvantages of each?
3. What are steps used in the merit system?
4. What does the Constitution say about choosing judges?
5. What is the role of the American Bar Association (ABA) in selecting federal judges?
6. What is the controversy over the ABA role?
7. How do senators dominate the process of selecting federal judges?
8. What is the process for removing federal judges?
9. Why is the prosecutor the most powerful person in criminal justice?
10. What is the role of the solicitor general?
11. In most states, what is the primary responsibility of the attorney general?
12. What is the difference between horizontal and vertical prosecution?
13. Why do prosecutors handle most cases horizontally?
14. How do the prosecutor and defense attorney differ on the issue of justice?
15. What are the three ways to accomplish the right to counsel?
16. What are the difficulties encountered by private attorneys who handle criminal cases?
17. Why is it necessary for private defense attorneys to be friendly with prosecutors?
18. Why is the public defender usually not elected?
19. What is the basis of mistrust by clients of the public defender?
20. What are the advantages of being represent by the public defender?
21. Why would assigned counsel be used when there is public defender?
22. Why would a private attorney request to be assigned counsel?

INTERNET CONNECTIONS

American Association for Justice: http://justice.org/cps/rde/xchg/justice/hs.xsl/default.htm

American Judges Association: aja.ncsc.dni.us

American Judicature Society: http://ajs.org

Center for Competitive Politics: http://www.campaignfreedom.org

Council for Court Excellence: http://courtexcellence.org

Justice at Stake: http://www.justiceatstake.org

Money in State Politics: http://followthemoney.org

National Criminal Justice Reference Service: https://ncjrs.gov

National District Attorneys Association: http://ndaa.org

National Institute of Justice: http://www.nij.gov

National Judicial College: http://judges.org

Office of the U.S. Solicitor General: http://www.usdoj.gov/osg

PART III

Justice

8

Criminal Justice

In the last chapter we examined the key actors in the legal system, all of whom are attorneys, and in previous chapters we looked at the role of attorneys in the appellate process. In this chapter we will look at the public stage on which attorneys are the stars and at the scenarios of criminal trials. The trial brings together two opposing attorneys whose combat in an adversarial system is refereed by a judge. In some cases, the judge also acts as a finder of fact; in other cases, this responsibility is left to a jury. We will begin with an examination of the criminal justice system.

American Criminal Justice

The administration of criminal justice in the United States reflects the highly decentralized nature of our governmental structure. Although policing is basically a municipal responsibility, there are also county and state police agencies. A county may have dozens of police agencies—more than 125 in Cook County (which includes Chicago), Illinois—and a single municipality may have specialized police agencies for public housing and/or mass transit. Federal law enforcement agencies such as the Federal Bureau of Investigation and Drug Enforcement Administration have responsibilities that often overlap with those of state, county, and municipal police.

Research has revealed that most crimes are not reported to, or discovered by, the police, and of those that are reported, about one in five is cleared by an arrest. Thus, persons entering the criminal justice system represent the least skilled criminals and/or those whose sheer number of offenses has sufficiently enhanced the probability of detection and arrest.

The prosecutorial function, as discussed in Chapter 7, is usually a county responsibility, but New York City has an elected district attorney in each of its five boroughs. The jail is usually a responsibility of the county sheriff, but many large municipalities (and any number of counties) have their own department of corrections. **Probation** may be administered at any level of government, in either the judicial or executive branch, whereas prisons and **parole** are a state responsibility. And, of course, there is a separate federal system of criminal justice.

Corpus Delicti

Basic to criminal process is the rule of *nullum crimen sine lege*: "No crime without a law." The Constitution (Article 1, Section 9) prohibits the passage of an *ex post facto* **law**, and (case law) requires "fair warning" (*McBoyle v. United States* [1931]) that the behavior is proscribed: A court has no jurisdiction in a criminal case unless there is a statute making the behavior a crime (Berman and Saliba 2009). When statutory jurisdiction exists, the state must prove the *corpus delicti* ("the body of the crime"), referring to the sub-

Figure 8.1   The Criminal Justice Process

stance (or body) of the alleged violation of the criminal law. It includes two elements that must be proved in order to **sustain** a criminal charge: *actus reus* and *mens rea*.

Actus reus means a wrongful act or deed; it refers to the need to prove that a violation of the criminal law—a crime—actually occurred. *Actus reus* consists of a description of the criminal behavior and evidence that the accused acted accordingly. For example, according to the Illinois Criminal Code of 2012 (Chapter 38: para. 19-3a), "A person commits residential burglary who knowingly and without authority enters the dwelling place of another with intent to commit therein a felony or theft." Thus, it must be proved that the defendant entered the dwelling place of another without permission of the legal occupant for the purpose of committing a felony, harming the occupant, for example, or taking something of value. The defendant's fingerprints found inside a dwelling, to which he or she had never been given legal access, may be sufficient as proof of *actus reus*—that is, burglary—while possession of jewelry belonging to the occupant, which the defendant had not been given permission to possess, would constitute evidence of *mens rea*: **intent** to commit theft.

Mens rea, "guilty mind," is a legal standard referring to the question of *intent*—the mental state accompanying an illegal act. In order to prove the *corpus delicti*, the prosecutor must show that the defendant had a wrongful purpose—willfulness—in carrying out the *actus reus*. Thus, a person lawfully employed by a moving company who mistakenly entered the wrong apartment and mistakenly removed household items was devoid *of mens rea*. *Mens rea* may also be absent as a result of **infancy** or mental incapacity. However, a person who injured or killed another by accident has (general) *mens rea* if he or she was acting in a reckless manner, for example, driving under the influence of alcohol or drugs. Behavior that is a gross deviation from the standard of care expected of a reasonable person may constitute *mens rea* if it involves a conscious and unjustifiable risk of harm to others: for example, backyard target practice in an urban area.

Some offenses do not require a showing of *mens rea*. In cases of *strict* or **absolute liability**, the intentions of the perpetrator are irrelevant. If the law prohibits possessing a concealed firearm, a claim of ignorance—not knowing that it is illegal in that jurisdiction—is not an acceptable defense. Persons accused of violating federal environmental protection laws can be prosecuted without regard to intent.[1] Except in drug, weapons, and certain pollution cases, however, the penalties in **strict liability** cases are usually fines and not imprisonment.

A defendant can also raise an **affirmative defense**: He or she can claim **self-defense** or **entrapment**, that government trickery induced him or her to commit a crime that he or she was otherwise not independently predisposed to commit. Prosecutors, however, have wide latitude in demonstrating an "independent predisposition," and it is one of the exceptions to the hearsay rule (discussed later).

Due Process

Due process is one of the rare legal terms that is meant to be understood literally: the process that is due; procedures to which a person is entitled. Due process was origi-

---

[1] In civil cases, strict liability dispenses with the need to prove fault. In tort cases involving extremely hazardous activities, such as the lawful use of explosives, the actor is accountable for any reasonably related injuries, even in the absence of a showing of negligence. For an examination of strict liability, see Vandall (1989).

nally derived from English common law dating back to the twelfth century. The concept serves to restrain government from arbitrarily depriving a person of life, liberty, or property (Abraham 2003). The Supreme Court has ruled that a public high school student is entitled to some sort of hearing before being suspended from school (*Goss v. Lopez* [1975]), and students at a *public* university also have rights based on the **due process clause** of the Constitution. The amount of due process required in a particular setting is dependent on what is at stake: Whereas a college student's challenge to a course grade is entitled to only minimal due process, a criminal defendant can lose liberty or even life and is thus provided with the maximum amount of due process available under our system of justice. At private schools, however, student disciplinary procedures typically afford few of the rights that attach in criminal cases, and this has been a source of increasing controversy. Students at private colleges can often be expelled on the basis of flimsy evidence, and they are not usually permitted to be represented by counsel at disciplinary hearings (Pérez-Peña 1994a; see Stevens 1999 for a discussion of this issue).

In a criminal action, the state is arrayed against an individual defendant. This inherent inequality requires that certain specific procedures be followed, or the defendant cannot be found guilty and punished according to law. There is an inherent tension between society's desire for security and safety and the value we place on liberty. Herbert Packer (1968) refers to this as a conflict between two conceptual models of criminal justice: *crime control* and *due process*. (A conceptual model is a way of representing an idea that allows for discussion and understanding of the reality represented by the model.)

The **crime control model** "is based on the proposition that the repression of criminal conduct is by far the most important function to be performed by the criminal justice process" (Packer 1968: 158). The stress is on achieving the greatest amount of societal security and safety. Effective crime control requires a high level of efficiency: The system must be able to apprehend, prosecute, and convict a large proportion of criminal offenders. However, the system must respond to these cases with only limited resources. Consequently, efficiency demands that cases be handled speedily, with a minimum of formality and without time-consuming challenges. This efficiency can be accomplished only by a presumption of guilt: "The supposition is that the screening processes operated by the police and prosecutors are reliable indicators of probable guilt" (1968: 160). To maximize crime control after this screening, the system must move expeditiously to conviction and sentencing. (Efficient case processing is discussed in more detail in "Rough Justice," later in the chapter.) The crime control model is characterized by a high level of confidence in the ability of police and prosecutors to separate the guilty from the innocent. It is a model that tends toward an inquisitorial system of justice and conflicts with the due process model.

The **due process model** stresses the need to protect individual liberty. It assumes that the criminal justice system is deficient, and it stresses the possibility of error:

> People are notoriously poor observers of disturbing events—the more emotion-arousing the context, the greater the possibility that recollection will be incorrect; confessions and admissions by persons in police custody may be induced by physical or psychological coercion so that the police end up hearing what the suspect thinks they want to hear rather than the truth; witnesses may be animated by a bias

Crime Control v. Due Process

The conflict between the crime control and due process models of criminal justice can be conceived of as a zero-sum continuum: Court decisions or legislation that move criminal justice toward one model do so at the expense of the other. Exceptions to the exclusionary rule, e.g., while they may increase police efficiency in certain instances, also lessen the ability of the courts to control police misconduct.

Crime Control   **Due Process**

◀──▶

efficiency   liberty

or interest that no one would trouble to discover except one specially charged with protecting the interests of the accused (as the police are not). (Packer 1968: 163)

Due process confronts crime control and its need for efficiency and speed with an obstacle course of formalities, technicalities, and civil rights: "Power is always subject to abuse—sometimes subtle, other times, as in the criminal justice process, open and ugly. Precisely because of its potency in subjecting the individual to the coercive power of the state, the criminal justice process must . . . be subjected to controls that prevent it from operating with maximal efficiency" (Packer 1968: 166). The due process model requires the system to slow down until it "resembles a factory that has to devote a substantial part of its input to quality control" (1968: 165)—due process guarantees.

The government's response to the challenges posed by the terrorist attacks of 9/11 continue to test the limits of due process. As noted in Chapter 6, there are decisions limiting the government's response to terrorism, in particular, the indefinite detaining of suspects without a hearing (*Rasul v. Bush*; *Hamdi v. Rumsfeld*).

Due Process Guarantees

A finding of guilty requires a level of certainty referred to "as beyond a reasonable doubt," as opposed to the standard in a civil case of "preponderance of the evidence" (something over 50 percent). Although this legal concept cannot be quantified, it would certainly be far in excess of 50 percent: The juror must be fully satisfied or entirely convinced of the defendant's guilt. In *Sandoval v. California* (1994), the Supreme Court defined **reasonable doubt** as "not a mere possible doubt . . . [but] that state of the case which after the entire comparison and consideration of all the evidence, leaves the minds of the jurors in that condition that they cannot say they feel an abiding conviction, *to a moral certainty*, of the truth of the charge." If a juror cannot conclude, based only on the evidence presented and admitted at trial, beyond any reasonable doubt that the defendant committed the crime alleged, the juror must vote for a verdict of "not guilty." In 1993, the Supreme Court (*Sullivan v. Louisiana*) ruled that if a judge failed to instruct the jury properly on this issue, a guilty verdict is invalid (it is not a **harmless error**).

There is a series of guarantees that are part of the Constitution or Supreme Court rulings (case law) based on the Constitution. Although the Constitution provides a

---

Reasonable Doubt

While criminal statutes, e.g., Illinois (Ch. 38: 3-1), typically declare "no person shall be convicted of any offense unless his guilt thereof is proved beyond a reasonable doubt," the term reasonable doubt is not defined. Like other legal standards, reasonable doubt defies quantification. It infers a degree of certainty that is conclusive and complete. It is, however, less than certainty—no possibility of error—since that would be an impossible standard to expect of a human tribunal.

---

number of due process rights, particularly in the first ten amendments (Bill of Rights), these were not automatically applicable to the states, although many states have similar provisions. Slowly, over a considerable period of time, the Supreme Court has applied many of these rights to the states, usually through the vehicle of the Fourteenth Amendment (discussed in Chapter 6).

While the Supreme Court determines the minimum level of due process to which a defendant is entitled, states have the sovereign power to provide rights beyond those embodied in the Constitution, and most states provide additional rights by statute or as a result of judicial interpretation of a state constitution. Thus, while the Supreme Court has ruled that six-person juries and less than unanimous decisions by 12-member juries are constitutional, most states require unanimous decisions by 12-member juries—Louisiana and Oregon are the exceptions. In New York, the state's highest court (court of appeals) has ruled in more than a dozen cases that the state constitution extends protections to individuals beyond those granted by the US Supreme Court. "The Court of Appeals has ruled, e.g., that the state demands a more stringent standard for searching a car or closing an adult bookstore" (Kolbert 1990: 12). "State courts . . . have been interpreting state constitutions more broadly than the U.S. Supreme Court interprets the federal Constitution" ("State Courts Providing Broader Constitutional Protections" 1993: 1), a process known as *judicial federalism* (Jones 1997). This has been particularly true in the area of criminal due process (Coffin 1994; Gardner 2005).

Right to Remain Silent. According to the Fifth Amendment, a person cannot "be compelled in any criminal case to be a witness against himself." Thus, the government must prove the allegation beyond a reasonable doubt, and the defendant is protected from having to assist in this endeavor. The basis for providing this protection is the long history of coerced confessions, which undermined justice in a number of respects, the most obvious of which is coercion can involve physical and psychological torture—the infamous police "third degree"—which, in turn, can lead to false confessions. The innocent may falsely admit guilt; in addition to the obvious moral dimension, coercion also permits the guilty to escape sanctions. Since confessing to a crime is counter to the defendant's interests, it is the strongest evidence that can be offered. Yet, the false admission of guilt is a serious problem: Gisli Gudjonsson (2011) states that false confessions are typically the result of manipulative and coercive interrogation techniques and suspects' vulnerabilities in interviews. With the evolution of

DNA use in the courts, which began in England in 1986, DNA evidence now allows experts to identify false confessions in hundreds of cases (Kolker 2010). The Fifth Amendment, however, protects only against verbal testimony. The government may compel a defendant to provide blood, hair, voice, and handwriting samples, participate in a lineup, or put on articles of clothing. Even a defendant's diary can be used against him or her.

In 1966, the Supreme Court interpreted the Fifth Amendment (*Miranda v. Arizona*) to require that before a suspect can be questioned by the police, he or she must be informed of the right to remain silent as well as the right to counsel during any questioning. Since that time, however, the Court has restricted the application of *Miranda* in number of ways. In 1984, the Supreme Court, in a 5–4 decision (*New York v. Quarles*), ruled that "overriding considerations of public safety" may justify questioning a suspect in **custody** without providing the warnings contained in *Miranda*. The **public safety exception** was the result of a woman's complaint to two New York City police officers that she had been raped and that the suspects had entered a nearby supermarket. The officers entered the store and apprehended one of the suspects, who was found to be wearing a shoulder holster. One of the officers asked whether he had a gun. The suspect nodded toward a pile of boxes and said, "The gun is over there." The Court ruled that the unattended firearm represented an immediate danger to public safety, and the gun and the statement were admitted into evidence.

In 1985, the Court handed down a decision in the case of *Oregon v. Elstad* that affected the *Miranda* decision. Pursuant to an arrest **warrant**, the police went to the home of an 18-year-old suspect and explained to him that they thought he was involved in a burglary. He responded, "Yes, I was there." An hour later at the police station, the officers informed the suspect of his *Miranda* rights. He indicated that he understood and gave a full confession. On appeal the Court ruled that the statement "I was there" was **inadmissible**; however, the Court ruled that the second confession was valid despite defense arguments that it was an extension of the original inadmissible confession and was thereby tainted.

In a 1986, decision (*Moran v. Burbine*) the Court ruled that a suspect's *Miranda* rights were not violated when the police misled his attorney. Brian Burbine had been arrested for the brutal murder of a woman. An assistant public defender telephoned the police station where Burbine was being held and was told that there would be no questioning until the next day. The suspect was not informed of the call. About an hour later, Burbine was advised of his rights and confessed to the murder. The Court ruled that "events occurring outside of the presence of the suspect and entirely

Miranda v. Arizona

"The current [1966] practice of incommunicado interrogation is at odds with one of our nation's most cherished principles—that the individual may not be compelled to incriminate himself. Unless adequate protective devices are employed to dispel the compulsion inherent in custodial surroundings, no statement obtained from the defendant can truly be the product of his free choice."

unknown to him, surely can have no bearing on the capacity to comprehend and knowingly relinquish a constitutional right." In that same year, the Court ruled (*Colorado v. Connelly* [1986]) that confessions of mentally ill defendants are admissible: A criminal suspect's "perception of coercion flowing from the 'voice of God,' however important or significant such perception may be in other disciplines, is a matter to which the United States Constitution does not speak."

In 1990, the Court upheld a murder confession given by an inmate to an undercover police officer posing as a fellow inmate. In an 8–1 decision, the Court ruled that the *Miranda* decision prohibits *coercion*, not *deception*. In this case, the inmate confessed to an unsolved murder for which he had not been charged (*Illinois v. Perkins*). In a 6–2 decision, that went in the other direction, the Court ruled that once a suspect in custody has asserted his right to an attorney, the police may no longer question him or her unless counsel is actually present. The decision overturned a murder conviction based on questions asked of the suspect after he had consulted with an attorney (*Minnick v. Mississippi* [1990]). The following year, in a narrow (5–4) decision (*Arizona v. Fulminante*), the Court held that even when a confession is coerced or involuntary, its admission into trial can be a "harmless error" that need not reverse a finding of guilty if the remainder of the evidence was sufficient beyond a reasonable doubt.

In addition to Supreme Court decisions limiting the application of *Miranda*, there are reports that police tactics are routinely chipping away at the Fifth Amendment rights of suspects (Hoffman 1998a, 1998b). In 2001, the Court ruled on such an issue (*Texas v. Cobb*). In this case, the defendant was free on bail for burglary and denied knowing anything about two apparent murders. After confessing to his father that he had committed the murders, the defendant was arrested and questioned by the police who obtained a written confession in the absence of counsel. The Court ruled 5–4 that the right to counsel is "offense specific." That is, police can question a suspect without his or her lawyer present even if the suspect is being represented by counsel in a closely related crime. In 2000, the Court affirmed the *Miranda* decision by a vote of 7–2 (*Dickerson v. United States*). In 2013, the Court ruled (*Salinas v. Texas*) the right to remain silent is not self-executing—unless a suspect explicitly invokes the right to remain silent in the face of police questioning before an arrest, prosecutors can use that silence as evidence of guilt at trial.

Right to Counsel. At the time of the American Revolution, defendants in England were not entitled to be represented by counsel, even at their own expense, except in cases of treason (McIntyre 1987). The right to counsel became part of the Constitution through the Sixth Amendment, which guarantees the accused "the assistance of Counsel for his defence." But it was not until 1963 that the Supreme Court ruled that states must provide counsel for all indigent defendants in felony cases (*Gideon v. Wainwright*). In the opinion of Justice Hugo Black: "That government hires lawyers to prosecute and defendants who have the money hire lawyers to defend are the strongest indications of the widespread belief that lawyers in criminal courts are necessities, not luxuries. The right of one charged with a crime to counsel may not be deemed fundamental and essential in some countries, but it is in ours."[2] Subsequently, this right was

---

[2] Plaintiff Clarence Gideon, of course, was indigent. He was represented by Abe Fortas, who was appointed by the Supreme Court to act pro bono.

extended to misdemeanor cases where imprisonment might result (*Argersinger v. Hamlin* [1972]). In 2002, the Court ruled (*Alabama v. Shelton*) that in the absence of counsel, the state cannot impose a suspended sentence in which imprisonment at a future date is possible. In 1979 (*Scott v. Illinois*), the Court ruled that the sentence actually imposed rather than the one authorized by statute determines whether the state needs to provide counsel. The right to appointed counsel is not limited to court but extends to any time the police wish to ask a suspect questions (*Miranda*).

Although the criminal defendant has an absolute right to counsel, the question of attorney competency is not as clear. Defendants often challenge their convictions by arguing on appeal that they were represented by ineffective counsel. In general, for the defendant to prevail, he or she must show that counsel made errors that were so serious as to deny the constitutional right to representation and that the deficient performance prejudiced the defense (*Strickland v. Washington* [1984]). Serious questions about the adequacy of indigent defense counsel remain (Liptak 2003). The Harvard Law Review Association (2000: 2062) reported that "decades after *Gideon*, the states have largely, and often outrageously, failed to meet the Court's constitutional command. . . . The political process failure in this area is unsurprising, for indigent defendants, by definition, lack the financial and political capital necessary to pursue effective reform efforts." In 2006, New York State's chief judge decried the condition of legal services for criminal defendants and recommended a state takeover (Hakim 2006).

Right to Bail.   The Constitution is vague on a number of important issues, one of them is bail. Although the Eighth Amendment prohibits "excessive bail," no definition of "excessive" is provided. For a person without means, a bail of even $25 can be excessive, whereas some major drug dealers find no difficulty raising $1 million for bail. In 1987, the Supreme Court ruled that defendants found to constitute a danger to public safety may be held without the setting of bail (*United States v. Salerno*), and persons charged with murder are generally held without bail. In some states, bail bondsmen, who are privately licensed entrepreneurs, provide a defendant's bail for a fee, generally 10 percent of the bail amount. If the defendant fails to return to court as required in the bail agreement, the money is forfeited. Bail bondsmen employ skip tracers ("bounty hunters") to apprehend bail jumpers. Jumping bail is an additional criminal offense for which a judge issues an arrest warrant providing law enforcement agents (and bounty hunters) with authority to arrest the wayward defendant.

Many defendants are released without the need for a cash **bond** or its equivalent (e.g., title to a car or house); known as **release on recognizance (ROR)**, this is an unsecured pledge to return to court on the appointed date to stand trial. In some jurisdictions there are programs designed to maximize the number of persons who can qualify for ROR. The best known of these programs, the Manhattan Bail Project, was developed by the Vera Foundation in New York City and has been copied by many jurisdictions. Defendants are interviewed by pretrial investigators (who are sometimes law students), and the results are entered on a point scale:

> A number of items dealing with the defendant's ties in the community (e.g., employment, residence and family ties) and relevant criminal justice factors (such as prior record, current charge or prior bail violations) are included in the scale. Normally a defendant is given plus or minus points for each item. The information

> obtained in the interview is then verified by referring to records, employers and family members. If the defendant has attained a certain number of points, a recommendation is made to the court for release. (Kirby 1977: 1)

Persons who are unable to effect a release on bail are held in custody in a jail. This subjects legally innocent persons to punishment; separates them from family, friends, and employment; limits them in assisting their attorneys in the defense process—because of security procedures, attorney visits to clients in jail can be quite time-consuming; and adds to the severe overcrowding that is characteristic of most jails. Although incarceration is always an unpleasant experience, it is even more so in a jail. Most provide few opportunities for recreation, and they are usually understaffed and overcrowded, subjecting the inmates to the possibility of physical and/or sexual assault by other prisoners.

The basic purpose of bail is to guarantee a defendant's return to court, but it is often used as a form of **preventive detention**. When there is strong belief that the defendant will return to crime, a judge, often on the recommendation of the prosecution, will set bail at a level that is impossible for the defendant to make. The use of bail in this manner, though not illegal, is controversial. It involves predictions of future behavior, always a questionable undertaking with important moral and legal dimensions. The judge's bail decision is influenced by the defendant's previous criminal record, previous behavior while out on bail, roots in the community, the attitude of the prosecutor, and publicity that the case may have generated. Some jurisdictions are using house arrest with electronic monitoring in "bail or jail" decisions. Electronic monitoring often uses a transmitter strapped to the defendant's ankle that sends an alert if he or she leaves home.

Right to a Speedy and Public Trial.   Again we are confronted with constitutional vagueness. The Sixth Amendment guarantees: "In all criminal prosecutions, the accused shall enjoy the right to a speedy and public trial, by an impartial jury." But the term "speedy trial" is not defined in the Constitution. In 1972, the Supreme Court (*Barker v. Wingo*) ruled that determination of whether a particular defendant has been denied a speedy trial is to be made on a case-by-case basis, and the Court established several tests by which to judge the delay: (1) length of the delay, (2) reasons for the delay, (3) timely assertion of the right to a speedy trial, and (4) prejudice to the defendant as a result of the delay. The Court indicated an interest in preventing oppressive pretrial incarceration, minimizing the anxiety and hardship of the defendant, and avoiding hampering the defense: Delay that hampers the defense can result in the denial of a fair trial, which violates the Fifth and Fourteenth Amendments. In response to *Barker*, states and the federal government enacted statutes specifying the amount of time allowed from arrest to trial. The U.S. Code (Sec. 3161) provides: "In any case in which a plea of not guilty is entered, the trial of a defendant charged in an **information** [an accusatory document detailing the charges; emphasis added] or **indictment** with the commission of an offense shall commence within seventy days from the filing date (and making public) of the information or indictment, or from the date the defendant has appeared before a judicial officer of the court in which such charge is pending, whichever date last occurs." In Illinois, statutes require that the defendant be brought to trial within 120 days if incarcerated, or 160 days if free on bail; in New York, it is 180 days after an indictment; delays caused by the defense stop the clock.

While the Sixth Amendment protects criminal defendants from being tried in secret, can a defendant **waive** this right or demand a closed trial?[3] In 1986, the Court ruled that the First Amendment's freedom of the press cannot be overcome by a defendant's assertion that a public trial will be prejudicial. In 1986 (*Press-Enterprise Company v. Superior Court of California*), the Court ruled that judges may bar the press and the public from pretrial hearings in criminal cases only as a last resort to ensure a fair trial, and only after stating why it is necessary to conduct the hearings in secret. Chief Justice Warren E. Burger, writing for the majority, pointed out that "one of the important means of assuring a fair trial is that the process be open to neutral observers." In addition to the trial itself, in 1984 the Court ruled unanimously that trial judges must also ordinarily permit the public and news media to attend jury selection proceedings (*Press-Enterprise v. Superior Court*).

The televising of trials has also added new meaning to the term "public." Almost all states permit television coverage of at least some of their judicial proceedings, and the federal courts have experimented with broadcasting civil cases. Although no problems had been reported, in 1994 the Judicial Conference of the United States Courts voted to end the practice. In 2005, New York's highest court ruled that televising or making movies of proceedings in which witnesses may be forced to testify is off limits. That made New York the only state with an outright ban on televising trials (Baker 2005).

Right to Confront Witnesses.   The Sixth Amendment requires that the defendant "be informed of the nature and cause of the accusation; to be confronted with the witnesses against him; to have compulsory process for obtaining witnesses in his favor." Thus, the defendant can subpoena a witness to testify in his or her defense and has the unlimited right to cross-examine adverse witnesses (discussed later in this chapter).

Double Jeopardy Prohibited.   The Fifth Amendment forbids **double jeopardy**, stating that no person shall "be subject for the same offence to be twice put in jeopardy of life or limb." Once a defendant has been acquitted (not guilty), he or she can never be tried again for the same crime. Jeopardy attaches when the jury is **impaneled** and sworn, or, in a **bench trial**, when the judge begins to hear evidence. (Jeopardy issues are not relevant in civil or administrative proceedings.) The Court has permitted separate trials in federal and state courts based on the same act (e.g., murder in a state court and civil rights violations based on the murder in federal court), and in more than one state. In the case of four Los Angeles police officers accused of beating Rodney King, they were acquitted in state court and tried again in federal court for civil rights violations based on their actions in the same incident.

In *Heath v. Alabama* (1985), the Court ruled that two states may prosecute a defendant for the same criminal act without violating the Fifth Amendment. Larry Heath was sentenced in Alabama and Georgia for hiring two men to kidnap and kill his pregnant wife. She was kidnapped from their home in Alabama and shot to death in Georgia. In order to avoid a possible death sentence, Heath pled guilty in Georgia to a noncapital crime. He was subsequently tried and convicted of the same charges in

---

[3] This is an issue only for criminal trials, because the public has no constitutional right to attend a civil trial.

Alabama and sentenced to death. The Court ruled that because each state is sovereign, the defendant had committed separate offenses against the law of each and, therefore, the convictions were an exception to the double jeopardy clause.

The double jeopardy clause also prohibits multiple punishments for the same offense. However, in 1997, the Court ruled 9–0 in favor of the imposition of both criminal and civil sanctions on an offender for the same behavior. *Hudson v. United States* involved three bank officers who had agreed to pay civil fines to the government for making illegal loans from banks they had run in the 1980s. The government subsequently indicted them, which the Court, reversing a precedent established eight years before (*United States v. Halper* [1989]), ruled permissible.

Exclusionary Rule

This legal principle, sometimes referred to as the "poisoned fruit doctrine," is based on the Fourth and Fourteenth Amendments and prohibits evidence obtained in violation of the Constitution from being used at trial—if the tree (the search) is poisoned, so by logical extension is its fruit (the evidence). Thus, even evidence proving a defendant's guilt **beyond** a **reasonable doubt** cannot be entered into evidence if it was secured in an unconstitutional manner (*Weeks v. United States* [1914]; *Mapp v. Ohio* [1961]). The **exclusionary rule** is the Court's way of controlling the behavior of law enforcement agents: It renders certain improper activities not worth the effort (since the results will be inadmissible). A great deal of criticism has been leveled at the exclusionary rule, particularly by persons in law enforcement and political conservatives. They have argued that the proper remedy for unconstitutional activity by the police is a tort, not the suppression of evidence; to paraphrase Justice Cardozo, why should the criminal go free because the police blundered. Supporters of the rule contend that a tort action is an awkward mechanism for controlling police behavior, and it assumes that the victim of police misconduct will be able to secure adequate legal assistance. On the other hand, personal liability may actually prove too great a restraint on police activity, police officers being reluctant or unwilling to act even when they have lawful authority.

Since the Court's decision in *Mapp*, a series of (often confusing) cases has limited its application without overturning its basic premise—controlling police behavior. In 1968, the Court ruled that with "reasonable suspicion" a police officer is permitted to stop and frisk a suspect even in the absence of probable cause—for the officer's protection (*Terry v. Ohio*). In 2000, the Court ruled (*Illinois v. Wardlow*) that flight at the mere sight of a police officer is sufficient to justify a stop-and-frisk search. Later that year, however, the Court ruled (*Florida v. J. L.*) unanimously that an anonymous tip that a person is carrying a gun, absent any further sign that the information is reliable, is not sufficient to justify a stop and frisk.

In 1984 (*United States v. Leon*), the Court ruled that when the police act on a defective search warrant, the exclusionary rule need not apply, since its purpose is control of the behavior of police, not of judges (who issue warrants). In the same year, the Court established the doctrine of **inevitable discovery** as an exception to the exclusionary rule in *Nix v. Williams* (a continuation of a famous 1977 case, *Brewer v. Williams*). Robert Williams was suspected of killing a 10-year-old girl, and 200 volunteers combed the Des Moines, Iowa, area searching for her body. The police promised the

Mapp v. Ohio

In 1914, the Supreme Court ruled (*Weeks v. United States*) that if federal agents seize evidence in violation of the Fourth Amendment, it can be (on a motion by the defense) excluded from use at trial. For more than 40 years, this exclusionary rule did not apply to state officials.

On May 23, 1957, three Cleveland police officers arrived at the home of Dollree Mapp and demanded admittance because they believed that a "wanted for questioning" numbers operator, as well as a large amount of illegal lottery paraphernalia, was being hidden in the house. After telephoning her lawyer, Mapp refused to let the police into her house. The officers conducted a surveillance and three hours later, with additional officers, they forced their way into the house. Mapp and her attorney, who had arrived at the scene, demanded to see the search warrant. One of the officers held up a piece of paper. Mapp seized the paper and was arrested and handcuffed. The numbers operator was taken into custody—he was never charged—the entire house was thoroughly searched, and police discovered "obscene materials"—four smutty books. No evidence that a search warrant had ever been issued was presented at the subsequent trial. Despite this apparent violation of the Fourth Amendment, Mapp was convicted of possessing obscene materials and sentenced to a prison term of up to seven years.

On appeal, the Supreme Court held that "the State, by admitting evidence unlawfully seized, served to encourage disobedience to the Federal Constitution which it is bound to uphold." The Court concluded, "The ignoble shortcut to conviction . . . tends to destroy the entire system of constitutional restraints on which the liberties of the people rest." Through the Fourteenth Amendment, the Court applied the exclusionary rule to the states.

suspect's attorney that they would not question Williams, but as they were driving Williams across the state, they asked him to think about the fact that "the parents of this little girl should be entitled to a Christian burial" for their daughter. His response led police to the victim's body.

In the 1977 case decision, the Court ruled that the "Christian burial" speech had violated the suspect's constitutional rights by inducing him to incriminate himself outside his lawyer's presence. Williams was tried again, and the prosecutors did not offer into evidence any incriminating statements of the defendant, nor did the state attempt to show that Williams had directed police to the body. The trial judge admitted the prosecution's evidence as to the condition of the body and related physical evidence on grounds that the prosecution had shown that, even if Williams had not been improperly interrogated, the victim's body would nevertheless have been found by the search party. In its decision, the Court gave recognition to the principle of inevitable discovery.

In *Colorado v. Bertine* (1987), the Court created an inventory exception to the exclusionary rule when it stated that police need not secure a search warrant to look into closed containers found in a confiscated vehicle. Police found illegal drugs in a closed backpack after a drunk-driving arrest. The Court ruled that police were following standardized procedures by opening closed containers and listing their contents during a vehicle inventory. The Court noted that knowledge of the precise nature of property found in vehicles for which the police have a responsibility helps to guard against claims of theft, vandalism, or negligence.

In *Maryland v. Garrison* (1987), the Court established a **reasonable mistake exception** to the exclusionary rule. Police officers in Baltimore, acting on a valid search warrant, entered the wrong apartment in a multiunit dwelling, where they found illegal drugs. The Court ruled that under the circumstances—two apartments on a floor that the police reasonably believed contained only one apartment—the Constitution had not been violated. Later in 1987 the Court appeared to move in a different direction. In *Arizona v. Hicks*, the Court ruled that police officers acting on a warrant to search for illegal weapons could not move stereo equipment suspected of being stolen to check the serial numbers.

In 1989 the Court ruled that without a warrant, a police helicopter could hover over a home at an altitude of 400 feet and take pictures without violating the owner's rights. The decision (*Florida v. Riley*) did not indicate how low the helicopter could fly before it engaged in an impermissible search. A 1990 case dealt with a long-standing exception to the exclusionary rule: Prosecutors have been allowed to use illegally obtained evidence to impeach the testimony of a defendant (*Harris v. New York* [1971]). In an Illinois case, that state's highest court ruled that even when a defendant chooses not to testify, illegally secured evidence could be used to impeach the testimony of defense witnesses. The Supreme Court, in a 5–4 decision, refused to allow the Illinois exception (*James v. Illinois* [1990]). In 1990, the Court ruled 6–3 that the Constitution does not prohibit American law enforcement agents operating outside the United States from warrantless searches and seizures of property owned by foreigners. The decision appears to prohibit similar searchers of property owned by American citizens in other countries (*United States v. Verdugo-Urquidez*). In 1991, in a 7–2 decision, the Court held that evidence, such as drugs, discarded by a fleeing suspect, can be admitted into trial even in the absence of evidence that police had a sufficient basis for their original suspicion leading to the pursuit. The Court ruled that a chase is not a seizure within the meaning of the Fourth Amendment (*California v. Hodari D.*). In 1995, in a unanimous decision (*Wilson v. Arkansas*), the Court ruled that the police must "knock and announce" their presence when executing a valid search warrant. Unless there are specific exigent circumstances—e.g., imminent peril or destruction of evidence—the Court found that the Fourth Amendment does not permit a "no knock" entry. However, in a 5–4 decision in 2006 (*Hudson v. Michigan*), the Court's new conservative majority refused to extend the exclusionary rule to "no knock" violations. In other words, when the police violate the Constitution and the *Wilson* decision, any evidence seized can be used at trial thus rendering the "knock and announce" rule meaningless.

In a 5–4 decision, in 2001, the Court ruled that absent a search warrant, law enforcement officers could not point a heat sensing device at a home to detect evidence of illegal activity—marijuana growing. The decision, *Kyllo v. United States*, was written by Justice Scalia who based it on his view of *original intent* (discussed in Chapter 5): Technology allowing intrusion into space that would have otherwise necessitated physical entry requires a warrant. To rule otherwise, he argued, "would leave the homeowner at the mercy of advanced technology."

Joinder of Offenses

An issue related to double jeopardy, **joinder of offenses**, occurs whenever a defendant is alleged to have violated several statutes based on the same act, or several acts that are somehow connected: "Most often, local law grants the prosecutor the option to bring either separate prosecutions or a single prosecution when the several charges arose from the same criminal episode" (Israel and LaFave 1980: 31). However, a prosecutor who opts for separate prosecutions runs the risk of crossing the somewhat nebulous line that constitutes double jeopardy and, in any event, state law and court decisions will typically bar cumulative sentences: "the maximum sentence will be limited to that available for the highest offense on which a conviction is obtained" (1980: 34). At times the court will order two or more indictments or informations to be tried together (joined) if they could have initially been the subject of a single indictment/information. In 1992, however, the Court ruled 9–0 that the Fifth Amendment is not violated by successive prosecutions for committing a crime and then for conspiring to commit that crime. *United States v. Felix* involved prosecutions for the illegal manufacture of methamphetamine and for *conspiracy* to manufacture and distribute the drug.

Pretrial Procedures

Before we look at the steps in the process used in the adjudication of criminal defendants, we need to note that its details vary from state to state and even between jurisdictions in the same state. Therefore, this chapter will present a generalized version of the criminal trial process that may not match exactly that of every jurisdiction, as shown in Figure 8.2 on the following page.

Criminal cases usually begin with a summary arrest (that is, an arrest without a warrant) by a police officer acting on his or her own—having seen a crime committed—or on behalf of a civilian complainant, usually the victim of a crime. In either event, the evidence needed to effect a lawful arrest is known as **probable cause**: "That set of facts or circumstances based on reliable information or personal knowledge or observation by an officer which reasonably show and would warrant an ordinary prudent man in believing that a particular person has been guilty of, is threatening, or is about to commit some offense against the law" (Texas Criminal Justice Council 1974: 161; for a history of probable cause, see Oliver 2010). Less frequently an arrest is made pursuant to a warrant issued by a judge based on information provided by police or based on an indictment by a grand jury.

Once arrested, the perpetrator, except in some minor offenses (usually involving a motor vehicle), will be transported to a police facility, fingerprinted, photographed, and given the opportunity to make one or more telephone calls. (At this point the procedures vary, and the following are those most frequently encountered.) If the charge

---

Conspiracy

Conspiracy is an agreement between two or more persons to commit a criminal act; it is the agreement that becomes the *corpus* (body) of the crime. Conspiracy requires proof (beyond a reasonable doubt) that two or more persons planned to violate the law and (in many but not all jurisdictions) that at least one overt act in furtherance of the conspiracy was made by a conspirator, e.g., the purchase of materials to aid in the transportation or dilution of the drugs. There are several different types of conspiracy (see Abadinsky 2013).

is a misdemeanor, a lesser crime for which most jurisdictions provide a penalty of no more than one year of imprisonment, the suspect may be allowed to post bail and appear in court on a subsequent date. If the subject is unable to post bail, or if the charge is a felony, that is, a crime punishable by more than one year of imprisonment, he or she will be transported to a lower court for an initial appearance, or (in misdemeanor cases) **arraignment** usually within 24 hours after the arrest: The charges will be read, the need for assigned counsel considered (in a misdemeanor case a plea is entered), and bail will be set. In misdemeanor cases, the charge(s) may be disposed of at this stage in a process often referred to as *rough justice*.

Rough Justice in the Lower Courts

Most criminal cases begin and end in the lower courts. Because of the large volume of cases entering this part of the criminal justice system, efficient case processing is the primary focus. Efficiency requires speed, but the various due process guarantees to which every criminal defendant is entitled slow down the process considerably. In an effort to avoid delay, judges in the lower courts typically disregard the niceties of due process, and they are assisted in this process by both prosecutor and defense counsel. Defendants may be processed collectively, or at such high rates of speed that individualization is virtually impossible. **Dismissals** and pleas of guilty predominate, and to the casual or uninformed observer the scene is confusing and not at all resembling popular portrayals of justice—it is rough justice (Feeley 1992).

INITIAL APPEARANCE
- Counsel
- Charges
- Bail

PRELIMINARY HEARINGS
- Probable cause
- Bail review

INFORMATION / GRAND JURY

ARRAIGNMENT
- Plea
- Bail

TRIAL
- Pretiral motions
- *Voir dire* hearing
- Opening statements
- Examination of witnesses
- Motions
- Summation
- Charge to the jury
- Deliberations
- Verdict—not guilty *or* guilty

PRESENTENCE REPORT

SENTENCING
- Probation
- Fine / jail
- Prison . . . . parole

Figure 8.2   The Flow of Felony Cases

A study by the chief administrative judge in New York revealed that, on average, lower-court judges in that city spend a mere 3.4 minutes on each case ("No Trial—and No Punishment Either" 1986). A study in Florida revealed that in 2010, 70 percent of misdemeanor defendants pled guilty or no-contest at court appearances that lasted less than three minutes (Caplan 2013). An editorial in the *New York Times* (August 18, 1986: 22) referred to the lower courts in New York as dispensing "cattle car" justice. In Chicago (where I worked for the sheriff), processing occurs so swiftly that defendants are often unaware of the fact that their cases have been dismissed—the inconvenience of being housed in dank and often foul-smelling police and court lockups being viewed as sufficient punishment for innocent and guilty alike. And there is a class-linked dimension to this process: "Pretrial incarceration is the most punitive form of procedural punishment imposed by the lower courts. Specifically, its imposition primarily is caused by poverty, thus generating 'punishment,' through confinement, on the basis of class rather than guilt" (Blackwell and Cunningham 2004: 64). In 1991, the Supreme Court ruled that detention prior to appearance before a judicial officer may not exceed 48 hours (*Riverside v. McLaughlin*).

In order to avoid legal complications that cause delay, the key actors must gain the cooperation of the defendant. This is accomplished by treating him or her in a lenient manner. Thus, defendants who waive their rights and who do not object to the speedy processing receive an outcome considerably more lenient than that to which they might otherwise be entitled. The rare defendant who insists on the full array of due process rights will get them, but there is often a price. Such defendants may be viewed as disruptive, as lacking in any show of contrition and, therefore, deserving of more severe treatment. If convicted they will receive a sentence in excess of the norm, and, in the meantime, they may be subjected to relatively high bail and a stay in jail awaiting trial. It is no small irony that offenders who raise no **objections** and quickly plead guilty are often able to avoid incarceration, while those who insist on their innocence may be incarcerated, even if only for a short period of time. A former assistant district attorney in Manhattan reports:

> For the down and out, even a hundred dollars' bail guaranteed their waiting in Rikers Island Prison for a trial that might easily be six months away. The message was loud and clear: take my reasonable offer of five days or you're going to rot in Rikers fighting the issues. . . . Strong-arming defendants into a plea was rough justice, but it kept the number of dispositions up, the numbers of 'bodies in the system' down, and sped cases along to a conviction. (Heilbroner 1990: 58)

Felony Cases

In felonies, the prosecutor may send a case to the grand jury or present evidence at a preliminary (probable-cause) hearing and file an information setting forth the details of the alleged offense, such as date, time, and place.

Grand Jury

The use of a grand jury dates back to King Henry II in twelfth-century England, when it was called the "accusing jury." The king used it to seize jurisdiction of cases handled by the church and baronage, enhancing the royal treasury by claiming fines and forfeitures that flowed from the jury's proceedings. The grand jury was also used to terrorize political enemies (Armstrong 1998). Over the centuries it remained an arm of the king, part of his law enforcement and prosecutorial authority.

In the American colonies, however, grand juries were not an arm of executive power and routinely defied governmental authority. As revolution approached, these juries were generally sympathetic to those resisting British rule; they refused, for example, to indict opponents of the Stamp Act. It was during this period that the grand jury gained a reputation as a protector of the individual against unwarranted prosecution and, as a result, was incorporated into the Fifth Amendment: "No person shall be held to answer for a capital, or otherwise infamous crime, unless on a presentment or indictment of a Grand Jury." England, which originated the grand jury, abolished it in 1933, and the Supreme Court has ruled that this Fifth Amendment requirement does not apply to the states (*Hurtado v. California* [1884]). Thus, whereas the federal government operates under the grand jury requirement, states differ in their use of this body. "While most states retain the option of a grand jury indictment, few require it to begin felony proceedings. A diminished role for the state grand jury in processing felony cases can be seen early in this century. Grand jury indictments were largely replaced by the practice of prosecutors filing a document called a criminal information" (Rottman and Strickland 2006: 213).

Many states follow the federal practice of requiring that indictments be used to charge serious crimes but allowing informations to be used to bring charges for lesser felonies and misdemeanors. In many states, the use of indictments is a prosecutor's option. Connecticut and Pennsylvania abolished the use of grand juries to return indictments but kept the investigating grand jury. Even where the use of a grand jury for bringing charges is optional,

> under certain circumstances prosecutors may prefer to use the grand jury or be forced to do so by events outside their control. For example, a grand jury indictment may be used to file charges when the defendant cannot be located and the time limits allowed for prosecution under the statute of limitations are about to be exceeded. Similarly, the secrecy of the grand jury may allow defendants to be charged and taken into custody before they can pose potential danger to a witness's safety or flee from the jurisdiction. In addition, the need to protect the identity of undercover agents, the ability to test a witness before a jury, or the opportunity to involve the community in case screening may be contributing factors. (Emerson 1983: 13)

In the federal system, a grand jury is a body of 16 to 23 citizens empowered to operate with a quorum of 16; 12 votes are required for an indictment. In the 50 states, however, although the minimum varies considerably, nowhere does the maximum number of grand jurors exceed 23. Although some states adhere to the federal rule of 12 for an indictment, in others the range is anywhere from four to nine. Like those serving on a petit (also known as trial) jury, grand jurors are generally selected from the voting rolls. Because grand jury terms usually last 18 months or more, they tend to include mostly retired persons who may volunteer for service. A panel may have no meetings for lengthy periods when prosecutors have no need for them. Sometimes, a grand jury may be involved in more than one case at a time.

A grand jury meets in secret sessions in a court building to consider evidence presented by the prosecutor in the absence of a judge, defendant, or defense attorney. Secrecy prevents subjects from escaping before arrest or tampering with witnesses, and encourages witnesses to speak freely without fear of retaliation. Testimony is recorded by a court stenographer and the transcript can be used at trial if the witness dies or cannot be called to testify for some other reason. If the witness testifies at trial, but says something different than what he or she said before the grand jury, the prosecutor or defense attorney can use the transcript to impeach trial testimony.

A presiding judge convenes the grand jury, usually at the request of the prosecutor, selects the jurors, and rules on any motions that are brought by witnesses who do not want to testify. The judge will also rule on any other legal matters and, at the request of the prosecutor, will provide immunity from prosecution in order to compel testimony that would otherwise be barred by the Fifth Amendment. Although a witness can refuse to reply to any questions if the answers may be incriminating, he or she can be granted immunity and, under the threat of being jailed for contempt, be required to answer all questions.

There are two types of immunity:

1. *Transactional immunity* provides blanket protection against prosecution for crimes about which a person is compelled to testify.

2. *Use immunity* prohibits the information provided by a person from being used against him or her, but the person can still be prosecuted based on evidence obtained independently of his or her testimony before the grand jury.

Since the members of a grand jury (at least in theory) are not agents of the government—they act as representatives of the citizenry—the extensive due process rights typically enjoyed by a criminal defendant are not relevant to grand jury proceedings. The grand jury meets in secret and its activities and hearings can be kept secret until its term (e.g., 18 months) expires. (In 1990, the Supreme Court ruled in *Butterworth v. Smith* that statutes prohibiting grand jury witnesses from ever making their testimony public violate the First Amendment.) Sixteen states permit the subject of a grand jury inquiry to have an attorney present at the hearing, but counsel is permitted only to give advice. In the other states and the federal system, an attorney is not even permitted to accompany his or her client at the hearing. There is no right to present evidence or to cross-examine adverse witnesses.

In most jurisdictions, the grand jury can receive virtually any type of information, even that which would not be admissible at trial, such as certain types of **hearsay** and evidence that was secured in violation of the Fourth Amendment—the exclusionary rule does not apply to the grand jury (*United States v. Calandra* [1974]). If a majority of grand jury members vote in support of an indictment, they return a **true bill**; a failure to indict (**no true bill**) is a relatively rare event, since jurors have only heard the prosecutor's version of the case.

In every state and the federal system, the grand jury may also be used for investigation. The California constitution, for example, requires that each county impanel a grand jury every year. Such grand juries have the power to, among other things, investigate and report on the conduct of local government. Investigative grand juries typically have broad investigative authority, including the power to subpoena persons

Virginia Grand Jury

There are three types of grand juries in the commonwealth: regular, special, and multi-jurisdiction. A regular grand jury is convened at each term of the circuit court of each city and county, to attend to the usual matters needing grand jury action. On infrequent occasions a court will convene a special grand jury to investigate some particular matter. Multijurisdiction grand juries involve more than one jurisdiction and are primarily used to investigate drug law violations.

(*subpoena ad testificandum*) and documents (**subpoena** *duces tecum*). In those states where statutes permit and in the federal system, the grand jury is used to investigate the operations of law enforcement and other government agencies (particularly when corruption is suspected) and the activities of **organized crime**. In addition to handing down indictments, a federal grand jury (impaneled under the Organized Crime Control Act of 1970) and those of several states are permitted to issue reports. Federal organized-crime grand juries have the power to publish reports at the completion of their terms on certain types of noncriminal misconduct by public officials, although on the state level the practice varies. "Many states prohibit grand jury reports, and those that permit them commonly circumscribe the grand jury's power. Grand juries are generally prohibited from commenting on purely private activity, and reports criticizing publicly elected officials tend to be allowed only where statutory authority exists. Finally, as a rule, grand jury reports may be disclosed only with court approval" (Frankel and Naftalis 1977: 32). Although grand jury reports cannot command any particular performance, the widespread publicity they receive usually encourages action by government officials.

The original purpose of the grand jury in the United States was to protect a person from being subjected to prosecution in the absence of sufficient evidence. Because the grand jury hears only one side of the case, however, it seldom votes for no true bill, and there are many observers who feel that its original purpose has been distorted into being a tool of the prosecutor. The former chief judge of New York State called the requirement for a grand jury indictment a waste of scarce resources. In addition to grand juror fees, he argued, are untold additional and duplicative expenses borne by the taxpayers for court officers, police officers, and prosecutorial resources diverted from other activities. Furthermore, he notes, the public often equates an indictment with guilt because it is ignorant of the difference between grand and **petit juries**, notwithstanding the constitutional presumption of innocence (Wachtler 1990). And, as noted, the subject of a grand jury inquiry is not entitled to the due process guarantees that are normally attached in any other judicial proceeding, such as a preliminary or probable cause hearing. Indeed, federal—and most state—prosecutors are not required to disclose **exculpatory evidence** to the grand jury (Brenner 1995).

Judge's Charge to a Grand Jury, Mississippi

As members of the Grand Jury, you are a part of the judicial branch of state government and have the power of indictment or presentment in a crime and the additional authority to issue reports. The grand jury is the means, not only of bringing to trial persons accused of crime, but also to protect persons from unfounded accusations whether presented by legal officers or by others who may be motivated by public clamor or private malice. Your duty is to allow or to deny issuance of an indictment. There are from 15 to 20 members of a grand jury and 12 members must agree before you can approve an indictment. You will hear only one side of a case. It is not your duty to decide the guilt or innocence of the accused. It is your duty to determine whether there is sufficient evidence or probable cause to require an accused to stand trial. If the evidence establishes a probability that a crime was committed and that the defendant committed the crime, then you should return a "true bill." If the evidence fails to establish a probability that a crime was committed and that the defendant is guilty of that crime, then you must refuse to return a "true bill."

You are cautioned that rumor and hearsay testimony are unreliable. Also, that no person may be compelled to be a witness against himself/herself. A witness who testifies about his/her own participation in crime must first be advised in your presence of his/her constitutional rights by the prosecuting attorney(s) before you may accept such evidence. You determine what witnesses you will permit to appear and testify before you. It is the duty of the prosecutor to be present with the grand jury in the room to present the evidence, to examine the witnesses, and to give advice on any matter of law which may be raised. You are entitled to the legal advice of the prosecutor on matters of law unless you are instructed to the contrary by the court. You are, however, the sole judges of the facts and the prosecutor may not influence you as to whether an indictment will be approved. After the testimony is taken and you are discussing what action you will take, the prosecutor will withdraw from your jury room. Prosecutors are not permitted to be present during your deliberations nor when a ballot is taken and they may not influence your decision on any question of fact. You may request the advice and assistance of the attorney general of the state. You are also at liberty at any time to call for further instructions from the court. You are an independent body. You, as well as the prosecutor, have the right to require the clerk of this court to issue subpoenas for witnesses to be brought before you to testify.

The **oath** is your promise that you will keep secret what takes place in the grand jury room. A grand juror, except when called as a witness in court, shall not disclose any proceedings or action in relation to offenses brought before it for six months after the **adjournment** of the grand jury upon which the juror served. A grand juror shall not disclose the name or testimony of any witness who has been before the grand jury. Any disclosure of secrets within the six month period is punishable by fine or imprisonment for contempt of court.

Preliminary/Probable Cause Hearing

If the grand jury is not used, the lower-court judge will have witnesses sworn and hear testimony from both the prosecution and the defense. This process is similar to, but more informal than, the trial process, since its only purpose is to allow a judge to determine whether there is enough evidence (probable cause) to justify continuing the case. In effect, a **probable cause hearing** reviews the sufficiency of evidence used by the police to justify an arrest. If no probable cause is found (an infrequent occurrence), the subject is released. If probable cause is found, the prosecutor will file an information and the defendant will be arraigned in superior court. In a few jurisdictions, such as Ohio, both a preliminary hearing and a grand jury indictment are required before a case can be transferred to superior court (Boland et al. 1988).

Arraignment

After a probable cause hearing and the filing of an information and/or a grand jury indictment, an arrest warrant is issued, and the subject is brought before a judge in superior court for arraignment. He or she is informed of the charges and, if the subject is indigent, an attorney will be appointed; bail is set or (if previously set) reviewed; and the subject enters a plea: (1) not guilty, (2) not guilty by reason of **insanity**, (3) **guilty but insane** (14 states), (4) guilty, or (5) *nolo contendere*. Literally meaning "I choose not to dispute," and commonly referred to as "no contest," ***nolo contendere*** pleas are allowed in all federal courts, but only about half the states allow them, and in state courts, both the prosecutor and the judge must agree to the plea. A *nolo contendere* plea has the same effect as a plea of guilty, but it cannot be used as evidence of a criminal conviction at any subsequent civil trial related to the criminal act.

Persons who plead "guilty but insane" are sentenced as would be any other defendant guilty of the same offense. They do receive mental health attention and treatment if necessary. Persons who refuse to enter a plea have a plea of not guilty automatically entered for them. In practice, many pleas at arraignment are "guilty," since there has often been an agreement to enter a plea of guilty in exchange for some form of leniency. (Plea bargaining is discussed in Chapter 9.) Defendants who plead not guilty or not guilty by reason of insanity are ready to be tried. (Those who plead guilty or *nolo contendere* are ready for a sentencing hearing.)

The (Peitit) Jury

The origins of the jury system date back to the early Middle Ages and the *inquisitio*, "which consisted in having the inhabitants of an area interrogated under oath by royal agents. It mainly related to questions of landed property in which the king or the church had an interest" (van Caenegem 1994: 26). The use of citizens summoned by the Crown to render verdicts became popular after Pope Innocent III in 1215 prohibited ecclesiastical officiation at trials by combat and ordeal. "This step effectively

---

Nolo Contendere

Critics argue that the *nolo contendere* plea leaves the public confused about the defendant's guilt, leads to light sentences, and allows some guilty defendants to avoid collateral consequences of their guilt. Supporters argue that "it conserves judicial and systemic resources, because removing the threat of collateral civil consequences encourages criminal defendants to capitulate and accept punishment. This is especially true in the anti-trust context where the threat of private civil trials, including treble damage actions, could make criminal penalties insignificant in comparison" (Gurevich 2005: 1).

undermined the existing procedural alternatives to the jury and opened the way for its rapid expansion" (Landsman 1993: 26). At first, juries were composed of knowledge-able witnesses who relied on their own knowledge. Gradually, the jury became a dis-interested body of laypeople that was to draw its own conclusions based solely on testimony provided by witnesses. But this transformation took place over several cen-turies. By the last third of the eighteenth century juries were required to base their decision solely on evidence presented at trial (Sward 2003). As these changes occurred, so did other aspects of legal procedure. Factual questions were strictly sepa-rated from legal questions, "so a juror would address only those questions he could comprehend" (Llewellyn 1989: 34).[4]

Juries were available in virtually all civil and criminal cases in Virginia no later than 1624, and they were specifically provided for in the 1641 Massachusetts Body of Liberties (Landsman 1999). In the years prior to the Revolutionary War, the Crown prosecuted American colonists for revenue violations in admiralty courts without juries, rather than risk an acquittal in common pleas courts. Trials for treason were conducted in England, thus removing them entirely from the scrutiny or participation of colonists, practices which helped precipitate the Revolution. Even before the Decla-ration of Independence, each of the 12 states that had adopted a written constitution included the right of the accused to a jury trial (King 1999).

The jury trial was eventually made part of the Constitution for criminal cases by Article III, Section 2, and the Sixth Amendment; but no details were provided. As a result, for nearly two centuries, judges interpreted the jury provisions in Article III and the Sixth Amendment to govern only prosecutions in federal courts for violations of federal criminal law. However, most crimes were state offenses and only a tiny frac-tion of all criminal prosecutions took place in federal court. Even though every state guaranteed the right to a jury trial for at least some criminal charges, state law differed as to what that right entailed. This patchwork system of justice, with the state and fed-eral courts following separate laws, sometimes resulted in striking differences in jury procedures. It was not until 1968 (*Duncan v. Louisiana*) that the Supreme Court applied the Sixth Amendment's right to a jury trial to the states (King 1999).

The Supreme Court has interpreted the Constitution as requiring a jury trial only when the possible sentence is imprisonment for six months or more, although some states provide jury trials for all criminal defendants. In 1898, the Supreme Court ruled (*Thompson v. Utah*) that a jury must be "composed of not less than 12 persons," but this was not applied to the states. The Supreme Court has determined that the number 12 was an "historical accident" and has ruled that juries with as few as six persons are con-stitutionally permissible except in cases involving a capital crime (*Williams v. Florida* [1970]). The Court has ruled that jury verdicts of 10–2 and 9–3 are constitutionally per-mitted (*Apodaca v. Oregon* [1972]; *Johnson v. Louisiana* [1972]). Most states permit juries of less than 12 to decide misdemeanors, while all require 12-person juries for felony cases. In some states, if both sides agree, a six-person jury is permitted. The Court ruled against a five-member jury even in misdemeanor cases (*Bellew v. Georgia* [1978]). In all states, jury decisions (verdicts) in felony cases are required to be unanimous (Malega and

---

[4] In England, devoid of a constitution, "the nature and extent of the right to trial by jury are governed by ordinary parliamentary statute, which can be altered by a simple act of Parliament" (Lloyd-Bostock and Thomas 1999: 11).

Cohen 2013); otherwise, the result is a hung jury and a retrial or dismissal of the charges. The Supreme Court has ruled that if six jurors are used, the decision must be unanimous (*Burch v. Louisiana* [1979]). In a small number of criminal trials, when evidence admissible against one defendant is inadmissible against another, two juries may be utilized. Both juries are present only during testimony admissible against both defendants.

Selection and Retention of Jurors

The jury selection process involves seven steps:

1. *First master list.* The voting rolls, by their very nature, contain the names of citizens over the age of 18. In some jurisdictions, the rolls of the motor vehicle bureau or tax rolls are used because some persons choose not to register to vote in order to avoid jury duty.

2. *First juror list.* Names are selected at random from the master list.

3. *Questionnaires.* Persons on the first juror list are mailed questionnaires to determine if they are qualified. Most jurisdictions require that the jurors be citizens of at least 18 years of age who are able to read, write, and understand the English language; have been residents of the court's jurisdiction for at least one year; and are free of felony convictions and physical or mental handicaps that would make them unable to render jury service. Persons otherwise qualified (e.g., law enforcement officers, doctors, lawyers, and mothers of infants) may be exempted for a variety of reasons, depending on the statutes and customs of the jurisdiction. More than two dozen states have eliminated all automatic exemptions—those summoned can be excused on a case-by-case basis. Persons may also receive a temporary postponement based on a hardship that is time-limited (e.g., teachers during the school year or farmers during the harvest season).[5] Evasion of jury service is a significant problem in the United States, and sometimes trial courts have to shut down because not enough of those summoned appear for service—another reason for prosecutors to avoid a jury trial in favor of negotiation.

4. *Second master list.* Based on the questionnaires, a second master list is developed, and jury service summonses are sent out. Those responding are screened as disqualified, exempt, excused, or qualified.

5. *Report for service.* Those who are qualified are directed to report to a central jury room, where they constitute the **jury pool**.

6. *Impaneled.* The members of the jury pool are sworn in as jurors.

7. *Voir dire.* A panel of jurors is brought into a large courtroom in which the key actors are present in addition to the defendant. Each member of the panel is questioned by the judge, prosecutor, and defense counsel. (In some jurisdictions, only the judge questions the jurors, although attorneys may submit questions to the judge.)

There are two purposes for the *voir dire* (pronounced vwor deer—an Old French term meaning "say the truth") **hearing**: first, to determine if a juror is unfit to serve on

---

[5] In 1999, the mayor of New York, a former federal prosecutor, was selected as a juror in a civil case.

this particular jury, for example, if he or she is familiar with the defendant or victim, is prejudiced, or has heard a great deal about the case as a result of pretrial publicity; and second, to allow the attorneys for the prosecution and defense some discretion in determining who will serve on the jury. These goals are achieved by use of the **challenge for cause** and the peremptory challenge.

Either attorney can argue that a juror is not fit to serve based on certain information that is revealed as a result of the questions asked by the judge or the attorneys. A challenge for *cause* must be upheld by the judge, in which case the juror is excused. **Peremptory challenges** can be used by either attorney to excuse any juror without having to state a reason. Their number of peremptory challenges is limited from two to 26 depending on the statutes and the seriousness of the charges. Some jurisdictions (and England) do not permit peremptory challenges. The hearing continues until a jury is chosen and impaneled, which means they are administered an oath by the court clerk "to well and truly try the case." In many jurisdictions, one or two additional, or alternate jurors, are chosen in the event that a regular juror becomes ill or cannot serve for some other reason.

In 1986, the Supreme Court ruled that prosecutors may not use their peremptory challenges to exclude blacks from juries because they believe that such persons may favor a black defendant. In *Batson v. Kentucky*, the Court overruled a 1965 decision on the same issue. The Court determined that "although a prosecutor ordinarily is entitled to exercise permitted peremptory challenges 'for any reason at all, as long as that reason is related to his view concerning the outcome,' the Equal Protection Clause [Fourteenth Amendment] forbids the prosecutor to challenge jurors solely on account of their race or on the assumption that black jurors as a group will be unable to impartially consider the state's case against a black defendant."

The decision also made it easier for a defendant to raise the issue. The Court's decision noted, "Once the defendant makes a *prima facie* [sufficient on its face] showing [that black jurors were excluded], the burden shifts to the state to come forward with a neutral explanation for challenging black jurors." This decision may hasten the move to abolish the peremptory challenge, a position that was supported by Justice Thurgood Marshall in his concurring opinion. In *Griffith v. Kentucky* (1987) and *Brown v. United States* (1987), the Court ruled that the decision in *Batson* would apply retroactively. (The ruling for retroactivity represents a significant shift from the Court's previous approach to rulings on criminal procedure.) In 1992, the Court ruled 7–2 that the defense, also, cannot exclude jurors based on race (*Georgia v. McCollum*). In a 1994 case that involved paternity and child support issues (*J.E.B. v. T.B.*), the Court extended the prohibition in *Batson* to include gender. Later that year, however, the Court refused to grant certiorari in a case that involved the prosecutor's removal of a juror because he was a Jehovah's Witness (*David v. Minnesota*).

In 1990, the Court ruled 5–4 against a white defendant's claim that he was denied the right to an impartial jury because the prosecutor used peremptory challenges to remove the only two members of the jury pool who were black. The decision (*Holland v. Illinois*) states that the Sixth Amendment requires an impartial, not a representative, jury. In 1991, the Court, by a vote of 7–2, extended the defendant's right to object to the prosecution's use of peremptory challenges based on race. In this case (*Powers v. Ohio*), the defendant was a white man accused of murdering two white people; the excluded

In Support of the Peremptory Challenge

Peremptory challenges will make the verdict more acceptable to the losing party while assuring the public that the case has been decided based on the evidence, not the personal biases of the jurors.

Because there are limits on the use of challenges for cause, some jurors, even though biased, will otherwise remain on the jury because the attorney is unable to prove that the juror is not impartial. The peremptory challenge enables the screening out of suspected, but unprovable bias.

Peremptory challenges are also essential in order to protect effective *voir dire*. An attorney does not know, until he or she asks questions, if a particular juror is biased. Although questioning may reveal suspected bias, there may not be sufficient proof of bias to satisfy a challenge for cause. However, by questioning a potential juror's impartiality, an otherwise impartial juror may be insulted and develop a bias against the attorney. Without peremptory challenges, such persons could not be excluded. Therefore, an attorney may opt to refrain from asking potentially offensive questions rather than risk insulting a prospective juror (Henley 1996).

jurors were black. Writing for the majority, Justice Anthony Kennedy stated that race cannot be a criterion, regardless of the race of the defendant or the jurors.

The Court has ruled that prospective jurors who state that they could not under any circumstances vote for imposition of the death penalty could be excluded for cause. In *Lockhart v. McCree* (1986) the Court stated that the so-called death-qualified jury, "unlike the wholesale exclusion of blacks, women or Mexican-Americans from jury service, is carefully designed to serve the state's concededly legitimate interest in obtaining a single jury that can properly and impartially apply the law to the facts of the case at both guilt and sentencing phases of a capital crime." (In most states that authorize the death penalty, the jury first decides on guilt, and then, after a hearing, determines whether the death sentence should be imposed.)

Scientific Jury Selection and Trial Consultants

Scientific jury selection refers to the use of tools of the social sciences to assist attorneys in the jury selection process. A number of

> sociologists, psychologists, market researchers and others use public opinion surveys, in-depth interviews, computer analyses correlating jurors' backgrounds and attitudes and laboratory simulations of impending trials to help lawyers select jurors likely to favor their side, exclude those likely to be hostile to it, and present their cases in ways psychologically designed to benefit from the unconscious needs and motives of the jurors. (Hunt 1982: 70)

Consultants are used in about 6,000 mostly civil trials annually. The American Society of Trial Consultants has more than 400 members, some of whom are employed by companies that offer jury consultation services (Gavzer 1997).

Social scientists attempt to identify the type of person most likely to be favorable to their side, as well as those most likely to be hostile, for use at *voir dire* hearings. In some programs, a simulated jury selection process is conducted and the "jurors" selected are paid to participate in a mock trial that helps to prepare attorneys for the actual case being litigated. After the mock trial, the "jurors" are interviewed to determine the best trial approach, the one most likely to convince a real jury—what questions should be asked, how to speak, what clothes to wear—all in an effort to enhance the attorney's influence on the prospective jury, to provide an "edge." They may also assist attorneys in preparing questions for potential witnesses and evaluate pretrial statements.

A number of firms will provide this service, and it is expensive. For that reason, except in isolated cases, social scientific assistance usually occurs only in civil cases where the outcome can involve millions of dollars. The best-known criminal case where this approach was used (by the defense)—it would be too costly for the prosecution—(the O. J. Simpson case being a noted exception) involved a 20-year-old black female inmate, Joan Little. In 1974, while being held in the rural Beaufort, North Carolina, jail on a burglary charge, Little stabbed a white, 62-year-old night jailer to death with an ice pick. Little claimed that the jailer had used the ice pick to force her to commit an act of oral sodomy, and while there was conclusive evidence of a sex act, it could not be determined if the jailer had perpetrated a rape or had been lured to his death.

Because of racial and gender implications, Joan Little received assistance that she would not have otherwise been able to afford. Social scientists conducted a public opinion poll among residents in the counties of the Beaufort area, and the degree of prejudice uncovered caused the court to grant a **change of venue** to Raleigh (Wake County). Subsequent surveys of a sample of Wake County voters revealed a profile of friendly and unfriendly jurors that assisted lawyers at the *voir dire* hearing. The five-week trial ended with a jury deliberation that lasted only 78 minutes—Joan Little was acquitted. The cost of the scientific jury services contributed to the Little defense is estimated at more than 1.2 million in today's dollars. The potential for exacerbating already existing inequities in our system of justice is obvious.

In addition to firms that provide jury selection services, the American Society of Trial Consultants represents hundreds of trial consultants in the United States. These persons, most frequently psychologists and a few lawyers, usually work for defendants at fees of about $200 an hour.

Instructions to the Jury

The members of a jury are given specific instructions by the judge about their responsibilities as jurors. The judge cautions them against discussing the case with anyone,

Social Media and the Jury

In recent years, ubiquitous social media sites, such as Facebook and Twitter, have added an additional complication to the jury trial. Some states have put limits on lawyer interaction with jurors through social media—sending them a Facebook "friend" request, for example. Mistrials have resulted from jurors using social media to discuss a case with their friends and engaging in online research on defendants. Some states have responded by adding language to their jury instructions barring all forms of electronic communication once a case begins (Urbina 2014).

including fellow jurors, and against reading or listening to anything pertaining to the case. They are directed to report any person who attempts to discuss the case with them, since this may constitute a crime—jury tampering. In particularly sensitive cases, or when there is a great deal of news coverage of a case, the jurors may be sequestered. This can happen from the time the jury is impaneled or after the trial is over and they are sent to deliberate. In such cases, jurors are held in a form of protective custody in a hotel or motel guarded by court officers, bailiffs, deputy sheriffs, or marshals. What they read or view on television is monitored and subject to censorship, and their telephone conversations with family or friends are restricted accordingly. Each court day they are transported by a special bus to and from the courthouse under guard. The **sequestering** continues until the jury reaches a verdict or until they are dismissed by the judge if they are a **hung jury**—unable to reach a verdict.[6]

Under our system of adversarial justice, members of a jury are observers who, until they begin deliberations, must remain silent and passive. However, in selected cases in a number of states, such as New York and California, civil and criminal jurors are being allowed to question witnesses and inform judges when they want more information. Juror participation is an extension of the growing restlessness of trial judges, who have frequently interrupted lawyers to question witnesses directly—inquisitorial in style. Generally, jurors are permitted to ask questions when opposing lawyers agree and only after they are finished questioning a witness. "The guidelines sent to participating judges suggest that jurors submit written questions to lawyers on both sides and that a lawyer submit any evidentiary objections in a handwritten note to the judge" to avoid slighting a juror (Wiehl 1989b: 20). This might help keep jurors interested in the case—or at least keep them awake, something that has become a problem at marathon trials (Pallasch 1998).

Evidence

Evidence secured in an unconstitutional manner cannot be admitted at trial (exclusionary rule). Jurors must also be protected from evidence that may be misleading or prejudicial. This includes *hearsay*: an assertion made by a testifying witness about a statement made out of court by someone else. Hearsay is generally considered unreliable, if not prejudicial, because opposing counsel does not have an opportunity to test the reliability of the evidence by cross-examining the person who allegedly made the original statement. "The speaker may have been joking, or guessing, or even deliberately lying" (Friedenthal, Kane, and Miller 1985: 464). The jury, after all, is made up of laypeople, and it is the responsibility of the judge, acting on motions or objections from counsel, to prevent improper testimony from being entered as evidence. There are many exceptions to the general prohibition against hearsay evidence, more than 30 in the *Federal Rules of Evidence*.

---

[6] There has been concern over jurors selling, or offering for sale, their experiences on highly publicized trials—fear that jurors will be influenced in favor of a case outcome that has greater commercial appeal. It became known that in at least one case, the "Howard Beach trial," which concerned a racially motivated killing in New York, a juror attempted to sell the story even while deliberations were in progress. For an examination of various aspects of this issue, see Cunningham (1989), Nagel (1989), and Lomasky (1989).

Hearsay

The following are not excluded by the hearsay rule in the *Federal Rules of Evidence* if the declarant is unavailable as a witness:

- **Former testimony.** Testimony given as a witness at another hearing of the same or a different proceeding, or in a deposition taken in compliance with law in the course of the same or another proceeding, if the party against whom the testimony is now offered, or, in a civil action or proceeding, a predecessor in interest, had an opportunity and similar motive to develop the testimony by direct, cross, or redirect examination.

- **Statement under belief of impending death.** In a prosecution for homicide or in a civil action or proceeding, a statement made by a declarant while believing that the declarant's death was imminent, concerning the cause or circumstances of what the declarant believed to be impending death.

- **Statement against interest.** A statement which was at the time of its making so far contrary to the declarant's pecuniary or proprietary interest, or so far tended to subject the declarant to civil or criminal liability, or to render invalid a claim by the declarant against another, that a reasonable person in the declarant's position would not have made the statement unless believing it to be true. A statement tending to expose the declarant to criminal liability and offered to exculpate the accused is not admissible unless corroborating circumstances clearly indicate the trustworthiness of the statement.

- **Statement of personal or family history.** (a) A statement concerning the declarant's own birth, adoption, marriage, divorce, legitimacy, relationship by blood, adoption, or marriage, ancestry, or other similar fact of personal or family history, even though declarant had no means of acquiring personal knowledge of the matter stated; or (b) a statement concerning the foregoing matters, and death also, of another person, if the declarant was related to the other by blood, adoption, or marriage or was so intimately associated with the other's family as to be likely to have accurate information concerning the matter declared.

There are two fundamental types of evidence, direct and indirect:

1. *Direct evidence* is testimony provided by an eyewitness (which in law also includes hearing and the senses of taste, smell, and touch). An example of **direct evidence** would be a statement such as, "I observed the defendant exit the liquor store with a firearm in his right hand and a paper bag in his left hand."

2. *Indirect or circumstantial evidence* does not prove a proposition directly. An example is a bullet recovered from the body of the victim that matches those fired from a revolver owned by the defendant. Jon Waltz states that **circumstantial evidence** "is frequently far more persuasive than direct evidence" (1997: 12). Evidence such as fingerprints and hair samples are often more reliable than that provided by an eyewitness, particularly when the latter is based on the testimony of an untrained civilian, often the victim. Persons who are threatened or otherwise subject to the trauma of a crime are notoriously poor observers (Engelhardt 1999). "Witnessed events often occur under less than optimal viewing conditions. Moreover, witnesses to crimes often experience high levels of stress or emotional arousal"

(Stanny and Johnson 2000: 359). "The major problem is that people are not very good at recognizing other people. Especially strangers. Especially strangers of a different race. Especially strangers of a different race seen briefly under stress" (Uviller 1996: 55). In studies of persons wrongfully convicted, but later exonerated by DNA testing, the most common cause was eyewitness error (Gawande 20001; see Cutler and Penrod 1995 for a discussion of this issue; also Huff, Rattner, and Sagarin 1996 for a discussion of the issue of "convicted but innocent").

These two types of evidence come in three basic forms (Waltz 1997):

1. *Testimonial evidence* is that presented orally by a witness in court and under oath, although occasionally it takes the form of a sworn pretrial written deposition, common in civil cases. A few states do not require a court order for taking depositions in criminal cases; a few allow them with a court order; while most allow depositions if a witness will not be available for trial.

2. *Tangible evidence* is any physical **exhibit**, which can be:

   (a) *Real evidence*, such as the actual murder weapon, fingerprints, drugs; or

   (b) *Demonstrative evidence*, usually a visual aid such as a drawing of the crime scene or an anatomical model.

3. *Judicial notice* refers to those matters that are subject to common knowledge or certain verification through reference to such highly reliable sources as calendars or medical dictionaries. Such matters need not be proved, but the judge will instruct the jurors to take them as fully established without any necessity of witnesses or exhibits.

Court Personnel

Before proceeding to the trial, we should note the presence of persons other than the key actors. There will be one or more bailiffs (deputy sheriffs, court officers, marshals) responsible for maintaining order, security, and guarding prisoners. There will be a clerk who maintains records and may call cases. There will be a court reporter who records all proceedings in the courtroom, especially testimony of witnesses. The reporter uses a small, typewriter-like stenographic device, which in the hands of a skilled operator permits simultaneous recording at about 250 words per minute. The stenographic record is transcribed and becomes the official record of the trial. In some jurisdictions, a tape recorder may be used in addition to the court reporter.

The Trial

The centerpiece of the adversarial process is the trial, a highly structured battle between two attorneys and accomplished in accord with established rules of procedure under the stewardship of a judge.

Pretrial Motions

Before the jury is brought into the courtroom to hear **opening statements** and to hear or observe the presentation of evidence, the defense attorney has an opportunity to make pretrial motions—oral and/or written pleadings. The most common are:

- *Motion to dismiss.* This motion is routinely made and routinely denied. Defense counsel claims that the information or indictment is insufficient to justify a trial.

- *Motion for a change of venue.* The defense argues that a fair trial is not possible in the current jurisdiction because of the amount of pretrial publicity. If the judge agrees, the trial will be moved to another jurisdiction.

- *Motion for a bill of particulars.* This motion is an attempt by the defense to obtain a **bill of particulars**—details of the prosecution's charges and of the occurrences to be investigated at trial. The defense is then able to place limits on evidence offered by the prosecution; it must be **material** (that is, clearly related to the items in the bill of particulars), or it will be excluded as immaterial on an objection by defense counsel.

- *Motion for discovery.* This is a request for access to the evidence the prosecution plans to use at trial, allowing counsel to prepare his or her defense. Although statutes and practices governing **discovery** differ considerably between states, and in the federal system (Middlekauff 1994), in many, if not most, jurisdictions, discovery is informal, and opposing counsel is routinely allowed to review evidence, which facilitates plea bargaining. The deliberate withholding of exculpatory evidence by a prosecutor is an unconstitutional denial of due process (*Brady v. Maryland* [1963]). The state, however, is obligated to disclose only that evidence for which there is a reasonable probability that the trial outcome would have been different had the defense obtained the evidence in time for trial (*United States v. Bagley* [1985]).

- *Motion to suppress.* This motion seeks to invoke the exclusionary rule. If successful, it often leaves the prosecution without important evidence and requires a *nolle prosequi* or dismissal of the charges.

- *Motion for severance.* Defendants charged with multiple counts may move to have them severed—require separate trials for various offenses that can be bundled together in a logical manner—or request separate trials (rejoinder) for two or more defendants.

Sidebars

At times during a trial, the prosecution or defense will approach the bench and request a sidebar, a private conference with the judge. This is usually done at the side of the bench away from the jury, and opposing counsel must be present because any *ex parte* (having only one party present) discussion with the judge is considered improper. This brief conference, conducted so jurors cannot hear what is being said, usually involves the question of admissibility of certain evidence, or it may be used to inquire if certain questions can properly be asked of a witness. If the issue cannot be decided quickly, the judge will have the jury removed and hear arguments in open court on the matter.

Opening Statements

The method of presentation by a prosecutor parallels that of good scholarly paper. As in a scholarly paper, the trial begins with an introduction. Before any evidence is presented, each side is allowed to address the jury in the form of a general outline of the case he or she intends to present. The prosecutor formally introduces him- or herself (and any colleagues) to the court and states his or her intentions and the nature of the evidence to be presented: "Ladies and gentlemen of the jury, the state intends to prove that on . . ." The defense may decline to present an opening statement; it is up to the prosecution to prove the defendant guilty beyond a reasonable doubt, and the defendant has no corresponding responsibility. An opening statement also provides advance notice to the opposition of the line of prosecution or defense. There is no time limit for an opening statement; it is at the discretion of the judge. The defense may object to any overstatements by the prosecutor, or the prosecutor's opening statement may be used by the defense at summation to bring the prosecutor's credibility into question for failing to prove what was set forth in the opening statement. At the conclusion of opening statements, it is time for the prosecutor's case-in-chief: the presentation of evidence. In a scholarly paper, this would be the research narrative.

Prosecutor's Presentation of Evidence

Evidence must be presented by a witness who is called, sworn in by the court clerk or bailiff, and directed to take the witness stand, a raised chair at the side of the judge's bench. A witness may testify on matters he or she saw, heard, or has knowledge of by one or more of the senses. As mentioned previously, third-party testimony is hearsay and generally not admissible. For example, a witness who testifies, "I was told by the defendant's girlfriend that he robbed . . ." will not normally be permitted to continue because defense counsel cannot test the reliability of the girlfriend's statement. As also noted earlier, there are many exceptions to the hearsay rule (e.g., hearsay evidence is admissible in conspiracy cases for the purpose of tying together defendants who comprise the combination or confederation that is the basis for the criminal allegation.) In general, a witness cannot offer an opinion or conclusion unless it has been established that he or she is an "expert." However, lay opinion with respect to matters such as duration of time, height, weight, or the speed of a vehicle is commonly allowed into evidence. Expert witnesses—scientists, medical doctors, handwriting analysts—can offer their professional opinions and conclusions, or they can be asked to respond to a hypothetical question that has a bearing on the case. Thus, a pathologist can testify as to the cause of death.

Witnesses, particularly police officers, are used to identify physical (or forensic) evidence such as documents, photos and diagrams of the crime scene, fingerprints, bloodstains, and weapons. Without such identification, an item cannot be admitted

---

Types of Witnesses

There are two main types of witnesses in a criminal (or civil) trial:

1. **Witness of fact.** Using the senses, this person has heard, seen, felt, or smelled something that has a bearing on the matter being litigated.
2. **Expert witness.** Persons who by virtue of education, training, and/or experience are able to form an (expert) opinion that is beyond the scope of the average person.

into evidence as "Exhibit A" or "B" or "C." This involves the **chain of custody**: The prosecutor must be able to prove that the piece of forensic evidence being presented to the jury is without any doubt the same item that was retrieved at the scene of the crime or during a subsequent investigation. This is not as easy as it may sound. The trial usually occurs months, if not years, after the crime. The evidence has passed through a number of hands—the police officer(s) who responded to the scene; the technician(s) who analyzed it; and other police officers or clerks involved in transporting, filing, and storing it for use at the trial. Each person handling the evidence must record that fact by writing out his or her name, the date, time, and purpose. It must be shown that the evidence was properly secured, that only authorized persons had access to it, and that they properly recorded every time they had custody of the item. Each person in the chain can be required to testify, and any broken link can render the evidence inadmissible. Poor police practices (e.g., failing to properly secure the crime scene from the public and/or other police officers) can raise doubts about evidence. If many police officers were walking around the crime scene, each can be called to testify by the defense. This can be problematic for the prosecution because the jury can grow quite bored, and the more officers, the greater the chances of contradictory testimony.

When introducing physical/forensic evidence, the prosecutor shows the evidence to the judge and to the opposing counsel and asks that it be marked (by the clerk) for identification (e.g., "Prosecution's Exhibit A"). The prosecutor then shows the marked evidence to the witness for proper identification: "Officer, do you recognize this firearm marked as 'Prosecution's Exhibit A'?" A positive response will result in the prosecutor asking the witness to identify the firearm for the court and then requesting that it be admitted into evidence. Opposing counsel can object to the offering. The witness is then asked a series of questions about the evidence. (In some jurisdictions, these questions come before moving to have the evidence admitted.)

In the adversarial system of justice used in this country (as opposed to an inquisitorial system), the examination of a witness involves a series of questions. The questions and the responses must be narrow enough for opposing counsel to have the opportunity to object—to claim that the jury is about to hear testimony that is inadmissible. If such testimony does occur and the attorney objects, the judge will order it stricken from the record and instruct the jury to disregard it, which may be easier said than done. Questions cannot be *leading*, that is, queries that suggest their own answer, such as "Isn't it true that the defendant owned a firearm?" as opposed to the more permissible question, "To your knowledge, did the defendant own a firearm?" The exceptions are preliminary questions to establish some basic facts, such as, "You reside at 1492 Columbus Avenue?" or "Is it correct that you are employed as a manager by the Howell Strident Corporation?" During a sidebar, counsel may request permission from the judge to ask a leading question and state the reason for wanting to ask such a question—to help the witness remember an item, for example. In any event, direct questioning has as its purpose getting the witness to tell a story without wandering.

Opposing counsel can object to any question or answer on grounds the attorney is leading the witness or for any other procedural defects (e.g., that it is immaterial and irrelevant or that it requires an opinion or conclusion that only an "expert" witness can offer). The judge determines whether to uphold the objection or to overrule. If the objection is sustained, opposing counsel may make an offer to prove, which is dictated

Perjury

Perjury is a crime committed when a person, under oath in a judicial proceeding, willfully makes a false statement in a material (that is, relevant to the issue) matter. The statement may be oral (e.g., court testimony) or written (e.g., an **affidavit**). Some jurisdictions use a broader concept, false swearing, in which case the falsehood need not be in a judicial matter or even material. According to the U. S. Code (Sec. 1621): "Whoever (1) having taken an oath before a competent tribunal, officer, or person, in any case in which a law of the United States authorizes an oath to be administered, that he will testify, declare, depose, or certify truly, or that any written testimony, declaration, deposition, or certificate by him subscribed, is true, willfully and contrary to such oath states or subscribes any material matter which he does not believe to be true; or (2) in any declaration, certificate, verification, or statement under penalty of perjury as permitted under . . . [law] willfully subscribes as true any material matter which he does not believe to be true; is guilty of perjury and shall, except as otherwise expressly provided by law, be fined under this title or imprisoned not more than five years, or both. This section is applicable whether the statement or subscription is made within or without the United States."

In Illinois, perjury is a Class 3 felony punishable by a term of imprisonment for two to five years.

to the court reporter out of hearing of the jury. If an objection is overruled, the attorney may make an **exception**, which has the effect of arguing that the court made an error, thereby preparing the record for a possible appeal.

Lawyers must not only seek to win their cases at trial but also do everything they can to generate a record of the trial that will convince an appellate court that justice did or did not prevail. Since an appellate court can consider only the formal record generated at trial, attorneys must be careful to create a complete and accurate record of the trial. An action to which an objection was not raised at trial is not preserved for appellate review. "Appellate courts, except in cases of egregious error that led to fundamental injustice, take the position that any issue not timely raised in the earlier proceedings has been lost by 'procedural default'" (Hughes 1996: 22). This process is an effort to foreclose on a strategy of avoiding objections at trial, when they should be made, in order to use them as a weapon on appeal. It would also open the floodgates to indeterminate appeals (Coffin 1994).

Cross-Examination

After the prosecutor has completed the direct examination of a witness that he or she has called, the defense has an opportunity to cross-examine. During this phase of the trial, the attorney can ask **leading questions**: "Isn't it true that on the night of December 30th, you consumed at least five glasses of alcoholic beverages?" **Cross-examination** has several purposes. It is used to challenge a witness' testimony (e.g., by questioning his or her memory or vision). The attorney may attempt to impeach the credibility of the witness (e.g., by asking questions about any criminal record, history of mental illness, or alcoholism, any information that will tend to blemish the reputation of the witness in the eyes of the jury). The attorney may ask for details of any previous relationship with the defendant. As with direct examination, the prosecutor can object to any questions. In some states, "rape shield laws" have placed restrictions on the type of personal questions that can be asked of a rape victim.

Redirect and Recross-Examination

After defense counsel has had an opportunity to cross-examine an adverse witness, the prosecution can ask additional questions of the witness about any new matters that have been brought out during the cross-examination, in an effort to reestablish the testimony or rehabilitate the witness. Questions that go beyond those new areas raised on cross-examination can be objected to by defense counsel. After the prosecution has completed redirect examination, defense counsel can recross-examine. This process can continue until both sides have no further questions or the judge intervenes.

After all prosecution witnesses have been subjected to direct and cross-examination, and to redirect and recross-examination, the state rests; the prosecution's case-in-chief has been presented. At this point, defense may ask for a **directed verdict**: The jury is removed from the courtroom, and the judge is requested to render a verdict of not guilty based on insufficient evidence having been presented by the prosecution. Rarely does a judge agree to a directed verdict; the motion usually is made to preserve some legal rights on appeal. The judge, however, may dismiss certain counts of a multicount indictment or information based on insufficient evidence, but the trial will continue on the remaining counts.

Defense Attorney's Response

In many jurisdictions, particularly if defense counsel declined to make one earlier, he or she may now present an opening statement summarizing evidence that will be used to counter the prosecution's case. Defense counsel now has an opportunity to present witnesses, who may or may not include the defendant. According to the Fifth Amendment, a defendant cannot be forced to testify and the decision to not testify cannot be used against him or her when considering the question of guilt or innocence; this will be explained to the jury by the judge.

If the defendant decides to testify, the defendant-as-witness can be subjected to vigorous cross-examination by the prosecutor, who will attempt to impeach the defendant's credibility. As part of the **impeachment** process, questions about past criminal behavior, as well as alcohol or drug abuse, which would not ordinarily be permitted, are relevant and permissible. As a witness on his or her own behalf, the defendant can refuse to answer any question. Such a refusal, however, can be used as evidence, an issue the prosecution will usually stress to the jury during **closing arguments**. Allowing a defendant with a serious criminal history to testify is, obviously, a calculated risk for the defense. In most cases, the defendant's criminal history will be placed before the jury during direct examination by his or her attorney in order to blunt the issue.

Witnesses called by the defense are questioned by direct examination and subjected to cross-examination by the prosecution. Redirect and recross-examination continue as with the witnesses called by the prosecution. After the defense has rested, the prosecutor is permitted to call further witnesses for the purpose of **rebuttal**, testimony designed to refute the testimony of defense witnesses. If the prosecutor has introduced new evidence or has delved into new matters, the defense is entitled to a rejoinder, testimony restricted to new defense evidence to refute the prosecutor's rebuttal. In practice, however, a judge seldom allows a **rejoinder**. On the rare occasions when there is a surprise witness, it is during rebuttal or rejoinder that he or she is usually called to testify.

Final Motions and Closing Arguments

After both sides rest, and without the jury present, the defense can renew the motion for a directed verdict of acquittal, a pleading that the prosecution has not provided sufficient evidence—e.g., failed to prove the *actus reus* to allow the case to be decided by the jury. If the motion is sustained, the trial is over and the defendant is acquitted. If the motion is denied by the judge, summations or closing arguments are in order.

As in a good scholarly paper, the prosecution's case ends with a summary and conclusion. The prosecutor is allowed to address the jury, presenting remarks that summarize the case he or she has presented, usually highlighting important testimony. Summations are not evidence, and the jury is informed of this by the judge. The defense is provided with the same opportunity, typically stressing the weakness of the state's case and the need to find a defendant guilty beyond a reasonable doubt. Attorneys for the state and for the defendant are allowed considerable leeway during summations, which can sometimes be quite dramatic. However, improper remarks by the prosecutor (e.g., those that are inflammatory) can provide a basis for appealing an adverse jury decision. After the defense closes, the prosecutor is permitted a rebuttal. This is typically limited to those areas discussed by the defense in summation; new lines of argument are not permitted. In some states, if the defense has not called any witnesses, he or she is entitled to first and last closing arguments. There are no specific time limits for closing arguments, which may last only a few minutes or, in complex cases, run for a few days.

Charge to the Jury

The judge now charges the jury—explains their responsibilities and the options they have as jurors.[7] In a multiple-count indictment or information, for example, in addition to a verdict of guilty or not guilty, they can find the defendant guilty on some counts and not guilty on others. The judge will carefully cover the law applicable in the case, stating the issues and defining terms that may be unfamiliar to a layperson. This task can be difficult—terms such as reasonable doubt, malice aforethought, and mayhem are not exemplars of clarity even for lawyers (Tiersma 1999). Miller Shealy, Jr. (2013: 225) notes that "the Supreme Court has failed to define the concept of 'reasonable doubt' with any precision." In many states, attorneys are permitted to submit suggestions to be included in the instructions to the jury, and the judge will indicate those that are acceptable and those that are not. Defense counsel may object to any ruling on suggestions; the objection is recorded by the court reporter, providing the basis for an appeal in the event of an adverse verdict.

The judge instructs the jurors in two areas: what their task consists of during deliberation and what procedures they should employ in reaching a verdict.

---

[7] In some jurisdictions, such as Missouri, the judge reads instructions to the jury before the closing arguments are made.

The procedures defined by the judge generally include the instruction that the juror is to regard the defendant as innocent until proven otherwise; that the burden of proof is on the prosecution; that the juror's task is to determine the facts on the basis of credible evidence; that certain information may be regarded as evidence, such as direct testimony of witnesses, charts and exhibits, observations of the witnesses, and reasonable inferences drawn from the testimony; that other information may not be regarded as evidence, such as statements and questions posed by the attorneys, or the race and background of defendant; how to assess the credibility of testimony, such as each witness' opportunity to observe, possible bias, character, and contradictions in testimony; what constitutes a reasonable inference as opposed to unwarranted speculation; and what is the meaning and application of the standard of proof, namely beyond a reasonable doubt, in assessing the truth of allegations. The second portion of the judge's instructions defines for the jurors a complete set of possible verdicts, of which they must choose one. (Hastie, Penrod, and Pennington 1983: 17)

As in the English system, in some jurisdictions, particularly federal district courts, the judge is permitted to comment on the evidence, although the judge's opinion is not binding on the jurors. Most jurisdictions, however, prohibit judges from commenting on witness credibility.

Jury Deliberations

The jury retires to the jury room and elects a foreperson (unless the trial takes place in one of the states where the foreperson is automatically the first juror chosen). The room is guarded by a bailiff, and no one is permitted to enter without an explicit request from the foreperson, via the bailiff, to the judge. At times, jurors may request the court reporter to read some testimony or to review some forensic evidence. The manner in which the jury proceeds is not governed by law or custom; each jury is independent and not bound by precedent. Deliberations may take less than an hour or as long as a few days, or even weeks. As noted earlier, jurors may be sequestered, or they may leave at the end of the court day, even when they have not reached a verdict.

If all jurors agree on a verdict, it is signed by the foreperson and read aloud in court by the foreperson, the bailiff, or the court clerk. The jurors may be polled, each asked by the judge if this is his or her decision. After the verdict is read, the jury is dismissed by the judge "with thanks." Jurors are now free to discuss the case with anyone they choose—the press, the prosecutor, or the defense. (Five states and 18 federal districts prohibit trial lawyers from speaking with jurors at the end of a trial.) In a Connecticut rape case in which the jury was deadlocked, the defense attorney hired a member of the jury to act as a consultant at the retrial. The attorney was interested in finding out what arguments had been most effective. Nevertheless, the defendant was convicted at the second trial (Johnson 1986).

If, despite repeated encouragement from the judge, jurors cannot reach a unanimous decision, it is a hung jury. The prosecutor must decide if he or she wishes to retry the case. This often depends on the number of jurors who voted for a conviction. For example, an 11–1 vote for conviction would almost invariably result in a retrial or a plea bargain.

Sentencing

If the defendant is found guilty, or pleads guilty, he or she enters the sentencing stage. Sentencing in the United States can be *indeterminate* or *determinate*.

Indeterminate Sentencing

While the **indeterminate sentence** can be traced back to the nineteenth century, contemporary use dates back to the years following the Second World War. Toward the end of the war, Governor (and later Chief Justice) Earl Warren of California, responding to a prison scandal, instituted a new approach to penology: corrections. Instead of punishing criminals, the California system would attempt to rehabilitate offenders using the latest scientific approaches: Prisons became correctional institutions, wardens became superintendents, and guards became correction officers. "Treaters" (psychiatrists, social workers, teachers) were sent to the correctional institutions. Since it is not possible to know in advance how much time will be needed to "correct" a specific offender, the indeterminate sentence was instituted and became the cornerstone of the corrections approach.

Under the indeterminate sentence, an offender is sentenced to a minimum and a maximum number—the judge sets the parameters—of years. For example, a sentence might be three years to nine years—written 3-0-0/9-0-0. It is the **parole board**, not the judge, who determines when the offender is to be released from prison (correctional facility) in 3-0-0, or 4-0-0, or 5-0-0, all the way up to 9-0-0. Members of the parole board review an inmate's record, efforts at rehabilitation, past criminal history, and future plans and make a release decision within the parameters set by the judge's sentence. Inmates not paroled become eligible for release prior to the expiration of their sentence through the mechanism of "time off for good behavior" (**good time**) usually one-third off the maximum. Thus, an inmate serving 3-0-0/9-0-0 could be paroled after serving three years, but in any event, assuming good behavior, the inmate would be released after six years (6-0-0). Persons paroled or released on good time come under the supervision of a parole officer for the remainder or a portion of the unserved sentence.

> *Persons serving a prison sentence in states that have a parole board,*
> *or who have been denied release by a parole board,*
> *usually qualify for release prior to the expiration of their sentence*
> *for good behavior, referred to as "good time."*

The California system of corrections spread to every state in the nation. It was criticized by those on the right of the political spectrum for releasing criminals before the expiration of their sentence. But critics on the left argued that the indeterminate sentence actually kept persons in prison longer than they would have been made to serve if punishment had been the sole basis of incarceration. Critics pointed out that under the indeterminate sentence, persons sent to prison for crimes of similar severity would not all serve the same amount of time—some would be paroled before others—which amounts to unequal justice. Furthermore, parole boards often returned offenders to prison for violating the conditions of their release, meaning the rules of parole (see Figure 8.3). By

1. RELEASE: Parolee shall report to:

_____

2. RESIDENCE: Parolee shall establish a residence of record and shall reside at such residence in fact and on record shall not change this place of residence without the consent of his Parole Officer; and shall not leave the area paroled to nor the State paroled to without the permission of the Parole Officer.

3. CONDUCT: Parolee shall obey all State and Federal laws and Municipal ordinances at all times. Parolee shall follow the directives of the Parole Officer.

4. REPORT: Parolee shall make written and in-person reports as directed by the Parole Officer and shall permit visits to place of residence as required by the Parole Officer.
   a. Parolee further shall submit urinalysis or other tests for narcotics or chemical agents upon the request of the Parole Officer, and is required to pay for all tests.
   b. Parolee further agrees to allow the Parole Officer to search his person, or his residence, or any premises under his control, or any vehicle under his control upon request.

5. WEAPONS: Parolee shall not own, possess, nor have under his control or in his custody firearms or other deadly weapons.

6. ASSOCIATION: Parolee shall not associate with any person with a criminal record without the permission of the Parole Officer.

7. EMPLOYMENT: Parolee shall seek and obtain employment or shall participate in a full-time education or vocational program, unless waived by the Parole Officer.

8. ALCOHOL/DRUGS: Parolee shall not abuse alcoholic beverages or use illegal drugs.

9. ADDITIONAL CONDITIONS:

I have read the foregoing document or have had it read to me and I have full and intelligent understanding of the contents and the meaning thereof, and I have received a copy of this document.

I hereby affix my signature of my own free will and without reservation or coercion.

_____   _____
Parole Officer   Parolee

                                                          _____
                                                          Date

Figure 8.3   Parole Rules

the mid-1970s, criticism of indeterminate sentencing increased as research into rehabilitative efforts failed to reveal any significant level of success in preventing recidivism (a reversion to criminal behavior). By 1980, a number of states, including California, had switched back to determinate sentencing, a trend that continues.

Determinate Sentencing

In response to criticism of indeterminate sentencing—that it results in dangerous criminals being released early or leads to disparate sentences for similar crimes (Abadinsky 2015)—a variety of so-called flat or **determinate sentence** schemes have been adopted. Although each requires the setting of a specific sentence—no minimum or maximum—they differ according to the amount of discretion left to the judge. Determinate sentencing requires a judge to impose a specific number of years for each particular crime, e.g., nine years (9-0-0) for robbery. The offender is required to serve the entire sentence minus time off granted for good behavior in prison (usually a maximum of 50 percent off the sentence; much less in the federal system). In practice, no state has adopted a strict egalitarian approach. Instead, determinate sentences can be classified according to the amount of discretion enjoyed by the judge.

- *Determinate sentence/wide discretion.* The legislature provides for a range of sentences for each level of offense. For example, a Class 2 felony would be punishable with a sentence of between 3-0-0 to 9-0-0. Under this system the judge retains discretion to sentence a Class 2 offender to 3-0-0, or 4-0-0, or more all the way up to 9-0-0. The sentence imposed is definite, for a specific number of years, but the judge's discretion is quite wide.

- *Presumptive/narrow discretion.* The legislature limits discretion to a narrow range of sentences for each level of offense. For each level there is a presumed sentence from which the judge cannot deviate except if there are aggravating or **mitigating circumstances**, and then only in a very limited manner. If a defendant is convicted of a Class 2 felony, the judge would be required to set a sentence of (for example) 5-0-0. On a showing of aggravation by the prosecutor, however, the judge could increase the presumptive sentence to (for example) 6-0-0; on a showing of mitigation by the defense, the judge could decrease the presumptive sentence to (for example) 4-0-0. In some states, e.g., Minnesota, the presumed sentence is increased by a fixed amount based on the severity of any prior convictions (see Figure 8.4).

- *Presumptive/wide discretion.* As in the presumptive sentence with narrow discretion, the legislature provides three possible terms for each class of felony. However, while each class has a presumptive sentence, the judge may decrease (for mitigation) or increase (for aggravation) by significant amounts, a few months or several years (depending on the class of offense). A departure from the presumptive sentence usually requires a written statement of factual findings and reasons for the departure.

In 2004, the Supreme Court, 5–4, declared unconstitutional a Washington State determinate **sentencing guidelines** scheme, dooming that and other similar sentencing systems used by federal courts and about 20 states (*Blakely v. Washington*, 542 U.S. 296). The Court ruled that any findings that increase the penalty for a crime beyond

Presumptive sentence lengths are in months. Italicized numbers within the grid denote the discretionary range within which a court may sentence without the sentence being deemed a departure. Offenders with stayed felony sentences may be subject to local confinement.

SEVERITY LEVEL OF CONVICTION OFFENSE		0	1	2	3	4	5	6 or more
Murder, 2nd Degree (intentional murder; drive-by shootings)	11	306 *261–367*	326 *278–391*	346 *295–415*	366 *312–439*	386 *329–463*	406 *346–480²*	426 *363–480²*
Murder, 3rd Degree Murder, 2nd Degree (unintentional murder)	10	150 *128–180*	165 *141–198*	180 *153–216*	195 *166–234*	210 *179–252*	225 *192–270*	240 *204–288*
Assault, 1st Degree Controlled Substance Crime, 1st Degree	9	86 *74–103*	98 *84–117*	110 *94–132*	122 *104–146*	134 *114–160*	146 *125–175*	158 *135–189*
Aggravated Robbery, 1st Degree Controlled Substance Crime, 2nd Degree	8	48 *41–57*	58 *50–69*	68 *58–81*	78 *67–93*	88 *75–105*	98 *84–117*	108 *92–129*
Felony DWI	7	36	42	48	54 *46–64*	60 *51–72*	66 *57–79*	72 *62–84²*
Controlled Substance Crime, 3rd Degree	6	21	27	33	39 *34–46*	45 *39–54*	51 *44–61*	57 *49–68*
Residential Burglary Simple Robbery	5	18	23	28	33 *29–39*	38 *33–45*	43 *37–51*	48 *41–57*
Nonresidential Burglary	4	12¹	15	18	21	24 *21–28*	27 *23–32*	30 *26–36*
Theft Crimes (Over $5,000)	3	12¹	13	15	17	19 *17–22*	21 *18–25*	23 *20–27*
Theft Crimes ($5,000 or less) Check Forgery ($251–$2,500)	2	12¹	12¹	13	15	17	19	21 *18–25*
Sale of Simulated Controlled Substance	1	12¹	12¹	12¹	13	15	17	19 *17–22*

☐ Presumptive commitment to state imprisonment. First-degree murder has a mandatory life sentence and is excluded from the Guidelines under Minn. Stat. § 609.185. See Guidelines section 2.E. Mandatory Sentences, for policies regarding those sentences controlled by law.

▨ Presumptive stayed sentence; at the discretion of the court, up to one year of confinement and other non-jail sanctions can be imposed as conditions of probation. However, certain offenses in the shaded area of the Grid always carry a presumptive commitment to state prison. Guidelines sections 2.C. Presumptive Sentence and 2.E. Mandatory Sentences.

¹ 12¹ = One year and one day

² Minn. Stat. § 244.09 requires that the Guidelines provide a range for sentences that are presumptive comitment to state imprisonment of 15% lower and 20% higher than the fixed duration displayed, provided that the minimum sentence is not less than one year and one day and the maximum sentence is not more than the statutory maximum. Guidelines section 2.C.1–2. Presumptive Sentence.

Source: http://mn.gov/sentencing-guidelines/images/2013%2520Standard%2520Grid.pdf

Figure 8.4   Minnesota Sentencing Guidelines

Sentencing	
Equality/punishment	Discretion/rehabilitation
Determinate sentencing	**Indeterminate sentencing**
(specific term of years, e.g., 5-0-0)	(minimum/maximum, e.g., 3-0-0/9-0-0)

the prescribed statutory maximum must be submitted to a jury and proved beyond a reasonable doubt.

The rationale behind determinate sentencing was to reduce judicial discretion and promote less **disparity in sentences** for crimes of equal severity. As noted already, however, determinate sentencing schemes often maintain wide discretion and even those with narrow discretion cannot control the prosecutor's role in determining the charges. A study of federal determinate sentencing found great variation in sentences for crimes of equal severity (Lacasse and Payne 1999). Determinate sentencing has been criticized for failing to deal adequately with the issue of disparity due to the influence of a prosecutor in determining the sentence via plea bargaining. It has also led to the demise of rehabilitative programming in many prisons and exacerbated problems arising from overcrowding. Determinate sentencing systems usually include a provision for "good time" in order to promote prison discipline and keep down the prison population. Good time is typically deducted in advance, when the offender is first received at the institution; misbehavior results in time being added. In some states an inmate may be entitled to additional time off the sentence for exemplary performance: "meritorious good time" or "industrious good time." Enhanced good-time schemes are usually a response to court orders that flow from prison overcrowding. Good-time provisions have come under severe political assault and many public officials are advocating or enacting "**truth in sentencing** laws," which reflect the actual amount of time each sentenced offender will serve—or provisions requiring the serving of at least 85 percent of the sentence. Of course, this can increase prison overcrowding and new schemes for releasing inmates early.

Presentence Investigation Report

In some states, before imposing a sentence, the judge is required to order a **presentence investigation (PSI) report**; in other jurisdictions, it is discretionary. The presentence investigation report has several purposes: Most important, it serves as a guide for the judge in the exercise of sentencing discretion, especially when a sentence of probation instead of imprisonment is being considered. In most jurisdictions, the report is given to the judge, prosecutor, and defense counsel and becomes a subject at the sentencing hearing. (The PSI also assists correctional authorities to classify prisoners and probation and parole agencies to supervise offenders.)

In some jurisdictions (e.g., Illinois) the judge has very wide discretion, and therefore the presentence investigation report may be quite important. In other states, such as California, the judge has limited discretion, which renders the presentence investigation report relatively unimportant. Most cases end not with a trial but with a negotiated plea of guilty. This makes the presentence investigation report unnecessary,

Presentence Investigation Report

The primary purpose of the probation department's presence investigation (PSI) is to assist the judge in rendering a sentencing decision based not only on the criminal record but also on the social and psychological background of the offender. The PSI report typically contains information on the following items:

- **Offense**
  - Official version
  - Statement of police officer, complainants, victims
  - Defendant's version
- **Prior Juvenile and Criminal Record**
- **Family History**
  - Defendant
  - Parents and siblings
  - Spouse and children

- **Education**
- **Health**
  - Physical
  - Mental
- **Employment History**
- **Financial Condition**
- **Victim Impact Statement**
- **Evaluation and Summary**
- **Recommendation**

although in some jurisdictions a similar (pre-plea) report is submitted to provide a basis for plea bargaining.

Sentencing Hearing

In some states, sentencing authority rests with the jury in all serious criminal cases, and in a few others that authority is restricted to particular types of cases. The Supreme Court ruled that the death penalty must be imposed by a jury and not a judge. There are also statutes that require a sentence of life without parole on conviction for a third felony: "three-strikes-and-you're-out" (actually "in") laws.

The Supreme Court has ruled that a defendant who has been convicted has a right to be represented at sentencing by an attorney. Counsel can muster facts and present them in a manner most likely to benefit the defendant in his or her attempt to win some form of leniency from the court. The prosecutor and the defense are permitted to address the court, each advocating an outcome in this final scene of the long adversarial process. The judge's degree of discretion varies depending on the statutes and the particular sentencing scheme used, indeterminate or determinate. Generally the judge can impose a fine and/or, if the subject is eligible, a sentence of probation. The judge can impose a sentence of incarceration in the county or the local jail (for terms of one year or less) or in a state prison for felony convictions. For some offenses in various jurisdictions, there is a mandatory sentence for certain crimes. In 2003, the Supreme Court upheld California's "three-strikes" law that mandates a life sentence on conviction for a third felony even if it is a nonviolent crime. In this case (*Ewing v. California*), the appellant, who had a long criminal record, received a sentence of 25-years-to-life for the theft of three golf clubs. The "three-strikes" law in California now requires that the "third-strike" be for a serious felony. The Court found that the state's legitimate goal of deterring and incapacitating repeat offenders means the sentence is not grossly disproportionate to the offense and therefore does not violate the Eighth Amendment's prohibition on cruel and unusual punishments. (For an analysis of this issue, see Frase 2005.)

Probation and Parole

Persons sentenced to probation and those released from prison by a parole board or based on time off their sentence for "good behavior" typically come under the supervision of a probation or parole officer. The former is usually part of the judicial branch; the latter is part of the executive branch, although some states combine probation and parole (P/P) in the same agency under the executive branch. P/P officers have responsibility for enforcing the rules and regulations by which a probationer or parolee/conditional releasee is required to abide. If the P/P officer alleges that the rules have been violated, a violation process will be implemented.

Because the amount of due process required is dependent on what is at stake, persons on probation and parole have already been convicted and, therefore, are not entitled to the same rights as a criminal defendant. But while supervision in the community curtails freedom, it is valuable—less restrictive than incarceration. This provides a **liberty interest**, and therefore due process rights before probation or parole can be revoked. For probation violations, a preliminary hearing (as per *Gagnon v. Scarpelli* [1973]) will take place before a judge—if possible, the one who imposed the original sentence of probation. At the preliminary hearing, the judge will determine if there is sufficient evidence (probable cause) to indicate that the probationer violated one or more of the conditions of probation in an important respect. If so, the probationer can be held in custody for 60 days pending a revocation hearing. At the preliminary and revocation hearings, the probationer will have an opportunity to confront and question adverse witnesses, be represented by counsel, and provide evidence on his or her own behalf. At the revocation hearing, the judge considers the probationer's entire record while under supervision (e.g., employment record), in addition to the rule violations, and makes a decision (based on the preponderance of the evidence) whether to continue probation or revoke supervision and order the offender to serve his or her sentence in jail or prison.

For parole violations, the process is similar, except that the hearing is not part of the judicial system; rather it is held under the administrative authority of the parole board (as per *Morrissey v. Brewer* [1972]). The preliminary hearing is usually conducted by a hearing officer, and the revocation hearing by members of the parole board. At the revocation hearing, members of the parole board determine whether the violation is serious enough to warrant returning the parolee to prison. Probation and parole agencies may use a brief term of local incarceration as an alternative to prison.

Executive Clemency

All states and the federal government (Article II of the Constitution) have provisions for **clemency**. In 31 states and the federal government, the chief executive holds the final clemency power, and in most of these states, the parole board or a clemency board appointed by the governor investigates clemency applications at the request of the governor. Clemency consists of the **reprieve**, the commutation, and the **pardon**. A reprieve is a temporary suspension of the execution of sentence. Its use today is quite limited and usually concerns cases in which capital punishment has been ordered. In such cases, a governor or the president of the United States can grant a reprieve—a stay of execution—to provide more time for further legal action or other deliberations. A commutation is a modification of sentence to the benefit of an offender. Commutation has been used when an inmate provided some assistance to the prison staff, such as during prison riots. It may also be granted to inmates with a severe illness, like AIDS or cancer. Laws governing commutation differ from state to state, and it is traditionally granted at Christmastime. A pardon is an unconditional forgiveness for any crimes committed and, in addition to a release from a prison sentence, can restore civil/legal rights lost as a result of a criminal conviction.

Appeals

The American system of justice is unique in the extensive postconviction review procedures to which a defendant is entitled. A convict may petition the trial court for a new trial or take an appeal to the state's intermediate appellate court and, if unsuccessful there, can still appeal to the state court of last resort. If unsuccessful in state court, he or she can petition the US Supreme Court for certiorari. The convict can also attack the conviction "collaterally" (using indirect means by way of a writ of *habeas corpus*), claiming that his or her constitutional rights were violated in some way by the state court conviction. *Habeas corpus* requires authorities holding a prisoner to produce him or her and justify custody. Having exhausted direct and indirect appeals in state courts, he or she can move over to the federal courts, claiming again that the conviction was unconstitutional, usually on grounds of lack of due process.

The appeal of a guilty verdict requires submitting a notice of appeal and elaborate documents, including a trial transcript. In 1963 (*Douglas v. California*) the Supreme Court ruled that an indigent defendant is entitled to state-appointed counsel on the first appeal following a felony conviction. Court rulings in 1990 curtailed the right of state prison inmates to appeal in federal courts using favorable rulings that have been issued since their own convictions (*Butler v. McKellar*; *Saffle v. Parks*).

An appeal—criminal or civil—is a separate proceeding, rather than a continuation of the trial. The appellate court cannot act as a trial court (i.e., receive new evidence concerning facts already established at the original trial). It is limited to addressing new theories or legal arguments regarding the law applicable to these facts or challenges to a verdict based on "errors of procedure"—e.g., the misapplication of the rules of evidence. As noted above, in order to preserve the right to appeal, defense counsel is required to raise objections to errors committed at trial, objections that allow problems to be corrected immediately by the trial judge. These objections become part of the trial record on which the appeal is based. Although, in general, appellate courts will review only those claims that were properly presented at trial, there are a number of exceptions designed to protect defendant rights (Israel and LaFave 2006). The appellate court can uphold the verdict, overturn it, or order it reversed and remanded to the trial court for a new trial.

SUMMARY

- The prosecutor must prove the *corpus delicti* that has two elements: *actus reus* and *mens rea*.

- *Actus reus* consists of a description of the criminal behavior and evidence that the accused acted accordingly.

- *Mens rea*, "guilty mind," is a legal standard referring to the question of *intent*.

- In cases of *strict or absolute liability*, the intentions of the perpetrator are irrelevant.

- An affirmative defense represents a denial of *mens rea*: claim of self-defense or entrapment.

- Due process is one of the rare legal terms that is meant to be understood literally: the process that is due; procedures to which a person is entitled: right to remain silent; right to counsel; right to bail; right to a speedy and public trial; right to confront witnesses; double jeopardy prohibited.

- The *crime control model* is based on the proposition that the repression of criminal conduct is the most important function of the criminal justice process and presumes the guilt of defendants.

- The exclusionary rule prohibits evidence secured improperly from being used at trial, but there are numerous exceptions.

- The *due process model* stresses the need to protect individual liberty and assumes that the criminal justice system is deficient and stresses the possibility of error.

- A finding of guilty requires a level of certainty referred to "as beyond a reasonable doubt."

- Criminal cases usually begin with a summary arrest.

- Most criminal cases begin and end in the lower courts, and due to the large volume of cases, efficient case processing is the primary focus.

- In an effort to avoid delay, judges in the lower courts typically disregard the niceties of due process and gain the cooperation of the defendant by leniency in misdemeanor cases.

- The federal government operates under the grand jury requirement, but states differ in their use of this body.

- A grand jury meets in secret sessions in a court building to consider evidence presented by the prosecutor in the absence of a judge, defendant, or defense attorney.

- Because the grand jury hears only one side of the case, it rarely votes for "no true bill."

- Instead of a grand jury, some jurisdictions hold probable cause hearings.

- In addition to handing down an indictment, the grand jury may be used for investigation.

- A defendant may choose not to dispute the charges, referred to as "no contest," *nolo contendere*, pleas.

- The Supreme Court has interpreted the Constitution as requiring a jury trial only when the possible sentence is imprisonment for six months or more, although some states provide jury trials for all criminal defendants.

- The Constitution lacks details about jury trials.

- While most states use 12-member juries and require a unanimous verdict, the Supreme Court ruled that juries with as few as six persons are permissible except in cases involving a capital crime, and verdicts of 10–2 and 9–3 are permitted.

- The purpose of a *voir dire* hearing is to determine if a juror is unfit to serve and to allow the attorneys for the prosecution and defense some discretion in determining who will serve on the jury.

- An attorney can argue that a juror is unfit to serve based on certain information—a challenge for *cause*; a peremptory challenge allows and attorney to excuse any juror without having to state a reason.

- Scientific jury selection refers to the use of tools of the social sciences to assist attorneys in the jury selection process.

- A jury unable to reach a verdict is referred to as a *hung jury.*

- *Hearsay* is an assertion made by a testifying witness about a statement made out of court by someone else. Hearsay is generally considered unreliable because opposing counsel does not have an opportunity to cross-examine the person who allegedly made the original statement.

- Direct evidence is testimony provided by an eyewitness; forensic experts often provide indirect evidence.

- The most common pretrial motions are: motion to dismiss; motion for a change of venue; motion for a bill of particulars; and motion for discovery.

- The *chain of custody* requires the prosecutor to prove that the piece of forensic evidence being presented to the jury is without any doubt the same item that was retrieved at the scene of the crime or during a subsequent investigation.

- Direct questioning cannot be *leading*, that is, queries that suggest their own answer.

- An action to which an objection was not raised at trial is not preserved for appellate review.

- The purpose of cross-examination is to challenge a witness' testimony and credibility.

- If the defendant decides to testify, the defendant can be subjected to vigorous cross-examination by the prosecutor, who will attempt to impeach his or her credibility.

- There are no rules for the manner in which a jury deliberates.

- Depending on state statutes, sentencing may be determinate or indeterminate.

- In some states, before imposing a sentence, the judge is required to order a presentence investigation report; in other jurisdictions, it is discretionary.

- Because the amount of due process required is dependent on what is at stake, persons on probation and parole have already been convicted and, therefore, are not entitled to the same rights as a criminal defendant.

- If an offender has a liberty interest, he or she is entitled to limited due process.

- The amount of due process to which as person is entitled is based on what is at risk.

KEY TERMS

absolute liability
actus reus
adjournment
affidavit
affirmative defense
arraignment
bench trial
beyond reasonable doubt
bill of particulars
bond, personal recognizance/
   release on recognizance (ROR)
chain of custody
challenge for cause
change of venue
circumstantial evidence
clemency
closing arguments
corpus delicti
crime control model
cross-examination
custody
determinate sentence
direct evidence
directed verdict
discovery
dismissal
disparity in sentences
double jeopardy
due process
due process clause
due process model
entrapment

evidence, circumstantial
evidence, direct
ex post facto law
exception
exclusionary rule
exculpatory evidence
executive clemency
exhibit
good time
guilty but insane
harmless error
hearsay
hung jury
impanel
impeachment
inadmissible
indictment
inevitable discovery
infancy
information
insanity
intent
joinder of offenses
jury pool
leading question
liberty interest
material
mens rea
mitigating circumstances
no true bill
nolo contendere
oath

objection
opening statements
organized crime
pardon
parole
parole board
peremptory challenge
petit jury
presentence investigation
   (PSI) report
preventive detention
probable cause
probable cause hearing
probation
public safety exception
reasonable doubt
reasonable mistake
   exception
release on recognizance
reprieve
self-defense
sentencing guidelines
sequestering
service of process
strict liability
subpoena *duces tecum*
sustain
true bill
truth in sentencing
voir dire hearing
waive
warrant

REVIEW QUESTIONS

1. What is the *actus reus* that a prosecutor must prove?
2. How does an affirmative defense challenge *mens rea*?
3. What is meant by due process?
4. How does the crime control model differ from the due process model?
5. What is the exclusionary rule and what its purpose?
6. Why are the lower courts referred to as dispensing "rough justice"?
7. Why do defendants in lower courts go along with a judge's disregard for due process?

8. What is the role of a grand jury?

9. Why is it unusual for a grand jury not to indict (no true bill)?

10. Why would a defendant choose a "no contest" (*nolo contendere*) plea?

11. What has the Supreme Court ruled with respect to the size of a jury?

12. What has the Supreme Court ruled about jury unanimity?

13. What is the purpose of a *voir dire* hearing?

14. How does the challenge for cause differ from the peremptory challenge?

15. What is meant by scientific jury selection?

16. What is a *hung jury*?

17. Why is hearsay generally not permitted at a trial?

18. Why is indirect evidence often more reliable that direct evidence?

19. What are the common pretrial motions?

20. What does a prosecutor have to show in order to prove the chain of custody?

21. What is a *leading* question?

22. Why won't appellate courts consider an issue that was not raised during trial, usually in the form of an "objection"?

23. What are the purposes of cross-examination?

24. What are the rules for the manner in which a jury deliberates?

25. What are the differences between a determinate and indeterminate sentence?

26. What is the purpose of a presentence investigation?

27. Why are persons on probation and parole not entitled to the same rights as criminal defendants?

28. How is the amount of due process to which a person is entitled determined?

INTERNET CONNECTIONS

American Bar Association Criminal Justice: http://www.americanbar.org/groups/criminal_justice.html

American Probation and Parole Association: http://www.appa-net.org/eweb

American Society of Trial Consultants: http://astcweb.org/public/index.cfm

Criminal justice links: http://lawguru.com/ilawlib/96.htm

Legal Resource Center: http://crimelynx.com/research.html

National Association of Pretrial Services: http://www.napsa.org

National Criminal Justice Reference Service: https://www.ncjrs.gov

National Institute of Justice: http://www.nij.gov/Pages/welcome.aspx

U.S. Department of Justice Links: http://www.justice.gov/agencies

9

Negotiated Justice

Most court cases in the United States, criminal and civil, are settled not by trial but by negotiation (or dropping of the action). Only about 3 to 4 percent of all civil filings and criminal cases are disposed of by trial. Negotiation in criminal cases is referred to as **plea bargaining**, an ad hoc exchange between a defendant who agrees to plead guilty to a criminal charge and a prosecutor who offers leniency in return. As we shall see in this chapter, conventional views of plea bargaining are often oversimplified and misunderstood.

Plea Bargaining

Plea bargaining in the United States dates back more than 100 years (Friedman 1979) and "appears to have become fairly well entrenched in a number of United States jurisdictions by the 1880s" (Sanborn 1986: 134). In New York City, for example, guilty pleas composed as much as 85 percent of the total number of convictions during the last two decades of the nineteenth century (Sanborn 1986). At this time, "judges found themselves confronted by an onslaught of new, and newly complex, civil suits brought on by the ravages of industrial machinery," and they embraced the expediency of negotiating outcomes in civil and criminal cases (Fisher 2000: 1074).

In the 1920s, plea bargaining was criticized as a device for enabling politically connected defendants to gain preferential treatment; when it emerged as an issue again during the 1950s, however, its condemnation centered around the coercion involved in "forcing" a defendant to plead guilty (Nardulli 1978). In more recent debates, plea bargaining has been criticized for providing criminals with excessive leniency and coercing defendants to waive their constitutional rights to a trial. Nevertheless, in more than 90 percent of felony cases the defendant pleads guilty, and this is most likely to be the result of some sort of plea bargain, explicit or implicit (Dawson 1992). Gerald Lynch (2003: 401) points out, however, "in a system where ninety percent or more of cases end in a negotiated disposition, it is unclear why the 'discounted' punishment imposed in that ninety percent of cases should not rather be considered the norm." Comparing it to selling new cars, Lynch continues: "Where almost no one pays the 'manufacturer's suggested retail price,' and almost everyone buys the item at a 'discounted' price, no one really gets a 'bargain,' and the product's real price is what is actually charged in the marketplace."

Plea bargaining occurs "when a defendant enters a guilty plea with the reasonable expectation of receiving some consideration from the state" (McDonald 1985: 6). Ronald Wright and Marc Miller (2002) distinguish plea bargaining from **open pleas**. The former involves a negotiated outcome; in the later, defendants plead guilty as charged without any prior negotiated agreement with the prosecutor, often because they have obtained information from judges about a likely sentence, and in some cases they actually negotiate with the judge. In some jurisdictions, however, a trial can be more like a plea bargain than the adversarial proceeding it is supposed to symbolize: "Defendants learn that if they agree not to contest the trial they will receive more lenient sentences than they might if they challenge the cases against them." Although such cases are essentially plea bargains, they are counted as trials and help maintain the appearance of a trial system. Paul Wice notes that consideration from the state can take two forms, "being charged with a less serious crime, which will usually result in a lighter sentence, or receiving the minimum punishment allowable for the originally charged offense" (1985: 24).

Plea bargaining is often criticized as an abuse of discretion that results in leniency for serious criminals. On the other hand, it is also criticized as unfair to defendants who must either waive their constitutional rights or run the risk of a substantially higher sentence if found guilty after a trial: The significant sentencing differences between guilty pleas and jury trials support the idea that the defendant who plea-bargained got away with something (Guidorizzi 1998). Popular perceptions of plea bargaining, however, fall far short of reality. In order to better understand the reality of plea bargaining, we will examine two opposing views.

The Negative View

Critics argue that plea bargaining is a symptom of a system operated to further the needs of principal actors rather than the needs or interests of justice or the public. Heavily funded police departments bring an abundance of cases into a judicial system that does not have the resources necessary to provide individualized justice. Justice requires a deliberately slow and exacting concern for due process; it is a luxury the system cannot afford—cases resulting in trials take about twice as long as cases disposed of by guilty pleas. In response to this dilemma, the key actors—judges, prosecutors, defense attorneys—disregard the goal of justice and, instead, tailor their activities to enable the system to function with a minimum of difficulty or disruption.

In the United States, justice is ensured through the adversarial method, an ideal characterized by a vigorous prosecutor for the state who is opposed by an equally vig-

---

Politics of Plea Bargaining

"Demagogues seek to establish that they are tough on crime and that others are not, thereby harnessing for themselves the tremendous public emotion that the crime issue generates. It is thus in the self-interest of entrepreneurial politicians to portray the criminal justice system as worse than it is—and to preach against plea bargaining as a particularly odious part of that system" (McCoy 1993: xvi).

The Theory and the Practice

"In theory, every person accused of a serious crime comes to court protected by the pre-sumption of innocence and the promise of effective representation by a well-prepared and experienced defense counsel supported by investigators, experts, and other resources needed to mount an effective defense. Today our system has broken faith with that basic premise and forgotten its primary mission, often operating under a presumption of guilt in which processing the 'presumed guilty' as cheaply as possible has been made a higher prior-ity than concern for the possibility of innocence" (Benner 2011: 1).

orous advocate for the defendant in a courtroom battle staged before judge and jury. In the view of Abraham Blumberg, the requirements of the judicial system have led to an abandonment of the adversarial ideal—justice—because the practice of criminal law has been reduced to a *confidence game*.

> Organizational goals and discipline impose a set of demands and conditions of practice on the respective professions in the criminal court, to which they respond by abandoning their ideological and professional commitments to the accused cli-ent, in the service of these higher claims of the court organization. All court person-nel, including the accused's own lawyer, tend to be co-opted to become agent-mediators who help the accused redefine his situation and restructure his percep-tions concomitant with a plea of guilty. (1967: 19–20)

How does the system "help" defendants "redefine" their situation in a manner that induces a plea of guilty? The scenario begins with criminal statutes that prescribe lengthy terms of imprisonment for many felony crimes. Although these sentences are rarely imposed, they serve to generate a great deal of fear in a defendant. This fear is aided by police and prosecutors who engage in **overcharging**, vertical and horizontal. *Vertical overcharging* means charging a single offense at a higher level than the circum-stances in the case would appear to support, such as charging murder in a case where the evidence seems to indicate manslaughter, or charging as a felony the kind of case routinely disposed of as a misdemeanor. *Horizontal overcharging* means charging the arrestee with every conceivable crime even remotely related to his or her actions, even though the actual sentence will usually be limited to that available for the highest offense on which a conviction is obtained (see *joinder of offenses* in Chapter 8). Twenty-seven years later, David Lynch, who served as both a public defender and a prosecu-tor, supported Blumberg's assertions: "It has been my experience that judges, lawyers, and even police officers often love plea bargaining. They love it not because it pre-vents the breakdown of the criminal justice system but because it helps them avoid work and stress" (1994: 122).

What about Blumberg's charge that defense counsel is, in effect, a "double agent"? In his investigation of the charge, Rodney Uphoff (2002: 88) found that low-income defendants who do not qualify for a public defender or assigned counsel often cannot obtain adequate legal representation. They are advised by defense counsel that the meager retainer paid will only cover a negotiated plea. "The economic realities of the system, not the defense lawyer's lack of zeal, frequently pressure the defendant to accept a plea." He concludes that "unless we give defense lawyers the necessary resources and incentives to challenge the state, our adversarial system indeed will drift further toward the co-optive system Blumberg described" (2002: 98).

In order to better manipulate the client, Michael Cox points out, the defense counsel is assisted by the prosecutor:

> Prosecutors have great leverage; they draft the charges and generally make recommendations on sentencing. These prosecutorial prerogatives put the defendant at a disadvantage. A prosecutor may "overcharge," either horizontally (e.g., in a bad check case charge uttering, obtaining by false pretenses, and forgery, even though they may overlap and be multiplicious [excessive] for sentencing), or vertically (e.g., always charge homicides as first degree murder). Through overcharging, an accused is immediately put on the defensive. If the case is tried on the merits, a jury will often react by thinking (even if only subconsciously), "There are so many charges and they are so serious; the defendant must be guilty of something." The number of charges/specifications and the "degree" [e.g., robbery in the first degree or burglary in the second degree] are at the heart of plea negotiations. As an added incentive to deal, a prosecutor may threaten to recommend a high sentence if conviction is obtained after a trial on the merits. (1975: 34; bracketed material added)

Thus, at their first meeting the defense counsel informs the defendant that if convicted on the highest count or on all of the counts alleged by police, he or she will be ready for Social Security before being released from prison. The unsettling prospect of a lengthy prison term signals the beginning of a softening-up process. As a part of this, overcharging results in higher bail, which can cause the defendant to remain in jail while awaiting adjudication. Even when compared to prisons, most jails are unpleasant places, leaving defendants desperate to get out.

If the system is to function efficiently, the occasional recalcitrant defendant must be made to serve as an example for others who might be contemplating a jury trial. Thus, "after Ron Baker was arrested for robbery, prosecutors offered him probation in return for a guilty plea. The public defender assigned to handle his case urged him to accept the offer. But Baker, a deliveryman with no criminal convictions, pleaded innocent and asked for a chance to prove it in a jury trial. Eventually he was convicted, and the same judge who had earlier approved the probation offer sentenced Baker to six years in prison" (Tybor and Eissman 1985: 1). In another county, a defendant refused to be intimidated by the judge into accepting a plea bargain, and lost at trial. "He received a 30-year sentence, one so harsh (though perfectly legal) for the crimes committed that attorneys reacted with stunned disbelief about it. . . . That was the last time any defense attorney dared to have a trial before that judge for a long, long time" (Lynch 1994: 120). Timothy Sandefur (2006: 49) argues that "if defendants are so afraid

---

Plea Bargaining as Disaster

"Constitutional and doctrinal objections aside, plea bargaining seriously impairs the public interest in effective punishment of crime and in accurate separation of the guilty from the innocent" (Schulhofer 1992: 1979).

The Downside

"The public in general, and victims in particular, lose faith in a system where the primary goal is processing and the secondary goal is justice. The public doubts justice has been done when the sanction in a negotiated plea case does not match the actual behavior. Defendants and defense attorneys also consider bargaining for pleas to be dishonest, even when the bargain inures to their benefit. Defendants develop the cynical belief that they have received some undeserved favorable treatment because of a skillful defense lawyer or a sloppy or harried prosecutor. Defense attorneys in systems driven by bargains believe that they must convince most of their clients—even innocent defendants—to accept lesser punishments to avoid a substantial risk of much greater punishment" (Wright and Miller 2002: 33).

of trials that they regularly plead guilty to crimes they did not commit in order to avoid trial, then that is an indictment of the trial system, not plea bargaining."

In Tulsa, Oklahoma, the 38-year-old defendant declined a plea bargain for sentences totaling 10 years for marijuana possession. After a trial, he was convicted. Noting that the defendant had rejected a plea agreement that would have allowed a much lighter punishment, the judge imposed prison sentences totaling 93 years (Braun 1997).

The judicial attitude behind such treatment is summed up in the statement: "He takes some of my time; I take some of his" (Uhlman and Walker 1980). In many instances, however, mandatory sentencing—legislators "getting tough"—means a judge is without the discretion to mitigate overly harsh sentences. In Polk County, Florida, Orville Wollard said he fired his registered handgun into his living room wall to scare his daughter's boyfriend into leaving the house because of threats he made against the family. Wollard turned down a plea offer of five years probation. After being convicted at trial, the judge imposed the mandatory sentence for aggravated assault with a firearm—20 years (Oppel 2011).

If a defendant is able to secure private counsel, in addition to being concerned about the outcome of the case, he or she must be concerned about paying legal fees. As noted in Chapter 7, criminal attorneys depend on quantity rather than quality and demand "upfront money" because their clients are generally poor and unreliable. In most cases this will not be sufficient for the hours typically required for a jury trial. "Most attorneys who specialize in criminal cases depend on a high turnover of clients

Criminal (In)Justice

In 1990, after his first trial ended in a hung jury, the defendant, insisting that he was innocent, refused a plea bargain that would have resulted in a sentence of time already served—despite being tried for murder, he would have been a free man. He was retried, convicted, and sentenced to 20 years. After spending five years in prison, his conviction was overturned. The appellate court found that the only evidence against him was a witness whose testimony was permitted despite the fact that the prosecutor knew it was perjured. The defendant received compensation of $300,000 (Elliott and Weiser 2004).

The Innocent Pleading Guilty

- On September 22, 2011, Kenneth Kagonyera and Robert Wilcoxson were freed and found innocent of any involvement in the 2000 murder of Walter Bowman. The two men maintained their innocence throughout their incarceration, but had pled guilty to second-degree murder charges to avoid the death penalty or life in prison. In 2003, after the defendants had entered pleas, a federal inmate confessed to the homicide and named two accomplices. Tests on DNA from the crime scene generated a DNA profile, resulting in a match to one of the named accomplices, and excluded both Mr. Kagonyera and Mr. Wilcoxson.

- On December 16, 2010, John Watkins was released from custody after serving 7.5 years in prison for a sexual assault he did not commit. Mr. Watkins had accepted a plea offer of 14 years for sexual assault and a nonviolent felony to avoid a potential life in prison sentence. No semen or sperm was detected on the rape kit items and, thus, in 2003, no DNA testing was conducted on this evidence.

---

who can afford only modest fees. Without high volume and the investment of a modest amount of time in each case, many a private defense counsel would go broke" (Jacob and Eisenstein 1977: 26). Most work for a flat fee paid in advance. "Since court rules usually prohibit defense counsel from withdrawing once an appearance has been entered, a retained attorney is obliged to take her case to trial if settlement negotiations fail, and in that event, her additional services are rendered free of charge" (Schulhofer 1992: 1988). Under such circumstances, a private defense counsel is likely to recommend that the client plead guilty in exchange for leniency. For a defendant facing the prospect of a lengthy term of imprisonment, this may appear to be sound advice. Summarizing the purpose of these plea bargaining practices, Albert Alschuler states that "overcharging and subsequent charge reduction are often the components of an elaborate sham, staged for the benefit of defense attorneys. The process commonly has little or no effect on the defendant's sentence, and prosecutors may simply wish to give defense attorneys a 'selling point' in their efforts to induce defendants to plead guilty" (1968: 95).

In some states, insisting on a trial could mean a life sentence; hence, the attraction of the plea bargains. Avoid the trial altogether. Accept a lower sentence and live to walk the streets again. "Except that what gets lost in the shuffle is the case of the occasionally innocent defendant who takes the deal rather than face the prospect of what will happen if he loses at trial" (Ted Koppel, "Crime and Punishment: Let's Make a Deal," *ABC News Nightline*, May 12, 2000).

The Role of the Public Defender

The prosecutor can keep a private attorney hopping by objecting to continuances when the lawyer overbooks. Usually, if counsel requests a continuance, and the prosecutor does not object, it will be routinely granted. If the prosecutor objects, however, and the judge is also opposed, an attorney with several cases scheduled for the same day is in serious trouble. The prosecutor can make the defense attorney's life pleasant or miserable, "by agreeing to or opposing continuances; by opening or closing files for discovery; by waiving or insisting on technical requirements; by recommending or denigrating the attorney to prospective clients; by being generally agreeable or disagreeable" (Dershowitz 1983: 355).

Thus, defense attorneys are forced to abandon their adversarial stance in favor of accommodation. Alschuler states that the system of plea bargaining "leads even able, conscientious, and highly motivated attorneys to make decisions that are not really in their clients' interests" (1975: 1179). Defendants are finessed or coerced, sometimes both, into cooperating with a system that not only is seeking to inflict punishment on them but also lacks the resources to ensure that the innocent do not plead guilty. Prosecutors whose cases pass initial screening have no option other than to ignore claims of innocence: They have an incentive to avoid any reduction in the penalty for the possibly innocent that might lead to strategic behavior—"I'm innocent and deserve a break"—by guilty defendants (Scott and Stuntz 1992).

Whereas private defense counsel must depend on client fees, the public defender is a salaried employee who is paid regardless of how many cases he or she handles. Nevertheless, "public defender organizations charged with representing all indigent defendants prefer a quick disposition because their manpower barely suffices to handle their caseload" (Jacob and Eisenstein 1977: 26). A report for the City Bar Association revealed that indigent defendants in New York City were not being adequately represented; legal aid lawyers in the criminal division were seeking to process as many cases as possible instead of providing vigorous advocacy for clients. The report stated that "barely 5 percent of the cases handled by society attorneys resulted in a trial and more complex cases were referred to court-appointed counsel, many of whom were incompetent, if not senile" (Margolick 1985: E4).

Although the public defender is a salaried employee, he or she may experience pressure from trial judges concerned with disposing of as many cases as possible and as quickly as possible. Trial judges are under pressure from the chief administrative judge who is anxious to move cases so they do not exceed speedy trial requirements and thus require dismissal. In 1999, in Baltimore, for example, a judge dismissed first-degree murder charges against four men who had been awaiting trial for almost three years. The delay was a result of a massive backlog in the criminal courts because of aggressive policing designed to reduce the rate of homicides (Janofsky 1999).

Pressure from a trial judge may begin with a judge's suggestion that a certain plea agreement would be fair and if a defender accepts this suggestion, the matter is at an

---

Right to a Speedy Trial

The Sixth Amendment guarantees, "In all criminal prosecutions, the accused shall enjoy the right to a speedy and public trial, by an impartial jury." In 1972, the Supreme Court (*Barker v. Wingo*) ruled that determination of whether a particular defendant has been denied a **speedy trial** is to be made on a case-by-case basis, In response to *Barker*, states and the federal government enacted statutes specifying the amount of time allowed from arrest to trial. The failure to meet speedy trial requirements means the case must be dismissed, an action for which presiding judges have a strong aversion.

end. Defenders who resist judicial suggestions too often, however, are frequently forced to endure abusive remarks from the bench (Alschuler 1975: 1237):

> "You're a quasi-public agency. You should be interested in justice."
> "Haven't you got any client control?"
> "You spend too much time on hardened criminals."
> "No private attorney would take this case to trial."
> "You must be awfully eager for experience."
> "When will you guys bend to reality?"
> "You guys believe your clients too much."
> "You're acting like a private lawyer."

The counsel for the defense—whether private, public defender, or assigned—shares a great deal in common with prosecutors and judges: a similar educational, professional, and often political background. Defense attorneys are socialized into a closed system, and they learn that a price must be paid for failing to understand and abide by system norms. Milton Heumann describes how this socialization takes place: "In the process of handling their cases, new defense attorneys learn that the reality of the court differs from what they had expected; through rewards and sanctions, they are taught to proceed in a certain fashion" (1978: 57). In particular, he points out, they learn to avoid legal challenges that can gain the enmity of both prosecutors and judges and may be seen as frivolous. "The hostility of prosecutors and judges to these time-consuming motions is communicated to the new attorney. First, the prosecutor or judge may simply call the defense attorney into his office and explain that the motions are needless formalities. If this advice is insufficient to dissuade the newcomer, sanctions such as 'hassling' the attorney by dragging the case out over a long period of time, closing all files to the attorney, and even threatening to go to trial on the case, ensue" (1978: 62). Lynch states that many defense attorneys fear trials because they lack trial experience, and this fear "not only causes attorneys to talk clients into plea bargaining when their clients really want to go to trial but also can negatively affect their ability to negotiate, since they know in their hearts that they fear going to trial" (1994: 1270).

Conformity is rewarded; attorneys who cooperate, who do not raise time-consuming motions or engage in frivolous behavior, can expect to build "credit" that can be drawn on in time of need, as one public defender points out: "Everybody, by virtue of being a good guy, has so many chips a year that he can cash in. You go in to a judge and you say, 'Look, judge. I'm busting my buns every day in this dang court, and I need a break on this case.' It has nothing to do with justice, nothing to do with law. I need a break. Okay! You get so many chips a year that you can cash in" (quoted in Eisenstein, Flemming, and Nardulli 1999: 30).

The Benign or Positive View

When asked to explain the existence of plea bargaining, even informed observers point to the amount of cases that threaten to overwhelm the judicial system; they say, "Nobody likes plea bargaining, but it's the only way the system can survive." Candace McCoy argues that the "caseload pressure" explanation is a ploy by court workers to avoid blame for the perceived leniency of plea bargaining: "No court worker wants to be blamed for sentencing leniency, and the caseload hypothesis shifts the blame from criminal justice decision makers to their supposedly overloaded working conditions" (1993: 69). Malcolm Feeley (1997) refers to this as the "functional fallacy," and Milton Heumann (1978) points out that guilty pleas have been the outcome of most criminal cases for almost 100 years, even when courts were not overburdened with too many cases. Indeed, trials have not been the central means for resolving criminal or civil cases for more than a century. In New York, for example, in 1839, guilty pleas were 25 percent of convictions; by 1869, that figure had jumped to 70 percent, and they increased every year until leveling off to around 90 percent in the 1920s (Guidorizzi 1998). It was similar in New Haven, Connecticut, during roughly the same period (Feeley 1997).

Heumann states that defense and prosecution have a preference for guilty pleas because they "recognize the factual culpability of many defendants, and the fruitlessness, at least in terms of case outcome, of going to trial. From these perceptions flows the notion that if the obviously guilty defendant cops a plea, he will receive some reward. Whether the defendant believes this results from his show of contrition, or, more prosaically, from saving the state time and money," is irrelevant. "Similarly, prosecutors and judges do not believe that they accord this reward simply to 'move the business'" (1978: 156). By rewarding the defendant who pleads guilty, prosecutors believe they are furthering their own professional goals by sorting serious cases from nonserious ones and obtaining certain prison time in serious cases—it is not simply an expedient to dispose of onerously large caseloads.

William McDonald (1985) corroborates this view. His research indicates that, contrary to popular belief, prosecutors are not concerned with the question of case backlog or caseload when they evaluate what to do with specific cases. With respect to overcharging, he points out that it is considerably easier to drop or reduce charges than to add or increase them. Police are likely to charge up—bring the highest possible charges—not simply to provide room for bargaining, but because the amount of information available early in a case is often limited. (It should also be noted that the credit received by an officer who makes an arrest is dependent on the seriousness of the charges, another reason for charging up.) Kyle Graham (2013: 8) states, "Most prosecutors understand that it is unethical to bring charges on patently inadequate grounds." Thus, "overcharging" may be nothing more sinister than the prosecutor's inability to accurately gauge the strength of a case. Graham notes, however, that "high-profile cases invite overreaching by prosecutors. In these matters, a prosecutor may succumb to public clamor and charge a relatively serious offense, even upon only marginal proof" (2013: 10).

Lynch points out that in the suburban county in which he worked, the "evidence against most defendants was overwhelming, and many defendants, realizing this, probably would have pled guilty eventually without a bargain. To go to trial when the evidence is overwhelming would invite public humiliation." But more important, it would indicate an obvious lack of remorse to the judge, who presides not only at the trial but at the sentencing. "Defendants who had little hope of winning at trial generally recognized that trials were not in their best interests and correctly guessed that judges would usually reward a plea of guilty (even one entered without a bargain) with a greatly reduced sentence" (1994: 118). The obviously guilty who insist on a jury trial raise the ire of a judge: "Not only does the SOB fail to show contrition, but he is trying to escape without any penalty for his behavior."

Malcolm Feeley (1979) explains the prevalence of plea bargaining by noting that one of the norms of the legal profession is a preference for events that have a relatively high level of **predictability**. (This is not unique to lawyers; in most businesses, from grocery stores to auto manufacturers, uncertainty is problematic.) But the trial process lacks predictability; it requires professionals (prosecutor and defense counsel) to relinquish control over the outcome of a case to a jury, a panel of 12 persons (typically) without any legal training. Whether it is a civil or criminal matter, lawyers do not normally find this situation appealing. Research by Celesta Albonetti revealed that "prosecutorial screening following felony indictment is influenced by decision makers' attempts to avoid uncertainty" (1986: 640).[1]

The prosecutor has additional concerns. First, the longer a case takes, the greater the likelihood of an outcome in favor of the defendant. Witnesses may fail to appear, die, or forget important facts, and files are sometimes misplaced or lost. Gathering necessary elements for the trial, including the defendant and witnesses, all at the same time in the same courtroom, can be troublesome. In Los Angeles County, California, for example, the sheriff's office must move more than 1,000 defendants a day from their cells to various courthouses scattered throughout this very large county (Shuster 2001). Nancy Jacobs and Ellen Chayet found that in New York City "trouble in delivering an incarcerated defendant, while not a regular occurrence, consumes nearly two months, on average, when it is a factor. Witness production problems, for either the prosecution or defense, typically add an average of a month to case processing time" (1986: 15). And producing physical evidence is sometimes a problem. In Chicago, for example, the police department's Evidence and Recovered Property Section has a history of losing evidence, including millions of dollars in narcotics and thousands of dollars in jewelry (Ferkenhoff 2001; Hanna and Ferkenhoff 2001).

Research indicates that "in cases where the scientific evidence strongly associated the defendant with the crime, prosecutors were *less* inclined to offer a plea bargain" (Peterson et al. 2010: 16). But the mishandling of physical evidence at the crime scene and crime-lab shortcomings can impede the certainty of plea bargaining. In 1985, the state of Illinois ordered the shutdown of a laboratory that regularly botched tests involving drug and drunk-driving cases (Franklin 1985). A study by the Chicago Crime Commission in 1986 revealed that failure to complete tests on suspected contraband drugs substantially hampered prosecution of drug cases in that city (Tybor and Eissman 1986). A three-year study of 240 government-operated crime laboratories at the federal, state, county, and municipal levels revealed that 70 percent failed to perform even a simple blood test correctly (Grunson 1983). As if to underscore this problem, in 1994 authorities arrested a forensic chemist for falsifying evidence that led to the conviction of dozens of persons in several states, some of whom have already been freed from prison as a result of disclosures of impropriety (Associated Press 1994). In

---

[1] P. S. Atiyah and R. S. Summers state that "in England the gradual decline in the civil jury over the last fifty years is itself partly due to the fact that barristers actually prefer trial by judges to trial by jurors in civil cases. And this in turn is due to the fact that barristers prefer more rational, and less emotional, fact-finding procedures, and have greater confidence in the fact-finding ability of judges" (1987: 166).

2013, a state crime lab chemist in Massachusetts was sentenced to prison for tampering with evidence, forging signatures, perjury, and falsifying drug tests, an action that may have tainted more than 40,000 samples involving thousands of cases (Seelye and Bidgood 2013).

In 1997, the forensic laboratory of the FBI, long considered exemplary, was criticized by the Department of Justice inspector general for lax procedures in handling evidence (Johnston 1997; Navarro 1997). In recent years, shoddy crime lab procedures have been uncovered in Ohio, Texas, and Virginia (Blumenthal 2005), and New York's Nassau County, one of the wealthiest counties in the country, closed its crime lab in 2011 because of inaccurate measurements in drug cases; a national accreditation agency had twice placed the lab on probation for its shoddy work. In 2012, the Suffolk County (Boston) crime lab was closed after a chemist was arrested for misconduct that tainted hundreds of cases. The trial of a West Virginia state police lab serologist for falsifying test results in at least 134 cases ended with his death in 2002. His misconduct came under scrutiny as the result of a DNA exoneration of a rapist he had positively identified as the perpetrator.

Investigations of the medical examiner's offices in New York and Chicago revealed numerous errors in determining causes of death. And in some counties investigations into causes of death are conducted by elected, nonphysician coroners. As a result, an undetermined number of deaths are misdiagnosed, leading to acquittals for the guilty and convictions for the innocent (Baden and Hennessee 1989). In 1992, a Texas pathologist was convicted of faking autopsies—at least 20 death penalty convictions were obtained with the aid of his testimony (Giannelli 1994).

The norms of the legal profession require cordiality between adversaries. As in the case of professional boxers, attorneys are expected to (at least figuratively) shake hands before and after a bout, an act that does not reduce their efforts to emerge victorious. David Neubauer explains that "if defense and prosecution are on good terms, this does not mean the adversary process has broken down. It may be only a reflection of the normal rules of conduct expected of lawyers. The 'cooperation' of defense and prosecution is a product of such general expectations about how lawyers should conduct themselves" (1974: 78).

Although defense attorneys, private or public defenders, are typically on good terms with their counterparts in the prosecutor's office, each is a professional who is

Botched Evidence

A prosecutor in Arkansas who admitted the FBI tested the wrong strand of hair from the 1991 murder of a schoolgirl, said he would drop charges against the suspect. Prosecutors originally said DNA testing done on a hair tested by the FBI had linked the defendant to the victim. But they later determined that the tested hair had been taken from the girl during her autopsy, rather than from the defendant's car during the investigation. That left no physical evidence to link the defendant to the death of the nine-year-old (Associated Press 2000a).

An FBI audit revealed that the national DNA database contains dozens of profiles containing mistakes due to inaccurate handwriting or interpretation errors by lab technicians. Authorities in New York found similar errors in the state's DNA database (Goldstein 2014).

expected by the other, as well as by the rest of his or her legal peers, to behave in a professional manner. And the norms of professionalism require a lawyer to engage in vigorous advocacy; anything less can lead to a loss of respect that can devastate a legal career. And reputation among the principal players is an important dynamic in maintaining respect:

> Members of the criminal defense bar are in constant contact with local prosecutors. Reputations are valuable in markets characterized by repeat dealing. A good part of the practice of many defense lawyers, especially in the period before indictment, is supplying information to prosecutors. Prosecutors take seriously information coming from reputable counsel. Guilty defendants cannot copy the signal of innocence sent by careful, honest lawyers. . . . Lawyers with the best evidence of innocence secure the dismissal of charges (or attractive pleas) even though they do not succeed in "proving" innocence. (Easterbrook 1992: 1971–72)

In place of a trial as the epitome of the adversarial ideal, private plea negotiation has evolved, and as Suzann and Leonard Buckle (1977) argue, plea negotiation is adversarial. Thus, in place of two opposing attorneys meeting in a highly dramatic and time-consuming courtroom confrontation, they negotiate in private settings such as the judge's chambers. Each attorney reviews the case, pointing out the strengths of his or her position as opposed to the weaknesses of his or her opponent's position. The process continues until an agreement—a "deal"—can be struck; it is like a minitrial without the time-consuming formalities required in a courtroom.

During plea bargain conferences with prosecutors in a California municipal court, defense attorneys presented case narratives that highlighted salient characteristics that were advantageous to clients. In effect, they were rehearsing their likely courtroom presentations for the benefit of the prosecutor. Through this approach, attorneys attempted to gain the best possible outcome for clients by portraying their cases as strong relative to the evidence available to the state (Maynard 1988; Emmelman [1996] found a similar approach in the county she studied).

In Alameda County, California, Pamela Utz (1979) found that early discussion between defense and prosecution was encouraged by an informal discovery process during which both sides reviewed the case together before the preliminary hearing. It was understood that cases that were not prison material should not go to trial, while serious cases with good evidence were inappropriate for plea bargaining—nonnegotiable cases. The prosecutor met with the defense attorney as a collegial professional, rather than as an adversary, ready to share in reviewing and evaluating cases. "Using the facts of the case, including what is known about the offender, the two sides try to determine 'what really happened,' and what is an equitable disposition for the particular defendant." According to the unwritten policy that evolved,

> the parties must assess the evidence according to the norms of rational inquiry, and each side is there to hold the other accountable. Thus, negotiation continues to presume vigorous advocacy, although the assessment binds both sides who must refrain from threatening a trial. If, after settling the facts, the defendant is judged guilty, the seriousness of the offense is judged according to community interests and a penalty that is realistically related to seriousness and case worth is jointly decided on the basis of established norms. (Utz 1979: 112)

In the jurisdiction she studied, Debra Emmelman (1996) found that public defenders frequently used veiled or explicit threats of going to trial as part of their negotiating techniques.

Does the prevalence of plea bargaining indicate that the adversarial method has been abandoned in favor of expediency in the attempt to reduce uncertainty? Feeley states an emphatic no! "To infer the lack of an adversarial stance and the existence of bargained settlements—for the pure purpose of administrative convenience—from the absence of trials is to ignore altogether the importance of these other 'truthtesting' and highly combative processes. . . . [In other words] combativeness—short of trial—does in fact exist" (1979: 29).

Plea Bargaining: The Process

The accomplishment of a plea bargain depends on many factors, particularly the prosecutor's assessment of the case and agreement among judicial actors about the appropriate charges. When a prosecutor receives a case from the police, its strengths and weaknesses are evaluated. This is usually done by an assistant prosecutor assigned to an intake (screening) unit. A prosecutor's office frequently has to deal with dozens of state, county, and municipal police agencies (and even more in some metropolitan areas). As would be expected, some agencies perform better than others. Some police officers are well-trained and conscientious; some are poorly trained and lack motivation. The prosecutor receives cases from them all.

Rather than waste scarce resources prosecuting petty or weak cases, prosecutors employ a screening system that generally follows a scheme with four categories for rating cases, as shown in Figure 9.1.

Figure 9.1   Variables Influencing a Prosecutor's Charging Decision

- *Category I.* A case in which the charges are not serious and the evidence is weak will usually not be prosecuted.

- *Category II.* A case in which the charges are not serious but the evidence is strong is a good candidate for plea bargaining.

- *Category III.* A case in which the charges are serious but the evidence is weak is a good candidate for rejection, dismissal, or plea bargaining.[2]

- *Category IV.* A case in which the charges are very serious and the evidence is strong is a candidate for vigorous prosecution.

One research effort found that in cases in which the prosecutor believes the defendant to be guilty but the legally admissible evidence does not support successful prosecution, "using the threat of a prison or jail sentence as a lever, the prosecutor may bargain with defense counsel and defendant for a reduced charge or a suspended sentence in return for a plea of guilty" (Winfree and Kielich 1979: 176). Another researcher found "an overwhelming propensity to moderate the harshness of plea bargain terms to defendants if the government had a weak case against them" (Champion 1989: 257).

In addition to legal factors that influence a prosecutor's charging decision, there are extralegal factors such as the defendant's prior criminal record, age, health, marital status, and work history; publicity about the case; and the background and status of the victim. Donald Black refers to the social structure of a case: Are the differences in *social status* between perpetrator and victim upward or downward? Is there a low-status defendant and high-status victim (more favorable to the prosecutor), or vice versa? What is the relationship, if any, between victim and perpetrator? And what about the probable judge and jury? In one study, for example, white judges were found

> more likely than black judges to convict defendants of serious crimes (felonies). White judges handling black defendants have the highest conviction rate, and black judges handling white defendants have the lowest conviction rate. A comparison of sentencing in two cities indicates that judges of northern European ancestry and those from a middle-class background are more legalistic and severe than ethnic judges (such as Jews and Italian-Americans) and those from a low-income background. (Black 1989: 16)

An experimental study revealed that white jurors are more likely than black jurors to find a criminal defendant guilty, and even more likely to do so when the defendant is black (Black 1989). Another study found that "a defendant's socioeconomic condition influences his/her chances regarding plea bargain agreements," and that "prosecutors appear to be most sensitive about who represents an alleged offender" (Champion 1989: 262). In some cases the defendant will assist police or the prosecutor, such as by providing information about other criminals. These factors combine with evidentiary aspects of a case to determine the charging decision.

The degree of case screening accomplished by a prosecutor's office differs from jurisdiction to jurisdiction. A jurisdiction that subjects cases to an early and vigorous

---

[2] According to the Bureau of Justice Statistics, "evidence-related deficiencies and witness problems account for more than half the rejections by prosecutors at screening. In most jurisdictions, evidence and witness problems are also the most common reasons for dismissals in court" (1986: 14).

review "increases the degree of confidence we can have that the guilty plea process is convicting probably guilty defendants" (McDonald 1985: 46). Where such screening is not used, guilty pleas may be made without those "values associated with ideas about legality and the requirement of proof beyond a reasonable doubt." On the other hand, vigorous screening programs "reject cases that could have been convicted through plea bargaining. For those who believe that a little bit of punishment for a lot of offenders, regardless of the seriousness of their crimes or their prior records, deters more crime than the selective prosecution of a smaller number of serious offenders, rigorous screening is not regarded as positive reform" (McDonald 1985: 46–47). There exist many difficulties when evaluating prosecutorial performance on the basis of a conviction rate since "it may be a sign of excellent prosecutorial performance or a sign of overly conservative charging policies" (Feeney, Dill, and Weir 1983: 243).

Strong cases are built on quality investigations—all the available evidence has been gathered and all the witnesses have been found and interviewed. Cases brought in by police may fail to meet the evidentiary standard necessary to justify prosecution and are rejected at screening. A high rejection rate "may be a sign of lax performance by either the police or the prosecutor, illegal or highly aggressive police work" (Feeney, Dill, and Weir 1983: 243). Research indicates that only a small fraction of police officers (8 to 19 percent) account for about half of the arrests that end in convictions. These officers are apparently more adept at gathering evidence than their peers (Boland et al. 1983).

Serious cases that appear strong at intake can begin to weaken as time passes. They are either dropped after charges have been filed or negotiated down to secure a guilty plea. The Vera Institute of Justice found the main reason that many of the cases that begin as felonies are not prosecuted as felonies is because "a high percentage of them, in every crime category from murder[3] to burglary, involve victims with whom the suspect has had prior, often close relations. Logically, suspects who are known to their victims are more likely to be caught than strangers because they can be identified more easily by the complainants. And this very fact of a previous personal relation-

Two Questions Guiding Discretion

Researchers studying prosecutorial discretion in two counties found that decisions were guided by two basic questions: "'Can I prove the case?' and 'Should I prove the case?' The relative influence of these questions was found to shift over the course of the case. The first question was most influential at the outset of a case, where the objective strength of evidence was the determining factor in most screening decisions. Later, factors such as the seriousness of the offense, the defendant's criminal history, characteristics of the defendant and victim, and contextual factors became increasingly influential, as prosecutors evaluated whether a case should go forward" (Frederick and Stemen 2012: iii).

---

[3] "From 1993 to 2008, among homicides reported to the FBI for which the victim-offender relationship was known, between 21% and 27% of homicides were committed by strangers and between 73% and 79% were committed by offenders known to the victims" (Harrell 2012: 1)

ship often leads a complainant to be reluctant to pursue prosecution through adjudication" (1977: 134). This reluctance can be the result of tempers that cool with the passage of time; or informal mediation, conciliation and/or restitution may have been effective; or the complainant may have been intimidated.

Because criminal conduct is often the explosive spillover from ruptured personal relations among neighbors, friends, lovers, and spouses, prosecutors are sometimes reluctant to prosecute as full-scale felonies cases that erupted from quarrels between persons with close prior relationships. Often the primary purpose of an arrest in such situations is to defuse a potentially violent situation, and these cases are frequently candidates for rejection at screening or subsequent dismissal in court (Vera Institute 1977).

Prosecutors who utilize a more intensive case-screening policy drop fewer charges after filing:

> One effect of a rigorous screening policy is that crimes that are in essence private disputes are prevented from taking up costly court time and resources. Studies have shown that many crimes against persons involve individuals who had some kind of prior relationship. At the time of the incident, police intervention may be necessary to quell a potentially explosive situation. But by the time the case is brought to court, the victim often no longer wants to prosecute. With experience, prosecutors learn to identify such cases and can prevent them from getting into the court system only to be dropped later in the proceedings. (Boland et al. 1983: 6)

An overwhelming majority of assault cases investigated in New York City "were alleged to have occurred between friends and relatives." These cases were usually treated quite leniently (Bernstein et al. 1977: 374).

Many states have statutes that provide victim input into the plea bargaining process. This may take the form of an impact statement, which is sometimes prepared by a **probation officer**, and/or the prosecutor may be required to consult with the victim, and/or the victim may be given an opportunity to address the court before any plea agreement is accepted by the judge. "Because most states provide no consequences for non-compliance with such laws, however, crime victims are still frequently left out of the plea agreement process" (*Victim Input Into Plea Agreements* 2002: 2).

Plea bargaining may result from a prosecutor's perception that the case is unlikely to be won at trial because of the failure of a complainant to cooperate because of intimidation, or

> because the burden of further cooperation exceeds his ebbing anger, or his sense of civic duty, or his tolerance of the treatment he received in court. He . . . may live far from the courthouse, and his presence is required on a great many occasions along the enforcement route—when he files the complaint, at the preliminary hearing, before the grand jury, and finally at trial. While not all cases travel the whole route, some of these occasions require repeated appearances because of unforeseen adjournments and other managerial obstacles. (Zeisel 1982: 27)

These adjournments may be the result of a paucity of attorneys to represent indigent defendants. As noted in Chapter 7, some jurisdictions have a difficult time finding attorneys who will accept assignments to represent indigent defendants because of the low compensation. As a result, cases are repeatedly delayed because assigned counsel are overloaded with cases that are scheduled for trial.

Reduced charges, however, often are "not the result of negotiations between prosecutor and defense counsel but, rather, reflect the unilateral decision on the part of the prosecutor that the appropriate conviction charge should be a less serious crime than the initial arrest or court charges" (Boland and Brady 1985: 18; also Winfree and Kielich 1979). Such decisions are normally made early in case processing.

Normal Crimes

The outcome of cases not screened out at intake or dropped after charges have been filed is usually a guilty plea, the result of some form of negotiation, implicit or explicit, based on one of two models (Eisenstein et al. 1999: 243):

1. *Concessions model* "emphasizes explicit bargaining over the terms of the agreement, haggling in the style of a middle-eastern bazaar."

2. *Consensus model* "likens agreement to a shopper's acceptance of a supermarket's posted prices. Once the nature of the item is known, the posted price, the 'going rate,' prevails."

Although the guilty plea is most often a result of some form of exchange, the actual process may be so simple that it cannot be accurately described as "negotiation." David Sudnow (1965) explains such transactions by introducing the concept of **normal crimes**: those that have common features (the ways they usually occur, the characteristics of persons who commit them, as well as the typical victims) and can be classified as "normal." For example, a "normal burglary" involves a nonprofessional violator who is black or Latino, no weapons, low-priced items, little property damage, and a lower-class victim. However, possession of firearms, harm to the occupants, victims who are not lower class, indications of professional criminality (see Abadinsky 1983), or organized crime (see Abadinsky 2013), for example, would remove the incident from the category of "normal burglary." If the defense attorney and prosecutor agree that a burglary is a normal one, custom and precedent provide for a settlement without the need for negotiation. Although the statutes provide a penalty for each crime, judicial actors have established their own unwritten penalties for each "normal crime," which, because they mitigate statutory penalties, serve to encourage pleas of guilty and thus ensure a penalty for the perpetrator at a minimum expenditure of scarce legal resources.

This procedure is made possible by the reality that "core members of the [court] community usually develop a common understanding of what penalties ought to be attached to which crimes and defendants" (Eisenstein et al. 1988: 203). "Through daily wrangling, court workers generally agree on a baseline, expected sentence for each category of crime" (McCoy 1993: 55). During his research, Dean Champion found "considerable agreement among prosecutors concerning the going rate for various offenses" that facilitated plea bargain agreements (1989: 256–57). Serious crimes, however, especially those likely to be tracked by the news media, are less likely to fall into a "going rate" category—cases that Sudnow might view as not "normal." Most defense attorneys will candidly admit that virtually all of their felony clients are undoubtedly guilty, and the cases against them are usually conclusive. Under such conditions, forcing a trial makes little sense. As one Cook County assistant public defender comments:

"You get a guy who was caught red-handed with the proceeds, with the stuff, and he's already confessed. . . . The state's attorney offers a good deal, and my guy's happy with it. As long as my client is happy with it, and especially as long as I can't see how by pushing it we could do better, then I tell him go ahead and cop, and take the plea. So, essentially the case is over. It maybe only took a half hour; hell, it maybe only took five minutes. But why should I spend any more of my time on it? Sometimes I pick up maybe fifteen cases like that in one morning. Sometimes more." (quoted in McIntyre 1987: 64)

I recall, while working for the county sheriff, a plea bargain "negotiated" in a courthouse men's room where an assistant prosecutor asked a private defense attorney: "What are you planning to do with the Benny Smith case?" The attorney's reply completed the "negotiations": "We'll take the usual."

Emmelman (1996) found that cases are often not immediately subjected to plea bargaining, and some involve multiple episodes of plea bargaining in which the negotiations entail a wide array of formal litigation proceedings. The public defenders "generally believe that unless an initial offer is better than average, offers for guilty pleas will not get any worse and could become more favorable to the defendant further along in the adjudication process. They explain that this occurs because either the prosecutor loses witnesses or better evidence eventually turns up on behalf of the defense" (1996: 342–43). Sometimes they miscalculate: the prosecution's case gets stronger "and the prosecutor will offer a defendant less incentive to plead guilty than previously" (1996: 343). Defense counsel, of course, is gambling with the defendant's prison time.

A study of the Los Angeles Superior Court found that public defenders (PDs) determined which cases to settle without a trial based on predictions of case outcome:

In making these predictions, PDs investigated their client's version of what happened, the arrest report made by police, the transcript of the preliminary hearing, testimony of possible witnesses, any physical evidence, and other pertinent information. There was a staff of investigators for attorneys in the public defender's office to help check out evidence and interview witnesses, and the PDs themselves had one day a week with no cases assigned to allow them time for investigations in the field. The PDs then evaluated all of the strengths and weaknesses in each case against perceived judge and jury behavior on the issue of reasonable doubt. (Mather 1988: 256)

The majority of felony cases, however, were "dead bang" with little chance of an acquittal. Cases won at trial were usually the result of sloppy prosecution.

When presented with the same hypothetical cases, "prosecutors and defense counsel were in remarkable agreement in their estimates of the probability of conviction in those versions of the cases where the evidentiary strength of the case was strong" (McDonald 1985: v). In weaker cases, however, there were significant differences between them.

In order to facilitate plea bargaining, judges, prosecutors, and defense attorneys must constitute a *workgroup* (Jacob and Eisenstein 1977) in which people work together and cooperate in a cordial fashion. Cooperation requires regular players who interact frequently and share the common goal of disposing of cases with a minimum of resource expenditure and uncertainty. Only a stable workgroup can develop the patterns necessary to make behavior predictable. Judicial systems in which personnel

> ## The Courtroom Workgroup, Essex County, New Jersey
>
> "Public defenders and prosecutors are assigned to a particular judge and his or her court-room for approximately a year. Prosecutors and public defenders combined with judges, clerks, case managers, stenographers, and bailiffs form the courtroom workgroup. This mod-est-sized group develops a unique behavior pattern that can directly affect criminal case dispositions. The speed with which decisions are made as well as the specific case outcomes reached either through pleas bargaining or trial are all influenced by the interaction of this collection of courtroom officials" (Wice 2005: 124).

(judges, assistant prosecutors, defense attorneys) are frequently shifted lack the stability necessary for the formation of workgroups, and plea bargaining will be more difficult to accomplish. In a Cook County (Chicago) courtroom, I once observed both prosecutor and public defender deliberately put off cases through postponements and other devices. The courtroom deputy sheriff explained to me this seemingly puzzling behavior: "Regular judge is out today and the guys don't know his replacement very well. They'll hold off cases until he returns tomorrow." In the North Carolina county where I taught criminal justice, judges were rotated, presiding over criminal cases in different courts from month to month. This weakened the **courtroom workgroup** and affected plea bargaining, the reason for the practice.

The Role of the Judge

The role of the judge in plea bargaining differs from jurisdiction to jurisdiction and may depend on the type of sentencing scheme used (discussed in Chapter 8) and rules governing their behavior. Federal district court judges are prohibited by the *Federal Rules of Criminal Procedure* from participating in plea negotiations. In Mississippi, while "the prosecuting attorney is encouraged to discuss and agree on pleas which may be entered by the defendant," the rules of procedure add that "the trial judge shall not participate in any plea discussion." In Illinois, however, circuit court judges are routinely involved in plea negotiations. In states where judges exercise a great deal of discretion in the sentencing process, they tend to be more involved in plea negotiations. Where judges have only limited options, their role is far less important. For example, Illinois utilizes a determinate sentencing system in which the judge has wide discretion. The charging decision, which is controlled by the prosecutor, does not carry with it a specific sentence. Therefore, before a prosecutor can offer a sentence to the defendant in return for a plea of guilty, the judge must be in agreement. A pre-plea conference must be requested by defense counsel. When agreement is reached, a sentence is conveyed to the defendant by his or her counsel. If the defendant accepts, the principals return to the courtroom and formalize the agreement on the record. In many cases the judge will request from the probation department a **pre-plea report**, which provides background information—social, psychological, and criminal—on the defendant, before agreeing to a particular sentence.

A Minneapolis study found plea negotiations did not involve the prosecutor, who is present but merely as a "third party" witness. Instead, the judge led discussions centering on the sentence, not the charges. The same situation obtained in Pittsburgh, where negotiations centered on the sentence, instead of the charges, and typically involved the judge and defense counsel (Levin 1977). In the county she studied, Emmelman (1996: 338) found that judges encourage case settlements, so when both sides agree on the terms of plea bargains, judges generally accept those terms. "When the attorneys encounter problems in reaching agreements, however, the judges act as arbiters. In this arbitration, the judge typically exerts pressure on, or makes promises regarding sentencing to, either attorney in order to reach a settlement."

In 1984, when federal legislation established a guideline system that significantly reduced the sentencing discretion of judges, the prosecutor gained de facto sentencing power by determining the charges linked to specific sentences. Plea bargaining shifted accordingly, from *sentence bargaining* to *charge bargaining* (Nasheri 1998): "By assigning a narrow range of sentencing options to virtually every criminal violation and by giving judges only limited power to impose a sentence below that range, guideline systems have invested prosecutors with the power to dictate almost every sentence by choosing one set of charges over another" (Fisher 2000: 1072).

In some jurisdictions, there is a "plea court," an arrangement whereby one or more judges who specialize in "moving cases" preside at calendar hearings; their purpose is to dispose of as many cases as possible by pleas of guilty. In New York City, Judge Harold J. Rothwax of the supreme court (a trial court) developed a reputation for moving cases, usually one every two to 10 minutes. As each case is called, an assistant district attorney hands the judge a sheet indicating the details of the crime, the recommended bail, and the plea offer. As an example of how the judge expedited the cases before him, reporter Sam Roberts provides this vignette:

> Two repeat felons appear before Judge Rothwax, one without counsel. Instead of adjourning the case he assigns a lawyer sitting in the front row reserved for attorneys. The district attorney's offer was a sentence with a minimum of two years and a maximum of four years. "After today," the judge states, "it's three to six; after that it's four to eight." To the lawyer he states: "If they're ever going to plead, today is the time to do it." (1985: 13)

The wide discretion over sentencing enjoyed by judges in New York obviously facilitates plea bargaining. And without plea bargaining New York's system would quickly come to a halt: "The strain on New York City's system could be seen one morning in December [1998] in the Jury 7 courtroom of the sprawling Manhattan Criminal Courts building. At 9:30, Judge Robert A. Sackett tried to urge dozens of defendants and prosecutors into beginning trials or agreeing to plea bargains that would resolve the 64 cases on the docket that day. Five cases dated to 1996. Twelve dated to 1997" (Rohde 1999: 19).

The number of cases disposed of by a judge is one important indicator of productiveness. In Cook County, Illinois, judges are under scrutiny by the chief judge with respect to how many cases they dispose of every year; a "scorecard" is kept and judges strive to avoid coming in at the close of the year with a "low score." This typically results in a scramble to dispose of large numbers of cases in December, with judges pressuring prosecutors to speed up the plea bargaining process in order to clear their dockets before the new year begins. Prosecutors, fearful of jurors experiencing "holiday time mercy," also wish to avoid jury trials during the Christmas season. The need for judges to dispose of large numbers of cases was evidenced in Kings County (Brooklyn), New York, where in the first 11 months of 1989, judges assigned to the supreme court received 13,460 felony cases. A little more than 6 percent ended in a trial (Glaberson 1990).

Federal appellate judge Frank Easterbrook (1992: 1976) states, "Critics of plea bargaining commit the Nirvana Fallacy, comparing an imperfect reality to a perfection achievable only in imaginary systems." H. Richard Uviller (1996: 198) concludes that the "prevailing system of plea bargaining seems both better and worse than its popular image." He argues "It is better because by and large it neither cheapens crime by overgenerous allowances nor discriminates against the poor and friendless defendant." It is difficult to determine if it induces guilty pleas from the innocent, "but it is probably true that most of those who plead guilty would be convicted on trial. At the same time, the system is worse than its image because it unavoidably levies a tax on those who elect to exercise their constitutional right to trial by jury" (Uviller 1996: 198). But there is no reason to believe that, absent plea bargaining, innocent defendants would be any better off (Scott and Stuntz 1992).

Legal Issues

In general, plea bargaining has been supported by legal decisions basing their logic on contract law (Easterbrook 1992). Just as two parties are entitled to enter into a contractual relationship in a noncriminal matter, so too is plea bargaining supported as simply the criminal justice system's extension of this law of contract. "Just as there is no inherent conflict between a tort plaintiff's right to a day in court and his ability to trade that right in settlement negotiations, there is no inherent conflict between the right to a criminal trial and the ability to sell that right for sentencing concessions" (Scott and Stuntz 1992: 1916). Of course, contracts are invalid if they are the result of *duress*. Although improper coercive behavior invalidates a contract, the mere fact that a person enters into a contract as a result of pressure or undesirable circumstances is not sufficient: People in financial distress may sell their homes or cars or settle a tort for less than the "fair value."

In order for a plea bargain agreement to be legally binding on a defendant, the trial judge is required to determine if the defendant understands the ramifications of a plea of guilty. The plea must be "informed" since information deficits can invalidate a contract (Scott and Stuntz 1992). The *Federal Rules of Criminal Procedure* require that a judge determine the defendant understands:

- The nature of the charge to which the plea is offered, the mandatory minimum penalty provided by law, if any, and the maximum possible penalty provided by law including the effect of any special parole terms
- If the defendant is not represented by an attorney, that he or she has the right to be represented by an attorney at every stage of the proceeding against him or her and, if necessary, one will be appointed
- That he or she has the right to plead not guilty or to persist in that plea if it has already been made, and that defendant has the right to be tried by a jury and at

that trial has the right to the assistance of counsel, the right to confront and cross-examine adverse witnesses and the right not to be compelled to incriminate him- or herself

- That if he or she pleads guilty or *nolo contendere* (no contest) there will not be a further trial of any kind, so that by pleading guilty or *nolo contendere* the defendant waives the right to a jury trial
- That if the defendant pleads guilty or *nolo contendere*, the court may ask questions about the offense to which he or she has pleaded, and if defendant answers these questions under oath, on the record, and in the presence of counsel, the answers may later be used against him or her in a prosecution for perjury or false statement

In 1970, the Supreme Court ruled (*Brady v. United States* and *North Carolina v. Alford*) that a determination must be made as to the voluntary nature of a plea of guilty and, furthermore, the plea must be made knowingly and intelligently (*Boykin v. Alabama* [1969]). Accordingly, Federal Rule 11(d) provides that "the court shall not accept a plea of guilty or *nolo contendere* without first, by addressing the defendant personally in open court, determining that the plea is voluntary and not the result of force or threats or of promises apart from a plea agreement. The court shall also inquire as to whether the defendant's willingness to plead guilty or *nolo contendere* results from prior discussions between the attorney for the government and the defendant or his attorney." Figure 9.2 (on the following page) is an example of the document used by the judge to prove that a guilty plea is voluntary and intelligent.

When a plea agreement is reached, there is a **stipulation** of the factual underpinning for the guilty plea—the defendant generally must state the details of his or her culpability in court for the record (Palermo et al. 1998). However, the court can permit an *Alford* **plea** allowing a defendant to plead guilty while asserting innocence as long as the plea is a voluntary and intelligent choice (*North Carolina v. Alford* [1970]).

If a defendant refuses a prosecutor's offer of leniency in return for a plea of guilty, can the prosecutor reindict the defendant on more serious charges? In 1978, the Supreme Court (*Bordenkircher v. Hayes*) said *yes*. In this case, Paul Hayes declined to plead guilty to a lesser charge in return for a sentence of five years. He was subsequently convicted of forgery and sentenced under Kentucky's "habitual offender" statute to a term of life imprisonment. The Court reasoned that since plea bargaining had been ruled constitutional in prior decisions, the Court must also accept the "simple reality that the prosecutor's interest at the bargaining table is to persuade the defendant to forego his right to plead not guilty." As long as procedural safeguards have been adhered to, charging the defendant with a more serious crime when he or she declines to plead guilty does not violate the Due Process Clause of the Fourteenth Amendment.

In 1989, in an 8–1 decision, the Court ruled that when a defendant withdraws an initial plea of guilty and is convicted after a trial, the judge may impose a longer sentence than the earlier plea agreement had called for. In *Alabama v. Smith*, a plea agreement called for a sentence of no more than 30 years; after withdrawing his plea and being convicted for burglary, sodomy, and rape, the defendant was sentenced to 150 years.

Can a defendant contest a plea agreement on the grounds that his or her lawyer was ineffective? In order to do so, the Supreme Court has ruled (*Hill v. Lockhart* [1985])

GUILTY PLEA PROCEEDING

The defendant personally appearing before me, I have ascertained the following facts, noting each by initializing it.

Judge's
Initials

_____ 1. That the defendant understands the nature of the charges against him.

_____ 2. That the defendant understands the range of possible sentence for the offenses charged, from a suspended sentence to a maximum of _____ and that the mandatory minimum (if any) is _____.

_____ 3. That the defendant understands the following constitutional rights which he gives up by pleading guilty:
  (a) His right to trial by jury, if any.
  (b) His right to the assistance of an attorney at all stages of the proceeding, and to an appointed attorney, to be furnished free of charge, if he cannot afford one.
  (c) His right to confront the witnesses against him and to cross-examine them as to the truthfulness of their testimony.
  (d) His right to present evidence on his own behalf, and to have the state compel witnesses of his choosing to appear and testify.
  (e) His right to remain silent and to be presumed innocent until proven guilty beyond a reasonable doubt.

_____ 4. That the defendant wishes to give up the constitutional rights of which he has been advised.

_____ 5. That there exists a basis in fact for believing the defendant guilty of the offenses charged.

_____ 6. That the defendant and the prosecutor have entered into a plea agreement and that the defendant understands and consents to the terms.

_____ 7. That the plea is voluntary and not the result of force, threats or promises other than a plea agreement.

On the basis of these findings, I conclude that the defendant knowingly, voluntarily, and intelligently pleads guilty to the above charges, and accept his plea.

_____   _____

Date   Judge

Certification of Defendant

I certify that the judge personally advised me of the matters noted above, that I understand the constitutional rights that I am giving up by pleading guilty, and that I desire to plead guilty to the charges stated.

_____   _____

Defense Counsel, if any   Defendant

Figure 9.2   An Example of a Document Used to Prove That a Judge Has Ascertained That a Defendant Understands the Ramifications of a Guilty Plea

there must be a reasonable probability that, but for counsel's errors, the defendant would not have pled guilty and would have insisted on going to trial—that he or she would have gotten a better deal is not sufficient. In 2012, the Court ruled (*Missouri v. Frye* and *Lafler v. Cooper*) that defendants have a constitutional right to be represented by *effective* counsel during plea negotiations.

In *Frye*, a defense attorney failed to convey prosecution's offer to reduce a driving-with-a-revoked-license for the third time to a misdemeanor with a 90-day sentence. The offer subsequently expired and the defendant pled guilty to a felony for which he received a sentence of three years. In *Frye*, the Court (5–4) noted, "97 percent of federal convictions and 94 percent of state convictions are the result of guilty pleas. Plea bargains have become so central to today's criminal justice system that defense counsel must meet responsibilities in the plea bargain process to render the adequate assistance of counsel that the Sixth Amendment requires at critical stages of the criminal process."

In fact, it may be impossible to distinguish between good and bad bargaining: "A two-minute conversation with the prosecutor in the hallway with only slight advance preparation may represent evidence of sloppiness and sloth. Or it may be that defense counsel, who has a great deal of experience in dealing with similar cases, knows the market price, realizes that investigation is extremely unlikely to lead anywhere, and understands how to get the best offer expeditiously" (Scott and Stuntz 1992: 1959). Presumably, the judge knows the "market price" and has discretion to revise the agreed-on sentence accordingly.

Does a prosecutor have to live up to the terms of a plea bargain? In 1971, the Supreme Court (*Santobello v. New York*) said *yes*. In this case, the assistant district attorney agreed to permit the defendant to plead guilty to a gambling misdemeanor charge that would carry a maximum prison sentence of one year. The prosecutor agreed to make no recommendation as to the sentence. After the plea of guilty was entered, a sentencing hearing was scheduled at which a different assistant district attorney appeared. In violation of the agreement, this district attorney recommended the maximum sentence. The Court ruled that "when a plea [of guilty] rests in any significant degree on a promise or agreement of the prosecutor, so that it can be said to be part of the inducement or consideration [to plead guilty], such promise must be fulfilled." State appellate courts have ruled that prosecutors violate plea agreements when they convey an impression that the sentence should be more severe than that called for in the plea agreement or indicate reservations about the plea agreement sentence recommendation (Palermo et al. 1998). In 1984, however, the Supreme Court (*Mabry v. Johnson*) ruled unanimously that a defendant has no constitutional right to enforcement of a proposed plea bargain that a prosecutor withdraws before it becomes official.

During the discovery phase of a criminal trial, the prosecution is obligated to reveal any information that may be exculpatory (*Brady v. Maryland* [1963]). Does the government have a corresponding obligation with respect to plea bargaining? The Supreme Court, in a unanimous decision (*United States v. Ruiz* [2002]) said *no*: The Constitution does not require the government to disclose impeachment evidence prior to entering a plea agreement with a defendant.

Limiting or Abolishing Plea Bargaining

Attempts to limit or exclude plea bargaining from criminal justice have had mixed results. In New York, for example, laws passed at the behest of Governor Nelson Rockefeller, known locally as the "Rockefeller Laws," severely limited the ability of prosecutors to plea-bargain. According to the legislation, once charges were filed, the prosecutor was quite limited in lowering them. The result was a substantial increase in the number of defendants demanding jury trials, and prosecutors and judges soon found ways to circumvent the law. They initiated *front-loading*—plea bargaining at an early stage of the criminal justice process, prior to the filing of formal charges (Joint Committee on New York Drug Law Evaluation 1977; Aaronson et al. 1977). This tactic brings with it all of the dangers of "justice" done in haste. In Alaska, on the other hand, when the attorney general (that state's chief prosecutor) issued an order prohibiting the state's district attorneys from engaging in plea bargaining, the number of defendants pleading guilty remained about the same. Prosecutors did not have to waste time on negotiations, and the system became more efficient. There were, however, unanticipated results of the policy (Rubinstein, Clarke, and White 1980):

- There was absolutely no change in sentences for cases involving violent crimes such as rape, robbery, and felonious assault.

- There was very little change in sentences for most serious property offenders, particularly those with prior felony convictions.

- The major change was longer sentences for less serious property offenders.

In 1993, the attorney general removed the ban on plea bargaining (Guidorizzi 1998), and plea bargaining has returned to most areas of Alaska. Nevertheless, because of statutory changes—the state now uses determinate-presumptive sentencing (discussed in Chapter 8)—instead of bargaining over the sentence, plea bargaining is likely to focus on the charges (Carns 1992; Carns and Kruse 1991).

Belinda McCarthy and Charles Lindquist (1985) found that robbery defendants in Jefferson County (Birmingham), Alabama, frequently pled guilty even in the absence of significant benefits. Martin Levin (1977) found that in Minneapolis judges discouraged plea bargaining, but defendants pled guilty at a very high rate nevertheless. A study in Cook County (Chicago) revealed no significant difference between the penalties given to violent offenders who entered pleas of guilty and those convicted by judges at **bench trials** (Eissman and Tybor 1985). However, bench trials may actually be the result of the "slow plea." The defendant waives the right to a jury trial in exchange for an expected leniency and the case is recorded as a trial, providing considerable cover for prosecutors and judges (Guidorizzi 1998).

In California, voters in 1982 approved the "Victims Bill of Rights" to, among other things, curtail plea bargaining in cases of serious crimes. A study by Candace McCoy and Robert Tillman (1986) revealed, however, that this did not happen. Pursuant to a plea agreement, in felony cases defendants pled guilty in lower (municipal) court, and the case was then "certified" to superior court for review and sentencing. In practice, the superior court rarely overturned a certified (plea bargain) case. The 1982 proposition increased front-loading through the use of plea certification: "Court professionals learned to accept disposition of serious felony cases through guilty pleas to 'normal'

Mississippi Code: Plea Bargaining Prohibited

"Under no circumstances shall the party or the prosecutor engage in discussion for the purpose of agreeing to exchange concessions by the prosecutor for the party's admission to the petition."

---

sentences at much earlier stages of prosecution than had been usual before Proposition 8" (McCoy 1993: 131). As in the New York situation, however, front-loading had some distinct disadvantages: "Neither defense counsel nor prosecutors can fully examine the strengths of the case. Similarly, lower court judges have little information on legal points or on the defendant's background so as to inform the sentencing decision—and a sentencing decision it is, even though superior court later reviews it very quickly" (McCoy and Tillman 1986: 6).

Now that we have completed our examination of criminal justice, in the next chapter we will turn to the civil side of justice.

SUMMARY

- Plea bargaining has been criticized for providing criminals with excessive leniency and coercing defendants to waive their constitutional rights to a trial.
- An "open plea" involves defendants pleading guilty without negotiating with the prosecutor because they can reasonably expect a particular sentence.
- Critics of plea bargaining argue that it is a symptom of a system operated to further the needs of principal actors rather than the needs or interests of justice or the public.
- Critics argue defense attorneys are forced to abandon their adversarial stance in favor of accommodation.
- Defendant compliance with a plea deal is promoted by police and prosecutors who engage in overcharging, vertical and horizontal.
- Most private attorneys who specialize in criminal cases depend on a high turnover of clients who can afford only modest fees.
- Speedy trial requirements influence plea bargaining because failure to meet speedy trial requirements means the case must be dismissed.
- The prevalence of plea bargaining can be explained by a preference by attorneys for high levels of predictability.
- Plea bargaining can resemble a minitrial without the time-consuming formalities required in a courtroom.
- Most defendants are guilty and the evidence is usually sufficient to prove guilt.
- Rather than waste scarce resources prosecuting petty or weak cases, prosecutors employ a screening system for rating cases.
- The most important factor for prosecutors in screening a case is strength of the evidence.

- Prosecutors who utilize a more intensive case-screening policy drop fewer charges after filing.
- Suspects known to their victims are more likely to be caught, and having a previous personal relationship often leads a complainant to be reluctant to pursue prosecution.
- As a result of "normal crimes," the process involved in plea bargaining may be so simple that it cannot be accurately described as "negotiation."
- The "courtroom workgroup" promotes plea bargaining.
- The role of the judge in plea bargaining differs from jurisdiction to jurisdiction and may depend on the type of sentencing scheme used.
- A pre-plea report may be used in states using a determinate sentencing system in which the judge has wide discretion.
- In general, plea bargaining has been supported by legal decisions basing their logic on contract law.
- Supreme Court decisions on plea bargaining require that a determination be made as to the voluntary nature of a plea of guilty and the plea must be made knowingly and intelligently,
- The Court has ruled that when a defendant withdraws an initial plea of guilty and is convicted after a trial, the judge may impose a longer sentence than the earlier plea agreement had called for.
- A prosecutor must live up to the terms of a plea bargain.
- Attempts to limit or abolish plea bargaining can result in unintended consequences.

KEY TERMS

Alford plea	open plea	pre-plea report
bench trial	overcharging	probation officer
courtroom workgroup	plea bargaining	speedy trial
front-loading	predictability	stipulation
normal crimes		

REVIEW QUESTIONS

1. What are the contradictory criticisms of plea bargaining?
2. How is plea bargaining similar to buying a new car?
3. What is an "open plea"?
4. What are the arguments of the "negative view" of plea bargaining?
5. How does overcharging encourage defendants to accept a plea deal?
6. Why do private attorneys who specialize in criminal cases want to avoid trials?
7. How does the right to a speedy trial influence plea bargaining?
8. What are the arguments of the "benign or positive view" of plea bargaining?
9. How does a preference for predictability influence plea bargaining?

10. How can plea bargaining be like a minitrial without the time-consuming formalities required in a courtroom?

11. Why would defendants plead guilty in the absence of a negotiated deal?

12. What is the most important factor for prosecutors in screening a case?

13. How does the degree of case screening influence what will happen to a case?

14. How does a prior relationship between victim and defendant often influence a case?

15. How do "normal crimes" promote plea bargaining?

16. How does the "courtroom workgroup" facilitate plea bargaining?

17. What is the connection between a state's sentencing scheme and the judge's role in plea bargaining?

18. Why would some jurisdictions use a pre-plea report?

19. In general, what have legal decisions determined with respect to plea bargaining?

20. What do Supreme Court decisions require in order for a plea bargain to be proper?

21. What were the unintended consequences of Alaska abolishing plea bargaining?

INTERNET CONNECTIONS

American Bar Association Criminal Justice: http://www.americanbar.org/groups/criminal_justice.html

Legal Resource Center: http://crimelynx.com/research.html

National Criminal Justice Reference Service: https://www.ncjrs.gov

10

Civil Justice

In contrast to criminal justice, in which the government has a compelling interest, there is not a corresponding interest in private disputes, save the avoidance of criminal retribution. The government does, however, provide a forum for settling private disputes that disputants are under no legal obligation to utilize.

In this chapter we will look at the procedures used to resolve civil disputes, issues surrounding the contingency fee, class action lawsuits, and the conflict between trial attorneys, insurance companies, corporations, and medical doctors. As in the criminal justice system, very few civil cases are adjudicated with a formal trial. About 90 percent of the approximately one million lawsuits filed each year are settled[1] at the earliest stages of the process, somewhere between filing a complaint or petition and the first scheduled appearance before a judge. In fact, civil cases concluded at trial have declined to below 2 percent in the federal courts and below 1 percent in state courts (Langbein 2012).

In some jurisdictions, extensive activity takes place before a complaint is ever filed with the court, and the "case," usually a **tort**, is frequently settled or abandoned without any court involvement. In one 12-month period, jury cases were 2 percent of the 762,000 tort, contract, and real property cases disposed by state courts of general jurisdiction in the nation's most populous counties (DeFrances et al. 1995). In numerous cases, a trial is not the goal; instead, there is a need for a judicial declaration, for example, in uncontested divorces or probate proceedings (Galanter 1989).

According to Herbert Kritzer, criticisms of settlement in the civil justice system neatly parallel those of plea bargaining:

> Some people attack the deals that are made by way of settlement as evidence that victims of legally compensable injuries are forced (by delay, uncertainty, and the like) to accept resolutions far short of what the law entitles them to. Others see the civil justice process as a vehicle by which undeserving persons (and their contingent-fee lawyers) extort payments by filing frivolous lawsuits which defendants choose to settle because of the cost of defending the case in court exceeds the amount that the plaintiff is willing to accept in settlement. (Kritzer 1991: 5)

---

[1] When parties settle, they will usually ask the court for a consent order: judicial recognition of the agreement that cannot then be nullified without the consent of both parties.

The major difference, of course, is that in a civil action a defendant's freedom is not at stake.

> *"A striking trend in the administration of civil justice in the United States in recent decades has been the virtual abandonment of the centuries-old institution of trial" (Langbein 2012: 524).*

Civil Litigation

Whereas a criminal action can only be brought by the government (municipal, county, state, or federal prosecutor), most civil actions are brought by private parties, although the government is sometimes a plaintiff or a defendant. Cases typically handled by the civil justice system involve:

- *Torts.* Injury that did not involve a contract
- *Contracts.* Violation of an agreement (about a third of all civil trial cases)
- *Property.* Disputes relating to the exclusive right to possess, use, or dispose of an item: real property refers to land and buildings (or crops) on that land; personal property is everything else
- *Succession/estate.* Issues relating to the right to pass along property after death: inheritance, probate
- *Family relations.* Issues related to marriage, children, and divorce
- *Civil rights.* Violation of federal or state constitutions or statutes designed to protect individuals from the abuse of power by public and nonpublic officials

There are common elements in a civil case:

> [Each] involves a complaining party who demands a remedy from the courts for an asserted legal wrong. Every case involves a defending party who denies having a legal obligation in the matter, or at least contends that its legal obligation is different or less than the complaining party contends. In any particular case, the facts may be contested, compelling the tribunal to resolve conflicting evidence in making a determination of the facts. In addition, the meaning or application of the law may be contested, in which event the tribunal must resolve conflicting interpretations of the law. Many cases involve disputes of both fact and law. (Hazard and Taruffo 1993: viii)

Several important distinctions between civil and criminal justice exist. For example, the doctrine of *nullum crimen sine lege* (no crime without law; discussed in Chapter 8) is not applicable in civil litigation, and the *ex post facto* law prohibited by the Constitution (Article IX, Section 1) is limited to criminal cases (*Calder v. Bull* [1798]). Courts accept jurisdiction in civil cases, although the legislature has not specifically declared that the wrong allegedly committed by the defendant is the basis for a civil action, and (noncriminal) statutes and case law may be applied retroactively. One important guarantee that does apply—*res judicata*—is similar to the prohibition against double jeopardy. Once a plaintiff loses a suit, he or she cannot raise the same cause of action again even if there are new grounds for the claim. The defendant, likewise, is prevented from bringing a new action to defeat an adverse judgment. Plaintiff and defendant can of course, appeal an adverse decision, but as discussed in Chapter 5, new issues or new evidence cannot be raised on appeal. Chapter 8 discussed *joinder of offenses*, and in civil actions there is a parallel device, **joinder of parties/claims**. Rules governing these devices allow the plaintiff to name as defendants any/all persons allegedly responsible in any way for injuries or **damages**. The joinder of claims allows the court to consolidate claims if they arose out of the same incident and are too complex/interdependent to be considered separately.

In addition to narrowly drawn conflicts, the courts are often called on to decide broad issues of public policy, such as school desegregation, legislative reapportionment, and antitrust actions (discussed in Chapter 5). Civil litigation can accomplish three desirable goals (Lieberman 1981):

1. Provide for the compensation of those who have been injured

2. Serve to deter future harms or actions that are potentially harmful by the knowledge that some types of behavior can result in costly suits

3. Cause the termination of ongoing harms or the reformation of institutional systems that perpetuate them

The resolution of a dispute between private parties involves a lawsuit that has several key elements (Holland 1982):

- A lawsuit is a conflict about private rights motivated by self-interest. A typical civil action involves a *tort*, a lawsuit based on allegations of damages caused to the plaintiff by the defendant.

- The dispute is about events that happened in the past—events that disturbed a preexisting social harmony.

- A third party stands as a passive and impartial umpire who, after hearing arguments offered by each party in the presence of the other, resolves the dispute in accordance with preexisting legal rules.

- The court must hear the plaintiff's claim, and the parties initiate and control the definition of the issues, the development of facts, and the presentation of law.

"To prevail in a lawsuit, the plaintiff must prove both that the defendant committed an act that caused injury and that the act was a legal wrong" (Lieberman 1981: 18). However, modern litigation often involves the transformation of once lawful acts into legal wrongs: "Through a steady stream of legislative enactments and judicial pronouncements [case law], the citizen's right to redress has grown apace," replacing, for example, "the doctrine of *caveat emptor* (let the buyer beware) and related rules, with stringent duties of care on those who act," such as manufacturers, hospitals, and units of government (Lieberman 1981: 19).

The expansion of the role of the judiciary has also led to an increase in lawsuits whose primary purpose appears to be the harassment of opponents. In an effort to thwart these "frivolous" lawsuits, the federal judiciary toughened Rule 11 of the *Federal Rules of Civil Procedure* to ensure that every legal filing is grounded in fact and not designed "for any improper purpose such as to harass or to cause unnecessary delay or needless increase in the cost of litigation." If a judge finds that a lawyer has violated Rule 11, the plaintiff can be forced to pay the costs and legal fees expended by his or her opponents in defending against the improper action—an incentive to avoid cases that do not fit into established legal concepts.

The amended Rule 11 requires attorneys to inquire into the merits of their cases before proceeding, invalidating a "pure heart, empty head" defense. Critics argue that the amended rule has created just another means of harassing opponents through the use of civil litigation, increasing the amount of time required for litigation, generating a great deal of additional legal work, and thereby increasing costs accordingly—the opposite of what was intended. Indeed, the rule has spawned treatises and newsletters on this area of jurisprudence (Labaton 1992). There is also fear that the possibility of sanctions for bringing a legal action may frighten off aggrieved parties with legitimate claims, while serving to keep attorneys from filing innovative cases with legal theories that require the passage of time before being accepted (Lewin 1986b).

The Civil Process

For the most part, the adversarial process used in criminal trials is also used in civil trials, with some important differences. Judges have more leeway in civil cases to interpret statutes broadly to remedy wrongs not previously recognized as such. Although the rules of evidence are generally the same, "the law of criminal evidence has more restrictions favoring the accused" (Hazard and Taruffo 1993: 132).

Standing

In a noncriminal case, a litigant must have **standing**—meaning he or she must have a personal stake in the outcome of the controversy so that the adversarial model will be fully operative. For example, in order to challenge the constitutionality of a particular statute or executive action, a litigant must be prepared to show that he or she has been or will be harmed—an *injury in fact*—unless the court provides a remedy. The party who seeks to invoke the court's authority must show that he or she has suffered, not in the abstract but personally, some actual or threatened injury as a result of allegedly illegal conduct on the part of the defendant (Schwartz 1988). In 1991, for example, a lawsuit filed by a group of Harvard law students accusing their school of discriminating against women and minorities in faculty hiring and promotion was dismissed in state court because the plaintiffs lacked standing—they could not show direct harm ("Judge Voids Suit on Harvard Hiring" 1991). Standing is particularly important when

---

Standing

"Have the appellants alleged such a personal stake in the outcome of the controversy as to assure that concrete adverseness which sharpens the presentation of issues upon which this court so largely depends for illumination of difficult questions? This is the gist of the question of standing" (William J. Brennan, Jr., *Baker v. Carr* [1962]).

the case **at issue** may provide precedent, thereby influencing other disputes not before the court. It is generally believed in the legal community that a party with an immediate personal stake is more likely to present the court with a specific and well-developed fact situation on which law (that is, precedent) can be made (Marvell 1978).

Ideological opposition or a general grievance against a particular policy of government—military intervention Iraq or Afghanistan—for example, is not sufficient to provide standing, and a plaintiff will be told that since the injuries alleged are not personal, the suit will be dismissed for lack of standing. The Court "will not even examine the accusation that tax money is being illegally spent, although this may well be the case" (Lempert and Sanders 1986: 23–24). In 1923 (*Frothingham v. Mellon*), the Court ruled unanimously against taxpayer suits as a device for limiting the manner in which federal funds are spent; the Court stated that the plaintiff must show that he or she sustained "some direct injury." Being one of millions of taxpayers creates a minute, indeterminable, and remote effect, and not interest sufficient to support standing. In 1968, however, the Court limited the application of *Frothingham* by recognizing standing in the case of a challenge to congressional funding that conflicts with a constitutional limitation, in this case (*Flast v. Cohen*) aid to parochial schools as a violation of the First Amendment. And, as noted in Chapter 5, the courts have granted standing to groups with generalized claims on behalf of the "public interest." Liberalizing the rules governing standing has been subjected to severe criticism by persons on the right of the American political spectrum, such as James Q. Wilson (1989, Chapter 15).

Federal Standing

"According to the Supreme Court, the Federal Constitution limits not only the types of matters that federal courts can adjudicate, but also the parties who can bring those matters before them. In particular, the Court has held that private citizens who have suffered no concrete private injury lack standing to ask federal courts to redress diffuse harms to the public at large. When such harms are **justiciable** at all, the proper party plaintiff is the public itself, represented by an authorized officer of the government" (Woolhandler and Nelson 2004: 689; emphasis added).

Moot Cases

If the outcome of a case will have no significant impact on the litigants, it is moot—"neither side would gain in the immediate dispute no matter how the court ruled"—and the case will generally be thrown out. Typically, the case begins with a real dispute, but changed circumstances have resolved the issue and the adversarial system will no longer be operative. At times, however, an appellate court will decide a **moot case** if the issue is one likely to come before the court again (Marvell 1978: 43). For example, in *Bowers v. Hardwick* (1986), the Supreme Court ruled that the Constitution does not prohibit a state from criminalizing homosexual acts between consenting adults, despite Georgia's decision not to prosecute Bowers, making the case moot.

Jury Issues

In 1970, the Supreme Court upheld a Florida statute mandating six-person juries in criminal cases (*Williams v. Florida*), and in 1973, *Colgrove v. Battin* extended this ruling to federal civil trials. Accordingly, civil juries frequently have fewer than 12 members, and they are not sequestered. Most states do not require unanimity in civil verdicts; in California, for example, only nine of 12 jurors have to agree on a verdict. In actions involving issues of equity (nonmonetary matters requesting specific performance—discussed in Chapter 1), there is not a constitutional right to a jury trial. The Seventh Amendment guarantees the right to a jury trial only in common-law suits "where the value in controversy shall exceed twenty dollars." Although the Seventh Amendment has not been made applicable to the states, almost all states have similar constitutional provisions (Friedenthal et al. 2013).

As in criminal cases, *voir dire* remains an important aspect of the civil jury process. "Lawyer-conducted *voir dire* is the traditional American method of screening the members of the panel called for jury service. In some states, *voir dire* has been left so completely in lawyers' hands that the judge does not even preside at the sessions in which opposing lawyers question potential jurors" (Landsman 1999: 292).

Criticism over alleged lawyer abuse of *voir dire*—e.g., lawyers using the *voir dire* to indoctrinate the jury and to cultivate friendly relationships with individual jurors; lawyer-directed questioning veering into inappropriate areas touching on jurors' private lives and specific views about evidence they have not yet heard—has led various courts to impose restrictions on lawyer participation in the questioning process. In the federal courts, civil rules authorize judges to conduct the entire *voir dire* themselves. In many jurisdictions, lawyers are permitted to supplement the judge's questioning, making it possible to secure the benefit of both judicial restraint and lawyer probing. Sometimes an oral *voir dire* is supplemented with a written questionnaire answered by each potential juror (Landsman 1999).

Once *voir dire* has been concluded, each side is allowed to exercise its peremptory challenges—federal rules entitle each side to three, and states vary in their number. Either attorney can use peremptory challenges to excuse any juror without having to state a reason, In 1991, the Supreme Court ruled (*Edmonson v. Leesville*) that the prohibition against prosecutors using peremptory challenges to exclude blacks from juries because they believe that such persons may favor a black defendant (*Batson v. Kentucky* [1986]) also applies to both the plaintiff and defendant in civil actions. When the complaining party makes a **prima facie case** of discriminatory challenges, the burden shifts to the party who exercised the peremptory strikes to articulate a "neutral explanation" for his or her selections. The trial judge decides if unlawful discrimination has been proven.

Evidence

In civil cases, a finding for the plaintiff—the party bringing the action—is based on a **preponderance of the evidence** and, sometimes (e.g., for punitive damages in some states or for involuntary civil commitment), **clear and convincing evidence**, not the more stringent criminal standard of *beyond a reasonable doubt* (Figure 10.1 on the following page). Because of the lower standard of proof, a defendant can be found not

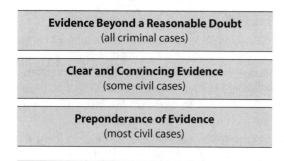

Figure 10.1   Levels of Trial Evidence in Order of Stringency

guilty of criminal charges but liable for damages in a civil proceeding. Thus, in 1995, Hall of Fame football star O. J. Simpson was found not guilty of double homicide but, nevertheless, found liable in 1997 for the *wrongful death* of his victims.

Many of the extensive due process guarantees that accrue to a defendant in a criminal case are not applicable in a civil proceeding, in particular:

- *Counsel:* Neither plaintiff nor defendant is constitutionally entitled to an attorney; government has no legal obligation to provide an attorney to an indigent party involved in a civil action.

- *Remain silent:* There is no Fifth Amendment right to remain silent, and defendants are often called on to testify.

- *Confront witnesses:* The right to cross-examine an adverse witness is circumscribed in civil cases: In the absence of a witness, his or her **deposition** (discussed below) may be read into evidence. When a witness is outside of the jurisdiction of the court, the party seeking testimony can apply to the court for *letters rogatory.* This commission is directed to an official or an attorney in the proper jurisdiction empowering him or her to take the witness' deposition and forward it to the court. In some states, court intervention is not necessary, only notice to opposing counsel of the intention to take a deposition.

Jurisdiction

There is a code of civil procedure governing noncriminal disputes, and the first issue to be determined is jurisdiction, which can at times be quite complex. Is the case a proper one for federal or state court? What if the plaintiff and defendant live in different counties, different states, or even different countries? What if the damages occurred in a third county or state? Some actions are local, for example mortgage foreclosure, and can be brought only in the county where the property is located. Other actions can be transitory, meaning they may be brought wherever the defendant is found and served with the summons, such as a tort action for personal injuries. There are also specialized courts such as domestic relations, chancery, and small claims. The plaintiff is required to establish that the court has jurisdiction to rule on the issue being presented. Under Article IV, Section 1, of the Constitution, a judgment rendered by a state court is enforceable in all states: "**Full faith and credit** shall be given in each State to the public Acts, Records, and judicial Proceedings of every other State" (emphasis added).

In 1998, the Supreme Court ruled 9–0 that despite Article IV, one state's court system cannot bind another's to an agreement barring particular testimony or evidence from a trial. In this case (*Baker v. General Motors*), as a result of a settlement, a former employee who had testified as an expert witness against General Motors agreed to an injunction barring him from testifying in further lawsuits against the company. A Michigan court issued an order putting the settlement into force. When the employee was subpoenaed to testify in a suit against General Motors in Missouri, the company invoked the Michigan injunction, but the trial judge invoked Missouri law and permitted him to testify. The plaintiffs—survivors of a woman who died when her Chevrolet Blazer caught fire after a crash—were awarded $11.3 million.

Jurisdiction can be exercised over the defendant: *in personam* jurisdiction empowers the court to issue judgments against the defendant personally, seizing the person's assets, for example, to satisfy a judgment. Or, jurisdiction can be exercised over things and status: *in rem* jurisdiction empowers the court to dissolve a marriage or adjudicate the disposition of real estate (Emanuel 2008).

Filing a Civil Complaint

A typical civil case is either *ex delicto*, a tort or action alleging a wrong committed by the defendant against the plaintiff, or *ex contractu*, an action alleging a breach of a promise set forth in a contract. A civil action is known by the name of the plaintiff and the name of the defendant—*Smith v. Jones*; the plaintiff's name appears first. The case typically begins (see Figure 10.2 on the following page) when the plaintiff's attorney pays a fee and files a complaint or petition with the clerk of the proper court, setting out the facts on which the action is based, the damages alleged, and the remedy or relief being sought, generally called a *prayer*. The petition may consist of a simple court form requiring only that blanks be filled in, or it may be a long, printed document. The clerk issues a summons, which is attached to a copy of the complaint or petition, and personnel from the sheriff's office, a US marshal, or a private process-serving agency serve both on the defendant.

The summons directs a defendant to file a response—*pleading*—within a certain time, usually 30 days, or suffer a judgment of default. A **default judgment** requires that the defendant be served personally and not by proxy. There are some alternative methods, for example, registered mail accompanied by an announcement in the legal section of a newspaper or a copy affixed to the defendant's residence or business, a form of service known as "nail and mail." It is not necessary that the defendant actually have notice of the action being brought, so long as the method of service is reasonably calculated to give notice and an opportunity to defend (Berman and Saliba 2009). The defendant's attorney can now respond to the allegations, sometimes alleging wrongdoing on the part of the plaintiff (a counterclaim), moving to dismiss, or filing a claim against another party whom he or she alleges should be held accountable.

Pretrial Activities

Activities prior to a civil trial are extensive and, in practice, usually lead to an out-of-court settlement. Settlements have been aided by services available to attorneys. One firm, for example, provides computerized data on jury verdicts nationwide. The data is used to predict the statistical probability of a plaintiff winning a personal injury case and the likely award (Hinds 1994). The employment of specialized assistants has become routine. These persons, trained in a particular area of litigation (e.g., nurses who analyze medical records and interview victims) aid in analyzing the *value* of cases.

The delay after filing and preliminary motions may last several months, and roughly 75 percent of cases are resolved during that time without a trial. (An unknown number of cases are settled before any court filing actually occurs.) Depending on how cases are calendared in the particular jurisdiction, a judge may first become involved within two to four months after the complaint is filed, or the judge may wait until a certificate of readiness, at-issue memo, or similar document is filed by one or both of the attorneys signifying that the case is ready to be placed on the trial calendar (Mahoney 1988). In some jurisdictions, there may be an initial conference with the attorneys in order to set a schedule for future events in the case. In any event, there are usually pretrial conferences with the judge to facilitate a settlement. As opposed to criminal cases, the litigants, not the court, have primary responsibility for control of the case (speedy trial requirements apply only to criminal cases).

Figure 10.2   The Flow of Civil Cases

Motions

Defense counsel can make a number of pretrial motions:

- *Motion to quash* asks the court to void the summons as not having been properly served.

- *Motion to strike* asks the court to excise parts of the petition as irrelevant, improper, or prejudicial.

- *Motion to make more definite* asks the court to require the plaintiff to be more specific about the complaints that are alleged, for example, to describe the injuries in greater detail so the defense will be better able to respond.

- *Motion to dismiss* argues that the court lacks jurisdiction, or that the plaintiff did not present a legally sound basis for a cause of action against the defendant even if, in fact, the allegations are true (known as a *demurrer*).

- *Motion for* **summary judgment** is based on a claim that there is no genuine issue of material fact and, therefore, the undisputed portion of the case should be eliminated from trial; if the undisputed issues are crucial, the entire case may be determined without a trial.

Additional motions may be made subsequent to discovery (discussed below), for example, adding another person/corporation as a defendant—*motion for permission to join*.

The defendant's response can be to deny the allegations, admit some and deny others, or admit them all and plead **extenuating circumstances**—an excuse. The defendant may also file a counterclaim, which may be part of the response (cross-claim) or filed independently (counterclaim). It asks for relief or damages from the plaintiff and sometimes from others. The plaintiff may then file any of the above motions against the cross-complaint, except the motion to **quash**. Either party can now file a reply in answer to any new allegations raised by the other party. The plaintiff's answer to the defendant's plea is referred to as a *replication*; the defendant's response to a replication is called a *rejoinder*.

Discovery

"In the early days of the American legal system, a party had to prove its case with evidence that it obtained on its own, without help from the other side" (Morrison 1996: 70). "The term '**discovery**' encompasses the methods by which a party or potential party to a lawsuit obtains and preserves information regarding the action" which "should permit parties to obtain a fair understanding of all relevant evidence before the trial begins, thereby avoiding 'trial by ambush'" (Friedenthal, Kane, and Miller 1985: 380 [emphasis added]; Alliance of American Insurers 1987: 19). Because it is presumed that litigants act in their own self-interest, discovery rules "compel the disclosure of evidence that would not—were it not for the fact of pretrial disclosure itself—emerge at trial . . . Discovery adds to the accuracy of outcomes not only by eliminating surprises about the evidence, but also by expanding the quality of evidence" (Hay 1994: 482; 498). Discovery seeks to make decision making more accurate. It should help the parties avoid a trial and evaluate settlement conditions. Discovery rules empower judges to punish false or incomplete disclosure by attorney fee awards, contempt **citations**, and default judgments. Doctored evidence or false denials about the existence of relevant evidence exposes a litigant to civil and criminal liability, and attorneys to professional discipline, **disbarment**, and prosecution (Hay 1994).

The discovery phase of civil litigation differs considerably from its criminal counterpart. The civil process utilizes extensive discovery procedures, whereas "even in 'liberal' jurisdictions, [criminal] attorneys can get only a fraction of the information that is routinely available in civil litigation" (Schulhofer 1994: 137)—noncriminal defendants have no Fifth Amendment protection against extensive requests for information. The discovery phase of litigation can be lengthy and costly, providing an advantage to those litigants who can afford to absorb such costs. "There are attorneys," notes Roy Grutman (with Thomas 1990: 60), "who are assigned to do nothing but create correspondence and bury the opposition in paperwork. The issues in the case become secondary." Although rules of evidence require attorneys to prove the need for particular discovery information, this is rarely enforced by judges (Linowitz 1996). Some jurisdictions have limited the number of witnesses who can be deposed or the number of interrogatory questions that can be propounded, or the amount of documents required. "Thus, while discovery is often criticized because of the burdens it imposes, a reasonable amount of discovery is essential if informed decisions are to be made about settlement. The problem is drawing the line between reasonable and excessive discovery" (Morrison 1996: 73).

Discovery in a civil action includes interrogatories, depositions, and requests to produce, enter, or inspect documents.

Interrogatories.   If relevant answers are not forthcoming, either side can submit written questions (known as interrogatories) for the other side to answer under oath. Although a respondent need not answer a question deemed improper, the interrogating party can seek a court order to compel an answer. In particularly acrimonious situations, the court can appoint a referee to handle the discovery phase. A variation of the interrogatory is the **request for admission**: Written statements of material facts or allegations at issue are submitted to opposing counsel for a response—admission or denial. Those that are admitted need not be proved at trial.

Interrogatories are considered very useful for obtaining information from the other side, at quite modest cost, since the only expense is the writing of the questions. They are particularly useful when the other side is an organization, such as a corporation or government agency, because the rules require the organization to make reasonable inquiries to all persons in the organization who might have information about the subject, and it cannot reply based on one person's knowledge or lack of it. The principal difficulty in using interrogatories is if the question is not precisely phrased, clever counsel on the other side can respond in a way that, while literally true, does not provide information of the kind the requesting party was actually seeking and would have obtained if the question had been framed slightly differently (Morrison 1996: 72).

Depositions.   As part of the discovery stage, the civil process utilizes a legal device, the deposition, which is generally absent from criminal cases. (Most states allow criminal depositions only if a witness will not be available for trial.) The deposition is an out-of-court procedure whereby plaintiff, defendant, and any witnesses are placed under oath and asked questions by opposing counsel on matters not otherwise privileged and that relate to the pending case. The questions and their answers are recorded by a private court reporter engaged for this purpose. If a witness lives a considerable distance from where the case is being tried, typically 100 miles or more, and is not a party to the dispute, that person cannot be subpoenaed to testify. A deposition, however, may be taken and read into the record, often by a professional deposition reader—there are firms that provide this service.

Depositions are particularly useful for narrowing down the issues involved, and they provide each side with an opportunity to evaluate the case and better prepare for trial (or settlement). The deposition can also be used in court as a basis for impeaching subsequent testimony in conflict with the sworn out-of-court record. Although many of the rules that apply in court are in effect, a deposition is not a matter of public record and, thus, the press has no right of access until it is released by virtue of a court order. The deposition process can be expensive, since both sides and their lawyers have a right to be present and the sessions must be recorded by a legal stenographer and/or on videotape.

Documents.   Discovery may also involve the production and inspection of documents, such as a contract or lease, and may require the plaintiff to undergo an examination by a medical doctor chosen by the defendant or the court in order to substantiate claims of injury.

The *Federal Rules of Civil Procedure* require lawyers to furnish opponents with basic factual information at the onset of litigation, including relevant documents and lists of witnesses: "Litigants seeking information need do nothing but wait for it. The party possessing the information has the burden of marshaling the relevant documents and determining which witnesses have relevant information, and then producing this information to his or her opponent" (Koski 1994: 85). In addition to other penalties, the failure to disclose relevant information precludes its use at trial.

Pretrial Conference

After discovery, but before trial, the attorneys appear before the judge, usually without their clients, in order to agree on certain uncontested factual issues (*stipulations*) such as the date and time of the incident, photos, sketches, and other routine evidence. The purpose of stipulations is to make the trial process more efficient and cut down on the time necessary for completion. (Often, this part of the process can result in a settlement without the need for a trial.) The judge enters a pretrial order, which may specify the witnesses to be called and the documents to be offered at trial. The order governs the conduct of the trial. "A pretrial conference is a regular procedure in federal courts, but many state courts hold pretrial conferences only in complex cases" (Hazard and Taruffo 1993: 122).

Trial

Civil and criminal trials (discussed in Chapter 8) are conducted in the same manner: selection of a jury/*voir dire*, opening statements, witnesses called by the plaintiff and then the defense, direct examination, cross-examination, redirect, recross-examination, closing arguments, charge to the jury, deliberations, and verdict. A judge may preclude the case being sent to the jury by ruling in favor of a motion for a *directed verdict*—at the close of the presentation of the opponent's evidence, either defense or plaintiff can argue that the evidence is either so compelling or so weak that only one outcome would be proper. If the plaintiff fails to present sufficient evidence from which a jury could reasonably find a verdict for the plaintiff, the judge dismisses the case for **failure of proof**.

At the beginning of the trial, after seating the jury, the judge usually provides an orientation to the case, introducing the parties and their counsel, describing the general subject of the case, and outlining the duties of the jury, the judge, and counsel (Hazard and Taruffo 1993). The plaintiff's attorney typically makes the first opening statement and the final closing argument (paralleling the role of the prosecutor in criminal trials). Usually the plaintiff is a witness, and the defendant may also opt to testify or be called as a witness by the plaintiff. In closing arguments, the plaintiff's attorney summarizes the case in a manner that points to the defendant's liability and stresses the losses that the plaintiff has suffered. Defense counsel claims that the defendant is not responsible for the injury or loss, or that the compensation claimed is too high. The plaintiff's attorney is usually permitted a brief rebuttal. The judge, depending on the complexity of the case, typically limits closing arguments.

Civil trials may involve complex legal and scientific matters (e.g., medical or engineering testimony) presented by expert witnesses, which need to be simplified to be understood by the jury. Attorney Roy Grutman (and Thomas 1990: 117) recalls such a case, when Memorex sued IBM for unfair competition: "The billion-dollar lawsuit was a test of physical stamina as well as the jurors' grasp of economics, engineering and corporate psychology. The trial lasted three months, as jury members listened to eighty-seven witnesses, examined three thousand exhibits, and then spent nineteen days in deliberation before informing the judge they were too confused to reach a verdict."

Under such circumstances, the judge may utilize a legal device known as the **special verdict**. Instead of a verdict for or against the defendant, the jury responds to a series of written questions of fact posed by the judge. Based on the jury's answers, the judge determines the outcome of the case. A verdict in favor of the defendant by judge or jury ends the trial; a finding for the plaintiff requires a judgment. A trial judge may reduce a jury award that is excessive, order a new trial when the verdict goes against the clear weight of the evidence, or reverse a verdict that is unreasonable given the facts presented at trial and the legal standard to be applied (known as a *judgment notwithstanding the verdict*).

Whereas some states require unanimity, the decision rule in others requires only a supermajority—five out of six or nine out of 12. Research shows little effect of jury size or decision rule on outcomes (Feigenson 2000).

In the civil jury verdict, must all of the jurors agree on each of the issues? "Consider, for example, a personal injury action in which the plaintiff alleges three separate factual bases for finding that defendant was negligent. Suppose that the jurors split eight to four against a finding of **negligence** on each of these bases, but as to every determination, different four jurors thought that negligence had been established. Thus, despite their disagreements on the specific factual issues, all twelve jurors find defendant at fault and return verdict for plaintiff" (Friedenthal, Kane, and Miller 1985: 461). The judge may become aware of this situation as the result of a post-verdict **poll of the jury**, and courts have split on the matter of letting the verdict stand. The trend seems to be in favor of upholding the verdict. "The result turns on whether the particular jurisdiction views the proper role of the jury merely to decide specific factual issues or to determine the overall outcome of the case" (1985: 461–62).

In cases of equity, or when both sides waive a jury trial, the judge will often interject his or her own questions to witnesses, and when all evidence is received, the judge may ask the parties for written briefs on issues of fact and law. The judge may reserve rendering a decision until he or she has had an opportunity to review the trial transcript (Hazard and Taruffo 1993).

There is no sentence in a civil case; the next step is a determination by judge or jury of the remedy or damages to be assessed. Once the judge enters a judgment against the defendant, if appropriate, the plaintiff can ask to have the court clerk issue an order to **execute** the judgment. This document commands the sheriff or US marshal to take possession of the defendant's property and sell it at auction to satisfy the judgment, or a lien (**garnishment**) can be placed against the defendant's salary and a certain amount of money taken out each payday by the employer for the plaintiff. If the defendant fails to carry out the provisions of the judgment, the plaintiff can ask for a contempt order that can result in arrest and imprisonment. In cases where there is concern that a defendant may move or otherwise dispose of his or her property prior to the outcome of a trial, the plaintiff can request an **attachment** preventing any disposition of property that may thwart satisfaction of an adverse judgment. In practice, enforcement of a judgment can be complex. For example, most states immunize some of the property of debtors from attachment or seizure, such as the debtor's home and a vehicle required for employment (Hazard and Taruffo 1993).

In the civil process, as opposed to the criminal process, there is a peculiar practice known as *vacating* a decision. Vacating typically refers to setting aside or rescinding a (faulty) judgment. In this case, it means that the losing party and the winning party have struck a deal, perhaps in exchange for extra compensation, asking the court to vacate the decision as if it never existed. The decision is stricken from the record and is no longer available to serve as a precedent. Although it doesn't actually disappear (the records can be found in the courthouse where the judgment was issued), few lawyers would ordinarily be aware of it (Kolata 1993).

Small-Claims Courts and Administrative Bodies

Civil courts are handicapped by an oppressive caseload, and it is not unusual for a tort action to take as long as five years before reaching the trial stage. In the nation's largest court system, Cook County, Illinois, the average length of time it takes for a lawsuit to reach trial is six years. When plaintiffs have a choice of courts, they usually select the one with the least amount of delay, although travel considerations will also be taken into account; the court of choice may be located some distance from the plaintiff and his or her attorney. Efforts to deal with the problem of delay have included the establishment of specialized courts and administrative bodies (as well as alternative dispute resolution discussed in Chapter 12). The civil division of a state court system frequently has specialized courts for such matters as equity (chancery court), divorce (a family or domestic relations court), settlement of estates (probate court), cases of juveniles (discussed in Chapter 11), and small-claims cases. The discussion of small-claims courts serves as an example of specialized courts.

Small-Claims Courts

Small-claims courts have jurisdiction to decide cases when the money being contested is not above a certain dollar amount, depending on the statutes of the jurisdiction, ranging from $5,000 (Florida), to $10,000 (Illinois), to $25,000 (Tennessee). The first small-claims court was established in 1913 by the Cleveland Municipal Court. The simplified process required no pleadings and only a nominal filing fee, and participation of lawyers was discouraged. By 1920, other cities—Chicago, Minneapolis, New York, and Philadelphia—had established small-claims courts based on the Cleveland model. In that year, Massachusetts adopted a statewide small-claims court; every lower court judge was required to establish special sessions for hearing all claims under $35 (Harrington 1985). Contemporary small-claims courts siphon off less complex cases for handling in a less formal manner than is typical in most other trial courts. The court's rules of procedure and evidence are relaxed to make it easier for persons to represent themselves without hiring attorneys. Filing fees vary—$15–$20 in New York, $119–$247 in Cook County (Illinois), and as high as $225 in Los Angeles County (California)—and a summons can often be served by certified mail or by the sheriff for a small fee. The plaintiff need not engage an attorney, and counsel rarely represents defendants. Some states, for example, California, generally do not allow the use of attorneys.

Although these courts were supposedly designed for the "little man," the citizen whose case does not involve enough money to interest a lawyer on a contingency basis (discussed later), they have frequently been used by collection agencies, utility companies, and retailers as a relatively cheap and efficient way to move against persons allegedly owing small amounts of money. This use of small-claims court is controversial, and some states, such as New York, have enacted legislation prohibiting this use of small-claims courts.

Administrative Bodies

In addition to specialized courts, governmental agencies have established administrative bodies (a number of these were mentioned in Chapter 1) that have quasi-judicial authority to adjudicate certain types of cases. For example, a workers' compensation board determines whether an employee's injury was job-related, thus qualifying him or her for workers' compensation. Motor vehicle departments may have hearing boards that make determinations about revoking driving licenses, and many states have boards that rule on matters involving civil rights and cases of alleged discrimination.

Administrative agencies hold evidentiary hearings before administrative decisions that adversely affect private individuals are made. Although procedures vary

---

Small-Claims Court, San Joaquin County, California

Small-claims court is a special court where disputes are resolved quickly and inexpensively. The rules are simple and informal. In small-claims court, you may ask a lawyer for advice before you go to court, but neither party can have a lawyer in court. Your claim cannot be for more than $5,000.

from agency to agency, these hearings follow most of the elements of civil trial procedure, including the calling and cross-examination of witnesses by opposing counsel,
but they exclude juries. The agency must explain the basis for the decision it makes at
the conclusion of the hearing (Schwartz 1996).

Appeals

Within a specified length of time, usually 30 days, a losing litigant can appeal an
adverse decision. However, under our adversarial system it is the obligation of the
appellant's lawyer to draw the court's attention to relevant portions of the trial record
in his or her brief. The appellate court does not independently search the record for
trial court errors, "but leaves the decision of what needs review to the litigants" (Friedenthal, Kane, and Miller 1985: 601). In general, appellate review is limited to errors
that were objected to by the aggrieved party's attorney at trial and, thus, appear in the
trial record; attorneys cannot offer new evidence. "Errors that are not objected to
before or arguments that are not raised at trial generally cannot be raised for the first
time on appeal" (Friedenthal, Kane, and Miller 1985: 598). The appellate court must
determine if the judge's ruling was incorrect and, if so, whether or not the error(s) was
serious enough to justify a new trial or if it was a "harmless error" not affecting the
outcome of the trial. In cases involving money damages, the defendant can also appeal
the jury award: The court can lower the amount (*remittitur*) or order a new trial on the
single issue of the amount of damages.

Torts and the Contingency Fee

The **contingency fee** offers a partial answer to the problem of providing legal assistance to persons without financial means who have suffered a tort. In this scheme, the
plaintiff's attorney in a personal injury case receives no retainer (compensation paid in
advance). If the case is lost, the lawyer receives no payment. If the lawyer is successful,
the plaintiff shares a percentage, generally one-third, of the compensation with his or
her attorney.

The Supreme Court declared the contingency fee legal in 1877 (*Stanton v. Embry*).
Nevertheless, the American Bar Association challenged it on grounds of propriety and
recommended that the judiciary supervise contingency fees. Fees received by law
firms from corporate interests would, of course, remain free of any scrutiny. Corporate
lawyers argued that because contingency fees would cause spurious lawsuits insti-
gated by shyster lawyers, contingency contracts required supervision. The same lawyers who argued that legislation providing a minimum wage or maximum hours of
employment (e.g., a 40-hour workweek) was an infringement on the freedom of contract found no contradiction with their stand on contingency contracts. Critics also
argued that a lawyer should not have a personal, as opposed to a professional, interest
in a client's case. Sol Linowitz argues that this was not a matter of class prejudice but
"was a rule the leaders of the bar applied to themselves in their corporate practice.
[Paul Cravath, for example,] forbade anyone who worked at Cravath, Swaine &
Moore from owning stock in any client corporation" (Linowitz and Mayer 1996: 29).
"One of the traditional criticisms of the contingent fee is that, by having an interest in
the outcome of the cases, lawyers are hindered in providing the kind of dispassionate

professional advice they should be rendering to their clients" (Kritzer 1991: 99). (In medicine, this is why physicians do not treat persons close to them for a serious medical condition.) And, in some cases, "it is more beneficial financially for the lawyer to secure a quick settlement, even if the amount paid is much lower than what could be achieved by going to trial" (Kritzer 1991: 100).

In the personal injury area, the plaintiff's lawyers may have a number of cases against a single insurance company; in this situation the lawyer may try to negotiate settlements for several cases at the same time. Given the lawyer's interest in maximizing the return from the complete set of cases, it may be expedient to forego a maximum return in any single case in order to achieve the best aggregate result (Kritzer 1990: 10): "Regular players in the system—attorneys who handle a great deal of personal injury litigation—may approach cases with a future orientation (such as relationships with other attorneys) rather than securing the best possible outcome for the instant case. A refusal to accept a settlement in a current case, while it may be in the best interest of a client, may harm future settlements."

Of no small historical interest is the current controversy pitting trial lawyers and the contingency fee against the insurance industry and its clients. Both sides have sought to claim the high ground by using terms such as "reform," "justice," and "fairness." They typically attempt to mask the substantial self-interest inherent in their respective positions. Both sides have buttressed their arguments with dubious statistics and anecdotal evidence (Daniels and Martin 1995). In 1994, a number of prominent legal scholars urged reform of the contingency fee to prevent windfalls for what amounts to nothing more than routine legal services. In 1989, a soft-drink delivery truck crashed into a school bus killing 21 children and injuring dozens of others. Because fault was never really in doubt, insurance companies settled for $122 million, and the plaintiff's attorneys received one-third, which amounted to $25,000 an hour.

The United States is a litigious society. In state courts, "Litigants sought punitive damages in 12 percent of the estimated 25,000 civil trials concluded in 2005.... The median punitive damage award was $64,000, and 13% of cases with punitive awards had damages of $1 million or more.... In 76 percent of the 632 civil trials with both punitive and compensatory damages, the ratio of punitive to compensatory damages was 3 to 1 or less" (Cohen and Harbacek 2011: 1). Some punitive damages cases make headlines because of the large dollar amounts imposed. In 1997, for example, a jury awarded $2.5 billion dollars in punitive damages against the CSX Corporation for a railroad fire in New Orleans in 1987, despite the fact that the federal National Trans-

Punitive and Compensatory Damages

Damages awarded in civil trial litigation can take the form of compensatory or punitive awards. **Punitive damages** are awarded for willful, malicious, or fraudulent conduct that exceeds the legal criteria for negligence or gross negligence. Awards are in addition to compensatory damages and serve to punish the plaintiff while deterring others from similar behavior (Cohen 2005). **Compensatory damages** are awarded to compensate the plaintiff for financial losses, pain, suffering, or emotional distress resulting from a defendant's negligence.

Chaotic Justice?

"Numbers have been, along with horror story anecdotes, one of the main tools used in the strategic representation of the civil justice system as a system in chaos. This is despite the limited amount of data actually available and the question of how to interpret them." And the "opponents of civil justice reform have not been idle. There is an antireform rhetoric that is equally problematic because of its use of horror stories, appeals to passion over reason, misuse of quantitative data, and so on" (Daniels and Martin 1995: 53, 246).

portation Safety Board determined that CSX had not caused the accident and no serious injuries had resulted (Salpukas 1997; Broder 1997).

In 1986, insurance companies began a vigorous lobbying campaign for a statutory cap on tort judgments, particularly for "punitive damages" that are supposed to serve as a deterrent. The campaign to impose caps is supported by local governments and doctors, as well as a variety of business and charitable organizations, all of who have to pay high insurance premiums. In response to caps on punitive damages, however, the plaintiff's attorneys have been shifting their claims to "pain and suffering," which has no legal limits. For example, in 1999, a jury in Detroit awarded a female assembly plant worker $20 million for the pain and suffering she endured as the result of sexual harassment (Liptak 2002).

Increasing rates have caused some local governments to drop their insurance coverage (and, correspondingly, public services). Insurance companies claim that the increase in rates is a result of defending against lawsuits and, most importantly, against judgments that are out of step with the tort concepts of fault and wrongdoing. They claim that judges and juries often hold "deep-pocketed" defendants liable simply because they have the resources to compensate plaintiff victims. However, a study of 9,000 trials throughout the country found that judges award punitive damages about as often as juries. Punitive damages are awarded in about 4 percent of the cases won by plaintiffs (Glaberson 2001b).

In 1987, the American Bar Association endorsed a controversial plan that would place some limits on the rights of injured parties to sue for damages, and the association endorsed greater discretion for trial judges to reduce awards they consider excessive. Some critics of the current system argue for the **English Rule**, a system in Great Britain that requires the losing side in a lawsuit to pay the winning side's attorney costs (Samuelson 1992).[2] In 1989, the Supreme Court ruled that unlimited awards for punitive damages do not violate the Eighth Amendment's prohibition against "excessive fines." In a 7–2 decision, the Court ruled that the limitation on fines applied only to government and not to private lawsuits. In this case, a jury awarded compensation of $51,146, but set punitive damages at $6 million (*Browning-Ferris Industries v. Kelco Disposal*). In 1991, the Court upheld a $1 million jury award to a poor woman with $3,800 in medical bills that an insurance company had refused to pay (*Pacific Mutual*

---

[2] Contingency fees are illegal in England (Linowitz 1996: 175), which is offset by the "existence of more tax-supported legal assistance programs."

Life Insurance Co. v. Haslip). In 1993, the Supreme Court ruled again on the issue of excessive punitive damages: in a 6–3 decision the Court refused to overturn a $10 million award for a $19,000 injury (*TXO Production v. Alliance Resources*). In 1994, however, the Court set aside a damage award of $5 million for an Oregon man who was injured when his three-wheeled vehicle overturned on him. In *Honda Motor Co. v. Oberg*, the Court ruled 7–2 that punitive damages pose a risk of being arbitrary and, therefore, some judicial review of jury awards is constitutionally required—Oregon was the only state that failed to provide for such review. In 1996, in a 5–4 decision (*BMW v. Gore*), the Court ruled that punitive damages can be so "grossly excessive" as to be unconstitutional. Evidence had been presented that BMW repainted at least 1,000 cars sold as new, a violation of Alabama law, but not illegal in every state. An Alabama state court jury found the damage and repair diminished the value of the plaintiff's car's value by $4,000, and multiplied that by 1,000 to arrive at a punitive award (which was cut in half by the Alabama Supreme Court). The US Supreme Court ruled that state courts could not use punitive damages for conduct that may be legal in another state. In an elaboration of *BMW v. Gore*, the Supreme Court ruled 8–1 (*Cooper Industries Inc. v. Leatherman Tool Group Inc.* [2001]) that federal and state appellate courts must apply scrutiny when deciding if a jury award for punitive damages is excessive. The decision was seen as a victory for opponents of punitive damage awards (Greenhouse 2001b).

In 1999, Alabama joined about two dozen states in placing a ceiling on punitive damages—this, after a jury awarded $581 million to a family that had been overcharged $1,200 for two satellite dishes. The Alabama law limits punitive damages in noninjury cases against large corporations to three times the compensatory damages or $500,000, whichever is greater. In injury cases, the caps are three times the compensatory damages or $1.5 million, whichever is greater (Firestone 1999). However, top state courts in more than a half-dozen states have struck down laws placing limits on liability awards as contrary to state constitutions (Glaberson 1999). In 1997, for example, the Illinois Supreme Court struck down a $500,000 cap on noneconomic damages. The court ruled that the legislature had violated the separation of powers by assuming powers reserved for the judicial branch to reduce excessive jury awards.

Critics argue that fear of potential liability claims caused one company to shelve an asbestos substitute, and the American Medical Association complains that lawsuits have forced all but one pharmaceutical firm out of birth-control research (Rengel 2000). In 1996, President Bill Clinton vetoed a bill that would have placed caps on the

"Caps" on Legal Representation

Kimberly, 41, died after hernia surgery during which it was confirmed that she had uterine cancer, a condition that doctors suspected but left untreated for months despite continued internal bleeding. Her mother wanted to know why doctors failed to act on her daughter's cancer symptoms or to adequately monitor the drugs given to prevent the bleeding and clotting that ultimately caused her death. But Arkansas has a $250,000 cap on pain and suffering that is awarded only if the plaintiff can prove malicious intent or recklessness, which is very hard to do. So Kimberly's mother was unable to find an attorney to represent her (Lieberman 2006).

The Drunk, the Train, the Award

In 1980, Francisco M. entered a New York City subway station. He was apparently intoxicated. A subway employee notified the police that an intoxicated man was on the platform. Before the police arrived, Mr. M. fell on the tracks, was hit by a train, and lost his arm. A jury awarded him $3.6 million, but a state appeals court dismissed this in 1996.

amount of money people injured by faulty products could win in lawsuits. The bill was part of a measure that had been included in the "Contract with America," the manifesto of Republican members of the House of Representatives (Lewis 1996). (In 1995 the president vetoed a bill to make it harder for stockholders to file lawsuits against corporations for securities fraud. Congress, however, overrode this veto.)

Trial lawyers argue that increases in tort litigation have been proportionate to the increase in population. "Sue the bastards" is apparently an old American tradition, and there are more lawyers than ever apparently eager to carry the tradition forward. Ironically, lawyers have increasingly become a target of **malpractice** suits, and many attorneys can no longer afford the cost of malpractice insurance (Talbac 1987). Some firms devote their entire practice to suing or defending attorneys in malpractice cases (Pérez-Peña 1994b). Personal injury lawyers, and those involved with securities and real estate syndication, have been the primary targets. The single most important factor in the increase of such suits is that lawyers are no longer seen simply as advocates, "but as advisers, deal makers and, in some instances, investors. And as they have become more versatile, they have also become more vulnerable" (Margolick 1988c: 25). But many malpractice lawsuits are the result of attorneys failing to meet filing deadlines and other routine matters (Pérez-Peña 1994b).

Malpractice and "Tort Reform"

The controversy over liability awards and the contingency fee has been particularly intense in the matter of medical malpractice, pitting doctors, hospitals, and their insurance companies against trial lawyers. Malpractice insurance premiums for obstetrics in some states reach $200,000 per year, and it sometimes takes three years to resolve these lawsuits, which means physicians must take time from their practices to do so. To avoid suits, doctors may order more tests to avoid being the target of a lawsuit (Furchtgott-Roth 2009). The rising cost of malpractice insurance has had an impact on health clinics, causing many to cut back or eliminate services for low-

Recklessness v. Negligence

In 2006, New York State's highest court ruled in favor of a $1.4 million award to the plaintiff who lost both his legs below the knee when hit by a subway train. The victim, 18 at the time of the accident, had been drinking with friends when they mistakenly concluded that trains were not running and jumped onto the catwalk (Donohue 2006).

> ### Malpractice
>
> "The average doctor in a high-risk practice like surgery or obstetrics is sued about once every six years. Seventy percent of the time, the suit is either won by the defendant or dismissed in court. But the cost of defense is high, and when doctors lose, the average jury verdict is half-a-million dollars. General surgeons pay anywhere from thirty thousand to two hundred thousand dollars a year in malpractice insurance premiums, depending on the litigation climate of the state they work in; neurosurgeons and obstetricians pay upward of fifty percent more" (Gawande 2005: 63).

income patients. These clinics treat high-risk patients such as pregnant women whose circumstances may cause them to neglect prenatal care until problems become acute. "Data from the American College of Obstetricians and Gynecologists (ACOG) projects a shortfall of between 9,000 and 14,000 obstetrician-gynecologists (ob-gyns) in the next 20 years" (Anderson 2013). The decrease in the number of ob-gyns is because of the high cost of insurance premiums. "Rising malpractice premiums are associated with an increased rate of exit and a reduced rate of entry for obstetricians" (Polsky, Marcus and Werner 2010: 61). "In many cases, ob-gyns can reduce their malpractice premiums in half by eliminating their obstetrical duties" (Anderson 2013). It is often rural and inner-city areas where low-income women are more likely to experience high-risk pregnancies that experience a shortage of obstetrical care.

One study revealed that out of 46 malpractice suits resolved after 10 years, in 13 cases where the records showed that there was no malpractice, litigants were nevertheless awarded an average of $98,192. In 10 cases, where injuries to the patient were clearly caused by the underlying disease, litigants received an average of $28,760 each from insurance companies eager to avoid the costs of a trial (Reuters 1996). But suing physicians and hospitals requires the use of use of expensive medical experts whose role colleagues may criticize and whose testimony is subject to critical scrutiny by medical society committees (Andrews 2003).

Some states have enacted legislation limiting pain-and-suffering awards, and congressional Republicans have endorsed "capping" legislation for the federal system. The cases of Harry Jordon and Agnes Mae Whitaker exemplify the difference that such legislation can make. Harry was a Californian with a malignant kidney. His Los Angeles surgeons accidentally removed the healthy one, relegating him to a short and painful life. The victim's award was reduced to $256,000 as the result of a California statute that limits pain and suffering awards (Quinn 1986). On the other hand, a jury in New York awarded Agnes Mae Whitaker, a victim of medical malpractice, a compensatory award of $7 million: Doctors had failed to diagnose an intestinal constriction that caused an infection requiring the removal of most of her small intestine. The jury also awarded Agnes an additional $58 million for pain-and-suffering (Editorial, *New York Times*, July 24, 1986: 22). New York subsequently enacted legislation that limits the amount of a single payment to a successful plaintiff to $250,000, with the remainder paid out over 10 years.

How Much Is a Career Worth?

The team surgeon for the New York Rangers operated successfully on the knee of a 43-year-old dance choreographer. Unfortunately, it was the wrong knee and the resulting arthritis ended his dancing career. He received a jury award of $450,000 (Peterson 2005).

By 1989, 23 states had enacted legislation placing caps on malpractice awards. In 2003, Texas voters approved a constitutional amendment limiting the amount a patient injured by faulty medical practice can receive to $250,000 from a doctor and $500,000 from a medical facility for pain and suffering, disfigurement, and other compensation. The amendment does not limit awards for loss of income and medical expenses (Blumenthal 2003).

President George W. Bush proposed a cap of $250,000 for noneconomic damages—despite the fact that defendants win nearly 80 percent of malpractice trials (Lohr 2005). In 2006, federal legislation to impose payments by individual doctors to $250,000 and health care institutions to $750,000 failed to pass the Senate (Stolberg 2006). A cap of $250,000 for noneconomic damages discourages attorneys from representing injured children since they have no economic value and the cost of employing experts would typically be in excess of the cap. In 2004, while campaigning for a cap on malpractice claims, President George W. Bush introduced an obstetrician/gynecologist who he said had been driven from his practice by frivolous lawsuits. In fact, the doctor had been driven from his practice by such malpractice as leaving a sponge inside a patient that subsequently adhered to her internal organs and required removal of part of her intestines (Herbert 2004).

A study by the *New York Times* (Steinhauer and Fessenden 2001: 24) revealed, "many New York hospitals routinely hire and retain doctors with bad records—especially those who bring a lot of money." A comprehensive study by the New York State Department of Health revealed that although thousands of deaths and tens of thousands of injuries are tied to medical negligence each year, relatively few result in any court action (Sack 1990). The National Academy of Sciences reports that in addition to those permanently disabled by in-hospital medical errors, errors kill 44,000 to 98,000 people a year (Pear 1999), figures that have been challenged by the medical establishment. A study of lawsuits against physicians in New Jersey (Taragin et al. 1993) found that the defensibility of a case generally determines outcome: The researchers (medical professionals) found that in 25 percent of the cases physician error was clear and

Oops!

A study by nine physicians (Stahel et al. 2010) of medical errors involving wrong-site and wrong-patient procedures concluded that the data are shocking: there is a high frequency of doctors operating on the wrong patient or on the wrong body part—errors termed *never events* because they should *never* happen.

in more than 90 percent of these cases judgments were (appropriately) for the plaintiffs. In the 62 percent of cases they considered defensible, physicians prevailed 80 percent of the time. In the remaining cases, it was not clear if physician care was defensible. They conclude: "Our findings suggest that unjustified payments are probably uncommon" (1993: 780). For a decade, the number of malpractice lawsuits filed has remained constant; two-thirds are dropped or dismissed, while fewer than 10 percent produce jury verdicts for patients claiming injury. A little less than one-third of the cases filed end with settlements that can be driven by the fear of a big jury verdict (Schmitt 2003).

An extensive research effort into medical malpractice, product liability, and punitive damage lawsuits concludes:

> The characterization of juries and the civil justice system animating the tort reform movement is at odds with the findings of systematic empirical research or is based

How Much Is a Death Worth?

While the controversy over "just" compensation for victims in tort cases continues, insurance companies are also concerned about the cost of "death compensation." Their attorneys argue that frequently "large jury verdicts include compensation for intangible non-economic injuries, like the decedent's pre-death fear or decedent's loss of enjoyment of life (hedonic damages) or for decedent's family's grief, anguish, mental distress, and loss of nurture, companionship and love. Without in any way questioning the significance of injuries, the fact is that money does not alleviate them." Therefore, "judges and juries should not be permitted to make financial awards for intangible non-economic losses [since] the law does not and cannot give juries and judges any legal principles or other useful yardsticks to determine how to evaluate these losses" (Craft 1989: 2).

Trial lawyers respond: "Money can make family members who have suffered a grievous loss feel better. The recognition by the law that they have suffered such a grievous loss at the hands of a negligent defendant gives rise to an expectation of damages. The recovery of these damages does fulfill a psychological need. And while it is true that revenge and punishment are not parts of compensatory damages, the fact is that aggrieved family members do derive satisfaction that the negligent defendant has been caused to pay for the loss. Furthermore to deny the victims adequate damages would only reward the defendant's wrongdoing" (Kreinler 1989: 2).

Tort Reform

"The genius of tort reform, which focuses on putting a cap on the awards from malpractice suits, is that it offends only one big-money lobbying group: trial lawyers who are important financial supporters of the Democratic Party. Meanwhile, it helps or holds harmless Republican special interests in the insurance, drug and health care industries" ("Malpractice Mythology" 2005: 12).

on claims about things for which there is little or no systematic research. This is especially true in terms of systematic evidence for the causal connections linking the legal system to a host of social and economic ills. Consequently, we are skeptical of the efficacy of enacted reforms and concerned about the possible unintended consequences of those measures. Beyond the self-interest of those groups lobbying for reform, we can see little reason for continuing or endorsing this reform movement. (Daniels and Martin 1995: 249)

Caps on awards for noneconomic damages such as "pain and suffering" have not necessarily translated into lower insurance rates for doctors, and some are calling, instead, for state regulation of medical insurance (Schmitt 2003; Springer 2005). California, for example, prohibits insurers from raising malpractice insurance rates more than 15 percent a year without a public hearing (Treaster and Brinkley 2005).

There has been what some call "silent tort reform." At the urging of industry groups, federal regulatory agencies have been promulgating rules that thwart efforts by trial lawyers and state attorneys general from applying higher state standards. Claiming a need for uniformity, federal agencies have been overriding states' rights in areas such as consumer safety and protection and discriminatory lending practices (Labaton 2006).

How Much Is *Your* Brain Worth?

Sylvia Richardson, 35, married with one daughter, went into a university medical center to have her wisdom tooth removed. The resident gave her 10 times the intended amount of anesthesia resulting in a 10-day coma and brain damage—she requires around-the-clock care. Indiana, which limited malpractice awards to $500,000, no matter how serious the incident, increased the amount to $750,000 as a result of this case (Wilkerson 1990).

The man who successfully lobbied for the Indiana cap on damage awards became the victim of medical malpractice that left him confined to a wheelchair and kept alive by a respirator. At age 49 and in constant pain, he was given less than two years to live. Like Mrs. Richardson, Frank Cornelius (1994) was limited to a damage award of $750,000, while his medical bills were in excess of $5 million.

Who Is Concerned with Justin?

In 1985, when he was 26 months old, Justin was rushed to a Florida public hospital suffering an asthma attack. He never left. By the following day, mistakes admitted to by the hospital left the boy with severe brain damage: He cannot walk, talk, breathe, or take nourishment without the aid of tubes. His mother wants Justin home, but she cannot afford to pay for the cost of care this would entail—Florida law limits the liability of state agencies to $200,000 (Navarro 1995; Rall 2010). "Throughout America there are thousands of doctors—working in hospitals, clinics and private offices—who hurt and even fatally injured patients through incompetence or carelessness yet remain in active practice" (Gavzer 1996: 4) because they are often protected by caps on liability in the name of "reform."

Too Little or Too Much?

A jury in Tampa, Florida, awarded $3.3 million to a man whose doctor fused the wrong vertebrae in his neck during surgery (Associated Press 2000b).

Class Action Lawsuits

The **class action lawsuit** is traditionally used when there are many parties involved to prevent the inconvenience of a multiplicity of lawsuits. "An early but important principle applied to class actions was that judgment would apply to absentee class members who were not parties in the court" (Alliance of American Insurers 1987: 39). The current controversy over class action lawsuits is the result of a 1966 change in Rule 23 of the *Federal Rules of Civil Procedure*, which most states copied. This statute authorizes the filing of a lawsuit brought by one plaintiff or a small number of persons on behalf of a larger number of persons, which the plaintiffs believe themselves to represent, such as Vietnam veterans exposed to Agent Orange, a toxic herbicide; industrial workers injured by exposure to toxic chemicals; prison inmates physically abused by prison employees; recipients of silicone breast implants found to cause systemic health problems; and shoppers whose personal and financial information was stolen due to a data/security breach at Target stores. The 1966 revision did away with the requirement that all individuals seeking money damages with class action lawsuits need to "opt in": sign on affirmatively. Instead, those whom the plaintiffs claim to represent are deemed to be part of the lawsuit unless they specifically "opt out": withdraw (Hensler et al. 1999).

Plaintiffs have standing as a group much as other recognized collectivities such as labor unions and corporations, but without the need for organization. "*Interest* provides the substitute for individual initiative and consent; the class action justifies action that legally binds another without his consent by pointing out that his interest is represented in a situation in which it is inconceivable that he would not wish his interest to be so pursued" (Yeazell 1987: 15).

But this presents a legal problem: Under our system of due process each individual is entitled to control the destiny of his or her own litigation. Generally, if the court certifies the lawsuit as a class action, all members of the class must be notified and given an opportunity to opt out of the class or lose the ability to bring an individual action. In some cases, however, notification is not required, and a person who may not be aware of the lawsuit loses the ability to bring an individual action at some later date.

Public interest groups frequently bring class action lawsuits on behalf of consumers or environmental concerns, and to protect minorities, women, the handicapped, and the elderly against discriminatory practices. In 1996, the Republican-controlled Congress banned class action suits by the federally funded Legal Services Corporation, eliminating "the most effective tool at the disposal of legal services lawyers for attacking systemic problems in government institutions and benefit programs" (Greenhouse 1996b: E5). There are also class action cases brought by lawyers for pecuniary reasons.

There are a few nominal plaintiffs who are members of the class, but the suit is usually the entrepreneurial undertaking of a law firm for a contingent fee. In class action cases the most important decision the court must make is whether the alleged claims can be combined into one lawsuit. A decision that the claims cannot be combined will inevitably cause the whole matter to go away because no one plaintiff has enough at stake to justify bringing the suit. Certification of the class, on the other hand, may allow the aggregation of small claims to the tune of millions of dollars—and a 30 percent contingent fee interest in an award of that size definitely justifies some real care and attention by the plaintiffs' law firm. (Neely 1985: 45)

In many cases "opportunistic lawyers themselves initiated litigation and used the club of costly adversarial legalism to extract settlements that primarily benefited the lawyers themselves" (Kagan 1994: 42). A growing number of companies are taking advantage of class action rules to immunize themselves against future litigation—they are initiating class action lawsuits against themselves. The firms encourage the litigation that they subsequently settle with inflated legal fees. This enriches plaintiff attorneys while limiting the ability of those harmed to subsequently litigate claims against the company (Meier 1996).

In order for their claims to be accepted, "litigants must show that they are proper representatives for the class of persons they seek to champion, that the type of issues they wish to raise are common to the class, and they must be able to demonstrate how a remedy can be formed that will meet the needs of the class" (Cooper 1988: 15). If the class prevails in the tort, "it is entitled to a remedy that embraces all its members, even though only one or two have participated actively in the lawsuit" (Yeazell 1987: 1).

While Scott Baldwin (1984), former president of the Association of Trial Lawyers of America (changed to American Association for Justice in 2006), argues that the class action contingency fee is the only sure way to protect the "little guy." Wall Street attorney Stephen Case (1984) responds that plaintiff attorneys are grossly overcompensated in class action suits. Case notes that in every tort case two issues must be resolved: (1) Did the defendant commit a wrong? (e.g., market an unsafe product), and (2) how much money should the claimant receive? In mass torts there can be dozens, and sometimes hundreds or thousands, of claimants represented by a single attorney

"Winners" and Lawyers

A real estate broker in Portland, Maine, discovered he had won $2.19 in a class action lawsuit brought against his bank, an action he knew nothing about until he spotted a $91.33 miscellaneous deduction from his escrow account—it went to pay an $8.5 million fee for "his" lawyers (Meier 1995). The broker brought a lawsuit against the lawyers, an action supported by the attorney generals of several states (Meier 1997a). The case was dismissed in federal court and the Supreme Court refused to consider his appeal.

In 2001, lawyers earned $22 million in the settlement of a class action lawsuit against a consumer electronics company; consumers received $50 rebate coupons on future purchases. That same year, as a result of a suit against Blockbuster over its late fee policy, consumers received coupons for free movie rentals—lawyers earned $9.25 million (Lavelle 2005).

Class Action: Opposing Views

"Conservatives and business groups say class actions are a form of regulation through litigation and insert courts into matters better left to administrative bodies [or legislators]. Consumer and civil rights lawyers counter that without class action treatment, grave but widely dispersed wrongs would never be addressed" (Liptak 2011b: WK 5).

or small law firm. Contingency fees in such cases can range in the millions, although the work involved is not significantly more complex than in single-plaintiff cases.

Baldwin (1984) counters that references to the mass tort by attorneys representing corporate interests are merely a smokescreen to divert attention from the real damages, pain, and suffering inflicted on real persons who, without the class action contingency fee, would not have the funds necessary to deal with the legal resources of corporate law firms. Trial lawyers involved in class action lawsuits often expend considerable resources over many years in a venture that may yield no profits. In cases such as those involving the Dalkon Shield, asbestos, and Rely tampons, there were thousands of clients and complex scientific questions that had to be dealt with (e.g., see Bacigal 1990). In some cases they required an investment by the lawyers of several million dollars. For example, in the "Agent Orange" case, five lawyers each contributed more than $250,000 to a common defense fund (Wagner 1986). A cap on judgments would make such cases not worth the gamble, leave injured parties without legal representation, and reduce the incentive to deal with the negligence that is at the root of personal injury judgments.

While class action lawsuits can provide impressive contingency fees for attorneys, individual claimants may actually derive very little, because the settlement has to be shared among so many persons. Without going to trial to fight for a better deal, class action lawyers can settle for a few cents on the dollar for their clients while earning millions of dollars in legal fees for themselves (Eichenwald 1993). In 1994, about a dozen law firms, serving as class action counsel, shared $22 million dollars in a settlement with a major securities company, while defrauded investors received about $679 each. Ironically, the lawyers originally settled for a lesser amount, which was rejected by the court. Those who opted out of the class action did considerably better in their settlements (Eichenwald 1994). For more than three decades, however, judges have usually employed the *lodestar formula* to determine attorney fees in class action cases.

In the **lodestar method**,

> the court makes a determination of the number of hours that were "reasonably" spent on the case by the plaintiff class attorney (usually a matter of some dispute) and multiplies this by the going hourly billing rate for lawyers of "comparable" skills (another area of dispute). This product is called the "lodestar" and reflects roughly what the lawyers would have received had they been paid contemporaneously on an hourly rate. The lodestar is then adjusted upward by various multipliers to reflect such factors as the risk of losing the case (in which event there would be no fee at all) and the delay between the effort and deferred compensation. The final result is the attorney fee award. (Lynk 1994: 187–88)

> **Lawsuit Lending**
>
> During the past decade financial institutions, banks, hedge funds, and private investors have been financing lawsuits. Trial attorneys seek investments—loans—to cover the expenses of litigation, hiring expert witnesses, for example. Similar to mortgage lending, investors hire experienced attorneys to appraise the strength of the lawsuit. Interest, usually 15 to 20 percent, is billed to the client, who may not be aware of the arrangement until the case is concluded; accumulated interest can exceed the benefits of winning. There is also the issue of confidentiality when attorneys provide client information to the lender (Applebaum 2010). A powerful opponent of lawsuit lending is the United States Chamber of Commerce that argues the practice could encourage frivolous lawsuits, while the American Bar Association has remained neutral (Alden 2012).

In response to criticism, the "Class Action Fairness Act of 2005" requires that (except in securities cases) class action lawsuits involving more than 100 plaintiffs and $5 million be filed in federal rather than state courts. Removing the state courts from class action jurisdiction is problematic because federal courts are notoriously slow: Thus, in 2005, Exxon Mobil was continuing to appeal a $4.5 billion judgment lodged against it in 1994 on behalf of fishing and other businesses destroyed by the *Exxon Valdez* oil spill off of the coast of Alaska in 1989 (Lavelle 2005). In an editorial, the *New York Times* noted that the federal courts are already stretched thin and the Class Action Fairness Act is destined "to delay or deny justice in many cases, and to discourage plaintiffs and plaintiffs' lawyers from pursuing legitimate claims in the first place" ("Class Action Lawsuits" 2005: 20). There remain "carve-outs," exceptions ensuring that certain cases remain in state court, such as class actions that involve a local controversy (Wenger 2010).

The 2005 act also states that if a settlement provides for coupons, the portion of any attorney's fee award attributable to the coupons shall be based on the value to class members of the coupons that are actually redeemed or "upon the amount of time class counsel reasonably expended working on the action." If any settlement would result in a net loss to the class member, the court must determine "if the nonmonetary benefits to the class member substantially outweigh the monetary loss." Consumer contracts often require arbitration and include waivers of the right to bring a class action lawsuit, a practice upheld by the Supreme Court (*AT & T Mobility v. Concepcion* [2011]).

Legal Aid

While a criminal defendant facing incarceration is entitled to be represented by competent counsel, persons with civil grievances or defendants in a noncriminal action have no such constitutional entitlement. Justice has a price that most Americans cannot afford to pay (unless there is a contingency fee): "Throughout most of our history, few of the poor have been able to turn to the courts for redress of their grievances and participate in judicial development of law and policy" (Lawrence 1990: ix).

The European Convention on Human Rights recognizes the right to counsel in civil cases as a fundamental human right, and all Western democracies furnish counsel for those who cannot afford their own in civil litigation. According to English law, "no one needing the protection of an English Court should be denied this for lack of means," and "the courts can fulfill their function of administering the law effectively, [only] through the parties coming before them on equal terms, irrespective of their financial resources" (Ritchey 2001: 333).

In the United States, in the years just before and immediately after the First World War, there was fear of civil unrest that intensified with the Bolshevik Revolution in Russia. Immigrants who had fueled the Industrial Revolution were now seen as potential revolutionaries. Strikes and mass demonstrations for higher wages, better working conditions, and a 40-hour workweek were viewed as the forerunner of radical upheavals. The American Bar Association argued that the influx of foreigners was at the heart of the problem. It was important to educate these alien elements, to show them that they had a stake in the American system. Law and courts, not strikes and violence, are the American way, said the ABA. The bar had a responsibility, a *noblesse oblige*, to promote justice under law (Auerbach 1976).

Legal Aid Societies

German Americans founded the Legal Aid Society in New York in 1876 to assist their compatriots, many of whom were being preyed on by confidence men. The society subsequently expanded its services generally to the poor, and other cities followed the New York example. A society was formed in Chicago in 1886 to aid young women who were being lured into prostitution with duplicitous offers of legitimate employment. By the turn of the century, there were legal aid societies in six cities, and in 1909, the first bar association-sponsored Legal Aid Society was established. Most societies, however, were supported by private contributions, and expansion of legal aid was primarily the result of the efforts of Arthur von Briesen, a Prussian immigrant who served the Union during the Civil War. He warned potential contributors that the alternative to legal aid was civil strife and political disorder—given the times, a very realistic approach to raising money. As fear of social unrest increased, so did the expansion of legal aid societies. Although there were only 15 by 1910, that number increased to 41 in the next decade, and by 1923 there were 61. In 1914, Reginald Heber Smith, a young Harvard Law School graduate, became the head of the newly formed Boston Legal Aid Society. He was appalled by the lack of legal services for the poor. Traveling on a Carnegie Foundation grant, Smith toured the United States visiting legal aid societies and courts. The result was a book, *Justice and the Poor* (1919). Because of his efforts, the National Organization of Legal Aid Organizations (now known as the National Legal Aid & Defender Association) was formed, and the ABA established a standing committee on legal aid.

Legal aid societies limited their assistance to the "deserving poor," those who were employed, and cases accepted were too petty for any private attorney—the societies wanted to avoid competing with the private bar. They did not involve themselves in law reform, rarely engaging in the appellate process. The continuing inability of legal aid even to begin to address the issue of equal justice under law eventually led to the establishment of the Legal Services Corporation and public interest law firms.

Federal Legal Services

In 1965, as part of President Lyndon B. Johnson's "War on Poverty," Congress autho-rized funding for legal aid for the poor in civil and criminal cases under the Office of Economic Opportunity (OEO). The program came in the wake of urban riots, much as the impetus for earlier legal aid was the unrest a half century earlier. Legal services had the support of the president of the ABA, Lewis F. Powell, Jr., who was later appointed to the Supreme Court by President Richard Nixon. Bar groups, however, wanted assurance that the legal services attorneys would not compete with local pri-vate practitioners. Under OEO legislation, local groups with federal funding opened neighborhood law offices. They were soon swamped by more needy clients than the lawyers could properly represent (Johnson 1974).

A review of program goals led to the conclusion that funding provided by the fed-eral government could not even begin to meet the legal needs of the poor. A new strat-egy was developed. Instead of handling the problems of the poor simply on an individual basis, legal services attorneys would work for law reform that could affect large numbers of poor persons—the instrumental use of law. The legal services lawyer would move from a client server role to that of a law reformer:

> Prior to the establishment of the Legal Services [Corporation], the [Supreme] Court had seldom addressed the civil claims of the poor. There is a very simple explana-tion for this. The de facto assistance of counsel requirement had prevented those poor whose legal claims did not fit into an interest group's litigation strategy from bringing their cases to the Court. The philosophy of the legal aid societies pro-duced a set of lawyers representing the poor who had little interest in litigation and even less in appellate advocacy. The poor's claims were rarely placed on the Court's jurisdictional agenda. (Lawrence 1990: 149)

As a result of legal services litigation, the Supreme Court began to focus on poverty issues outside of criminal justice, using the due process and equal protection clauses to supervise the state's interaction with the less fortunate.

The goal of law reform was advanced by the quality of attorney attracted to the legal services program; elite law school graduates who would normally be destined for corporate practice were energized by the prospects of social action through law. During the entire history of the Legal Aid Society, no staff attorney had ever taken a case to the Supreme Court, but between 1967 and 1972, legal services attorneys took 219, 136 of which were decided on their merits, and 73 of these were won (Johnson 1974). Federal legal services had a dramatic impact on legislative and executive branch policy. Casebooks on poverty law were published and law schools began pre-senting courses on poverty law (Lawrence 1990).

By 1973, there were more than 900 legal services offices around the country employing close to 5,000 lawyers. They initiated class action suits against powerful interests. Without an overall national strategy, they forced federal and local govern-mental agencies to pay benefits to poor persons as mandated by welfare legislation; they forced the public schools to admit children of illegal aliens; they forced public hospitals to provide free abortions to indigent women; and they initiated litigation to force officials to improve jail conditions. The legal services attorneys upset business and farming communities by litigating to enforce state and federal statutes with respect to wages and working conditions. In addition to its efforts on behalf of farm-workers, California Rural Legal Assistance forced the state to increase Medicaid and other welfare payments. (For a discussion of major legal services cases and strategies, see Lawrence 1990.) Then-Governor Ronald Reagan was unsuccessful in his efforts to cut off funding for the group.

In 1974, President Nixon signed legislation creating the Legal Services Corpora-tion (LSC) to insulate the activities of legal services lawyers from increasing political pressures. Soon after Ronald Reagan was elected president, however, he moved to abolish the program, asking Congress to cut out all appropriations. Congress refused, although funding was cut back 25 percent, and significant restrictions were placed on the types of cases legal services lawyers could handle. The 1974 legislation provided for a governing board of 11 members appointed by the president, and in his continu-ing efforts to destroy the program, President Reagan nominated opponents of legal services to the governing board. In the first three years of his presidency, he nomi-nated 26 people for the board, all opponents of legal services, none of whom were con-firmed by the Republican-controlled Senate. Under President George H. W. Bush, this policy continued. Both Reagan and Bush resorted to recess appointments in order to delay Senate confirmation, and over a period of a decade they were successful in stacking the board with legal services opponents. Two presidents of the American Bar Association, in 1986 and 1988, called for the removal of the chair of the Legal Services Corporation because of his hostility toward the mission of the very agency that he was chosen by the president to head (Raven 1988). The LSC chairman, a former aide to Senator Jesse Helms (R-NC), hired an attorney to draft a brief contending the corpora-tion unconstitutional, and he hired lobbyists to convince Congress to cut the corpora-tion's budget (Lewis 1989a).

The battle over the role of government in providing legal assistance for the poor continues, with the ABA on the side of continued funding and many political conser-vatives and the US Chamber of Commerce in opposition. The latter have accused the LSC of being antibusiness and "part of a political movement that views the American free enterprise system as a grand conspiracy" (DiLorenzo 1988: 3). Maggie Gallagher, a syndicated columnist and senior fellow at American Principles Project, a conserva-tive nonprofit organization, refers to the LSC as "a $300-million cornucopia for rebel lawyers with a cause. In the guise of helping the poor," she argues, "taxpayers' money goes to radical legal think-tanks, strategy sessions, and class action lawsuits that have sought, in many cases successfully, to expand the welfare state and undermine bour-geois social values" (1988: 42).

With the election of Bill Clinton as US president, a new board, with members com-mitted to the concept of Legal Services Corporation, was chosen. Nevertheless, in 1996 a Republican-controlled Congress succeeded in slashing the program's budget by 30 percent and enacted a ban on LSC lawyers bringing class action lawsuits, an impor-tant tool in policy-oriented litigation (Bernstein 1996).

Many of the most far-reaching LSC lawsuits had involved welfare cases, so the 1996 Congress "also prohibited the lawyers from taking part in any cases challenging the administration of welfare laws" (Greenhouse 1996b: E5). In addition, the legisla-tion limited the freedom to represent client interests before legislative and administra-tive bodies. In 2001, the Supreme Court, in a 5–4 decision, ruled that this legislation violated the First Amendment by denying LSC attorneys the right to act as advocates (*Legal Services Corporation v. Velasquez*), But the irony continues: America has a glut of lawyers and an absence of affordable legal services.

In an effort to provide funds for legal services for the poor, every state has adopted a program known as "Interest on Lawyers' Trust Accounts (IOLTA)." Lawyers are usually required to hold their client's money, such as escrow for real estate closings, in short-term accounts on which no interest is paid. With support from the ABA, these accounts are now pooled, and the net interest diverted to help support legal services programs. Opposing legal services for the poor, the conservative Washington Legal Foundation brought suit against IOLTA, arguing that diverting the interest was a "taking of private property without just compensation," a violation of the Fifth Amendment. In a 5–4 decision, the Supreme Court ruled that transaction costs on individual accounts would have wiped out any interest so there was no issue of "just compensation" (*Brown v. Legal Foundation of Washington* [2003]). Significant declines in bank interest rates have impacted the IOLTA program.

> "A panoply of fundamental rights is rendered inconsequential
> if people lack the resources and access to vindicate them.
> Yet in a system that lauds its adherence to the rule of law, the
> inattention to equal access to justice is shameful" (Carasik 2011: 798).

Public Interest Law

Public interest law is the name given to the provision of legal representation to interests that historically have been unrepresented and underrepresented in the legal process (Council for Public Interest Law; hereafter CPIL 1976). Along with civil rights and civil liberties organizations, public interest lawyers "share an enthusiasm for using the legal system to redress social and economic injustices" (Aron 1989: 3).

There are two kinds of public interest law programs:

1. Programs established to "focus on policy-oriented cases, where a decision will affect large numbers of people or advance a major law reform objective." Test cases are selected because they have the potential to extend beyond the particular litigants, e.g., those involving the environment or civil rights (CPIL 1976: 7). The interest group controls the arguments advanced in an attempt to affect policy. Instead of direct representation, public interest firms may submit *amicus curiae* briefs.

2. Programs "designed to provide legal services to underserved groups on matters of immediate concern only to the parties directly involved," such as those provided by legal aid societies, public defenders, and neighborhood legal services offices (CPIL 1976: 7).

The first type of public interest law is of rather recent vintage. As noted in Chapter 5, historically, the judicial branch often thwarted legislative efforts designed to improve the situation of disadvantaged portions of our population, such as blacks, workers, children, the mentally ill, and the poor. While those on the left of the political spectrum advocated legislative remedies, those on the right found comfort in the courts. Over the years, however, the legislative branch became increasingly tolerant of activities that often denied equal protection and due process to less powerful elements in society. The Supreme Court, headed by Earl Warren, gave impetus to those seeking to use the judicial branch to advance liberal causes that had failed in the legislative branch. Policy-oriented public interest law emerged from this perspective and from the political activism of the civil rights and Vietnam War era.

> Influenced by the activism of the antiwar, civil rights, feminist, and environmental movements of the late 1960s and early 1970s, public interest lawyers have developed a common set of goals: to make government more accountable to the public and more responsive to the concerns and needs of unrepresented persons; to increase the power of citizens' groups; to insist on a place at the bargaining table; and to ensure that the development of public policy is open to public scrutiny. (Aron 1989: 3–4)

The public interest law firm is generally an independent, tax-exempt corporation operating under a board of trustees and funded chiefly by foundation grants and individual contributions. These firms usually combine traditional legal activities with research, publication, organizing, and public education. One of the best known public interest firms is the Legal Defense Educational Fund of the National Association for the Advancement of Colored People (NAACP): "Virtually all subsequent public interest legal endeavors have followed in some respects the early example of the NAACP" (CPIL 1976: 34).

Public interest law firms usually specialize in a particular area of advocacy and litigation. Public Justice, a Washington-based public interest law firm, seeks damages on behalf of victims of government and corporate misconduct. Cases accepted by the firm must have a far-reaching effect on public interest litigation and set precedents for similar actions. Such cases generally have the potential for large monetary damage awards to alleviate the suffering of the victim and punish the wrongdoer. The cases must involve unique legal issues that demonstrate a creative use of law for the public good. The firm has brought suit against a number of companies on behalf of persons harmed from exposure to toxic chemicals and against government officials for failing to protect persons from contaminated water. Public Justice has utilized the federal Clean Water Act, which allows citizens to file suit against companies to force compliance with federal law. This is designed to improve water quality through punishing polluting companies with steep fines. The firm's activities are supported by private contributions, settlement fees, and pro bono work by numerous attorneys. Public Justice attorneys have been fighting against legislative efforts to limit the size of awards in personal injury cases.

The Washington-based Center for Law and Social Policy was established in 1969 by four attorneys in the District of Columbia to work on behalf of the poor and the physically and mentally disabled. In addition to its advocacy efforts, the center sponsors a law school clinic, for which approximately 20 law school students a year receive academic credit. Equal Rights Advocates of San Francisco specializes in cases involv-

National Association for the Advancement of Colored People

Founded in 1909, the NAACP was originally a lobbying and educational group. It gradually increased its activities to include litigation through its Legal Defense Educational Fund (LDEF), which became independent in 1939. By 1921, the NAACP had won court cases on voting, housing, and grand juries; it was the LDEF (with lead attorney and later Supreme Court justice Thurgood Marshall) that litigated the issue of school segregation culminating in the decision of *Brown v. Board of Education*. The strategy used by the NAACP to challenge segregation was based on two major points, which are described by Rosemary Salomone: "First sue for equal schools [as per the *Plessy* decision] on the theory that the cost of maintaining a dual system would prove so prohibitive as to speed the abolition of a segregated system. Second, pursue desegregation on the university level where it was likely to meet the least resistance. Then proceed incrementally to the elementary and secondary level" (1986: 41).

The CPIL (1976) lists the elements of the model developed by the LDEF:

- Used full-time, salaried staff attorneys
- Avoided routine service cases and took on those that affected issues beyond the immediate concern of individual litigants
- Assumed a proactive posture, seeking out cases with issues that could bring about changes in the ways in which political and social institutions dealt with blacks
- Raised funds from widespread membership efforts
- Rejected the accumulation of big cases in favor of incremental victories that built a favorable legal climate and fostered a positive public and legislative climate that could be converted into changed behavior patterns
- Created a network of private attorneys to follow up on court victories and convert the rights won in court into practical substantive benefits

ing employment and employment-related discrimination against women. The firm chooses cases that will have an impact—either because of the number of people who will be affected by the results or because of the legal principle that will be established—with respect to pay equity, sexual harassment, access to nontraditional jobs, or pregnancy-based discrimination.

The Economic Justice Institute (EJI) is headquartered in Madison, Wisconsin, where it operates a clinical program with the University of Wisconsin Law School. EJI specializes in issues relating to health care cost containment, particularly for senior citizens. Founded in 1972, the Bazelon Center for Mental Health Law (BCMHL) is a public interest law firm that litigates on behalf of children and adults with mental disabilities. BCMHL litigation has improved conditions for persons confined to institutions and resulted in the establishment of community care for those inappropriately confined. The Washington-based center is supported by foundation grants, government contracts, sales of publications, and income from an endowment.

With the establishment of the Pacific Legal Foundation in 1973, a new development in the field of public interest law emerged—firms with expressly conservative or probusiness agendas. They hold the more traditional public interest legal firms largely responsible for overregulation of business "and see themselves as a balance to the influence such groups exercise over public policy" (Aron 1989: 74). Conservative public interest law firms receive most of their financial support from corporations or corporate foundations.

The Washington Legal Foundation (WLF) was established in 1977 to promote "free enterprise and economic growth." The Washington Legal Foundation defends and promotes the principles of free enterprise and individual rights by shaping public policy through aggressive litigation and advocacy, publishing timely legal studies, and educating policy makers and the public through extensive communications outreach, including media briefings and web seminars. Its 2012 Annual Report sates:

> Our litigation team, with the help of scores of prestigious law firms nationwide, rigorously monitors and intervenes in any case, action, or complaint that threatens the fundamental rights of hard-working Americans and the integrity of the country's legal system. When government agencies interfere with those rights in a manner we deem unwarranted, WLF's litigation team does not hesitate to challenge those agencies in court.

The National Chamber Litigation Center (NCLC) was founded in 1977 as a public policy law firm for the US Chamber of Commerce. The NCLC represents the business community in issues of national concern before the courts and regulatory agencies. The Mountain States Legal Foundation is a public interest legal center, which, according to its website, is "dedicated to individual liberty, the right to own and use property, limited government and the free enterprise system."

According to their literature, the Thomas More Law Center (TMLC) is a not-for-profit public interest law firm whose "mission is to restore and defend America's Judeo-Christian heritage and moral values, and to preserve a strong national defense, and a free and sovereign United States of America." TMLC is dedicated to defending religious freedom of Christians; restoring family values; defending the sanctity of human life on issues such as abortion, pornography, and same-sex marriage; defending national security; and confronting the threat of radical Islam. Their avowed purpose is to be "the sword and shield for people of faith," providing legal representation without charge to defend and protect Christians and their religious beliefs in the public square. They achieve this goal principally through litigation by seeking out cases that align with their mission.

In the next chapter, we will turn to the justice system used for juveniles.

SUMMARY

- The major difference between civil and criminal actions is that a defendant's freedom is not at stake.
- The government provides a forum for settling private disputes that disputants are under no legal obligation to utilize.
- Few civil cases are adjudicated with a formal trial.
- A trial may not be the goal; instead, there is a need for a judicial declaration.
- A civil case involves a complaining party who demands a remedy from the courts for an asserted legal wrong, and a defending party who denies having a legal obli-

gation or contends that its legal obligation is different or less than the complaining party contends.

- A civil case may involve disputes of both fact and law.
- There are important distinctions between civil and criminal justice.
- To prevail in a lawsuit, the plaintiff must prove both that the defendant committed an act that caused injury and that the act was a legal wrong.
- While the rules of evidence are generally the same, the law of criminal evidence has more restrictions favoring the defendant.
- In a civil case, a litigant must have *standing* so that the adversarial model will be fully operative.
- Civil juries frequently have fewer than 12 members, and unanimity is often not required.
- In civil cases, jurisdiction can be quite complex.
- The Constitution provides that judgments rendered by a state court are enforceable in all states.
- Jurisdiction can be exercised over the defendant, *in personam*, or over things and status, *in rem*.
- The civil process utilizes extensive *discovery* procedures, and defendants have no Fifth Amendment protection against extensive requests for information.
- The discovery phase of litigation can be lengthy and costly, providing an advantage to those litigants who can afford to absorb such costs.
- Civil and criminal trials are conducted in the same manner.
- The civil division of a state court system has specialized courts, such as chancery, family, probate, juvenile, and small-claims.
- The contingency fee offers a partial answer to the problem of providing legal assistance to persons without financial means who have suffered a tort.
- The *contingency fee* is criticized because it hinders lawyers in providing the kind of dispassionate professional advice they should be rendering to their clients.
- Damages awarded in civil trial litigation can take the form of compensatory or punitive awards.
- Some jurisdictions have caps on awards for pain and suffering.
- The contingency fee has pitted trial lawyers against insurance companies.
- A class action lawsuit is used when there are many parties whose individual loss is not sufficient to justify a lawsuit.
- The Legal Aid Society represents an effort to provide legal representation in civil cases that do not offer a significant contingency fee.
- Federal legal services attracted the opposition of political conservatives by engaging in policy-oriented litigation.
- Public interest law firms provide legal representation to interests that historically have been unrepresented and underrepresented in the legal process.
- Public interest law firms focus on cases that have a policy impact.

KEY TERMS

at issue
attachment
citation
class action lawsuit
clear and convincing evidence
compensatory damages
contingency fee
damages
default judgment
demurrer
deposition
disbarment
discovery
English rule
ex contractu
ex delicto

execute
extenuating circumstances
failure of proof
full faith and credit
garnishment
in personam
in rem
interrogatories
joinder of parties/claims
justiciable
legal aid
lodestar method
malpractice
moot case
negligence

nullum crimen sine lege
poll of the jury
preponderance of
  the evidence
prima facie case
public interest law
punitive damages
quash
remittitur
request for admission
res judicata
special verdict
standing
summary judgment
tort

REVIEW QUESTIONS

1. What is the primary difference between a civil and a criminal case?
2. What are the common elements in a civil case?
3. What are important distinctions between civil and criminal justice?
4. Why does a litigant in a civil case need standing?
5. Why is jurisdiction complex in a civil case?
6. How is *in personam* jurisdiction distinguished from *in rem* jurisdiction?
7. How does discovery in a civil differ from that in a criminal case?
8. How can discovery be used as a tactical tool in civil litigation?
9. What are the differences in how civil and criminal trials are conducted?
10. What is the purpose of a small-claims court?
11. What is the purpose of the contingency fee?
12. What is the conflict of interest problem with the contingency fee?
13. How does a compensatory award differ from a punitive award?
14. What are the arguments for and against caps on medical malpractice awards?
15. What are the arguments for and against a cap on pain and suffering?
16. What are the arguments over contingency fees that have pitted trial lawyers against insurance companies?
17. What is a class action lawsuit?
18. What are the criticisms of class action lawsuits?
19. What are the arguments in favor of class action lawsuits?

20. What is the role of the Legal Aid Society?

21. What was the activity of federal legal services that attracted the opposition of political conservatives?

22. What are the characteristics of a public interest law firm?

INTERNET CONNECTIONS

American Association for Justice: http://justice.org/cps/rde/xchg/justice/hs.xsl/default.htm

Bazelon Center for Mental Health Law: http://www.bazelon.org

Center for Law and Social Policy: http://www.clasp.org

Equal Rights Advocates: http://www.equalrights.org

Law Guru: http://www.lawguru.com

Legal Sites on the Web: http://ih2000.net/ira/legal.htm

Public Justice: http://publicjustice.net

Thomas More Public Interest Law Center: http://www.thomasmore.org

Washington Legal Foundation: http://wlf.org

11

Juvenile Justice

The goals of **juvenile** justice and the procedures of the juvenile court are so different from both the criminal *and* the civil processes that juvenile justice warrants its own coverage. We will review the historical development and legal foundations of juvenile justice, procedures of the juvenile court, and juveniles prosecuted in criminal court.

History and Philosophy

In Europe, from Roman times to the late eighteenth century, children were routinely abandoned by their parents; the classical philosopher Rousseau, for example, boasted of abandoning five of his children to foundling homes (Boswell 1989). Abandoned children were subjected to extreme levels of deprivation and exploitation. English common law considered children as chattel, and a rather indifferent attitude toward children became characteristic of America, where children became creatures of exploitation. Child labor remained an important part of economic life into the twentieth century. Children of the poor labored in mines (where their size was an advantage), mills, and factories with unsanitary and unsafe conditions. As noted in Chapter 6, the Supreme Court reflected the prevailing belief in *laissez-faire* capitalism and would not intervene—statutes prohibiting children under 12 from employment and limiting the workday of youngsters over 12 to 10 hours were ruled unconstitutional or routinely disobeyed. Increased immigration, industrialization, and urbanization drastically altered American society. The 10- and 12-hour workday left many children without parental supervision, and family disorganization became widespread. Many children lived in the streets, where they encountered the disorder and rampant vice of the urban environment.

In the early days of colonial America, the family remained the mainstay of social control, "although by 1700 the family's inability to accommodate and discipline its young was becoming more apparent" (Mennel 1973: xxii). Numerous laws began to appear, threatening parents for failing to properly discipline their children. Furthermore, the British practice of transporting wayward young to America for indenture, which often involved neglect, cruelty, and immorality, left many youngsters without supervision as they fled from these onerous circumstances. By the end of the eighteenth century society began to realize that a "system of social control would have to be developed apart from the family which would discipline homeless, vagrant, and destitute children—the offspring of the poor" (1973: xxvii). This need led to the rise of houses of refuge.

The first house of refuge opened in New York in 1825 and was quickly followed by one in Boston (1826) and another in Philadelphia (1828). These institutions provided housing and care for troublesome children who might otherwise be left in the streets or, if their behavior brought them into serious conflict with the law, sent to jail or prison. The house of refuge was used "not only for the less serious juvenile criminal, but for runaways, disobedient children or vagrants" (Empey 1979: 25–26). Orphan asylums were used for abandoned or orphaned children, for the children of women without husbands, or for children whose parents were "unfit." These institutions "were established to inculcate children with the values of hard work, orderliness, and subordination and thereby ensure their future good behavior" (Mennel 1973: 8). To achieve these ends, however, discipline and punishments were often brutal, and the house of refuge in New York experienced group escapes and inmate uprisings.

Although these institutions were run by private charities, their public charters included the first statutory definitions of juvenile delinquency and provided the basis for the state to intervene in the lives of children who were neglected or in need of supervision, in addition to those youngsters who had committed crimes (Walker 1998). Within these charters was embodied a "medieval English doctrine of nebulous origin and meaning" (Schlossman 1977: 8) known as **parens patriae**, originally referring to the feudal duties of the overlord to his vassals and later the legal duties of the king toward his subjects who were in need of care, particularly children and the mentally incompetent. In its original form, *parens patriae* provided the Crown with authority to administer the estates of landed orphans (Sutton 1988). The legal system's exercise of jurisdiction over families and children in the United States is founded on principles of equity (National Council of Juvenile and Family Court Judges 1988).

"With the independence of the American colonies," states Herbert Lou, writing in 1927, "and the transplanting of the English common-law system, the state in this country has taken the place of the crown as the *parens patriae* of all minors" (1972: 4). This concept gave almost complete authority over children to the state—the Bill of Rights simply did not apply to children (*Ex parte Crouse* [1838])—and *parens patriae* became the legal basis for the juvenile court. Although *parens patriae* has become identified with the rehabilitation of juvenile delinquents, it originally applied only to dependent children.

As the end of the nineteenth century approached, both immigration and urbanization continued unabated, and the specter of masses of undisciplined and uneducated children gave rise to the child-saving movement. Led by middle- and upper-class women of earlier American stock, the child savers were influenced by nativist prejudices of their day and, later, by social Darwinism (discussed in Chapter 6), in addition to more humane motivations. The juvenile court was the result of their efforts, although controversy surrounds the interests and motivations of the child savers.

Anthony Platt argues that these women, although they "viewed themselves as altruists and humanitarians dedicated to rescuing those who were less fortunately placed in the social order," were actually motivated by boredom and middle- and upper-class social, economic, and political interests (1977: 3). "The child-savers were concerned not with championing the rights of the poor against exploitation by the ruling class but rather integrating the poor into the established social order and protecting 'respectable' citizens from the 'dangerous classes'" of people, who might otherwise be drawn into social revolution, if not criminality (Platt quoted in Empey 1979: 31). According to Platt, the juvenile court would serve to protect propertied and commercial interests from the predations of lower-class youngsters while ensuring an adequate supply of disciplined and vocationally trained labor. In fact, however, many states had already separated juvenile cases from those of adults without establishing a distinct juvenile court. And the movement to establish a juvenile court was part of a larger program of social reform advocated by the Progressives of the late nineteenth and early twentieth centuries. David Rothman (in Empey, 1979: 37) places the issue in perspective: The juvenile court movement "satisfied [both] the most humanitarian of impulses and the most crudely self-interested considerations."

Something had to be done to save the children from their environment of ignorance and vice, or they would become progenitors of the same. The asylum, the house of refuge, and the reformatory were all part of this movement, but the most important accomplishment was the establishment of the juvenile court.

Juvenile Court

Although common law did not differentiate between adults and minors, in most states a minor was 10 to 12 years of age (McMillian 1999). A minor might be sent to the house of refuge or the reformatory instead of jail or prison, but he or she could be arrested, detained, and tried like any adult accused of a crime. A few jurisdictions modified their trial process for children in the decades after the Civil War in an attempt to separate them from adult offenders, but "it was left to Illinois to pass the first comprehensive law to create the first specially organized juvenile court" (Lou 1972: 19). That this occurred in Chicago was no coincidence. Chicago was the scene of rapid urbanization. From 1890 to 1900, the population increased almost 50 percent, with 70 percent of the residents being foreign born (Pettibone et al. 1981). In 1893, there was an economic panic, and as conditions of the poor continued to deteriorate, reforming juvenile justice became the primary goal of the child savers, women who "were generally well educated, widely traveled, and had access to political and financial resources" (Platt 1977: 77).

The first juvenile court was established in Cook County (whose county seat is Chicago) on July 1, 1899, the result of the Juvenile Court Act of April 14, 1899. In addition to children who were delinquent (persons under 16 who violated the law), and consistent with the concept of *parens patriae*, the juvenile court was given jurisdiction over neglected and dependent children, and over children who presented "behavior problems," such as truancy and running away from home. Children who are not considered **delinquent** but who have these behavior problems are labeled as status offenders. Within 30 years, all but two states had a separate court for juveniles operating under the concept of *parens patriae* (Finckenauer 1984).

Parens patriae *provided the legal basis for the juvenile court.*

As noted in Chapter 8, the amount of due process is directly related to what is at risk. In juvenile court children were not at risk—the court only wanted to help, as per *parens patriae*. Thus, the due process guarantees of the adult criminal court were absent. With its informal and unstructured system of justice, the juvenile court quickly became the standard for similar courts established throughout the United States. The noncriminal nature of the proceedings even extended to the nomenclature used, as shown in Figure 11.1.

Adult Criminal Court	Juvenile Court
defendant	respondent
information/indictment	petition
arraignment	hearing
prosecution	adjudication
verdict	finding
presentence report	predisposition report
sentence	disposition
parole	aftercare

Figure 11.1   Adult and Juvenile Court Terms Compared

The juvenile court typically handles four types of cases:

1. *Delinquency,* or behavior that, if engaged in by an adult, would constitute a crime. In the case of certain very serious criminal behavior (e.g., murder), the law may require a transfer of the case for prosecution in adult criminal court.

2. *Status offense,* or behavior that would not constitute a crime if engaged in by an adult, but that (based on *parens patriae*) provides the basis for governmental intervention in the life of a child, such as truancy, being beyond the control of parents, addiction to drugs or alcohol, running away from home, and sexual promiscuity (almost invariably referring to the behavior of girls).

3. *Neglect or abuse,* or the cases of children who are neglected or abused by parents or **guardians**.

4. *Dependency,* or the cases of children who do not have parents or guardians available to provide proper care.

In some jurisdictions, the functions of a juvenile court are encompassed in a **family court** that also considers issues such as divorce and child support. Using a **"one family, one judge"** approach, "any case related to a family is sent before the same judge to ensure that overlapping issues related to the family are addressed in a consis-

Juvenile Court Stats

More than 30 million youth are under juvenile court jurisdiction. More than 1.5 million youth are referred to juvenile court each year, about 25 percent for offenses against persons, 40 percent for property offenses, 10 percent for drug law violations, and about 25 percent for public order offenses. Other youth are charged with status offenses such as truancy and underage drinking. Approximately 60 percent of all adjudicated delinquents are placed on probation; about 25 percent are placed in a residential facility. Other dispositions include restitution, community service, or referral to another agency (Puzzanchera, Adams, and Sickmund 2011; Leone and Weinberg, 2010).

tent manner. It also diminishes the need for families to appear in multiple courtrooms on multiple days to address those overlapping issues" (Spinak 2008: 261).

Legal Developments

The nature of the juvenile court process remained unchanged into the 1960s, when the Warren Court began to pay increasing attention to questions of due process as indicated by decisions in the cases of *Gideon*, *Mapp*, and *Miranda* (discussed in Chapter 8). In 1966, the Court granted certiorari in the case of *Kent v. United States*.

Kent v. United States.   Morris Kent, age 16, had been convicted in criminal court of raping a woman in her Washington, DC, apartment. He was sentenced to a term of 30 to 90 years in prison. Following federal statutes, the case had first been referred to the juvenile court where, over the objections of defense counsel, jurisdiction was waived to the criminal court. The Supreme Court ruled that before a juvenile can be tried in adult court, he or she is entitled to a waiver hearing with counsel and, if jurisdiction is subsequently waived, a statement of the reasons must be provided by the judge for the record.

Although this decision had only limited application, the Court noted a problem in applying *parens patriae*. In past decisions, the Court had interpreted the Fourteenth Amendment to mean that certain classes of persons, such as juveniles, could receive less due process if accompanied by a compensating benefit—in the case of juveniles, greater concern for the youngster's interests. Noting that this benefit may not actually exist, the Court stated that a juvenile might receive the worst of both worlds: that is, "neither the protections accorded to adults nor the solicitous care and regenerative treatment postulated for children." *Parens patriae* assumes that the state, "acting as a substitute parent, will act considerately and in the best interests of the child" and that "the interest of the state and the welfare of the child are in harmony" (McMillian 1999: 6). When this harmony is not present, when the state fails to fulfill its obligations under *parens patriae*, serious issues of due process emerge as the next case reveals.

In re Gault.   In 1967, less than a year after *Kent*, the Supreme Court decided the most important case affecting the juvenile court when it agreed to consider a writ of *habeas corpus* in the case of *In re Gault*.[1]

Gault was an Arizona case that reached the Court without benefit of a lower court review. In general, an appellate court will not consider a case unless all other remedies have been exhausted. However, Arizona law did not permit a review of juvenile court decisions, and furthermore, no record had been made of the juvenile court proceedings on which to base an appeal.

Gerald Gault, age 15 at the time, and a friend were arrested by police on the complaint of a female neighbor that they had made lewd and indecent remarks over the telephone. Neither youngster's parents were notified of their son's arrest and did not receive a copy of the **petition**. Juveniles were not entitled to many due process guarantees in Arizona juvenile court proceedings, and Gerald was not advised of his right to remain silent or his right to counsel. At a second hearing, Gerald was declared to be a juvenile delinquent and committed to the state industrial school for a maximum of

---

[1] In states that do not provide an appellate process for juvenile court cases, such as Arizona, they are cited as *In re* (in the matter of), as opposed to the more conventional format of *Gault v. Arizona*.

six years—until his 21st birthday. Had Gerald been over the age of 18, the maximum sentence would have been a fine of not more than $50 or imprisonment for up to 60 days. The complainant was not present at either hearing; the judge did not speak with her on any occasion; and no record was made of the court proceedings.

Until *Gault*, juvenile court operations were based on principles set out in a book published in 1927 (Lou, 1972: 2):

> These principles upon which the juvenile court acts are radically different from those of the criminal courts. In place of judicial tribunals, restrained by antiquated procedure, saturated in an atmosphere of hostility, trying cases for determining guilt and inflicting punishment according to inflexible rules of law, we have now juvenile courts, in which the relations of the child to his parents or other adults and to the state or society are defined and are adjusted summarily according to the scientific findings about the child and his environments. In place of magistrates, limited by the outgrown custom and compelled to walk in the paths fixed by the law of the realm, we have now socially-minded judges, who hear and adjust cases according not to rigid rules of law but to what the interests of society and the interests of the child or good conscience demand. In the place of juries, prosecutors, and lawyers, trained in the old conception of law and staging dramatically, but often amusingly, legal battles, as the necessary paraphernalia of a criminal court, we have now probation officers, physicians, psychologists, and psychiatrists, who search for the social, physiological, psychological, and mental backgrounds of the child in order to arrive at reasonable and just solutions of individual cases.

In its decision, the Supreme Court acknowledged the helping (noncriminal) philosophy that led to the establishment of the juvenile court. But it also revealed a sense of outrage over what had transpired in this case: "Under our Constitution, the condition of being a boy does not justify a kangaroo court." The Court ruled that a youngster being adjudicated in juvenile court is entitled to certain rights and procedures, which include the following:

1. *Notice.* The child and parents or guardians shall receive a notice "in writing, of the specific charge or factual allegations to be considered at the hearing, and . . . such written notice [shall] be given at the earliest practicable time, and in any event, sufficiently in advance of the hearing to permit preparation."

2. *Right to counsel.* This requires that "the child and his parents must be notified of the child's right to be represented by counsel retained by them, or if they are unable to afford counsel, that counsel will be appointed to represent the child."

3. *Protection against self-incrimination.* This guarantee "is applicable in the case of juveniles as it is with respect to adults." The Court added, "It would be surprising if the privilege against self-incrimination were made available to hardened criminals but not to children."

4. *Right to confront and cross-examine adverse witnesses.* This, like the right to remain silent, was found to be essential: "No reason is suggested or appears for a different rule in respect to sworn testimony in juvenile courts than in adult tribunals."

5. *Right to appellate review and transcripts of proceedings.* The Court held that this cannot be denied: "As the present case illustrates, the consequences of fail-

ure to provide an appeal, to record the proceedings, or to make findings or state the grounds for the juvenile court's conclusion may be to throw the burden upon the machinery for *habeas corpus*, to saddle the reviewing process with the burden of attempting to reconstruct a record, and to impose upon the Juvenile Judge the unseemly duty of testifying under cross-examination as to the events that transpired in the hearings before him."

Other Juvenile Justice Decisions

Twelve-year old Samuel Winship was charged with stealing $112 from a woman's purse in a store. No one actually saw him take the money but he was seen running from the scene just before the woman noticed the money was missing. Because of the noncriminal nature of the juvenile court, instead of the proof-beyond-a-reasonable-doubt standard, the level of evidence required for a **finding** of delinquency was the civil standard of the preponderance of evidence. Based on that standard, Winship was adjudicated a delinquent and sent to a New York State training school. In 1970, the Supreme Court (*In re Winship*) overturned the adjudication and ruled "the reasonable-doubt standard plays a vital role in the American scheme of criminal procedure. It is a prime instrument for reducing the risk of conviction resting on factual error." Accordingly, the Court determined that "the constitutional safeguard of proof beyond a reasonable doubt is as much required during the adjudicatory stage of a delinquency proceeding as those constitutional safeguards applied in *Gault*."

At age 16, Joseph McKeiver was charged with robbery, larceny, and receiving stolen goods. It was alleged that he and 20 to 30 youths chased three youngsters, taking 25 cents from them. His lawyer requested a jury trial, which was denied by the juvenile court judge. McKeiver was adjudicated a delinquent and placed on probation. In 1971, in *McKeiver v. Pennsylvania*, the Court ruled that a juvenile court proceeding is not a criminal prosecution within the meaning of the Sixth Amendment and, therefore, a child is not entitled to a jury trial. Nevertheless, about a half dozen states recognize a juvenile's right to a jury trial in delinquency cases either by law or court decisions (Possley 1999).

In 1975, the Court (*Breed v. Jones*) ruled on the issue of double jeopardy for juveniles. Gary Jones was 17 years old when he was arrested for armed robbery, and a juvenile petition alleging the original charge and two other robberies was filed. After taking testimony from two witnesses presented by the prosecutor and the **respondent**, the judge sustained the petition. At a subsequent disposition hearing, however, the judge ruled that the respondent was not "amenable to the care, treatment and training program available through the facilities of the juvenile court" and ordered that he be prosecuted as an adult. Jones was subsequently found guilty of armed robbery in superior court. In its decision, the Supreme Court held "that the prosecution of respondent in Superior Court, after an adjudicatory proceeding in Juvenile Court, violated the Double Jeopardy Clause of the Fifth Amendment, as applied to the States through the Fourteenth Amendment."

In 1984, in a strong affirmation of the concept of *parens patriae*, the Court upheld the constitutionality of a New York statute that permits the preventive detention of juveniles when there is a "serious risk" that the juvénile may commit an act before trial that, if committed by an adult, would constitute a crime. Gregory Martin, age 14, was charged with robbery, assault, and possession of a weapon after he and two other

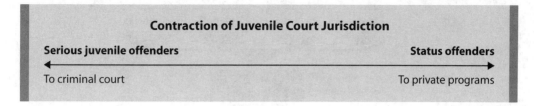

youths hit a boy on the head with a loaded gun and stole his jacket and sneakers. Martin was held in detention pending adjudication. Martin's attorney filed a writ of *habeas corpus*. In *Schall v. Martin*, the Supreme Court found that juveniles, unlike adults, "are always in some form of custody," and that by definition, they "are not assumed to have the capacity to take care of themselves."

Adherence to almost all of the criminal justice system's due process guarantees has made the juvenile court—like its criminal counterpart—adversarial, helping to facilitate a dramatic shift away from the concept of *parens patriae* (what the juvenile needs) and toward a model based on *just deserts* (what the offender deserves—punishment) for juvenile offenders. This clearly defeats the purpose of a separate court for juveniles where the *raison d'etre* is help, not to punish, yet this movement has proven politically popular. Although *parens patriae* is paternalistic and not inconsistent with the concept of punishment (Weisheit and Alexander 1988), the use of a punitive approach in juvenile court converts it to a criminal court for children and therefore is without grounding as a separate system of justice. At the same time, some states have relinquished juvenile court jurisdiction over status offenders. Jurisdictional modifications have narrowed "the scope of juvenile courts at the 'hard' end through the removal of serious juvenile offenders and at the 'soft' end through the removal of noncriminal status offenders" (Feld 1992: 59).

Juvenile Court Process

While the juvenile court process differs from state to state and jurisdiction to jurisdiction—even the name can vary, and in most states/jurisdictions it is not even called juvenile court—all approximate the model presented in Figure 11.2 on the following page.

The definition of a juvenile is statutory; meaning the age of adulthood is determined by the legislature. In most states it is 15 to 17, although the juvenile court may retain jurisdiction for additional years. Unlike adult courts, in most states juvenile proceedings are closed to the general public,[2] and the records and transactions are confidential. In most states, the records of a juvenile court proceeding are sealed, and access to them requires a court order. Juveniles are not routinely fingerprinted and photographed, and their names are usually not printed in newspapers.[3] This confidentiality is

---

[2] The original Cook County Juvenile Court was by law open to the public in an effort to have court activities monitored to ensure that private organizations would not gain custody of children and profit by "selling" them as had occurred with juveniles in New York City (Snyder and Sickmund 2006).

[3] The Supreme Court has ruled that newspapers cannot be prevented from publishing the names of juveniles if they obtained the information legally from noncourt sources—the First Amendment trumped the need for confidentiality (*Oklahoma Publishing Co. v. District Court in and for Oklahoma City* [1977]; *Smith v. Daily Mail Publishing Co.* [1979]).

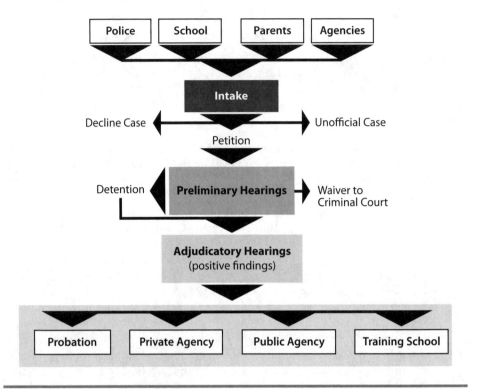

Figure 11.2   Juvenile Court Process

under severe attack, especially for more serious juvenile offenders, and all states now permit the fingerprinting and photographing of juveniles who have been arrested for felonies or have reached a certain age (Snyder and Sickmund 2006). Until 1992, the FBI collected records only of juveniles tried as adults. In that year, however, new regulations gave the FBI's National Crime Information Center (NCIC) authority to receive juvenile court information. Although states do not have to submit juvenile court records to the FBI, the NCIC can transmit instantly to law enforcement agencies, and within days to some employers, juvenile court records that were formerly kept confidential.

The juvenile court may be part of a division of superior court, but more frequently it is a lower court. Judges usually sit at a table, instead of the more traditional high bench, and they usually do not wear judicial robes.

Intake

Cases referred to the juvenile court enter by way of the **intake** section, which is usually staffed by probation officers (POs). The intake officer determines if the court has jurisdiction, if the case is to be referred to a courtroom for a hearing, or if services should be provided by another source. He or she will interview the child and the child's parents or guardians, and any other interested parties, for example, a victim or witness. The files of any previous court contact will be reviewed, and the intake officer will often consult (especially in serious cases) with the prosecutor's office before making a determination. "Since the mid-1990s, 'zero tolerance' policies in public schools have led to children being criminally charged for minor misbehavior that in the past would likely have only been addressed internally through school disciplinary procedures" (Birckhead 2013: 3–4).

Most of the cases that come to the attention of the juvenile court involve delinquent acts. "In 2009, juvenile courts in the United States handled an estimated 1.5 million delinquency cases that involved juveniles charged with criminal law violations, and law enforcement agencies were the primary source of referrals. . . . In 2009 more than 31 million youth were under juvenile court jurisdiction" (Puzzanchera, Adams, and Hockenberry 2012: 31, 8), and 280,200 (19 percent of all delinquency cases) were dismissed at intake, generally for lack of legal sufficiency (Knoll and Sickmund 2012). Status offenders—over 142,000 in 2009—are called MINS, Minors in Need of Supervision, or **PINS, Persons in Need of Supervision**, or **CHINS, Children in Need of Supervision**. They are referred to juvenile court by law enforcement agencies, social service agencies, schools, parents, probation officers, and victims (Puzzanchera, Adams, and Hockenberry 2012).

Most cases involving abused, neglected, or dependent children are referred to juvenile court by the department of child welfare after it has been notified by the police, neighbors, or certain responsible professionals. The law requires certain persons—such as medical doctors, nurses, teachers, and social workers—to report cases of suspected abuse or neglect to the child welfare agency for investigation. A caseworker may then draft a petition and refer the case to juvenile court, which has the authority to ensure the protection and treatment of the child through various judicial orders. In order to qualify for certain federal funds, states must appoint an attorney (**guardian** *ad litem*) to represent and act as an advocate on behalf of an abused or neglected child. A juvenile court judge may also appoint a special advocate to advise the court about the best interests of an abused or neglected child. Every state uses volunteer nonattorney advocates who investigate the child's situation and report back to the court with a recommendation. They may also be appointed to monitor compliance with court orders (*Court Appointed Special Advocates* 1997).

Instances of less serious delinquency and status offenses and instances of neglect, abuse, or dependency that come to the attention of the authorities are often handled in a manner that does not involve the formal justice apparatus. School officials or police, for example, may refer such cases directly to public or private social welfare or child protective agencies without any juvenile court involvement. In less serious cases, a nonjudicial alternative is often the first choice, making it an unofficial case. If all parties are amenable, the child and parents/guardians will be referred to a social service agency, and/or the youngster may be placed on unofficial probation for 90 days.

If unofficial handling is not successful or if the case is too serious for such treatment, it will be sent to court by way of a petition—in 2009, 55 percent of delinquency cases were handled by petition (Puzzanchera, Adams, and Hockenberry 2012). The petition sets out the allegations in the case, and filing a petition results in a court hearing at which an assistant corporation counsel (municipal attorney) or assistant prosecutor represents "the people." Children whose families are unable to pay for legal services are represented by an assistant public defender. Respondents can waive their

Intake in Texas

It is 1:15 AM in Texarkana. James, 15 years of age, and an adult male have been arrested for aggravated robbery. Police are taking the juvenile to the detention center intake unit at the Bowie County Juvenile Probation Department. Harold Harlston, a probation officer on duty, has just been called to the intake office where he must decide if James will be detained or released. In checking the records, Harlston finds that James has a prior arrest for theft, but the initial police report suggests that this time James was influenced to participate in the robbery by the older man. Harlston awakens James' parents with a phone call. They are quite upset and head for the center. While continuing to interview James, the PO is interrupted by a call alerting him that the police are bringing in a girl involved in a street fight. She is being charged with assault—again. Harlston anticipates a long, busy night.

The girl being brought in is 14 and goes by her street name, "Decca." Street wise, she has learned to cover her vulnerability with a defiant attitude and abusive vocabulary. She fidgets nervously as she waits for her intake interview. A file check reveals that Decca lives with her mother and several siblings. The father does not live in the home, and the family has a history of court referrals.

Harlston learns that James' parents have just arrived. He tells them their son will be held until his detention hearing, usually occurring within 48 hours. His parents express their disappointment; they would like to take James home tonight. The PO explains the seriousness of the charges and the state law allowing juveniles to be tried in adult court for offenses as serious as aggravated robbery. If James is transferred to adult court, he could be sentenced to prison. The young man is lucky; his parents express their love and pledge to stand by him. Decca is not so fortunate. When her mother is contacted, she tells the probation officer: "Do whatever you want with her—I'm tired."

The night is young, and Harlston learns the police are bringing in two more youths. Detention center staff prepare for overcrowding by placing temporary cots in the dining area of the 10-bed facility.

right to counsel in about 20 states without consulting parents or an attorney, while a few states require juveniles to have representation whenever they appear before a judge. Based on *Scott v. Illinois* (1979), status offenders for whom an out-of-home placement is not being considered need not be represented by counsel.

Intake in the juvenile court is unique: It permits the court to screen cases not only on jurisdictional and legal grounds but also on social dimensions. The PO interviews the presenting agent, the young person, and the child's parents or guardians. The PO then reviews court files for previous records concerning the child. If the case involves a serious crime or child abuse and has not already been screened by the prosecutor, the PO consults with that office. At this stage, the probation officer has a dual function: legal and social service.

The *legal function* requires that the PO determine if the juvenile court has jurisdiction and also requires that the child and parents be advised of the right to counsel and the right to remain silent during the intake conference. There is criticism that defense attorney participation at an intake conference—and in juvenile proceedings in general—is rare, waivers of rights tend to be finessed, and the norm is for parents to encourage the child to discuss his or her participation in the alleged offense with the intake officer (Rubin 1998: 304; Feld, 1992; Berkheiser 2002). A study in Missouri, for example, found "youth are discouraged from and systematically denied counsel throughout the state" (Scali and Tandy 2013: 7). When defense attorneys are present in juvenile court, tension is inherent in their responsibilities to the client: "a choice between the traditional adversary role (or the procedural model that regulates professional behavior in the criminal court) and the historic treatment or rehabilitative concerns of the family [juvenile] court" (Fabricant 1983: 41). Barry Feld reports that even when juveniles are represented by counsel, "attorneys may not be capable of or committed to representing their juvenile clients in an effective adversarial manner. Organizational pressures to cooperate, judicial hostility toward adversarial litigants, role ambiguity created by the dual goals of rehabilitation and punishment, reluctance to help juveniles 'beat a case,' or an internalization of a court's treatment philosophy may compromise the role of counsel in juvenile court" (1992: 395). Indeed, he notes that the presence of counsel may actually be disadvantageous to the juvenile—those represented by attorneys tending to receive more severe dispositions. Nevertheless, Feld, a law professor, advocates legislation that mandates counsel and does not permit a waiver of this important constitutional right.

The *social service function* involves an assessment of the child's situation—home, school, physical, and psychological—and can provide the basis for *adjusting* the case, handling it informally without the filing of a petition. This happens in about one-half of the cases reaching the juvenile court, when the situation is not serious, when the matter can best be handled by the family, and when neither the child nor the public is in any danger. When the child is in conflict with parents or school officials, the worker may serve as a mediator. If the young person and parents agree to informal processing, the juvenile can be placed under supervision of a probation officer, usually for a period of 90 days. Although this may save the young person and his or her parents from the trauma of court action, unofficial handling has its critics. Informal processing requires an explicit or tacit admission of guilt. The substantial advantages that accrue from this admission (the avoidance of court action) also act as an incentive to confess. This approach casts doubt on the voluntariness and truthfulness of admissions of guilt.

Preliminary Hearings

A preliminary hearing is held to inform parties of the charges in the petition and of their rights in the proceedings as per the *Gault* decision. If the case involves an abused, neglected, or dependent child, a guardian will be appointed to act as an advocate for the child, usually a social worker from a child welfare agency. If appropriate, the hearing will be used to determine whether an alleged delinquent child should remain in detention or custody. This custody hearing is usually held within 24 hours of the apprehension. If it is determined that there is an "urgent and immediate necessity" to continue detention, the judge issues a hold in custody order. Otherwise, the child is released to parents or guardians or to shelter care.

Dependent, neglected, or abused children and status offenders may be placed into foster care or a residential shelter. Within a few days, a shelter hearing is held at which a judge determines whether continued out-of-home placement is necessary. If it is, the judge will appoint a temporary guardian for the child, usually someone from a child welfare agency, but sometimes a relative or family friend. The judge may also issue an order of protection, which allows the penalties for contempt of court (summary imprisonment) if violated. An order of protection will usually contain specific restrictions on a potential abuser or assailant to refrain from further abuse and/or contact with the child or others in danger. During a custody or shelter hearing, probable cause must be established: that is, the judge must determine whether there is enough evidence to believe that the allegations stated in the petition justify an **adjudicatory hearing**.

Adjudicatory Hearings

The adjudicatory hearing parallels an adult trial. Its purpose is to provide the judge with a basis for determining whether the child should be made a ward of the juvenile court because he or she is a delinquent, a status offender, abused, neglected, or dependent. There are three phases common to adjudicatory hearings:

1. A plea is entered in the form of an admission or denial of the allegations made in the petition.

2. If a denial is made, then evidence must be presented to prove beyond a reasonable doubt that a delinquent act was committed by the respondent—more than half of the cases result in a positive finding—or, in the case of a status offense, with a preponderance of the evidence that the child is a MINS (or CHINS or PINS), or abused, neglected, or dependent.

3. If the allegations are sustained, the judge enters a finding that the child is an adjudicated delinquent, a MINS (or CHINS or PINS), abused, neglected, or dependent and declares him or her to be a ward of the court (see Figure 11.3).

Despite its noncriminal nature, with the exception of a jury, the procedures of an adjudicatory hearing are the same as a criminal trial (discussed in Chapter 8).

Predisposition Report

The goal of the juvenile court is to provide services. To do so on the basis of the best available information, if the judge makes a positive finding, the probation department prepares a predisposition or **social investigation** report containing the social and psychological factors affecting the child and his or her family (it parallels the presentence report used in criminal court).

The PO who conducts the investigation will present his or her findings in a report that includes the sociocultural and psychodynamic factors that influenced the juvenile's behavior, providing a social history that is used by the judge to determine a disposition for the case. The report will typically include:

- Review of court records
- Review of school records
- Review of police records
- Interviews with the respondent
- Interviews with family members
- Interviews with teachers and school officials

- Interviews with employers, youth workers, and clergy whenever appropriate
- Interviews with complainant, police officer, or witnesses
- Results of any psychological or psychiatric examinations
- Recommendation, which should include the available treatment alternatives

Sometimes the recommendation of the PO is not included in the report, but is transmitted orally to the judge. The completed report should enable the judge to make the best disposition available based on the individual merits of the case and the service *needs* of the young person. One problem encountered at the disposition stage is the paucity of available alternatives for helping a youngster. A youngster will often be placed on probation because of a lack of feasible alternatives.

adoption: Custody hearings which grant custody to the prospective adoptive parents, and adoption hearings, which grant final adoption.

adjudication: (1) Hearing at which the minor enters a plea to one or more allegations of the petition and at which the judge pronounces the child a delinquent minor; (2) contested hearing (trial) at which witnesses testify and evidence is presented, at the conclusion of which the judge determines whether or not the child has been found to be a delinquent minor

advisory: Hearing for youth paperreferred to court at which the petition detailing the delinquent allegations is presented, a determination is made whether the minor qualifies for appointed counsel, and a trial review date is selected

detention: Hearing held within 24 hours of the filing of a petition for a detained youth at which counsel is appointed and the court considers whether the minor should be detained or released from custody

disposition: Hearing, analogous to the adult court sentencing, for which the probation officer prepares a comprehensive report of the adjudicated child's background and at which the judge determines what action(s) the court will take

restitution: Hearing at which the judge determines what restitution to a victim the child must pay to satisfy the conditions of probation

review: Review of the child's adherence to probation conditions to consider revising these conditions or terminating the minor from probation

revocation: Hearing to determine if the minor has violated probation by failure to adhere to the conditions of probation or by committing a delinquent act

transfer: Hearing to determine if the juvenile court should retain jurisdiction for the allegations set forth in the petition or whether the matter should be transferred for prosecution to the adult court

trial review: Hearing at which the child requests that the charges be set for a contested adjudication (trial), or at which he/she admits one or more allegations of the pending petition

Figure 11.3   Guide to the Most Common Hearings Held in Juvenile Court

Disposition Hearing

The purpose of the disposition hearing is to determine what outcome will best serve the interests of the child, his or her family, and the community. A number of different dispositions are available to a juvenile court judge, but some depend on the resources available in the jurisdiction. Basic to dispositions in the juvenile court is the concept of *least restrictive alternative*, meaning that a disposition should not be more restrictive than that which will adequately serve the needs of the child. In cases of delinquency, these include:

- *Commitment* to a state youth authority or the juvenile division of the department of corrections for children who are at least 13 and whose offense would be punishable with incarceration if tried under the criminal law. The period of this commitment is indeterminate, but it may not extend past the delinquent youth's 21st birthday. (The actual date of release is determined by youth authority or department of corrections juvenile officials.) A few states (e.g., Oregon, Wisconsin) have extended the age to 25 years (Torbet et al. 1996).

- *Probation* for adjudicated delinquent children of any age for a period not beyond the age of 21. A child placed on probation will be released to parents or placed out of the home and receive supervision and services by a probation officer. As a condition of probation, juveniles are usually required to obey their parents, attend school regularly, be home at an early hour in the evening, avoid disreputable companions and places, and refrain from alcoholic beverages and controlled substances. In some cases there will also be a requirement for restitution and/or community service.

- *Conditional discharge* and release to parents on the condition that no further delinquent acts will take place.

- *Out-of-home placement*, often in the form of a commitment to the child welfare agency, which will arrange for a foster home, group home, or residential treatment setting that can provide counseling and education to help the child to behave in a more constructive manner.

- *Referral* to a public or private agency with specialized services such as a drug treatment program for children who are addicted to controlled substances or alcohol.

- *Detention*, usually for no more than 30 days, in a juvenile facility and then release to probation supervision, perhaps in combination with one of the other alternatives listed above. If appropriate, the judge may also order protective supervision of the parents or guardians to whose custody the child was released.

A **blended sentence** law in Minnesota created a new category of serious juvenile offender. Serious juvenile offenders are tried as juveniles but given full due process protections, including the right to a jury trial. If convicted, they are given an adult sentence that is applied *only* in the event the juvenile does not satisfactorily complete the juvenile court disposition (Griffin et al. 2011). In some states (e.g., California, Florida), the case is tried in criminal court, which has the authority to impose a juvenile or adult sanction.

The dispositional alternatives for status offenders include probation supervision, out-of-home placement, referral, and emancipation of the child as a mature minor. The federal Juvenile Justice and Delinquency Act of 1974 states that in order to qualify for

Juvenile Court Dispositions

Basic to dispositions in the juvenile court is the concept of *least restrictive alternative*, meaning that a disposition should not be more restrictive than that which will adequately serve the needs of the child. These dispositions generally follow this principle, progressing from the less to the more restrictive.

- Reprimand with unsupervised probation
- Probation with supervision
- Foster care with or without probation
- Community-based day treatment
- Group home
- Private school or residential treatment
- Community-based secure facility
- Training school

funding, juveniles not charged with acts that would be crimes for adults "shall not be placed in secure detention facilities or secure correctional facilities." For children who are abused or neglected, the court will choose the disposition that is best able to provide protection and overcome the ill effects of neglect or abuse. The dependent child is by definition without parents or guardians available to provide proper care, and dispositions are limited to an out-of-home placement with the assignment of a guardian or emancipation. As in cases involving other categories of children, the judge may also order protective supervision. In many jurisdictions, particularly those that utilize a family court, the court may also have jurisdiction over cases of adoption, child support, paternity disputes, and related "family" issues, in addition to cases of juveniles.

Problems with Disposition. The disposition stage of the juvenile court process has typically been based on the concept of *parens patriae*. Distinctions between dispositions have been based on the needs of the child and not necessarily on the behavior that brought a case to the attention of the juvenile court—in other words, based not on justice but on rehabilitation, positivism rather than classicalism. Although the Supreme Court ruled that the juvenile court must adhere to due process, it continued to be a vehicle for providing social services to children in need. As noted earlier, in some states the line between adult criminal court and juvenile court has become blurred as the latter moves toward a justice (or classical) model (what the youngster deserves) and away from *parens patriae* (what the youngster needs). "The concept of *parens patriae* has largely disappeared from the political and public agenda. The delinquency courtrooms now work more like the criminal system that the juvenile court was supposed to counter" (Kiernan, 1997: 12).

This disturbing trend is exacerbated by the lack of effective legal representation in most jurisdictions. Public defenders in juvenile court are unable to handle caseloads that are often in excess of 500 cases. Often, they have no time to meet with clients prior to the detention hearing. Resources are often inadequate to investigate the charges or gather critical information from families, schools, or social service agencies. Accordingly, there is a reduction in the accuracy of judicial decision making, inappropriate disposition, and the unnecessary transfer of juveniles to the adult criminal justice system (Puritz and Shang 1998).

Juveniles are sometimes released in the custody of their parents for placement in private boarding schools, military academies, and so on. This disposition is most often limited to children from at least middle-income status, and Dale Mann notes: "One obvious effect is to guarantee that public institutions for juvenile offenders serve an underclass population" (1976: 12). Jerome Miller (1992: 5) refers to a

> two-tiered system of residential care [that] has grown up across the country with a dramatic surge in short-term hospitalization in private psychiatric hospitals for recalcitrant, disobedient, or drug-abusing suburban adolescents. Whether or not this approach works, the effect is to spare these youngsters the correctional diagnosis and the labels which undermine hope—"psychopath," "sociopath," "unsocialized aggressive." Such terms apply only to the children of the poor and the racial minorities who populate our youth correctional institutions.

In many states, although a judge can order an adjudicated youth committed to the department having responsibility for institutional care, the judge cannot determine the type of institution to which he or she will be confined. In Idaho, for example, youth placed in Department of Juvenile Corrections custody go through an observation and assessment process to determine the best placement; a judge may not specify secure confinement or make any recommendations for placement of adjudicated youth.

Disposition of Juvenile Female Offenders.   Female offenders often receive harsher treatment in juvenile court because of culturally fostered attitudes and the lack of alternative programs for them. Judges may feel it is necessary to intervene in these girls' lives; that is, judges use the authority of the juvenile justice system to try to "save" these females. Magnifying the problem is that status offenders have reduced due process rights, so they may not have recourse against such attitudes (Shelden 2012). With regard to sentencing, Laura Barnickol found:

> Although female offenders are generally brought into the system for lesser offenses than most male offenders, their case dispositions are often as severe or more severe than their male counterparts. Research has shown that delinquent adolescent females receive longer sentences than delinquent adolescent males adjudicated for the same offenses. In addition, they receive worse treatment throughout their incarceration. In particular, the system treats adolescent females who exhibit promiscuous behavior more harshly than adolescent males. (Barnickol 2000: 429)

"Rehabilitation can be a difficult struggle for girls as they enter a system of treatment and controls created for a male juvenile delinquent population" (Miazad 2002: 3).

Juveniles in Criminal Court

During the 1970s, there was increasing public concern over juvenile crime and the juvenile justice system, which was frequently attacked as too lenient. Enter Willie Bosket. His first contact with the juvenile system occurred at age nine when his mother complained to the court that she could not control him. Willie remained in state agency placements for the next several years. At age 15, six months after being released from a maximum security youth facility, he shot and killed two New York City subway passengers. Labeled "the Baby-Faced Butcher," he was subject only to juvenile court jurisdiction—the maximum sentence was a placement with the Division for Youth until he was 21.

In the midst of a tough campaign for reelection, New York's liberal governor called the legislature into special session to pass the "Willie Bosket law" which provides for the automatic transfer of children as young as 13 to criminal court if charged with murder; children as young as 14 would automatically be transferred if charged with various crimes of violence. Many states followed New York's lead, and the jurisdiction of juvenile courts over serious crimes was cut back in state after state (Klein 1998). The pool of cases eligible for criminal court handling vastly expanded and critical decision-making power in this area shifted away from judges and toward prosecutors (Torbet et al. 2000).

It should be noted that the possibility of transfer to adult criminal court is not an invention of the late twentieth century. Since the establishment of the juvenile court, judges have retained the discretion to waive jurisdiction over serious young offenders and allow them to be prosecuted in criminal court. In Cook County, the juvenile court typically waived about 15 boys a year. These were usually juveniles age 16 or older arrested for violent crimes (Klein 1998).

"All states have transfer laws that allow or require criminal prosecution of some young offenders, even though they fall on the juvenile side of the jurisdictional age" (Griffin et al. 2011: 2). There are three basic mechanisms for accomplishing the transfer of a juvenile to criminal court:

1. *Legislative exclusion.* Some states and the District of Columbia exclude certain categories of juveniles from juvenile court jurisdiction. Some states have enacted some form of "once an adult, always an adult" provisions, requiring that once a juvenile has been prosecuted in criminal court, all subsequent cases involving the juvenile will be in criminal court (Griffin et al. 2011). To mitigate automatic transfer statutes, most states have *reverse waiver* provisions, whereby prosecutors in criminal court can move to have a juvenile case sent back to juvenile court.

2. *Judicial waiver.* Virtually every state and the federal system permit juvenile court judges to "waive" (transfer) their jurisdiction over certain juvenile offenders.

3. *Prosecutorial discretion.* Some states empower prosecutors to charge juveniles in either juvenile or adult courts. This discretionary power may be limited by statutory criteria with regard to age and type of offense.

Juveniles and Capital Punishment

In 2005, the Supreme Court ruled 5–4 that the Eighth Amendment to the Constitution categorically bars capital punishment for crimes committed before the age of 18 (*Roper v. Simons*). A dissent filed by Justice Antonin Scalia that was joined by three other justices decried the use of foreign sources in the majority decision.

Researchers have reported a lack of any significant difference in sentence outcome for youngsters adjudicated in juvenile court and those tried in criminal court after statistically controlling for the severity of offense. They point out that "minors are likely to be looked upon as special persons by prosecutors, probation officers, and judges in the criminal courts. They are younger than the main population of defendants before the criminal courts. Even jurors may view the young person in criminal court differently." Thus, in the cases they examined, "there were more findings of 'not guilty' in the criminal court than in the juvenile court. The labeling process may be different in the two courts. While a minor may be looked upon as a hardened criminal in the juvenile court, (s)he may be viewed as a mere innocent youngster in criminal court" (Sagatun, McCollum, and Edwards 1985: 87).

There has been a dramatic reversal of "tough on crime" statutes that moved more juveniles into the adult criminal court. About half of the states have enacted laws keeping more juveniles in the juvenile system and preventing them from being incarcerated in adult jails and prisons (Schwartz, 2013).

Issues of Controversy

A great deal of controversy has been generated over juvenile justice, particularly with respect to the role of juvenile court judges, defense attorneys, status offenses, and treatment.

Judges

While a judicial post requires knowledge of law and legal procedure, the juvenile court judge also needs a working knowledge of several other disciplines, including psychology, sociology, and social work. Judges in general come to the bench without any special training for the position, and this can be a particular problem in juvenile court. Legal education provides very little in the way of training for practice in juvenile justice, and the judge typically comes to a juvenile court bench with a background in civil or criminal law and with little knowledge of the philosophy and practice of the juvenile court. Furthermore, many if not most judges have little or no experience with children of poor or otherwise marginalized groups, which are most likely to be found in juvenile court.

In many jurisdictions, the juvenile court is a bench with relatively low prestige. Those receiving juvenile court appointments often aspire to a higher court, one with more prestige (and perhaps a higher salary). This can have a destabilizing influence on the juvenile court (one that could be corrected by a unified court system; see Chapter 4). In order to deal with the other shortcomings, some states have mandated training for juvenile court judges. The National Council of Juvenile and Family Court Judges (NCJFCJ) participates with the University of Nevada, Reno, and The National Judicial College in the Master and Doctorate of Judicial Studies degree program, the only such program of its kind in the country offering advanced degrees to trial court judges. Some jurisdictions are utilizing referees or masters, specialists trained in law and juvenile justice who hold hearings and make recommendations to juvenile court judges.

Defense Attorneys

In juvenile court, there is frequently a waiver of the right to counsel and this raises serious questions. The validity of a waiver rests on knowledge and intent: "Many minors who become involved with the juvenile justice system never realize these basic rights because they ill-advisedly waive their right to counsel, inappropriately accept plea bargains, or receive substandard services. In some jurisdictions, as many as 80 to 90 percent of youth waive their right to an attorney because they do not know the meaning of the word 'waive' or understand its consequences" (Jones 2004: 2).

When defense counsel is present, their role in juvenile court can be fraught with ambivalence. In a criminal case, the role is clear: advocacy, bringing to bear all of one's professional skills to gain the best possible outcome for a client. The "best possible outcome" in juvenile court, however, is often a matter of opinion, and the role of the attorney in a *parens patriae* proceeding is not clear. Most children entering juvenile court are in need of help. Should defense counsel become an agent mediator between the court, the youngster, and his or her parents, so that the client receives this help? Or should the lawyer argue vigorously against the allegations in the petition in order to free the client of all judicial encumbrances? Although the canons of legal ethics do not require an attorney to accept the client's view of a particular situation, how far can counsel go in disregarding the wishes of a youngster facing action in juvenile court?

For youngsters automatically transferred to adult criminal court, defense attorneys are often ill-prepared. "They, like judges, prosecutors, and probation officers assigned to criminal courts, are generally untrained and inexperienced in recognizing the needs and characteristics of young defendants" (Young 2000: 1). Defense attorneys working with children encounter problems that their adult clients have compensated for or overcome. Many have suffered trauma or abuse, which may not have been diagnosed, and which may interfere with their ability to communicate, to aid in their own defense. "They often suffer from behavioral problems, family crises, poverty, learning disabilities, asthma or other health problems, alcohol or drug abuse, or emerging mental illness." Adequate representation requires attorneys to understand and explain a child's competency to waive his or her rights, to make an admission, or to confess. "An attorney representing a child must be able to explain how child development issues apply to the case as part of a defense." Yet most lawyers trained for practice in adult criminal court are unfamiliar with the field of child development (Young 2000: 4).

Status Offenses

Juvenile court jurisdiction over status offenders has long been controversial. In 1976, I argued against such jurisdiction, and similar positions have been taken by the National Council on Crime and Delinquency and the American Society of Criminology. Since, by definition, a status offender has not been accused of a crime, punitive intervention—arrest, detention, the court process, training schools—is inappropriate, and the stigma is potentially harmful. Edwin Schur states that an initial appearance in juvenile court can set in motion a potentially damaging series of events, "a complex process of response and counterresponse beginning with an initial act of rule-violation and developing into elaborated delinquent self-conceptions and a full-fledged delinquent career" (1973: 120). In Scandinavian countries and in Belgium, social agencies have responsibility for status offenders without the need for court intervention. As already noted, some states, such as Illinois, have relinquished juvenile court jurisdiction over status offenders.

Proponents of continued juvenile court jurisdiction over status offenders argue that these youngsters are not essentially different from those youngsters committing delinquent acts. They are all children in need of services, and without the intervention of juvenile court, they argue, these services would not be forthcoming. Indeed, in cases of delinquency a finding of status offense may result from "plea bargaining."

Treatment

In the field of juvenile justice there is general agreement that services for children are inadequate. Judges are often faced with few options at dispositional hearings, something that accounts for the frequent use of probation even when this is not in the best interests of the child and the community. Treatment facilities for children are quite expensive, especially residential facilities, which have to be staffed 24/7 and contain a full school system—operating expenses can easily cost $50,000–100,000 per year per youngster. This unfortunate situation shows no signs of improving in the future.

In the next chapter we will examine alternative justice.

SUMMARY

- *Parens patriae* gave almost complete authority over children to the state and became the legal basis for the juvenile court.
- Controversy surrounds the interests and motivations of the child savers.
- In addition to children who were delinquent, the juvenile court was given jurisdiction over neglected and dependent children, and *status offenders*.
- Because the juvenile court sought only to help children, there was no need to provide due process.
- The juvenile court typically handles four types of cases: delinquency, status offense, neglect or abuse, and dependency.
- The family court operates in about 20 states and is a single forum in which all legal matters relating to children can be decided.
- During the 1960s, a number of Supreme Court decisions affected juvenile justice, the most important being *In re Gault*.
- The Court subsequently ruled that in cases of delinquency the standard of evidence is "beyond a reasonable doubt."
- In 1975, the Court (*Breed v. Jones*) ruled on the issue of double jeopardy for juveniles.
- In 1971, the Court (*McKeiver v. Pennsylvania*) ruled against the need for juries in juvenile court.
- There has been shift away from the concept of *parens patriae* and toward a model based on *just deserts* for juvenile offenders.
- The juvenile court may be part of a division of superior court, but more frequently it is a lower court.

- Juvenile court judges usually sit at a table, instead of the more traditional high bench, and they usually do not wear judicial robes.
- In most states juvenile proceedings are closed to the general public, and the records and transactions are confidential.
- The intake officer, usually a probation officer, determines if the court has jurisdiction, if the case is to be referred to a courtroom for a hearing, or if services should be provided by another source.
- Every state uses volunteer nonattorney advocates who investigate the child's situation and report back to the court with a recommendation.
- Instances of less serious delinquency and status offenses, neglect, abuse, or dependency are often handled in a manner that does not involve the formal justice apparatus.
- Informal processing requires an explicit or tacit admission of guilt.
- Different dispositions are available to a juvenile court judge, but some depend on the resources available in the jurisdiction.
- In a blended sentence juveniles are tried as juveniles but given full due process protections, and if convicted, they are given an adult sentence that is applied *only* in the event the juvenile does not satisfactorily complete the juvenile court disposition.
- All states have transfer laws that allow or require criminal prosecution of some young offenders, even though they fall on the juvenile side of the jurisdictional age.
- There are three basic mechanisms for accomplishing the transfer of a juvenile to criminal court: legislation exclusion; judicial waiver; prosecutorial discretion.
- Juvenile court judges frequently lack an adequate background for the position.

KEY TERMS

adjudicatory hearing	family court	juvenile
blended sentence	finding	*parens patriae*
child savers	guardian	person in need of supervision (PINS)
children in need of supervision (CHINS)	guardian *ad litem*	petition
delinquent	indeterminate sentence	respondent
	intake	social investigation

REVIEW QUESTIONS

1. What is the controversy surrounding the interests and motivations of the child savers?
2. Who are *status offenders*?
3. Why were the due process guarantees of the adult criminal court absent in juvenile court?
4. What are the four types of cases typically handled by the juvenile court?
5. What did the Supreme Court rule in the case of *In re Gault*?
6. What is the standard of evidence in a delinquency case?
7. What did the Supreme Court rule in the 1975 case of *Breed v. Jones*?

8. What has the Supreme Court ruled with respect to the use of a jury in juvenile court?

9. What is the role of an intake officer in juvenile court?

10. What is the role of a nonattorney advocate in juvenile court?

11. Why is unofficial handling in juvenile court criticized?

12. What dispositions are available to a juvenile court judge?

13. What is a blended sentence?

14. What are three basic mechanisms for accomplishing the transfer of a juvenile to criminal court?

15. Why do juvenile court judges typically lack what the position requires?

16. What is the role ambivalence that confronts defense attorneys in juvenile court?

INTERNET CONNECTIONS

Council of Juvenile Correctional Administrators: http://cjca.net
National Council on Crime and Delinquency: http://nccdglobal.org
National Council of Juvenile and Family Court Judges: http://www.ncjfcj.org
Office of Juvenile Justice and Delinquency Prevention: http://www.ojjdp.gov

Alternative Justice

The complexity and formalism of American law, courts, and justice, as well as their attendant expense, have led to a search for alternatives, particularly for those matters that appear unsuitable for, or less relevant for adjudication by, traditional adversarial systems. This chapter will explore this issue by examining alternative dispute resolution and an expanded role for the judicial branch represented by therapeutic jurisprudence, community courts, and restorative justice.

Alternative Dispute Resolution (ADR)

"ADR—an umbrella term for a range of dispute resolution processes that occur largely outside the courts and includes negotiation, conciliation, mediation, dialogue facilitation, consensus- building, and arbitration—has emerged as a principal mode of legal practice in virtually every legal field and in virtually every country in the world" (Tokarz and Hollander-Blumoff 2012: 2).

Alternative Dispute Resolution (ADR)

ADR "is the resolution of disputes by means other than litigation" (Mills 1991: 1), and it often derives from dissatisfaction with the administration of justice in the United States: "The processes [of the traditional judicial system] themselves are described as incomprehensible, the products of lawyers who profit from obfuscation and complexity so that the layperson is incompetent to seek redress in the courts without professional guidance" (Cooke 1982: 3). Even lawyers find the system problematic: "Attorneys more frequently are considering alternatives such as mediation in divorce cases, arbitration in commercial cases, and private courts or rent-a-judge programs in cases where there is a need for speedy resolution or confidential treatment of certain matters" (Alfini 1986: 252). "Alternative dispute resolution is conducted in a manner that is more businesslike than litigation. Each party tells its side of the story to the arbitrator in an atmosphere that is less formal than a court proceeding" (American Arbitration Association n.d.: 3).

> *"Civil jury trials continued at multi-decade lows, both absolutely and as a percentage of dispositions. And alternatives to those trials have become mainstream" (Philbin, Maness, and Loree 2010: 758).*

In practice, few persons make use of the entire process of justice; most cases, criminal or civil, are settled without resorting to trials. On the civil side, a trial can be painstakingly slow and expensive, and the outcome may create new problems for the principals. These outcomes are always zero-sum decisions; that is, a win for one side in the dispute results in a loss for the other side. On the other hand, cases that do not go to trial—the minor cases, both civil and criminal—are typically given short shrift as part of the mass of cases that enter the justice system. For these reasons, Supreme Court Justice Sandra Day O'Connor urged that "the courts of this country should not be the places where the resolution of disputes begins. They should be places where the disputes end—after alternative methods of resolving disputes have been considered and tried" (quoted in Roehl and Ray 1986: 2).

Whereas the adjudication of serious criminal behavior would be inappropriate for any forum other than the criminal court, civil disputes and interpersonal disputes that do not involve serious criminal behavior are candidates for alternative processing—that is, for utilizing a forum other than the formal justice system. David Aaronson and his colleagues (1977: 3) argue that alternative processing can be beneficial in criminal cases:

> A central thesis of the alternatives movement is that our criminal courts, patterned on an adversary model for the resolution of social conflicts, are an imperfect—and often inappropriate—societal response to the processing of many offenders, especially those charged with minor criminal offenses or offenses involving no substantial factual disputes. In many lesser criminal cases the process of conventional adjudication may be too time-consuming, too expensive, somewhat irrelevant to, or even inconsistent with, achieving effective dispositions. . . . Alternatives seek immediate relief for the overburdened criminal justice system: through simpler, less expensive, more effective and fairer dispositions.

The ADR movement is a response to "(1) criticism of lower courts for not providing procedural or substantive justice to minor offenders, and (2) the claim that courts cannot effectively address social demands expressed in complex disputes because such disputes require a more flexible negotiation process that involves the parties more directly in decision making" (Harrington 1985: 34). ADR can move beyond the symptoms of conflict, establishing "an outlet for the discussion of larger issues than can be covered in a court of law" (Kennedy 1990: 84). ADR programs can also be a way of alleviating court delay by moving less-serious cases out of the formal system: "An underlying premise of many of the programs has been that removing a significant volume of particular types of cases from the courts would help reduce backlogs and improve the speed with which the remaining cases are processed" (Mahoney 1988: 63, 66).

Whereas dissatisfaction with the courts as a vehicle for adjudicating minor criminal matters is often due to the need to expedite the handling of such cases—rough justice—dissatisfaction in civil disputes is usually due to the inability of persons with grievances to afford access to the courts. Most people cannot manage the cost of litigation unless there is a provision for a contingency fee. In cases that do not promise a financial settlement or where the amount of money in dispute is relatively small, such as in tenant–landlord or consumer–merchant disputes, litigants have no easy way to gain satisfaction. The frustrations arising out of this reality can result in bitter resignation, alienation, or even violence.[1] In addition to the interpersonal level, ADR is used extensively at the corporate and government regulatory levels.

Under an **adversarial system** of law, "the lawyer is not supposed to see the resolution of these disputes as a question of what might be best for the society as a whole. He is an advocate; his function is to see the possible resolution of a controversy in terms of his client's best interests (though he is not obliged to accept his client's view of what these best interests might be)" (Mayer 1969: 82). As mentioned previously, the goal of both inquisitorial and adversarial systems is the determination of "truth" so that blame or guilt can be assigned. The outcome clearly favors one or the other side of the dispute—a zero-sum outcome. There are, however, systems of law whose goal is the resolution of disputes in terms of what might be best for the society as a whole, or at least what is best for both disputants: **mediation** and **arbitration**. These alternatives to formal adjudication of civil and criminal disputes share a common goal, "trying to resolve the underlying problems that exist between parties in a manner that will result in an avoidance of future disputes" (DeLappa 1983: 9). Although these systems, which focus on harmony as opposed to vindication, predominated in preindustrial societies (e.g., Elias 1956; Gluckman 1955; Newman 1983), only since the 1970s have they been studied and adapted to industrial societies such as the United States.

In some instances, the use of mediation has been established by law, such as the Federal Mediation and Conciliation Service, which provides for the mediation of labor–management disputes arising out of the Labor-Management Relations Act of 1947. The Civil Rights Act of 1964 created the Community Relations Service (CRS) of the Department of Justice to resolve disputes relating to discrimination based on race, color, national origin, gender, gender identity, religion, sexual orientation, or disability. CRS provides communities with highly skilled conciliators to bring community-wide conflicts to peaceful closure. The agency uses impartial mediation practices and conflict resolution procedures to solve problems that might otherwise be solved on the streets or in the judicial system (Moore 2014).

Expansion of ADR in the federal system occurred in 1988 when Congress authorized 10 district courts to implement mandatory arbitration programs and an additional 10 to establish voluntary arbitration programs. Many courts require mediation in domestic relations cases and custody and visitation disputes. "After an agreement is worked out, the contract is brought to the judge, who then issues a court order to make it enforceable" (Kassberg 1989: 4). A further impetus came with the passage of the Civil Justice Reform Act of 1990, which requires all district courts to develop, with the help of an advisory group of local lawyers, scholars, and other citizens, a district plan to reduce cost and delay in civil litigation. ADR is one of the six civil case management principles recommended by the statute (Plapinger and Stienstra 1996). The

---

[1] Richard Posner states that the surprises and confrontations—adversary zeal—that occur in a trial "all seem related to the function of judicial dispute resolution as a substitute for retribution" (1985: 6).

Federal Alternative Dispute Resolution Act of 1998 requires each district court to establish at least one ADR program. The statute also requires federal district courts to authorize the use of ADR in civil actions and bankruptcy proceedings. Before their cases can proceed to trial, litigants must consider the use of court-based or private ADR. North Carolina operates court-related mediation programs and requires superior court litigants and their attorneys to participate in a settlement conference with a paid mediator before their case can be tried in court (Administrative Office of the Court 2007). In California, any case with claims less than $50,000 per plaintiff is eligible for referral or court order for mediation or arbitration. For claims that exceed $50,000, the parties can agree to participate in ADR voluntarily.

Mediation

In our society, many disagreements are sometimes handled through suppressed anger or avoidance. When these methods are not effective, tensions may force action, formal or informal. Formal action ranges from filing complaints with administrative agencies to instituting a tort. Informal action includes unlawful coercion or violence. Formal action may be time-consuming and/or expensive; informal action is obviously dangerous to the persons involved and to society in general. No matter which course of action is utilized, there is a strong possibility that the outcome will leave a great deal of unresolved acrimony. Mediation provides an alternative avenue of resolving disagreements that is both informal and prosocial and that strives to alleviate or obviate bitterness.

Mediation is nonadversarial—devoid of any attempt to determine right or wrong; the process utilizes an impartial third party (a mediator) to assist disputants in reaching a voluntary settlement of their differences. "The best mediations involve *collaboration at every level*. Disputants work together and with the mediator to create outcomes beneficial to all" (Domenici and Littlejohn 2001: 2). "In a broad sense, mediation encompasses a form of communication that breaks through barriers and builds bridges . . . *mediation is a process where parties are encouraged to make clear, deliberate choices while acknowledging the perspective of the other. In this process, mutually acceptable agreement is one possible outcome. . . .* The mediation process empowers individuals by giving them choices" (Domenici and Littlejohn 2001: 32). "The mediator . . . works to reconcile the competing interests of the two parties [and] to assist the parties in examining their interests and needs, to help them negotiate an exchange of promises, and to redefine their relationship in a way that will be mutually satisfactory and meet their standards of fairness" (Moore 2014: 18). It is the mediator's role to reconcile differences between the parties to the dispute.

Mediation

"*Mediation* is an extension or elaboration of the negotiation process that involves the intervention of an acceptable third party who has limited (or no) authoritative decision-making power. This person assists principal parties to voluntarily reach a mutually acceptable settlement of the issues under dispute" (Moore 2014: 8). While the mediator may offer suggestions, resolution of the dispute rests with the parties themselves (American Arbitration Association n.d.).

The typical mediation process begins with an introduction by the mediator, who explains the procedures and attempts to establish some rapport with the two parties. The complaining party is then asked to present his or her story. The mediator takes copious notes, sometimes asking for restatement or clarification of material from the complainant. At the conclusion of the statement, the mediator summarizes the presentation, omitting any disparaging remarks, and determines if the responding party understands the complaining party's story. The second party is then asked to present his or her story, and the mediator once again takes notes, asks for restatement or clarification, and summarizes (Cooley 1986).

The mediator now attempts to clarify the underlying issues in the dispute by talking privately (*ex parte*) with each party (something not permitted in an adversarial process). In subsequent joint sessions, the mediator summarizes areas of agreement and disagreement, carefully avoiding disclosure of material given in confidence. The mediator then employs two fundamental principles of effective mediation: "creating doubt in the minds of the parties as to the validity of their positions on issues; and suggesting alternative approaches which may facilitate agreement" (Cooley 1986: 267). He or she continues meeting individually and collectively with the disputants to narrow the areas of disagreement and to urge a settlement with which each side can live more harmoniously.

The popularity of mediation has led to the establishment of mediation/ADR centers throughout the United States. Some have government sponsorship, others are attached to a university; some function under the aegis of the Better Business Bureau or a similar entity, while others are independent not-for-profit corporations.

Community Mediation Movement

Since the 1970s, there has been a movement to encourage the establishment of community mediation centers. The National Association for Community Mediation (NAFCM) reports on the types of cases that are typically handled by such centers:

- *Neighborhood and community disputes* consist of cases involving neighbors or family members or others who have a fairly close relationship. They can range from noise complaints, landlord–tenant and consumer–merchant disputes, to assaults, threats, and harassment problems.

- *Family/custody disputes* are viewed broadly, beyond divorce/custody, to include grandparent visitation and disputes involving family members other than the husband and wife.

- *Juvenile and school mediation* seeks to address issues of conflict and violence in schools by establishing school conflict resolution programs. Most community mediation programs believe that the sooner people learn basic problem-solving and communication skills, the sooner they can solve their own problems and improve their relationships.

- *Victim–offender mediation* programs offer an opportunity for victims and offenders to participate in a dialogue with each other (see, for example, Umbreit 2001). Most of these programs do not handle extremely serious cases such as rapes and armed robberies. This type of mediation is an effort to humanize the situation and increase sensitivity to the victim, thus creating the potential of restorative justice (discussed later).

- *Courts/legal system referrals to mediation* are the result of case referrals from court clerks, prosecutors, judges, and the police. These cases are generally referred for one of two reasons: either no law is being broken and the conflict involves quality-of-life issues (e.g., noise which does not rise to the level of a public disturbance but keeps a neighbor awake), or the referring agency recognizes that issuing citations or judgments might make the conflict worse.

- *Civil litigation mediation* is offered for those cases that have already entered the litigation process. Cases must be deemed appropriate for mediation and attorneys must represent each side. These mediations utilize an attorney-mediator who is skilled in the use of joint and individual sessions.

Beyond these types of cases, community mediation programs are involved in parent–child disputes and school conflicts including truancy and gang mediation. Programs throughout the country are involved in a wide, diverse variety of innovative applications involving such issues as construction sites, prison, AIDS, race relations, boycotts, migrant workers, agriculture, clean air/water rights, public policy, farm grazing rights, employment, as well as religious disputes. We will examine two different community mediation programs.

Exemplary Program: Dispute Settlement Center of Durham, NC

Established in 1983, the Dispute Settlement Center of Durham (DSCD), North Carolina, originally accepted only minor criminal cases referred by the district court. The center now provides family and divorce mediation, school and workplace mediation, and conflict resolution training. Volunteer mediators are selected through the general training the center offers to the public. Once selected, volunteers receive more rigorous training, a combination of discussions about conflict resolution strategies and hands-on experience through simulated mediation sessions, which are critiqued by experienced staff members and mediators. In addition, new mediators observe a series of mediation sessions before mediating alongside an experienced mediator.

Minor criminal cases referred by the Durham County District Court dominate the center's caseload. Typical cases include harassment, assault, and related problems among relatives, neighbors, and acquaintances. Referrals come from a daily review of new warrants issued at the court clerk's office. Incoming complaints at the district attorney's office are also reviewed because warrants will not be issued in all cases, and some rejected cases may be highly suitable for mediation. The police department occasionally refers disputes to the center.

Specially trained mediators handle divorce cases, which typically require several sessions. At the initial meeting, which lasts about an hour, the parties present the general issues that need to be addressed. The parties are asked to bring relevant information for subsequent sessions designed to clarify issues in conflict and enable them to deal with property, custody, and visitation matters. The parties are asked to obtain legal counsel prior to signing the final agreement arising from mediation. All aspects of the hearings and agreements are confidential.

In addition to handling routine interpersonal disputes referred from the courts, the center processes a large number of worthless-check cases filed in the courts. Judges may make referrals during court proceedings and typically provide the parties with a 30-day continuance of the case. The center sends disputants letters suggesting a date and time for the mediation session. If mediation is successful, the charges are dropped.

Program officials consider several types of disputes as inappropriate for mediation, such as cases involving domestic violence, child abuse, alcohol and drug abuse, a marked imbalance of power between the parties, parties suffering from serious and untreated mental illness, and the potential for setting significant legal precedents. Also excluded are shoplifting cases, as the district attorney's office mandates that all shoplifting offenses must be prosecuted.

Once a case is selected for referral to mediation, a form letter is sent to the disputants advising them that they have the option of engaging in mediation. The level of pressure applied to disputants to attend mediation sessions varies depending on the nature of the referral agency. Referral letters from the district attorney's office have a stronger tone and are sent by the center on official stationery from the district attorney's office. The center also uses form letters that can be sent when disputants contact the program directly to request mediation. The letter informs them that mediation services are free and confidential and that mediators are neutral and do not act as judges but, instead, seek to help the parties resolve their conflict. The letter indicates who has made a complaint and why the complaint was made and suggests a time for a mediation session.

At the center, two mediators mediate each session. The parties are asked at the outset to sign an agreement indicating that all discussions during mediation are confidential and that the parties will not seek a subpoena to use information from the sessions in any legal action. To underscore the confidentiality of the mediation process, all written notes developed by the mediators and the parties are collected and destroyed at the end of the sessions.

The mediation procedure used by the center is common to many programs across the country. Mediators begin by establishing the ground rules for the mediation session—for instance, do not interrupt and be respectful when stating your concerns. Complainants are then asked to describe the problem from their perspective. Respondents are asked to respond to complainants' comments and to indicate their views regarding the dispute. Mediators focus on having the parties clearly state their positions and on exploring common perspectives and areas of disagreement.

If a mediation does not appear to be leading to a mutually agreed upon definition of the problem and a potential resolution to the conflict, the parties may be asked to meet separately with mediators to discuss their perceptions of issues and possible solutions. Such private caucuses may reveal issues that one party is hesitant to present in a session with the other party present. A caucus discussion may also reveal areas of potential agreement that can be pursued. Mediators may also ask the parties to consider future steps, which can disengage the parties from any dead-end discussions. In some cases, when a deadlock occurs, a second mediation session is scheduled to give the parties time to further consider the issues. In other instances, an interim agreement that identifies the issues the parties agree on is drafted to illustrate that common ground exists.

If disputants arrive at an agreement, the terms are written down and signed by the parties. This written agreement, when signed by the parties, may have the same legal status as any other written contract. Approximately 90 percent of mediation sessions result in such agreements (Dispute Settlement Center of Durham website).

Exemplary Program: Neighborhood Dispute Settlement (Harrisburg, PA)

The Neighborhood Dispute Settlement (NDS) mediation center is an alternative dispute resolution tool for police, police administrators, and lower court judges for minor, but annoying and potentially volatile, incidents:

- Family conflicts including custody of children
- Conflicts with a neighbor
- Conflicts between coworkers
- Disputes between an employer and an employee
- Issues between landlords and tenants
- Conflicts between groups in a community
- Disagreements between merchants and consumers

Offending behavior between neighbors may fall just short of being criminal and/ or be inappropriate for resolution through criminal process. Police and other public authorities are usually limited by time/priority constraints in how they can respond to what are essentially private disputes early on. Calls to police and other local authorities are all too frequent responses from bickering neighbors—and perhaps the most perplexing matters to resolve. Too often, authorities have to wait until enough substantiation to support a charge exists before being able to intervene. Utilized properly, community mediation can provide another tool for public authorities to deal with neighbor conflict very early on and conserve limited, expensive resources.

NDS gives police officers another tool to address first-time and chronic disputes between neighbors and other individuals. The program is a front-end approach to community problems, in that it seeks to address incidents before anything is defined as a "crime" and anyone a "victim" or "offender." It serves as an alternative to issuing citations, or making an arrest, or canceling the call—when any of these is likely to leave the situation unresolved.

On responding, the police officer explains the NDS mediation process and the "complainant" (usually the person[s] who called the police) agrees to accept it as an alternative to prosecution for a minor offense or no prosecution for incidents where the officer otherwise may not be able to do anything. A three-part form is completed and one copy given to the "complainant" and one copy given to the "respondent" (usually the person who is alleged to have offended); the third copy is provided to NDS. The form provides NDS with sufficient contact information on the parties and a brief summary of the incident(s) that occurred.

A respondent is required to contact NDS within five days and cooperate with arranging mediation; the complainant has the responsibility to follow through with trying mediation or the matter is entirely dropped. In this manner, both parties have some responsibility in attempting to reach a resolution through mediation. Once the cooperation of both sides is obtained, a mediation session is scheduled at the site (church or other building) nearest the residences of both disputants. Two mediators, who are trained volunteers from the community, arrange for scheduling letters to be sent to all concerned and reminder calls are made the day before or day of the mediation. All parties within the disputants' households or neighbors who have experienced direct conflict with the other side are requested to attend in order to prevent flare-ups from surrogates acting on behalf of the original disputants.

If the parties reach an agreement that resolves the matter, a copy is provided to both sides. The NDS office retains one copy and another sent to the referring police officer. This is the only document or information that is disclosed out of the mediation. A follow-up letter is sent to the police department to have any pending complaint canceled or initiated (if not resolved or no show), whichever is appropriate. If the mediators suspect that the disputants have not completely resolved the matter, they will often urge the parties to agree to reconvene in thirty to sixty days after some history with the agreement has developed. The NDS mediation center has documented a reduction of calls for police service by more than 77 percent in chronic neighbor disputes (Neighborhood Dispute Settlement, Harrisburg, PA, website).

Arbitration

In the last quarter of the nineteenth century, many states enacted legislation governing arbitration, and by the end of the century it was a common practice in the United States (MacNeil 1992). The Federal Arbitration Act (FAA) was passed in 1925 without a single negative vote in either the House or the Senate. The purpose of the act was primarily to make arbitration agreements enforceable in federal court, and secondarily to provide procedures that would make this enforcement process simple and expeditious, thereby enabling merchants to resolve their disputes more cheaply and easily.

The statute was limited in scope, intended to apply to disputes between merchants of approximately equal economic strength over questions arising out of their daily relations. The bill was not the result of trade-offs or strategic compromises, because it was essentially unopposed. The FAA applied only when the parties voluntarily agreed to arbitration. Enacted as a procedural statute effective only in federal court, the FAA has been interpreted to apply to states and to preempt state law that conflicts with the Supreme Court's interpretation of the FAA. Thus, the FAA preempts state law on the use of arbitration unless a specific arbitration clause can be shown to be unconscionable. Margaret Moses (2006) is critical of Supreme Court decisions that she argues go far beyond the scope of the statute, substantially reducing access to the court system, particularly for consumers, workers, and those with little economic power. Any employer, hospital, bank, telecommunications company, transportation company, and scores of other businesses can prevent those with less economic power from ever having access to state court to hold them accountable.

FAA makes arbitration clauses in contracts specifically enforceable, and such provisions are standard in labor–management agreements (Leeson and Johnston 1988; for a history of arbitration law, see MacNeil 1992). The New York arbitration law of 1920 provided a basis for the model Uniform Arbitration Act (UAA) of 1955. Of the 49 jurisdictions that have arbitration statutes, 35 have adopted the UAA and 14 have adopted

---

The Uniform Arbitration Act: Section 1

"Validity of Arbitration Agreement; A written agreement to submit any existing controversy to arbitration or a provision in a written contract to submit to arbitration any controversy thereafter arising between the parties is valid, enforceable and irrevocable, save upon such grounds as exist at law or in equity for the revocation of any contract. This act also applies to arbitration agreements between employers and employees or between their respective representatives."

---

substantially similar legislation. Promulgated by the National Conference of Commissioners on Uniform State Laws, the act provides legal recognition of the inclusion of arbitration provisions in a contract for resolving disputes arising out of the agreement. The UAA was revised in 2000 and makes some procedural changes to better meet the needs of arbitration in the twenty-first century. The 1990 Administrative Dispute Resolution Act requires federal agencies to consider ADR for resolving disputes, and a 1991 executive order directs agencies to consider ADR as a method for improving civil justice. A number of agencies, many with the assistance of the Administrative Conference of the United States, have developed ADR programs for internal as well as external disputes (Stienstra and Willging 1995).

The arbitration process utilizes one or more (sometimes panels of three) persons whose decision is binding on both parties. Although arbitration is less formal than the judicial process, it is nevertheless "a formal proceeding following the standard adversary process, often involving rules of evidence and written briefs" (DeLappa 1983: 9). Parties present evidence and testimony to the arbitrator in a format that is similar to, but less formal than, a court proceeding. The hearings conclude when the arbitrator determines that each side has had a full opportunity to present its evidence. Arbitration promises a more speedy resolution of a dispute than could be expected in the judicial process. It is also conducted in private, an important advantage for parties who wish to preserve confidentiality.

Arbitration

Arbitration is a private adjudication (Anderson 2003) that involves an agreement between (or a requirement that) parties to submit their dispute to a person(s) chosen by them for determination. "The arbitrators may be attorneys or businesspersons with expertise in a particular field. The parties control the range of issues to be resolved by arbitration, the scope of the relief to be awarded and many of the procedural aspects of the process" (American Arbitration Association n.d.: 1). The arbitrator's decision, or award, is made in writing and is enforceable in court under state and federal statutes.

"Arbitrators can summon before them any person with information or materials relevant to the controversy. If the witness refuses to comply, a civil court can compel the witness to appear before the arbitrator or punish the witness for contempt as though they had refused to appear in a civil court" (Baker 2012: 161).

Many companies opt for arbitration because it is faster and cheaper than going to court. Instead of months of depositions, the process of discovery is normally limited to each side turning over requested documents. Arbitrating a dispute might be over in a few months rather than the several years a lawsuit often takes. And instead of trying to educate a jury, you present the case to arbitrators who are already familiar with your industry and with the issues involved—and less likely to issue a runaway verdict. (Bahls and Hauls 2000: 106)

The American Arbitration Association, the Federal Mediation and Conciliation Service, the National Mediation Board, and the Bureau of National Affairs produce directories from which arbitrators can be selected. These may be non- or for-profit firms, and fees range from several hundred dollars an hour to a flat charge of several thousand dollars. The American Arbitration Association is a nonprofit organization established in 1926. It has offices throughout the country and more than 25,000 ADR specialists and handles more than two million arbitrations a year. The International Institute for Conflict Prevention & Resolution (CPR) is the leading nonprofit independent resource helping global business and their lawyers resolve complex commercial disputes cost effectively and efficiently.

As in the handling of civil cases in the judicial process, there may be discovery, typically referred to as "information exchanges," prehearing conferences, submission of briefs, and oral arguments in an adversarial spirit. The UAA provides subpoena power for arbitrators. Arbitration rules typically disavow strict adherence to hearsay rules, but the arbitrator can bar certain hearsay testimony or simply disregard it (Sabatino n.d.). As opposed to the mediation process, *ex parte* conferences (i.e., with only one party present) are not permitted. At the conclusion of the arbitration process, the arbitrator(s) makes a decision orally and usually in writing. On occasion, these may be accompanied by lengthy opinions of the basis (*ratio decedendi*) for the decision (Cooley 1986), but other arbitrators are under no obligation to follow them. Courts have shown a reluctance to overturn voluntary arbitration awards, except when fraud or other unethical conduct is proven, and they generally enforce arbitration rulings as they would judicial judgments (Leeson and Johnston 1988).

Court-Annexed ADR

In some jurisdictions, all civil cases involving disputes under a certain fixed amount must be submitted to arbitration. In 1952, the Pennsylvania legislature granted trial courts the power to establish compulsory arbitration programs (Johnson 1977). In Philadelphia, for example all cases (except real estate and equity) under $50,000 are referred to panels of three attorney-arbitrators. The panel awards are binding unless the loser requests a trial, and the litigant whose trial does not improve the size of the award is penalized. "Other jurisdictions employ mandatory screening panels in particular subject areas, such as medical malpractice. These panels listen to informal presentations of both sides' cases and recommend settlements" (Marks, Johnson, and Szanton 1985: 31). At least 16 states have authorized court-ordered arbitration programs, as have a number of federal judicial districts.

In the federal system, the small percentage of cases that are tried indicates that ADR procedures serve primarily as alternatives to traditional forms of pretrial dispute resolution, and not as alternatives to trial. In administering a court-based ADR program, the court generally provides a roster of mediators who conduct the sessions, establishes criteria for inclusion on the roster, and adopts rules regarding such matters as case selection, methods for assigning mediators or arbitrators to cases, confidentiality guarantees, and guidelines for conducting the ADR session.

Some programs automatically refer certain types of cases to the ADR process, a so-called "mandatory" referral; the parties can request that their cases be removed from the program. In other programs, cases enter the ADR process only after referral by a judge or at the request of the parties. In all federal court ADR programs, the outcome is nonbinding (Stienstra and Willging 1995).

Exemplary Program: The Mediation Program of the United States District Court for the District of Columbia

The Mediation Program of the United States District Court for the District of Columbia was created in 1989 as a faster, less expensive, and more appropriate method for addressing underlying issues than traditional litigation. All civil cases in which parties are represented by counsel are eligible for mediation. While not appropriate in all cases, mediation can benefit many litigants: it can lead to resolutions more quickly, with less expense, and with results that are more satisfying to the litigants than those that result from judicial disposition of a claim.

Mediation services are available to litigants on a pro bono basis. Participation is voluntary, requested by the parties or suggested by the presiding judge at a status hearing. If all parties consent, the judge issues an order referring the case to the Office of the Circuit Executive, where the program is administered. Rule 206 requires counsel to meet within 15 days after the defendant enters an appearance in a case, to discuss, among other things, whether mediation is appropriate.

Within 10 days following this meeting, the parties must submit a joint report to the court describing their views on the application of mediation to their case and outlining the steps that might be taken to facilitate that process. The report must also tell the court whether counsel discussed mediation with their clients before filing the report. Thus, even if the presiding judge does not suggest that counsel consider mediation, Rule 206 requires them to do so.

Cases seen as appropriate candidates often involve parties who have a business or other ongoing relationship and/or when emotions are so high that the intervention of a third person would help the parties communicate. Litigation may not be able to provide a satisfying remedy, for example, when the plaintiff may want an apology—courts generally do not order litigants to apologize, but some form of apology might be available through a mediation.

Mediators have been admitted to the practice of law for at least 10 years and are knowledgeable about civil litigation in federal court. Those selected by the court are trained by professional trainers; the court typically maintains a roster of approximately 150 mediators. Mediators with particular expertise in the subject matter of the lawsuit are available if the judge and the parties believe a neutral evaluation of the case is needed. In such a case the mediator not only assists the parties in identifying their interests and the options for settlement, she or he can also give them an informal, nonbinding assessment of the merits of the action. That assessment may be given to each side privately or to all parties in a joint mediation session.

Mediation proceedings are confidential, and even the assigning judge is not told of the identity of the mediator or any information of what transpired. Mediation ends when the parties settle their dispute, or the mediator believes further discussions would be fruitless, or when a date established by the judge's order is reached. Agreements reached during mediation are reduced to writing and signed by counsel and the parties (United States District Court for the District of Columbia mediation booklet).

Other Means of Dispute Resolution

Stephen Ware refers to two types of arbitration: (1) general and (2) intragroup. The first involves parties who share no membership in any small cohesive group and is more "lawyerized" and legalistic. For example, as noted above, a variety of standard contracts contain clauses requiring the parties to submit disputes to general arbitration. The second "resolves disputes among members of a small, cohesive group"—it is only for members of the groups involved (1999: 1057). In cities with an organized Jewish community, there is often a rabbinical court (*bet din*) or mediation forums for the private resolution of personal disputes involving members of the community. Chinese communities have similar systems. A variety of organizations provide mediation or arbitration in specific disputes; the Chamber of Commerce, Better Business Bureau, and trade associations may sponsor forums for settling certain types of consumer disputes. "Countless trade associations," Ware notes, "arbitrate disputes among their members. In many trade association arbitrations the parties have no lawyers representing them and the arbitrator is not a lawyer. The arbitrator may have a similar background to the parties, or be engaged in the same business; he is likely, then, to be familiar with the presuppositions and understandings of the trade" (1999: 1057–58). For the decisions of these various groups to be enforceable in court, their procedures must conform to the Federal Arbitration Act, discussed earlier.

California enacted legislation in 1872 providing for a "private" judicial system, although it has only been since the 1970s that the law has been extensively utilized. Los Angeles uses dozens of retired superior court judges as arbitrators for civil litigants who opt for a more speedy resolution of their claims. In California, however, these arbitrators have judicial authority and their decisions are enforceable by the state (Chambers 1986). The parties involved pay the arbitrators who set their own fees, which can be as much as $10,000 for a one-day trial. The most famous of these "private justice" judges was Joseph Wapner, star of television's *The People's Court* (Judge Marilyn Milian now presides), which is limited to disputes in which damages do not exceed $1,500.

There are firms that specialize in alternative dispute resolutions services. For a fixed fee they can provide a "one-day trial" with each side paying one-half of the cost; or a "mock trial" with only one side participating. If two parties are involved, they can decide if the outcome will be binding or advisory. The one-side mock trial is an effort to gain insight into the likely outcome of a case should it be litigated. A similar approach, the **summary jury trial**, requires the parties make to make a condensed presentation of their evidence to a jury of persons recruited (and paid) for this service.

The jury then delivers a verdict, but it is nonbinding. If the parties are unhappy, they can still have a regular trial. Summary jury trials encourage settlement because the parties can see how the jury evaluates the case.

Attorneys are frequently turning to mediators to resolve family disputes over questions such as: Should an elderly relative be placed in a nursing home? What happens when three siblings inherit a piece of property? Should a child attend a private or public school? (Dullea 1986). In 2001, the ABA House of Delegates developed the *Model Standards of Practice for Family and Divorce Mediation*. The overview states:

> Family and divorce mediation is a process in which a mediator, an impartial third party, facilitates the resolution of family disputes by promoting the participants' voluntary agreement. The family mediator assists communication, encourages understanding and focuses the participants on their individual and common interests. The family mediator works with the participants to explore options, make decisions and reach their own agreements.
>
> Family mediation is not a substitute for the need for family members to obtain independent legal advice or counseling or therapy. Nor is it appropriate for all families. . . .
>
> Effective mediation requires that the family mediator be qualified by training, experience and temperament; that the mediator be impartial; that the participants reach their decisions voluntarily; that their decisions be based on sufficient factual data; that the mediator be aware of the impact of culture and diversity; and that the best interests of children be taken into account. Further, the mediator should also be prepared to identify families whose history includes domestic abuse or child abuse. (Symposium on Standards of Practice 2001: ii)

One type of ADR used by businesses is known as the **corporate minitrial**, a mix of the adversarial approach, mediation, and negotiation:

> The mini-trial is a nonbinding settlement procedure structured to convert a legal dispute into a business problem. Lawyers make abbreviated presentations exposing the strengths and weaknesses of the case to an audience of business executives from both sides, rather than a judge or jury. These summaries are often heard by a neutral advisor, who may be a retired judge or an authority on the technical issues in the case. The neutral advisor presides at the hearing and may offer suggestions and opinions. After the attorneys for each party present their case, the business executives meet in private to negotiate an agreement. This meeting frequently resembles a practical business deal rather than a legal settlement. (Henry 1985: 114)

This approach can offer considerable savings on legal fees, while resolving issues that can easily drag out into several years of litigation.

Criticism of ADR

A less positive view of ADR centers is expressed by Stephen Schulhofer who declares that, although the idea of "neighborhood justice," a collaborative problem-solving approach to dealing with quality-of-life offenses, is appealing, "what we have learned about the operation of these centers does not afford much basis for an optimistic assessment of their potential" (1986: 86). According to Schulhofer, there are no significant differences in satisfaction levels expressed by those using a neighborhood justice center (NJC), such as the Neighborhood Dispute Settlement (NDS) mediation center discussed above, and those resorting to the courts. "There is no evidence," he states, to indicate "neighborhood mediation, when it occurs, has been more successful than adjudication in reaching the underlying causes of conflict. In practice, mediators have tended to deal only with the superficial aspects of disputes" (1986: 88). He points to the professionalization of mediators, who tend to be lawyers (the ABA is quite interested in mediation programs—they have a section on dispute resolution) and notes that dispute resolution is fast becoming another specialty for attorneys. Indeed, there are many lawyers offering ADR services on the Internet.

Thomas Stipanowich (2010) decries the "legalization" of arbitration. At one time, advocates promoted arbitration as a means of avoiding the contention and expense of a court trial; arbitration represented economy, efficiency, and the opportunity to fashion true alternatives to litigation. While these conventional perceptions are still associated with arbitration,

> business arbitration is more and more frequently described in terms similar to civil litigation—"judicialized," formal, costly, time-consuming, and subject to hardball advocacy. The "legalization" of commercial arbitration is increasingly a leading cause for complaint among business users; at the same time, paradoxically, lawyers are seeking ways of making arbitration even more like court trial, most notably through contractual provisions for expanded judicial review of arbitration awards. (Stipanowich 2010: 1)

There is a problem with participation, of creating dispute processes in which both parties will participate. Whereas it is often the complainant who withdraws from participation in the lower criminal court, in the ADR programs, it is frequently the respondent who withdraws. Christine Harrington observes "the coercion and authority of police, prosecutors, and judges are essential elements to the institutional existence of neighborhood justice centers" (1985: 170). The need to resort to these coercive elements "suggests that mediation reproduces the participation problems reformers sought to resolve with alternatives" (Harrington 1985: 170).

Some critics argue that informal justice systems merely result in **net-widening**—bringing more people into and keeping them longer in the justice system than would otherwise be the case—without reducing the burden on formal systems; persons who would not have been subjected to litigation or prosecution find themselves involved in a similar, albeit informal, system. Indeed, a majority of cases in the neighborhood justice systems would not have received a hearing in the formal courts. In many instances, however, the alternative to informal justice may be a simmering dispute leading to interpersonal intimidation and/or violence (Matthews 1988). Tony Marshall responds that the "provision of dispute settlement services, just like social work or psychiatric services, can therefore be justified in terms of public good as well as compassion for human suffering. Moreover, it may not just be suffering that is saved, but also the resources of citizens released from debilitating and fruitless conflict" (1988: 42).

Other criticisms center on the question of disparity: forcing the poor to resolve disputes in lesser forums while the wealthy continue to have access to, and make use of, the formal systems of justice. "By diverting poor people's cases to less formal forums do we lessen the chance that the courts will be made fairer to poor people—as by requiring that adequate representation be provided to those who cannot afford to hire their own lawyers?" (Marks et al. 1985: 52). On the other hand, there is also concern "that corporations and other major litigants will create 'luxury class justice' outside the courts." Freed from having to deal with cumbersome delays and the other shortcomings of formal justice, elite litigants will desert the courts, and "just as public schools deteriorate when affluent parents send their children to private schools, so the argument goes, court performance will deteriorate further when affluent litigants no longer have to face delays and costs which burden the rest of the litigating populace" (1985: 52).

Businesses have been inserting clauses into retail contracts mandating arbitration, "often in ways that are nearly invisible to all but the most conscientious consumers" (Meier 1997b: C7). Such clauses have long been routine in certain businesses, such as brokerage firms and health plans. Now they are frequently found in many routine transactions such as those involving computer purchases, doctor–patient relationships, and bank credit cards. These clauses require the consumer to give up the right to sue in favor of arbitration. "A person cannot open a bank account, obtain a credit card, buy a car, or use a cell phone without contracting away the Seventh Amendment right to a jury trial." The practical effect of these provisions "is a paradigmatic shift in our civil justice system—no longer is it based upon the fundamental right of trial by jury" (Smith and Moye 2011: 282). In 2013, in a 5–3 decision (*American Express Co. v. Colors Italian Restaurant*), the Supreme Court upheld contracts requiring individual arbitration, thereby precluding class actions. The potential reward of individual arbitration is typically too small to justify the cost.

Corporations have added arbitration clauses to their employment contracts in order to ease the burden of discrimination lawsuits—almost 100,000 discrimination cases were filed in 2010 (U.S. Equal Employment Opportunity Commission 2011). Federal employment law, such as the Americans with Disabilities Act of 1990 and the Civil Rights Act of 1991 have fueled a dramatic increase in employment-related litigation, particularly discrimination and wrongful discharge claims. "If you don't waive your right to sue, you don't get the job" (Kaufman and Underwood 1997: 48). Many of these mandatory arbitration clauses are heavily weighted in favor of the employer: for example, the employer can opt for court; the employer has the sole right to pick the arbitrator(s); employees are not permitted outside counsel; caps are placed on punitive damages. Arbitrators are neither licensed nor regulated, and companies can choose anyone to serve in the position (Furchgott 1997). The Supreme Court has been generally supportive of these arbitration clauses in employment contracts (*Circuit City Stores v. Adams* [2001]; Walsh 2001). In 2011, the Supreme Court (*AT&T Mobility v. Concepcion*) upheld the practice of including waivers of the right to proceed as a class action and requiring arbitration in routine consumer agreements.

"Thank You Member Account" (CitiBank)

"Claims brought as part of a class action, private attorney general or other representative action can be arbitrated only on an individual basis [and the] arbitrator may award relief only on an individual basis."

Another issue is that of uncertainty. As noted in Chapter 1, a rational system of law promotes commerce and industry, which require a high level of predictability—capitalists require a reasonable expectation of a particular outcome for the myriad transactions with which they are involved. Alternative dispute resolution mechanisms, often informal justice, render decisions on a case-by-case basis and not necessarily according to legal norms—"but mediate mutually acceptable agreements or apply common notions of justice to decide disputes" (Marks et al. 1985: 55). Arbitration panels decide cases based on the information presented, without complex rules, and precedent is absent since the arbitrators do not have to explain their decisions (Fatsis 1990). Alternative dispute mechanisms represent a move toward *kadi* or ad hoc justice. "Court decisions are supposed to be consistent with objective legal standards that are applied consistently to individual cases." Outcomes reached through ADR, however, may be tailored to particular circumstances based on personal conceptions of fairness (Crowne 2001: 1777–1778)—*kadi* justice is discussed in Chapter 5.

An extension of the "alternatives" approach will be examined under the rubric therapeutic jurisprudence.

Therapeutic Jurisprudence

Like law and economics (discussed in Chapter 2), therapeutic jurisprudence (TJ) is concerned with consequences. Whereas the law and economics perspective favors an analysis along the dimension of efficiency, a cost-benefit analysis, TJ prefers to focus on consequences as either enhancing or detracting from psychosocial well-being. Originating in the early 1990s in the area of mental health law, TJ "seeks to apply social science to examine the law's impact on mental and physical health of the people it affects" (Winick 1997: 187). According to one of its primary proponents, Bruce J. Winick (1997: 188), TJ "suggests that, *other things being equal*, positive therapeutic effects are desirable and should generally be a proper aim of law, and that antitherapeutic effects are undesirable and should be avoided or minimized." "TJ doesn't necessarily dominate, but rather informs and in so doing provides insight and effective results. Such considerations enter into the mix to balance when considering a law, or a legal decision, or course of legal action" (Schma 2000: 4).

This would include those matters that come before the courts as well as those consigned to the lawyer's office and his or her responsibilities as a counselor for the client's *total* welfare (Stolle et al. 1997). According to Winick (1997), this approach can be incorporated in many types of cases, ranging from personal injury to domestic violence, to discrimination, to estate planning. David Wexler (1999: 696) notes the types of questions TJ can address: "How the criminal justice system might traumatize sexual battery victims, how workers' compensation schemes might create the moral hazard of prolonging work-related injury, how a fault-based (rather than a no-fault) tort compensation scheme might enhance recovery from personal injury, and how the current law of contracts might operate to reinforce the low self-esteem of disadvantaged contracting parties."

> Legal rules, legal procedures, and the roles of legal actors (such as lawyers, judges, and often therapists) constitute social forces that, like it or not, often produce therapeutic or antitherapeutic consequences. Therapeutic jurisprudence proposes that we

be sensitive to those consequences, rather than ignore them, and that we ask whether the law's antitherapeutic consequences can be reduced, and its therapeutic conse- quences enhanced, without subordinating due process and justice values. Therapeu- tic jurisprudence does not suggest that therapeutic considerations should trump other considerations; therapeutic considerations are but one category of important considerations, as are autonomy, integrity of the fact-finding process, and commu- nity safety. Therapeutic jurisprudence also does not purport to resolve the value questions; instead, it sets the stage for their sharp articulation. (Wexler 1999: 696)

Judge William Schma (2000) provides some examples. In busy dockets, he notes, it is common for judges to accept *nolo contendere*—no contest—pleas in sex offense cases in lieu of a guilty plea. A TJ approach asks the judge to consider the therapeutic effects that may follow as a consequence of such a plea. A *nolo* plea can reinforce a process of denial that will frustrate the offender's rehabilitation. "If the offender does not have to admit the crime to the judge, he or she may more easily deny it later to a probation offi- cer or sex abuse counselor. Anti-therapeutic consequences such as frustration of reha- bilitation and return to abusive behavior may result from the judge's acceptance of the plea" (Schma 2000: 1). An *Alford* plea (discussed in Chapter 9)—allowing a defendant to plead guilty while asserting innocence—is seen as particularly antitherapeutic since it allows an offender to remain in denial and resist any treatment. "These pleas are most attractive to those who deny guilt to others and perhaps themselves. But these are precisely the offenders who need help to break down their illusions, excuses and pride. If they cannot remember the past, they are doomed to repeat it" (Bibas 2003: 172). And the victim's need to hear an apology is denied by a *nolo contendere* or *Alford* plea.

Judge Schma (2000: 1) continues: "Consider this final example: the role of apology in tort law. Practitioners familiar with medical malpractice cases know that many plain- tiffs only want an apology from their health care provider for the adverse outcome they experienced. A lawsuit is the furthest action on their mind. And for negligent care pro- viders, an apology for a regrettable mistake would be a therapeutic event." However, insurance companies usually prohibit an insured health care provider from having any contact with a patient who may file a claim. And, while there is a sound legal basis for this practice—fear that a nonprivileged admission could adversely impact the case— the antitherapeutic result is that the patient is deprived of what the patient may want most, and the health care provider cannot take necessary steps to cleanse his or her mind and return to productive work. Moreover, because the insurance provider forces a defendant into a position of denial, the likelihood of reoccurrence increases.

To promote healing for the victim, a therapeutically oriented judge could allow crime victims to speak in open court. Since perpetrators of domestic violence often deny responsibility, TJ would require offenders to provide details about their offenses, thereby ensuring that they accept responsibility for their crimes (Berman and Feinblatt 2005).

Therapeutic jurisprudence is the "theoretical foundation for **problem-solving courts**" (Winick and Wexler 2003: 7; emphasis added).

Problem-Solving Courts

Problem-solving justice can trace its theoretical roots to innovations in policing, partic- ularly community and problem-oriented policing, which attempt to "replace tradi- tional law enforcement's focus on responding to individual offenses with a focus on identifying and addressing patterns of crime, ameliorating the underlying conditions that fuel crime, and engaging the community as an active partner" (Wolf 2007: 1).

In recent decades, in addition to their traditional dispute-resolving function, there has been a trend toward using law and the courts as problem-solving entities. A range of problems—substance abuse, domestic violence, certain kinds of criminality, child abuse and neglect, and mental illness—which are often social and psychological in nature, have appeared before the courts. "These cases require the courts to not only resolve disputed issues of fact, but also to attempt to solve a variety of human problems that are responsible for bringing the case to court. Traditional courts limit their attention to the narrow dispute in controversy. These newer courts, however, attempt to understand and address the underlying problem that is responsible for the immediate dispute, and to help the individuals before the court to effectively deal with the problem in ways that will prevent recurring court involvement" (Winick 2003a: 1055).

This is sometimes accomplished in traditional court settings, although specialized courts are proliferating. "The purpose of the new specialized courts is to qualitatively improve outcomes for litigants and society in cases involving individuals with underlying social and emotional problems" (Rottman 2000: 22). Domestic violence courts, for example, are an effort to provide a more comprehensive approach to this critical problem, beyond the traditional "order-of-protection" response (Tsai 2000). Criminal court processing of domestic violence cases is event focused. But domestic violence is a process not an event, and a problem-solving court can respond accordingly (Winick 2003b). "While drug courts and community courts aspire to help offenders change their behavior, domestic-violence courts are almost single-mindedly focused on simply insuring that defendants abide by protective orders. If they have any interest in treatment at all, it's focused on the victim, providing her with the services she needs to be protected from future harm" (Berman and Feinblatt 2005: 102–3). Previously, specialized courts were intended to enhance efficiency by using differentiated case management techniques. The TJ approach is seen as more appropriate and effective than the traditional adversarial process for these types of cases. In past decades, the juvenile court would clearly have been included under the rubric "therapeutic jurisprudence." However, as noted in Chapter 11, the juvenile court has moved in the direction of the criminal court, considerably lessening its therapeutic goals.

TJ involves explicit use of judicial authority to motivate individuals to avail themselves of needed programs and services and to monitor their compliance and progress. It places the trial judge in a new role: director. He or she coordinates the role of many actors involved in the therapeutic process. "Therapeutic jurisprudence uses insights from psychology and the behavioral sciences to critique legal and judicial practices, and to suggest how they can be reshaped to increase their therapeutic potential and avoid the risk of psychological harm" (Winick 2003a: 1064).

Although therapeutic jurisprudence can include the use of mediation and arbitration in court-annexed programs, it is designed to extend beyond this realm and address a wide range of social problems that affect individuals in a community, paralleling the goals of community policing. The impetus for this trend are societal changes "that placed courts in the frontline of responses to substance abuse, family breakdown, and mental illness. Courts cannot restrict the flow of such problems into the courtroom, and often such problems stand in the way of effective adjudication of cases" (Rottman and Casey 1999: 13). Therapeutic jurisprudence "directs the judge's attention beyond the specific dispute before the court and toward the needs and circumstances of the individuals involved in the dispute." According to TJ, attending to the individuals as well as the issues involved in the case will lead to more effective dispositions (Rottman and Casey 1999: 14). The TJ court "is in a better position to mobilize and coordinate treatment and social service providers in a locality, providing the court with access to skilled resources" (Rottman 2000: 23).

> Problem-solving justice is dedicated to the notion that defendants should be treated as individuals not numbers on a docket. Indeed, one of the primary forces that have driven the expansion of problem-solving courts is the frustration of many front-line judges and attorneys, who have vowed not to practice "assembly-line justice." In contrast, problem-solving courts seek to move away from a one-size-fits-all approach to justice. Many court cases are not complicated in a legal sense, but they involve individuals with complicated lives. Problem-solving justice recognizes this and seeks to give judges the tools they need to respond appropriately. . . .
>
> Many initiatives, especially domestic violence courts, also provide services to victims, including links to shelter and safety planning as well as advocacy. The goal is to prevent "re-victimization" (the sense that victims are abused twice: once by the batterer and again by the system), to encourage involvement in the court case (including corroborating affidavits), and to reduce the likelihood of continued abuse. (Wolf 2007: 7)

Among the approaches that fall under this trend are drug courts and domestic violence courts.

Drug Courts

"When drug courts first began, their immediate goal was to address a case-overload crisis in the courts resulting from punitive 'War on Drugs' laws and the ensuing expensive prison population. Only later did the therapeutic and problem-solving nature of the reform begin to take hold" (Spinak 2008: 260). When the "war on drugs" policy of the 1980s (see Abadinsky 2014) exacerbated already overcrowded prisons and court dockets, new methods were devised to divert drug abusers from the criminal justice process and into treatment (Gebelein 2000). Judges increasingly made participation in drug treatment a condition of probation, as did parole boards. In 1989, treatment and punishment were melded in the form of a specialized "drug court" in Miami, Florida (Boldt 1998). This high-volume court expanded on traditional drug-defendant **diversion** programs by offering a year or more of court-run treatment; defendants who completed this option have their criminal cases dismissed. Between 1991 and 1993, Miami influenced officials in more than 20 other jurisdictions to establish drug courts (*The Drug Court Movement* 1995). The 1994 Crime Act provided federal funding to establish or expand drug courts, and by the end of 1999 they were available in almost every state. In 1994, the National Association of Drug Court Professionals (NADCP) was formed by about a half-dozen judges; about 20 years later, its annual training meeting drew 4,200 attendees (National Association of Drug Court Professionals 2013). There are currently about 2,700 drug courts operating in the US.

Drug courts typically target nonviolent drug abusing offenders and in a "slow track process" retain jurisdiction over the case until the defendant satisfactorily completes the treatment or, if he or she fails, is returned to court for further processing—prosecution and possible incarceration. "Some Drug Courts serve only individuals charged with drug-possession offenses or may disqualify offenders who are charged with or have a history of a serious felony" (National Association of Drug Court Professionals 2013: 7). "Drug courts funded by the 1994 Crime Act may process only nonviolent offenders, but many drug courts that are wholly State funded or locally funded accept some violent offenders" (Gebelein 2000: 4).

The preadjudication model of drug court emphasizes immediate treatment-driven intervention and due process, and adversarial defense lawyer conduct is seen as counterproductive. "When weighing conflicting values the emphasis on treatment may be understandable when the only consequence of failure is to return to a neutral starting point." The postadjudication model includes defendants accused of felonies and the courts "often insist on a guilty plea and may not set aside the plea, hence leaving the defendant with a permanent record" (Reisig 2002: 3).

Domestic Violence Courts

Throughout most of the twentieth century domestic violence was viewed a private matter; police officers typically avoided making arrests, and their goal was to extricate themselves from the scene as quickly as possible. Since the late 1990s, a key development in state courts has been the institution of specialized structures, processes, and practices to address not only rising domestic violence caseloads but also the distinct nature of these cases and the need to give them special attention. "These specialized approaches have collectively come to be called domestic violence courts. There is, however, great variation among these courts and in the specialized processes they use" (Keilitz 2004: III-9-3).

In the past two decades "a growing number of jurisdictions have established specialized domestic violence courts. With more than 200 such courts operating in the United States, they represent an important new strategy for handling the massive number of domestic violence cases that flood state courts nationwide. Domestic violence courts typically handle a jurisdiction's domestic violence cases on a separate calendar, presided over by a specially assigned judge who gains expertise in the unique legal and personal issues that these cases pose" (Cissner, Labriola, and Rempel 2013: iv).

"While some jurisdictions have created courts that handle only domestic violence cases, others have altered court processes to ensure more effective processing of domestic violence matters; yet others have specialized staff that provide support to victims" (Advocates for Human Rights 2010: 1). In Quincy, Massachusetts, "the cooperating parties include judges, clerks, prosecutors, police, probation officers, social service providers, and community agencies. In the New York court, courtrooms are staffed by specially trained judges, prosecution teams, and domestic violence personnel including a resource coordinator, victim advocate, and defendant monitor" (Shaffer 2004: 992).

In domestic violence courts, the same judges and prosecutors who gain expertise in the issues and ensure consistency in how cases are treated usually handle cases. "They will be more sensitive to the needs of victims and be able to direct them to additional community resources. Dedicated courts or prosecution teams may also be able to process cases more quickly, thus reducing the opportunity a batterer has to intimidate his partner into abandoning the charges" (Advocates for Human Rights 2010: 1).

Domestic Violence: New York State

The State of New York defines domestic violence as "a pattern of coercive tactics, which can include physical, psychological, sexual, economic and emotional abuse, perpetrated by one person against an adult intimate partner, with the goal of establishing and maintaining power and control over the victim."

Domestic Violence Courts: Idaho

"Domestic Violence Courts assign families with a criminal domestic violence case and a divorce, custody, or child protection case to a single judge. This practice ensures accurate information for judicial decisions; compatible, consistent court orders; and improved outcomes for families. Violence against women can be enmeshed with child abuse and neglect issues, often because batterers also are abusing children in the home or children are suffering from the secondary effects of the violence committed against their mothers.

"A fast-track criminal case disposition is combined with ongoing judicial reviews. This process enhances victim and children safety while holding offenders accountable. Domestic violence courts hold offenders to a higher level of accountability by concentrating responsibility for defendant oversight in the hands of a single judge who can monitor compliance with court orders and program mandates. In addition, victims gain a greater voice in their cases and are better able to address critical family issues—such as safe visitation—that often impede safety and independence. Additionally, resources and referrals for victims are coordinated early in the court process."

Many domestic violence courts integrate their civil and criminal caseloads; victims can address all legal issues uniformly in one or two dedicated courtrooms, including petitions for protection orders and participation in criminal proceedings against their batterers (Maytal 2008). While retaining the power to issue civil protection orders and prosecute abuse cases, the court works with and refers batterers, victims, and their families to a variety of programs, including victim counseling, batterer treatment, and substance abuse treatment (Keilitz 2004).

Therapeutic Justice Issues

Colorado district court judge Morris Hoffman (2002: 2066) is critical of what he sees in drug courts:

> Defendants are "clients"; judges are a bizarre amalgam of untrained psychiatrists, parental figures, storytellers, and confessors; sentencing decisions are made off-the-record by a therapeutic team or by "community leaders"; and court proceedings are unabashed theater. Successful defendants—that is, defendants who demonstrate that they can navigate the re-education process and speak the therapeutic language—are "graduated" from the system in festive ceremonies that typically include graduation cake, balloons, the distribution of mementos like pens, mugs,

or T-shirts, parting speeches by the graduates and the judge, and often the piece de resistance—a big hug from the judge.

And Hoffman notes, similar scenarios are being played out in misdemeanor and even civil courts, which he considers dangerous: "Constitutional principles, based on our founders' profound mistrust of government, and including the commands that judges must be fiercely independent, and that the three branches of government remain scrupulously separate, are being jettisoned" (2002: 2071–72). He concludes that TJ involves judges in areas beyond their competence and, moreover, beyond their assigned role in our system of government. If judges want to act as social workers, they should at least get a graduate degree in that discipline (MSW)—indeed, there are a few schools that offer combined degrees JD/MSW, such as Chicago's Loyola University.

Inherent in therapeutic jurisprudence is an altering of the adversarial configuration characteristic of a traditional criminal proceeding, in favor of an ethic of cooperation (Boldt 1998; Winick 1997). Abandonment of the adversarial justice role by defense lawyers is reminiscent of the pre-*Gault* juvenile court (discussed in Chapter 11); a *juvenilization* of the adult criminal court. Instead of their traditional neutral and passive role in adversarial justice, therapeutic jurisprudence moves judges in the direction of the inquisitorial approach used in civil-law systems (discussed in Chapter 1) or perhaps *kadi* justice (discussed in Chapter 5). Problem-solving courts engage in judicial activism, albeit on a picayune level, for which the judicial branch has often been criticized.

In drug court, lawyers are frequently not even present during regular drug court sessions. Instead, the main courtroom drama is between the judge and the client, both of whom speak openly and freely in the drug court setting. Instead of defense counsel, a treatment provider often accompanies the defendant, advising the judge and reviewing the *client's* treatment progress. The various problem-solving courts, notes James Nolan, Jr. (2003), have adopted this nonadversarial approach. Nevertheless, terms such as "paternalism" are applied when government is seen as acting in the capacity of "Big Brother." In systems that screen cases and share information among government agencies, mothers who seek relief from the court risk becoming the target of dependency proceedings that can lead to their losing custody of their children (Keilitz 2004: III-9-4).

Judge Peggy Hora (with Theodore Stalcup 2008: 811) presumes the propriety of American drug policy that has been rejected in much of the Western world, arguing that drug court participants "are not forced to leap blindly but instead are given a choice between the traditional and time-honored criminal justice system and treatment for their addiction." Critics respond that such choice presumes the propriety—if not the "success"—of coerced treatment. Drug courts are seen by some as an extension

---

Biting Off More than You Can Chew

"Addressing significant societal problems through court-based and court-structured solutions—in particular the burgeoning problem-solving court movement—requires us to ask whether courts are the best places to solve some of the most intractable social problems of our time" (Spinak 2008: 271).

of an irrational policy wherein the users of psychoactive substances such as marijuana or cocaine are subject to the criminal justice system—albeit a "therapeutic" one—while users of nicotine and alcohol, despite the serious dangers inherent in these substances, avoid coerced therapy. A failure to distinguish drug use from drug abuse is at the center of a debate on drug policy with the drug court approach taking a position that has a paucity of empirical support (Abadinsky 2014). We do not expect attorneys—judges, prosecutors, defense counsel—to be familiar with the scientific literature on drug use; yet they are making decisions about persons whose drug use may be explained by a physical or psychological disorder.

Domestic violence "courts which have both civil and criminal jurisdiction could potentially violate the defendant's constitutional right against self-incrimination" (Maytal 2008: 231). In addition, "if the defendant is aware that his testimony in a civil case (i.e., protective order requests) could be used against him later in a criminal case, he might invoke his right to remain silent immediately" (Maytal 2008: 231). This would serve to derail the civil proceedings intended to quickly provide victims the safety and resources they need and could be remedied through state legislation forbidding the use of a defendant's civil court testimony in a criminal proceeding.

Community Courts

The courts have become distant from the public, both physically and psychologically. The lack of connection between the public and the courts results in the latter being seen by the former as irrelevant to solving the problems of pressing concern to most citizens (Rottman and Casey 1999). Thus, in the early 1990s, the idea of **community courts** was born to develop collaborate problem-solving approaches to neighborhood quality-of-live offenses without bypassing the traditional adjudicatory function of the courts.

"Community courts differ from drug courts and other specialized courts in that the former focus on the community's 'quality of life,' whereas specialized courts focus on specific problems (drugs, domestic violence and mental health)" (Malkin 2003: 1587). As a result, low-level offenses such as prostitution, street-level drug possession,

---

Community Courts

"Community courts seek to fix problems in the courts by developing legal forums that are unique in three ways. First, these institutions bring citizens and defendants closer in a jurisprudential process that is both therapeutic and accountable. Legal responses to families and individuals with multiple legal problems are coordinated, and ideally, unified. Some community courts are multi-jurisdictional courts that link typically separate court parts into one location and under one administrative umbrella. Second, community justice centers and community courts link service providers to the court and, in turn, to families in a way that is responsive to their perceived needs. It brings the court closer—both physically and administratively—to the social and behavioral origins of the problems that it seeks to address, and it seeks to bring services to bear on these problems under the administrative aegis of the court. Third, these justice centers bring the courts and their service adjuncts into a community with limited access to both public and private services" (Fagan and Malkin 2003: 898).

The Midtown Community Court Model

- Locating the court in the community, close to where crimes take place.
- Repaying a community damaged by low-level crime by requiring offenders to compensate neighborhoods through community service.
- Using the leverage of the court to sentence offenders to complete social services that will help them address problems such as drug addiction or involvement in prostitution.
- Bringing the court and the community closer by making the courthouse accessible, establishing a community advisory board, and publishing a quarterly newsletter.
- Using the court as a gateway to treatment and making social services available to offenders right at the courthouse.

Source: Lee (2000: 3).

and vandalism erode the quality of life and create an atmosphere in which serious crime flourishes (Sviridoff, Rottman, and Curtis 1997). Premised in large part on the philosophy developed in the ground-breaking article "Broken Windows" (Wilson and Kelling 1982), the "quality-of-life" approach of community courts has its parallel in policing in what has become known as the "broken windows" approach—leave one broken window unattended, and they will soon all be broken. "Community courts have been promoted as both a way to enable communities to maintain control over their neighborhoods and as mechanism to imbue the judicial system with a degree of legitimacy that it had recently lost" (Thompson 2002: 66).

New York State has been a pioneer in the community court approach where the Center for Court Innovation (CCI) and then-chief judge of the New York Court of Appeals, Judith Kaye, designed a new court to handle arraignments for pervasive misdemeanor crimes, such as prostitution, illegal vending, graffiti, shoplifting, and turnstile-jumping in the city's subway system. Judge Kaye made clear that the new court would focus on quality-of-life crimes and would implement the broken windows methodology (Thompson 2002).

There are more than two-dozen community courts in a number of states, including Colorado, Connecticut, Maryland, and Minnesota. Instead of the traditional adversarial system, neighborhood justice asks judges to play new roles, lessening their judicial detachment and actively engaging defendants, victims, and community members. But adversarial justice is not discarded—the district attorney prosecutes each case and each defendant is represented by counsel (Feinblatt, Berman, and Sviridoff 1998).

Exemplary Program: Midtown Community Court

Opened in New York in 1993, the Midtown Community Court (MCC) seeks to honor the idea of community by making justice restorative and accountable to neighborhood residents. The court is located in one of the busiest commercial districts in the country. The catchment area includes four police precincts and is home to approximately 750,000 people, in addition to more than three million commuters who work in Midtown. In the 1990s, the area was besieged by low-level crime such as drug dealing, graffiti, illegal street vending, shoplifting, street prostitution, and vandalism—offenses and offenders that interfered with business and tourism.

Offenders are sentenced to pay back the community through work projects such as caring for streets and trees, removing graffiti, cleaning subway stations, and sorting cans and bottles for recycling. The court also links offenders to health care, education, job training, and other social services in order to address the root causes of their criminal behavior. The center staff includes a resource coordinator who serves as a link between the court, attorneys, and social service providers, keeping track of sentencing options and making sentencing recommendations to judges based on the results of defendant assessments carried out by the city's pretrial services agency (Feinblatt, Berman, and Sviridoff 1998).

After an arrest in the area covered by MCC, the individual is booked and is either issued a desk appearance ticket to appear in court at a future date or detained by the police and escorted to court. All arrestees are interviewed by the city's pretrial services agency to help create a detailed portrait. This information is bundled with the defendant's rap sheet and made available to the judge, defense attorney, and prosecutor through the court's computer system. Color-coded information highlights problems such as homelessness and drug use. Each defendant is interviewed by a public defender. The resource coordinator reviews the information and makes a recommendation to the judge. If the defendant makes a request for a particular service, drug treatment, for example, the coordinator will have the defendant interviewed by a court-based counselor.

When the defendant appears in an MCC courtroom, the judge already has considerable information about him or her. In 80 percent of the cases, the defendant pleads guilty and the judge is able to construct a sentence that takes into account personal circumstances, past criminal history, and compliance with prior sentences at Midtown Community Court. Approximately 70 percent of defendants receive community service or social service sentences; the rest are disposed of with jail or fines. Those sentenced to community and/or social services are immediately escorted by a court officer to the alternative sanctions floor devoted to the scheduling and monitoring of alternative sanctions and the provision of court-based social services. They are interviewed by nurses from the city's health department, who provide referrals for health services and on-site testing for HIV, TB, and STDs. Community service clients are divided into those requiring low, medium, and high supervision, and the work includes cleaning streets, removing graffiti, and assignments under direction of the Salvation Army and similar service agencies. Social services are provided by a number of public and private agencies, all of who have personnel on site (Center for Court Innovation website).

Community Courts Issues

Community courts reconceptualize the judicial branch. "It is no longer an impartial arbiter of state power, but instead seeks to serve a victimized community that is in need of repair. The judicial branch now becomes an activist pressing for social transformation and neighborhood healing. It pushes for the mobilization of social services under the auspices of the court" (Fagan and Malkin 2003: 902). Question: Is this a proper role of the judicial branch of government? Or does it represent a paternalistic force acting beyond the judicial powers envisioned by the framers of our Constitution? Are community courts being used to usurp roles traditionally assigned the executive and legislative branches? And is it proper that an offender is required to plead guilty so that he or she can receive the services that a community court has available? (Thompson 2002).

Businesses—not community residents—have often been the driving force behind the design and establishment of these courts (Thompson 2002). By focusing on the individual, systemic problems such as homelessness, lack of accessible social services, and employment training and assistance are ignored.

Restorative Justice

"Restorative Justice is a problem-solving approach to crime which involves the parties themselves, and the community generally, in an active relationship with statutory agencies" (Marshall 1998: 1). Although there are important differences between therapeutic jurisprudence and **restorative justice**, the two have much in common. First, both are not merely analytical frameworks but propose to alter legal practices in accordance with new ways of thinking about justice. Second, both are therapeutic in the sense that they place an emphasis on emotions, empathy, healing, and the psychological well-being of individuals encountering the legal system (Nolan 2003). However, central to restorative justice (RJ) is restoration of violated or ruptured human relationships, and "direct participation by victim, offender, and community becomes normative as the way to achieve this restoration" (Olson and Dzur 2003: 62).

In the United States, criminal law views the state as the victim, with the victim in fact placed in a passive and secondary (at best) role (Carlson 1993). Instead, RJ "views crime as a violation of one person by another, rather than against the state" (Maloney and Umbreit 1995: 43). Emerging during the 1970s as part of the victim's movement, restorative justice is the guiding philosophical framework for a paradigm that seeks to promote maximum involvement of the victim, the offender, and the community (Bazemore and Maloney 1994). Instead of simply punishing those who commit crimes—*retributive justice*—the focus is on allowing the offender an opportunity to make amends to his or her victim (Umbreit 2001; Wright 1991).

Restorative justice is the name given to a variety of different practices, including apologies and restitution and acknowledgments of harm and injury, as well as to other efforts to provide healing and reintegration of offenders into their communities, with or without punishment. RJ usually involves direct communication, often with a facilitator, between victims and offenders to provide a setting for acknowledgment of fault by the offender and apologies and restitution of some sort to the victim (Menkel-Meadow 2007).

Although there is some variation, proponents of RJ agree on its core principles (Kurki 1999: 2):

- Crime consists of more than violation of the criminal law and defiance of government authority.
- Crime involves disruptions in a three-dimensional relationship of victim, community, and offender.

Restorative Justice

"Crime is a violation of people and relationships. It creates obligations to make things right. Restorative Justice involves the victim, the offender, and the community in a search for solutions which promote repair, reconciliation, and reassurance" (Zehr 1990: 181). "Restorative justice views crime as a violation of one person by another, rather than a violation against the state" (Umbreit and Carey 1995: 47).

- Because crime harms the victim and the community, the primary goals should be to repair the harm and heal the victim and the community.
- The victim, the community, and the offender should all participate in determining the response to crime; government should surrender its monopoly over that process.
- Case disposition should be based primarily on the victim's and the community's needs—not solely on the offender's needs or culpability, the dangers he or she presents, or his or her criminal history.

As Jim Sinclair points out, the depersonalized mechanisms of criminal justice "fail to deliver the message to the offender that by his/her actions s/he has harmed another human being; and that part of the offender's habilitation or rehabilitation should be geared toward making the victim whole again. The evolution of the criminal justice system in this country has resulted in a de-emphasis on the responsibility of the offender toward the victim(s) of his/her wrongful acts" (1994: 16). Thus, there is a perception that neither punishment nor rehabilitation provide adequate means for an offender to take responsibility for his or her actions: Punishment "may have several counterdeterrent effects on offenders, including stigmatization, humiliation, and isolation, that may minimize prospects for regaining self-respect and the respect of the community," while a rehabilitation response provides little in the way of a message that the offender has harmed someone and should take action to repair damages to the victim (Bazemore and Umbreit 1995: 300).

Restorative justice offers a way to look at the response to crime and criminal behavior beyond the traditional debate over punishment and rehabilitation. RJ holds offenders more directly accountable for their actions. Perpetrators must listen to the human side of the injuries they have caused and must begin to take some responsibility for repairing the damage they caused. In some cases, that might also include offering genuine expressions of remorse (Gehm 1998). Instead of advocating more/better rehabilitation or greater punishment, the RJ model seeks system-wide change, a new philosophical framework in which the victim is at the center. RJ argues not only for bringing the victim back into the criminal justice system but also for including all parties—victim, offender, community—in the response to crime (Umbreit 2001).

RJ is accomplished by means of victim–offender mediation through which the parties are given a human face: "Facing the person they violated is not easy for most offenders. While it is often an uncomfortable position for offenders, they are given the equally unusual opportunity to display a more human dimension to their character.

> ## Restorative Justice in Vermont
>
> In Vermont, restorative justice is a statewide mandate by statute. Persons convicted of nonviolent offenses and placed on probation are required to appear before the local reparative board. Each town has its own volunteer board and larger municipalities have several. Victims and other affected parties are invited to appear, and a reparative plan to be completed in 90 days is negotiated. The offender may listen to the victim's account or to the reactions of victims of similar offenses. He or she may be required to write an essay describing the harm that was done. The plan may include victim restitution, a letter of apology, and community service. Counseling and educational opportunities are offered to the offender with the goal of reducing the likelihood of reoffending (Karp 2001).

For many, the opportunity to express remorse in a very direct and personal fashion is important. The mediation process allows victims and offenders to deal with each other as people, oftentimes from the same neighborhood, rather than as stereotypes and objects" (Umbreit 1994: 9).

Restorative Justice Issues

Although the RJ approach appears appropriate for less-serious crimes and offenders (Levrant et al. 1999), particularly when there is a prior relationship between victim and offender, it is with more serious crimes and more hardened criminals that RJ appears more complex. When either victim or offender is unwilling to participate, or when the offense is too heinous or the suffering too severe, the offender meets with other victims, often through victim advocate organizations, rather than his or her own victim(s) as a step toward assuming responsibility (Zehr 1990).

Victim rights advocacy groups have been critical of restorative justice, particularly those programs operated by community corrections—probation and parole—agencies "whose habits are offender focused." The RJ process "can cast victims as little more than props in a psychodrama focused on the offender, to restore him (and thereby render him less likely to offend again)." A victim "while engaged in restorative conferencing and feeling genuinely free to speak directly to the offender may press a blaming rather than restorative agenda." Attempts to script victim participation are destructive of the RJ process. And "restorative processes depend, case by case, on victims' active participation, in a role more emotionally demanding than that of complaining witness in a conventional prosecution—which is a role avoided by many, perhaps most victims" (Smith 2001: 5).

RJ suffers from the same net-widening accusation leveled at informal justice systems. Thus, in Vermont and Salt Lake City RJ programs, "many of the low-risk offenders for whom the programs are designed might not have had any contact with a probation worker at all, but would have just paid a fine, in the absence of these restorative justice programs" (Olson and Dzur 2003: 74). Since outcomes in RJ are inconsistent, there is conflict with a most basic tenet of American justice: equality. "The traditional criminal justice system aims at uniformity, employing a system of graded offenses and sentencing guidelines designed to assure that like cases are treated alike.

Although far from perfect in realizing this goal, the system at least holds consistency up as an ideal and includes measures designed to bring it about" (Delgado 2000: 751). This is exacerbated in victim–offender mediation forms of RJ by an absence of the panoply of procedural devices that serve to limit state power such as a public forum, defense counsel, and (neutral) judge (Delgado 2000). But as discussed in chapter 8, in the lower courts there is often an absence of procedural due process.

For offenders who have not already pled guilty, participation in RJ could result in the disclosure of incriminatory information protected by the Fifth Amendment (Reimund 2005). There is always a chance that the restorative process may break down, the offender will be prosecuted, and what is said in the restorative justice process has the potential to be used against the offender in a later criminal proceeding. "Self-incrimination is also problematic when offenders discuss unrelated crimes they have committed Even if the offense at issue is resolved in the restorative process, there is still the problem that statements made in the proceedings could be used against the offender in prosecutions for other crimes" (Ikpa 2007: 312).

Full Circle

In the United States, case law and the attendant system of adversarial justice have become so complex, time-consuming, and expensive that they have led to a renewed interest in more informal systems of resolving disputes: mediation and arbitration. Thus, our examination of law, courts, and justice has taken us from a fledgling country's more primitive and informal systems of justice to its use of the complexities and strictures of common law, which later gave rise to the need for a system of equity. We have come full circle in our examination of courts and justice.

SUMMARY

- A trial can be painstakingly slow expensive, and the outcome and outcomes are always zero-sum decisions; that is, there is a winner and a loser.

- Civil disputes and interpersonal disputes that do not involve serious criminal behavior are candidates for utilizing a forum other than the formal justice system.

- Alternative dispute resolution (ADR) can move beyond the symptoms of conflict to a discussion of larger issues than can be covered in a court of law.

- ADR tries to resolve the underlying problems that exist between parties in a manner that will result in an avoidance of future disputes.

- ADR can remove a significant volume of cases from the courts, which would help reduce backlogs and improve the speed with which the remaining cases are processed.

- Dissatisfaction in civil disputes is usually due to the inability of persons with grievances to afford access to the courts unless there is a provision for a contingency fee.

- Some jurisdictions require mediation prior to litigation.

- Mediation is a nonadversarial process using a neutral third party to assist disputing parties in reaching their own mutually acceptable settlement of issues in dispute.

- The mediator attempts to clarify underlying issues by talking privately (*ex parte*) with each party, something not permitted in an adversarial process.
- Since the 1970s, there has been a movement to encourage the establishment of community mediation centers.
- The Federal Arbitration Act (FAA) makes arbitration clauses in contracts enforceable in federal court.
- Almost all jurisdictions have statutes based on the Uniform Arbitration Act that provide legal recognition of the inclusion of arbitration provisions in a contract for resolving disputes arising out of the agreement.
- The arbitration process is adversarial, using one or more persons whose decision is binding on both parties.
- In contrast to litigation, arbitration is speedy and private, and discovery is normally limited to each side turning over requested documents.
- In some jurisdictions, all civil cases involving disputes under a certain fixed amount must be submitted to arbitration.
- In some jurisdictions, trial courts have the power to order cases be submitted to arbitration, and some programs automatically refer certain types of cases to the ADR process.
- The *summary jury trial* requires the parties make to make a condensed presentation of their evidence to a jury of persons recruited (and paid) for this service. The jury then delivers a verdict, but it is nonbinding.
- The *corporate minitrial* uses a mix of the adversarial approach, mediation, and negotiation and can offer considerable savings on legal fees, resolving issues that can easily drag out into several years of litigation.
- Neighborhood mediation has been criticized as no more successful than adjudication in reaching the underlying causes of conflict.
- Business arbitration has been criticized for becoming another legal specialty without providing benefits of economy and efficiency.
- Critics argue informal justice systems merely widen the net without reducing the burden on formal systems.
- ADR is criticized from two directions: forcing the poor to resolve disputes in lesser forums while the wealthy continue to use the formal system of justice; and creating "luxury class justice" for elites who are freed from having to deal with cumbersome delays and the other shortcomings of formal justice.
- *Therapeutic jurisprudence* is concerned with consequences as either enhancing or detracting from psychosocial well-being.
- Therapeutic jurisprudence is the theoretical foundation for problem-solving courts.
- Problem-solving justice can trace its theoretical roots to community and problem-oriented policing, which attempt to ameliorate underlying conditions that fuel crime and engage the community as an active partner.

- Traditional courts limit their attention to the narrow dispute in controversy. Problem-solving courts attempt to understand and address underlying causes of the problems.
- TJ alters the role of the judge, who, using judicial authority, motivates individuals to accept needed services and monitors their compliance and progress.
- Drug courts target mostly nonviolent drug abusing offenders and retain jurisdiction over the case until the defendant satisfactorily completes the treatment or, if he or she fails, is returned to court for further processing.
- In domestic violence courts, the same judges and prosecutors who gain expertise in the issues and ensure consistency in how cases are treated usually handle cases.
- TJ is criticized for judges acting beyond their competence and their assigned role in our system of government.
- TJ involves abandonment of the adversarial justice role by defense lawyers reminiscent of the pre-*Gault* juvenile court.
- There is concern that TJ results in net widening, bringing more people into and keeping them longer in the justice system than would otherwise be the case.
- Neighborhood justice is a collaborative problem-solving approach to quality-of-life offenses.
- Community courts focus on the whole community's quality of life and allow communities to maintain control over their neighborhoods.
- Neighborhood justice has been criticized for usurping roles assigned to other branches of government, and by focusing on the individual, ignores systemic problems such as homelessness, lack of accessible social services, employment training and assistance.
- Restorative justice emphasizes the well-being of individual victims and the obligation of offenders to repair damages he or she caused.
- Restorative justice frequently depends on active victim participation, a role avoided by many, perhaps most victims.

KEY TERMS

adversarial system	diversion	problem-solving courts
arbitration	*ex parte*	restorative justice
community courts	mediation	summary jury trial
corporate minitrial	net-widening	therapeutic jurisprudence

REVIEW QUESTIONS

1. What are the advantages of alternative dispute resolution (ADR)?
2. How does mediation differ from arbitration?
3. What are the types of cases typically handled by community mediation centers?
4. What is the primary purpose of the Federal Arbitration Act?
5. What does the Uniform Arbitration Act provide?

6. What are the advantages of arbitration over litigation?

7. What is court-annexed arbitration?

8. What is intragroup arbitration?

9. What is a *summary jury trial*?

10. What is the *corporate minitrial*?

11. What are the criticisms of ADR?

12. What is the net-widening issue of informal justice?

13. What is the disparity criticism of ADR?

14. What is the "luxury class justice" criticism of ADR?

15. What do problem-solving courts share with community and problem-oriented policing?

16. How does therapeutic jurisprudence alter the traditional role of a judge?

17. How do drug courts differ from traditional courts?

18. What are the advantages of domestic violence courts?

19. What are criticisms of therapeutic jurisprudence?

20. What are the goals of community courts?

21. What are the criticisms of community courts?

22. How does restorative justice differ from traditional justice?

23. What are the criticisms of restorative justice?

INTERNET CONNECTIONS

American Arbitration Association: http://www.adr.org

American Bar Association Section on Dispute Resolution: http://www.abanet.org/dispute

Association for Conflict Resolution: http://www.acrnet.org

Center for Court Innovation: http://www.courtinnovation.org

Mediators and Everything Mediation: http://mediate.com

National Association for Community Mediation: http://www.nafcm.org

Restorative Justice Online: http://www.restorativejustice.org

Glossary

absolute liability   Without the need to prove *mens rea*/intent.

accomplice   Partner in a crime.

accord   When an agreement has been carried out, thus barring the right of further action.

acquittal   When a defendant is found not guilty.

accreditation   Recognition by an official accrediting body.

action   Proceeding or dispute before the court.

action *in personam*   Legal action founded on personal liability.

action *in rem*   A legal action for the recovery of property possessed by another.

actus reus   Behavior that constitutes a specific crime.

adjournment   A delay in trial ordered by the judge, usually at the request of one of the lawyers.

adjudication   A judgment or decision.

adjudicatory hearing   Trial in juvenile court.

administrative agencies   Created by the legislative branch to carry out an executive branch responsibility.

administrative law   Body of law created by administrative and regulatory bodies.

adversarial system   System of fact-finding used in American trials in which each side is represented by an attorney who acts as an advocate.

affidavit   A sworn, written statement of facts.

affirm   Uphold the decision of a lower court.

affirmative defense   Without denying the charge, defendant raises extenuating or mitigating circumstances such as insanity, self-defense, or entrapment.

aid and abet   Actively assist another person in the commission of a crime.

Alford **plea**   Allows a defendant to plead guilty while maintaining innocence.

alternative dispute resolution (ADR)   Alternative to courtroom litigation such as mediation and arbitration.

amicus curiae   Latin, "friend of the court;" refers to allowing parties who are not litigants to participate in arguments before the court.

answer   Formal response by defendant to plaintiff's allegations.

appeal   Legal challenge to a decision by a lower court.

appearance   Formal proceeding by which a defendant submits to the jurisdiction of the court.

appellate jurisdiction   A court having authority to review and modify the decision of a lower court.

appellate review   The consideration of a case by a court of appeals.

arbitration   The submission of a dispute to a nonjudicial third party for binding judgment.

arraignment   Early stage in the judicial process when the defendant is informed of the charges and enters a plea of guilty, *nolo contendere*, or not guilty.

arrest   The physical taking into custody of a suspected law violator or juvenile.

arrest warrant   A document issued by a judicial or administrative officer authorizing the arrest of a specific person.

Articles of Confederation   Document providing for government after the Revolution, but before the Constitution was ratified.

Article III   The part of the Constitution dealing with the judicial branch.

assigned counsel   Private attorney appointed to represent an indigent defendant.

assumption of risk   Doctrine according to which a person cannot collect damages for injuries to which they voluntarily expose themselves.

at issue   The point in the civil pleadings when one side affirms what the other side denies; thus, the case is ready for trial.

atavism   Reversion or "throwback" to a primitive or prehistoric state.

attachment   An order by which a plaintiff can secure a lien on the property of the defendant prior to a judgment.

attorney of record   The attorney whose name appears on the permanent case files.

bail   Money or other security placed in custody of the court in order to ensure the return of a defendant to stand trial.

bailiff   Court officer who keeps order in the courtroom and has custody of the jury.

bankruptcy   Legal process by which persons or businesses that cannot pay their debts can seek the assistance of bankruptcy court.

bar   Partition separating the general public from lawyers commonly refers to the whole body of attorneys.

bench trial   A trial conducted without benefit of a jury.

bench warrant   Judge's order for the arrest of a person.

beyond reasonable doubt   Standard of proof required to find a person guilty of a crime or a delinquent.

bill of particulars   Details of the charge(s) against the defendant.

Bill of Rights   First 10 amendments to the Constitution.

bind over   To hold for trial or send to grand jury.

Black Codes   Statutes enacted by Southern states after the Civil War designed to deny blacks many of their basic rights.

Blackstone's Commentaries [*on the Laws of England*]   William Blackstone (1723–1780) divided common law into four volumes that influenced legal education.

blended sentence   A combination of juvenile and criminal sanctions given to young offenders.

bond, personal recognizance/release on recognizance (ROR)   Document signed by a defendant in which he or she agrees to return to court at a subsequent date to stand trial.

bond hearing   An appearance before a judicial officer who determines the conditions of release—bail—pending trial.

booking   The process of photographing, fingerprinting, and recording of identifying data subsequent to a suspect's arrest.

Brady rule   Based on *Brady v. Maryland*, prosecutors must disclose exculpatory material evidence to the defense upon request.

Brandeis brief   An appellate brief that, in addition to conventional legal citations, contains extensive social and economic data.

breach of contract   Wrongful failure to carry out one or more promises in contractual agreement.

brief   Report prepared by an attorney and filed in court setting forth facts and applicable law in support of a case.

burden of proof   The need to establish a claim or allegation; in a criminal case, the state has the burden of proof.

calendar   A list of cases to be heard in a trial court on a specific date, containing the title of the case, the lawyers involved, and the case number.

capital crime A crime punishable by death.

case law Previous decisions of appellate courts, particularly the Supreme Court.

case method Teaching device using case law and the Socratic method to educate students in law school.

case reporter Series of books containing court decisions of a particular court(s).

cause Any question/action subject to litigation before court.

cause of action Facts that give rise to a matter before the court.

caveat A warning.

caveat emptor "Let the buyer beware"; relieves the seller of liability for a defective product.

certification (1) Process of transferring a minor's case from juvenile to adult (criminal) court. (2) A request from a federal court asking the Supreme Court to rule on a legal question in a pending case that the federal court cannot resolve.

certiorari Writ issued by an appellate court accepting a case for review; requirement that four justices must agree to hear a case before it can be considered by the Supreme Court.

certiorari before judgment Supreme Court rule that permits an immediate hearing upon a showing that the case is of such public importance as to require prompt resolution.

chain of custody Record of continuity of possession of physical evidence.

challenge Legal objection raised by opposing attorney.

challenge for cause Objection to using a prospective juror raised by counsel at a voir dire hearing.

chambers Judge's office.

change of venue Moving a trial to a county where the crime did not occur in order to avoid an unfair trial due to pretrial publicity.

charge Accusation against the accused that he or she violated a specific criminal law(s).

charge to the jury The instructions of a judge to the jury after the trial is complete and deliberations are about to begin.

chief judge Judge who has primary responsibility for court administration.

children in need of supervision (CHINS) Status offenders.

child savers Middle- and upper-class women of the late nineteenth century active in establishing the juvenile court.

circumstantial evidence Indirect evidence, such as fingerprints, from which an inference can be drawn.

citation Reference to a legal authority; written directive to appear in court in place of arrest.

civil law A system of law using statutes or codes in which precedent is absent as a legal concept; statutes and court decisions that involve noncriminal matters.

class action lawsuit A tort action brought by one person or a small number of persons on behalf of a larger number of persons, of which the plaintiffs believe themselves to be representative.

classical theory An outgrowth of Enlightenment philosophy that stresses free will and equality before law—"all men are created equal"—and provides a basis for determinate sentencing.

clear and convincing evidence Standard of evidence for certain civil cases that exceeds preponderance of evidence but is lower than beyond a reasonable doubt.

clemency Grant of mercy, such as a pardon, by a chief executive.

clerk of the court Official responsible for managing the flow of cases and maintaining court records.

closing arguments Summary statements to a judge or jury by opposing attorneys at the end of a trial.

code A compilation of laws arranged by chapters.

code of procedure Provides directions for carrying out criminal and noncriminal statutes.

collateral action Challenging a judgment indirectly, rather than through direct action of an appeal (e.g., claiming that the court lacked jurisdiction).

collateral estoppel Rule that bars raising a claim in a judicial proceeding that has already been adjudicated in another proceeding.

color of law   Acting in an official capacity.

comity   Without being bound by precedent, one court follows the decisions of another court in a similar case.

commit   Court order sending a person to an institution such as a prison, a hospital, or reformatory.

common law   A legal system inherited from England based on tradition or precedent rather than statutory law or fixed legal codes; law the result of judicial decisions as opposed to legislative enactment.

community courts   Courts that focus on minor or quality-of-life crimes.

commutation   A shortening of sentence provided by a governor or president as part of the powers of executive clemency.

comparative negligence   A system whereby blame and therefore damages are apportioned on a percentage basis.

compelling government interest   Sufficient reason for government action that overrides otherwise fundamental rights.

compensatory damages   An award to compensate plaintiffs for financial losses, pain, suffering, or emotional distress resulting from defendants' negligence.

complaint   Means of initiating a criminal or noncriminal case by setting out the cause of action.

concurrent jurisdiction   That shared by different courts.

concurrent sentence   Sentences for more than one crime that are served simultaneously.

concurring opinion   Agreeing with the decision, but not the rationale.

condemnation   Legal process by which the government pays the owner a fair price and takes private land for public use.

conditional releasee   Person released from prison based on the accumulation of time off for good behavior and requiring him or her to abide by certain regulations.

consecutive sentence   A sentence beginning at the expiration of another.

consensual crime   An offense that has no complaining victim but has nevertheless been outlawed, such as the possession of heroin or certain sexual activities.

constitutional courts   Federal courts created as per Article III of the Constitution.

construction   The process of interpreting or determining the real meaning of a statute, legal document, or agreement.

contempt of court   A summary judgment holding that a person has willfully disobeyed a lawful order of the court.

contingency fee   A portion of the settlement in a tort action received by an attorney, generally one-third.

continuance   A delay in trial granted by the judge at the request of either attorney in a case; an adjournment.

contract   An agreement between two or more parties that creates an obligation to do or not do a particular thing.

contributory negligence   Plaintiff's failure to exercise care, which contributed to the damages he or she sustained.

conviction   Judgment of guilt against a criminal defendant.

corporate counsel   Employee of a corporation who handles routine legal matters.

corporate minitrial   Informal device by which corporations can test a case.

corpus delicti   Proof that a crime has been committed: *actus reus* and *mens rea*.

corroboration   Supplementary evidence that tends to strengthen or confirm other evidence previously introduced.

counsel   Attorney; legal advice.

counterclaim   Claim made by defendant against plaintiff; counter lawsuit.

court   Government entity authorized to resolve legal disputes; used by judges to refer to themselves in the third person.

court of general jurisdiction   Trial court that can adjudicate any type of case.

court of last resort   Highest appellate court in a jurisdiction.

court of limited jurisdiction   Court that can only adjudicate certain minor cases.

court manager   An administrative employee responsible for nonlegal matters.

court reporter   Skilled stenographer who makes a word-by-word record of what is said in court.

courtroom workgroup   Participants with shared norms who interact regularly.

court unification   Entails a simplified state trial court structure, rule-making centered in the supreme court or judicial council, system governance authority vested in the chief justice of the supreme court, and state funding of the judicial system with a statewide judicial system budget.

courtroom workgroup   The regular participants in the day-to-day activities of a particular courtroom: judge, prosecutor, defense attorney. Clerks and bailiffs may also be included.

Cravath system   A method used by national law firms to train the graduates of elite law schools in the practice of corporate law.

crime   Any violation of the criminal law.

crime control model   A theoretical construct that emphasizes efficiency as a vital factor in the detection, apprehension, and conviction of criminal offenders and views due process as impeding this efficiency.

criminal intent   *Mens rea*; necessary element to be proved in a criminal trial.

criminal law   Statutes defining certain acts of commission or omission as crimes.

criminal negligence   Crime based on failing to exercise the necessary degree of care.

criminalistics   The science of crime detection; refers to the examination of physical evidence of a crime such as footprints, weapons, and bloodstains.

criminology   The scientific study of criminal law, criminal behavior, and the system of criminal justice.

critical legal studies   View of law as a device for protecting capitalism.

cross-claim   Lawsuit by co-defendants or co-plaintiffs against each other and not persons at the opposite side of the lawsuit.

cross-examination   The questioning of a witness by the attorney who did not call the witness; questions aimed at discrediting the courtroom testimony of an opposition witness.

custody   Detaining a person by lawful authority.

cyberlaw   Legal issues involving the Internet.

damages   Compensation paid by defendants to successful plaintiffs in civil cases.

death-qualified jury   Jury panel whose members do not oppose the death penalty.

declaratory judgment   Judgment that expresses an opinion without the need for enforcement.

decree   An order of the court.

de facto   In fact; actual (as contrasted with *de jure*).

default judgment   Judgment in favor of plaintiff because the defendant failed to answer or appear to contest the plaintiff's claims.

defendant   Person accused of a crime or against whom the plaintiff brings suit.

definite sentence   *See* determinate sentence.

de jure   By law (as contrasted with *de facto*).

delinquent   A person found to have violated the law, but whose age prevents defining him or her as a criminal.

demurrer   A motion to dismiss based on the charge that, even if the facts alleged are true, the defendant's behavior does not constitute the basis for legal action.

de novo   Anew; for a second time.

deposition   The testimony of a witness not taken in open court; used extensively during the preliminary stages of a civil case.

derivative evidence   That derived from or obtained only as a result of other evidence.

determinate sentence   A term of imprisonment, imposed by a judge, that has a specific number of years, for example, 9-0-0 (nine years), as opposed to indefinite/indeterminate sentences.

determinism   A construct stressing the lack of choice, particularly the belief that one's behavior is "determined" by physiological or environmental variables, devoid of *mens rea*.

dicta   Explanatory comments in a ruling that are not part of the *ratio decedendi* and, thus, do not establish precedent.

diploma privilege   Admitting the graduates of law school to the bar without further examination.

direct evidence   That which stands on its own to prove an allegation; usually eyewitness testimony.

direct examination   Questions asked of a friendly witness by counsel at trial.

directed verdict   An instruction by the judge to the jury to return a specific verdict. In criminal cases, a judge may not direct a guilty verdict.

disbarment   Disciplinary action that disqualifies an attorney from practicing law.

discovery   A pretrial procedure allowing access to the information held by opposing counsel.

discretion   The lawful ability of an agent of government to exercise choice in making a decision.

dismissal   Termination of a case before trial.

disparate impact   Law or practice that, while apparently neutral in theory, has an differential and adverse impact in practice.

disparity in sentences   The phenomenon of offenders committing similar crimes receiving vastly different sentences.

disposition   The decision of a juvenile court judge after a positive finding has been made (e.g., placing the respondent on probation).

dissent   A minority opinion in an appellate case.

distinguish away   To disregard an apparently relevant precedent by narrowly confining the case to its particular facts.

diversion   Permitting a person charged with an offense to avoid prosecution in exchange for participation in a rehabilitative or restitution program.

diversity of citizenship   Provides the basis of federal jurisdiction in disputes between citizens of different states and/or foreign nations.

diversity jurisdiction   Federal court authority to decide cases with litigants from different states.

docket   Log containing the complete history of each case in the form of a brief chronology.

domicile   The place where a person has his or her permanent legal home. A person may have several residences, but only one domicile.

double jeopardy   Trying a defendant a second time for the same offense after he or she has already been found not guilty.

dual federalism   Concept that federal and state governments are sovereign and each exercises its own authority.

due process   Those procedural guarantees to which every criminal defendant is entitled under the Constitution and its interpretation by the Supreme Court (e.g., the right to remain silent, to a trial by jury).

due process clause   Fifth and Fourteenth amendments which prohibit government from taking life, liberty, or property without due process of law.

due process model   A theoretical construct which brings into question the ability of law enforcement officials to correctly identify criminals; it stresses painstaking procedures to ensure that errors are avoided, that the innocent are not found guilty, and that the police do not abuse their authority. This restrictive approach places roadblocks in front of the efficiency of the crime control model.

due process, substantive   *See* substantive due process.

Durham rule   A test of responsibility that maintains a defendant cannot be held legally accountable if his or her criminal behavior was the product of a mental disease.

elements of a crime   Specific factors in the law that define a crime which the prosecution must prove beyond a reasonable doubt in order to obtain a conviction.

elite law schools   The most prestigious university law schools.

eminent domain   Power of the government to take private property for public use through *condemnation*.

en banc   All of the judges of an appellate court collectively deciding a case.

English rule   Losing side in a lawsuit must pay the legal costs of the winner.

enjoin   Issue an injunction.

entrapment   The behavior of an agent of government that encourages the committing of a criminal act by a person who was not predisposed to do so. Constitutes an affirmative defense.

Equal Protection Clause   That part of Section 1 of the Fourteenth Amendment prohibiting states from denying persons their right to equal protection of the law (discriminating).

equity   Legal standard that refers to a concern for fairness of outcome. Often implemented through the use of injunctive relief and judicial review.

equitable   Referring to civil suits in equity.

et al.   And others.

estate   Property left by the deceased.

estoppel   Acknowledgment of facts that bars making subsequent claims to the contrary.

estoppel doctrines   Application of equity to avoid unfair outcomes.

evidence, circumstantial   That from which something can be inferred (e.g., fingerprints).

evidence, direct   Eyewitness testimony.

exception   A formal objection to the action of the court during trial; provides the basis for an appeal.

exclusionary rule   A legal doctrine prohibiting evidence secured in an improper manner from being used at a trial.

ex contractu   Action alleging breech of a promise set forth in a contract.

exculpatory evidence   That which casts doubt on a defendant's guilt.

ex delicto   A tort; an action alleging a wrong committed by the defendant against the plaintiff.

executive clemency   Refers to the power of a governor or president to grant pardons, commutations, and reprieves.

executive privilege   Power of an executive branch member to resist a subpoena.

exhibit   Document or other item introduced as evidence during a trial or hearing.

execute   To complete the legal requirements; to execute a judgment means to put the final judgment of the court into effect.

exigent circumstances   Conditions permitting an exception to the need for a search warrant.

ex parte   Discussion having only one party present.

ex post facto **law**   After the fact; statute making an already completed behavior a criminal act.

expunge   Official erasure of court record in whole or part.

extenuating circumstances   Rendering a crime less reprehensible than it would otherwise be.

extradition   Surrendering a fugitive to another jurisdiction.

extralegal   Beyond the formal legal process.

failure of proof   Basis for a dismissal when the plaintiff or (with affirmative defenses and counterclaims) defendant fail to present sufficient evidence.

family court   Court having jurisdiction over juvenile cases as well as issues such as divorce and custody.

Federal Register   Government publication containing all rules/regulations proposed and promulgated by federal agencies.

fellow servant rule   Doctrine according to which an injured employee cannot recover damages against an employer as the result of actions by another worker.

felony   The more serious of the two basic types of criminal behavior, usually bearing a possible penalty in excess of one year in prison.

fiduciary   The obligation of a trustee to act according to scrupulous good faith.

file   Place a document in official custody of the clerk of the court to enter into the files or records of a case.

finding The verdict in a juvenile court.

flat sentence *See* determinate (definite) sentence.

forum non conveniens A legal action that could be dismissed because it is inconvenient for the defendant and/or witnesses to try a case so far away, provided the plaintiff has an alternative forum.

fraud Misrepresentation of the nature of a person, product, or service.

free will According to classical theory, each person has the opportunity to be law-abiding or criminal (*mens rea*) and, therefore, the person who opts to commit a crime is deserving of punishment commensurate with the offense.

front-loading Plea bargaining at an early stage of the criminal justice process, prior to the filing of formal charges.

full faith and credit The constitutional requirement that the official judicial acts of one state will be respected by every other state.

garnishment Collection of a portion of the earnings of a debtor to satisfy a debt.

general jurisdiction The ability of a trial court to hear any type of case.

good faith exception Exception to the exclusionary rule that allows the admission of evidence based on the officer's reasonable, but mistaken, belief that his/her action was proper.

good time A reduction of the time served in prison as a reward for not violating prison rules; usually one-third to one-half off the maximum sentence.

grand jury A group of citizens, usually numbering twenty-three, who are assembled in secret to hear or investigate allegations of criminal behavior.

guardian Person appointed to assume responsibility for incompetent adults or minor children.

guardian *ad litem* Person appointed by a court to look after the interests of a minor during the course of a judicial proceeding.

guilty but insane A legal concept according to which a person who is suffering from a mental illness is not relieved of criminal responsibility.

habeas corpus A legal document challenging custody and designed to force authorities holding a prisoner to produce him or her and justify the custody. Often used as an alternate method of appealing a conviction.

harmless error Error that does not affect that outcome of a judicial proceeding.

hearsay Statement by a witness who did not hear or see the incident but heard about it from someone else; a statement whose veracity cannot be subjected to cross-examination and is therefore generally not admissible (although there are many exceptions).

holding Principle that may reasonably be drawn from a case, in the case law process.

horizontal prosecution Organized on the basis of a division of functions.

hostile witness A witness whose testimony is not favorable to the side that called him or her; can then be subjected to cross-examination by the party who called the witness.

hung jury A jury that cannot reach a verdict.

immunity Exemption from a civil or criminal responsibility.

impanel Select and swear in a jury.

impeachment Official accusation against a public official brought by a legislative body seeking his or her removal; impugning the credibility of a witness at trial.

impeachment of a witness An attack on the credibility of a witness during cross-examination.

inadmissible Cannot be admitted under the rules of evidence.

in camera In private, referring to a judge's chambers.

indefinite sentence A sentence that has both a minimum and maximum term of imprisonment, the actual length determined by a parole board.

indeterminate sentence Same as an indefinite sentence.

indictment Formal criminal charge issued by a grand jury.

indigent Unable to afford counsel.

indirect evidence   Circumstantial evidence, such as fingerprints, from which an inference can be drawn.

inevitable discovery   A legal doctrine that permits the use of evidence even though it was secured in an improper manner on the belief that it would have eventually been discovered anyway—an exception to the exclusionary rule.

infancy   A legal age at which a person cannot be held criminally responsible.

inflammatory remarks   Impermissible remarks by counsel at trial designed to inflame the jury.

in forma pauperis   Being able to bring an action without payment of legal fees.

information   Accusatory document, detailing the charges and filed by the prosecutor, which serves to bring a defendant to trial.

infraction   Minor violation of law not punishable by incarceration.

injunction   Court order prohibiting a threatened or continuing act.

Inns of Court   English law schools.

in personam   *See* action *in personam*.

inquisitorial system   System in which in judges are at the center of the fact-gathering process.

In re   In the matter of.

in rem   *See* action *in rem*.

insanity   In law, refers to lack of criminal responsibility.

insanity defense   Affirmative defense offered to avoid being held accountable for criminal behavior.

intake   Where juvenile cases enter the juvenile/family court.

integrated bar   Membership in a state bar association is required (compulsory) in order to practice law.

intent   *Mens rea*; state of mind that must be proved in a criminal trial.

interlocutory appeal   An appeal raised prior to the completion of a trial alleging errors by the judge which must be corrected if the trial is to proceed in a just and proper manner.

intermediate court of appeals   Appellate court located between trial courts and the court of last resort.

interrogatories   In a civil case, written questions submitted to opposing counsel for answering out of court and under oath. While a respondent need not answer a question deemed improper, the interrogating party can seek a court order to compel an answer.

interstate commerce   Business that transcends state boundaries.

irrational law   System in which the outcome of a case is not based on general principles and is thus unpredictable.

jail   Local, municipal, or county, institution used to house those awaiting trial, those convicted of a misdemeanor, and those convicted of a felony and awaiting transfer to a prison.

joinder of claims   Allows the court to consolidate claims if they arose out of the same incident and are too complex/interdependent to be considered separately.

joinder of offenses   A single prosecution when the several charges arose from the same criminal episode.

joinder of parties/claims   Allows the court to consolidate claims if they arose out of the same incident and are too complex/interdependent to be considered separately.

judgment   Official decision of a court resolving the dispute.

judgment notwithstanding the verdict   A trial judge may reduce a jury award that is excessive, or order a new trial when the verdict goes against the clear weight of the evidence, or reverse a verdict that is unreasonable given the facts presented at trial and the legal standard to be applied.

judicial activism   Pejorative term referring to a court overstepping its authority.

judicial comity   A courtesy according to which the courts of one state defer to the laws and judicial decisions of another state. As contained in the Eleventh Amendment, serves to protect the independence of the state courts from federal intervention.

Judicial Conference   A body of judges established to provide uniformity of policy and to consider matters of judicial discipline.

judicial federalism   Refers to state courts providing due process rights beyond those required by the Supreme Court.

judicial restraint   Belief that judges should exercise power cautiously and within strict parameters set by precedent and/or deference to the other branches of government.

judicial review   The power of the judicial branch to declare acts of the executive and legislative branches unconstitutional.

jurisdiction   The authority to adjudicate a case based on a variety of factors such as geography, seriousness of the crime, or the value of the amount in dispute.

jurisprudence   Study of law and the structure of the legal system.

jury pool   Those persons who have been summoned and sworn to serve on a jury, but who have not yet been subjected to a *voir dire* hearing.

justiciable   Issues and claims capable of being properly examined in court.

juvenile   Person who has not achieved an age set by law.

laissez-faire **capitalism**   Economic theory that argues against government intrusion in the marketplace.

law and economics   View that courts should consider the economic consequences of their decisions.

law clerk   Law school graduates who assist judges with research.

law review   Legal journal edited by law school students.

Law School Aptitude Test (LSAT)   Exam used to determine fitness for law school.

leading question   During the examination of a witness at trial, a question that suggests an answer.

legal aid   Legal services provided by an agency to indigent persons.

legal realism   View that appellate courts should go beyond precedent to consider the societal impact of decisions.

legislative courts   Federal courts created by Congress as per Article I of the Constitution.

legislative intent   Interpreting a statute based on what the legislature was trying to accomplish.

legislative supremacy   Recognition of courts as an inferior branch of government.

legitimacy   Recognition that a public official or branch of government is entitled to exercise authority on a particular matter or issue.

letters rogatory   A court-issued document enabling a party in a civil action to secure testimony from a witness out of the court's jurisdiction; it empowers an official or attorney in the proper jurisdiction to take the witness's deposition and forward it to the court.

liable   Legally responsible.

liberty interest   When a minimum of due process is required.

lien   A legal claim against another person's property as security for a debt.

limited application   A narrow appellate court decision that provides little or no precedent.

limited jurisdiction   Refers to a trial court that can only hear certain types of cases.

litigant   Party to a lawsuit.

lodestar method   A general procedure used by judges to determine attorney fees in class action cases.

long-arm statutes   Allows jurisdiction over nonresidents if they have ties to that state when the cause of the action is local and affects local residents.

lynching   Extra-legal execution.

machine politics   Manner by which political parties assert domination of local government.

magistrate   Judicial officer in a court of limited jurisdiction.

mala in se   "Evil in itself"; behavior that is universally recognized as criminal.

mala prohibita   Behavior that is wrong because the law defines it so.

malfeasance   Official misconduct.

malicious prosecution   Improper action whose intention is injuring—not convicting—the defendant.

malpractice   Improper performance by a licensed professional that gives rise to a legal liability.

malpractice, medical   Personal injury or death caused by a medical professional's negligent care.

mandamus   *See* writ of *mandamus*.

mandatory release   The release of an inmate at the end of his or her sentence minus any good time.

material   Relevant.

mediation   Submitting a dispute to a nonjudicial third party who attempts to get the parties to agree on an outcome.

mens rea   The "guilty mind"—intent—necessary to establish criminal responsibility.

merit system   *See* Missouri Plan.

misdemeanor   Lesser of the two basic types of crime; usually punishable by no more than one year of imprisonment.

Missouri Plan, The   The "merit selection" of judges using a panel whose members are appointed by the governor or selected by the bar association; the panel submits a list of candidates to the governor who must pick one for a judicial vacancy. After serving for one year, the judge must stand for retention at a general election.

mistrial   Trial declared invalid, the result of a fundamental error or jury deadlock.

mitigating circumstances   While not an excuse for a crime, may be considered as reasons for reducing the degree of blame.

mittimus   A written judicial order directing the sheriff or other officer to convey a person to custody until his or her fate is determined by the court.

mixed prosecution   Vertical and horizontal handling of cases.

M'Naghten Rule   A test of criminal responsibility based on English common law; did the offender know that what he or she was doing was wrong?

moot case   If the outcome of a case will have no significant impact on the litigants, it is moot—already resolved. Typically it will be dismissed, but in some cases an appellate court may render a decision on a moot case if the issue is likely to come before the court again.

motion   Application to the court for the invoking of a rule or order.

national law firms   Large law firms whose clients are geographically diverse.

nativism   Antagonism toward recent immigrants.

natural law   Belief that there is a code that is higher/supersedes positive (man-made) law.

natural rights   Inherent rights which cannot be abridged by government.

negative contagion   When strong opposition to a law, such as that prohibiting manufacturing alcohol, leads to contempt for law in general.

negligence   Failure to exercise ordinary care.

net-widening   Unnecessarily extending the reach of the justice system.

nolle prosequi   A decision by the prosecutor declining to prosecute a particular defendant.

nolo contendere   A plea of "no contest" to criminal charges. Has the same effect as a plea of guilty, but cannot be used as evidence of a criminal conviction at any subsequent civil trial related to the criminal act.

normal crimes   A concept that recognizes that there are certain frequent and routine patterns that result in categories of crime being viewed as "normal" by prosecutors and defense attorneys.

notary public   Person authorized to administer oaths, certify signatures, and perform other minor official acts.

no true bill   Grand jury decision not to indict.

nullum crimen sine lege   "No crime without a law." The Constitution (Article I, Section 9) prohibits the passage of an *ex post facto* law.

oath   Written or oral pledge to speak the truth.

obiter dicta   Incidental statements contained in an appellate decision.

objection   The act of taking exception to a statement or procedure during a trial.

open plea   Defendant pleads guilty without a prior negotiated agreement.

opening statements   Remarks made to the jury by attorneys at the start of a trial.

opinion   Written opinion by which judges explain the decision of the court.

oral argument   Opportunity for lawyers to summarize their position before the court and respond to the judge's questions.

order   A written or oral command from a court directing or forbidding an action.

ordinance   A statute enacted by a municipality or county.

organized crime   Refers to persons involved in ongoing criminal conspiracies whose goals are personal gain and which may persist indefinitely.

original intent   Doctrine that the Constitution and statutes should be interpreted according to what their authors intended.

original intent   Doctrine that the Constitution and statutes should be interpreted according to what their authors intended.

original jurisdiction   Trial jurisdiction.

overbook   When the police charge a suspect with every possible violation of law.

overcharging   A practice of alleging an excessive number of criminal violations when charging a suspect.

overrule   Judge's decision not to allow an objection; decision by a higher court that a lower court decision was in error.

pardon   An act of executive clemency that has the effect of releasing an inmate from prison and/or removing certain legal disabilities from persons convicted of crimes.

parens patriae   Common law concept that refers to the obligation of the state toward persons who are unable to care for themselves, such as children or the mentally ill.

parole   The release of a prison inmate prior to the expiration of sentence by a board authorized to make such a decision, followed by a period of supervision by a parole officer.

parole board   An administrative body whose members are chosen to review the cases of prisoners eligible for release on parole. The board has the authority to release such persons and to return them to prison for violating the conditions of parole.

pat-down   Refers to frisking, placing the hands about the body of a suspect in order to detect any weapons that he or she may be carrying.

per curiam   A decision in which an appellate court states its opinion, but the author is not revealed.

peremptory challenge   The right of opposing attorneys to excuse prospective jurors without having to state a reason.

perjury   Deliberately testifying falsely under oath about a material fact; a criminal offense.

personal recognizance   Pretrial release without the need for bail.

personam, in   See action *in personam.*

persons in need of supervision (PINS)   Status offenders.

petit jury   Trial jury composed of six or twelve persons.

petition   Formal written request or "prayer" for action; form of complaint used in juvenile proceedings.

plain meaning   Narrow method of interpreting a statute.

plaintiff   Person initiating an action in a civil case or on appeal.

plea   Criminal defendant's response to the charges.

plea bargaining   Conducting a legal transaction in which a defendant pleads guilty in exchange for some form of leniency.

pleading   Written statements of contentions submitted by parties in a legal action, each responding to the other, until the points at issue are sufficiently narrowed to proceed to trial.

police powers   Authority of the state to enact law to further the public health, safety, and welfare.

poll of the jury   After a jury verdict, asking jurors individually whether they agree with the verdict.

positive law   Deliberately created law (as opposed to natural).

positivism   In criminology, the use of the scientific method to study crime; the belief that such methods will enlighten society about the nature of crime and criminals and that crime is not simply the result of free will.

precedent   Court decision in an earlier case that is relevant to subsequent cases, as per *stare decisis*.

predictability   Ability to anticipate the outcome of a potential legal issue or case.

pre-plea report   Similar to a presentence investigation report, this report provides information for the judge before accepting a plea bargain agreement.

preponderance of the evidence   Standard used to determine the outcome of a noncriminal action.

presentence investigation (PSI) report   A document submitted by a probation department to a judge containing information about the offender upon which the judge can base his or her sentencing decision.

presumptive waiver   Provisions according to which certain juvenile offenders must be waived to criminal court unless they can prove they are amenable to rehabilitation, shifting the burden from the prosecutor to the juvenile.

pretrial release   Setting free a defendant without requiring bail; ROR (release on recognizance).

preventive detention   Holding a defendant in custody pending trial on the belief that he or she is likely to commit further criminal acts.

private law   Civil action between two parties that does not involve government as a defendant or plaintiff.

prima facie **case**   A case that is sufficient (i.e., has at least the minimum amount of evidence necessary to allow it to continue in the judicial process).

privilege   An exceptional right.

privity of contract   Liability limited to the immediate party to a contract and not extending to any third party (who may be the actual manufacturer).

probable cause   The minimum level of evidence needed to make a lawful arrest or secure certain warrants; a level of information that would lead a prudent person to believe that a crime was being, or had been, committed by a specific perpetrator.

probable cause hearing   A court hearing to determine if an arrest was justified—did the officer have probable cause?

probate court   Court responsible for estate administration.

probation   A sentence in lieu of imprisonment under which a defendant is supervised in the community by a probation officer.

probation officer   Public official authorized to accomplish presentence reports and supervise probationers.

problem-solving courts   Nonadversarial tribunals that focus on helping defendants.

pro bono   Lawyer working without compensation.

procedural law   Specific instructions for invoking substantive law.

product liability   Personal injury or damage caused by the negligent manufacture or design of a product or exposure to toxic substances.

pro se   Latin for "on one's own behalf"; presenting a case without a lawyer.

prosecutor   A public official who represents the state in a criminal action.

protective search   A search by law enforcement officers without the benefit of a search warrant to ensure that there are no weapons about that could endanger them, or to secure items in possession of a suspect who has been placed under arrest.

public defender   An attorney employed by government to represent indigent defendants.

public interest law   Noncriminal action in which government is either a plaintiff or defendant.

public safety exception   An exception to the exclusionary rule on the grounds that the action which resulted in securing evidence that would normally be suppressed was necessary to protect the public from some immediate danger.

punitive damages   Award in excess of the loss sustained in order to punish the defendant and or for purposes of deterrence.

quash   To void or declare invalid; usually a summons or indictment.

ratio decedendi   The legal principle on which a case decision is based.

rational law   A system in which there is an application of general principles to specific facts.

reasonable doubt   Doubt that a reasonable person could have with respect to the evidence.

reasonable mistake exception   Legal argument raised to justify the admission of evidence that might otherwise be suppressed, as per the exclusionary rule.

rebuttal   The introduction of contradicting testimony.

recidivate   The repetition of criminal behavior.

recognizance   Obligation to perform some act, usually returning to court to stand trial.

recuse   A judge disqualifying him- or herself from a case because of some personal involvement or interest.

redirect   The questioning of a friendly witness after he or she has been subjected to cross-examination by opposing counsel.

regional law schools   University law schools drawing most of their students from the greater area in which the schools are located.

rejoinder   Defense response to prosecutor's rebuttal; defense response to plaintiff's answer to the defense plea.

release on recognizance   Releasing a defendant without the need to post bail; referred to as ROR.

remand   To send back, usually for a new trial or sentencing.

remedy   Means by which a court can enforce a finding.

remittitur   Procedure whereby the amount awarded by a civil jury is lowered, or a new trial on the issue of the amount of damages is ordered.

reporter system   Publications containing current appellate decisions from a specific region.

reprieve   A temporary stay of the execution of a sentence to allow more time for judicial review.

request for admission   Written statements of material facts or allegations at issue are submitted to opposing counsel for a response—admission or denial. Those that are admitted need not be proved at trial.

reserved powers   Those enjoyed by the state or the people under the Tenth Amendment.

res ipsa loquitur   "The thing speaks for itself"; if damages resulted, unless proven otherwise, negligence on the part of the defendant is assumed.

res judicata   A controversy that has already been adjudicated, thereby barring a new legal action.

respondent   Person against whom an appeal is taken; accused in juvenile court.

rest   After one party has presented all the evidence it intends to offer.

restorative justice   Approach to criminal justice in which the victim is at the center.

retainer   An advance paid by a client to an attorney in order to engage the attorney's services.

reverse   Act of an appellate court setting aside the decision of a trial court.

reversible error   A procedural error during a trial serious enough to justify reversing the judgment of a lower court.

rules of evidence   Standards governing the admission of evidence.

search warrant   A judicial order authorizing a law enforcement officer to search a specific area for a particular piece of evidence.

self-defense   Affirmative defense claiming that physical force was used to protect oneself or others in imminent danger.

self-incrimination   Forcing a suspect to provide evidence against him- or herself; prohibited by the Fifth Amendment.

senatorial courtesy   Tradition that allows a US senator to veto the appointment of a federal official in his or her state.

sentence disparity   *See* disparity in sentences.

sentencing guidelines   An attempt to reduce sentencing disparity by providing judges with a structure to guide their decisions.

separation of powers   The division of government into three branches: executive, legislative, and judicial.

sequestering   Placing a jury in protective custody until they complete their deliberations.

service of process   Delivery of writs or summonses to the appropriate party.

shelter   Temporary residential facility for children in need of emergency care.

sidebar   Conference between judges and attorneys in courtroom out of hearing by the jury.

small-claims court   Court having jurisdiction to adjudicate civil claims below a certain amount without a jury and in which parties usually appear without attorneys (*pro se*).

social investigation   A study prepared by a probation officer in juvenile court to provide the judge with information on which to base a disposition.

sociological jurisprudence   View that courts should consider the social implications of decisions.

Socratic method   Teaching method that challenges law students to "think on their feet."

solicitor general   Federal official who represents the government before the Supreme Court.

sovereign immunity   Rule of law that a nation or state is exempt from a lawsuit (unless legislation specifically waives immunity).

special verdict   In civil trials, when the issues involve complex legal and scientific (e.g., medical or engineering) matters that need to be simplified in order to be understood by the jury, the jury responds to a series of written questions of fact posed by the judge instead of delivering a verdict for or against the defendant. Based on the jury's answers, the judge determines the outcome of the case.

specific performance   An order under equity compelling the fulfillment of the terms of a contract where damages would be inappropriate or inadequate.

speedy trial   Sixth Amendment requirement for which states and the federal government have statutes specifying the amount of time allowed from arrest to trial.

standing   Having the right to bring a legal action by virtue of being personally harmed.

stare decisis (*stare decisis et non quieta movere*)   "Stand by the decision and do not disturb what is settled" is the basis for adhering to precedent in common/case law adjudications.

states' rights   View that certain powers are reserved to state authority.

status offense   Actions that would not constitute a crime if the actor were an adult (e.g., truancy) but, in accord with *parens patriae*, can subject the youngster to the juvenile court process.

statute   Law passed by a legislature.

statute of limitations   Period of time fixed by law within which a lawsuit or prosecution must be commenced, or it will be barred forever.

statutory law   The enactments of legislative bodies.

stay   A court order that temporarily stops a legal proceeding.

stipulation   An agreement between opposing counsel on certain uncontested factual issues, such as the date and time of the incident, photos, sketches, and other routine evidence.

strict liability   The absence of a need to prove *mens rea* (criminal intent) in a criminal action or fault (e.g., negligence) in a tort case; absolute liability.

strike   Highlighting evidence in the record of a case that has been improperly offered and will not be relied on.

subpoena *ad testificandum*   A court order requiring a witness to appear and testify.

subpoena *duces tecum*   "Bring with you"; a court order requiring a witness to bring all relevant documents that might affect the outcome of legal proceedings.

substantive due process   A vague concept, based on the Fourteenth Amendment, that there are individual rights which cannot be unreasonably or arbitrarily interfered with.

summary decision   Made by an appellate court without benefit of briefs or oral arguments.

summary judgment   A judgment rendered by the court on a motion by the plaintiff or defendant who claims that there is an absence of a factual dispute requiring a verdict.

summary jury trial   An unofficial proceeding before a mock jury to test evidence so that a trial might be avoided.

summons   Legal instrument used to notify a person that he/she is being named as a party in a legal action and requiring the defendant to appear and defend. Also used to notify a witness or juror to appear in court.

Supremacy Clause   Article VI, Clause 2, declares the federal Constitution and laws to be "the supreme Law of the Land," and provides the federal government powers that cannot be exercised by the states and which the states must heed.

suppress   Forbid the use of evidence at trial because it was improperly obtained.

sustain   Upholding an objection.

temporary restraining order   Judicial order in equity prohibiting a person from an action that is likely to cause irreparable harm that lasts only until a hearing can be held.

testimony   Oral evidence presented by witnesses.

textualist   A person who uses a method of judicial interpretation that stresses the plain meaning of words as they were understood at the time they were promulgated, as opposed to seeking out the intent of those who enacted the law.

therapeutic jurisprudence   Study of the role of law as a helping/treating agent.

tort   A private wrong that is the subject of a lawsuit; *ex delicto*.

transcript   Written word-for-word record of a judicial proceeding or oral deposition.

trial   A fact-finding process using the adversarial method.

trial *de novo*   A new trial in which the entire case is retried as if no prior trial had taken place.

true bill   The handing up of an indictment by a grand jury.

truth in sentencing   Statute requiring offenders to serve their entire sentence, usually with a small reduction for good behavior.

ultra vires   Acting beyond one's authority; typically applies to public officials and corporations.

unification   *See* court unification.

Uniform Commercial Code   Comprehensive laws relating to commercial transactions promulgated by the National Conference of Commissioners on Uniform State Laws and adopted by each state except Louisiana.

uphold   Appellate court agrees with the lower court.

vacating a decision   Setting aside or rescinding a faulty judgment or at the request of the winning litigant, usually for extra compensation to avoid making it part of the public record.

venire   Process by which jurors are summoned to service.

venue   Proper jurisdiction for considering a particular case.

verdict   A conclusion that forms the basis for the court's judgment.

vertical prosecution   Organized on a caseload basis.

vigilantism   Extralegal use of force.

***voir dire* hearing**   The judicial procedure by which opposing attorneys have an opportunity to question and/or challenge prospective jurors.

waive   To give up a personal right (e.g., to remain silent as per the Fifth Amendment).

warrant   Legal document authorizing a search or arrest.

witness   A person called to testify in a judicial proceeding.

writ   A court order commanding certain action(s).

writ of certiorari   Order of the US Supreme Court directing a lower court to transmit records for a case that it has agreed to hear on appeal.

writ of *mandamus*   From a Latin word meaning "to order"; an extraordinary court order compelling a public official to perform his or her duty.

writ of prohibition   Extraordinary writ forbidding a public official from performing some act.

References

Aaronson, David E., Nicholas N. Kittrie, David J. Saari, and Carolina Cooper
  1977   *Alternatives to Conventional Adjudication Guidebook for Planners and Practitioners*. Washington, DC: US Government Printing Office.
Abadinsky, Howard
  2015   *Probation and Parole: Theory and Practice*, 12th ed. Upper Saddle River, NJ: Pearson.
  2014   *Drug Use and Abuse: A Comprehensive Introduction*, 8th ed. Belmont, CA: Wadsworth.
  2013   *Organized Crime*, 10th ed. Belmont, CA: Wadsworth.
  2012   *Probation and Parole: Theory and Practice*, 11th ed. Upper Saddle River, NJ: Pearson.
  1983   *The Criminal Elite: Professional and Organized Crime*. Westport, CT: Greenwood.
Abel, Richard L.
  1989   *American Lawyers*. New York: Oxford University Press.
Abraham, Henry J.
  1998   *The Judicial Process: An Introductory Analysis of the Courts of the United States, England and France*, 6th ed. New York: Oxford University Press.
  1990   "Beneficial Advice or Presumptuous Veto? The ABA's Committee on Federal Judiciary Revisited." Pages 61–78 in *Judicial Selection: Merit, Ideology, and Politics*, edited by Henry J. Abraham, Eugene W. Hickok, Jr., and William Bradford Reynolds. Washington, DC: National Legal Center for the Public Interest.
Abraham, Henry J. and Barbara A. Perry
  2003   *Freedom and the Court: Civil Rights and Liberties in the United States*, 8th ed. Lawrence: University Press of Kansas.
Abrahamson, Leslie with Richard Flaste
  1997   *The Defense Is Ready: Life in the Trenches of Criminal Law*. New York: Simon and Schuster.
Adler, Matthew D. and Eric A. Posner
  2000   "Implementing Cost-Benefit Analysis When Preferences Are Distorted." *Law and Economics Working Paper No, 88*, University of Chicago Law School.
Administrative Office of the Court
  2007   *The Judicial System in North Carolina*. Raleigh, NC: Author. Available: http://euro.ecom.cmu.edu/program/law/08-732/Courts/NorthCarolinaJudicialSystem.pdf.
Advocates for Human Rights
  2010   *Specialized Domestic Violence Courts*. Available: www.theadvocatesforhumanrights.org/about_us.
Albonetti, Celesta A.
  1986   "Criminality, Prosecutorial Screening, and Uncertainty: Toward a Theory of Discretionary Decision Making in Felony Case Processings." *Criminology* 24 (Nov.): 623–44.

Alden, William
 2012 "Looking to Make a Profit from Lawsuits, Firms Invest in Them." *New York Times* (May 1): B3.

Aldisert, Ruggero J.
 1997 *Logic For Lawyers: A Guide to Clear Legal Thinking*, 3rd ed. South Bend, IN: The National Institute for Trial Advocacy.

Alexander, Gregory S.
 n.d. Property in the Two Legal Realisms." Cornell Law School Working Papers.

Alfini, James J.
 1986 "Alternative Dispute Resolution and the Courts: An Introduction." *Judicature* 69 (Feb.–March): 252–53, 314.

Alliance of American Insurers (AAI)
 1987 *Advancing Justice: May We Approach the Bench?* Schaumburg, IL: AAI.

Alschuler, Albert W.
 2000 *Law without Values: The Life, Work, and Legacy of Justice Holmes.* Chicago: University of Chicago Press.
 1975 "The Defense Attorney's Role in Plea Bargaining." *Yale Law Review* 84: 1179–314.
 1968 "The Prosecutor's Role in Plea Bargaining." *University of Chicago Law Review* 36: 50–112.

Alter, Jonathan, with Howard Fineman and Eleanor Clift
 1989 "The World of Congress." *Newsweek* (April 24): 28–34.

Amar, Akhil Reed
 2005 *America's Constitution: A Biography.* New York: Random House.

Amer, Mildred
 2006. "Membership of the 109th Congress: A Profile." CRS Report for Congress. http://www.senate.gov/reference/resources/pdf/RS22007.pdf.

American Arbitration Association (AAA)
 n.d. *Introductory Guide to AAA Arbitration and Mediation.* New York: AAA. Available: http://www.adr.org/aaa/ShowPDF?doc=ADRSTG_003835.

American Bar Association (ABA)
 n.d. *2012 Law Graduate Employment Data.* Available: http://www.americanbar.org/content/dam/aba/administrative/legal_education_and_admissions_to_the_bar/reports/law_grad_employment_data.authcheckdam.pdf.
 1980 *Law Schools and Professional Education: Task Force on Lawyer Competency and the Role of Law Schools.* Chicago: ABA.

American Bar Association Commission on Women in the Profession
 2013 "Women in the Law." Available http://www.americanbar.org/groups/women/resources/statistics.html.

American Friends Service Committee
 1971 *Struggle for Justice.* New York: Hill and Wang.

Anderson, James M. and Paul Heaton
 2012 *Measuring the Effect of Defense Counsel on Homicide Case Outcomes.* Washington, DC: National Institute of Justice.

Anderson, Richard E.
 2013 "Ob-Gyn Shortage Is Going to Get Worse." *livescience.* Available: http://www.livescience.com/37824-obgyn-shortage-looming.html.

Anderson, Van A.
 2003 "Alternative Dispute Resolution and Professional Responsibility South Carolina: A Changing Landscape." *South Carolina Law Review* 55 (Fall): 191–220.

Andreski, Stanislav, ed.
 1971 *Herbert Spencer: Structure, Function and Evolution.* New York: Scribner's.

Andrews, Michelle
    2003   "Making Malpractice Harder to Prove." *New York Times* (December 21): BU 8.

Applebaum, Binyamin
    2010   "Putting Money on Lawsuits, Investors Share in the Payouts." *New York Times* (November 15): 1, 20–21.

Archer, Pete
    1956   *The Queen's Courts: An Account of the History, Jurisdiction, and Procedure of the Various Courts and Tribunals Which Administer English Law.* Middlesex, UK: Penguin.

Armstrong, Ken
    1998   "The Verdict on the Accusers: Not So Grand." *Chicago Tribune* (September 27): Sec. 2: 1, 8.
    1997   "Injured Construction Workers Regain Right to Seek Damages." *Chicago Tribune* (September 12): Sec. 2: 6.

Armstrong, Ken and Andrew Fegelman
    1996   "Wayward Words Might Kill Workers' Suits." *Chicago Tribune* (December 13): B1, 2.

Armstrong, Ken and Maurice Possley
    1999   "The Verdict: Dishonor." *Chicago Tribune* (January 10): 1, 13.

Aron, Nan
    1989   *Liberty and Justice for All: Public Interest Law in the 1980s and Beyond.* Boulder, CO: Westview Press.

Aspen, Marvin E.
    1987   "Let's Select Judges on Their Merit, Not Their Politics." *Chicago Tribune* (Jan. 21): 17.

Associated Press
    2005   "Skipping Law School. Lincoln Did It. Why Not the Valoises?" *New York Times* (September 21): 23.
    2000a   "Prosecutor Admits Botched Evidence." June 14.
    2000b   "Jury Awards $3M in Botched Surgery." July 1.
    1994   "Accused of Falsifying Evidence in Criminal Cases, Chemist Surrenders." *Chicago Tribune* (August 5): 14.

Atiyah, P. S. and R. S. Summers
    1987   *Form and Substance in Anglo-American Law: A Comparative Study in Legal Reasoning, Legal Theory and Legal Institutions.* Oxford, UK: Oxford University Press.

Aubert, Vilhelm
    1983   *In Search of Law: Sociological Approaches to Law.* Totowa, NJ: Barnes and Noble.

Auerbach, Carl A.
    1983   "Administrative Agency." Pages 74–75 in *Guide to American Law.* St. Paul, MN: West.

Auerbach, Jerold S.
    1976   *Unequal Justice: Lawyers and Social Change in America.* New York: Oxford University Press.
    1971   "Enmity and Amity: Law Teachers and Practitioners, 1900–1922." Pages 549–601 in *Law in American History,* edited by Donald Fleming and Bernard Bailyn. Boston: Little, Brown.

Axelrod, David
    1983   "Judicial Bench No Place to Practice Party Loyalty." *Chicago Tribune* (August 28): Sec. 4: 4.

Bacigal, Ronald J.
    1990   *The Limits of Litigation: The Dalkon Shield Controversy.* Durham, NC: Carolina Academic Press.

Baden, Michael M., with Judith A. Hennessee
    1989   *Unnatural Death: Confessions of a Medical Examiner.* New York: Random House.

Bahls, Steven C. and Jane Easter Hauls
    2000   "And Arbitrated Justice for All." *Entrepreneur* 28 (December): 106.

Baker, Al
    2005   "Ruling Upholds Ban on Cameras in Court." *New York Times* (June 17): B3.

Baker, Amanda M.
    2012   "A Higher Authority: Judicial Review of Religious Arbitration." *Vermont Law Review* 37: 157–237.

Baldwin, Scott
    1984   "The Sure Way to Protect the 'Little Guy.'" *New York Times* (December 2): F2.

Bannon, Alicia
    2013   *Federal Court Vacancies: The Trial Courts.* New York: Brennan Center for Justice Analysis.

The Bar Examiner
    2013   "2012 Statistics." Available: http://www.ncbex.org/assets/media_files/Bar-Examiner/articles/2013/8201132012statistics.pdf.

Barnickol, Laura A.
    2000   "The Disparate Treatment of Males and Females within the Juvenile Justice System." *Journal of Law and Policy* 2: 429–457. Available: https://law.wustl.edu/journal/2/p429barnickol.pdf.

Barry, Dan
    2006   "In This Hall of Justice, One Case May Be Mice, the Next Cheese." *New York Times* (June 3): B1, 4.

Baudouin, Jean-Louis
    1974   Impact of Common Law on the Civilian Systems of Louisiana and Quebec." Pages 1–11 in *The Role of Judicial Decisions and Doctrine in Civil Law in Mixed Jurisdictions,* edited by Joseph Dainow. Baton Rouge: Louisiana State University Press.

Baum, Lawrence
    2013   *The Supreme Court,* 11th ed. Washington, DC: Congressional Quarterly Press.
    1994   *American Courts.* Boston: Houghton Mifflin.

Bazemore, Gordon and Dennis Maloney
    1994   "Rehabilitating Community Service: Toward Restorative Service Sanctions in a Balanced Justice System." *Federal Probation* 58 (March): 24–35.

Bazemore, Gordon and Mark S. Umbreit
    1995   "Rethinking the Sanctioning Function in Juvenile Court: Retributive or Restorative Responses to Youth Crime." *Crime and Delinquency* 41 (July): 296–316.

Becker, David M.
    1998   "Debunking the Sanctity of Precedent." *Washington University Law Quarterly* 76: 854–974.

Beckerman-Rodau, Andrew
    1999   "A Jurisprudential Approach to Common Law Legal Analysis." (Originally published in the *Rutgers Law Review* 269.) Available: http://www.lawprofessor.org/publications/articles.html&articlename=rutgers (accessed October 24, 2013).

Bellows, Randy I.
    1983   "Notes of a Public Defender." Paper prepared for the Program on the Legal Profession. Harvard University Law School.

Bendavid, Naftali
    2001   "Report: Public Should Finance Judge Elections." *Chicago Tribune* (July 23): 7.

Benner, Laurence A.
    2002   "Eliminating Excessive Public Defender Workloads." *Criminal Justice* 26 (Summer). Available: http://www.americanbar.org/content/dam/aba/publications/criminal_justice_magazine/cjsu11_benner.authcheckdam.pdf.

Benson, Michael L., Francis T. Cullen, and William J. Maakestad
  1993   *Local Prosecutors and Corporate Crime*. Washington, DC: National Institute of Justice.
Berger, Raoul
  1987   *Federalism: The Founders' Design*. Norman: University of Oklahoma Press.
  1977   *Government by Judiciary: The Transformation of the Fourteenth Amendment*. Cambridge, MA: Harvard University Press.
Berkheiser, Mary
  2002   "The Fiction of Juvenile Right to Counsel: Waiver in the Juvenile Courts." *Florida Law Review* 54 (September): 577–667.
Berman, Greg and John Feinblatt
  2005   *Good Courts: A Case for Problem-Solving Justice*. New York: The New Press.
Berman, Harold J.
  1958   *The Nature and Functions of Law*. Brooklyn, NY: Foundation Press.
Berman, Harold J. and Samir Saliba
  2009   *The Nature and Functions of Law*, 7th ed. New York: West/Thomson Reuters.
Bernstein, Illene N., Edward Kick, Jan T. Leung, and Barbara Schultz
  1977   "Charge Reduction: An Intermediate Stage in the Process of Labeling Criminal Defendants." *Social Forces* 56 (Dec.): 362–84.
Bernstein, Nina
  1996   "Curb on Class-Action Suits for the Poor Is Challenged." *New York Times* (August 1): 14.
Bibas, Stephanos
  2003   "Using Plea Procedures to Combat Denial and Minimization." Pages 169–76 *in Judging in a Therapeutic Key* edited by Bruce J. Winick and David B. Wexler. Durham, NC: Carolina Academic Press.
Birckhead, Tamar R.
  2013   "Closing the Widening Net: The Rights of Juveniles at Intake." *Texas Tech Law Review* 46: 1–28.
Black, Donald
  1988   *Sociological Justice*. New York: Oxford University Press.
Blackstone, Erwin A. and Gary W. Bowman
  1999   "Economics and the Law from Posner to Post-Modernism." *Atlantic Economic Journal* 27 (December).
Blakeslee, Sandra
  1996   "Genetic Questions Are Sending Judges Back to Classroom." *New York Times* (July 9): B7, 10.
Blackwell, Brenda Sims and Clark D. Cunningham
  2004   "Taking the Punishment out of the Process: From Substantive Criminal Justice through Procedural Justice to Restorative Justice." *Law and Contemporary Problems* 67 (Autumn): 59–87. Available: http://scholarship.law.duke.edu/cgi/viewcontent.cgi?article=1340&context=lcp.
Blumberg, Abraham S.
  1967   "The Practice of Law as Confidence Game: Organizational Cooptation of a Profession." *Law and Society Review* 1: 15–39.
Blumenthal, Ralph
  2005   "In Texas, Oversight for Crime Labs Is Urged." *New York Times* (January 5): 18.
  2003   "Malpractice Suits Capped at $750,000 in Texas Vote." *New York Times* (September 15): 12.
Blumrosen, Alfred W.
  1962   "Legal Process and Labor Laws." Pages 188–225 in *Law and Sociology: Exploratory Essays*, edited by William Evan. Glencoe, IL: Free Press.

Boland, Barbara and Elizabeth Brady
    1985   *The Prosecution of Felony Arrests, 1980.* Washington, DC: US Government Printing Office.
Boland, Barbara, Elizabeth Brady, Herbert Tyson, and John Bassler
    1983   *The Prosecution of Felony Arrests, 1979.* Washington, DC: US Government Printing Office.
Boland, Barbara, Catherine H. Conly, Lynn Warner, Ronald Sones, and William Martin
    1988   *The Prosecution of Felony Arrests, 1986.* Washington, DC: US Government Printing Office.
Boldt, Richard C.
    1998   "Rehabilitative Punishment and the Drug Treatment Court Movement." *Washington University Law Quarterly* 76: 1205–1306.
Bond, James E.
    1987   *The Art of Judging.* New Brunswick, NJ: Transaction Books.
Bordenhamer, David J.
    1992   *Fair Trial: Rights of the Accused in American History.* New York: Oxford University Press.
Bork, Robert H.
    1993   "The Senate's Power Grab." *New York Times* (June 23): 11.
    1989   *The Tempting of America: The Political Seduction of the Law.* New York: The Free Press.
Boswell, John
    1989   *The Kindness of Strangers: The Abandonment of Children in Western Europe from Antiquity to the Renaissance.* New York: Pantheon.
Bouchoux, Deborah E.
    2001   *Cite-Checker: A Hands-On Guide to Learning Citation Form.* Albany, NY: Delmar.
Boyle, James, ed.
    1992   *Critical Legal Studies.* New York: New York University Press.
Boyle, Joseph
    1992   "Natural Law and the Ethics of Traditions." Pages 3–30 in *Natural Law Theory,* edited by Robert P. George. Oxford, UK: Oxford University Press.
Braun, Bill
    1997   "Plea Offer Rejected, Defendant Given 93 Years." *Tulsa World On-Line,* February 28.
Brennan, William J., Jr.
    1986   "Guaranteeing Individual Liberty." *USA Today* (Sept.): 40–42.
Brenner, Susan W.
    1995   "The Voice of the Community: A Case for Grand Jury Independence." *Virginia Journal of Social Policy and the Law* 3 (Fall).
Breyer, Stephen
    2005   *Active Liberty: Interpreting Our Democratic Constitution.* New York: Knopf.
Broder, John M.
    2006   "States Curbing Right to Seize Private Homes." *New York Times* (February 21): 1, 17.
    1997   "Stares of Lawyerly Disbelief at a Huge Civil Award." *New York Times* (September 10): C1.
Bronner, Ethan
    2013a   "Law Schools' Applications Fall as Costs Rise and Jobs Are Cut." *New York Times* (January 30). Available: http://www.nytimes.com/2013/01/31/education/law-schools-applications-fall-as-costs-rise-and-jobs-are-cut.html.
    2013b   "To Place Graduates, Law Schools Are Opening Firms." *New York Times* (March 8): 14, 16.
    1989   *Battle for Justice: How the Bork Nomination Shook America.* New York: Norton.
Brown, Richard M.
    1971   "Legal and Behavioral Perspectives on American Vigilantism." Pages 103–44 in *Law in American History,* edited by Donald Fleming and Bernard Bailyn. Boston: Little, Brown.

Brownell, Emery A.
  1951   *Legal Aid in the United States: A Study of the Availability of Lawyers' Services for Persons to Pay Fees.* Rochester, NY: Lawyers Co-Operative Publishing.
Buckle, Suzann R. and Leonard Buckle
  1977   *Bargaining for Justice: Plea Disposition in the Criminal Courts.* New York: Praeger.
Buenker, John D.
  1973   *Urban Liberalism and Progressive Reform.* New York: Scribner's.
Bureau of Justice Assistance
  1988   *Court Unification.* Washington, DC: US Government Printing Office.
Bureau of Justice Statistics
  2007   *Special Report: State Organization, 1987–2004.* Available: http://www.bjs.gov/content/pub/pdf/sco8704.pdf.
  1986   *Crime and Justice Facts, 1985.* Washington, DC: US Government Printing Office.
Burt, Robert A.
  1995   "Alex Bickel's Law School and Ours." *Yale Law Journal* 104 (May): 1852–73.
Burton, Steven L.
  2007   *An Introduction to Law and Legal Reasoning,* 3rd ed. New York: Aspen.
  1985   *An Introduction to Law and Legal Reasoning.* Boston: Little, Brown.
Butler, Carolyn Kleiner
  2006   "Rethinking Law School." *U.S. News and World Report* (April 10: 54–58.
Calabresi, Guido
  1982   *A Common Law for the Age of Statutes.* Cambridge, MA: Harvard University Press.
Caldeira, Gregory A.
  1986   "Neither Purse nor the Sword: Dynamics of Public Confidence in the Supreme Court." *American Political Science Review* 80 (Dec.): 1209–26.
Cannon, Mark W.
  1982   "Innovation in the Administration of Justice, 1969–1981: An Overview." Pages 35–48 in *The Politics of Judicial Reform,* edited by Philip L. Dubois. Lexington, MA: D. C. Heath.
Canon, Bradley C. and Charles A. Johnson
  1999   *Judicial Policies: Implementation and Impact,* 2d ed. Washington, DC: Congressional Quarterly.
Caplan, Lincoln
  2013   "The Right to Counsel Badly Battered at 50." *New York Times* (March 10): SR 10.
  2012   "An Existential Crisis for Law Schools." *New York Times* (July 15): 10.
  1987   *The Tenth Justice: The Solicitor General and the Rule of Law.* New York: Knopf.
Carasik, Lauren
  2011   "Renaissance or Retrenchment: Legal Education at a Crossroads." *Indiana Law Review* 44: 735–818.
Cardarelli, Alpert P. and Stephen C. Hicks
  1994   "Radicalism in Law and Criminology: A Retrospective View of Critical Legal Studies and Radical Criminology. *Journal of Criminal Law and Criminology* 84: 502–53.
Cardozo, Benjamin N.
  1924   *The Growth of the Law.* New Haven, CT: Yale University Press.
Carlson, Jill M.
  1993   "Restorative Justice: Beyond Crime and Punishment." Master of Science Thesis, Mankato State University, Minnesota.
Carns, Teresa White
  1992   "Alaska's Ban on Plea Bargaining Reevaluated." *Judicature* 75 (April–May): 310–17.

Carns, Teresa White and John Kruse
   1991   *Alaska's Plea Bargaining Ban Re-Evaluated*, Juneau, AK: State Justice Institute.
Carp, Robert A., Ronald Stidham, and Kenneth L. Manning
   2014   *Judicial Process in America*, 9th ed. Washington, DC: Congressional Quarterly Press.
Carrington, Paul
   2011   "Business Interests and the Long Arm in 2011." *South Carolina Law Review* 63: 637–41.
Carson, Gerald
   1978   *A Good Day at Saratoga*. Chicago: American Bar Association.
Carter, Lief H.
   1984   *Reason in Law*, 2d ed. Boston: Little, Brown.
Carter, Leif H. and Christine Harrington
   2009   *Administrative Law and Politics*, 4th ed. Washington, DC: CQ Press.
Case, Stephen
   1984   "Lawyers Are Often Grossly Overpaid." *New York Times* (Dec. 2): F2.
Casey, Linda
   2012   "Money in Judicial Elections, 2009–2010." National Institute on Money in State Politics (April 6). Available: http://www.followthemoney.org/press/ReportView.phtml?r=485.
Casper, Jonathan
   1978   *Criminal Courts: The Defendant's Perspective*. Washington, DC: US Government Printing Office.
Central Office of Information
   1976   *The Legal System of Britain*. London: Her Majesty's Stationery Office.
Chambers, Marcia
   1986   "California's Private Courts Are Swift." *New York Times* (Feb. 24): 9.
Champion, Dean J.
   1989   "Private Counsels and Public Defenders: A Look at Weak Cases, Prior Records, and Leniency in Plea Bargaining." *Journal of Criminal Justice* 17: 253–63.
Chandler, Adam F.
   2011   "The Solicitor General of the United States: Tenth Justice or Zealous Advocate?" *Yale Law Journal* 121: 725–37.
Chapin, Bradley
   1983   *Criminal Justice in Colonial America: 1606–1660*. Athens: University of Georgia Press.
Chemerinsky, Edwin
   1998   "Prosecutorial Immunity: The Interpretation Continues." *Trial* 34 (3): 80–83.
Cherovsky, Erwin
   1991   *The Guide to New York Law Firms*. New York: St. Martin's.
Chira, Susan
   1987   "If You Insist on Your Day in Court, You May Wait and Wait and Wait." *New York Times* (Sept. 1): 4.
Choate, Rufus
   1962   "The Positions and Functions of the American Bar." Pages 258–73 in *The Legal Mind in America, From Independence to the Civil War*, edited by Perry Miller. Garden City, NY: Anchor.
Chroust, Anton-Hermann
   1965   *The Rise of the Legal Profession in America, Vol. 2*. Norman: University of Oklahoma Press.
Cissner, Amanda, Melissa Labriola, and Michael Rempel
   2013   *Testing the Effects of New York's Domestic Violence Courts: A Statewide Impact Evaluation*. New York: Center for Court Innovation.

"Class Action Lawsuits"
   2005   *New York Times* (February 2): 20.
Coffin, Frank M.
   1994   *On Appeal: Courts, Lawyering, and Judging.* New York: Norton.
Cohen, Adam
   2007   "Last Term's Winner at the Supreme Court: Judicial Activism." *New York Times* (July 9): 16.
Cohen, Thomas H.
   2005   *Punitive Damages Awards in Large Counties, 2001.* Washington, DC: Bureau of Justice Statistics. Available: http://www.bjs.gov/content/pub/pdf/pdalc01.pdf.
Cohen, Thomas H. and Kyle Harbacek
   2011   *Punitive Damage Awards in State Courts, 2005.* Washington, DC: Bureau of Justice Statistics. Available: http://www.bjs.gov/content/pub/pdf/pdasc05.pdf.
Collins, Kristin A.
   2010   "'A Considerable Surgical Operation': Article III, Equity, and Judge-Made Law in the Federal Courts." *Duke Law Journal* 60 (November): 249–343.
   2009   "Pro Se Trials and the Merging of Inquisitorial and Adversarial Systems of Justice." *Catholic University Law Review* 58: 445–500.
Cooke, Lawrence H.
   1982   "Mediation: A Boon or a Bust?" Pages 3–17 in *Mediation in the Justice System*, edited by Maria R. Volpe, Thomas F. Christian, and Joyce E. Kowalewski. Chicago: American Bar Association.
Cooley, John W.
   1986   "Arbitration vs. Mediation—Explaining the Differences." *Judicature* (Feb.–March): 263–69.
Cooper, Philip J.
   1988   *Hard Judicial Choices: Federal District Court Judges and State and Local Officials.* New York: Oxford University Press.
Coquillette, Daniel R., Mary P. Squiers, and Stephen N. Subrin
   1989   "The Role of Local Rules." *ABA Journal* (Jan.): 62–65.
Cornelius, Frank
   1994   "Crushed By My Own Reform." *New York Times* (October 7): 15.
Corriher, Billy
   2013   "Criminals and Campaign Cash: The Impact of Judicial Campaign Spending on Criminal Defendants." Center for American Progress. Available: http://www.americanprogress.org/wp-content/uploads/2013/10/CampaignCriminalCash-6.pdf.
Cosgrove, Richard A.
   1987   *Our Lady, the Common Law: An Anglo-American Legal Community, 1870–1930.* New York: New York University Press.
CPIL (Council for Public Interest Law)
   1976   *Balancing the Scales of Justice: Financing Public Interest Law in America.* Washington, DC: Council for Public Interest Law.
"Court Allows Challenge to Bias Ruling to Continue"
   1989   *New York Times* (June 6): 25.
Court Appointed Special Advocates: A Voice for Abused and Neglected Children in Court
   1997   Washington, DC: United States Department of Justice.
Court Statistics Project
   2013   "The Four Types of Appellate Court Structure." National Center for State Courts. Available: http://www.courtstatistics.org/Appellate/20122Appellate.aspx.

Cox, Archibald
    1987   *The Court and the Constitution*. New York: Houghton Mifflin.
Cox, Michael P.
    1975   "Discretion: A Twentieth Century Mutation." *Oklahoma Law Review* 28: 311–32.
Craft, Randal R., Jr.
    1989   "Put Limits on Death Compensation." *New York Times* (Oct. 8): Sec. 3: 2.
Criminal Defense Systems
    1984   Washington, DC: US Government Printing Office.
Crowne, Caroline Harris
    2001   "The Alternative Dispute Resolution Act of 1998: Implementing a New Paradigm of Justice." *New York University Law Review* (December): 1768–1818.
Cunningham, Richard F.
    1989   "Selling of Jury Deliberations: Commentaries on the Issue." *Criminal Justice Ethics* 8 (Winter/Spring): 27–30.
Curran, Barbara A.
    1986   "American Lawyers in the 1980s: A Profession in Transition." *Law and Society Review* 20: 19–52.
Curtis, Michael K.
    1986   *No State Shall Abridge: The Fourteenth Amendment and the Bill of Rights*. Durham, NC: Duke University Press.
Cutler, Brian L. and Steven D. Penrod
    1995   *Mistaken Identification: The Eyewitness, Psychology and the Law*. New York: Cambridge University Press.
Damâska, Mirjan R.
    1986   *The Faces of Justice and State Authority: A Comparative Approach to the Legal Process*. New Haven, CT: Yale University Press.
Daniels, Stephen and Joanne Martin
    1995   *Civil Juries and the Politics of Reform*. Evanston, IL: Northwestern University Press.
Darwin, Charles
    1871   *The Descent of Man*. London: John Murray.
    1859   *On the Origin of Species by Means of Natural Selection*. London: Murray.
Dawson, John M.
    1992   *Prosecutors in State Courts, 1990*. Washington, DC: Bureau of Justice Statistics.
DeFrances, Carol J. and Marika F. X. Litras
    2000   *Indigent Defense Services in Large Counties, 1999*. Washington, DC: Office of Justice Programs.
DeFrances, Carol J., Steven K. Smith, Patrick A. Langan, Brian J. Ostrom, David B. Rottman, and John A. Goerdt
    1995   *Civil Jury Cases and Verdicts in Large Counties*. Washington, DC: Bureau of Justice Statistics.
Degler, Carl N.
    1991   *In Search of Human Nature: The Decline and Revival of Darwinism in American Social Thought*. New York: Oxford University Press.
DeLappa, Fred
    1983   *Resolving Disputes: An Alternative Approach*. Chicago: American Bar Association.
Delgado, Richard
    2000   "Goodbye to Hammurabi: Analyzing the Atavistic Appeal of Restorative Justice." *Stanford Law Review* 52 (April): 751, 759. Available: http://papers.ssrn.com/sol3/papers.cfm?abstract_id=1328536.

Dershowitz, Alan M.
  2001   *Supreme Injustice: How the High Court Hijacked Election 2000*. New York: Oxford University Press.
  1983   *The Best Defense*. New York: Vintage Books.
De Tocqueville, Alexis
  1956   *Democracy in America*. New York: New American Library. (Originally published in 1835.)
Dictionary of Criminal Justice Data Terminology
  1981   Washington, DC: US Government Printing Office.
DiLorenzo, Thomas
  1988   *The Anti-Business Campaign of the Legal Services Corporation*. St. Louis, MO: Center for the Study of American Business.
Dobbins, Jeffrey C.
  2012   "New Evidence on Appeal." *Minnesota Law Review* 96: 2016–66.
Domenici, Kathy and Stephen W. Littlejohn
  2001   *Mediation: Empowerment in Conflict Management*, 2d ed. Long Grove, IL: Waveland Press.
Donohue, Pete
  2006   "Loses to Train and Wins Big." *New York Daily News* (March 25): 3.
Donovan, Karen
  2008   "From Making Cases to Challenging Them." *New York Times* (May 2): C6.
Dorsett, Lyle W.
  1968   *The Pendergast Machine*. New York: Oxford University Press.
Draper, Israel
  1989   *Crime and Punishment in the Ancient World*. Lexington, MA: D. C. Heath. (Originally published in 1865.)
"Drive-by Legal Defense"
  2001   *New York Times* editorial (April 12): 26.
The Drug Court Movement
  1995   Washington, DC: National Institute of Justice
Dullea, Georgia
  1986   "Using Mediators to Resolve Family Disputes." *New York Times* (April 21): 17.
Dworkin, Ronald
  1986   *Law's Empire*. Cambridge, MA: Harvard University Press.
  1985   *A Matter of Principle*. Cambridge, MA: Harvard University Press.
Earle, Edward M.
  1937   "Introduction" to *The Federalist*. New York: New Modern Library.
Easterbrook, Frank H.
  1992   "Plea Bargaining as Compromise." *Yale Law Journal* 101: 1969–78.
"Editorial"
  1964   *Journal of the American Judicature Society* 48: 124–25
Edmunds, Palmer D.
  1959   *Law and Civilization*. Washington, DC: Public Affairs Press.
Eichenwald, Kurt
  1994   "Lawyers Receiving $22.6 Million of Prudential Settlement." *New York Times* (May 20): C2
  1993   "Millions for Us, Pennies for You." *New York Times* (December 19): Sec. 3: 1, 12.
Eisenberg, Melvin A.
  1988   *The Nature of the Common Law*. Cambridge, MA: Harvard University Press.
Eisenstein, James
  1978   *Counsel for the United States: U.S. Attorneys in the Political and Legal Systems*. Baltimore, MD: Johns Hopkins University Press.

Eisenstein, James, Roy B. Flemming, and Peter F. Nardulli
  1999   *The Contours of Justice: Communities and Their Courts.* Lanham, MD: University Press of America.
Eissman, Mark and Joseph R. Tybor
  1985   "Plea Bargaining Declines." *Chicago Tribune* (Nov. 3): 1, 18.
Elias, Stephen
  1989   *Legal Research: How to Find and Understand the Law.* Berkeley, CA: Nolo Press.
Elias, T. Olawale
  1956   *The Nature of African Customary Law.* Manchester, UK: Manchester University Press.
Elliott, Andrea and Benjamin Weiser
  2004   "When Prosecutors Err, Others Pay the Price." *New York Times* (March 21): 25, 30.
Elliott, Catherine, Eric Jeanpierre, and Catherine Vernon
  2006   *French Legal System,* 2d ed. Essex, UK: Pearson.
Ellis, Michael J.
  2012   "The Origins of the Elected Prosecutor." *Yale Law Journal*: 1528–69.
Emanuel, Steve
  2013   *Constitutional Law,* 31st ed. Frederick, MD: Wolters Kluwer Law & Business.
  2008   *Civil Procedure,* 4th ed. Larchmont, NY: Aspen.
Elsing, Siegfried and John M. Townsend
  2002   "Bridging the Common Law Civil Law Divide in Arbitration." *Arbitration International* 18 (1): 1–7.
Emerson, Deborah D.
  1983   *Grand Jury Reform: A Review of Key Issues.* Washington, DC: US Government Printing Office.
Emmelman, Debra S.
  1996   "Trial by Plea Bargain: Case Settlement as a Product of Recursive Decision-Making." *Law and Society Review* 30 (No. 2): 335–60.
Empey, LaMar, ed.
  1979   *Juvenile Justice: The Progressive Legacy and Current Reforms.* Charlottesville: University Press of Virginia.
Engelhardt, Laura
  1999   "The Problem With Eyewitness Testimony: A Commentary on a Talk by George Fisher and Barbara Tversky." *Stanford Journal of Legal Studies* 1 (December): 25–29.
Epstein, Richard A.
  2005   "The Not So Minimum Content of Natural Law." *Oxford Journal of Legal Studies* 25 (Summer): 219–55.
Eskridge, William N., Jr.
  1994   *Dynamic Statutory Interpretation.* Cambridge, MA: Harvard University Press.
Fabricant, Michael
  1983   *Juveniles in the Family Courts.* Lexington, MA: D. C. Heath.
Fagan, Jeffrey and Victoria Malkin
  2003   "Theorizing Community Justice Through Community Courts." *Fordham Urban Law Journal* 30 (March): 897–956.
Failinger, Marie A.
  2005   "Can a Good Judge Be a Good Politician? Judicial Elections From a Virtue Ethics Approach." *Missouri Law Review* 70 (Spring): 433–526.
Falcone, Michael
  2006   "Stanford Law Students Get Early Supreme Court Duty." *New York Times* (March 15): B8.
Fallon, Richard H.
  2011   "Are Originalist Constitutional Theories Principled, or Are They Rationalizations for Conservatism?" *Harvard Journal of Law and Public Policy* 34: 5–28.

Farber, Daniel A. and Philip P. Frickey
  1991   *Law and Public Choice: A Critical Introduction.* Chicago: University of Chicago Press.
Farrand, Max
  1967   *The Records of the Federal Convention of 1787* (three volumes). New Haven, CT: Yale University Press.
Fatsis, Stefan
  1990   "Investor Challenges Arbitration Process on Losses." *Chicago Tribune* (Jan. 22), Sec. 4: 3.
Feder, Barnaby J.
  1993   "The Unorthodox Behemoth of Law Firms." *New York Times* (March 14): Sec. 3: 1, 6.
Federal Judicial Center (FJC)
  1985   *The Roles of Magistrates: Nine Case Studies.* Washington, DC: US Government Printing Office.
The Federalist Papers
  1937   New York: New Modern Library. (Originally published in 1788.)
Feeley, Malcolm M.
  1997   "Legal Complexity and the Transformation of the Criminal Process: The Origins of Plea Bargaining." *Israel Law Review* 31 (Winter–Summer): 183.
  1992   *The Process Is Punishment: Handling Cases in a Lower Court.* New York: Russell Sage Foundation.
  1984   "Legal Realism." Pages 129–31 in *The Guide to American Law: Everyone's Legal Encyclopedia.* St. Paul, MN: West.
Feeney, Floyd, Forrest Dill, and Adrianne Weir
  1983   *Arrests Without Conviction: How Often They Occur and Why.* Washington, DC: US Government Printing Office.
Feigenson, Neal
  2000   *Legal Blame: How Jurors Think and Talk About Accidents.* Washington, DC: American Psychological Association.
Feinblatt, John, Greg Berman, and Michele Sviridoff
  1998   *Neighborhood Justice.* New York: Center for Court Innovation.
Feld, Barry C.
  1992   "Criminalizing the Juvenile Court: A Research Agenda for the 1990s." Pages 59–88 in *Juvenile Justice and Public Policy: Toward a National Agenda,* edited by Ira M. Schwartz. Lexington, MA: Lexington Books.
Feldman, Noah
  2010   "What a Liberal Court Should Be." *New York Times Magazine* (June 27): 38–43.
  2008   "When Judges Make Foreign Policy." *New York Times Magazine* (September 25). Available: http://www.nytimes.com/2008/09/28/magazine/28law-t.html?pagewanted=all&_r=1&.
Feldstein, Thomas M. and Stephen B. Presser
  1984   "David Dudley Field." *The Guide to American Law: Everyone's Legal Encyclopedia.* St. Paul, MN: West.
Ferguson, Robert A.
  1984   *Law and Letters in American Culture.* Cambridge, MA: Harvard University Press.
Ferkenhoff, Eric
  2001   "Cops Find, Then Lose Widow's Jewelry." *Chicago Tribune* (March 3): 1, 8.
Feuer, Alan
  2011   "The Defense Can't Afford to Rest." *New York Times* (May 22): LI 1, 9.
Field, David Dudley
  1965   "The Index of Civilization." Pages 30–47 in *The Golden Age of American Law,* edited by Charles H. Haar. New York: George Braziller.

Finckenauer, James O.
  1984   *Juvenile Delinquency and Corrections: The Gap Between Theory and Practice*. New York: Academic Press.

Finegan, Sharon
  2009   "Pro Se Trials and the Merging of Inquisitorial and Adversarial Systems of Justice." *Catholic University Law Review* 58: 445–500.

Firestone, David
  1999   "Alabama Acts to Limit Huge Awards by Juries." *New York Times* (June 2): 14.

Fish, Stanley
  2005   "Intentional Neglect." *New York Times* (July 19): 21.

Fisher, George
  2000   "Plea Bargaining's Triumph." *Yale Law Review* 109 (March): 857–1086.

Fishman, James J.
  1979   "The Social and Occupational Mobility of Prosecutors: New York City." Pages 239–54 in *The Prosecutor*, edited by William F. McDonald. Beverly Hills, CA: Sage.

Flango, Victor E.
  2010   "Role of State Supreme Court Decisions in Law Development." Pages 142–46 in *Future Trends in State Courts 2010*, edited by Carol R. Flango et al. Williamsburg, VA: National Center for State Courts.

Flango, Victor E. and Carol R. Flango
  1997   "A Taxonomy of Appellate Court Jurisdiction." *Caseload Highlights* 3 (July): 1–4.

Flemming, Roy B.
  1988   "Client Games: Defense Attorney Perspectives on Their Relations with Criminal Clients." Pages 228–52 in *Criminal Justice: Law and Politics*, edited by George F. Cole. Pacific Grove, CA: Brooks/Cole.

Foschio, Leslie G.
  1999   "A History of the Development of the Office of United States Commissioner and Magistrate Judge System." *Federal Courts Law Review* 4. http://www.fclr.org/fclr/articles/html/1999/fedctslrev4.pdf.

Foster, James C.
  1985   "Legal Education and the Production of Lawyers to (Re)Produce Liberal Capitalism." *Legal Studies Forum* 9: 179–211.

Foster, Lawrence C.
  2001   "The Impact of the Close Relationship Between American Law Schools and the Practicing Bar." *Journal of Legal Education* 51 (September): 346–49.

Frank, Jerome
  1970   *Law and the Modern Mind*. Gloucester, MA: Peter Smith. (Originally published in 1930.)

Frankel, Marvin E. and Gary P. Naftalis
  1977   *The Grand Jury: Institution on Trial*. New York: Hill and Wang.

Franklin, Tim
  1985   "State to Seek Funds to Replace Bungling Lab." *Chicago Tribune* (Aug. 18): Sec. 3: 1.

Frase, Richard S.
  2005   "Punishment Goals, and the Eighth Amendment: 'Proportionality' Relative to What." *Minnesota Law Review* 89 (February): 571–669.

Frederick, Bruce and Don Stemen
  2012   *The Anatomy of Discretion: An Analysis of Prosecutorial Decision n Making—Technical Report*. Washington, DC: US Department of Justice.

Freedman, Monroe H.
  1975   *Lawyers' Ethics in an Adversary System*. Indianapolis, IN: Bobbs-Merrill.

Freitag, Michael
    1989   "Law Firms Lift Income Aided by Takeover Fees." *New York Times* (July 6): 25.
Freund, Paul A.
    1961   "The Supreme Court." Pages 71–84 in *Talks on American Law,* edited by Harold J. Berman. New York: Vintage Books.
Friedenthal, Jack H., Mary Kay Kane, and Arthur Miller
    1985   *Civil Procedure.* St. Paul, MN: West.
Friedenthal, Jack H., Arthur R. Miller, John E. Sexton, and Helen Hershkoff
    2013   *Civil Procedure,* 11th ed. St. Paul, MN: West.
Friedman, Lawrence M.
    2005   *A History of American Law,* 3rd ed. New York: Touchstone.
    1984   *American Law.* New York: Norton.
    1979   "Plea Bargaining in Historical Perspective." *Law and Society Review* 7: 247–59.
    1973   *A History of American Law.* New York: Simon and Schuster.
Friend of the Constitution
    1990   "Congress, the President, and Judicial Selection: Lessons from the Reagan Years." Pages 49–58 in *Judicial Selection: Merit, Ideology, and Politics,* edited by Henry J. Abraham, Eugene W. Hickok, Jr., and William Bradford Reynolds. Washington, DC: National Legal Center for the Public Interest.
Frug, Jerry
    1986   "Henry James, Lee Marvin and the Law." *New York Times Book Reviews* (Feb. 16): 1, 28–30.
Fuchs, Josef
    1965   *Natural Law: A Theological Investigation.* New York: Sheed and Ward.
Fuller Lon L.
    1961   "The Adversary System." Pages 30–43 in *Talks on American Law,* edited by Harold J. Berman. New York: Vintage Books.
Fund for Modern Courts
    1986   *The Illusion of Democracy: New York City Civil Court Elections, 1980–1985.* New York: Fund for Modern Courts, Inc.
Furchgott, Roy
    1997   "Opposition Builds to Mandatory Arbitration at Work." *New York Times* (July 20): F11.
Furchgott-Roth, Diana
    2009   "Reduce the High Cost of Medical Malpractice." *The Great Debate.* Reuters. Available: http://blogs.reuters.com/great-debate/2009/08/06/ reduce-the-high-cost-of-medical-malpractice/.
Gac, Edward J.
    1988   "The Socratic Method in Undergraduate Education: Overcoming the Law School Image." *Focus on Law Studies* 3 (Spring): 3, 5.
Galanter, Marc
    1989   "Adjudication, Litigation and Related Phenomena." Pages 106–11 in *American Court Systems: Readings in Judicial Process and Behavior,* edited by Sheldon Goldman and Austin Sarat. New York: Longman.
Galanter, Marc and Thomas Palay
    1991   *Tournament of Lawyers: The Transformation of the Big Law Firm.* Chicago: University of Chicago Press.
Gallagher, Maggie
    1988   "Legal Disservices: The New Serfs." *National Review* (August 5): 42–43, 56.
Gardner, James A.
    2005   *Interpreting State Constitutions: A Jurisprudence of Function in a Federal System.* Chicago: University of Chicago Press.

Gavzer, Bernard
    1997   "Are Trial Consultants Good for Justice?" *Parade* (January 5): 20.
    1996   "Why Some Doctors May Be Hazardous to Your Health." *Parade* (April 14): 4–7.
Gawande, Atul
    2005   "The Malpractice Mess." *New Yorker* (November 14): 63–71.
    2001   "Under Suspicion: The Fugitive Science of Criminal Justice." *New Yorker* (January 8): 50–53.
Gebelein, Richard S.
    2000   *The Rebirth of Rehabilitation: Promise and Perils of Drug Courts.* Washington, DC: Office of Justice Programs.
Gehm, John R.
    1998   "Victim-Offender Mediation Programs: An Exploration of Practice and Theoretical Frameworks." *Western Criminology Review* 1 (1). Available: http://wcr.sonoma.edu/v1n1/gehm.html.
George, Robert P.
    2000   "Introduction." *Great Cases in Constitutional Law.* Princeton, NJ: Princeton University Press.
Gerber, Richard Allan
    1981   "The Reinterpretation of the Due Process Clause of Fourteenth Amendment in the Age of Industrialization." Pages 143–209 in *American Industrialization, Economic Expansion, and the Law,* edited by Joseph R. Frese and Jacob Judd. Tarrytown, NY: Sleepy Hollow Press.
Gerber, Rudolph J.
    1989   *Lawyers, Courts, and Professionalism: The Agenda for Reform.* Westport, CT: Greenwood.
Gershman, Bennett L.
    2002   "A Moral Standard for the Prosecutor's Exercise of the Charging Decision." Pages 57–72 in *Criminal Courts for the 21st Century,* edited by Lisa Stolzenberg and Steward J. D. D'Alessio. Upper Saddle River, NJ: Prentice-Hall.
Gerwitz, Paul and Chad Golder
    2005   "So Who Are the Activists?" *New York Times* (July 6): 19.
Gest, Ted
    1993   "Doing Good Is Doing Well." *U.S. News & World Report* (March 22): 60–61.
Giannelli. Paul C.
    1994   "When the Evidence Is a Matter of Life and Death." *New York Times* (August 21): E15.
Gillers, Stephen
    1996   "The American Legal Profession." Pages 151–76 in *Fundamentals of American Law,* edited by Alan B. Morrison. New York: Oxford University Press.
Gilmore, Grant
    1977   *The Ages of American Law.* New Haven, CT: Yale University Press.
Ginsburg, Ruth Bader
    2012   "Foreword." Pages xi–xii in Kommers, Donald P. and Russell A. Miller, *The Constitutional Jurisprudence of the Federal Republic of Germany,* 3rd ed. Durham, NC: Duke University Press.
Glaberson, William
    2001a   "Juries, Their Powers under Siege, Find Their Role Is Being Eroded." *New York Times* (March 2): 1, 15.
    2001b   "A Study's Verdict: Jury Awards Are Not Out of Control." *New York Times* (August 6): 9.
    2000a   "Fierce Campaigns Signal a New Era for State Courts." *New York Times* (June 5): 1, 22.
    2000b   "A Spirited Campaign for Ohio Court Puts Judges on New Terrain." *New York Times* (July 7): 11.

2000c   "States Rein in Truth-Bending in Court Races." *New York Times* (August 23): 1, 16.

2000d   "To Bear or Not to Bear: It Depends on How You Read History." *New York Times* (September 24): WK 7.

1999   "State Courts Sweeping Away Laws Curbing Suits for Injury." *New York Times* (July 16): 1, 13.

1990   "Confronting Assembly-Line Justice: Tumult in New York's Courtrooms." *New York Times* (Jan. 16): 12.

Glater, Jonathan D.

2011   "Joseph H. Flom, Pioneering Lawyer in Mergers and Acquisitions, Dies at 87." *New York Times* (February 24): B12.

2005a   "Are Lawyers Being, Er, Overbilled?" *New York Times* (December 4): BU 1, 8.

2005b   "Linking Those in Need with Volunteer Lawyers." *New York Times* (December 16): C6.

2001   "Law Firms Are Slow in Promoting Minority Lawyers to Partner Role." *New York Times* (August 7): 1, C2.

Glendon, Mary Ann

1994   *A Nation under Lawyers*. Cambridge, MA: Harvard University Press.

Glenn, H. Patrick

2010   *Legal Traditions of the World*. 4th ed. New York: Oxford University Press.

2000   *Legal Traditions of the World*. New York: Oxford University Press.

Glick, Henry R.

1983   *Courts, Politics, and Justice*. New York: McGraw-Hill.

1982   "The Politics of State-Court Reform." Pages 17–33 in *The Politics of Judicial Reform*, edited by Philip L. Dubois. Lexington, MA: D. C. Heath.

Gluckman, Max

1955   *The Judicial Process among the Bartose of Northern Rhodesia*. Manchester, UK: Manchester University Press.

Goldman, Sheldon and Thomas P. Jahnige

1985   *The Federal Courts as a Political System*. New York: McGraw-Hill.

Goldstein, Joseph

2014   "F.B.I. Audit of Database That Indexes DNA Finds Errors in Profiles." *New York Times* (January 25): 15.

Goodman, James

1994   *Stories of Scottsboro*. New York: Pantheon.

Goodrich, Chris

1991   *Anarchy and Elegance: Confessions of a Journalist at Yale Law School*. Boston: Little, Brown.

Goozner, Merrill

1992   "Courts Add to Pain of Pollution Victims." *Chicago Tribune* (February 13): 23, 26.

Gordon, John Steele

1991   "Reforming the Law." *American Heritage* (September): 18–20.

Gould, Carole

1986   "When to Turn to a No-Frills Law Firm." *New York Times* (Nov. 9): F15.

Gourevitch, Philip

2001   "The Crime Lover." *New Yorker* (February 19 and 26): 160–73.

Graham, Kyle

2013   "Overcharging." Legal Studies Research Papers Series, Santa Clara University School of Law.

Granfield, Robert

1986   "Legal Education as Corporate Ideology." *Sociological Forum* I: 514–23.

Granfield, Robert and Thomas Koenig

1992   "Learning Collective Eminence: Harvard Law School and the Production of Elite Lawyers." *Sociological Quarterly* 33: 503–20.

Gray, Jerry
   1993   "Trenton Court Upholds Senate's 'Courtesy' Veto." *New York Times* (December 24): 10.
Green, Bruce A.
   2003   "Criminal Neglect: Indigent Defense From a Legal Ethics Perspective." *Emory Law Journal* 52: 1169–2005.
Greenhouse, Linda
   2005a   "William H. Rehnquist, Architect of Conservative Court, Is Dead at 80." *New York Times* (September 4): 38.
   2005b   "Justice Weighs Desire v. Duty (Duty Prevails)." *New York Times* (August 25): 1, 16.
   2002   "The Competing Visions of the Role of the Court." *New York Times* (July 7): 3.
   2001a   "The High Court's Target: Congress." *New York Times* (February 25): WK 3.
   2001b   "Punitive Damages Must Get a Searching Review on Appeal, Justices Rule." *New York Times* (May 15): 18.
   2000   "The High Court Rules: The Law of the Land Changes." *New York Times* (July 2): WK 1, 5.
   1999   "States Are Given New Legal Shelf by Supreme Court." *New York Times* (June 24): 1, 22.
   1996   "How Congress Curtailed the Courts' Jurisdiction." *New York Times* (October 27): E5.
   1994   "High Court Opens Its Fall Session by Refusing Cases. *New York Times* (October 4): 1, 10.
   1993a   "Life and Times." *New York Times Magazine* (March 7): 84.
   1993b   "Has the Supreme Court Become Irrelevant? Or Will History Again Demand to Be Written There?" *New York Times* (September 10): B10.
   1991a   "Justices Back Shareholders' Suits." *New York Times* (May 21): C7.
   1991b   "A Longtime Precedent for Disregarding Precedent." *New York Times* (July 21): E4.
   1991c   "Conservatively Speaking, It's an Activist Supreme Court." *New York Times* (May 26): E1, E3.
   1990   "As Curtain Is Lifted, Rehnquist Is Off Cue." *New York Times* (March 16): 8.
   1989   "High Court's Reticence Raises Questions of Rules." *New York Times* (Nov. 22): 11.
Griffin, Patrick, Sean Addie, Benjamin Adams, and Kathy Firestine
   2011   *Trying Juveniles as Adults: An Analysis of State Transfer Laws and Reporting.* Washington, DC: Office of Juvenile Justice and Delinquency Prevention.
Grossman, Joel B.
   1965   *Lawyers and Judges: The ABA and the Politics of Judicial Selection.* New York: Wiley.
Grunson, Lindsey
   1986   "Tiny Delaware's Corporate Clout." *New York Times* (June 1): F6.
   1983   "Second Opinions on Medical Examiners." *New York Times* (May 15): E6.
Grutman, Roy and Bill Thomas
   1990   *Lawyers and Thieves.* New York: Simon and Schuster.
Guamieri, Carlo
   2004   "Appointment and Career of Judges in Continental Europe: The Rise of Judicial Self-Government." *Legal Studies* 24: 169–87.
Gudjonsson, Gisli
   2011   "False Confessions and Correcting Injustices." *New England Law Review* 46: 689–709.
Guidorizzi, Douglas D.
   1998   "Should We Really 'Ban' Plea Bargaining? The Core Concerns of Plea Bargaining Critics." *Emory Law Journal* 47 (Spring): 754–83.
Guinier, Lani
   1997   *Becoming Gentlemen: Women, Law School, and Institutional Change.* Boston: Beacon Press.
Gulati, Mitu and C. M. A. McCauliff
   1998   "On *Not* Making Law." *Law and Contemporary Problems* 61 (3): 157–227. Available: http://scholarship.law.duke.edu/cgi/viewcontent.cgi?article=1101&context=lcp.

Gurevich, Mark
  2005   "Justice Department's Policy of Opposing *Nolo Contendere* Pleas: A Justification."
          California Criminal Law Review 2 (6): Available: http://www.boalt.org/bjcl/v6/
          v6gurevich.htm.
Haar, Charles M.
  1986   "Need Services? Try Common Law." *New York Times* (May 14): 25.
Haar, Charles M., ed.
  1965   *The Golden Age of American Law.* New York: George Braziller.
Haar, Charles M. and Daniel W. Fessler
  1986   *Fairness and Justice: Law in the Service of Equality.* New York: Touchstone.
Hakim, Danny
  2006   "Judge Urges State Control of Legal Aid." *New York Times* (June 29): B1, 5.
Haley, John Owen
  1991   *Authority without Power: Law and the Japanese Paradox.* New York: Oxford University Press.
Hall, Kermit L.
  1989   *The Magic Mirror: Law in American History.* New York: Oxford University Press.
Hall, Kermit, William M. Wiecek, and Paul Finkelman
  1996   *American Legal History: Cases and Materials,* 2d ed. New York: Oxford University Press.
Hamilton, Alexander, John Jay, and James Madison
  1937   *The Federalist Papers.* New York: New Modern Library. (Originally published in 1788.)
Hamilton, Walter H.
  1999   "The Path of Due Process of Law." Pages 3–19 in *The Lanahan Readings in Civil Rights
          and Civil Liberties,* edited by David M. O'Brien. Baltimore: Lanahan.
Handlin, Oscar and Lilian Handlin
  1982   *Restless People: Americans in Rebellion, 1770–1787.* Garden City, NY: Doubleday.
Hanna, Janan and Eric Ferkenhoff
  2001   "Hillard Orders Probe After Cocaine Evidence Disappears." *Chicago Tribune* (April
          21): 1, 18.
Harlow, Caroline Wolf
  2000   *Defense Counsel in Criminal Cases.* Washington, DC: Office of Justice Programs.
Harmon, Amy
  1998   "The Law Where There Is No Land." *New York Times* (March 16): C1, 9.
Harper, Robert Francis
  1904   *The Code of Hammurabi.* Chicago: University of Chicago Press.
Harrell, Erika
  2012   *Violent Victimization Committed by Strangers, 1993–2010.* Washington, DC: US Depart-
          ment of Justice. Available: http://www.bjs.gov/content/pub/pdf/vvcs9310.pdf.
Harrell, Mary Ann and Burnett Anderson
  1985   *Shadow Justice: The Ideology and Institutionalization of Alternatives to Court.* Westport,
          CT: Greenwood.
  1982   *Equal Justice under Law: The Supreme Court in American Life.* Washington, DC: The
          Supreme Court Historical Society.
Hartnett, Edward A.
  1999   "A Matter of Judgment: Not a Matter of Opinion." *New York University Law Review* 74
          (April): 123–60.
Harvard Law Review Association
  2000   "Gideon's Promise Unfulfilled: The Need for Litigated Reform of Indigent Defense."
          Harvard Law Review 113 (June): 2062–79.

Harvard Law School
  2011   "The Legal Profession of the United States." Cambridge: President and Fellows of Harvard College. Available: http://www.law.harvard.edu/programs/plp/pdf/United_States_Legal_Profession.pdf.

Hastie, Reid, Steven D. Penrod, and Nancy Pennington
  1983   *Inside the Jury.* Cambridge, MA: Harvard University Press.

Hay, Bruce L.
  1994   "Civil Discovery: Its Effects and Optimal Scope." *Journal of Legal Studies* 23 (January): 481–515.

Hazard, Geoffrey C., Jr. and Michele Taruffo
  1993   *American Civil Procedure: An Introduction.* New Haven, CT: Yale University Press.

Heilbroner, David
  1990   *Rough Justice: Days and Nights of a Young D.A.* New York: Dell.

Heinz, John P. and Edward O. Laumann
  1982   *Chicago Lawyers: The Social Structure of the Bar.* Chicago: Russell Sage Foundation and the American Bar Association.

Henderson, Thomas A., Cornelius M. Kerwin, Randall Guynes, Carl Baar, Neal Miller, Hildy Saizow, and Robert Grieser
  1984   *The Significance of Judicial Structure: The Effect of Unification on Trial Court Operations.* Washington, DC: US Government Printing Office.

Henley, Patricia
  1996   "Improving the Jury System: Peremptory Challenges." *Public Law Research Institute Reports* (Spring). Available: http://gov.uchastings.edu/public-law/docs/plri/juryper.pdf.

Henriques, Diana B.
  1995   "Top Business Court Under Fire." *New York Times* (May 23): C1, C6.

Henry, James F.
  1985   "Alternative Dispute Resolution: Meeting the Legal Needs of the 1980s." *Ohio State Journal on Dispute Resolution* 1 (Fall): 113–20.

Hensler, Deborah R., Bonnie Dombey-Moore, Beth Giddens, Jennifer Gross, Erik K. Moller, and Nicholas M. Pace
  1999   *Class Action Dilemmas: Pursuing Public Goals for Private Gain.* Executive Summary. Santa Monica: RAND.

Herget, James E.
  1990   *American Jurisprudence: 1870–1970.* Houston, TX: Rice University Press.

Herbert, Bob
  2004   "Not So Frivolous." *New York Times* (June 18): 31.

Heumann, Milton
  1978   *Plea Bargaining.* Chicago: University of Chicago Press.

Hinds, Michael deCourcy
  1994   "Compiling Data, and Giving Odds, on Jury Awards." *New York Times* (January 21): B12.

Hines, Crystal Nix
  2001a   "Competition Sprouts One-Stop Law Firms," *New York Times* (May 31): C1, 7.
  2001b   "Without a Lawyer." *New York Times* (July 31): C1.

Hobson, Wayne K.
  1986   *The American Legal Profession and the Organizational Society: 1890–1930.* New York: Garland Publishing.

Hoffer, Peter Charles
  1998   *The Law's Conscience: Equitable Constitutionalism in America.* Revised ed. Chapel Hill: University of North Carolina.

1992   *Law and People in Colonial America.* Baltimore: John's Hopkins University Press.

1990   *The Law's Conscience: Equitable Constitutionalism in America.* Chapel Hill: University of North Carolina.

Hoffman, Jan

1998a   "Police Tactics Chipping Away at Suspects' Rights." *New York Times* (March 26): 1, 21.

1998b   "Police Refine Methods So Potent, Even the Innocent Have Confessed." *New York Times* (March 30): 1, 17.

Hoffman, Morris B.

2002   "Therapeutic Jurisprudence, Neo-Rehabilitationism, and Judicial Collectivism: The Least Dangerous Branch Become the Most Dangerous." *Fordham Urban Law Journal* 29 (June): 2063–3002.

Hoffman, Paul

1982   *Lions of the Eighties: The Inside Story of the Powerhouse Law Firms.* Garden City, NY: Doubleday.

Hogue, Arthur R.

1966   *Origins of the Common Law.* Bloomington: Indiana University Press.

Holland, Kenneth M.

1982   "The Twilight of Adversariness: Trends in Civil Justice." Pages 17–29 in *The Analysis of Judicial Reform,* edited by Philip L. Dubois. Lexington, MA: D. C. Heath.

Holmes, Steven A.

1996   "Pact Overhauls Accreditation of Law Schools." *New York Times* (June 28): 1, 9.

Hora, Peggy Fulton and Theodore Stalcup

2008   "Drug Treatment Courts in the Twenty-First Century: The Evolution of the Revolution in Problem-Solving Courts." *Georgia Law Review* 42 (Spring): 718–811. Available: http://www.ndci.org/sites/default/files/ndci/Hora-Stalcup.pdf.

Horowitz, Donald L.

1977   *The Courts and Social Policy.* Washington, DC: Brookings Institution.

Horowitz, Morton J.

1977   *The Transformation of American Law, 1780–1860.* Cambridge, MA: Harvard University Press.

Howard, J. Woodford, Jr.

1981   *Courts of Appeal: A Study of the Second, Fifth, and District of Columbia Circuits.* Princeton, NJ: Princeton University Press.

Huff, C. Ronald, Arye Rattner, and Edward Sagarin

1996   *Convicted But Innocent: Wrongful Conviction and Public Policy.* Thousand Oaks, CA: Sage.

Hughes, Graham

1996   "Common Law Systems." Pages 9–25 in *Fundamentals of American Law,* edited by Alan B. Morrison. New York: Oxford University Press.

Hunt, Morton

1982   "Putting Juries on the Couch." *New York Times Magazine* (Nov. 28): 70–72, 78, 82, 86, 88.

Hurst, James W.

1950   *The Growth of American Law: The Law Makers.* Boston: Little, Brown.

Hutchinson, Allan C., ed.

1989   *Critical Legal Studies.* Totowa, NJ: Rowman and Littlefield.

1988   *Dwelling on the Threshold: Critical Essays on Modern Legal Thought.* Toronto, Canada: Carswell.

Hyman, Harold M. and William M. Wiecek

1982   *Equal Justice Under Law: Constitutional Development, 1835–1875.* New York: Harper and Row.

Ikpa, Tina S.
2007   "Balancing Restorative Justice Principles and Due Process Rights in Order to Reform the Criminal Justice System." *Washington University Journal of Law and Policy* 24: 301–25.

Israel, Jerold H. and Wayne LaFave
2006   *Criminal Procedure: Constitutional Limitations*, 7th ed. St. Paul, MN: Thomson/West.

Jacob, Herbert and James Eisenstein
1977   *Felony Justice*. Boston: Little, Brown.

Jacobs, Nancy F. and Ellen F. Chayet
1986   "Court Dynamics and Disposition Time: The Realities of Case Delay." Paper presented at the annual meeting of the American Society of Criminology, Oct. 30, in Atlanta, GA.

Jaffa, Harry V.
1988   "Judge Bork's Mistake." *National Review* (March 4): 38–40.

Janofsky, Michael
1999   "Baltimore's Push on Crime Creates a Backlog of Cases." *New York Times* (January 7): 14.

Jaschik, Scott and Douglas Lederman
2004   "If You Went Here, You'd Be Sitting Pretty Now." *New York Times* (April 25): Education Life 37).

Johnson, Earl, Jr.
1977   *Outside the Courts: A Survey of Diversion Alternatives in Civil Cases*. Denver, CO: National Center for the State Courts.
1974   *Justice and Reform: The Formative Years of the OEO Legal Services Program*. New York: Russell Sage.

Johnson, Kirk
1986   "Lawyer Hires an Ex-Juror for Retrial." *New York Times* (Jan. 31): 15.

Johnston, David
1997   "Report Finds F.B.I. Lab Slipping From Pinnacle of Crime Fighting." *New York Times* (January 29): 1, 12.
1989   "A.B.A. to Resume Rating of Judicial Nominees." *New York Times* (June 1): 7.

Joint Committee on New York Drug Law Evaluation
1977   *The Nation's Toughest Drug Law: Evaluation of the New York City Experience*. New York: Association for the Bar of the City of New York.

Jones, Ashby
2009   "Scalia: 'We Are Devoting Too Many of Our Best Minds to Lawyering.'" Law Blog, *Wall Street Journal* (October 1). Available: http://blogs.wsj.com/law/2009/10/01/scalia-we-are-devoting-too-many-of-our-best-minds-to-lawyering.

Jones, David M.
1997   "Judicial Federalism and Prosecutorial Vindictiveness: State Responses to Bordenkircher and Goodwin." *Journal of Criminal Justice* 20 (1): 73–90.

Jones, Judith B.
2004   "Access to Counsel." *Juvenile Justice Bulletin*. Washington, DC: US Department of Justice. Available: https://www.ncjrs.gov/pdffiles1/ojjdp/204063.pdf.

"Judge Voids Suit on Harvard Hiring"
1991   *New York Times* (February 26): 12.

Kaczorowski, Robert J.
1987   "To Begin the Nation Anew: Congress, Citizenship, and Civil Rights after the Civil War." *American Historical Review* 92 (Feb.): 45–68.

Kagan, Robert A.
1994   "Do Lawyers Cause Adversarial Legalism? A Preliminary Inquiry." *Law and Social Inquiry* 19 (Winter): 1–62.

Kahlenberg, Richard D.
1992   *Broken Contract: A Memoir of Harvard Law School*. New York: Hill and Wang.
Kahn, Joseph
2005   "Deep Flaws, and Little Justice in China's Court System." *New York Times* (September 21): 1, 14.
Kairys, David
1982   "Legal Reasoning." Pages 11–17 in *The Politics of Law: A Progressive Critique*, edited by David Kairys. New York: Pantheon.
Kalman, Laura
1986   *Legal Realism at Yale: 1927–1960*. Chapel Hill: University of North Carolina.
Kamisar, Yale, Wayne R. LaFave, Jerold H. Israel, Nancy J. King, Orin S. Kerr, and Eve Brensike Primus
2012   *Basic Criminal Procedure*, 13th ed. New York: West/Thomson Reuters.
Kang, Michael S. and Joanna M. Sherherd
2011   "The Partisan Price of Justice: An Empirical Analysis of Campaign Contributions and Judicial Decisions." *New York University Law Review* 86 (April): 69–130.
Kant, Immanuel
1949   *Critique of Practical Reason*. Translated by Lewis White Beck. Chicago: University of Chicago Press.
Karp, David R.
2001   "Harm and Repair Observing Restorative Justice in Vermont." *Justice Quarterly* 18 (December): 727–57.
Kassberg, Maria
1989   "Alternative Dispute Resolution to the Rescue." *Update on Law-Related Education* 13 (Winter): 3–4, 64.
Katz, Stanley M.
1971   "The Politics of Law in Colonial America: Controversies Over Chancery Courts and Equity Law in the Eighteenth Century." Pages 257–84 in *Law in American History*, edited by Donald Fleming and Bernard Bailyn. Cambridge, MA: Harvard University Press.
Kaufman, Irving R.
1986   "What Did the Founding Fathers Intend?" *New York Times Magazine* (Feb. 23): 42, 59–60, 67–69.
Kaufman, Leslie and Anne Underwood
1997   "Sign or Hit the Street." *Newsweek* (June 30): 48–49.
Kay, Fiona and John Hagan
1998   "Raising the Bar: The Gender Stratification of Law-Firm Capital." *American Sociological Review* 63 (October): 728–43.
Keeva, Steven
1993   "Unequal Partners." *ABA Journal* (February): 50–54.
Keilitz, Susan
2004   "Specialization of Domestic Violence Case Management in the Courts: A National Survey." Pages III-9-3–III-9-10 in *Violence against Women and Family Violence: Developments in Research, Practice, and Policy*. Edited by Bonnie S. Fisher. Washington, DC: National Institute of Justice.
Kelly, J. M.
1993   *A Short History of Western Legal Theory*. New York: Oxford University Press.
Kelman, Mark
1987   *A Guide to Critical Legal Studies*. Cambridge, MA: Harvard University Press.
Kendall, Peter
1991   "Indebted New Lawyers Shunning Public Service." *Chicago Tribune* (January 29): Sec. 3: 1, 2.

Kennedy, Duncan
  1982   "Legal Education as Training for Hierarchy." Pages 40–61 in *The Politics of Law: A Progressive Critique*, edited by David Kairys. New York: Pantheon.
Kennedy, Leslie W.
  1990   *On the Borders of Crime: Conflict Management and Criminology.* New York: Longman.
Kens, Paul
  1990   *Judicial Power and Reform Politics: The Anatomy of Lochner v. New York.* Lawrence: University of Kansas Press.
Kessler, Mark
  1993   "Legal Discourse and Political Intolerance: The Ideology of Clear and Present Danger." *Law and Society Review* 27 (3): 559–97.
Kiernan, Louise
  1997   "Trial: At Juvenile Court, an Ongoing Struggle to Mend Broken Lives." *Chicago Tribune Magazine* (January 19): 11–18.
Kimball, Bruce A.
  2002   "Young Christopher Langdell, 1826–1854: The Formation of an Educational Reformer." *Journal of Legal Education* 52 (March/June): 189–237.
King, Anthony
  1997   "Running Scared." *Atlantic Monthly* (January): 41–61.
King, Michael
  2008   "Restorative Justice, Therapeutic Jurisprudence and the Rise of Emotionally Intelligent Justice." *Melbourne University Law Review* 32: 1096–1126.
King, Nancy Jean
  1999   "The American Criminal Jury." *Law and Contemporary Problems* 62 (Spring). Available: http://scholarship.law.duke.edu/cgi/viewcontent.cgi?article=1125&context=lcp.
Kirby, Michael P.
  1977   *The Effectiveness of the Point Scale.* Washington, DC: Pretrial Services Resource Center.
Kirschenbaum, Aaron
  1991   *Equity in Jewish Law. Halakic Perspectives in Law: Formalism and Flexibility in Jewish Civil Law.* Hoboken, NJ: Ktav Publishing House.
Klein, Eric C.
  1998   "Dennis the Menace or Billy the Kid: An Analysis of the Role of Transfer to Criminal Court in Juvenile Justice." *American Criminal Law Review* 35 (Winter): 371–401.
Knoll, Crystal and Melissa Sickmund
  2012   "Delinquency Cases in Juvenile Court, 2009." *Juvenile Offenders and Victims National Report Series.* Washington, CD: Office of Juvenile Justice and Delinquency Prevention. Available: http://www.ojjdp.gov/pubs/239081.pdf.
Kolata, Gina
  1993   "When Court Decisions Vanish From the Record." *New York Times* (June 18): B12.
Kolbert, Elizabeth
  1990   "In Civil Liberties Cases, New York's Court Leans on the State Constitution." *New York Times* (January 8): 12.
Kolker, Robert
  2010   "'I Did It.' Why Do People Confess to Crimes They Didn't Commit?" *New York Magazine* (October 11): 22–27, 89–90.
Kommers, Donald P. and Russell A. Miller
  2012   *The Constitutional Jurisprudence of the Federal Republic of Germany,* 3rd ed. Durham, NC: Duke University Press.
Korobkin, Russell B. and Thomas S. Ulen
  2000   "Law and Behavioral Science: Removing the Rationality Assumption from Law and Economics." *California Law Review* 88 (July): 1051–1144.

Koski, John C.
 1994   "Mandatory Disclosure: The New Rule That's Meant to Simplify Litigation Could Do Just the Opposite." *ABA Journal* (February): 85–87.

Kötz, Hein
 2003   "Civil Justice Systems in Europe and the United States." *Duke Journal of Comparative and International Law* [Special Issue] 13: 61–77.

Kreindel, Burton, Robert H. Adams, Robert V. D. Campbell, Susan P. Hobart, and John P. Moreschi
 1977   *Court Information Systems.* Washington, DC: US Government Printing Office.

Kreinler, Lee S.
 1989   "Monetary Awards Can Soothe the Pain." *New York Times* (Oct. 8): Sec. 3: 2.

Kress, Jack M.
 1976   "Progress and Prosecution." *Annals* 423 (Jan.): 99–116.

Kritzer, Herbert M.
 1996   "Courts, Justice, and Politics in England." Pages 81–176 in *Courts, Law and Politics in Comparative Perspective,*" edited by Herbert Jacob et al. New Haven, CT: Yale University Press.
 1991   *Let's Make a Deal: Understanding the Negotiation Process in Ordinary Litigation.* Madison: University of Wisconsin Press.
 1990   *The Justice Broker: Lawyers and Ordinary Litigation.* New York: Oxford University Press.

Kronman, Anthony J.
 1993   *The Lost Lawyer: Failing Ideals of the Legal Profession.* Cambridge, MA: Harvard University Press.

Kumble, Steven J. and Kevin J. Lahart
 1990   *Conduct Unbecoming: The Rise and Ruin of Finley, Kumble.* New York: Carroll & Graff.

Kunkel, Wolfgang
 1972   *An Introduction to Roman Legal and Constitutional History.* Oxford, UK: Oxford University Press.

Kurki, Leena
 1999   *Incorporating Restorative Justice and Community Justice Into American Sentencing and Corrections.* Washington, DC: National Institute of Justice.

Kynge, James
 2001   "China's Amateur Judges in the Dock." *Financial Times* (July 14–15): 4.

Labaton, Stephen
 2006   "'Silent Tort Reform' Is Overriding States' Right." *New York Times* (March 10): C5.
 1992   "Solution to Wasteful Lawsuits Becomes a Problem." *New York Times* (June 14): E2.
 1988a   "Federal Court Rules Challenged After 50 Years." *New York Times* (Oct. 14): 23.
 1988b   "U.S. Law Firms Expand to Reach Global Clientele." *New York Times* (May 12): 1, 43.

Lacasse, Chantale and A. Abigail Payne
 1999   "Federal Sentencing Guidelines and Mandatory Minimum Sentences: Do Defendants Bargain in the Shadow of the Judge?" *Journal of Law and Economics* 42 (April): 245–68.

Ladinsky, Jack
 1963   "Careers of Lawyers, Law Practice, and Legal Institutions." *American Sociological Review* 28: 47–54.

Landon, Donald D.
 1990   *Country Lawyers: The Impact of Context on Professional Practice.* New York: Praeger.

Landsman, Stephen
 1999   "The Civil Jury In America." *Law and Contemporary Problems* 62 (Spring). Available: http://scholarship.law.duke.edu/cgi/viewcontent.cgi?article=1133&context=lcp.
 1993   "The History and Objectives of the Civil Jury System." Pages 22–60 in *Verdict: Assessing the Civil Jury System,* edited by Robert E. Litan. Washington, DC: Brookings Institution.

Lane, Eric
  1999   "How to Read a Statute in New York: A Response to Judge Kaye and Some More."
           Hofstra Law Review 28 (Fall): 86–125.
Langbein, John H.
  2012   "The Disappearance of Civil Trial in the United States." *Yale Law Journal* 122: 522–72.
Langdell, Christopher C.
  1871   *A Selection of Cases on the Law of Contracts.* Boston: Little, Brown.
LaPiana, William P.
  1994   *Logic and Experience: The Origin of Modern American Legal Education.* New York: Oxford
           University Press.
Lattman, Peter
  2013a   "Legal Merger Shows Rise in Criminal Defense Status." *New York Times* (July 1): B4.
  2013b   "Mass Layoffs at a Top-Flight Law Firm." *New York Times* (June 25): B1, 5.
  2013c   "Ex-U.S. Attorney to Join Law Firm in Washington." *New York Times* (November 21): B7.
Lavelle, Marianne
  2005   "Class Action Crackdown." *U.S. News and World Report* (February 21): 46–47.
Lawrence, Susan E.
  1990   *The Poor in Court: The Legal Services Program and Supreme Court Decision Making.*
           Princeton, NJ: Princeton University Press.
Law School Admission Council (LSAC)
  2012   *ABA-LSAC Official Guide to ABA Approved Law Schools 2013 Edition.* Newton, PA: LSAC.
  1996   *The Official Guide to U.S. Law Schools.* New York: Bantam.
Lee, Eric
  2000   *Community Courts: An Evolving Model.* Washington, DC: Office of Justice Programs.
Leone, Peer and Lois Weinberg
  2010   *Addressing the Unmet Needs of Children and Youth in Juvenile Justice and Child Welfare
           Systems.* Washington, DC: Center for Juvenile Justice Reform, Georgetown University.
Leeson, Susan M. and Bryan M. Johnston
  1988   *Ending It: Dispute Resolution in America.* Cincinnati, OH: Anderson.
Lefever, R. Dale
  2010   "The Integration of Judicial Independence and Judicial Administration: The Role of
           Collegiality in Court Governance." Pages 66–72 in *Future Trends in State Courts 2010,*
           edited by Carol R. Flango et al. Williamsburg, VA: National Center for State Courts.
Lempert, Richard and Joseph Sanders
  1986   *An Invitation to Law and Social Science.* New York: Longman.
Levi, Edward H.
  2013   *An Introduction to Legal Reasoning.* Chicago: University of Chicago Press.
Levin, Martin A.
  1977   *Urban Politics and the Criminal Courts.* Chicago: University of Chicago Press.
Levrant, Sharon, Francis T. Cullen, Betsy Fulton, and John Wozniak
  1999   "Reconsidering Restorative Justice: The Corruption of Benevolence Revisited?"
           Crime and Delinquency 45 (January): 3–23.
Levy, Clifford J., Kevin Flynn, Leslie Eaton, and Andy Newman
  2004   "A Bronx Judiciary Awash in Patronage, All Legal." *New York Times* (January 3): 1, B4.
Levy, Leonard W.
  1988   *Original Intent and the Framers' Constitution.* New York: Macmillan.
Lewin, Tamar
  1986a   "Leaving the Law for Wall Street: The Faster Track." *New York Times Magazine* (Aug.
           10): 14–19, 42, 48, 53.
  1986b   "A Legal Curb Raises Hackles: It Punishes the Frivolous." *New York Times* (Oct. 2):
           25, 31.

1983   "A Gentlemanly Profession Enters a Tough New Era." *New York Times* (Jan. 16): Sec. 3: 1, 10–12.

Lewis, Neil A.

2001   "White House Ends Bar Association's Role in Screening Federal Judges." *New York Times* (March 23): 13.

2000   "Edward H. Levi, Attorney General Credited with Restoring Order after Watergate, Dies at 88." *New York Times* (March 8): C25.

1996   "Clinton Vetoes Liability Limits in Product Suits." *New York Times* (May 3): 1, 8.

1989a   "Legal Panel, 6–5, Keeps Disputed Chief." *New York Times* (Dec. 16): 11.

1989b   "Legal Skills and Legislation: Washington Growth Industry." *New York Times* (Dec. 29): 1, 26.

Lewis, Peter W. and Kenneth D. Peoples

1978   *The Supreme Court and the Criminal Process: Cases and Comments*. Philadelphia: W.B. Saunders.

Lieberman, Jethro K.

1989   "What Courts Do and Do Not Do Effectively." Pages 18–33. In *American Court Systems: Readings in Judicial Process and Behavior*, edited by Sheldon Goldman and Austin Sarat. New York: Longman.

1981   *The Litigious Society*. New York: Basic Books.

Lieberman, Trudy

2006   "Righting Wrongs: The Truth about Medical Malpractice and the Law." *AARP Bulletin* (April): 10–11.

Linowitz, Sol, with Martin Mayer

1996   *The Profession Betrayed: Lawyering at the End of the Twentieth Century*. Baltimore, MD: Johns Hopkins University Press.

Lintner, Bertil

2002   *Blood Brothers: The Criminal Underworld of Asia*. New York: Palgrave Macmillan.

Lipson, Jonathan C., Beth Engel, and Jami Crespo

2012   "Who's in the House? The Changing Nature and Role of In-House and General Counsel." *Wisconsin Law Review*: 237–50.

Liptak, Adam

2013a   "The Lackluster Reviews That Lawyers Love to Hate." *New York Times* (October 22: 15.

2013b   "How Activist Is the Supreme Court?" *New York Times* (October 13): SR 4.

2011a   "A Sign of Court's Polarization: Choice of Clerks." *New York Times* (September 7): 1, 16.

2011b   "When a Lawsuit is too Big." *New York Times* (April 3): WK 1, 5.

2010a   "Justices Offer Receptive Ear to Business Interests." *New York Times* (December 19): 1, 26.

2010b   "For Some Orphaned Arguments, Court-Appointed Guardians." *New York Times* (December 4): 16.

2007   "When Rendering Decisions, Judges Are Finding Law Reviews Irrelevant." *New York Times* (March 19): 8.

2006a   "In Limelight at Wiretap Hearings: 2 Laws, but Which Should Rule?" *New York Times* (February 7): 1, 18.

2006b   "Nonlawyer Father Wins His Suit Over Education, and the Bar Is Upset." *New York Times* (May 6): 8.

2004   "Judicial Races in Several States Become Partisan Battlegrounds." *New York Times* (October 24): 1, 30.

2003   "County Says It's Too Poor to Defend the Poor." *New York Times* (April 15): 1, 14.

2002   "Pain-and-Suffering Awards Let Juries Avoid New Limits." *New York Times* (October 28): 14.

Litras, Marika F. X., Sidra Lea Gifford, and Carol J. DeFrances
   2000   *Tort Trials and Verdicts in Large Counties, 1996*. Washington, DC: Office of Justice Programs.
Liu, Goodwin, Pamela S. Karlan, and Christopher H. Schroeder
   2009   *Keeping Faith With the Constitution*. Washington, DC: American Constitution Society for Law and Policy,
Llewellyn, Karl N.
   1989   *The Case Law System in America*. Edited and translated by Paul Gewirtz. Chicago: University of Chicago Press.
   1960   *The Common Law Tradition: Deciding Appeals*. Boston: Little, Brown.
   1951   *The Bramble Bush*. Dobbs Ferry, NY: Oceana Press.
Lloyd-Bostock, Sally and Cheryl Thomas
   1999   "Decline of the 'Little Parliament': Juries and Jury Reform in England and Wales." *Law and Contemporary Problems* 62 (Spring). Available: http://scholarship.law.duke.edu/cgi/viewcontent.cgi?article=1124&context=lcp.
Locke, John
   1952   *The Second Treatise of Government*. Indianapolis, IN: Bobbs-Merrill. (Originally published circa 1688.)
Lofgren, Charles A.
   1987   *The Plessy Case: A Legal-Historical Interpretation*. New York: Oxford University Press.
Loh, Wallace D.
   1984   *Social Research in the Judicial Process: Cases, Readings, and Text*. New York: Russell Sage.
Lohr, Steve
   2005   "Bush's Next Target: Malpractice Lawyers." *New York Times* (February 27): Sec. 3: 1, 4.
Lomasky, Loren E.
   1989   "The Selling of Jury Deliberations: Commentaries on the Issue." *Criminal Justice Ethics* 8 (Winter/Spring): 33–34.
Lorch, Robert S.
   1980   *Democratic Process and Administrative Law*, revised edition. Detroit, MI: Wayne State University Press.
Lou, Herbert H.
   1972   *Juvenile Courts in the United States*. New York: Arno Press. (Reprint of a 1927 edition.)
Luban, David
   2010   "Conscience of a Prosecutor." *Valparaiso Law Review* 45: 1–31.
Lynch, David
   1994   "The Impropriety of Plea Agreements: A Tale of Two Counties." *Law and Social Inquiry* 19: 115–33.
Lynch, Gerald E.
   2003   "Screening Versus Plea Bargaining: Exactly What Are We Trading Off?" *Stanford Law Review* 55 (April): 1399–409.
Lynk, William J.
   1994   "The Courts and the Plaintiff Bar: Awarding the Attorney's Fee in Class-Action Lawsuits." *Journal of Legal Studies* 23 (January): 185–209.
Lyon, Jeff
   1991   "Chicago Law." *Chicago Tribune Magazine* (June 9): 14–21.
Ma, Yue
   2002   "Prosecutorial Discretion and Plea Bargaining in the United States, France, Germany, and Italy: A Comparative Perspective." *International Criminal Justice Review* 12 (1): 22–52.
Maag, Gordon E.
   2001   "Forum Non Conveniens in Illinois: A Historical Review, Critical Analysis, and Proposal for Change." *Southern Illinois University Law Journal* 25: 461–527.

Macaulay, Stewart
    2005   "The New Versus the Old Legal Realism: 'Things Ain't What They Used to Be.'" *Wisconsin Law Review* 365–408.
MacDonald, H. Malcolm
    1961   "Government under Law." Pages 3–21 in *The Rule of Law*, edited by Arthur L. Harding. Dallas, TX: Southern Methodist University Press.
MacFarquhar, Larissa
    2001   "The Bench Burner." *New Yorker* (December 10): 78–89.
MacNeil, Ian R.
    1992   *American Arbitration Law: Reformation, Nationalization, Internationalization.* New York: Oxford University Press.
Maggs, Gregory E.
    2011   "A Concise Guide to the Records of the Federal Constitutional Convention of 1787 as a Source of the Original Meaning of the U.S. Constitution." *George Washington Law Review* 80: 1707–52.
Mahoney, Barry
    1988   *Changing Times in Trial Courts.* Denver, CO: National Center for State Courts.
Maier, Pauline
    2010   *Ratification: The People Debate the Constitution, 1787–1788.* New York: Simon and Schuster.
Maine, Henry S.
    1861   *Ancient Law: Its Connection with the Early History of Society, and Its Relation to Modern Ideas.* New York: Cockcroft and Company.
Malega, Ron and Thomas H. Cohen
    2013   *State Court Organization, 2011.* Washington, DC: Bureau of Justice Statistics.
Malkin, Victoria
    2003   "Community Courts and the Process of Accountability: Consensus and Conflict at the Red Hook Community Justice Center." *American Criminal Law Review* 40 (Fall): 1573–97.
Maloney, Dennis M. and Mark S. Umbreit
    1995   "Managing Change: Toward a Balanced and Restorative Justice Model." *Perspectives* 19 (Spring): 43–46.
"Malpractice Mythology"
    2005   *New York Times* (January 9): 12.
Mann, Dale
    1976   *Intervening With Convicted Serious Juvenile Offenders.* Washington, DC: US Government Printing Office.
Manning, Jennifer E.
    2013. "Membership of the 113th Congress: A Profile." Congressional Research Service. Available: https://www.fas.org/sgp/crs/misc/R42964.pdf.
Manza, Jeff
    1990   "Critical Legal Studies." *Berkeley Journal of Sociology: A Critical Review* 35: 137–50.
Margolick, David
    1994   "At the Bar." *New York Times* (February 4): B9.
    1991a   "Target: Drexel. Weapon: Tom Barr." *New York Times* (April 7): F1, 6.
    1991b   "Address by Quayle on Justice Proposals Irks Bar Association." *New York Times* (August 14): 1, 9.
    1989a   "Annual Race for Clerks Becomes a Mad Dash, with Judicial Decorum Left in the Dust." *New York Times* (March 17): 24.
    1989b   "Glimpse at Secret System of Punishing Judges." *New York Times* (July 14): 1, 21.
    1988a   "For Trial Lawyers in Big Firms, Arguing a Case Can Be a Remote Possibility." *New York Times* (Sept. 9): 19.

1988b   "Turning Economic Theory into Legal Practice and Spectacular Profit." *New York Times* (June 17): 22.

1988c   "Increasingly, Legal Firms Find Themselves in the Dock as the Litigation Explosion Boomerangs." *New York Times* (Nov. 18): 25.

1985   "The Legal Aid Society on the Defensive." *New York Times* (Aug. 4): E4.

1983   "The Trouble with America's Law Schools. *New York Times* (May 22): 20–25: 30–37.

Markoff, John

2011   "Armies of Expensive Lawyers, Replaced by Software." *New York Times* (March 5): 1, 15.

Marks, Jonathan B., Earl Johnson, Jr., and Peter L. Szanton

1985   *Dispute Resolution in America: Processes in Evolution.* Washington, DC: National Institute for Dispute Resolution.

Marshall, Tony F.

1998   *Restorative Justice: An Overview.* London: Restorative Justice Consortium.

1988   "Out of Court: More or Less Justice?" Pages 22–50 in *Informal Justice*, edited by Roger Matthews. Beverly Hills, CA: Sage.

Marvell, Thomas B.

1978   *Appellate Courts and Lawyers: Information Gathering in the Adversary System.* Westport, CT: Greenwood.

Mather, Lynn M.

1988   "The Outsider in the Courtroom: An Alternative Role for Defense." Pages 253–70 in *Criminal Justice: Law and Politics*, edited by George F. Cole. Pacific Grove, CA: Brooks/Cole.

Matthews, Roger, ed.

1988   *Informal Justice?* Beverly Hills, CA: Sage.

Mayer, Martin

1969   *The Lawyers.* New York: Dell.

Maynard, Douglas W.

1988   "Narratives and Narrative Structure in Plea Bargaining." *Law and Society Review* 22 (3): 449–81.

Maytal, Anat

2008   "Specialized Domestic Violence Courts: Are They Worth the Trouble in Massachusetts?" *Public Interest Law Journal* 18: 197–235.

McCarthy, Belinda R. and Charles A. Lindquist

1985   "Certainty of Punishment and Sentence Mitigation in Plea Behavior." *Justice Quarterly* 2 (Sept.): 363–83.

McClosky, Robert G.

2010   *The American Supreme Court*, 5th ed. Chicago: University of Chicago.

McCollam, Douglas

2010   "Slick on Slick." *New York Times Magazine* (November 7): 44–51, 58, 62–63, 65.

McCormick, John P.

1999   "Three Ways of Thinking 'Critically' about the Law." *American Political Science Review* 93 (June): 413–24.

McCoy, Candace

1993   *Politics and Plea Bargaining: Victim's Rights in California.* Philadelphia: University of Pennsylvania Press.

McCoy, Candace and Robert Tillman

1986   *Controlling Plea Bargaining in California.* Sacramento: California Bureau of Criminal Statistics.

McDonald, William F.

1985   *Plea Bargaining: Critical Issues and Common Practices.* Washington, DC: US Government Printing Office.

1983   "In Defense of Inequality: The Legal Profession and Criminal Defense." Pages 13–38 in *The Defense Counsel*, edited by William F. McDonald. Beverly Hills, CA: Sage.

McDonald, William F., Henry H. Rossman, and James A. Cramer
1982   *Police-Prosecutor Relations in the United States: Executive Summary.* Washington, DC: US Government Printing Office.

McDowell, Gary L.
1990   "The Politics of Advice and Consent." Pages xiii–xix in *Judicial Selection: Merit, Ideology, and Politics*, edited by Henry J. Abraham, Eugene W. Hickok, Jr., and William Bradford Reynolds. Washington, DC: National Legal Center for the Public Interest.
1988   *Curbing the Courts: The Constitution and Limits of Judicial Power.* Baton Rouge: Louisiana State University.
1982   *Equity and the Constitution: The Supreme Court, Equitable Relief, and Public Policy.* Chicago: University of Chicago Press.

McGee, Jim and Brian Duffy
1996   *Main Justice: The Men and Women Who Enforce the Nation's Criminal Laws and Guard Its Liberties.* New York: Touchstone.

McGillis, Daniel and Joan Mullen
1977   *Neighborhood Justice Centers: An Analysis of Potential Models.* Washington, DC: US Government Printing Office.

McGough, Maureen
2011   "Indigent Defense: International Perspectives and Research Needs." *NIJ Journal* 268 (October): 36–39.

McGuire, Kevin T.
1993   *The Supreme Court Bar: Legal Elites in the Washington Community.* Charlottesville: University Press of Virginia.

McIntyre, Lisa J.
1987   *The Public Defender: The Practice of Law in the Shadows of Repute.* Chicago: University of Chicago Press.

McKean, Dayton
1963   *The Integrated Bar.* Boston: Houghton Mifflin.

McKenna, Marian C.
1986   *Tapping Reeve and the Litchfield Law School.* New York: Oceana.

McMillian, Theodore
1999   "Early Modern Juvenile Justice in St. Louis." *Federal Probation* 63 (December): 4–7.

McNamee, Kathleen
1998   "Another Chapter in the History of Scholia." *The Classical Quarterly* 48 (Jan–June): 269–89.

Meese, Edwin
1986   "Interpreting the Constitution." *USA Today* (September): 36–39.

Meier, Barry
2000   "Bringing Lawsuits to Do What Congress Won't." *New York Times* (March 26): WK 3.
1997a   "Class-Action Consciousness." *New York Times* (February 18): C1, 11.
1997b   "In Fine Print, Customers Lose Ability to Sue." *New York Times* (March 10): 1, C7.
1996   "Lawsuits to End All Lawsuits." *New York Times* (January 10): C1, 5.
1995   "Math of a Class-Action Lawsuit: 'Winning' $2.19 Costs $91.33." *New York Times* (November 21): 1, C4.

Melville, Herman
1961   *Billy Budd.* New York: New American Library. (Originally published in 1924.)

Menand, Louis
2001   "Civil Actions: *Brown v. Board of Education* and the Limits of Law." *New Yorker* (February 12): 91–94.

1986   "What Is 'Critical Legal Studies'? Radicalism of Yuppies." *New Republic* (March 17): 20–23.

Menkel-Meadow, Carrie
  2007   "Restorative Justice: What Is It and Does It Work?" *Annual Review of Law and Social Science* 13 (July): 10.1–10.27.

Mennel, Robert M.
  1973   *Thorns and Thistles: Juvenile Delinquents in the United States, 1825–1940.* Hanover, NH: University Press of New England.

Mercuro, Nicholas and Steven G. Medema
  1997   *Economics and the Law: From Posner to Post-Modernism.* Princeton, NJ: Princeton University Press.

Merryman, John H.
  1985   *The Civil Law Tradition: An Introduction to the Legal Systems of Western Europe and Latin America,* 2d ed. Stanford, CA: Stanford University Press.

Merryman, John H. and Rogelio Pérez-Pedomo
  2007   *The Civil Law Tradition: An Introduction to the Legal Systems of Western Europe and Latin America,* 3rd ed. Stanford, CA: Stanford University Press.

Miazad, Ossai
  2002   "The Gender Gap: Treatment of Girls in the U.S. Juvenile Justice System." *Human Rights Brief* 10. Available: http://digitalcommons.wcl.american.edu/cgi/viewcontent.cgi?article=1391&context=hrbrief.

Michalowski, Raymond J.
  1985   *Order, Law and Crime: An Introduction to Criminology.* New York: Random House.

Middlekauff, William Bradford
  1994   "What Practitioners Say about Broad Criminal Discovery Practice. More Just—Or Just More Dangerous?" *Criminal Justice* 9 (Spring): 14–19, 54–58.

Milford, Maureen
  2001   "New Home for Delaware Chancery Court." *New York Times* (February 4): 38.

Miller, Jerome
  1992   *Last One Over the Wall: The Massachusetts Experiment in Closing Reform Schools.* Columbus: Ohio State University Press.

Miller, Perry, ed.
  1962   *The Legal Mind in America: From Independence to the Civil War.* Garden City, NY: Anchor.

Mills, Miriam K., ed.
  1991   *Alternative Dispute Resolution in the Public Sector.* Chicago: Nelson-Hall.

Montesquieu, Charles de
  1949   *The Spirit of the Laws.* Trans. by Thomas Nugent. New York: Hafner Publishing.

Moore, Christopher W.
  2014   *The Mediation Process: Practical Strategies for Resolving Conflicts,* 4th ed. San Francisco: Jossey-Bass.

Morris, Richard B.
  1964   *Studies in the History of American Law.* New York: Octagon Books.

Morrison, Alan B.
  1996   "Litigation." Pages 61–81 in *Fundamentals of American Law,* edited by Alan B. Morrison. New York: Oxford University Press.

Moses, Margaret L.
  2006   "Statutory Misconstruction: How the Supreme Court Created a Federal Arbitration Law Never Enacted by Congress." *Florida State University Law Review* 34: 99–159. Available: http://www.law.fsu.edu/journals/lawreview/downloads/341/moses.pdf.

Müller, Ingo
    1991   *Hitler's Justice: The Courts of the Third Reich.* Cambridge, MA: Harvard University Press.
Murphy, Dean E.
    2005   "The New Language for Jurors in California: Plain English." *New York Times* (August 28): 12.
Murphy, Walter F. and C. Herman Pritchett
    1986   *Courts, Judges, and Politics.* New York: Random House
Nagel, Robert F.
    1989   "The Selling of Jury Deliberations: Commentaries on the Issue." *Criminal Justice Ethics* 8 (Winter/Spring): 31–33.
Nardulli, Peter F.
    1978   "Plea Bargaining: An Organizational Perspective." *Journal of Criminal Justice* 6 (Fall): 217–31.
Nasheri, Hedieh
    1998   *Betrayal of Due Process: A Comparative Assessment of Plea Bargaining in the United States and Canada.* Lanham, MD: University Press of America.
National Association of Drug Court Professionals (NADCP)
    2013   *Adult Drug Court Best Practice Standards: Vol. 1.* Alexandria, VA: NADCP.
National Association of Women Lawyers
    2012   "Report of the Seventh Annual NAWL National Survey on Retention and Promotion of Women in Law Firms." NAWL Foundation. Available: http://www.nawl.org/p/cm/ld/fid=82#surveys.
National Conference of Bar Examiners
    2013   "2012 Statistics." http://www.ncbex.org/assets/media_files/Bar-Examiner/articles/2013/8201132012statistics.pdf.
National Council of Juvenile and Family Court Judges
    1989   *Court-Approved Alternative Dispute Resolution: A Better Way to Resolve Minor Delinquency, Status Offense and Abuse/Neglect Cases.* Reno, NV: National College of Juvenile and Family Law.
    1988   *Glossary of Selected Legal Terms for Juvenile Justice Personnel.* Reno, NV: National College of Juvenile and Family Law.
Navarro, Mireya
    1997   "Doubts about F.B.I. Lab Raise Hopes for Convict." *New York Times* (April 22): 8.
    1995   "Entangled by Law, Boy Stays in Hospital That Failed Him." *New York Times* (March 10): 1, 13.
Neely, Richard
    1985   *Judicial Jeopardy: When Business Collides with the Courts.* Reading, MA: Addison-Wesley.
    1981   *How the Courts Govern America.* New Haven, CT: Yale University Press.
Neubauer, David W.
    1974   *Criminal Justice in Middle America.* Morristown, NJ: General Learning Press.
Neubauer, David W. and Stephen S. Meinhold
    2006   *Battle Supreme: The Confirmation of Chief Justice John Roberts and the Future of the Supreme Court.* Belmont, CA: Wadsworth.
Newman, Katherine S.
    1983   *Law and Economic Organization: A Comparative Study of Preindustrial Societies.* Cambridge: Cambridge University Press.
Newman, Richard J.
    2006   "Can America Keep Up?" *U.S. News and World Report* (March 27): 48–56.
Newmyer, R. Kent
    1987   "Harvard Law School, New England Legal Culture, and the Antebellum Origins of American Jurisprudence." *Journal of American History* 74 (Dec.): 814–35.

Nolan, James L., Jr.
  2003   "Redefining Criminal Courts: Problem-Solving and the Meaning of Justice." *American Criminal Law Review* (Fall): 1541–66.
Noonan, John T., Jr.
  1976   *Persons and Masks of the Law.* New York: Farrar, Straus and Giroux.
"No Trial—and No Punishment Either"
  1986   *New York Times* (March 17). Available: http://www.nytimes.com/1986/03/17/opinion/no-trial-and-no-punishment-either.html.
Novak, William J.
  1996   *The People's Welfare: Law and Regulation in Nineteenth Century America.* Chapel Hill: University of North Carolina Press.
Novick, Sheldon M.
  1989   *Honorable Justice: The Life of Oliver Wendell Holmes.* Boston: Little, Brown.
O'Brien, Timothy L.
  2006   "Up the Down Staircase." *New York Times* (March 19): Sec. 3: 1, 4.
Ohlendorf, John David
  2011   "Textualism and the Problem of the Scrivener's Error." *Maine Law Review* 64: 119–64.
Oliver, Wesley MacNeil
  2010   "The Modern History of Probable Cause." *Tennessee Law Review* 78: 377–429.
Olson, Susan M. and Albert W. Dzur
  2003   "Reconstructing Professional Roles in Restorative Justice Programs." *Utah Law Review*: 57–92.
Oppel, Richard A., Jr.
  2011   "Sentencing Shift Gives New Clout to Prosecutors." *New York Times* (September 26): 1, 18.
Orlando, Leoluca
  2001   *Fighting the Mafia and Renewing Sicilian Culture.* San Francisco: Encounter Books.
Orth, John V.
  1987   *The Judicial Power of the United States: The Eleventh Amendment in American History.* New York: Oxford University Press.
Packer, Herbert L.
  1968   *The Limits of the Criminal Sanction.* Stanford, CA: Stanford University Press.
Palermo, George B., Maxine Aldridge White, Lew A. Wasserman, and William Hanrahan
  1998   "Plea Bargaining: Injustice for All?" *International Journal of Offender Therapy and Comparative Criminology* 42 (2): 11–19.
Pallasch, Abdon M.
  1998   "Napping Juries Giving Courts a Wakeup Call." *Chicago Tribune* (April 16): 1, 17.
Parsa, T. Z.
  1999   "The Drudge Report." *New York* (June 21): 24–31.
Parsons, Christi
  1997   "Constitution Shmonstitution." *Chicago Tribune* (June 8): Sec. 2: 1, 7.
Patterson, James T.
  2001   *Brown v. Board of Education: A Civil Rights Milestone and Its Troubled Legacy.* New York: Oxford University Press.
Paul, Jeremy
  2001   "CLS 2001." *Cardozo Law Review* 22: 701–20.
Pear, Robert
  1999   "Group Asking U.S. for New Vigilance in Patient Safety." *New York Times* (November 30): 1, 18.

Pérez-Peña, Richard
  2002   "Passing a Health Measure without a Second Thought." *New York Times* (January 17): 27.
  1994a   "Private Colleges Are Criticized for Their Brand of Justice." *New York Times* (June 1): B8.
  1994b   "When Lawyers Go after Their Peers: The Boom in Malpractice Cases." *New York Times* (August 5): B12.
Perry, H. W.
  1991   *Deciding to Decide: Agenda Setting in the United States Supreme Court.* Cambridge, MA: Harvard University Press.
Pertschuk, Michael and Wendy Schaetzel
  1989   *The People Rising: The Campaign against the Bork Nomination.* New York: Thunder's Mouth.
Petak, Lisa Faye
  2010   "Paid to Defer Employment at Big Firms, Young Lawyers Turn to Public Service." *New York Times* (August 20): 14.
Peterson, Helen
  2005   "Rangers Doc Whacked 450G in Wrong-Knee Op." *New York Daily News* (January 21): 3.
Peterson, Joseph, Ira Sommers, Deborah Baskin, and Donald Johnson
  2010   *The Role and Impact of Forensic Evidence in the Criminal Justice Process.* Washington, DC: US Department of Justice. Available: https://www.ncjrs.gov/pdffiles1/nij/grants/231977.pdf.
Pettibone, John M., Robert G. Swisher, Kurt H. Weiland, Christine E. Wolf, and Joseph L. White
  1981   *Major Issues in Juvenile Justice Information and Training: Services to Children in Juvenile Courts: The Judicial-Executive Controversy.* Washington, DC: US Government Printing Office.
Philbin, Donald R., Jr., Audrey L. Maness, and Philip J, Loree, Jr.
  2010   "Alternative Dispute Resolution: Litigating Arbitration Slows as Mediation Becomes More Popular." *Texas Tech Law Review* 43: 757–820.
Pierce, Richard J., Jr., Sidney A. Shapiro, Paul R. Verkuil
  2014   *Administrative Law and Process,* 6th ed. New York: Foundation Press.
Pileggi, Nicholas
  1982   "The Last Liberals." *New York Magazine* (Sept. 13): 28, 30–35.
Plapinger, Elizabeth and Donna Stienstra
  1996   *ADR and Settlement in the Federal District Courts: A Sourcebook for Judges and Lawyers.* Washington, DC: Federal Judicial Center.
Platt, Anthony M.
  1977   *The Child Savers: The Invention of Delinquency.* Chicago: University of Chicago Press.
Pohlman, H. L., ed.
  1993   *Political Thought and the American Judiciary.* Amherst: University of Massachusetts Press.
Polin, Raymond
  1986   "The Supreme Court's Dilemma and Defense." *USA Today* (Sept.): 43–45.
Polsky, Daniel, Steven C. Marcus, and Rachel M. Werner
  2010   "Malpractice Premiums and the Supply of Obstetricians." *Inquiry* 47(1): 48–61.
Posner, Richard A.
  2013   *Reflections on Judging.* Cambridge, MA: Harvard University Press.
  2001   *Breaking the Deadlock: The 2000 Election, the Constitution, and the Courts.* Princeton, NJ: Princeton University Press.
  1995   *Overcoming Law.* Cambridge, MA: Harvard University Press.
  1990   *The Problems of Jurisprudence.* Cambridge, MA: Harvard University Press.
  1987   "The Decline of Law as an Autonomous Discipline: 1962–1987." *Harvard Law Review* 100 (February): 761–80.
  1985   *The Federal Courts: Crisis and Reform.* Cambridge, MA: Harvard University Press.

Possley, Maurice
    1999   "Kids Get Right to Murder-Trial Jury." *Chicago Tribune* (April 13): Sec. 2: 1, 4.
Post, Robert C.
    1995   *Constitutional Domains: Democracy, Community, Management*. Cambridge, MA: Harvard University Press.
Pound, Roscoe
    1975   *An Introduction to the Philosophy of Law*. New Haven, CT: Yale University Press.
    1953   *The Lawyer from Antiquity to Modern Times*. St. Paul, MN: West.
Powell, Michael J.
    1988   *From Patrician to Professional Elite: The Transformation of the New York City Bar*. New York: Russell Sage Foundation.
Pre-law Handbook 1982–1983
    1983   Washington, DC: Association of American Law Schools.
President's Commission on Organized Crime
    1986   *The Impact: Organized Crime Today*. Washington, DC: US Government Printing Office.
Protess, Ben and Peter Lattman
    2013   "A Legal Bane of Wall Street Switches Sides." *New York Times* (July 23): 1, B4.
Provine, Doris Marie
    1996   "Courts in the Political Process in France." Pages 177–248 in *Courts, Law and Politics in Comparative Perspective*, edited by Herbert Jacob et al. New Haven, CT: Yale University Press.
Puritz, Patricia and Mary Ann Scali
    1998   *Beyond the Walls: Improving Conditions of Confinement for Youth in Custody*. Washington, DC: Office of Juvenile Justice and Delinquency Prevention.
Puritz, Patricia and Wendy Wan Long Shang
    1998   *Innovative Approaches to Juvenile Defense*. Washington, DC: Office of Justice Programs.
Puzzanchera, Charles, Benjamin Adams, and Sarah Hockenberry
    2012   *Juvenile Court Statistics 2009*. Pittsburgh, PA: National Center for Juvenile Justice. Available: http://www.ojjdp.gov/pubs/239114.pdf.
Puzzanchera, Charles, Benjamin Adams, and Melissa Sickmund
    2011   *Juvenile Court Statistics 2008*. Washington, DC: Bureau of Justice Statistics. Available: http://www.ojjdp.gov/ojstatbb/njcda/pdf/jcs2008.pdf.
"Q & A."
    1991   *Chicago Tribune* Magazine (June 16): 6.
Quillen, William T. and Michael Hanrahan
    1993   "A Short History of the Delaware Court of Chancery." Widener University School of Law. Available: http://courts.delaware.gov/chancery/history.stm (accessed October 24, 2013).
Quinn, Jane B.
    1986   "Cutting Back Verdicts." *Newsweek* (July 7): 44.
Rabkin, Jeremy
    1989   *Judicial Compulsions: How Public Law Distorts Public Policy*. New York: Basic Books.
Rakove, Jack N.
    1996   *Original Meanings: Politics and Ideas in the Making of the Constitution*. New York: Knopf.
Rall, J.
    2010   "2010 State Legislation Concerning State Liability and Sovereign Immunity." National Conference of State Legislators. Available: http://www.ncsl.org/documents/transportation/StateImmunityLeg0810.pdf.
Rampell, Catherine
    2011a   "At Well-Paying Law Firms, a Low Paid Corner." *New York Times* (May 24): 1, 17.
    2011b   "Judges Compete for Clerks in Lawless Terrain." *New York Times* (September 24): B1, 7.

Ramseyer, J. Mark and Eric B. Rasmusen
   2010   "Lawyers per 100,000 People." Cambridge, MA: Harvard Law School. Available: http://www.law.harvard.edu/programs/olin_center/papers/pdf/Ramseyer_681.pdf.
Raven, Robert D.
   1988   Letter to the Editor: "In Legal Aid Chicken Coop, the Fox Is King." *New York Times* (Dec. 9): 30.
Rawls, John
   1999   *A Theory of Justice*, revised edition. Cambridge, MA: Harvard University Press.
Re, Edward D.
   1975a   *Stare Decisis*. Washington, DC: Federal Judicial Center.
   1975b   *Appellate Opinion Writing*. Washington, DC: Federal Judicial Center.
Rehnquist, William H.
   1999   *All the Laws but One: Civil Liberties in Wartime*. New York: Knopf.
   1996   "Remarks of the Chief Justice at the Washington College of Law Centennial Celebration Plenary Academic Panel: The Future of the Federal Courts." American University, April 9.
   1987   *The Supreme Court: How It Was, How It Is*. New York: William Morrow.
Reich, Cary
   1986   "The Litigator." *New York Times Magazine* (June 1): 18–24, 48, 50, 70, 74–76, 84.
Reimund, Mary Ellen
   2005   "The Law and Restorative Justice: Friend or Foe? A Systematic Look at Legal Issues in Restorative Justice." *Drake Law Review* 53 (Spring): 667–97.
Rengel, Marian
   2000   *Encyclopedia of Birth Control*. Phoenix, AZ: The Oryx Press.
Reisig, Martin
   2002   "The Difficult Role of the Defense Lawyer in a Post-Adjudication Drug Treatment Court: Accommodating Therapeutic Jurisprudence and Due Process." Reprint from the *Criminal Law Bulletin* (March/April): 1–8.
Rembar, Charles
   1980   *The Law of the Land: The Evolution of Our Legal System*. New York: Simon and Schuster.
Reuters
   1996   "Malpractice Awards Tied to Disability." *New York Times* (December 26): 11.
Richert, E. Susanne
   1987   *Equal Justice Under Law*. Washington, DC: Judicial Conference of the United States Committee on the Bicentennial of the Constitution.
Ritchey, Joan Grace
   2001   "Limits on Justice: the United States' Failure to Recognize a Right to Counsel in Civil Litigation." *Washington University Law Quarterly* 79: 317–41.
Roberts, Sam
   1985   "For One Zealous Judge, Hard Bargaining Pushes Cases through the Courts." *New York Times* (April 29): 13.
Roehl, Janice and Larry Ray
   1986   "Toward the Multi-Door Courthouse—Dispute Resolution Intake and Referral." *NIJ Reports/SNI* 198 (July): 2–7.
Rohde, David
   1999   "A Glut of Minor Cases Swamps City's Courts." *New York Times* (February 2): 19.
Rosen, Jeffrey
   2008   "Supreme Court Inc." *New York Times Magazine* (March 16): 38–45, 66, 68, 71.
Roithmayr, Daria
   2005   "A Dangerous Supplement." *Journal of Legal Education* 55 (March/June): 80–93.

Rommen, Heinrich A.
   1998   *The Natural Law: A Study in Legal and Social History and Philosophy.* Indianapolis, IN: Liberty Fund. (Originally published in 1936.)

Ronner, Amy D. and Bruce J. Winick
   2000   "Silencing the Appellant's Voice: The Antitherapeutic Per Curiam Affirmance." *Seattle University Law Review* 24 (Fall): 499–511.

Rosen, Jeffrey
   2005   "So, Do You Believe in 'Superprecedent'?" *New York Times* (October 30): Sec. 4: 1, 3.

Rottman, David B.
   2000   "Does Effective Therapeutic Jurisprudence Require Specialized Courts (and Do Specialized Courts Imply Specialist Judges)?" *Court Review* 37 (Spring): 22–27.

Rottman, David and Pamela Casey
   1999   "Therapeutic Jurisprudence and the Emerging of Problem-Solving Courts." *NIJ Journal* (July): 12–19.

Rottman, David B. and William E. Hewitt
   1996   *Trial Court Structure and Performance: A Contemporary Reappraisal.* Arlington, VA: National Center for State Courts.

Rottman, David B. and Shauna M. Strickland
   2006   *State Court Organization, 2004.* Washington, DC: National Institute of Justice. Available: http://www.bjs.gov/content/pub/pdf/sco04.pdf.

Rubin, Emily
   1998   "Ineffective Assistance of Counsel, and Guilty Pleas: Toward a Paradigm of Informed Consent." *Virginia Law Journal* 80: 1699–1722.

Rubin, Phillip A.
   2011   "War of the Words: How Courts Can Use Dictionaries in Accordance with Textualist Principles." *Duke University Law Review* 60: 167–206.

Rubinstein, Michael L., Stevens H. Clarke, and Teresa J. White
   1980   *Alaska Bans Plea Bargaining.* Washington, DC: US Government Printing Office.

Ryan, John
   2006.   "New York Story: Evan Chesler." LAWDRAGON (March 6). Available: http://www.lawdragon.com/feature-articles/new-york-story.

Saari, David J.
   1985   *American Court Management: Theories and Practice.* Westport, CT: Quorum Books.

Sabatino, Jack M.
   1998   "ADR as 'Litigation Lite': Procedural and Evidentiary Norms Embedded within Alternative Dispute Resolution." *Emory Law Journal* 47: 1290–1350.

Sack, Kevin
   1990   "Thousands of Medical Errors, but Few Lawsuits, Study Shows." *New York Times* (Jan. 29): 15.

Sagatun, Inger, Loretta McCollum, and Michael Edwards
   1985   "The Effect of Transfers from Juvenile to Criminal Court: A Loglinear Analysis." *Journal of Crime and Justice* 8: 65–92.

Salomone, Rosemary C.
   1986   *Equal Education under Law: Legal Rights and Federal Policy in the Post-Brown Era.* New York: St. Martin's Press.

Salpukas, Agis
   1997   "CSX and Others Ordered to Pay Billions in '87 Rail Chemical Fire." *New York Times* (September 9): C1.

Samuelson, Robert J.
   1992   "I Am a Big Lawyer Basher." *Newsweek* (April 27): 62.

Sanborn, Joseph B., Jr.
   1986   "A Historical Sketch of Plea Bargaining." *Justice Quarterly* 3 (June): 111–38.
Sandefur, Timothy
   2006   "In Defense of Plea Bargaining: The Practice Is Flawed, but Not Unconstitutional."
            Pages 44–50 in *Taking Sides: Clashing Views in Public Policy, Justice, and the Law*, edited
            by Marie Natoli. New York: McGraw Hill.
Sanders, Joseph
   1996   "Courts and Law in Japan." Pages 315–88 in *Courts, Law and Politics in Comparative
            Perspective*, edited by Herbert Jacob et al. New Haven, CT: Yale University Press.
Savage, David G.
   1991   "Supreme Court Rulings Rankle Business Lawyers." *Los Angeles Times* (March 10): D1.
Scali, Mary Ann and Kim Tandy
   2013   *Missouri: Justice Rationed*. Washington, DC: National Juvenile Defender Center.
Scalia, Antonin
   1997   *A Matter of Interpretation: Federal Courts and the Law*. Princeton, NJ: Princeton Univer-
            sity Press.
   1996   "Speech before The Catholic University of America," October 18.
Scalia, Antonin and John F. Manning
   2012   "A Dialogue on Statutory and Constitutional Interpretation." *George Washington Law
            Review* 80: 1610–19.
Schlossman, Steven L.
   1977   *Love and the American Delinquent: The Theory and Practice of "Progressive" Juvenile Jus-
            tice, 1825–1920*. Chicago: University of Chicago Press.
Schma, William
   2000   "Judging for the New Millennium." *Court Review* 37 (Spring): 4–6.
Schmetzer, Uli
   1991   "China Judges Hail Imprisonments." *Chicago Tribune* (April 4): 5.
Schmitt, Christopher H.
   2003   "A Medical Mistake." *U.S. News and World Report* (July 7): 24–27.
Schubert, Frank A.
   2012   *Introduction to Law and the Legal System*, 10th ed. Boston: Houghton Mifflin.
Schulhofer, Stephen J.
   1994   "A Wake-Up Call From the Plea Bargain Trenches." *Law and Social Inquiry* 19: 135–44.
   1992   "Plea Bargaining as Disaster." *Yale Law Journal* 101: 1979–2009.
   1986   "The Future of the Adversary System." *Justice Quarterly* 3 (March): 83–93.
Schur, Edwin M.
   1973   *Radical Non-Intervention: Rethinking the Delinquency Problem*. Englewood Cliffs, NJ:
            Prentice-Hall.
   1968   *Law and Society: A Sociological View*. New York: Random House.
Schwartz, Bernard
   1996   "Administrative Law." Pages 129–50 in *Fundamentals of American Law*, edited by Alan
            M. Morrison. New York: Oxford University Press.
   1993   *A History of the Supreme Court*. New York: Oxford University Press.
   1988   *The Unpublished Opinions of the Burger Court*. New York: Oxford University Press.
   1974   *The Law in America: A History*. New York: McGraw-Hill.
Schwartz, John
   2013   "Bid to Keep Youths Out of Adult Prisons." *New York Times* (October 29): 12, 14.
Scott, Robert E. and William J. Stuntz
   1992   "Plea Bargaining as Contract." *Yale Law Journal* 101: 1909–68.

Seelye, Katherine Q. and Jess Bidgood
    2013   "Prison for State Chemist Who Faked Drug Evidence." *New York Times* (November 23): 9, 15.
Segal, David
    2011   "What They Don't Teach Law Students: Lawyering." *New York Times* (November 20): 1, 22.
Seligman, Joel
    1978   *The High Citadel: The Influence of Harvard Law School.* Boston: Houghton Mifflin.
Seymour, Christopher
    1996   *Yakuza Diary.* New York: Atlantic Monthly Press.
Shaffer, Catherine
    2004   "Therapeutic Domestic Violence Courts: An Efficient Approach to Adjudication?" *Seattle University Law Review* 27 (Spring): 981–97.
Shaibani, Sahand
    1999   "Psychodynamics of the Judicial Process." *Stanford Journal of Legal Studies* 1 (December): 1–10.
Shaman, Jeffrey M.
    1992   "Interpreting the Constitution: The Supreme Court's Proper and Historic Function." Pages 37–55 in *Judicial Politics: Readings From Judicature*, edited by E. E. Slotnick. Chicago: Nelson-Hall.
Shamir, Ronen
    1995   *Managing Legal Uncertainty: Elite Lawyers in the New Deal.* Durham, NC: Duke University Press.
Shapiro, Martin
    1988   *Who Guards the Guardians? Judicial Control of Administration.* Athens: University of Georgia Press.
    1981   *Courts: A Comparative and Political Analysis.* Chicago: University of Chicago Press.
Shealy, Miller W., Jr.
    2013   "A Reasonable Doubt about 'Reasonable Doubt.'" *Oklahoma Law Review* 65: 225–302.
Shelden, Randall G.
    2012   *Delinquency and Juvenile Justice in American Society,* 2d ed. Long Grove, IL: Waveland Press.
Shepherd, George B.
    2000   "Cartels and Controls in Legal Training." *Antitrust Bulletin* 45 (Summer): 437–66.
Sherry, Suzanna
    1998   "Independent Judges and Independent Justice." *Law and Contemporary Problems* 15 (Summer): 15–20.
Shesol, Jeff
    2010   *Supreme Power: Franklin Roosevelt v. the Supreme Court.* New York: Norton.
Shih, Gerry
    2009   "Downturn Dims Prospects Even at Top Law Schools." *New York Times* (August 26): B1, B7.
Shinall, Jennifer Bennett
    2010   "Slipping Away from Justice: The Effect of Attorney Skill on Trial Outcomes." *Vanderbilt Law Review* 63: 267–96.
Shuster, Beth
    2001   "The Science of Getting Inmates From Jail to Court." *Los Angeles Times* (August 3). Available: http://articles.latimes.com/2001/aug/03/local/me-30187.
Sigmund, Paul E.
    1971   *Natural Law in Political Thought.* Cambridge, MA: Winthrop.

Simmons, Omari Scott and James D. Dinnage
    2011   "Innkeepers: A Unifying Theory of the In-House Counsel Role." *Seton Hall Law Review* 41: 77–152.
Simon, James F.
    1989   *The Antagonists: Hugo Black, Felix Frankfurter and Civil Liberties in America.* New York: Simon and Schuster.
Sinclair, Jim
    1994   "APPA's Public Hearings Explore Probation and Parole's Response to Victims of Crime: Speakers Call for a New Approach to Victim Issues." *Perspectives* (Special Issue): 15–17.
Sinha, Surya Prakash
    1990   *What Is Law? The Differing Theories of Jurisprudence.* New York: Paragon House.
Slade, Margot
    1993   "Billable Hour, a Centerpiece of American Law, Is Fading." *New York Times* (October 22): 1, B9.
Slotnick, E. E., ed.
    1992   *Judicial Politics: Readings From Judicature.* Chicago: Nelson-Hall.
Smigel, Erwin O.
    1964   *The Wall Street Lawyer: Professional Organization Man.* Glencoe, IL: Free Press.
Smith, Christopher E.
    1997   *Courts, Politics, and the Judicial Process,* 2d ed. Chicago: Nelson-Hall.
    1993a   *Courts, Politics, and the Judicial Process.* Chicago: Nelson-Hall.
    1993b   *Courts and Public Policy.* Chicago: Nelson-Hall.
Smith, Craig and Eric V. Moye
    2011   "Outsourcing American Civil Justice: Mandatory Arbitration Clauses in Consumer and Employment Contracts." *Texas Tech Law Review* 44: 281–301.
Smith, Michael E.
    2001   *What Future for "Public Safety" and "Restorative Justice" in Community Corrections?* Washington, DC: National Institute of Justice.
Smith, Reginald H.
    1919   *Justice and the Poor.* New York: Carnegie Foundation.
Smith, Rogers M.
    1985   *Liberalism and American Constitutional Law.* Cambridge, MA: Harvard University Press.
Smith, Steven K. and Carol J. DeFrances
    1996   *Indigent Defense.* Washington, DC: Bureau of Justice Statistics.
Snyder, Howard and Melissa Sickmund
    2006   *Juvenile Offenders and Victims: 2006 National Report.* Washington, DC: US Department of Justice Office of Justice Programs.
Solomon, Harvey E.
    1987   "The Training of Court Managers." Pages 15–20 in *Court Administration: Issues and Responses,* edited by Charles R. Swanson and Susette M. Talarico. Athens: University of Georgia Press.
Spaeth, Harold J.
    1979   *Supreme Court Policy Making: Explanation and Prediction.* San Francisco: Freeman.
Spangenberg, Robert L., Marea L. Beeman, David J. Carroll, David Freedman, Evelyn Pan, David J. Newhouse, and Dorothy Chan
    2000   *Contracting for Indigent Defense Services: A Special Report.* Washington, DC: Office of Justice Programs.
Spangler, Eve
    1986   *Lawyers for Hire: Salaried Professionals at Work.* New Haven, CT: Yale University Press.

Spencer, A. Benjamin
    2012   "The Law School Critique in Historical Perspective." *Washington and Lee Law Review* 69: 1949–2063.

Spencer, Herbert
    2002   *Principles of Biology.* Haddonfield, NJ: Ross & Perry, Inc. (Originally published in 1864.)
    1961   *The Study of Sociology.* Ann Arbor: University of Michigan Press. (Originally published in 1871.)

Spinak, Jane M.
    2008   "Romancing the Court." *Family Court Review* 46 (April): 258–74.

Springer, John
    2005   "Malpractice Made Perfect." *Men's Health* (June): 170–76, 216

Stanny, Claudia J. and Thomas C. Johnson
    2000   "Effects of Stress Induced by a Simulated Shooting on Recall by Police and Citizen Witnesses." *American Journal of Psychology* 113 (Fall): 359–86.

Stahel, Philip F., Allison L. Sabel, Michael S. Victoroff, Jeffrey Varnell, Alan Lembitz, Dennis J. Boyle, Ted J. Clarke, Wade R. Smith, and Philip S. Mehler
    2010   "Wrong-Site and Wrong-Patient Procedures in the Universal Protocol Era: Analysis of a Prospective Database of Physician Self-reported Occurrences." *Archives of Surgery* 145 (10): 978–84.

"State Courts Providing Broader Constitutional Protections in Criminal Cases than U.S. Supreme Court"
    1993   *NCJA Justice Bulletin* 13 (No. 7): 1, 6, 9–12.

Steinberg, Allen
    2003   "The Public Prosecutor as Representational Image: The 'Lawman' in New York: William Travers Jerome and the Origins of the Modern District Attorney in Turn-of-the-Century New York." *University of Toledo Law Review* 34 (Summer): 753–82.

Steinhauer, Jennifer and Ford Fessenden
    2001   "Doctors Punished by New York Are Still Prized by Hospitals." *New York Times* (March 27): 24.

Stevens, Ed
    1999   *Due Process and Higher Education: A Systemic Approach to Fair Decision Making.* Washington, DC: Washington University, Graduate School of Education and Human Development.

Stevens, Robert
    1983   *Law School: Legal Education in America from the 1850s to the 1980s.* Chapel Hill: University of North Carolina Press.
    1971   "Two Cheers for 1870: The American Law School." Pages 403–548 in *Law in American History,* edited by Donald Fleming and Bernard Bailyn. Boston: Little, Brown.

Stewart, James B.
    1987   *The Prosecutors: Inside the Offices of the Government's Most Powerful Lawyers.* New York: Simon and Schuster.
    1984   *The Partners: Inside America's Most Powerful Law Firms.* New York: Warner.

Stienstra, Donna and Thomas E. Willging
    1995   *Alternatives to Litigation: Do They Have a Place in the Federal District Courts?* Washington, DC: Federal Judicial Center. Available: http://www.fjc.gov/public/pdf.nsf/lookup/altlitig.pdf/$File/altlitig.pdf.

Stipanowich, Thomas J.
    2010   "Arbitration: The 'New Litigation.'" *University of Illinois Law Review* 1: 1.

Stolberg, Sheryl Gay
    2006   "Senate Rejects Award Limits in Malpractice." *New York Times* (May 9): 25.

Stolle, Dennis F., David B. Wexler, Bruce J. Winick, and Edward A. Dauer
  1997   "Integrating Preventive Law and Therapeutic Jurisprudence: A Law and Psychology Based Approach to Lawyering." *California Western Law Review* 34: 15–51.
Stone, Geoffrey R.
  2012   "*Citizens United* and Conservative Judicial Activism." *University of Illinois Law Review* 2012: 485–500. Available: http://illinoislawreview.org/wp-content/ilr-content/articles/2012/2/Stone.pdf.
Story, Joseph
  1962   "Discourse Pronounced Upon the Inauguration of the Author." Pages 176–90 in *The Legal Mind in America: From Independence to the Civil War*, edited by Perry Miller. Garden City, NY: Anchor.
Stott, E. Keith, Jr.
  1987   "The Judicial Executive: Toward Greater Congruence in an Emerging Profession." Pages 21–36 in *Court Administration: Issues and Responses*, edited by Charles R. Swanson and Susette M. Talarico. Athens: University of Georgia Press.
Stout, Ronald
  1986   "Planning for Unified Court Budgeting." *Judicature* 69 (Dec.–Jan.): 205–13.
Stover, Robert V.
  1989   *Making It and Breaking It: The Fate of Public Interest Commitment during Law School.* Urbana: University of Illinois Press.
Strauss, Peter L.
  1990   "Too Often, the Buck Stops in the Appeals Court." Letter to the *New York Times* (April 14): 14.
  1989   *An Introduction to Administrative Justice in the United States.* Durham, NC: Carolina Academic Press.
Stryker, Robin
  1989   "Limits on the Technocratization of the Law: The Elimination of the National Labor Relations Board's Division of Economic Research." *American Sociological Review* 54 (June): 341–58.
Stumpf, Harry P.
  1998   *American Judicial Politics*, 2d ed. Upper Saddle River, NJ: Prentice-Hall.
Stumpf, Harry P. and John H. Culver
  1992   *The Politics of State Courts.* New York: Longman.
Subin, Harry I.
  1990   "Why the Bar Exam Is Absolutely Crucial." Letter to the *New York Times* (August 3): 10.
Sudnow, David
  1965   "Normal Crimes: Sociological Features of the Penal Code." *Social Problems* 12 (Winter): 255–64.
Sumner, William Graham
  1992   *On Liberty, Society, and Politics: The Essential Essays of William Graham Sumner*, edited by Robert C. Bannister. Indianapolis, IN: Liberty Fund.
Sunstein, Cass R.
  2005   *Radicals in Robes: Why Extreme Right-Wing Courts Are Wrong for America.* New York: Basic Books.
  2002   "Taking over the Courts." *New York Times* (November 9): 29.
  2000a   "*Dred Scott v. Sandford* and Its Legacy." Pages 64–89 in *Great Cases in Constitutional Law*, edited by Robert P. George. Princeton, NJ: Princeton University Press.
  2000b   "Cognition and Cost Benefit Analysis." *Law and Economics Working Paper No. 85*, University of Chicago Law School.
  1996   *Legal Reasoning and Political Conflict.* New York: Oxford University Press.

Sutherland, Arthur E.
 1967 *The Law at Harvard: A History of Ideas and Men, 1819–1967*. Cambridge, MA: Harvard University Press.
Sutton, John R.
 1988 *Stubborn Children: Controlling Delinquency in the United States, 1649–1981*. Berkeley: University of California Press.
Sviridoff, Michele, David Rottman, and Richard Curtis
 1997 *Dispensing Justice Locally*. New York: Center for Court Innovation.
Sward, Ellen E.
 2003 "A History of the Civil Trial in the United States." *Kansas Law Review* (May): 347–418.
Sweet, Alec Stone
 2007 "The Politics of Constitutional Review in France and Europe." *I•CON* 5 (January): 69–92.
Symposium on Standards of Practice
 2001 *Model Standards of Practice for Family and Divorce Mediation*. Available: http://www.americanbar.org/content/dam/aba/migrated/family/reports/mediation.authcheckdam.pdf.
Talbac, William L.
 1987 "Crossfire at the Bar." *New York Times Magazine/Business World* (May 3): 30–31, 47, 50, 55.
Tabarrok, Alexander and Eric Helland
 1999 "Court Politics: The Political Economy of Tort Awards." *Journal of Law and Economics* 42 (April): 157–88.
Tamanaha, Brian Z.
 2012 *Failing Law Schools*. Chicago: University of Chicago Press.
Taragin, Mark I., Laura R. Willett, Adam P. Wilczek, Richard Trout, and Jeffrey L. Carson
 1993 "The Influence of Standard Care and Severity of Injury on the Resolution of Medical Malpractice Claims." *Annals of Internal Medicine* 117 (November 1): 780–84.
Tarr, G. Alan
 2014 *Judicial Process and Judicial Policymaking*, 6th edition. Boston: Wadsworth.
 1999 *Judicial Process and Judicial Policymaking*. Belmont, CA: Wadsworth.
Taylor, C. James, ed.
 2008 *The Adams Papers Digital Edition*. Charlottesville: University of Virginia Press, Rotunda.
Taylor, Stuart, Jr.
 2000 "*Bush v. Gore* May Be Just the Beginning." *Newsweek* (January 1): 50.
 1988 "The 'Judicial Activists' Are Always on the Other Side." *New York Times* (July 3): E5.
 1986a "Vigor in the Court, Laughter in the Court." *New York Times* (Oct. 14): 12.
 1986b "Tasting the Salty Air of Politics and Criticism." *New York Times* (July 18): 8.
 1986c "An Inside Look at Supreme Court and Its Cases." *New York Times* (June 24): 10.
Texas Criminal Justice Council
 1974 *Model Rules for Law Enforcement Officers: A Manual on Police Discretion*. Gaithersburg, MD: International Association of Chiefs of Police.
Thomas, Landon, Jr.
 2004 "Need a Superlawyer? Take a Number." *New York Times* (June 13): BU 1, 4.
Thompson, Anthony C.
 2002 "Courting Disorder: Some Thoughts on Community Courts." *Washington University Journal of Law and Policy* 10: 63–103.
Tiersma, Peter M.
 2011 "The Role of Text: Is It Possible to Govern Using (Only) Statutes?" *New York University Journal of Law and Liberty* 6: 260–89.
 1999 "Jury Instructions in the New Millennium." *Court Review* 36 (Summer): 28–36.

Timmons, Heather
    2010   "Due Diligence from Afar." *New York Times* (August 5): B1, B2.

Toch, Hans
    1982   "The Role of the Expert on Prison Conditions: The Battle of Footnotes in *Rhodes v. Chapman*." *Criminal Law Bulletin* 18: 38–49.

Todd, A. L.
    1968   *Justice on Trial: The Case of Louis D. Brandeis*. Chicago: University of Chicago Press.

Toedt, D. C., III, Robert R. Robinson, and Randy S. Segal
    2005   "GC Rules: Over 350 Things I Knew My First Year as General Counsel." *ACC Docket* (May): 1–25.

Tokarz, Karen and Rebecca Hollander-Blumoff
    2012   "New Directions in Negotiation and ADR: Introduction." *Washington University Journal of Law and Policy* 39: 1–12.

Toobin, Jeffrey
    2012   "Money Unlimited." *New Yorker* (May 21): 36–47.

Torbet, Patricia, Richard Gable, Hunter Hurst IV, Imogene Montgomery, Linda Szymanski, and Douglas Thomas
    1996   *State Responses to Serious and Violent Juvenile Crime*. Washington, DC: Office of Juvenile Justice and Delinquency Prevention.

Torbet, Patricia, Patrick Griffen, Hunter Hurst, Jr., and Lynn Ryan MacKenzie
    2000   *Juveniles Facing Criminal Sanctions: Three States that Changed the Rules*. Washington, DC: Office of Juvenile Justice and Delinquency Prevention.

Treaster, Joseph B. and Joel Brinkley
    2005   "Behind Those Medical Malpractice Rates." *New York Times* (February 22): C1, 3.

Tribe, Laurence H.
    1985   *God Save This Honorable Court: How the Choice of Supreme Court Justices Shapes Our History*. New York: Random House.

Tribe, Laurence and Michael C. Dorf
    1991   *On Reading the Constitution*. Cambridge, MA: Harvard University Press.

Tsai, Betsy
    2000   "The Trend Toward Specialized Domestic Violence Courts: Improvement on an Effective Innovation." *Fordham University Law Review* 68: 1285–1327.

Turkel, Gerald
    1996   *Law and Society: Critical Approaches*. Needham Heights, MA: Allyn & Bacon.

Turow, Scott
    1977   *One L: An Inside Account of Life in the First Year at Harvard Law School*. New York: Penguin.

Tushnet, Mark
    2000   "*Marbury v. Madison* and the Theory of Judicial Supremacy." Pages 17–54 in *Greatest Cases in Constitutional Law*, edited by Robert P. George. Princeton, NJ: Princeton University Press.

Tybor, Joseph R. and Mark Eissman
    1986   "Study Confirms Crime Lab's Lag Let Drug Cases Fail." *Chicago Tribune* (March 3): 11.
    1985   "Judges Penalize the Guilty for Exercising the Right to Trial." *Chicago Tribune* (October 13): 1, 6.

Uhlman, Thomas M. and N. Darlene Walker
    1980   "He Takes Some of My Time, I Take Some of His: An Analysis of Judicial Sentencing Patterns in Jury Cases." *Law and Society Review* 14 (Winter): 323–41.

Umbreit, Mark S.
    2001   *The Handbook of Victim Offender Mediation*. San Francisco: Jossey-Bass.
    1994   *Victim Meets Offender: The Impact of Restorative Justice and Mediation*. Monsey, NY: Willow Tree Press.

Umbreit, Mark S. and Mark Carey
 1995   "Restorative Justice: Implications for Organizational Change." *Federal Probation* 59 (March): 47–54.

Uphoff, Rodney J.
 2002   "The Criminal Defense Lawyer: Zealous Advocate, Double Agent, or Beleaguered Dealer?" Pages 84–117 in *Criminal Courts for the 21st Century*, edited by Lisa Stolzenberg and Stewart J. D'Alessio. Upper Saddle River, NJ: Prentice-Hall.

Urbina, Ian
 2014   "Social Media, a Trove of Clues and Confessions." *New York Times* (February 16): SR 5.
 2006   "Ohio Supreme Court Rejects Taking of Homes for Project." *New York Times* (July 27): 18.

U.S. Equal Employment Opportunity Commission
 2011   "EEOC Reports Job Bias Charges Hit Record High of Nearly 100,000 in Fiscal Year 2010." Available: http://www.eeoc.gov/eeoc/newsroom/release/1-11-11.cfm.

Utz, Pamela
 1979   "Two Models of Prosecutorial Professionalism." Pages 99–124 in *The Prosecutor*, edited by William F. McDonald. Beverly Hills, CA: Sage.

Uviller, H. Richard
 1996   *Virtual Justice: The Flawed Prosecution of Crime in America*. New Haven, CT: Yale University Press.

Van Alstyne, W. Scott, Jr., Joseph R. Julin, and Larry D. Barnett
 1990   *The Goals and Missions of Law Schools*. New York: Peter Lang.

van Caenegem, R. C.
 1994   *A Historical Introduction to Private Law*. Cambridge: Cambridge University Press.

Vandall, Frank J.
 1989   *Strict Liability: Legal and Economic Analysis*. New York: Quorum Books.

Van Hoy, Jerry
 1997   *Franchise Law Firms and the Transformation of Personal Legal Services*. Westport, CT: Quorum Books.

Vera Institute of Justice
 1977   *Felony Arrests: Their Prosecution and Disposition in New York City's Courts*. New York: Vera Institute of Justice.

Vermeule, Adrian
 2000   "Interpretive Choice." *New York University Law Review* 75: 74–149.

Victim Input into Plea Agreements
 2002   Washington, DC: Office for Victims of Crime.

Volcansek, Mary L., with Elisabetta de Franciscis and Jacquiline Lucienne Lafon
 1996   *Judicial Misconduct: A Cross-National Comparison*. Gainesville: University of Florida Press.

Wachtler, Sol
 1990   "Grand Juries: Wasteful and Pointless." *New York Times* (Jan. 6): 15.

Wagner, Diane
 1986   "The New Elite Plaintiff's Bar." *ABA Journal* (Feb. 1): 44–49.

Walker, Samuel
 1998   *Popular Justice: A History of American Criminal Justice*, 2d ed. New York: Oxford University Press.
 1980   *Popular Justice: A History of American Criminal Justice*. New York: Oxford University Press.

Wall, Joseph F.
 1981   "*Lochner v. New York*: A Study in the Modernization of Constitutional Law." Pages 113–41 in *American Industrialization, Economic Expansion, and the Law*, edited by Joseph R. Frese and Jacob Judd. Tarrytown, NY: Sleepy Hollow Press.

Walsh, Mary Williams
   2001   "Ruling Likely to Bring Changes to Many Jobs." *New York Times* (March 22): C6.
Waltz, Jon R.
   1997   *Introduction to Criminal Evidence*, 4th ed. Chicago: Nelson-Hall.
Ware, Stephen J.
   1999   "Arbitration and Assimilation." *Washington University Law Review* 77: 1053–63.
Warren, Charles
   1966   "The Supreme Court in United States History." Pages 941–953 in *The Historian's History of the United States*, edited by Andrew S. Berk and James P. Shenton. New York: Capricorn Books.
Wasby, Stephen L.
   1993   *The Supreme Court in the Federal Judicial System*, 4th ed. Chicago: Nelson-Hall.
Washington Legal Foundation
   2012   *Annual Report*. Available: http://www.wlf.org/pdf/WLF2012AnnualReport.pdf.
Wasserstrom, Richard A.
   1961   *The Judicial Decision: Toward a Theory of Legal Justification*. Stanford, CA: Stanford University Press.
Weber, Max
   1967   *On Law in Economy and Society*, edited by Max Rheinstein. New York: Simon and Schuster. (Translated from the 1925 German edition.)
   1958   *The Protestant Ethic and the Spirit of Capitalism*. New York: Scribner's. (Originally published in German in 1905.)
Weisberg, Richard H.
   1997   *Vichy Law and the Holocaust in France*. New York: New York University Press.
Weisheit, Ralph H. and Diane M. Alexander
   1988   "Juvenile Justice and the Demise of Parens Patriae." *Federal Probation* 52 (Dec.): 56–63.
Weiss, Debra Cassens
   2012   "Scalia Denies Abortion Views Influenced by Religion, Calls His GPS Opinion 'Defendant Friendly.'" *ABA Journal* (February 4). Available: http://www.abajournal.com/news/article/scalia_denies_abortion_views_influenced_by_religion/
Wenger, Kristen L.
   2010   "The Class Action Fairness Act of 2005: The Limits of Its Text and the Need for Legislative Clarification, Not Judicial Interpretation." *Florida State University Law Review* 38: 679–707.
Westin, Alan F.
   1990   *The Anatomy of a Constitutional Law Case:* Youngstown Sheet and Tube Co. v. Sawyer, *the Steel Seizure Decision*. New York: Columbia University Press.
Wexler, David B.
   1999   "The Development of Therapeutic Jurisprudence: From Theory to Practice." *Revista Jurídica* 68: 691–705.
Wheeler, Russell R.
   1992   *Origins of the Elements of Federal Court Governance*. Washington, DC: Federal Judicial Center
Wheeler, Russell R. and A. Leo Levin
   1979   *Judicial Discipline and Removal in the United States*. Washington, DC: Federal Judicial Center.
White, G. Edward
   2000   *The Constitution and the New Deal*. Cambridge, MA: Harvard University Press.
   1980   *Tort Law in America: An Intellectual History*. New York: Oxford University Press. (Paperback edition 1985).
   1976   *The American Judicial Tradition*. New York: Oxford University Press.

Whitehead, Jason E.

    1999   "From Criticism to Critique: Preserving the Radical Potential of Critical Legal Studies Through a Reexamination of Frankfurt School Critical Theory." *Florida State University Law Review* 27: 701–42.

Whitman, Mark, ed.

    1993   *Removing a Badge of Slavery: The Record of* Brown v. Board of Education. New York: Markus Wiener.

Whittington, Keith E. and Amanda Rinderle

    2012   "Making a Mountain Out of a Molehill? *Marbury* and the Construction of the Constitutional Canon." *Hastings Constitutional Law Quarterly* 39 (Summer): 823–59.

Wice, Paul B.

    2005   *Public Defenders and the American Justice System.* Westport, CT: Praeger.

    1985   *Chaos in the Courthouse: The Inner Workings of the Urban Municipal Courts.* New York: Praeger.

    1983   "Private Criminal Defense: Reassessing an Endangered Species." Pages 39–64 in *The Defense Counsel,* edited by William F. McDonald. Beverly Hills, CA: Sage.

    1978   *Criminal Lawyers: An Endangered Species.* Beverly Hills, CA: Sage.

Wiecek, William M.

    1988   *Liberty under Law: The Supreme Court in American Life.* Baltimore, MD: Johns Hopkins University Press.

Wiehl, Lis

    1989a   "New Law Erects Barriers to the Federal Docket." *New York Times* (May 12): 22.

    1989b   "After 200 Years, the Silent Juror Learns to Talk." *New York Times* (July 7): 20.

Wiencek, Henry

    2012   "Master of Monticello." *Smithsonian* (October): 40–49, 92–97.

Wilder, Gita Z.

    2007   "Women in the Profession: Findings from the First Wave of the After the JD Study." The NALP Foundation for Law Career Research and Education and the National Association for Law Placement Inc. Available: http://www.nalp.org/assets/863_ajdgendermonograph2007.pdf.

Wilkerson, Isabel

    1990   "As Indiana Debates Its Malpractice Law, So Does the Country." *New York Times* (August 20): 11.

Wilkinson, J. Harvie, III

    2012   *Cosmic Constitutional Theory.* New York: Oxford University Press.

Wilson, James Q.

    1989   *Bureaucracy.* New York: Basic Books.

Wilson, James Q. and George Kelling

    1982   "Broken Windows: The Police and Neighborhood Safety." *Atlantic Monthly* (March): 29–38.

Wines, Michael

    1989   "Thornburgh Abandons Choice for Top Justice Post." *New York Times* (July 7): 1, 9.

Winfree, L. Thomas and Lawrence Kielich

    1979   "The Prosecuting Attorney and the Labeling Process: An Analysis of the Application of Official Sanction." Pages 161–79 in *Legality, Morality, and Criminal Justice,* edited by Nicholas Kittrie and Jackwell Susman. New York: Praeger.

Winick, Bruce J.

    2003a   "Therapeutic Jurisprudence and Problem Solving Courts." *Fordham Urban Law Journal* (March): 1055–96.

2003b   "Domestic Violence Court Judges as Risk Managers." Pages 201–11 in *Judging in a Therapeutic Key: Therapeutic Jurisprudence and the Courts*, edited by Bruce J. Winick, and David B. Wexler. Durham, NC: Carolina Academic Press.

1997   "The Jurisprudence of Therapeutic Jurisprudence." *Psychology, Public Policy, and Law* 1: 184–206.

Winick, Bruce J. and David B. Wexler, eds.

2003   *Judging in a Therapeutic Key: Therapeutic Jurisprudence and the Courts*. Durham, NC: Carolina Academic Press.

Wold, John T. and John H. Culver

1989   "The Defeat of the California Justices." Pages 323–29 in *American Court Systems: Readings in Judicial Process and Behavior*, edited by Sheldon Goldman and Austin Sarat. New York: Longman.

Wolf, Robert V.

2007   *Principles of Problem-Solving Justice*. New York: Center for Court Innovation.

Wolfe, Christopher

1986   *The Rise of Modern Judicial Review: From Constitutional Interpretation to Judge-Made Law*. New York: Basic Books.

Woolhandler, Ann and Caleb Nelson

2004   "Does History Defeat Standing Doctrine?" *Michigan Law Review* 102 (February): 689–739.

Woodiwiss, Anthony

1990   *Rights v. Conspiracy: A Sociological Essay on the History of Labour Law in the United States*. New York: Berg Publishers.

Wright, Martin

1991   *Justice for Victims and Offenders: A Restorative Response to Crime*. Philadelphia: Open University.

Wright, Ronald F.

2010   "Public Defender Elections and Popular Control over Criminal Justice." *Missouri Law Review* 75: 803–29. Available: http://law.missouri.edu/lawreview/files/2012/11/Wright.pdf.

Wright, Ronald and Marc Miller

2002   "The Screening/Bargaining Trade-off." *Stanford Law Review* 55 (October): 29–127.

Yarbrough, Tinsley E.

1995   *Judicial Enigma: The First Justice Harlan*. New York: Oxford University Press.

Yardley, Jim

2008   "Beijing Suspends Licenses of 2 Lawyers Who Offered to Defend Tibetans in Court." *New York Times* (June 4): 12.

2005   "A Judge Tests China's Courts, Making History." *New York Times* (November 28): 1, 12

Yeazell, Stephen C.

1987   *From Medieval Group Litigation to the Modern Class Action*. New Haven, CT: Yale University Press.'

Yellin, David S.

2011   "The Elements of Constitutional Style: A Comprehensive Analysis of Punctuation in the Constitution." *Tennessee Law Review* 79: 687–756.

Yiannopoulos, A. N.

1974   "Jurisprudence and Doctrine as Sources of Law in Louisiana and France." Pages 69–90 in *The Role of Judicial Decisions and Doctrine in Civil Law and in Mixed Jurisdictions*, edited by Joseph Dainow. Baton Rouge: Louisiana State University Press.

Young, Malcolm C.

2000   *Providing Effective Representation for Youth Prosecuted as Adults*. Washington, DC: Office of Justice Programs.

Zane, John Maxcy
    1998   *The Story of Law*, 2d ed. Indianapolis: Liberty Fund. (Originally published in 1927.)

Zarchin, Tomer
    2011   "Israel First in World for Lawyers Per Capita, Study Finds." *Haaretz* (August 3). Available: http://www.haaretz.com/print-edition/news/israel-first-in-world-for-lawyers-per-capita-study-finds-1.376646.

Zehr, Howard
    1990   *Changing Lenses: A New Focus for Crime and Justice*. Scottdale, PA: Herald Press.

Zeisel, Hans
    1982   *The Limits of Law Enforcement*. Chicago: University of Chicago Press.

Zobel, Hiller B.
    1991   "Naming a Justice Has Always Been Political as Usual." *American Heritage* (October): 94–101.

Zweigert, Konrad and Hein Kötz
    1998   *An Introduction to Comparative Law*, 3rd ed. Oxford, UK: Oxford University Press.
    1987   *An Introduction to Comparative Law*, 2d ed. Oxford, UK: Oxford University Press.

Case Index

In an appellate court citation, the first name is that of the party making the appeal; the second name is the party against whom the appeal is directed. The first number(s) is the volume of the court reports in which the decision may be found, followed by the name of the reporter system, with the second number(s) designating the first page of the decision. The year of the decision is always in parentheses.

For example, in the famous school desegregation case, *Brown v. Board of Education*, 347 U.S. 483 (1954), Brown refers to the appellant, the party who lost in a lower court and is appealing the decision; Board of Education refers to the school board of Topeka, Kansas, the respondent who won at the lower court level; 347 is the volume number of *United States Supreme Court Reports* (U.S.), and 483 is the page on which the case, which was decided in 1954, begins. There are also three private reporter systems for Supreme Court cases: *Supreme Court Reporter* (abbreviated S.Ct.), *Supreme Court Reports, Lawyer's Edition* (abbreviated L.Ed.), and *United States Law Week* (abbreviated LW). There are also some discontinued systems: Cranch, Wharton, Pet. (Peters), Wall. (Wallace's), Dall. (Dallas'), Wheat. (Wheaton's). A Supreme Court case may also be cited by its original Court number (No.) until the reporter systems provide a citation. Each case submitted to the Supreme Court—whether or not it is granted certiorari—is assigned a docket number. The first two digits indicate the calendar year in which the matter was brought to the Court, while the next set of digits represents the case's sequential position among cases presented that year. In states that do not provide an appellate process for juvenile court cases, they are cited as *In re* (in the matter of); thus *In re Gault* instead of *Gault v. Arizona*.

Citations of state appellate cases follow the same format except the abbreviated name of the state, for example, Mass., will appear with the year in parentheses; if the date is preceded by a number such as 2d Cir., (Second Circuit), it is a U.S. Court of Appeals case. In some cases, there is only one federal district in a state so the reporter system, such as F.Supp (Federal Supplement) would reveal the type of case, state or federal. (For a useful summary guide to legal citations, see Bouchoux 2001).

Author Index

Subject Index